1.S 94 —
↳ 12 n   KU-629-796

Travellers
Survival
Kit

turn off on
left
Grashet

U.S.A. &
Canada

SIMON CALDER
with additional research by Emily Hatchwell

Published by
VACATION WORK, 9 PARK END STREET, OXFORD

First published February 1985
Second edition January 1989
Third edition February 1993

TRAVELLERS SURVIVAL KIT — USA AND CANADA
by Simon Calder

Copyright © 1993

ISBN 1 85458 089 2

Cover Design

Mel Calman

Miller Craig & Cocking Design Partnership

Maps and illustrations by William Swan

Printed by **Unwin Brothers**, Old Woking, Surrey

Contents

U.S.A.

MAPS

CANADA

Regional Chapters

MAPS

Acknowledgements

A book of this nature involves contributions from dozens of travellers. In particular we wish to thank the following individuals for significant contributions:

New York	Marilyn Rubinstein and Hamish Mykura
Washington DC	Catherine Boardman
Chicago	Graham Pickup
New Orleans	Janet Morrison
Hawaii	Frank Partridge
Montréal	Elizabeth Strobel
Toronto	Cheryl Gasparet
Vancouver	Maire Guest and Jo Calder

In addition, Shirley Devlin, Alan Gibson, Tim James, Michael McDonnell, Mark Horobin, Mark Lawler, Julie Hunnisett, Alison Camp, Beverley Purcell, Julie Ashburner and Lorraine Downing have provided valuable support. Finally, a substantial editorial contribution was made by Emily Hatchwell.

UK Telephone Numbers. At Easter 1994, dialling codes in the UK are due to change. An additional digit, usually a 1, will be added after the initial zero, so the code for central London becomes 0171 and for Oxford 01865.

Preface

Life for visitors to North America is by turns wonderfully rewarding and deeply confusing. This vast and wealthy continent is crammed with all sorts of wonders, natural and man-made, and is peopled by a fascinating ethnic mix. The USA and Canada specialize in extremes of climate, achievement and personality. One tricky feature of preparing this book was sorting out the conflicting rivals for busiest airports, largest Chinatowns and most dangerous cities. These superlatives reinforce the image of North America as the futuristic, wild and dangerous place depicted in the media. The USA and Canada have given the world much of its popular culture: Bryan Adams and Neil Young, Marilyn Monroe and Madonna, *Star Trek* and *Twin Peaks*. So strong is the North American influence abroad that first-time visitors may be forgiven for believing that they know how it all works

But much of North America is deeply mystifying. If you're driving along a freeway, how can you tell if you're in a HOV — and what might happen if you're not? In this highly automated continent, which are the correct buttons to press to get a Metro ticket in Washington DC or a cash advance in Ottawa? How should you tip a New York City taxi, and how can you reclaim the taxes that the Canadian government owes you? Such problems, and the more obvious travellers' needs such as finding a safe and reasonably priced bed for the night, a meal which won't bankrupt or poison you, and how to work the world's most baffling telephone system, are all dealt with in the *Travellers Survival Kit: USA & Canada*. This book sets out to guide the visitor through the continent's complexities.

Many people see the inauguration of President Clinton as a sign of a new dynamism and freshness lacking in the 1980s and early 1990s. With a constitutional crisis besetting Canada, these are interesting times in North America. Despite the speed of changes, the essential generosity of the people and the fascinating environment they occupy are more than ever worth experiencing. This book aims to help you get the most from the USA and Canada.

Simon Calder
Oxford
January 1993

BEFORE YOU GO
USA and Canada

RED TAPE

Passports. A full ten-year passport is required for travel to both the USA and Canada. Application forms are available from post offices and should be sent with the appropriate fee, photographs and supporting documents to your regional passport office. Allow at least one month for processing by mail. If you're in a tearing hurry or realize your existing passport is soon to expire, you can usually obtain one in person if you're prepared to queue all day at a passport office.

For visits to the USA, your passport must have a minimum of six months to run. This rule is not rigidly enforced but nonetheless could be used as a reason to deny you entry. If your passport is lost or stolen while travelling, contact first the police then your nearest Consulate. Obtaining replacement travel documents is easier if you have a record of the passport number and its date and place of issue.

Visas. For up-to-date information on US visa rules, call 0891 200290 (a premium-rate service). Most travellers to the USA are covered by the visa waiver scheme. Under it, British visitors to the USA who meet certain conditions need no visa for a leisure or business trip of up to 90 days. You must hold full British citizenship and have a ticket back to, and refundable only in, your home country. You must be travelling on a carrier which has agreed to take part in the scheme: this includes the main transatlantic airlines. When you check in for your flight you will be required to sign a declaration to the effect that you are of sound mind and body and have neither suspect political affiliation nor criminal convictions. Upon arrival in the USA you must expect to spend longer at immigration than travellers with visas. Another drawback for those without visas is that side-trips to Canada or Mexico are possible only if you travel across the border with a carrier participating in the scheme. Furthermore, in return for the US authorities waiving your need for a visa, you waive your right to any appeal against the immigration officer's decision.

If you do not meet the conditions, or if you want to smooth your progress through immigration, get a visa. You can apply by post, using an application form which is free from most travel agents or the US Embassy Visa Branch, 5 Upper Grosvenor Street, London W1A 2JB. You must supply two passport photographs, evidence of financial resources, and a good reason for leaving after a temporary stay. 'Financial resources' can take the form of a receipt

11

for travellers cheques, a photocopy of your credit cards or a statement from a US citizen assuming responsibility for you. 'A good reason to leave' might be a commitment to a job, a family or a pet. A letter from your employer, college or social security office outlining the commitment should be regarded as sufficient proof of your intention to return.

The form also asks if you intend to work or study in the United States. Whatever your intentions, the correct answer is 'no', which is also the appropriate answer when you are asked if you have a contagious disease, a serious mental illness or a criminal conviction, and whether you have been a member of a Communist organisation or participated in atrocities perpetrated by Nazi Germany.

These documents, plus your passport, should be posted to the above address; allow three weeks for processing. If there are any irregularities in your application (such as omitting to sign or date it) it may take at least another fortnight to sort it out. Assuming you get one, it will valid either indefinitely or for a specific time; and entitle you to wither one or multiple applications for entry, with a maximum stay of six months for each visit. The norm is to issue an indefinite multiple one, which lasts a lifetime. (Anyone who is limited to a single entry or a few months is likely to be regarded as suspect in some way.) If your old passport contains an indefinite multiple entry visa, hang on to it even after your passport expires — just carry the old expired passport with you.

It is important to note that an American visa is no more than a permit to apply for entry to the USA. It does not guarantee that you will have no problems when you reach American soil — see *Red Tape: Immigration*, pages 27–29.

British visitors to Canada do not need visas for stays of up to three months. For information about working visas see page 391.

INSURANCE

Numerous visitors to North America have become destitute after having to pay enormous medical bills because they had insufficient insurance. Although all North Americans enjoy free emergency treatment in Britain courtesy of the National Health Service, there is no reciprocal agreement for the benefit of travellers to North America. Health care in the USA and Canada is extremely expensive. All but the poorest natives belong to health insurance schemes, and it is imperative that you be covered.

Policies valid for the USA and Canada usually cost more than those the rest of the world, since the high cost of health care means that the level of medical cover is around twice that deemed necessary elsewhere. Select a policy which offers at least £500,000 of cover. Any less might cause your premature departure from hospital in the event of a serious accident or illness. The cover provided by most policies is fairly standard: delay and cancellation insurance of up to £2,500; around £500,000 for medical expenses and emergency repatriation; £500,000 for personal liability; £20,000 for permanent disablement cover; lost or stolen baggage up to £1,000 (sometimes valuable single items are excluded); and cash to a maximum of £250. Every airline, tour operator and travel agent is delighted to sell you insurance because of the high commission it yields. Shopping around can save you money or get better cover for the same premium.

Two good-value companies are Endsleigh Insurance (Cheltenham Spa, Glos GL50 3NR; 0242 258258) and Columbus Travel Insurance (17 Devonshire Square, London EC2M 4SQ; 071-375 0011). If you stay longer than expected, you can buy a new policy from any insurance broker in the USA or Canada, but note that these policies do not cover the cost repatriation to your home country. You can also insure yourself as required for risky activities such as skiing for which a more expensive policy covering dangerous sports is required.

Protection against claims for negligence could prove to be as valuable as health insurance. For instance, if you cross a road without looking and cause a driver to swerve, the owners of the dog that subsequently gets hit may sue you. They will no doubt claim that you have caused inestimable grief and a court might award huge damages against you. Fortunately, most travel policies cover third party liability of this kind. Note, however, that negligence while driving is not covered (see *Driving: Insurance*).

If you have to claim on your insurance, the golden rule is amass as much documentation as possible to support your application. In particular, compensation is unlikely to be paid for lost baggage or cash unless your claim is accompanied by a police report of the loss.

MONEY

Travellers Cheques. Dollar travellers cheques ('travelers checks') are readily accepted at face value by virtually every enterprise in North America. They are treated as cash, and real dollars and cents are given in change. With a sufficient supply of travellers cheques, it is possible to avoid banks completely. Travellers cheques are much more useful than sterling cash, since many small banks may lack facilities for changing sterling on the spot. The normal charge for travellers cheques is face value plus 1%, in addition to the currency exchange commission for changing sterling to dollars.

The easy acceptance of travellers cheques applies only if you have them in the right currency — Canadian or US dollars as appropriate. Travellers cheques in sterling or other currencies can be changed only at *bureaux de change* and big banks.

The most easily negotiable travellers cheques are American Express, MasterCard and Visa. Processing just one $10 American Express travellers cheque entitles you to use their customer mail service (addresses for mail collection given in regional chapters). They are sold by Lloyd's Bank and the Royal Bank of Scotland in Britain. Visa cheques are issued by Barclay's, the Co-op, Yorkshire and the TSB. Midland Bank and Thomas Cook issue MasterCard cheques.

Carry your passport as ID when paying for goods or services with travellers cheques, though you'll hardly ever be asked for it. Low denomination cheques (ideally $10) are more welcome than high ones, especially if you are buying an inexpensive item. Don't be put off by the signs in shops, gas stations and restaurants saying 'No Checks' this usually refers only to personal cheques.

Keep a separate note of the cheques you have, and where and when the last was cashed. Note the toll-free phone number provided with the cheques so that you can claim a refund quickly and easily. This usually involves a trip to the nearest branch of the issuing bank or travel agent; some also have emergency arrangements with hotels and car rental outlets to give you $200 to tide you over until the next working day. American Express normally issues replacement travellers cheques as soon as you have completed a detailed form at one of its offices, and can even have replacements sent by courier to you. But if you don't have the numbers of the cheques (or you have a less well-known brand), the process can take several days. There is no charge for replacing lost or stolen travellers cheques.

Cheques. A British cheque book will be virtually useless. Unless you have a charge card like American Express or Diners Club which allows you to cash cheques against it, leave your cheque book safely at home. Details of how to open a bank account in North America are given under *Money* in the USA and Canada sections.

Credit and Charge Cards. A reasonably civilised life in North America is impossible without a credit or charge card. You can use one to pay for goods and services almost anywhere whether a campground in Colorado or a phone call in Phoenix. More importantly, a card is the accepted guarantee of your financial reliability when hiring cars, booking rooms or clearing immigration. A visitor to the USA without a plastic card will not have an easy time.

Credit cards allow you to pay off the debt over a long period of time at a high rate of interest. The two main brands are MasterCard, known as Access in the UK, and Visa. Charge cards are issued by American Express and Diners Club. These companies impose a joining fee plus an annual subscription, and let you spend up to a discretionary limit which is not pre-set, as long as you pay it off in full each month.

Ask the credit card issuer to increase your credit limit before you leave for North America. Even if you think you can keep your spending under control, hotels and car rental companies often 'block out' hundreds of dollars of your account temporarily, in case you fail to pay your bill or steal the car. These amounts do not appear on your statement, but while your spending may be well inside the limit, you could find that your card is rejected the next time you try to use it.

It is therefore worth carrying at least two credit/charge cards, which also helps on the odd occasion when one or other of the main cards is not accepted. When buying fuel, be prepared to pay with cash or travellers cheques. Oil companies issue their own credit cards (which are difficult for temporary visitors to obtain) and most gas stations do not accept other cards.

When you use a card, don't be alarmed if you have to wait while the number is checked with the issuing company; checks for stolen or abused cards are much more frequent than in Britain. You may well be asked for supporting ID and for your address and telephone number. You might also be given the carbons from the credit card voucher, since a favourite scam among American villains is to use them to make counterfeit cards bearing your name and number. Keep all sales vouchers until you return home, since it is not unknown for unscrupulous traders to add an extra digit or two to their copies. Also, keep a separate record of the numbers of your cards and the emergency telephone line to call in case of loss or theft. Report any loss to the local police and immediately call the card company toll-free or collect.

EMERGENCY NUMBERS TO REPORT LOST OR STOLEN CREDIT CARDS

Access/MasterCard 1-800-826-2181 Diners Club 1-800-525-9135
American Express 1-800-528-2121 Visa 1-800-336-8472

You can use British credit cards to draw cash at most cash machines, banks or *bureaux de change* displaying the appropriate Visa or MasterCard symbol.

Emergency Cash. Running out of cash, travellers of cheques and available credit need not spell disaster. British Consulates can cash a personal cheques for up to £50 in an emergency, though they do so reluctantly. You can only do this once. If you can survive for a week or two, persuade a relative or friend to send you an International Money Order (IMO) in sterling or dollars, which costs around £5. Your friend then sends the IMO through the post. If you have funds in your bank account, you can cable the bank to telegraph cash to a specified North American bank. Choosing a bank associated with your own in Britain will save time but even so you must allow 48 hours in major cities and longer in the depths of North Dakota or Nova Scotia. If weekends or public holidays intrude, you may have to wait a week. If you have a refundable airline ticket, you could cash it in to sustain yourself until help arrives, and then buy another.

If you are near a branch of Thomas Cook (principal addresses in regional chapters) you can arrange for a telegraphic transfer from a Thomas Cook branch office in Britain via New York or Toronto. This takes 24-48 hours and costs approximately £25. If there is no real urgency, Thomas Cook can send a banker's draft in American or Canadian currency. This goes by ordinary airmail post (about seven days), costs around £10 and must be paid into a bank account in the USA or Canada.

Provided you have an interesting story to tell, you might approach a local small-town newspaper. If they print it, they might slant it in the form of a request for assistance. Soft-hearted North Americans will respond with cash and invitations.

The information under *Work* could suggest a solution to cash flow crisis. But, as a last resort, your government will get you home. Once their efforts to find someone to pay your fare have failed, then they will reluctantly put you on a plane. Your passport will be impounded upon your arrival, and will not be returned until you have paid the authorities for the flight plus handling charge.

PLANNING AHEAD

This book should give you some good ideas about where to go, how to travel and so on. But you can supplement this with information on specific interests — from American football to zoology — by contacting US or Canadian tourist offices before you go. Their London addresses are:

USTTA   Canada House
PO Box 1EN   Trafalgar Square
London W1R 1EN   London SW1Y 5BJ
071-495 4466   071-629 9492

They can also help with comprehensive lists of accommodation, details of available tours, etc., allowing you to plan some or all of your itinery. You might also want to contact state or province tourism authorities; addresses for the USA are shown on page 119, for Canada on page 408. In addition, members of motoring organisations should ask for free information on driving and services provided by affiliated organisations in North America.

The best unlimited travel deals by air and bus are available only to people who book and pay for them abroad. Look under *Getting Around* for each country to see the offers available and details of how to book.

Phoning Ahead. You can find most numbers in the USA and Canada from Britain by dialling international directory enquiries on 153. To call a number in North America from Britain, dial 0101 followed by the area code (for New York 212, for Toronto 416, etc.) and then the number. So to call the British Embassy in Washington (code 202) you dial 010-202-462-1340. Time zones and charges from the UK through BT International are as follows:

cheap (55p per minute):   8pm-8am UK time, and all weekend
peak (65p per minute):   3pm-5pm Monday-Friday
standard (60p per minute):   all other times.

Mercury charges significantly less: 37p, 53p and 49.5p respectively, so if you plan to make a lot of international calls it is well worth getting a Mercury account; call 0500 194 from the UK for details.

If you wish to make a collect (reverse-charge) call to the USA you can dial straight through from the UK to the American operator on one of several numbers, according to the long-distance carrier used:

AT&T 0800 89 0011   MCI 0800 89 0222
Sprint 0800 89 0877   Phone USA 0800 89 0456

The cheapest is MCI, through which a three-minute collect call costs around $8.25.

For Canada, the only choice at present is Canada Direct on 0800 89 0016.

Before ringing relations to announce your arrival, or calling a hotel to make a booking, estimate what the time is at your destination; see *Times*, below.

Travellers' Clubs. If you lack friends and relations in America, you might consider joining an organisation which arranges hospitality exchanges. For example members of the Globetrotters Club (BCM/Roving, London WC1N 3XX) can request a list of members in the USA, Canada and other countries who have expressed a willingness to provide hospitality to other globetrotters. Membership costs £12 (£9 for subsequent years) and the list of members costs £1.

Servas International is an organization begun by an American Quaker which runs a worldwide programme of free hospitality exchanges for travellers, to help the cause of peace and international understanding. To become a Servas traveller, it is necessary to be vetted by a member (to weed out freeloaders) and to pay a joining fee of about £10/$15. If you are interested, contact Servas at PO Box 885, London W13 9TH (tel: 081-352 0303) or, in the USA, at Room 406, 11 John St, New York, NY 10038.

Handicapped Travellers. Before your flight to North America you may wish to consult *Care in the Air,* a free booklet published by the Air Transport Users Committee, Kingsway House, 103 Kingsway, London, WC2B 6QX (071-242 3882); and a UK airports obtainable free from BAA, 130 Wilton Road, London SW1V 1LQ (tel: 071-834 9449). Every airline gives free assistance to handicapped travellers, and will provide a wheelchair at 24 hours notice. Some airlines, including British Airways, require a medical certificate of fitness to travel.

The Royal Society for Disability and Rehabilitation has a holidays officer who can provide specialist advice. Write to RADAR at 25 Mortimer Street, London W1N 8AB, or call 071-637 5400. Mobility International exists to promote integration through international travel and exchange; its UK office is at 228 Borough High St, London SE1 1JX (tel 071-403 5688; fax 071-378 1292). See *Help and Information* in the introduction to the USA and Canada for details of similar organisations at your destination.

WHAT TO TAKE

Maps. Free maps issued by the USTTA and Canada House are sufficient to locate most towns and establish the distance between them. Good state maps can be requested from Exxon Touring Service (1251 Avenue of the Americas, New York, NY 10020) or from the state tourism offices (addresses in *Help and Information*). If you plan to drive, see the section on Routes and Maps in the *Driving* chapter. For a larger selection of specific city and regional maps, visit Edward Stanford Ltd, 12-14 Long Acre, London WC2E 9LP (tel: 071-836 1321). The Map Shop, 15 High St, Upton-on-Severn, Worcestershire WR8 0HJ (tel 0684 593146) is agent for the North American survey authorities. It has large numbers of maps in stock, especially of National Parks, plus maps and atlases for individual states and provinces.

Electrical Items. If you're taking an electric razor, hair dryer or anything else electrical you'll need a plug adaptor and possibly a voltage transformer. The standard North American mains plug has two pins (live and neutral) plus an optional third (earth). Buy a suitable adaptor before leaving, since convertors which accept British three-pin plugs are difficult to find in North America. If the appliance does not have a voltage selector, you'll also need a transformer to step up the American 110 volts supply to operate 240 volt equipment.

Medications. Contraceptve pills are the only prescription drugs you can carry through customs without problems. Other prescribed drugs should be accompanied by a doctor's letter explaining why you need them. Take a good supply: drug prescriptions are expensive in North America and many insurance policies will not meet the cost of medication for pre-existing conditions.

Do not take any non-prescribed drugs stronger than Asprin or Alka-Seltzer, and then only in the original packs. Customs officers are highly sensitive about drugs of all kinds. Some of which can be bought over the counter in Britain (such as certain cough mixtures, any headache remedy containing codeine, and kaolin and morphine) are available only on prescription in the USA and Canada.

Other Necessities. If you want to keep in touch with the goings-on in the rest of the world, take a short-wave radio. The BBC World Service broadcasts on various frequencies to North America, predominantly in the 49 metre band. For programme information, contact World Service Publicity, PO Box 76, Bush House, Strand, London WC2B 4PH (tel: 071-257 2211).

Literary travellers should take plenty of reading matter with them. Although there are thousands of bookshops selling millions of books, it sometimes hard to find any English novel older than a year or two. So whether your tastes are for Iris Murdoch or Georgette Heyer, don't expect to find their complete works wherever you go.

What Not To Take. Leave your jewels and flashy clothes at home; they will only attract unwelcome attention from street criminals.

GETTING THERE

Air. A dozen scheduled airlines, and numerous charter carriers, operate non-stop flights from Britain to 30 North American cities. Dozens of wide-bodied jets — plus a couple of Concordes — fly between Britain and North America every day. Most of these operate from London's two main airports, Heathrow and Gatwick, but you can also fly direct from Birmingham and Glasgow to New York, and from Manchester to New York, Los Angeles, Chicago and Atlanta. Competition is fiercest — and fares lowest — on the main routes between London and New York, Miami and Los Angeles. Fares range from around £200 for a low season return flight to the East Coast, to £4,000 for the supersonic trip to Washington and back.

Finding the best-value ticket requires some research or the services of a reliable discount travel agent. Fares and conditions change constantly, but at the start of 1993 the following advice was correct. Start by checking official fares and conditions with the main airlines direct:

Air Canada 081-759 2636	TWA 071-439 0707
American Airlines 0800 010 151	United Airlines 0800 888 555
British Airways 0345 222 111	USAir 0800 777 333
Delta 0800 414 767	Virgin Atlantic 0345 747 747
Northwest 0345 747 800	

Cheap return fares bought direct are almost always subject to advance booking requirements of 14 or 21 days. If you fail to travel on your booked flight, you lose your money, and changes to your itinerary are either impossible or very expensive. Most operators allow open-jaw returns, where you fly out to one city and return from another. These are generally permitted only within the USA or within Canada: you can't fly out to San Francisco and back from Vancouver on a cheap ticket.

During the peak season (usually June to September plus the Christmas period) you will be hard-pressed to find anything to the East Coast USA or Montréal/Toronto at below these official rates. At other times of the year, most aircraft fly with empty seats and the airlines periodically compete to fill these seats at almost any price. In November 1992, two people could fly to Los Angeles and back for £155 each on Air New Zealand, probably the lowest long-haul air fare ever sold.

Until the present recession ends, airlines will be falling over each other to attract passengers. Most sell cut-price fares through agents. The following specialize in cheap return flights to North America: Major Travel (071-485 7707), Slade Travel (081 202 0111) and Unijet (0444 458611). Most tour operators have special deals such as car hire for a nominal $1 per week. Take this into account when choosing the best bargain. If you intend to travel to the West Coast and Hawaii, a round-the-world ticket might suit you better; prices start at around £700 from the discount travel agencies which advertise in *Time Out, The Times, The Guardian* and *The Independent*.

Airport Tax. Departure taxes from Britain and Canada are included in the fare you pay. Tickets to and from the United States are subject to all sorts of taxes, such as a $10 Federal Inspection Fee, a $5 Customs User Fee and a $3 Passenger Service Fee. The actual tax levied varies from one airline to another, so be sure to include these in your calculations.

Baggage. All transatlantic airlines allow two pieces of luggage to be checked in for free, as long as the dimensions of the larger (length plus breadth plus width) do not exceed 65 inches, and those of the smaller, 55 inches. You can load these with lead weights if you wish withour having to pay excess baggage; the usual charge is £50 for each additional case.

It is quite feasible to take your own bicycle to and around the USA. Airlines will accept bikes as checked baggage provided they are boxed (with pedals removed and handlebars placed at right-angles) and the tyres deflated to avoid mid-air explosions.

Schedules. Transatlantic flights from Britain depart between 10am and 7pm and arrive in North America in the afternoon or evening (apart from Concorde, when you arrive an hour or two before you set off). If you are taking an onward flight, clearly the earlier you arrive the better, to avoid expensive overnight stays en route.

On the return journey, all but a handful of flights depart in the afternoon or evening from North America and arrive in Europe the following morning.

Air Courier Flights. Acting as an air courier is not the bargain it was a decade ago, when you could fly on Concorde for £150 return. It can still allow you to make useful savings, however. Express delivery companies use casual couriers to provide a fast service at low cost. The best way to send urgent documents is as accompanied baggage on a scheduled flight. As personal luggage, the consignment can be checked in at the last moment, and whisked through customs with a minimum of fuss at the destination. This requires a fare-paying passenger to be on board the flight. Delivery companies do not recruit casual couriers direct. British Airways' Speedbird Express operation uses BA flights, but the airline does not advertise its courier fares. Instead, seats are sold through a specialist agency such as CTS (071-351 0300) and Polo Express (081-759 5383). Bookings are taken up to three months in advance, and early booking is essential for the most popular destinations.

The range of routes is restricted to the big US and Canadian cities such as New York, Chicago, Miami, Los Angeles and Toronto. The dates of both the outward and return sectors are fixed (a condition also applied to most ordinary cheap tickets). The courier's ticket appears only at the airport, which may mean you are excluded from cheap flights in your destination country; Visit USA fares, for example, give 30% off but only if you produce your transatlantic ticket a week ahead.

The flight itself is not without its problems. You must check in at least two hours in advance, and look reasonably smart — no jeans or training shoes. There may be a fair amount of hanging around at the far end, waiting for customs officials to compare the manifest with the cargo. And if your idea of a long-haul flight is a seven-hour drinking binge, you're in the wrong job: couriers undertake that they 'will not consume excess alcohol in flight'.

Sea. If economy is not essential, you might consider a sea voyage to North America. Cunard's *Queen Elizabeth II* plies between Southampton and New York about a dozen times a year taking five days. You are entitled to take a great deal of luggage free of charge on board, which can be an advantage for emigrants. It is also possible to book a berth on a freighter, though these are usually not much cheaper than luxury liners. For further information, you might refer to *Freighter Travel News* (1745 Scotch Avenue SE, Salem, OR 97309) or *Ford's Freighter Travel Guide* (22151 Clarendon Street, Woodland Hills, CA 91365).

Getting Back. Classified advertisements in local newspapers in the USA and Canada often quote 'bargain' flights from North America to Britain. Unfortunately most of these are heavily restricted, or available for round-trip travel only. The most reliable and efficient discount travel agents are those operated primarily for students, but which also offer good deals for normal people. In the USA, contact a branch of Council Travel (or its sister company Council Charter) or the Student Travel Network — STN. Within Canada, Travel CUTS has offices in most major cities.

TIME

Travelling across North America can be chronologically confusing. The continent straddles eight and a half time zones, which means 7.30pm in Newfoundland is only noon in the Aleutian Islands of Alaska. Most of the continent is divided into five zones; the maps of the USA and Canada show where the boundaries lie. Atlantic Standard Time is four hours behind GMT; Eastern five hours behind; Central six hours; Mountain seven hours; and Pacific eight hours. Noon in London is 8am in Nova Scotia, 7am in New York and Montréal, 6am in Chicago and Winnipeg, 5am in Denver and Calgary, 4am in Los Angeles and Vancouver. Bear in mind time zones not just from abroad, but also when calling within North America. You might be wide awake in Miami at 9am, but your friend in San Francisco may not be delighted to hear from you at 6am her time.

Travelling west across North America you gain time, so a coast-to-coast flight appears to take only three hours. The day is squeezed when you go east, so a transcontinental flight will take all day.

The USA has stubbornly opposed the 24-hour clock. In schedules, times printed in normal type are before noon, while those in **bold** are after noon. The usual way to ask the time is to enquire 'what time do you have?'. Do not answer 'well, my doctor's given me six months'. Furthermore, North Americans say 'before' and 'after' rather than 'to' and 'past'. So 1.10 is ten after one, while 1.50 is ten before two.

U.S.A.

THE PEOPLE

African-American	black American
buppie	black urban professional (see yuppy)
Canuck	Canadian
GLC	Gay and Lesbian Community
GOP	Republican Party (Grand Old Party)
hick	country bumpkin
honky	black term for a white man
hop	a dance
horsebag	derogatory term, usually (but not always) applied to women
jap	Jewish American Princess; any rich spoiled girl
klutz	a physically or socially inept person
limey	Englishman (comparable in tone to Yank)
Mister Charlie	black term for white man
Native American	American Indian
ofay	poor farmer (originally referred to Oklahomans who fled the dust bowl during the Depression
redneck	ignorant yokel, often violently right wing, prevalent in the South
school	university or college what British people understand as a 'school' is usually called a High School.
WASP	White Anglo Saxon Protestant
Yankee	usually a New Englander, but to Southerners, all Northerners
yuppie	young urban professional, who frequents single bars and psycho-analysts

At the last official count there were 245,110,000 Americans. You will be relieved to discover that not all American men dress in loud checks nor do they all have blue-rinsed wives who nag them to hurry and take a photo or gush all over the antiquity of 1920's architecture. On their home territory they can be the most open, generous, uncomplaining and relaxed people you could hope to meet, not to mention well-dressed and polite. The average American is reckoned to be a 32-year-old Protestant white woman, married with children.

Like every nationality, the people of the USA have their egocentricities. They take great pride in living in the richest country in the world with its much vaunted belief in freedom, democracy and justice. This sometimes blinds them to the abject poverty in which some of their fellow citizens live, and also to the dark side of American foreign policy. Of course there are many informed, well-balanced Americans with a keen interest in all things foreign, including you. But there is a certain narrow-mindedness which can be irritating and amusing by turns. Partly this is because relatively few Americans travel abroad, and many US citizens have a shaky grasp of the geography of the rest of the world; don't be unduly suprised to be asked 'what is the capital of London?'.

Some young people really do seem to exist on a diet of soft drinks and fast foods while shuttling between divorced parents who bicker over the orthodontist's bill (you will see many sets of metal braces called 'railroad tracks' in place of teeth). Thrusting young professionals exude self-confidence by day and consult psychoanalysts by night. The middle-aged and the elderly are kept busy by regular visits to plastic surgeons. Everybody seems to judge you (and each other) in terms of material wealth.

Americans seem more conformist than Europeans, perhaps because of the power of the media and advertising. But plenty of folks don't conform to these or any other norms. And while the stereotypes presented by television of Wall Street wheeler-dealers, Miami police and Chicago hustlers do exist, there are areas in the States just as remote as places in northern Scotland; where small villages have only a post office and gas station; where farmers are like farmers everywhere and where people work and go home to their family and friends; where crime is virtually unknown or treated with horror and shock.

ETHNIC BACKGROUND

The USA is the most cosmopolitan country in the world. Every shade of skin, each of the earth's 200-plus nationalities and scores of the world's languages are represented. But the nation is not quite the melting pot it might seem; although most citizens take pride in being American — they will describe themselves as Irish-American, Polish-American, Korean-American — there is not much large scale intermixing between racial groups. The neighbourhoods of every city are often delineated along ethnic lines, more so than in Britain. There is a clear racial heirarchy in terms of material wealth: the White Anglo-Saxon Protestants (WASPs) are at the top, followed by the descendants of other immigrants from Europe, then Asians and finally blacks and Hispanics (Spanish-speaking Americans) competing for last place. The number of Hispanics (including large numbers of naturalized Americans from Mexico known as Chicanos, and political refugees from Latin America) has risen steadily to 25 million. With high birth-rates among Spanish-speaking people in the USA, they could soon surpass blacks (currently numbering 27 million), and become the largest minority.

Racial sensitivity frequently surfaces, though rarely as viciously as during the Los Angeles riots of 1992. Racism can manifest itself as a casual racist comment made someone of your own race. Or you may witness iinterracial attacks (either verbal or physical) on the streets. Even among people who appear to be tolerant, you need to tread warily to avoid inflaming concealed prejudices.

Jewish people play a significant role in the ethnic composition of America, particularly in and around New York. Numbering around six million (more than in Israel), they exert a political, business, intellectual and artistic influence disproportionate to their numbers. Despite the valuable contribution made by Jewish people to American culture, there is still a strong streak of anti-Semitism running right through American society.

Native Americans. The first humans to reach what is now the USA are thought to have crossed over the Bering Strait from Asia many thousands of years before Europeans reached America, and wandered down settling the continent. Some tribes, such as the Sioux, settled in teepees on the plains of the Midwest. The Navajo, Ute and others chose to dwell in the caves of the Rockies and the west. As soon as the white man arrived, the native peoples (erroneously described as 'Indians') were successively invaded, murdered, killed off by epidemics and sequestered. At the end of the 19th century, the comparatively few survivors were dispossessed of their remaining land and shunted off to reservations designated by the federal government in desert and mountain regions. Although over half the states of the Union have Indian names (MiciZibi = 'great river', Iowa = 'one who puts to sleep'), Native Americans were not made US citizens until 1924.

Gradually the condition of the original inhabitants is improving. Having Native American blood is now a matter of considerable pride, and the first Native American congressman took his seat in Washington in 1993. In recent years, Native Americans have been politically active in securing land, money and official encouragement in their struggle to maintain their culture. Their traditional handicrafts are held in great esteem and marketed more fairly than they once were. the rest of America has become aware of the plight as the profile has increased.

Inevitably, traditional ways have been altered by contact with the 20th century. Most travel in pick-up trucks rather than on horseback, and live in houses or tar-paper shacks not wigwams. (Any wigwams you see are likely to be plastic tourist attractions.) All the same, Native American reservations can provide a fascinating insight into the lives of an aboriginal people. Three quarters of a million people still live on reservations. Although reservations are subject to federal law, they are intended to be autonomous communities. When a public highway enters a reservation, there are often signs saying something like 'You are now entering the exclusive Navajo nation, and your entrance constitutes consent to the laws of the Navajo people and the jurisdiction of their court'. In the Midwest, casinos are operated on Native American lands beyond the jurisdiction of anti-gambling laws. There is still one tribe in Florida (the Miccosukee) who have not formally made peace with the United States.

If possible get into the heart of a reservation — although entrance to certain villages is forbidden — and avoid the tourist-orientated periphery. Respect the practices of Native Americans. Do not take photographs or record videos without the permission of the subjects. Some who have absorbed enough of the market ethic will insist on payment for pictures; others will be offended. Behave circumspectly and be especially deferential to the elders. Many Native Americans feel resentment towards white people, and have no intention of compromising their beliefs and rituals for the sake of curious visitors.

MAKING FRIENDS

It is easy to make friends with Americans without resorting to the personal ads or contact phone lines (though these make fascinating entertainment). Most Americans are extremely friendly towards foreigners, and are happy to talk to strangers on trains, buses and in restaurants. Furthermore, they are not an overtly critical people and will accept overtures of friendship at face value. Especially if their own ancestry is British, they will be delighted to befriend people from the UK, perhaps because they regret the lack of history in their own culture.

So even if you don't start your trip with a list of friends, acquaintances and distant relations to visit, you'll soon meet the locals in the usual places — youth hostels, bars, national parks, etc. Sooner or later you will be invited into an American home. Try to be punctual, polite and full of praise for the United States. Although many Americans have a hearty sense of humour, they seldom direct it at themselves or their country.

Don't be suprised if you are continually addressed as 'sir' or 'ma'am', since Americans use these titles indiscriminately. After just one meeting they may greet you with an intimacy which seems to you inappropriate. Relax and enjoy these social differences. Be as outgoing and yet respectful as you can, and they will respond with a generosity second to none.

Sex. The media give the impression that Americans worship sex almost as much as money. Although some observers might place cars or food above both, it is not a great exaggeration to say that a 'meaningful relationship' and, more starkly, sex is of overwhelming importance to many Americans. To others the topic is anathema. Religous fundamentalists devote more energy to attacking pre-marital sex, contraception and homosexuality than any other subjects. Displays of affection between gay people which go unnoticed in New York and San Francisco could get the practioners shot by Southern rednecks.

If the opportunity for casual sex presents itself, you should be aware of some the possible consequences, notably Aids but including the whole spectrum of venereal diseases, most of which are curable if irritating

There are other hazards facing the prospective sexual athlete, notably legal difficulties. The age of consent for both males and females is 18 in some states. Intercourse with someone below the age of consent is known as 'statutory rape' and is not legally distinguished from forcible rape: 80% of men in American prisons for rape are there for statutory rape. There are also laws about transporting minors over state borders so be cautious of picking up adolescent hitch-hikers.

Gay People. Homosexual activity among both men and women is illegal in half the states, but rarely prosecuted. (Even heterosexual sex between people not married to each other is classified as 'unlawful intercourse', although convictions are virtually unknown.) The USA has a more vocal gay and lesbian community ('GLC') than any other country. President Bill Clinton — a hyper-active heterosexual — actively wooed gay people in his race for the White House. At the same election, however, anti-gay rights legislation was passed in Colorado, and only narrowly defeated in Oregon, where a motion described homosexuality as 'abnormal, wrong, unnatural and perverse'.

Gay visitors to the USA should have no trouble making contacts in the cities, and in established gay resorts such as Key West in Florida. Public displays of affection between people of the same sex are accepted in such places, but deplored in the 'redneck' South and Texas.

Prostitution. Paid sex exists as it does everywhere the cheapest variety is provided by sleazy massage parlours and the poorly-paid waitresses and dancers in topless bars. Hookers in the $25-$50 range work dingy hotels, motels and bars in every large city. In the even of a police crackdown (usually preceding a local election), the women suffer rather than their clientele. The customer risks disease and a possible mugging. One notable exception is an area in the state of Nevada, where there are licensed brothels and the staff undergo regular medical examinations.

Language. Americans have certainly done interesting things to the English language. Pedants will have to steel themselves. 'Tonite' is flashed up everywhere, accommodation has inexplicably become a plural, and so on. The energy associated with the American lifestyle seems to be reflected in their love of dynamic verbs ('grab forty winks', 'fire off an application') and of inventing verbs ('to gift', 'to emote'). The best example of this is the New Yorker who elevatored up to his penthouse, to wash and tuxedo before going theatering.

American slang can be a delight. Be sure to commiserate with someone who tells you that he has just 'struck out' (a baseball term meaning failed, often in the context of attracting a partner) and don't disagree when someone says of another that he or she is 'out-to-lunch' (i.e. wierd, inattentive). 'Chill out' means calm down and 'to spin your wheels' is to make no progress. The term 'yuppies' to refer to young urban professionals has spawned many variations: buppies (black urban professionals), guppies (gay), puppies (pregnant).

This book uses British words and spellings except for proper names such as the World Trade *Center*. To help overcome linguistic difficulties, each chapter in the first part of this book begins with a glossary.

In England, one's speech often identifies one's education and social class, but in America those distinctions are not nearly so obvious. Someone with a PhD in geology from the University of Washington in Seattle will sound very much like the blue-collar worker from the local Boeing aircraft factory. And don't panic if you are not understood right away. Speak slowly and distinctly; the natives are not used to your English either. Perhaps suprisingly, English is the official language in only 16 states. And as the Hispanic population increases, Spanish is becoming more widespread: in New York City, Texas and the Southwest USA, most signs are bilingual. Those who have learned Castilian Spanish in Europe should note that Spanish-speaking Americans have been just as disrespectful to their tongue as have English-speakers.

Listen also for the colourful slang employed by blacks, much of which is impenetrable. There are pockets of interesting dialects across the country such as the Cajun *patois* heard in Louisiana, and Gulla, a dialect spoken by blacks living on the coastal strip in South Carolina and Georgia which contains many West African words. There is also a theory that the American accent is closer to the way Elizabethan was spoken than is the present BBC accent, though of course this is difficult to prove. There is some American vocabulary which was in common or dialect usage in England several centuries ago, but is now archaic. For example Americans talk about 'shucking' peas (i.e. shelling) which is a 17th century English word. Or they talk of a 'whole slew of boats', meaning large numbers, from the Irish 'sluagh'. Cookie was originally a Scottish word for plain bun. Going on a drinking 'jag' (prolonged spree) was an English dialect word.

Religion. Church attendance is much higher in the USA than it is in Britain, and many Americans practise their religion with a fervour uncommon in Europe. One of the first things you may notice is that every hotel and motel room is equipped with a bible, placed there by the Gideon Society, an association of Christian commercial travellers. The 'Moral Majority' (a subspecies of Christian fundamentalists) uses a literal interpration of the Bible to denounce many liberal causes from racial integration to toleration of homosexuality. There are entire television and radio networks funded by private donation which broadcast the message of salvation 24 hours a day. Try to tune in to a televised faith healing or revival meeting. A source of considerable amusement to liberal Americans is the suseptibility of TV evangelists to sex and fraud scandals. Nevertheless viewers continue to send millions of dollars to preachers who use tactics such as the threat of their imminent demise to appeal for funds. A popular satirical postcard reads 'Honey — if God had meant us to be rich, He would have made us TV evangelists'.

Of course, there are many other influential religions. The Roman Catholic Church claims a membership of over 50 million. Much smaller in number but also influential (especially in Utah) is the Church of Latter Day Saints, better known as the Mormons, who derive their teachings from one Joseph Smith who had visions of the Angel Moroni in New York early in the nineteenth century. The closest approximation of the Church of England is the Episcopal Church which has around three million members.

Cult religions have suprisingly large and enthusicastic followings, from offbeat meditating sects in California to the Unification Church (Moonies). Since many of these groups have energetic recruitment policies, be wary of offers of meals and accommodation or the chance of having a personality test (this latter is a popular tactic of the Church of Scientology). Whereas it is usually not difficult to brush off religeous pitches in Britain, American zealots are not so easily deterred and you can soon become embroiled in an unpleasant contest of wills. On the other hand, Hare Krishna have free vegetarian restarants and take-away temples in most large cities, where you find delicious food in exchange for enduring half-hearted attempts to convert you.

If you wish to attend a church service, enquire at the local tourist office or consult the Yellow Pages.

Politics. The political system of the American democratic republic is highly complex and quite unlike Britain's consitutional monarchy or Canada's parliamentary democracy. Federal, state and local officials from US President to district Sanitation chiefs are all democratically elected.

The two main parties — the Republicans (officially called the Grand Old Party or GOP) and the Democratic Party — have dominated American politics for many decades, despite incusions made by candidates such as H Ross Perot, who took one-fifth of the vote in the 1992 presidential election. As you might expect from the party that produced Ronald Reagan and George Bush the Republican Party is fairly right wing. The Democrats have become considerably less radical, and President Clinton and his deputy Al Gore have retreated from traditional Democrat social policies; both men favour capital punishment, for example.

The federal legislature of the United States of America is Congress, and is composed of the Senate with 100 Senators (two per state) and the House of Representatives with 435 members. Every leap year there is a Presidential election, preceded by an interminably long campaign. The first stage is a series of primary elections during which party supporters vote for their favourite presidential candidate. One interesting feature of primaries — which applies equally to local representatives as much as Presidential hopefuls — is that the candidates spend a great deal of time slagging each other off, in a spectacle of internecine fighting which focusses on the rivals' negative points. This stage over, the party is expected immediately to patch up its differences and start working together against the opposing party.

The choice of presidential candidate is sealed at the two party conventions in summer, which are huge, colourful and expensive media events. After nearly a year of campaigning, the President is elected in November and formally inaugurated in January. Instead of electing the President and Vice President directly, the voters of the USA vote 535 non-office-holding people to make up the Electoral College which in turn elects the President and Vice President. A great deal of razzamatazz surrounds the election of politicians and politics seems increasingly to be just a branch of showbusiness.

Be sensitive when discussing politics, since the range of views is much more limited in the USA. Socialism, for example, just does not feature on the American political landscape except for a lone Vermont congessman who actually resembles a liberal democrat rather more than a real socialist. Any viewpoint which might be construed as anti-American is best kept to yourself unless you really want a heated argument. Radical politics do exist, but tend to be issue-based: political action commitees — PACs — exist for all sorts of causes, and lobby prospective politicians intensively.

'Political correctness' is a buzzword in American society, meaning never to behave in a sexist or racist manner. Critics of the phenomenon complain that normal human emotions are being stifled. As far as travellers are concerned, it is of course only good manners to fit in with the social customs of your hosts.

CLIMATE

America specializes in extremes, and this applies to climate as much as to other aspects of life. You can call the American Express weather line on 1-900-WEATHER and find out the forecast for Death Valley, Disneyland or the Moon. This costs $1 a minute; more cheaply, you can call the local numbers mentioned in the text or just watch mainstream television or listen to radio for about five minutes. Americans are obsessed with the weather. Air quality is also important, and you can expect to find out more than you want to about various pollutants.

IMMIGRATION

Lots of people want to live and work in the USA. Much of the country's bureaucracy, it seems, is devoted to stemming the flood of illegal immigrants. This process impinges upon the smooth passage of *bona fide* visitors.

For details of visas and visa-waivers, see page 11. If you arrive by public transport — air, sea, bus or train — you should be given an Arrival/Departure record card (called an 'I-94') and Customs declaration form to fill in before you arrive. If you drive or walk across an international border, you'll be asked to fill them in at the frontier. Try not to make any mistakes on the forms, and complete them only in blue or black ink: otherwise the officials will make you rewrite them. If you don't have a definite address in the USA, choose a hotel or hostel from this book rather than leaving the section blank.

The US authorities have instituted a system of 'pre-clearance' when travelling from some foreign airports: visitors arriving direct from some points in Canada and the UK proceed through immigration before take-off. This avoids the lengthy queues for immigration at most American airports.

The procedure is the same whether or not you enjoy pre-clearance. Hand the officer your forms with your valid passport, plus an old passport if it contains an unexpired American visa. Have ready any documents which you think may prove your status as a desirable alien, and be as polite as possible. It may be that they simply ask you: 'What is your job, Sir/Madam?' 'Accountant'. 'Do you enjoy it?' 'Yes'. Stamp. However, if they suspect you of trying to work illegally or to undermine the American Way of Life, or they simply don't like your face, the questioning will be more aggressive. Sadly, the chances of getting through easily are improved if you happen to be white, English-speaking and smartly-dressed. But short of changing your wardrobe or skin colour, it makes sense to have as much in your favour as possible. In descending order of effectiveness, this means having:

— an onward or return air ticket, essential for those entering under the visa waiver scheme.

— an official-looking letter from someone in your home country explaining why you will have to return home after a designated period

— travellers cheques (a wad of low denomination cheques looks more impressive than a few of higher value). Immigration officers will be looking for at least $200 for every week of the requested stay. It helps to flash a few credit cards. If necessary, you can buy travellers cheques up to your credit limit on credit card and then send the money home to pay off the loan as soon as you're through

— an invitation from an American citizen accepting full responsibility for your keep. Again, this should look as official as possible. (If he has reason to doubt you, the officer won't hesitate to telephone this person at any time of day or night)

— a large amount of American dollars or foreign currency (pounds not pesos)

Do not underestimate the thoroughness of immigration officials if they suspect you intend to work illegally. They will go through all your possessions, and discovering a *curriculum vitae* will lead them to assume you're looking for a job.

Assuming they admit you, one copy of the Arrival/Departure card will be stapled to your passport. The passport itself will be stamped, and the date to which you are allowed to remain in the USA written in. If you've done well, you will get six months; if the officer has admitted you grudgingly, you may get much less. This is entirely at the discretion of the immigration officer.

Overstaying. The chances of arrest for overstaying a week or two are remote, but your non-compliance will probably be noticed when you leave, and be noted on your file should you ever wish to return.

The alternative is to request a visa extension before your allotted time expires, which you may do at any office of the US Immigration and Naturalization Service. Look in the telephone directory to find the nearest, and phone first to check the opening hours. Take along all the evidence you can amass to justify your claim. They will probably assume that you are working illegally, so adequate proof of your means of support is essential. Taking along a US citizen who will vouch for you is recommended. Get an 'Application for Issuance or Extension of Permit to Re-enter the USA'. It may be sufficient to say simply that you want to continue your travels. Or it might be safer to invent a plausible excuse such as your parents are joining you so you wish to extend your stay. If you apply more than once, use a different regional office. Some people have remained in the country for as long as a year.

Departure. The are no passport controls upon leaving the USA. If you are flying out, the check-in clerk will remove the Departure card from your passport. Travellers who cross by land into Canada should surrender the card to the Canadian border officials; leaving for Mexico, hand it in at the US side of the frontier.

CUSTOMS

After surviving immigration and collecting your luggage, hand in your completed Customs declaration form to the inspector and hope that he will be content with this. There is no need to declare gifts whose total value does not exceed $400. The inspectors are naturally more concerned with rich returning Americans than with modest-looking British travellers. In addition to questions about the value of what you are bringing in, you will be asked whether you have any fresh foods (if you say yes, they'll probably confiscate them) and whether your footwear have been on a farm in the previous month (ditto). Do not be over-scrupulous in answering such questions.

Some airports have a 'red' and 'green' channel system, as in Europe. If you have goods to declare, go through the red channel and discuss terms with the officer; payment may be made in cash or by credit card.

Alcohol and Tobacco. Travellers who have been out of the USA for over 48 hours and have not imported goods duty free in the previous 30 days can bring in 200 cigarettes and 100 cigars (not Cuban, unless you bought them in Cuba). These may, however, be subject to a few cents state tax on each pack. Visitors over 21 may import one litre (34 fl oz, slightly more than the US quart) of any alcoholic drink, unless this is prohibited in the state you arrive in.

Prohibited Goods. Carol Hallett, Commissioner of the US Customs Service makes its purpose icily clear:

Together we can end the devastating impact of illicit drugs; maintain the integrity of our economy by protecting US products, trademarks and immigration laws;

support a healthy economy by depositing in the national treasury duties levied on foreign goods, and guard our agricultural well-being from contaminated products.

As well as drugs and anything vaguely agricultural, the following are prohibited: liqueur-filled chocolates, obscene publications, video tapes, pirated tapes or books, 'seditious and treasonable material', lottery tickets and anything made by forced labour.

Restricted Goods. The booklet *Know Before You go* is free from the US Customs service (PO Box 7407, Washington, DC 20044) and contains details of items which require a permit, for example guns, goods made in Cuba, North Korea, Vietnam, etc.

Other Goods. If you are seen to have over $400 worth of gifts, you may have to pay 10% duty, however there are discounts depending on the country of origin of your gifts. Under the Generalized System of Preferences, intended to aid the economies of developing countries, you can bring in handicrafts from most developing countries.

Currency. There are no restrictions on the amount of money you may take to or from Britain. If you take more than $10,000 into or out of the USA, you are supposed to declare the fact on a form which is supplied by customs officers at the border.

Returning to Britain. Apart from the culture shock induced by returning from southern California to a wet Monday morning at Gatwick, your biggest problem is likely to be bringing in exotic and expensive purchases. You are only allowed £32 worth of purchases duty free; beyond that you'll pay duty of around 15%. Custom officers in the USA have lists of the serial numbers of valuable items such as cameras with which you can trace the country of sale, so don't be to daring. If you pay duty on expensive purchases, retain the receipt for future use.

The duty-free alcohol limit is paltry in comparison with allowances within the European Community: one litre of spirits or sparkling wine, plus two litres of still wine. The standard size for spirits sold in North American duty free shops is 40 fl oz (1.4 litres). This is technically more than you are allowed, although you are unlikely to encounter problems. Similarly, bringing in three standard bottles (750 ml) of wine will take you marginally over the limit, but most customs officers turn a blind eye. You may also bring back 200 cigarettes or 50 cigars or 250g (9 oz) of tobacco.

A large number of visitors to the USA are not satisfied with a fortnight or a month's holiday. They find the American way of life so addictive that they look for ways of earning money in order to extend their stays and to get to know one place well. Unfortunately, with ever-rising unemployment (7.8% in mid-1992), the American Dream has become a nightmare for many and the authorities do all in their power to stem the tide of aliens looking for work. Even applications for tourist visas require proof of means of support and documentary evidence that the applicant will return home.

Working Visas. The J-1 visa, available to participants of government-authorized Exchange Visitor Programmes (EVP), is a valuable and coveted addition to any passport since it entitles the holder to take legal paid employment. You cannot apply for the J-1 without form IAP-66 and you cannot get form IAP-66 without going through a recognized Exchange Visitor Programme which have sponsoring organizations in the USA.

BUNAC (the British Universities North America Club; 16 Bowling Green Lane, London EC1R 0BD; 071-251 3472) is one of the few organizations which can arrange for large numbers of people to work legitimately in the USA.

BUNAC administers three basic programmes in the USA: one is the 'Work America Programme' which allows full-time university students to do any summer job they are able to find; the second is 'BUNACAMP' which is open to anyone over 19½ interested in working on a summer camp as a counsellor; the third is 'KAMP' (Kitchen & Maintenance Programme) which is open to students who want to work at a summer camp in a catering and maintenance capacity. All participants must join the BUNAC Club (£3), travel on BUNAC flights between June and October and purchase compulsory insurance (about £85). BUNAC runs a loan scheme.

Contacting BUNAC headquarters or your local branch (in most universities) for a brochure setting out the various and potentially confusing procedures as clearly as possible. There is no easy way of circumventing the red tape and accompanying uncertainty though BUNAC is experienced at guiding applicants through the process.

The *Work America Programme* provides over 5,000 places. Once you are accepted on to the Programme and obtain a J-1 visa, you can travel to the place of your choice in the States and look for any job. But the process of collecting the evidence necessary for participation is complicated. The earlier you start (preferably by early April) the better your chances. In addition to the programme fee of £75 and the flight cost (£370), you must submit evidence of full time student status (university or HND) and one of the following:

(i) a definite offer of employment in the USA plus proof that you have purchased $300 in American dollar travellers cheques

(ii) a letter of sponsorship from a responsible American — preferably a relative — who promises in writing to bail you out in a financial emergency, plus supporting funds of $500,

(iii) a vague letter of support from America plus $500 and proof of access to a further $200.

If you choose either of the latter methods you need not worry about finding a job until you arrive in the States and, just like finding jobs in any other country, it is much easier if you present yourself in person to prospective employers. BUNAC participants who go to the USA without a pre-arranged job (40% of the total on the programme) take anything from two days to two weeks to find a job.

Those without obliging friends or relatives residing in the USA must fix up a job ahead of time by writing to prospective employers. Over half of the BUNACers who are successful with this method use BUNAC's own list of jobs made available to Club members early in the year with a later supplement sent upon request. This is a useful listing of employers who know about the programme and who have hired British students before.

To widen your scope, look at an annually revised book called *Summer Jobs USA* published each December in the States by Peterson's Guides (202 Carnegie Center, Princeton, NJ 08543) and distributed in Britain by Vacation Work. Employers indicate whether applications from foreign students are encouraged.

Summer Camps Many American parents send their kids to camp for part of the summer. Thousands of young people are needed to teach them sports and other activities, feed them and prevent them from running riot at these quintessentially American institutions. None of these programmes pays high wages, but after your registration fee of about £50 has been accepted, your return air fare to the States will be paid for you, plus you receive $250-$400 pocket money at the end of the nine-week work period. It is an excellent way to make friends with young Americans who often invite their fellow camp counsellors to their homes after camp is finished.

Two organisations in Britain recruit camp staff on a large scale, both geared largely but not exclusively to students. BUNAC recruits anyone aged between 19 and 35 who is able to satisfy the counsellor requirements. It has a subsidiary programme, called 'KAMP' (which is primarily open to students) for people who prefer to do domestic work in summer camps rather than look after kids. Camp America (37A Queen's Gate, London SW7 5HR; 071-589 3223) accepts applicants who are 18 years and older as camp counsellors, kitchen/maintenance staff or family companions. Camp America offers two other summer programmes: Campower for students who would like to work in the kitchen/maintenance areas at camp and the International Family Companion Programme for applicants aged 18-24 who would like to spend 10 weeks looking after children in American homes (see *Childcare* section below). The pocket money for nine weeks on Campower is $350 and for ten weeks with families is $400.

Another Exchange Visitor Programme which deals exclusively with jobs in summer camps is organized by **Camp Counselors USA (CCUSA)**, 27 Woodside Gardens, Musselburgh, Lothian EH21 7LG; 031-665 5843. It places around 2,000 counsellors from 12 countries including 400 from the UK and a large number from Australia, New Zealand, Eastern Europe, etc.

Childcare and Domestic Work: in recent decades thousands of European nannies and mothers' helps have gone to the States to work, virtually all of them on tourist visas. This situation had long been recognized as unacceptable and eventually the US Government added several au pair placement programmes to its list of Exchange Visitor Programmes. The 'au pair' programmes allow young Europeans with childcare experience to work for an American family for one year on a J-1 visa.

The basic requirements are that you be between 18 and 25, speak English, have Western European nationality, have childcare experience, be a non-smoker and a car driver/learner. In fact many applicants have discovered at interview that childcare experience is interpreted fairly loosely to include babysitting. The majority of candidates are young women though men with relevant experience (e.g. teaching sports at a children's camp) may be placed.

The job entails working 40-45 hours a week (including babysitting) with one and a half days off per week plus one complete weekend off a month. You will have to put down a deposit (normally £300) as a pledge that you won't leave before completing your one-year contract. Successful applicants receive free return flights from one of many European cities, orientations and follow-up. The time lag between applying and flying is usually about 2 months.

The fixed amount of pocket money for au pairs is $100 a week, which is considerably lower than an American nanny would expect, though still a reasonable wage on top of room, board and perks. An additional $300 is paid by the host family to cover the cost of educational courses (up to 4 hours a week). The American Institute for Foreign Study or AIFS (37 Queens Gate, London SW7 5HR) runs the Au Pair in America programme which is by far the largest of the placement organizations, sending over 1,000 participants a year. It has representatives in all the countries of Western Europe and agent/interviewers throughout Britain. The other active au pair Exchange Visitor Programmes are Experiment in International Living (EIL, 'Otesaga', West Malvern Road, Malvern, Worcs WR14 4EN; 0684 562577), AuPairCare (34-36 South St, Lancing, West Sussex BN15 8AG; 0903 755433) and Au Pair USA (36 South State, Suite 3000, Salt Lake City, Utah 84111-1401, USA; 801-943-7788)..

The requirements of the 10-week International Family Companion Programme, also administered by AIFS, are less rigorous. A genuine interest in and positive attitude to children will suffice for this programme. A driving licence is not absolutely essential. Like camp counsellors, family companions get a free flight and then a lump sum payment at the end of the summer of $400. There are about 500 places altogether.

Other Ways to Work Legally. Apart from the J-1 visa available to people on approved EVPs, there are two possible visas to consider. The Q visa, introduced in 1991, is the 'International Cultural Exchange Visa' (affectionately dubbed the 'Disney' visa, since it was introduced partly in response to the Disney organization's lobbying). If you find a job in which it can be argued that you will be providing practical training or sharing the history, culture and traditions of your country with Americans (e.g. nanny, pub barman, chef, Morris dancing teacher), you might be eligible to work legally for up to 15 months. This must be applied for by the prospective employer in the US and approved in advance by an office of the Immigration and Naturalization Service.

The other possibility is the B-1 'Voluntary' visa. Applications must be sponsored by a charitable or religious organization which undertakes not to pay you but may remimburse you for incidental expenses.

In addition, the H-1B 'Temporary Worker' visa is available for 'prearranged professional or highly skilled jobs' for which there are no suitably qualified Americans. All the paperwork is carried out by the American employer. The H-3 'Industrial Trainee' visa is the other possibility. Applicants must indicate in detail the breakdown between classroom and on-the-job time, and why equivalent training is not available in his or her own country. H-visas are rarely relevant to the average traveller.

Internship is the American term for traineeship, providing a chance to get some experience in your career interest as part of your academic course. Several organizations arrange for small numbers of UK students and graduates to undertake internships in the US. Request details of the CIEE Internship Programme from the Council on International Educational Exchange, 33 Seymour Place, London W1, or for business internships from the Mountbatten Internship Programme, 16 Gloucester St, Oxford OX1 2BN. The Central Bureau (Seymour Mews, London W1H 9PE) administers a Career Development Programme and a Hotel & Culintary Exchange for British nationals aged 19-35 who have a suitable background in their field.

The book *Internships* published by Peterson's Guides (address above) lists intern positions which are paid or unpaid, can last for the summer, for a semester (term) or for a year. The book offers general advice (including a section called 'Foreign Applicants for US Internships') and specific listings organized according to field of interest, e.g. Advertising, Museums, Radio, Social Services, Law, etc. This annually revised book is available in the UK from Vacation Work for £15.95.

It is exceedingly difficult to get an immigrant visa or 'green card' (actually it's white) which allows foreigners to live and work in the US as 'resident aliens'. Nearly all the permanent resident visas which are issued each year are given to close relations of American citizens. Money and love are not the only reasons to marry, though this course of action is too drastic for most. If you can find an employer willing to state that no American is qualified to do the job and have $800-$1,000 for legal fees, you might have a chance, though the procedure is desperately slow.

A few Australian and New Zealand students are now permitted to work in the USA under the auspices of the Council of International Educational Exchange in New York (205 E 42nd St, New York, NY 10017). Antipodean participants must be full-time students with a minimum fund of $1,500 and a return ticket to Los Angeles on one of the group flights departing Australia in November or December. The worst restriction is that work can be accepted only between November 1 and March 19, though the organizers in Australia (Student Services Australia, PO Box 399, Carlton South, Victoria 3053) are trying to extend the dates so that the period extended until Easter to at least cover the entire ski season. The cost of registration is $180.

Casual Work. In 1986 a law was passed stipulating that all employers must physically examine documents of prospective employees within three working days, proving that they are either a US citizen or an authorized alien. All US employers are obliged to complete an I-9 form which verifies the employee's right to work. Employers who are discovered by the Immigration and Naturalization Service (INS) to be hiring illegal aliens are subject to huge fines. This has restricted the black market in casual jobs but be no means killed it off, especially outside areas which are favourite INS targets like California. The law is unenforceable in seasonal industries such as fruit growing and resort tourism where it is still not uncommon for more than half of all employees to be illegal. Farmers and restaurateurs have claimed that they would be put out of business if they didn't hire casual workers without permits.

However while the law remains in force, those who are caught working illegally run the risk of being deported and possibly banned from ever obtaining a US visa again.

Harvests: as in Europe, fruit and vegetable harvests across the United States rely on itinerant pickers from the citrus harvests of Florida (October to May especially in Desoto County) to the wheat harvests in the Great Plains (mid May to August). In the southern and eastern states, soft fruits (strawberries, peaches) are harvested in May and June, followed by tobacco in July and August. Apple-picking in September in the north-eastern USA can be lucrative. Any of the leading wine-producing states (California, Washington, Idaho, New York) have opportunities for grape-pickers: the further north the location, the later the harvest. Always enquire locally about possible openings.

Tourism: although some might consider the proliferation of fast food establishments a blight on the land, they are often useful places in which to pick up some extra cash. There is a high turnover of staff, and a methodical series of enquiries along a strip of hamburger and pizza restaurants — especially in a resort town like Myrtle Beach South Carolina, Ocean Beach Maryland, Ann Arbor Michigan, along Cape Cod, or the beaches of Southern California or Florida — should eventually be rewarded. The main disadvantages with this sort of job are erratic or insufficient hours, lack of accommodation and low wages. It is not uncommon to paid a fraction of the minimum hourly wage ($3.35 at the time of going to press) since employers exploit the fact that serving staff receive generous tips.

Ski resorts are also worth investigation over the winter season which lasts from November to April in the high Rockies. Large ski resorts include Vail and Aspen in Colorado, Big Sky Montana, Sun Valley Idaho and Stowe Vermont. Try to show up at least a few weeks before the first customers and ask in all the shops, bars, day care centres and hotels.

Fishing: without some mechanical skills, plenty of physical stamina and a little experience at sea, it is difficult to get a place on one of the West Coast shrimp, salmon or tuna boats. Earnings can be very high — over $1,000 a month — so you may decide it's worth the trouble of visiting the docks (and visiting them often) at Kodiak, Chignik, Petersburg, Ketchikan or Wrangell in Alaska, or Newport and Astoria in Oregon. You can also try at fishing ports along the Gulf of Mexico, though these are not so good a bet due to the competition from Hispanic immigrants.

You have a better chance of finding work in the fish processing plants in any of these towns. Alaska offers the best prospects because of the size of its fishing industry and the relatively low population. Although much of the recruitment is done through Seattle, there are still many last-minute on-the-spot opportunities. Ask at the seafood packing factories well before the seasons begin. Most fishing seasons peak in July and August, though shrimping begins in Kodiak in April when it is easier to land a job.

Parks: the national parks offer a great many seasonal jobs. Hiring is done months in advance by a government agency which take on Americans almost exclusively. The exceptions are in May/June when managers are keen to fill their quotas, and in September when US temporary staff are returning to school. Logging and forestry jobs are hard to get because of high wages and strong unions. You might, however, be able to get a job planting trees between February and April (try Alabama and Missisippi).

Chances are better in theme and amusement parks, which are so popular with Americans. Jobs at commercial attractions throughout the USA range from selling hotdogs at massive amusement parks to dismantling rides for small travelling carnivals. The earlier in the year can you present yourself to the Personnel Director or carnival owner the better, but it is always worth asking about any last-minute openings. Get a list of the local attractions from the tourist information office.

Doing something constructive for the environment might hold out more appeal. Volunteers are recruited in numbers by the American Hiking Society (PO Box 86, North Scituate, Massachusetts 02060) to build and maintain trails, etc. from the Daniel Boone National Forest of Kentucky to Volcanoes National Park in Hawaii. Camping accommodation is arranged and in most cases food and partial travel expenses are provided. There is a registration fee of $25. Other organisations worth contacting for similar programmes are AMS, Box 298, Gorham, New Hampshire 03581, and the Sierra Club Service Trips, 730 Polk St. San Francisco, CA 94109.

Selling: the 'Sales' section of the classified advertisement columns of most big city newspapers is usually larger than any other employment category, and if you are determined and outgoing you should be able to come up with something. Many people find that selling products over the telephone is less intimidating, but it is not potentially as high paying. Most selling jobs will pay on a commission basis so earnings will be unreliable and seldom turnout to be as high as the adverts imply. But your foreign charm may make you a more successful salesperson than you expected. Jobs on icecream vans are advertised nearly as often as encyclopedia-selling jobs, and should not be too difficult to obtain in large cities, assuming you can drive.

Medical Research. This is definitely the desperate end of the job market. For people with a more casual interest in medicine, you can test new drugs as well as donating blood. There are Drug Research Centers in many American cities. It helps if you are either in good health or suffering from a pre-existing condition into which research is being carried out. The amount you get paid depends on the discomfiture of the experiment: for just taking a drug and having you urine monitored, you would not earn nearly so much as having the contents of your stomach examined by naso-gastric intubation.

Opportunities are often advertised in the press; you could also find out about them by calling the hospitals mentioned in this book, since medical students often know about them as sources of funding themselves through college.

auto-teller	cash dispenser
buck	dollar
change purse	purse
check	cheque *or* bill in a restaurant or bar

checking account	current account
dime	ten-cent coin
greenback	dollar
make change	give change
nickel	five-cent coin
penny	cent
purse	handbag
quarter	twenty-five cent coin
savings account	deposit account
sawbuck	ten-dollar bill (slang)
smackers	dollars (slang)
two bits	twenty-five cents (slang)

Coins. 1c (penny), 5c (nickel), 10c (dime), 25c (quarter), 50c (half-dollar), $1. The terms penny, nickel, dime and quarter are not slang words but official names — rather like farthing, florin and crown. However, 'buck' or 'greenback' are pure slang for dollar. All but the penny — which is bronze - are silver in colour. Half-dollar coins are rare. Dollar coins (called 'Susan B. Anthony dollars', after America's first suffragette, whose image is shown on the reverse) are found almost exclusively in change machines and in gambling cities.

The nickel and quarter are similar in size, but the quarter has a serrated edge. Quarters are easily the most useful coins — for telephones, launderettes, coin-operated newspaper vending machines, luggage lockers and exact-change buses — so maintain a supply.

Notes. $1, $2, $5, $10, $20, $50, $100, $1,000, $10,000. Each denomination of note is the same size, exactly the same shade of green and of a broadly similar design. Check notes carefully, and keep denominations as low as possible to reduce the risk and consequences of errors. Notes above $20 may be treated with suspicion, as counterfeiting of high-value notes is commonplace.

BANKS

If you spend travellers cheques like cash, and make use of credit cards and automatic teller machines, you should never need to visit a bank.

Banks are normally open 9am-3pm. Monday-Friday. Many large banks in urban areas stay open later especially on Fridays, and operate for a few hours on Saturdays. At other times, you can change foreign currency only at a few hotels and at the *bureaux de change* in international airports. Be warned that the exchange rates offered at these places are often grossly unfavourable.

Cash Machines. Automatic teller machines (auto-tellers or ATMs) can be found in shopping malls, at airports and the lobby of almost every bank. When the rest of the bank is closed, you may have to insert your card into a slot at the door to the lobby in order to gain entry. As elsewhere in the world cash machines are linked together by computer into several networks, allowing customers of other banks to draw funds; this includes holders of Access and Visa cards who can get cash by keying in their Personal Identification Number (PIN) in machines belonging to the Plus syndicate (for locations of Plus machines, call 1-800-THE-PLUS). The system is not yet functioning perfectly, so, after successfully drawing cash from a machine in one city, your card may be rejected by a similar machine elsewhere. In addition, if your card is damaged or accidentally placed in a magnetic field, it will be unceremoniously rejected by all machines. Therefore do not rely upon this method alone for getting cash.

Drive-In Banks. Various systems are employed to serve those unwilling or unable to leave their vehicles. Sometimes an auto-teller is placed at car window height outside a bank. Or there may be a Heath Robinson network of pneumatic tubes to transfer cheques and cash, with negotiations carried on through microphones and loudspeakers. The most human version involves driving up to a window and conducting transactions face-to-face. Drive-in banks can also be used by cyclists, motorcyclists and even pedestrians.

Opening a Bank Account. The American banking system is disparate and relatively primitive. Most banks have only a few local branches, and there are no nationwide banks with the size and influence of British clearing banks; the nearest contender is the Bank of America. So choosing a bank for your account will probably depend on the enticements offered; interest on current accounts, for example, or free giveaways to new customers.

Opening an account in the USA is quick and easy. You need only pay in a few dollars, show some identification and provide a US mailing address. You may be asked for a reference, although many banks waive this requirement in ceaseless search for new clients. If you have opened a current account (called 'checking account'), you will soon receive a cheque ('check') book and an auto-teller card. Deposit accounts are called 'savings accounts'.

Statements are sent out monthly. You are not allowed to go overdrawn without prior negotiation with the bank; in the USA this is taken more seriously than in Britain, and bouncing cheques should be avoided.

Once you have a cheque book, you might be tempted to use it. Be warned that for any store, gas station or hotel to take a cheque, you must be able to produce two pieces of identification: a credit card, plus something with your photograph on (a passport will do if you don't have an American driving licence). You will be expected to give your home and local addresses, telephone number and even your social security number, and the assistant may circle one letter in the acronym COINS; this stands for Caucasian-Oriental-Indian-Negro-Spanish, and is designed to help the police to identify and trace fraudsters. Not surprisingly, most people prefer to use credit cards.

TIPPING

There is strong tradition of tipping for every service in North America, especially in restaurants and bars. Servers of food and drinks are notoriously underpaid (often below the statutory minimum wage), and it is common knowledge that most rely on tips for their livelihood. So, as a general rule, be as generous as you can, but don't go to the extremes of some Americans who even tip air stewardesses.

Most guidebooks recommend a tip of 15% or even 20% in all situations: taxi drivers, waiters, bartenders and so on. You will have to use your discretion, as Americans do, when deciding if this is excessive. Taxi drivers are usually content with 10% (although they are loath to admit it) and some passengers simply round up the fare to the nearest dollar. Restaurant customers who leave more than 17½% are usually on expenses. If you pay by credit card, often the 'total' box will be left ominously blank; the idea is that you add on the amount you wish to leave as a tip. Most restaurant staff prefer you to leave a cash tip (for tax purposes) so you should fill in the total amount as it appears above.

In bars you need to tread carefully. Often the waiter will present you with the bill ('check') as each round is delivered. You can guarantee that if you don't tip, or at least round up to a convenient amount, you will subsequently receive lousy service. (If you have the audacity to ask for change for a ten dollar not on a bill for $9.50, you are certainly in for a dreary evening). Should you merely be having a couple of beers and standing at the bar, no bartender should take offence if you choose not to tip. If you intend to make a night of it, however, placing a $5 or $10 bill on the bar at the start of the session should ensure good service. To avoid both social embarrassment and spending more than necessary, try to keep an eye on how the other customers are tipping. Many of the establishments we recommend are used to budget travellers, and so are not unaccustomed to people who can not afford to tip.

area code	dialling code
automated attendants	computer-generated telephone operators
busy signal	engaged tone
cable	telegram
call collect	reverse the charges
FedEx	common abbreviation for Federal Express, an overnight delivery company
general delivery	poste restante
letter carrier	postman or woman
long distance	trunk call
night letter	overnight telegram
special delivery	express post
telephone booth	phone/call box
toll-free number	numbers (beginning 1-800) which are free
unlisted number	ex-directory
wire (verb)	to send a telegram
zip code	postal code

TELEPHONES

The average American makes ten phone calls a day — far more than the citizens of any other country. The telephone system is mostly slick and efficient, except when it comes to using a coin-operated payphone to make a long-distance call (see below). In general, however, American phones are a pleasure to use. The traveller also benefits from the fact that almost every organization has a 'toll-free' number, beginning 1-800, which helps to conserve your change. If you ring directory enquiries ('information') you will not hear the riffling of pages, but rather a gentle keyboard tapping which can find the right number — and repeat it to you in a synthesized voice — almost before you've finished spelling the name. When you call a business, the reply is quite likely to be from an answering machine which plays canned music to keep you entertained until a human being comes on the line saying 'Hi, this is Betty Lou, how can I help you?'

Tones. The dial tone is a low-frequency continuous note. You should hear this as soon as you pick up the receiver. The ringing tone is long with pauses. The engaged tone (or 'busy signal') is a repeated short beep, with short pauses in between. The unobtainable tone — a piercing continuous note — is rare; you are more likely to get an electronic operator who offers an alternative number.

Interactive Telephones. The TouchTone system — whereby each key emits a different tone when pressed — is almost universal within North America. Push button phones have buttons bearing the symbol # and * in addition to the ten normal digits. Used in the right combinations, these enable your telephone to perform a variety of amazing tasks, such as calling back an engaged number automatically, or diverting incoming calls to another number. A telephone is no longer a telephone; it's a computer terminal. Some public payphones do actually have a computer keyboard attached, and a port for you to plug in your laptop computer.

You may be called upon (by an electronic voice) to perform a task before achieving the desired aim. for example, calling Amtrak for train information (on 1-800-USA-RAIL) you should press 1 for arrival times and 2 for other information. Interacting with a telephone is no more difficult than operating a cash dispenser. One feature which may confuse the British, is that you may be called upon to press the 'pound' key; in fact, this is the # key.

Numbers. All American telephone numbers take the form (111) 222-3333, where 111 is the area code and 222 is the exchange. These numbers are often replaced by the letters: for instance, the British Airways number is 1-800-AIR-WAYS. This presents no problem, since dials and push buttons are marked with both letters and numbers. Don't mistake the zero button 0 which calls the Operator for the letter O which coincides with the number 6, nor the numeral 1 for I. Note that it is not accepted practice to say 'double-three double-seven'. Americans expect to hear three-three-seven-seven.

Local calls are made by dialling the last seven digits. Calls to numbers within the same area code are not necessarily local: for a definition of 'local', consult the directory to call the operator. Any calls outside this local district are long-distance ('toll calls'). To call a long-distance number with the same area code, dial 1 plus the last seven digits, e.g. 1-222-3333. For long-distance calls to a different area, dial 1 plus the area code plus the seven digit number, e.g. 1-111-222-3333.

The international prefix is 011. This should be followed by the country code (44 for Britain), then the dialling code minus the first zero, then the number. So to call Vacation Work Publications in Oxford, you should dial 011-44-865-241978. For further information on international calls, dial 1-800-874-4000; this call costs nothing.

Coin-operated payphones. Because such a high proportion of Americans have their own telephones, public telephone booths in the US are not as numerous as in Britain, and virtually non-existent on residential streets. But you should be able to locate them downtown street corners, in laundromats, gas stations, bars, restaurants and shopping malls. Airports and bus stations have banks of them. Although most booths have doors (the kind of phone booth used by Superman to change clothes), others are fixed to a post, and enclosed in a clear plastic shell which affords little protection against noise and the elements.

Do not make the mistake of going to a post office to make a call as you would in Europe, since the post office and the various independent telephone companies are absolutely separate. Unfortunately there are no public telephone offices in the US and long-distance calls must be made from an ordinary phone booth.

Because of regional variations in the way payphones work, always read the instructions. For a local call you insert the minimum fee (usually 25c) in nickels, dimes or quarters. This allows a local call, which may or may not be of limited duration. If you don't get a reply, replace the receiver to get your money back. If you are calling the operator, directory enquiries, a 'toll-free' number or an emergency service, the machine will return your money as soon as the call connects.

Long distance numbers can be dialled direct: but you may have to select the telephone company you wish to use. Some payphones have half-a-dozen different possibilities. In general, AT&T is expensive, Sprint is cheap. Before the number is connected a voice (either human or computer-generated) will cut in to tell you the cost for the first three minutes. You should have a large pile of nickels, dimes and quarters handy; the pile will be enormous if you are making an international call. The call will finally be put through after all you money has dropped through, though some people have found that the operator's meter does not tally with the amount that they've put in. If no one answers, replacing the receiver will initiate a flood of loose change. Should you get a reply, then after three minutes the same voice will cut in to advise you the cost for extra minutes. If you continue to speak, the operator will wait until your conversation is finished before ringing you back immediately to ask for more money. They can be extraordinarily persistent, and will not allow you to make any other call from the same payphone until you have settled up. If you don't pay, then the cost will be charged the number you have called. All in all, it is a dismal and difficult business; credit card payphones are a much cheaper and easier proposition.

Credit Card Payphones. An increasing number of payphones accept credit cards, including Access or Visa. You lift the receiver, wipe your card through the electronic reader, and dial. Apart from saving you the bother of amassing coins, you can pay for as little time as one minute (rather than the minimum of three minutes for coin-operated phones). When you credit card statement appears it will show not just the call but also the number dialled; bear this in mind if you're calling someone you shouldn't be, or using someone else's card.

Some ordinary coin-operated payphones are able to process credit card calls; you dial the given number, and read over your card number to a real live operator.

Credit card payphones are fitted aboard some trains and many aircraft. Inflight phones are built into armrests and the wall of the cabin. To release the handset, you insert a credit card and dial in the normal manner for long distance calls. When you replace the receiver at the end of your call the credit card is automatically debited with the charge ($7.50 for the first three minutes, $1.25 for each minute thereafter) before being released. Directory enquiries are free.

Directories. The introductory pages of the phone book contain a wealth of useful information, such as street maps or the local team's baseball fixtures. Directories are made up of the 'white pages' (the regular alphabetical listing), the 'yellow pages' (the trade directory) and the 'blue pages' (a thin section listing government organizations). In large cities, the yellow pages usually constitute a separate volume and may be divided into two sections: Consumer & Household, which contains all the listing an individual might need, and Business & Industrial for commercial enterprises.

Information. The almost universal number for local directory enquiries is 411. To find a non-local number within your area, dial 1-555-1212. For numbers in another area, add the area code, e.g. 1-111-555-1212. If you don't know the area code, just dial 411. Local directory enquiries are free, but a charge is made — from payphones as well as private phones — for long-distance information.

Finding a number abroad is a tedious and expensive business, costing as much as the call itself. You have to begin the proceedings by dialling the local operator on 0. He or she will make contact with the overseas operator and return eventually with the number if you're lucky — if the number is not listed, or is ex directory, you still have to pay.

Operator Services. The universal number for the operator is 0. This can also be used to contact emergency services if you can't find the correct emergency number (normally 911). Dial direct, whenever possible: unless you can prove the direct-dial mechanism is faulty, going through the operator increases the cost of the call by a minimum of $1.75. If you get a wrong number, ring 211 immediately and explain the fault. They should credit your bill or allow a further call from a payphone.

Dial-a-Service. Every large city has an astonishing range of numbers to call for 'useful' services. The phone book will list the most helpful, but not necessarily the most exotic. For the price of a local call, you can find respectable information such as weather reports or transport timetables. But you can also dial-a-soap opera (one episode each day, sponsored by advertising), dial-a-prayer, dial-a-joke or even dial-a-heavy breather. Or try 'Tipster's Confidential' number, a hot line to the FBI which enables you to grass on your mates in complete secrecy.

Beware of numbers which begin 1-900, since these are 'premium information lines' which correspond with 0898 numbers in the UK. Commercial enterprises run 900 numbers to supply information such as share prices or soft porn.

Private Telephones. If you're staying in one place for a month or more, it may be worth getting a phone installed, since this process is simple, quick and cheap. You may even be assigned a telephone number on the spot when you ask for one to be installed. The cost of installation is around $60. Monthly charges, which are much lower than in Britain, usually entitle you to a certain number of free local calls, and sometimes an unlimited amount.

Having a phone of your own also helps when making calls from payphones. Subscribers can obtain a telephone 'calling card'. This looks just like a credit card, and bears a number which you key into virtually any payphone. The charges appear on your monthly bill.

Charges. The cost of using the telephone is low by international standards, unless you are in the unfortunate position of having to feed coins into a payphone — the minimum three-minute charge between Boston and New York, for example, is $2.40. But local calls from private telephones are either free or cheap (around 10c). Most householders, restauranteurs or barkeepers will let you use their phone to call a local number without a second thought. And if you need to make a long distance call from a friend's phone, you can be sure that the call will be individually itemized on their next monthly bill and reimbursement can be exact. Before you use a hotel telephone for long distance calls, ask the operator for the amount of the surcharge; sometimes this is astronomical (e.g. twice the actual call charge), or it can just be a supplement of a dollar or two.

Try to make long distance calls when cheap rates apply. There is an evening rate (35% discount) from 5pm-11pm Sunday to Friday. The night and weekend rate (50% off) is 11pm-8am daily, all day Saturday and 8am-5pm on Sundays. For example, a three minute call from New York to Los Angeles during the cheapest period costs around 60c, depending upon the network used. Calls to Alaska, Hawaii, Canada and Mexico cost slightly more, though off-peak calls can be made at substantial savings. No off-peak discounts apply to operator-assisted calls; direct-dial calls from payphones benefit from discounts, but cost more than private rates.

Calls made from a private telephone on the East Coast to the UK and Ireland are charged at the standard rate from 7am to 1pm, local time; the discount rate (25% off) operates 1pm to 6pm, and the 'economy' rate (40% off) from 6pm to 7am. A one-minute call dialled direct to Britain from a private phone during the cheapest period costs about $1.50, with additional minutes at $1 each; this is cheaper than using a coin payphone, when the minimum three-minute call would cost $6.

Toll-Free Calls. Take maximum advantage of free numbers to smooth your travel planning. A 'toll-free' number has the prefix 800 in place of the area code, and should be dialled as a long distance number, e.g. 1-800-IGO-HOJO for the Howard Johnson lodging chain. It is accepted practice to call businesses and government agencies toll-free. Many organisations advertise their toll-free numbers widely, and they are usually listed in telephone directories alongside the ordinary number. A free call to the 800 directory assistance number (1-800-555-1212) will get you any publicly available toll-free number. A toll-free number may change from area to area in order to minimise the cost to the business. For example, the toll-free number for the Nebraska Tourist Division differs depending on whether you're calling from inside or outside the state.

Because of the expense involved, organizations try to discourage callers from using toll-free numbers within the city in which they are based. a company based in San Francisco, for example, might advertise its numbers as '765-4321 within San Francisco, (800) 123-4567 elsewhere'. However, if you want to save the cost of a local call, you can always try the toll-free number or call the company collect.

About the only disadvantage of toll-free numbers is that they cannot be dialled from outside North America, even if you're prepared to pay for the call.

POST

The US Mail does not match the efficiency of the telephone system. There is usually only one daily delivery, and (in rural areas) sometimes none at all. A small (but alarming) proportion of mail arrives in tatters, accompanied by an apologetic note from the postal service.

Letters within the USA take two to four days, and air mail to Europe can take a week. Numerous private companies compete by offering guaranteed overnight delivery. The leading firm is Federal Express (often abbreviated to FedEx) which has offices in most large towns.

Post Offices. Since there are no sub-post offices of the kind found in Britain, post offices are thin on the ground and a little harder to find. They are identified by a blue sign bearing an eagle and the words US MAIL. Post offices are usually open 9am-5pm Monday to Friday, 9am-noon Saturday. Central post offices in most large cities offer a 24-hour lobby service where you will find change and stamp machines, mail boxes large enough to accept parcels, scales and tables of postal rates.

Larger post offices have a daunting array of counters which offer a bewildering variety of services. Read the signs listing the services offered by each window carefully, in order to avoid queuing at the income tax counter when you only want to buy a stamp. To order stamps by telephone (minimum $12.50), call 1-800-STAMP-24 at any time.

Mail Collection. Mail boxes are blue and look rather like rubbish bins. They are found on many downtown street corners, often positioned to allow drivers to post letters without leaving their cars. However, mail boxes are rare in the suburbs. Instead, each house has a delivery/collection box fixed to a post at the end of the drive: the postman picks up mail as well as delivering it. A flag attached to the box is raised to indicate that mail is waiting to be collected even if there is nothing to deliver. There is usually only one collection each day. Collections in city centres are more frequent, but the last is at around 6pm, earlier at weekends.

General Delivery. This is the American equivalent of *Poste Restante*. Letters should be addressed c/o General Delivery, City, State (plus zip code if known). They will arrive at the main post office, from where they can be collected upon production of ID. The service is free, but advance notification should be given, and mail will be held for a maximum of 30 days before being returned to sender.

Post Office Box Numbers. Many Americans rent boxes for incoming mail at post offices. This is not necessarily because they are transients, or because they want to keep their address a secret: in some country areas or small towns there are no door-to-door postal deliveries, and rural folk just pick up their mail from town along with their groceries. Boxes are cheap to rent. You are given a key which you can use whenever the post office is open.

Zip Codes. The Americans invented post codes. The zip code is supposed to speed mail to its destination, and is universally used. It is a five-digit number identifying a small town or area of a city, and runs from 00001 (in northeastern New England) to 99999 (in Alaska). Mail without a zip code will get through eventually, but may take a day or two longer. A statewide list of zip codes is included in the back of local telephone directories, but it does not always break down the cities that have more than one zip code. That type of street-by-street information is included in the official zip code directory which is available for reference at any post office.

Because of the relative unsophistication of the zip code, allowing this huge country to be divided into a maximum of only 100,000 areas, a sub-system is being introduced which adds a further four digits to the existing five. These four are not as important as the first five.

Stamps. Sold at post offices, from machines at airports and bus stations (where $1 buys you 95c worth of stamps) and at many shops which sell postcards. Some air mail stamps do not bear values, but instead use a code letter. You don't need to know what the codes mean: just ask for a stamp for an airmail letter to Britain, or whatever.

The 'first-class' letter rate is 39c for an ounce. This ensures that your mail is sent by air where this is beneficial, but does not necessarily mean next day delivery. Air mail letters to Europe cost 50c for half an ounce; postcards sent by air mail cost 40c. It is customary for the sender to add his or her name and address to every piece of mail. If you post a letter with insufficient stamps, you can expect to find it returned to your address with a demand for extra postage.

Parcels. All parcels must be securely wrapped and clearly addressed. The counter clerk at the post office will not hesitate to send you away to re-wrap a parcel if he considers it not to meet US Mail regulations. Charges increase according to distance: parcels to neighbouring states cost far less than those being sent across the country. All parcels are sent overland unless you pay a lot more for air mail. When sending parcels abroad you need to complete a customs declaration form, free from post offices.

FAX AND TELEGRAM

The US Mail has taken even more of a hammering recently due to the proliferation of facsimile machines, yet another disincentive for people to use the postal service. You can even send a fax from a payphone-type machine: the Pay Fax company has installed credit card operated machines in hundreds of public places.

Telegrams (cables) cannot be sent from Post Offices. Western Union handles all telegrams, and has branches in all but the smallest American towns. Call 1-800-325-6000 to send a domestic cable, 1-800-435-7984 for international. Within the USA, cables cost around 25c per word with a minimum of twelve words ($3). Abroad, a cable of the same length costs about $10. Each word of the address must be counted, apart from the name of the country.

boardwalk	raised wooden promenade by seaside
box car	goods wagon on a train
brakeman	guard on a train
caboose	last wagon on a goods train
coach class	economy class as opposed to first, club or custom
el	elevated railway running above a city street
freight car	goods wagon
freight-hopping	the practice of riding (illegally) on or between freight cars
first floor	ground floor (and hence the second floor is the same as the British first floor, etc.)
hack stand	taxi rank (from original name for taxi, *Hackney carriage*)
one-way ticket	single
ramp	slip road

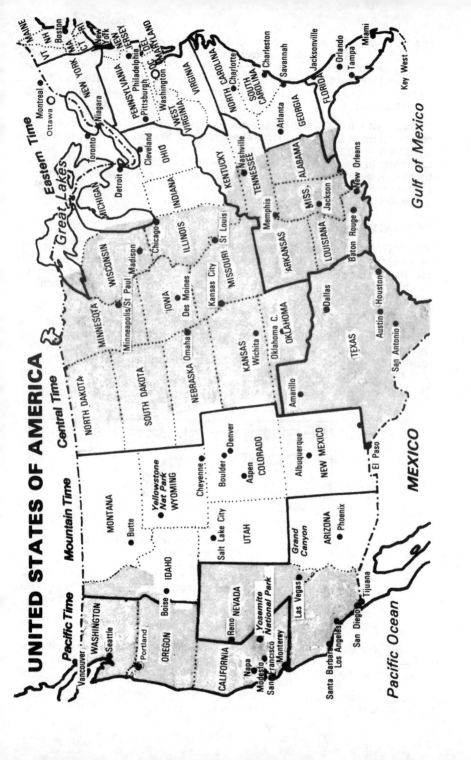

redcap	railway or airportporter
round trip	return ticket
sidewalk	pavement
smoky bears	policeman
streetcar	tram
subway	underground railway
tramway	cable car
truck	lorry
yard bull	railway yard patrolman

Never underestimate the size of the USA when planning your itinerary and choosing your modes of travel. It is over 3,000 miles by road from Miami to San Francisco or from Boston to Seattle. While part of the great American experience is to travel overland from coast to coast, do not undertake this lightly: whether driving, motorcycling or travelling by bus or train, you are not going to enjoy a trip telescoped into a few days. (If you try hitch-hiking, predicting if — and in what condition — you will arrive is arguably a more appropriate problem than 'when'). Flying is no way to get a sense of the vast expanses between urban America. But air travel is the fastest and most efficient way to visit cities far apart, and using one of the bargain airpasses on sale it can also be inexpensive. The range of unlimited travel tickets for the limited network of rail services are also well worth considering. Greyhound bus passes allow you to reach far more places. Or you may choose to visit just one region of the USA, in which case you might prefer to travel on ad-hoc basis. The following pages outline the options available.

AIR

Every day more than a million Americans catch a domestic flight. Often they give no more thought to boarding an aircraft than to catching a bus, and for many air journeys the fare will be similar. Airlines in the USA fly to more places more often than in any other country. For example between New York and Washington there are over 100 flights each way every day on a dozen different airlines. To find your way around the maze of services, consult the monthly *Official Airline Guide* at any library or travel agency, which will also give you some idea of the fares.

For visitors to the USA, air travel is a sensible way to cover the vast distances between interesting places. On heavily-travelled routes with competing airlines, fares are very low with extremely frequent flights. If you know your itinerary in advance, you can buy an airpass, some of which offer remarkably good value. Even if you plan to take only one or two flights, buy your domestic tickets before leaving Europe to qualify for the 30% Visit USA discount. Or if you want to fly free of charge you can try for a trip as an air courier. All of these ways of saving money are described below.

Fares. Air fares in the USA are crazy. The 20-mile hop between Los Angeles and Orange County airports in California costs $70, while for less than this you can fly 400 miles to San Francisco. Fares are determined much more by competition than by distance. The most heavily discounted routes are along the Eastern Seaboard (from Boston, New York and Washington as far south as Miami) and along the West Coast, and on coast-to-coast flights. To get the best fares you need to book a week or two in advance, and face a penalty of $25 if you need to change your reservation. Also, you can save around 30% by travelling off-peak (early morning, late evening, all day on Saturdays and Sundays before the evening rush) or 'night coach'.

There are many seemingly illogical bargains to be had. Sometimes it is cheaper to buy a return ticket and leave half unused than it is to buy the normal one-way ticket. Or if your flight continues beyond the city at which you want to disembark, it may cost less to buy a ticket to the aircraft's eventual destination and hop off when it touches down where you want to be (assuming you are carrying only hand luggage). Fares change literally daily and airlines which file low promotional fares boast loudly about them in the press. So keep your eyes open, try to find a sharp-witted travel agent or call the airlines for free. Foreign visitors can benefit from a range of cut-price deals, of which standby airpasses are the best buy for anyone planning extensive travelling.

Visit USA (VUSA). Most airlines offer reductions of about 30% on flights within the USA to visitors who buy tickets abroad at least a week before travelling to North America. You must provide proof of residence abroad and show your transatlantic ticket. VUSA tickets are most valuable on routes with little or no competition, which are unlikely to be discounted.

Airpasses. If you plan to travel extensively in the USA, an airpass can be invaluable. Most airlines sell you a pass for a specified number of flights, usually a minimum of three costing around £150. This in itself is excellent value since you could, for example, fly New York — Miami — Los Angeles — New York. Additional flight coupons usually cost only $25-$45 each, which makes a longer itinerary a bargain. Bear in mind that there are usually strings attached, such as you must buy the pass at least a week before you leave for the USA, and that you sometimes have to fly the Atlantic on a particular airline. In addition, no carrier has a truly comprehensive network within the USA.

Two of the larger airlines, Northwest and Delta, have unlimited travel passes valid for 30 days for $449. These involve travelling standby, but if you choose your flight times carefully to avoid peak periods you should rarely be disappointed. Fares and conditions change frequently, so call the airlines at their UK offices:

American Airlines	0800 010 151	TWA	071-439 0707
Continental	0800 776 464	United Airlines	0800 888 555
Delta	0800 414 767	USAir	0800 777 333
Northwest	0345 747 800		

Reservations. It is an easy matter to reserve a seat in advance for all domestic flights except the walk-on shuttle flights linking Boston and Washington with New York. You need not to pay for the ticket at the time of reserving a seat, and can pay later at any travel agency, at the airport or in some cases on board the aircraft. So if there is an outside chance you may wish to travel on a particular flight, phone the airline toll-free and reserve a seat as early as possible.

Call the following toll-free numbers for fares and reservations of flights within the USA:

American Airlines		TWA	1-800-221-2000
	1-800-433-7300	United	1-800-241-6522
Continental	1-800-525-0280	US Air	1-800-428-4322
Delta	1-800-221-1212		
Northwest	1-800-225-2525		

Reservations can also be made through the airline's office in Britain or through your transatlantic carrier. There is no penalty for failing to turn up. If you do not have a reservation, arrive at the airport well before departure time and ask to be put on the waiting list. On average, 15% of passengers booked on a domestic flight don't show up.

Overbooking. Because of their liberal reservations policies, airlines routinely overbook flights by 15%. If every passenger with a reservation shows up, some have to be turned away and put on a later flight. But all airlines offer 'denied boarding compensation' (DBC) to victims. This may be equivalent to the price of your ticket or a more exotic prize such as a return ticket to any destination on the airline's domestic network. If the airline staff ask for volunteers to be 'bumped', don't hesitate to step forward. If, however, you fail to show up by the time specified for check in, you forfeit your rights to a seat or DBC.

Smoking. Only flights scheduled to take six hours or more allow smoking, which in practice means only flights from Alaska and Hawaii to the Midwest or East Coast. Some airlines, notably Northwest, have banned smoking on all flights within North America. Pipes and cigars are prohibited on all airlines.

Coping with Airports. Some American airports are huge with separate terminals miles apart. Once you have successfully located the right terminal and checked in, don't sit about waiting for your flight to be announced; you're normally expected to turn up at the correct gate as shown on the numerous information screens. The absence of passport control means that friends, relations or belligerent Moonies can escort you all the way to the departure gate, where security checks take place. Don't be tempted to make jokes of the 'careful how you open that — there's a bomb inside' variety. Any such levity will be taken seriously and the FBI may be called in to question you while your plane takes off. Smokers may be dismayed to learn that smoking is either allowed only in specified areas, or banned entirely within the terminal building.

Baggage. The usual allowance is the same as on transatlantic flights, i.e. two reasonably-sized suitcases (or, indeed, a rucksack plus a bicycle box) with no weight restriction. Cabin baggage rules are not usually strictly enforced.

Frequent Flyer Schemes. Most American airlines operate a system to reward loyal customers for the amount of flying they do. If you fly 20,000 miles on United, for example, you qualify for a free ticket anywhere in the USA. Membership of all these schemes is free, and you can join at the check-in counter before you fly.

There is a booming business in selling the tickets which airlines give away to frequent fliers. Most cities have a 'coupon broker' who acts as a middleman between buyers and sellers and uses the classified sections of newspapers to advertise his wares. Note, however, that many airlines now insist upon ID for travellers using free tickets.

BUS

Bus travel is the cut-price alternative to flying in the USA. The network of long distance routes is dense, services are frequent, and journey times are as fast as the speed limits allow. It is also very easy to travel by bus: terminals are invariably in city centres, tickets may be bought at any time and reservations are not needed since relief buses are usually laid on when necessary. The vehicles — always called buses, never coaches — have reclining seats, air conditioning and a 'rest room'. So long-distance bus travel need not be an ordeal. There are also frequent rest stops where you can stretch your legs and your horizons. Smoking is forbidden.

By far the largest operator is Greyhound. Its UK address (for buying unlimited travel passes or other tickets in advance) is Greyhound International, Sussex House, London Road, East Grinstead RH19 1LD (0342 317317). Hundreds of other smaller bus companies serve individual areas, and your ticket or pass on Greyhound may be valid on their services. There seem to be no rules governing this, so it is always necessary to check locally.

Bus Passes. Greyhound offers a range of Ameripasses valid on all its services plus those of some other bus companies, which cost about $20 per day — decreasing for longer periods. To get the best deal, buy your bus pass before you fly to the USA from a travel agent or direct from the Greyhound office in the UK. If you just want to get from coast to coast as cheaply as possible, the four-day pass costing £50 is excellent value.

Joining a Tour. If your time is limited, you may prefer to take advantage of an organized tour rather than stitching together your own itinerary. These tours are designed to take you to the highlights without waiting around at bus stations. It is easy to meet like-minded people on these trips. Accommodation can be anything from camping to hotels, depending on the tour you choose. Two companies offering interesting itineraries are Contiki Travel, Bedford Way, London WC1H 0DG (071-637 0802), which organizes coach tours, and Suntrek, specializing in small group tours; these can be booked through Greyhound (address above).

Alternative Operators. In addition to conventional bus companies, there are a few more enterprising operators using imaginatively converted vehicles. In particular, *Green Tortoise* buys up obsolete Greyhound buses, rips out the seats and install matresses and bunk beds for about 30 passengers. Most of the driving takes place at night. The days are spent swimming, whitewater rafting or exploring canyons. As a result, progress is not rapid: the Boston-San Francisco route (via New York and Los Angeles) takes 11 days. Fares and frequencies vary wildly, but as a rough guide there are two transcontinental journeys per month in summer, with additional runs to the South in winter and up the West Coast as far as Alaska in summer. The coast-to-coast fare is about $350 one-way, plus an optional $50 for communal food. The free benefits such as side trips to hot springs, swimming holes and Caesar's Palace in Las Vegas make for a fascinating journey through the USA. Up-to-date fares and schedules are displayed at YMCAs and colleges, or contact Green Tortoise direct at Box 24459, 1667 Jerrold Ave San Francisco, CA 94124; (415) 821 0803 within California, 1-800-227-4766 from other states.

TRAIN

The American railroad system which encouraged the development and exploitation of an entire continent, is not what it once was. By the 1960s the nation's network of heroic proportions had become run down, bankrupt and in danger of total collapse. It was saved by a massive injection of federal funds and the creation in 1970 of the National Railroad Passenger Corporation — *Amtrak*. This nationalized concern operates a network that is thinly spread and little used by most Americans. Those who do travel by train tend to be more out-of-the-ordinary than most business travellers or

holidaymakers. This is not surprising since rail fares for long trips are often no cheaper than flying and take several days longer. The tracks upon which the modern carriages run are still owned by the old freight companies who show little enthusiasm for investing in new track. So journeys tend to be rather bumpy, and on routes in the West can be subject to improbably long delays.

However, trains score over planes in the fast, dense networks of the Chicago area and the Northeastern corridor. The Boston-New York-Washington line features 120 mph *Metroliners* and city centre-to-city centre journeys are often faster than by air. Trains are also a good way to view the country particularly from the double-decker *Superliners* used on long journeys. Instead of the endless freeways which comprise the view of most car drivers and bus passengers, railroads cut through dramatic scenery and America's backyards.

Reservations. Book before you leave for North America if you can plan ahead that far, especially for long distance trains in summer and around public holidays. Amtrak's General Sales Agents in the UK are:

Long Haul Leisurail
PO Box 113
Peterborough PE1 1LE
0733 51780

Thistle Air
22 Bank St
Kilmarnock KA1 1QJ
0563 31121

Within the USA, reservations can be made free at any time by calling (toll-free) 1-800-USA-RAIL or by personal application at travel agents, stations or city tickets offices. When you reserve a seat or sleeper by telephone, you'll be given a reservation number and a time limit by which you must pay for your ticket — usually you can negotiate to get one at the station. If you don't have a reservation but seats are still available, you'll be assigned a seat and sold a ticket at the departure station. Boarding a train without a ticket means you must pay the one-way fare plus a $10 charge. However, if the ticket office was closed at the time, you don't pay the charge and may buy a round-trip or discounted ticket. The Amtrak timetable (free from US travel agents or the Amtrak Distribution Center, Box 7717, Itasca, Il 60143) advises passengers to be at the station 30 minutes before departure. Arriving that early is necessary if you don't have a reservation or ticket, since queues can be long.

Fares. Regular one-way rail fares are slightly higher than on buses. Short journeys cost around 20c per mile. The rate decreases to 15c per mile over long distances. If you are able to travel outside peak periods, then return excursion fares offer a 35% reduction. For short journeys, the times to avoid are 1pm-7pm on Fridays and Sundays. On longer trips, peak times are usually at weekends and holidays.

Your ticket usually entitles you to an unlimited number of free stopovers, and it is much cheaper to buy a through ticket to your eventual destination rather than paying fares between intermediate points. Even so, $400 for the 2242 rail miles from Chicago to Los Angeles is an expensive way of travelling between the two cities. It is cheaper by air. Moreover, the basic price buys only a second class ('coach') reclining seat on the train. Pillows and blankets are provided free on overnight trains. For a proper sleeping berth, you must pay a supplement of between 25% and 100% of the regular fare. A similar premium is charged for custom class (first) or use of the club car. The high-speed Metroliners cost about 20% more than the corresponding coach fares. Advance reservations are essential for any of these special facilities.

You're also going to need refreshment. A federal law requires that food and drink be provided on any rail journey of over two hours, but does not specify that prices should be moderate. Most low-budget travellers take their own supplies. Alcohol is available on most trains, but its sale is subject to the licensing laws of the state through which the train is travelling.

Reduced Fares. Children under 16 pay half fare. Foreign visitors who buy tickets in advance can benefit from 'International Gateway' fares, e.g. $29 from Washington DC to Philadelphia, $59 from the capital to New York City.

Rail Passes. USA rail passes sold outside North America represent extremely good value for money. Each is valid for 45 days. They must be used within a year of the date of sale. The national pass costs from $299, i.e. less than $7 per day. There are also four regional passes. The Eastern pass (valid on all Amtrak services east of Chicago and New Orleans) is from $189. For everything west of Chicago and New Orleans, the Western pass costs $239, while a pass covering only the Far Western region (the west coast, plus lines inland as far as Denver and El Paso) is $189. Finally, 45 days travel around the (admittedly limited) Florida rail network costs $69, less than $1.50 a day.

These prices include only basic coach class travel; however, you can upgrade to custom class or Metroliner services upon payment of the appropriate supplement. Seat reservations (see above) are advisable for each journey and can be made at any time after purchase of the rail pass.

The rail pass sold within North America is not nearly such good value.

The All Aboard America fare allows three stopovers in 45 days in the west, central and/or eastern regions. The fare is $199 for one region, $279 for two and $339 for all three.

Baggage. Each fare-paying passenger can take three pieces of luggage, one of which may be a bicycle. Baggage is checked in airline-style and conveyed in a separate car, so make sure you have everything you need for the journey before you check in. The maximum liability for lost luggage is $500. Amtrak accepts bicycles as checked baggage when boxed; suitable boxes are sold at many stations for $5. You need not tip the station redcap who helps with your luggage, but he won't turn down a dollar or two.

Handicapped Travellers. Amtrak makes special provision for those with a travel-related handicap. Deaf people with access to a teletypewriter should call (toll-free) 1-800-523-6590 for information and reservations. Specially designed sleeping accommodation for overnight trains and assistance with wheelchairs are available upon request at the station or by calling 1-800-USA-RAIL.

GETTING AROUND CITIES

The public transport systems are described in detail under each *City* section. However, there are a few guidelines on finding your way around which are true for all American cities. American cities are not like their European namesakes. With a few notable exceptions (San Francisco, Boston) they consist of a central business district, where offices and condominiums tower over wasteground parking lots, an inner-city ring of menacing squalor punctuated by freeways and sprawling, identical suburbs. In all but the oldest or most hilly cities, streets are laid out in a strict grid pattern. They intersect at right angles and form squares or 'blocks'. Distances within cities are given in blocks; there are usually between ten and twenty blocks to a mile. The use of the grid system enables 'grid references' to identify easily a specific location. For instance, the Empire State Building is on the corner of 34th St and 5th Avenue in New York. For reasons of conciseness, Americans omit unnecessary words like 'street' or 'avenue'. Thus the above example will be abbreviated to '34th and 5th'.

Just because the street number in an American address is extremely high, e.g. 7765, it does not mean that the roads must be very long. Buildings in the first block of a street will be numbered from 1 to 99, but with random gaps in between: thus 99 Park Avenue could be next door to 80 Park Avenue. The second block is numbered from 100 to 199, the third 200-299 and so on. Occasionally the system breaks down: if a new building is erected between numbers 112 and 113, it will be numbered $112\frac{1}{2}$. Short streets follow the numbering system of the longer parallel road. So the numbers in a street could begin at 600 and run to 799. In most cities there is a mathematical formula to pinpoint street numbers to within a block: ask the locals.

Taxis. One popular image of American taxi drivers — as monosyllabic bruisers whose sole conversation consists of telling you they can't change a bill over $10 — is misplaced. Taxi driving is a common way for students to finance themselves through college, so your driver may be on the verge of qualifying for a PhD in Philosophy or Business Administration. Professional drivers, having 'seen life', are often fascinating characters and will take pride in pointing out places of interest in their city. They also rise to the occasion if you're in a hurry. Their motivation is not always financial: taxi drivers have been known to turn down tips if they sense you need the money more than they do, and even in New York City, taxis have stopped and offered a free trip to people who look as though they need a ride.

Finding a Cab. Taxis are large saloons, with the driver protected from passengers by a bullet proof screen and are usually either bright yellow or black and white checks. Taxis may be hailed in the street; their signs are illuminated when free, although you'll often find drivers who are not prepared to take you to an unfavourable location. 'Hack stands' (taxi ranks) are few and far between. This is relatively easy in affluent downtown areas, impossible in suburban and dangerous in inner city ghettos. Avoid unlicensed cabs at all costs. They are particularly prevalent at airports. At best, you'll be wildly overcharged; at worst, driven to an isolated patch of wasteground and robbed.

Fares. Expect to pay around $1.50 for the first quarter-mile and $3 a mile thereafter. Extras are charged for additional passengers, baggage, nights, Sundays and public holidays. Leaving the city limits increases the meter charge by 50-100%. This makes airport journeys particularly expensive; at some airports an official taxi-sharing scheme cuts the cost, and at others you can simply pair up with fellow travellers.

City Cycling. Many city cyclists wear smog-masks, and American drivers' ideas on how to share the roads with cyclists are not well-developed. Bicycle couriers have won a fearsome reputation for ignoring red lights, running into pedestrians and generally behaving abysmally. In cities some drivers seem to regard any cyclists as fair game. Even so, bicycles provide the visitor with a cheap and effective means of enjoying cities and the surrounding countryside.

Using a crash helmet in cities is not taking precautions too far; the majority of American cyclists wear them. Visitors unused to city traffic will find that a one- or three-speed bicycle with upright handlebars is safer than a ten-speed racer. Bad surfaces leave a lot to be desired; beware of potholes and streetcar tracks. It is essential to make yourself as visible as possibly to American motorists. Flourescent gear is particularly necessary at dawn or dusk. Although lights are not obligatory everywhere for night cycling, anyone who rides without them must have suicidal tendencies. Many Americans use lights strapped to an arm or leg, but the fixed variety are safer. Riding more than two abreast (or single file in cities) is foolhardly and illegal. Bicycles are not permitted to use freeways, and on strategic bridges must use the separate track provided. More and more cities are designating bicycle routes. American cyclists stick their left arm out to signal a left-hand turn, the same arm bent up at the elbow to indicate right and bent down to indicate an imminent stop.

DRIVING

beltway	ring road
divided highway	dual carriageway
expressway	motorway
fenders	wings
freeway	motorway
grade crossing	railway level crossing
gridlock	traffic jam in all directions
hood	bonnet
HOV	High Occupancy Vehicle, i.e. a car with at least three passengers, permitted to use special lanes
muffler	exhaust
no passing	no overtaking
no standing	no parking
parkway	yet another variation on the theme of motorway, landscaped with trees and grass
pavement	road surface
pull-off	lay by (on a motorway)
rotary	roundabout (very rare)
RV	recreational vehicle (camper van)
sedan	saloon car
sidewalk	pavement
smoky bear	highway patrolman (CB slang)
speed zone	a zone in which the speed limit is lower than 65 mph
station wagon	estate car
stop lights	traffic lights
stick shift	gear shift, or more broadly any car without automatic transmission
superhighway	motorway
tags	licence plates (slang)
thruway	motorway
trailer	caravan
trunk	boot
turnpike	toll motorway
U-Haul	small trailer, rather like a horse box, for moving goods
Winnebago	camper van (trade name that has become a generic term)

In America the car is king. Successive oil crises have encouraged the fashion for smaller vehicles at the expense of the gas-guzzling monsters of the 50s and 60s, but the cult of the automobile continues. A driving licence is regarded almost as a birthright and high school parking lots are jammed with the cars of 16-year-old commuters. Motorists guard their vehicles jealously, whether brand-new Cadillacs or dented pick-ups. One benefit of such fervour for the open road is the best highway network in the world, though coupled with one of the lowest speed limits: 65 mph. Despite this economy measure, the USA still manages to consume almost one-third of the world's petrol.

Licences. A full British licence is sufficient for up to a year. However, the police, and anyone else who asks for your licence as identification, are frequently surprised at the absence of a photograph, and astounded at an expiry date well into the 21st century. An International Driving Permit (obtainable from the AA or RAC) bears a photo and will enable you to go out without your passport. Remember to carry your licence with you whenever driving; unlike in Britain, you are required to produce it to police on the spot.

If you stay for a year or more you will need a licence issued by the state authorities, whereupon they may confiscate your British licence. To qualify, you must take a written examination based on state motoring law, have an eyesight test and undergo a road test. Apply for a test at the local office of the State Highway Department; it can be arranged within a few days, although some states require you to hold a learner's licence for a month before the test. The examination is usually pathetically easy, since a driving licence is regarded as an essential qualification. If you pass you pay between $5 and $25 for a licence valid for two, three or four years. Renewals are automatic upon payment for a further fee. Unlike in Britain, you are permitted to drive vehicles with manual transmission ('stick shift') even if you take the test in an automatic. Your licence will state whether or not you wear glasses. In big cities, there are agents who can issue an ID card to non-drivers. These official-looking documents cost $6 and may smooth the way for you in bars, etc.

The minimum age for holding a full licence is 15 in Mississippi, 21 in Colorado and Georgia, and 16, 17 or 18 in all other states. Under various schemes, learners as young as 14 are allowed on the road and people below the minimum state age can often drive as long as they have their parents' written permission.

Petrol. Fuel is sold in litres of US gallons (3.8 litres) which are 20% smaller than Imperial gallons (4.7 lites). There are wide variations in cost. Expect to pay $1-$1.40 per US gallon (26c-40c per litre). Prices are lowest among competing suburban gas stations, and highest on the freeways and in small towns where no competition exists. The most solid advice is to avoid places which do not boldly display their prices: they usually have something to hide. In a string of gas stations along a suburban highways, the first and last tend to be more expensive. Prices fluctuate continuously, so keep your eyes open for exceptionally good deals.

It is not always obvious whether a station is self-service or not. If you are served by an attendant, you might have to pay a little extra, but you'll get your windscreen cleaned and oil checked. Most late-night and 24 hour gas stations require you to pay the cashier before filling commences.

All vehicles must run on lead-free petrol ('unleaded gas'). This has a very low octane rating, but engines are fitted with a catalytic convertor which enables them to run without knocking.

ROAD SYSTEM

American roads vary in size from New Jersey Turnpike (with up to eight lanes in each direction) to the Ranch-to-Market roads in rural Texas. In quality, they range from the freeways of California (where the only imperfections are the lane studs designed to prevent drivers drifting side-ways) to the dirt-tracks of the Rockies and the mud-tracks of the Mississippi Delta.

Just as the Eskimo language is said to have 17 words for the word snow, so do Americans seem to have a large vocabulary for the word motorway. Roads are classified as freeways (which include Interstates, Turnpikes and some Federal Highways) or other roads. There are thruways, parkways, expressways, superhighways and beltways (i.e. ring roads). Like British motorways, freeways are dual-carriageways with 'grade-separated' junctions, i.e. entrance and exit is by slip road (ramp) leading above or below the freeway. On other roads, there are the usual impediments such as traffic lights, bicycles and pedestrians, but almost no roundabouts (called 'rotaries') as found in Britain.

American methods of numbering roads are not always logical. There are often optional variations to a particular route, identified by a variety of suffixes. Some will bear the suffix N,S,E or W (for north, south...). Or they may not give any geographical clue, and just be appended 'Alt' (alternative) or A,B,C, etc. Other sophistications include the alternatives 'Business' and 'Thru'. The sensible long-distance traveller will always choose the latter; business routes simply divert highways through industrial and commercial areas for the benefit of local traders. A good road map is essential for navigating through the myriad of choices.

Interstates. The Interstate and Defense Highway System (so called because the original funding came from the Defense Department) provides a comprehensive network of inter-urban roads of motorway standard i.e. with two lanes plus a hard shoulder in each direction. Some charge tolls, in which case they are known as Turnpikes. Each Interstate bears the prefix I- and is marked on maps and road signs with a red, white and blue shield. Those which run predominantly east-west are even-numbered, those running north-south are odd-numbered. The lowest numbers are in the south and west, the highest in the north and east. For example, I-5 runs up the West Coast and I-95 up the East Coast; I-10 crosses the country along its southern edge, I-90 along the northern border. Most Interstate numbers have one or two digits; three-digit Interstates are short urban spur motorways. The first digit is the prefix (eg I-610, a spur from I-10 around New Oleans) and theoretically denotes whether the spur goes around the city (even numberèd prefixes) or into the city (odd-numbered prefixes, eg I-395 into Washington DC). Three-digit interstates are not exclusively numbered; for example, I-295 recurs several times during the course of I-95.

Some interstates bear the names as well as numbers, such as the 'Golden State Freeway' or 'Dan Ryan Expressway'. Since these names are prone to change or vanish altogether after a few miles, they should be ignored in favour of numbers whenever possible. Names may, however, be unavoidable if they are part of local parlance. When giving directions, a native might say 'take the New England Thruway as far as Boston Post Road' and expect you to know he means 'I-95 as far as US 1'. A good map or road atlas will help with the translation.

Junctions are numbered in a way which Europeans may find curious, but which has some logic: starting at the state line, junctions take their numbers from the distance from the border. Therefore the first junction on I-5 in southern California is numbered 1, but the next is 7.

No interstates (unless they are also turnpikes — see below) have service areas of the kind that brighten the lives of European motorists. Instead, fuel and refreshments are obtainable at gas stations and restaurants located adjacent to junctions. The generic term for these is 'truck-stops'. They are easy to spot (look for a cluster of huge neon signs) and occur at reasonable intervals even in remote areas. Picnic sites and rest areas are becoming more common as part of a campaign to persuade drivers to rest more frequently.

Except in urban and strategic bridges and tunnels, emergency telephones are never provided. In the event of a breakdown you are supposed to wait (with hazard lights flashing) for a passing patrol car.

Turnpikes. These are toll motorways; some are part of the Interstate system, others not. They are found mostly in the northeast, although the states of Florida, Kansas and Oklahoma also have them. They are known by name for example the Will Rodgers Turnpike (Oklahoma) and the Garden State Parkway (New Jersey). Tolls are payable upon entry to or exit from the turnpike; the 900 miles from New York to Chicago via Philadelphia and Pittsburgh costs about $30. You will usually be given a card upon entrance to the turnpike and pay at tollbooths for the distance travelled.

Tolls on shorter turnpikes are often collected by throwing quarters into a basket, but usually need more than one: the New Hampshire Turnpike costs a dollar, for example. You may see the occasional driver go straight through without paying, but don't be tempted to follow suit. Some gates have concealed barriers which rise if the toll is not paid, and others operate police checks on non-payers; they note your licence plates and radio ahead to a waiting patrol car. Fines are heavy.

Federal Highways. These roads bear the prefix US, and are marked on maps and signs by a white shield with black lettering. They are equivalent to British 'A' roads, duplicating Interstates on some routes and providing links between them. They range in quality from fast dual carriageways, largely indistinguishable from Interstates (e.g. US 101 between Los Angeles and San Francisco) to little more than suburban streets; US 1, which runs down the east coast from Maine to Florida, is colloquially known as 'everybody's Main Street'. Adhering rigidly to the course of a Federal Highway is not recommended if you are in a hurry. Like Interstates, north-south Federal Highways are odd-numbered, east-west even numbered.

State Highways. These show an even greater variation in quality than Federal Highways. Some are almost of freeway standard, others simply gravel tracks. Road numbers on maps are marked in ovals, squares, circles, inside a printed outline of the state or even (in the state of Washington) inside a silhouette of George Washington's head. Since the numbering system is at the discretion of state authorities, numbers on through-routes often change at state borders.

Maps and Routes. To obtain maps in advance, you must write to the main tourist information office in each state (addresses on page 119). In addition, the more tourist-conscious states give away Official State Highway maps to personal callers at tourist offices, including the 'Welcome Centers' located on main routes just inside the state line. Many visitors find it easier to invest $6.95 in a Rand McNally road atlas; these are cheaper when combined with advertising material and sold by banks, insurance companies, etc. Most gas stations have a stock of good oil company maps, but these are not usually free. Cheaper maps are sold in supermarkets with their branch locations superimposed. Free maps can be picked up from car hire desks at airports: just ask.

Route advice can be obtained locally at tourist offices or simply by asking at gas stations. For those who prefer to plan in advance the AA and RAC will supply their members with a package containing a map of the USA, a catalogue of travel publications and a form for requesting route information. This information is supplied by their counterpart American Automobile Association (AAA, known as 'Triple A' in America). If you ask for advice about a specific journey, you'll be sent a strip map showing the recommended route. Do not write direct to the AAA: all requests must go through an affiliated motoring organisation in your own country, so letters to the AAA will go unanswered.

AAA Discounts: it is well worth showing an AA or RAC card when checking into a motel or paying at a museum, since discounts for AAA members are common. Note that an AA card may cause some hilarity since the acronym AA is universally recognized in the USA as representing Alcoholics Anonymous.

Road Signs. Signs giving instructions or warnings are usually spelt out explicitly: 'No U-Turns', 'Do Not Stop On The Tracks' for example. Some pictorial signs are being introduced, but there should be few problems for motorists familiar with European pictorial signs. One of the ones you may not be familiar with is a black X in a yellow circle with RR; this indicates a railway crossing which may or may not have an automatic gate.

Direction signposts are a different matter. Although main routes are well signposted for much of their courses, approach to cities leave a lot to be desired. For instance, driving to New York City is no problem until you get within ten or twenty miles of the city. Then the signs for New York disappear to be replaced by options like 'George Washington Bridge', 'Midtown Tunnel' and so on, which require you to have a thorough understanding of the city's road system. Plan your approach to large cities in advance with the aid of a good road map.

RULES OF THE ROAD

Drive on the right. Try not to get too annoyed when for the umpteenth time you hit the windscreen wipers instead of the indicator. Seat belts, where fitted, should be used at all times; at the start of 1993, all but seven states had made it compulsory to wear belts.

Freeways. Interstates, turnpikes and freeway-standard stretches of federal highways have the same rules. These include no stopping except in an emergency, no U-turns and a wide range of prohibited traffic: pedestrians, bicycles, animals, etc. Although technically you are not allowed to go slower than 40-50 mph, this is rarely enforced.

In urban areas there are no 'fast' or 'slow' lanes, so expect to be overtaken ('passed') on all sides. Furthermore slip roads sometimes join and leave the outside lane. When driving on a multi-lane freeway it is usually best to avoid the extreme nearside and outside lanes, since these have the unnerving habit of becoming exit lanes. On some stretches of urban freeways, one lane is reserved for buses and 'HOVs' during rush hours. A High Occupancy Vehicle is defined as any vehicle carrying the minimum number of passengers shown on the attendant road signs, usually three, driver included.

Although freeways outside cities technically have a through (slow) lane and a passing (fast) lane, many drivers choose a lane at random and stick to it. Others switch from one to another at will. Overtaking on the right is legal everywhere except in Connecticut, Maryland and Nebraska.

Other Roads. A single or double solid line along the centre of the road should not be crossed. U-turns are prohibited in city centres ('business districts') and elsewhere as posted.

The traffic light sequence is red-green-amber-red, or sometimes just red-green-red. At less busy times, there may simply be a flashing amber light which means 'proceed with caution'. In most places you are allowed to turn right against a red light, as long as you first come to a complete stop and give way to other cars, pedestrians, etc. Sometimes a sign may restrict this privilege to certain hours, or prohibit it entirely. You may be allowed to turn left from the extreme left lane of a one-way street into another one-way street. Before trying either of these manoeuvres, observe the practice of local drivers.

The octagonal STOP sign — or a flashing red light — instructs drivers to come to a complete standstill before proceeding. It is tempting not to bother. But the widely-pactised 'rolling stop' is a favourite target for traffic police keen to boost their takings. A common arrangement at crossroads is the 'four-way stop', where each road is controlled by a stop sign or flashing red light. The accepted convention is that the first vehicle to arrive and stop at the crossroads has priority. When you approach a road obstruction at the same time as another vehicle coming in the opposite direction, the first one to flash as meaning 'go ahead, pal' as it sometimes does in Europe!

School buses have absolute priority. They are bright yellow ('National School Bus Chrome' is the official colour) and are fitted with lights that flash when taking up or discharging passengers. When this happens, all traffic — whether travelling in the same or opposite direction — must stop and wait. This law is taken very seriously. The only exception to it is that vehicles travelling in the opposite direction on a divided highway do not have to stop. Other vehicles which will assert priority include streetcars (trams) and the cable cars of San Francisco.

Many railroad crossings are unguarded. Some have flashing lights and/or a bell to warn of approaching trains, but others rely upon the good sense of the motorist. If you stall on a crossing, your battery should have sufficient power to allow you to crawl out of danger using the starter motor.

Speed Limits. The usual 65 mph maximum on good roads in rural areas is not universally respected. Driving at around 70 mph seems to be the norm; many drivers of cars with cruise controls (which keep the speed constant until the accelerator or brake is operated) set them at about 72 mph, known as 'truckers speed'.

Of course, lower limits are often posted. Typically these are 55 mph on urban freeways, 50 mph for two lane highways in rural areas; 25-30 mph in residential districts; 15-25 mph in business districts; and 15 mph near schools when the kids are around. Watch for 30 mph and 35 mph zones just after you leave a freeway. Sometimes these speeds are enforced very strictly. Such zeal is usually attributed to traffic cops in small towns, especially in the southeastern USA, which reputedly depend upon speeding fines for a substantial part of their municipal revenue.

Detection techniques vary from state to state. They include the use of 'Vascar' speed guns (where a policeman points the device at your car and takes an instant reading), unmarked police cars, helicopters, aircraft and radar. Signs warning of these traps are usually posted. In Pasadena, California, for example, signs warn 'Smile — you're on photo radar', since cameras snapping speeding motorists are triggered by radar. Many states permit the use of in-car radar detectors, which sound an alarm when radar is in use; devices which jam the radar system are illegal. Some states are less than enthusiastic about the 65 mph limit: in Idaho the maximum fine for driving on freeways at over 65 mph but no more than 70 mph is a paltry $10 plus nominal $5 court costs.

The speed of trucks and cars equipped with CB radio should be closely observed, since their drivers are in contact with others who can warn of impending speed traps. These vehicles can be spotted by their distinctive antennae.

Penalties. If you are stopped for exceeding the limit, or for another 'minor violation' (such as an illegal turn, or failing to halt at a stop sign), be obsequious and show your passport: you might get away with a warning. Pleading unfamiliarity with American motoring practise may help. As with British traffic wardens, the most crucial point is to persuade police not to start writing. But don't despair, if the officer starts scribbling: he may only be filling out an official caution, described as a 'Friendly Warning' in some states.

If you do get a ticket, you have a choice of various course of action. Some states allow spot fines, others have to take you to court although the penalty is often fixed at the time of the offence. In the spot-fine states, you can elect to go to court if you wish. However, the spot fine — around $50 for up to ten miles over the limit, plus an additional $10 fine for each mile per hour — will usually be less than that per hour imposed by the court. In the court states, you can waive your right to a hearing by sending the amount of the fine to the court in advance.

Some travellers, particularly those about to leave the USA with no immediate plans to return, may be tempted to opt for a court appearance and then skip the hearing. An immediate impediment to this is that some states require a deposit to assure your appearance which is often more than the fine you face. A longer-term drawback is that disobeying the summons (the ticket issued at the time of the offence) is a much more serious crime in law than the one you were originally stopped for. Your non-appearance will forever remain on your record in some police computer, ready to haunt you next time you're in the country.

You might find your vehicle 'tagged', i.e. seen performing a traffic violation but not stopped, and later summonsed for the offence. If you are driving a rented car, the rental company will receive the summons and will debit your credit card account to cover the fine.

Parking. Most cities are divided into zones for the purposes of controlling parking. Generally, suburban areas are unrestricted, except for the main thoroughfares. Downtown, on-street parking is either metered or prohibited. Meters accept quarters; 25c buys up to half an hour with a maximum of two hours. Meter feeding is prohibited: the officers chalk the time they checked your car on the pavement, and therefore can tell if you have returned to insert some more coins. Erasing or amending the chalk mark will also incur a fine. Although you'll see plenty of cars parked illegally, it is not a good idea to join them unless you know the territory well.

There are certain places where you should never park. Avoid any stretch of kerb painted red, which means no parking at any time. You'll often see a tempting 20-foot gap between cars in an otherwise crowded street. The reason is probably the presence of a fire hydrant. Parking is prohibited within ten feet of hydrants, and this law is enforced strictly by towing offending vehicles away. Fire stations, ambulances and schools have a zone clearly marked on the roadway in front of them, which is similarly out-of-bounds. In addition temporary parking restrictions are often imposed in winter to allow snow ploughs to clear the streets.

Parking controls are enforced by city police together with private firms. The latter are paid on a piece-rate basis and hence are particularly zealous. Several techniques are employed. The most extreme is towing away; beware of signs showing a red axe embedded in a car. If your car is removed, the local police precinct station will tell you how to recover it and how much you will have to pay (at least $50).

Wheel clamps which immobilise cars are widely employed. Their colloquial name is the Denver Shoe, after the city in which they were first introduced. Details of where to go to pay the charge (about $50) for releasing your vehicle will be attached to the screen. You can expect to wait at least an hour or more at busy times for release.

Downtown parking lots cost upwards of $10 a day. Be warned that car parks which cater primarily for commuter traffic often lock their gates overnight. If using an automated car park, be sure to follow the instructions; if you try to leave by the wrong exit, spikes may be activated and do serious damage to your tyres.

Supermarkets, banks and other establishments often have free parking for customers's use only. They enforce the system by issuing a token with which you leave the car park at the conclusion of your business. Those who are not customers must pay a great deal to get out.

Parking a large American car can be tricky. Some drivers deliberately bump adjacent vehicles, relying on the law which requires that bumpers (fenders) be designed to withstand a 5 mph collision without damage.

Alcohol. Drunken driving is taken much more seriously than it is in Britain. Every state has an 'implied consent' law, whereby the act of driving implies a willingness to undergo a chemical test for drink. Some states set up road blocks to check every car and pick out drunk drivers. Otherwise, police must have some reason to stop you: if you drive with a blown headlight bulb, expect to be stopped and asked if you've been drinking. The officer will ostentatiously sniff the air around you, and may decide to administer a test. This may take the form of a breath test, or an analysis of blood, urine or saliva. The penalties for non-compliance are as serious as those for failing the test.

The blood-alcohol level above which you are deemed to be driving while intoxicated ('DWI' in highway patrol parlance) is 0.08% in most states. If your count is below the DWI level but above 0.05%, then you may still be charged with 'driving under impairment'. This is usually brought only as a secondary charge following an accident or a blatant case of reckless driving. However, DWI will earn you a heavy fine and withdrawal of your licence at the very least, possibly combined with some community service or treatment for alcoholism. Some states have mandatory 48-hour prison sentences for first offenders. If you hit someone while intoxicated, the penalties become much more severe. There is an extremely strong lobby against drunk drivers in the USA, comprised mainly of mothers who have lost children in road accidents where the offender was drunk.

Alcohol affects everyone differently according to their weight, metabolism and tolerance, and the only safe rule is to avoid drinking anything if you have to drive.

Carrying alcohol within the passenger compartment of a vehicle is a serious offence in most states. Alcohol must be transported in sealed containers which are locked in the boot ('trunk'). Some drivers attempt to circumvent the law by using the 'brown bag' technique, which involves taking surreptitious gulps from a bottle of liquor concealed in a brown paper bag. It is sometimes an offence to carry alcohol — even if locked beyond reach of the occupants — across state lines (particularly in the southern states) or city limits. However, this is one transgression which is unlikely to be detected.

Driving under the influence of illicit drugs, although harder to detect, incurs penalties similar to those for drunk driving.

HIGHWAY HAZARDS

Breakdowns. Drivers of rented cars should follow the procedure described by the company concerned on the rental agreement; if necessary, call the agency collect to negotiate repairs or a replacement vehicle. Those who have bought or borrowed vehicles should either join the AAA or be members of an affiliated motoring organisation. On production of a valid AA or RAC certificate members will receive the same privileges as full members of the AAA. These benefits include a limited breakdown service, activated by calling (toll-free) 1-800-336-HELP. Members are entitled to 30 minutes of mechanical help at the scene of the breakdown or towing to a garage up to two miles away. Additional charges for towing, labour and parts come out of the motorist's pocket.

Summer Driving. Air conditioning increases petrol consumption dramatically, as does the practice of driving with all the windows open or the roof down. For air conditioning to function properly, you must keep all the windows closed. Don't be alarmed at the drips of condensation when you stop.

Should your vehicle start to overheat, check the radiator level and turn the heater full on. Use the highest possible gear to keep your speed up but the revs down; this maximizes the cooling effects of the air. Always carry plenty of water to keep the radiator topped up — and to drink while you're waiting for help to arrive. If you do break down on a desert, stay in your vehicle until another car comes along.

Petrol expands with heat, so the energy value of a gallon bought at midday is less than that of a gallon bought early in the morning when temperatures are lower. Fill up early.

Winter Driving. Many of the same areas which suffer from excessive heat in summer are afflicted by severe snow and ice in winter. The most dangerous time to travel in snowy conditions is while the snow is actually falling. As soon as it stops, the ploughs (plows) come out in force. Don't park on main roads if there's a chance of snow, or your car may get ploughed away. The Interstate system is promptly cleared, although the passing lane may be slushy and a lower speed limit imposed. If you intend to drive on roads which may be cut off by snow, take sustenance, blankets, ccandles and a shovel.

Driving on ice is an altogether more frightening prospect. A warning that sometimes appears on signs is 'Bridges Freeze First': an apparently clear road can turn into an ice rink as you cross a bridge. The worst driving of all is in freezing rain (black ice). Traction is almost nil; you should brake, turn or accelerate only with the utmost care. The conditions for freezing rain — warm air at cloud level enclosing a patch of sub-freezing air at ground level — make it rare and usually short-lived. It eventually turns to snow, sleet or rain, depending on whether the warm air cools down or the cold air warms up.

Mountainous Areas. At high altitudes, engines function less efficiently and produce far more carbon monoxide due to the lower density of oxygen. Also, because there is less oxygen, people are more susceptible to the effects of carbon monoxide (which makes you first drowsy, then unconscious, then dead). If driving at altitude, keep a window partially open even in winter. Do not run your engine while stationary.

If two vehicles meet face-to-face on a single track mountain road, the convention is that the driver heading downhill must reverse back up the slope until a suitable passing place is reached.

Other Drivers. Many American motorists are on a short fuse, and on the road as elsewhere racial tensions exist; the car or truck is often used as an equalizer. So pay attention to other traffic at all times. Never stare at another driver, nor protest when a motoring discourtesy is committed against you that does not cause actual damage.

INSURANCE

Many visitors to the USA assume that American motor insurance policies include unlimited third party cover, as in Europe. They are wrong. There are very serious risks to British drivers without sufficient cover: you could be maimed yet unable to claim against an uninsured motorist, or — if you cause an accident — be crippled financially for life.

Vehicle insurance requirements vary greatly from state to state. In 12 states, insurance is not obligatory at all, subject to proof of financial resources sufficient to meet a moderate claim (say $20,000). In others, third party insurance is compulsory but with a similarly low level of cover. The lowest is $20,000 (Florida), the highest $50,000. So you must ensure that you and your passengers have sufficient medical insurance (see *Before You Go*). This will provide some compensation for being hit by an uninsured or hit-and-run driver. Wise American drivers buy 'uninsured motorist' insurance to protect themselves in such cases, but this is not easily available to foreigners.

You should have at least half a million dollars' worth of third party cover in case you cause an accident in which someone is injured. Law suits against negligent drivers can quite easily reach this level. A basic policy covering fire, theft, accident damage and third party claims up to the state minimum will cost about $100 for three months. The cost of increasing the third party cover to a more substantial amount is not expensive, costing around $20 for three months.

Before renting a car, find out the amount of third party cover. If it is below half a million dollars ask if you can extend it: some agencies increase the cover on payment of a dollar or two per day on top of the normal hire charge. If they do not, go elsewhere. The standard cover from Avis and Hertz is around $1 million.

Insurance policies of the cheapest car rental firms restrict the use of a hire car to one or several states. This is especially common for cars hired in Florida. Some policies are actually nullified if an offence is committed by the policyholder at the time of the accident. Since most accidents result from some transgression of the law, this is tantamount to driving without insurance. So read the small print. If someone offers to lend you a car, check their policy to make sure it extends to you and provides adequate cover; if in doubt, decline politely.

Some states have a 'no-fault' insurance law for accidental damage to vehicles. Each driver's insurers pay for his own damage, even if one party has absolutely no responsibility for the accident. This system does not encourage careful driving.

CAR HIRE

Every American city has a swarm of vehicle rental agencies. They range from small local outfits with a few beaten-up cars to the multinational chains of Avis, Budget and Hertz. Competition is intense. The cheapest regular rates for compacts are around $25 a day plus 15c per mile, or $35 unlimited. 'Standard' or 'full size' cars are most costly. Rates vary considerably from one state to another: New York is most expensive, Florida and California the cheapest. To these rates should be added around $12 per day for collision damage waiver (CDW) cover, plus local taxes. If you pick up the car at an airport, you can expect also to pay a surcharge of 10%.

Most hire cars have automatic transmission, which makes driving easy but increases petrol consumption. 'Stick-shift' (manual) rental cars are rare, but will save a few dollars if you find one. Air conditioning is an expensive extra, but may be worthwhile in summer. If you rent from a chain of agencies, it is possible to drop off the car at a different location but this can be expensive — especially if it is in another state. Hertz offers the best deals on one-way rentals.

You will be expected to produce a credit card. You must be at least 18 years of age for some companies, 21 for others. (Sometimes the insurance premiums are higher for younger drivers). A full British driving licence is sufficient, though you may be asked to show the photograph in your passport as well.

Don't try to avoid paying for any parking or speeding tickets; the hire company will simply charge the fine to your credit card. If you are going to be late returning the vehicle, let the hire company know. If you are late, you will be driving without insurance cover and may even be presumed to have stolen the car. Remember the possible gain or loss of an hour if you change time zones. Be sure to return the car with a full petrol tank (assuming you have taken the car on an 'out full, back full' basis) since rental agencies always charge dearly for fuel. One problem which befalls a lot of renters is finding the lever which releases the door to the filler cap. Look to the drivers left and right, and *in extremis* check inside the glove compartment on the passeneger side. Ideally, find out before you drive away.

Cheap Deals. For a real bargain, book ahead. Many fly-drive holidays sell flights and a week's car rental for little more than the cost of the air ticket. Off-season, a second week's rental may be thrown in free (but you still have to pay extra for adequate insurance and local taxes). Every package tour operator to the USA offers low cost car rental. Independent travellers can also benefit by booking ahead.

Once you are in the States, you can find the best deal by ringing around a few firms in the Yellow Pages. Most rental companies offer special weekend rates. You can also try for a cheap one-way deal: in a few locations (such as Florida) incoming one-way rentals drastically exceed those going the other way. It may be possible to hire a car for a nominal sum as long as you deliver it to, say, New York. Ring around the big companies and ask if they have any 'returns'. U-Haul (which rents out vans) is also worth a try. The company may even pay for fuel.

Rent-a-Wreck and Ugly Duckling are nationwide chains specialising in old, noisy and scruffy but mechanically sound cars at about half the rates charged by the other big companies. Call 1-800-228-5958 toll-free for Rent-a-Wreck reservations, 1-800-854-3380 for Ugly Duckling. One drawback is that the cars tend to be large 'gas-guzzlers' so what you save on rental you may squander on fuel. Another is the three-day minimum hire that some outlets impose. Local companies copying the idea, with names like 'Fender Benders' or 'Rent-a-Heap-Cheap', are usually cheapest of all.

Recreational Vehicles (RVs). To solve all your accommodation problems at a stroke, hire one of these camper vans. Rental charges will seem astronomical — at least $700 per week — but the freedom and flexibility they provide could offset this. Because of the limited availability of RVs, it is worth booking well in advance. The USTTA in London (address on page 117) will provide a list of agents who can arrange bookings. If you own a camper van at home, you can swap vehicles temporarily with an American family: contact Change Wheels at CW House, 84 Fallowcourt Avenue, London W12 OBG.

DRIVEAWAYS

Prosperous Americans and Canadians are prepared to pay several hundred dollars to companies such as Auto American Transport Inc. and Auto Driveaway who agree to arrange delivery of the car to a different city, usually because the car-owner wants his or her car available at their holiday destination but doesn't want to drive it personally. The companies find drivers, arrange insurance and arbitrate in the event of mishaps. You get free use of a car (subject to mileage and time restrictions) and pay for all gas after the first tankful and tolls on the interstates. Usually a deadline is fixed for delivery and a mileage limit is imposed. When the supply of drivers is greatest, the arrangement will be less flexible. When there is a shortage of drivers you may even get a fee.

The technique is this: decide where you want to go and then look up 'Automobile Transporters and Driveaway Companies' in the *Yellow Pages* of any big city. Alternatively ring a national toll-free number such as Auto American Transport (1-800 CAR SHIP), All American (1-800-942-0001), American International Delivery (1-800-248-0079) or Rent-a-Car Florida (1-800-GO ALAMO). Many companies impose a minimum age restriction of 21. An alternative to the *Yellow Pages* is to contact car rental agencies which arrange delivery of rental cars to the places where there is a seasonal demand, for example to Florida or to ski resorts in the winter. The colloquial expression for these cars is 'deadheads'.

If no company has what you want, then try to leave a number where they can reach you, or arrange to phone the most promising ones daily. Call in to register with the company, since they are more likely to take you seriously. When establishing your criteria, try not to be too fussy. The bigger the city you're in, the more vehicles there will be waiting to be delivered; and the greater your flexibility of destination, the quicker you'll be out of town. If you want to go coast to coast, it's probably worth waiting for a through vehicle; but if you have plenty of time and people and places to visit en route, you can piece together shorter runs which will eventually bring you to your destination.

If you are travelling with one or more people, you can save money by splitting the cost of the gas. The company allows you to take co-drivers and/or passengers provided they register for insurance purposes. This precludes the picking-up of hitch-hikers, so if you start alone, you should stay that way.

The type of vehicle you are assigned to drive can make a significant difference to the overall cost. Since you are paying for gas, the more fuel-efficient the car, the cheaper your trip will be. You should therefore try to find a modest sized car. This is difficult at the best of times in the United States but even harder among the kind of people who pay to have their cars moved for them. In fact you may not be able to avoid a Cadillac.

Eventually a company will have something going in the right direction and summon you to their office where you are told the details of pick-up, drop-off, time and distance restrictions. These are negotiable, depending on how desperate the company is to shift the vehicle, but reckon on 400 miles a day. You may have to produce two passport size photos, a returnable cash deposit ($250-$350) and your thumb prints. You will be given two copies of the way-bill, an insurance claim form and a notice informing you of the FBI's penalties for delay, diversion and other atrocities. In fact, the mileage limits are not usually enforced rigidly.

Few agencies store cars themselves so you will need to get a bus to the car's home. When you are introduced to the vehicle, check through a list of existing damage with the owner (or agent). Be thorough, since otherwise you may be held liable for existing damage or faults. If you do have mechanical problems on the road, you pay for any repairs costing less than a specified sum (perhaps $75), which you reclaim from the recipient of the vehicle. For more expensive work you should call the owner (collect) and discuss how he will arrange payment for the repairs. Ten minutes spent checking and going for a short test ride can save an awful lot later. Even if you know nothing about cars, you should be able to check the lights, oil, battery, brakes, and seat belts and also look for rust. If you do know some elementary mechanics, look for a worn fan belt and a leaky radiator which can cause serious problems during your trip. Point out to the owner/agent anything you are unhappy about. Also check that there is a full tank of petrol.

BUYING A CAR

A good way to see America is to buy a car and sell it at the end of your trip. Prices for decent secondhand cars start at about $500 and are generally much lower than in the UK. Readers have recommended buying a car in California and selling it in the East for a good premium due to the absence of rust problems on the West Coast.

Choosing a Car. A cheap, old model will minimize losses if resale should prove difficult. One of the better bets is a Volkswagen Beetle. They are economical to run, and reasonably reliable; if you do hit problems, then almost every mechanic will have some idea how to fix it. The air-cooled engine behaves very well in hot weather. There is a thriving trade in secondhand VWs which makes buying and reselling relatively straightforward. A 15-year-old Beetle will cost $300-$500, depending on condition, a VW Camper about twice that amount. Japanese cars are also good value. Old American cars offer greater space and comfort, but use more fuel and are prone to breakdowns. Unless you are an expert on a particular car, choose a popular model. Try to buy in an area of the USA not subject to snow. So much salt is used to clear it that rust is a serious problem even on newer cars.

The easiest way to get a car is to buy from one of the used car salesmen whose premises line the main highways out of every city. Unless a dealer is recommended to you by someone whose judgement you trust, you will have to gauge the dealer's honesty yourself. At least you are offered an immediate choice and can expect the paperwork to be completed with despatch. Transactions will normally be in cash, though in some cases a credit card will be accepted.

Cars sold privately are usually cheaper. Check advertisements in local newspapers and on college noticeboards. It is important to satisfy yourself that the seller actually owns the vehicle by checking the Certificate of Title against his driver's licence. You will probably never see the vendor again, so give the car a thorough going-over before parting with any money. The price of a vehicle is likely to come down rapidly if you can produce a bundle of ready cash. Some states impose a tax on the private sale of vehicles, and it is the purchaser's responsbility to pay this.

Legal Requirements. Every vehicle has a Certificate of Title, the American equivalent of the British 'log book' or Registration Certificate. The seller must endorse this across to you. You then send it to the Division or Registrar of Motor Vehicles for the state, who will issue you with a new certificate. There may be a small fee for this, and for the transfer of licence plates to your name. (Some states require only a rear number plate). However, the number plates may be retained by the vendor, particularly if they are the personalised variety (as found, for example, in California). You must then apply for new plates. This will cost you more, so take it into account when agreeing on the price of the vehicle.

Resale. Although it's probably better to buy a cheap heap and drive it into the ground, you may want to try to resell. If you are selling the car in the state (geographical, not mechanical or emotional) in which you bought it, there will be few problems. If you have sufficient time to sell privately, then wait for someone to answer your advertisement. Should you fail to find a buyer in time, your only choice is to hawk the vehicle around a few local dealers and accept the least derisory offer. Suntrek (represented in the UK by Greyhound, 0342 317317) offers a guaranteed repurchase scheme.

Many visitors who buy a car and drive across the continent will not want to return to the state or purchase just to sell their car. To sell legally in another state, you will normally have to re-register the vehicle in the state in which you wish to sell. This takes time and money, not least for buying new number plates. Once it is re-registered, proceed as above. The alternative is to sell to an individual or dealer who is prepared — for a suitable reduction in price — to accept the legal complications of buying an out-of-state car.

MOTORCYCLING

The Hell's Angels of the USA rejoice in the title of the 'one-per-centers', which arose from a claim that while 99% of American motorcyclists are law-abiding citizens, one per cent are troublemakers. Unfortunately for the remainder, they have earned all bikers an undeservedly poor reputation. Prejudice can manifest itself at truck stops, gas stations and — more worryingly — on the open road. Motorists probably won't actually try to run you down, but may well fail to give you due consideration. Even so, many visitors are prepared to put up with such ill-feeling in return for the freedom and economy that a motorcycle allows.

Buying a Motorcycle. When exchange rates are favourable, it is quite possible to buy a brand-new bike in the States, use it during your visit, then ship it back and pay import duty for less than the price of the same machine in Britain. If you intend to sell before returning, then buy secondhand to avoid the inevitable depreciation on a new motorcycle. Most dealers sell both new and used bikes. They charge state tax on sales. Buying privately may avoid tax and secure a better bargain. The legal requirements for buying and selling are the same as for *Buying a Car*, above. When you buy a bike, get a very strong lock at the same time.

The minimum age for riding a moped ranges from 12 in New Mexico to 16 in most other states. For motorcycles above 50 cc, the lower limit in between 14 and 18 years. Licences are required by motorcyclists in every state except Mississippi. A British motorcycle licence will suffice. In some states, helmets are obligatory and must be reflective. Elsewhere, helmets must be worn only by riders under 18 or 19. In Delaware, every biker must carry a helmet but only those under 19 need actually wear them. Any bike whose engine is larger than 50 cc is allowed on freeways. If you intend to ride a motorcycle, you are strongly advised to take out insurance well beyond the minimum level required by law.

HITCH-HIKING

The practice of thumbing a ride in the USA is not the smooth and pleasant experience usually found in Europe. It is harder to get lifts, the distances to be covered can be immense, police hassles are endless and a high proportion of drivers who give lifts can best be described as weird. Many lift-givers are drunk, or insist on smoking dope while driving, or are just plain crazy. It is questionable whether hitching in its traditional form is a worthwhile form of transport for anyone save inveterate hitchers and those down to their last few cents. As a result, an American definition of hitch-hiking now encompasses far more than thumbing lifts. It covers freight-hopping on the railways, getting rides on private yachts and aircraft, and the growing practice of ride-sharing.

Hitching out of Cities. Most American cities are criss-crossed by a maze of limited-access freeways, which are a nightmare for the hitcher. It is essential to have a good map to identify the road you want and to plan how to reach a suitable junction. Some hitchers specialize in asking drivers at downtown gas stations to recommend a suitable spot, and sometimes get a free ride out to the driver's choice.

Signs are essential for leaving large cities, and advisable elsewhere. A two-letter code is usually sufficient: NY, LA, SF etc. Add 'Please' if you're feeling polite and desperate. 'Home to Mom' has also been known to work. Brandishing a Union Jack usually helps even though many drivers may mistake it for the Canadian flag.

Cities are best avoided altogether by hopping from one truck stop to another. There is usually enough through traffic to guarantee a ride past big cities en route. Occasionally you may be seized by an urge to get out and visit a city; when you come to leave, directions to hitching spots are given under *Arrival and Departure* in each regional chapter.

Hitching on Freeways. It is universally illegal to hitch from the main carriageway of limited-access highways, and yet everyone does it until told to move on. The ramps are disputed territory; a sign saying 'No Hitch-hiking' at the start of a ramp is ignored at your peril. Turnpikes invariably have toll booths at junctions. If the toll collector is in a good mood, he will let you stand where the traffic is travelling slowly and may even solicit a ride on your behalf. More likely, though, he will warn you off his territory and not hesitate to call the police if you argue, so it's best to stay a few hundred yards up- or downstream.

Drivers. A fair amount of academic research into hitch-hikers has been carried out in the USA. Much of it is concerned with the kinds of drivers that hitchers attract, and the conclusion reached is that motorists generally pick up people like themselves. Experienced hitchers recommend three disguises; the casual-but-clean approach; wearing a suit and tie and carrying a suitcase rather than a backpack; or making the most of your European connections by wearing full Tyrolean mountain gear or a kilt and sporran, though this could well attract the weirdos. You then have some chance of being picked up by normal human beings. This can be a definite advantage in view of the many strange characters currently driving around America, many of them are religious cranks, drink or drug abusers or perverts of various kinds. If you do get a lift with a dubious character, you might try to gain your freedom by feigning sickness or slamming the gear lever into a low gear and leaping out. Beware of the central locking systems fitted to many American cars. The best policy is to avoid problems by turning down any drivers whose sobriety or motivation you suspect. Sometimes the motorist will be pleasant company but a dangerous driver; just ask to be set down if you're anxious.

Some drivers will demand payment for a ride before you get in. Whether or not you agree to this depends upon how desperate you are for a lift. If you do decide to pay, make sure you agree a figure in advance. Claim poverty and settle on a figure as low as possible in order to emphasize that you're not worth robbing. And don't hand over all the cash until you reach your agreed destination. It is not unknown for drivers to extract payment from hitchers, eject them after a few miles, then drive on to pick up the next unsuspecting victim. You should also be wary of a driver who asks you to step out to see if his tail lights are working. Many a hitcher has been left helpless on the road after the vehicle pulls away with his luggage.

The Law. Despite former FBI director J. Edgar Hoover's warning that 'the beckoning thumb of the hitch-hiker can be a lure to disaster in disguise', there is no federal law prohibiting hitching. Instead, there is a mass of piecemeal state and municipal legalisation. Some states ban the soliciting of rides entirely, although this is easily circumvented by the accepted local custom of just smiling at oncoming traffic (though of course this may label you as a weirdo). Other states permit thumbing except if you are standing on the road surface. In fact the laws are often vague, and many police officers use their powers of stop-and-search at their discretion to check for drugs and weapons, and often invoke local vagrancy laws to arrest hitchers carrying less than the statutory $10 or so. Penalties for contravening anti-hitching laws range from a $10 spot fine to 30 days in the local jail. If you are concerned, ring the local police and ask them what the local laws are.

Fortunately, foreign visitors — especially clean, tidy and polite foreign visitors — are frequently immune from the worst penalties of the law. Rather than fining or arresting you, the police will tend to warn you off a freeway ramp or order you to hitch outside the city limits. Some may decide to give you a ride, and you are not expected to decline this offer. This will usually be to the county or state line. In fact standing close to the state borders is a good idea since there is a real 'no man's land' in policing terms on interstates between the last exit in one state and the first in the next.

CB Radio. The use of citizen's band radio in the USA is more than a passing fad. Almost all trucks, and many private cars, are fitted with CB. Unfortunately truck drivers are far less prone to pick up hitchers due to strict company regulations. But if you are lucky, you'll get a ride in a truck and be able to listen to your driver talk about delays ahead, summon help to accidents, and warn of impending presence of 'smoky bears' (highway patrolman) looking for speeding vehicles. (However, the combination of CB jargon, radio interference and a southern drawl will render many conversations entirely incomprehensible). They also chat to one another to while away the endless hours of tedium on transcontinental freeways. In the course of such conversations, there is a chance that a driver who has picked you up will ask other drivers to take you further along your route, and arrange an exchange at a convenient truck-stop.

Boat Hopping. For a free ride on a private yacht, find a yacht marina and offer your services as a crew member. Any maritime experience will be valuable but not essential if you can offer another skill such as handyman, cook or cleaner. The best chances are at San Diego, San Francisco, the Chicago lakeside, Boston, Long Island Sound near New York, New Orleans and Miami. The last two are particularly promising for voyages around the Caribbean.

Hitching on Aircraft. There is a great deal of private aviation in the USA, made up of amateur pilots and corporations who fly executives around in private planes. Over 750,000 Americans have private pilots' licences. They operate mainly from the hundreds of small airfields dotted around the States. Many people have successfully hitched rides by the simple expedient of asking. The duty officer at an airfield should be able to tell you who is flying where, and it's up to you to use your powers of persuasion with the pilots concerned. Maximize your chances by travelling light and being slim: in small aircraft every pound in weight is significant. Pilots use the same criteria as drivers when choosing hitch-hikers, so be clean, tidy and a great conversationalist.

Ride Sharing. Most cities operate a car-pooling service for commuters, but since this is probably of little interest to long-distance traveller don't get excited when you hear about a municipal 'Ride Board'. More useful are the ad hoc systems which can be found in large cities. Community radio stations and college noticeboards are full of requests for passengers and drivers to share expenses on long journeys. Many cities have ride referral agencies (look for this heading in the local Yellow Pages) which charge a fee for matching drivers with passengers. Their advantage is that they have plenty of people on their books and so if you're not tied to an exact departure date, you'll probably find a suitable ride. There is one nationwide agency which deals in rides throughout the USA and Canada: Travel-Mate, which has offices in New York (1-800-243-8588) and Virginia (1-800-368-3137). One-off membership costs $20. They also deal in ride-sharing on private aircraft. Other agencies provide services whereby several riders deliver a driveaway car or club together to buy a cheap car, drive to their destination, then sell the car and split the proceeds.

However you fix up your ride, the customary arrangement is to divide the cost of oil and gas equally, and to share the driving; check that the owner's insurance covers you adequately before taking the wheel. If you register jointly for a driveaway, there is no problem about insurance.

Freighthopping. The art of riding illicitly on freight trains has enjoyed something of a renaissance recently, perhaps as a reaction to the increasing dangers of hitch-hiking. Although it is against federal law — and can be extremely dangerous — many railway employees are not averse to your hopping a lift. The idea is to find a railroad freight yard and identify a train to take you someway towards your destination. You do this by asking friendly-looking switchmen (the people who operate the points) or experienced hoboes. Your adversary is the yard bull, the security officer whose job consists of preventing theft and vandalism, but also of catching freighthoppers. Once you find a train, you must look for a safe place to hide, which with increasing containerization is becoming trickier. The ends of bulk grain loaders are reputed to be secure if uncomfortable. When you arrive at the next yard, you repeat the procedure until you finally reach your destination. For further information and an explanation of the jargon (e.g. 'hotshot' for express freight train and 'pussy' for hostile security guard) consult *The Freighthopper's Manual for North America* by Daniel Leen. The latest 1993 edition is available from the author at Box 191, Seattle, WA 98111 for $8.95 post paid.

apartment	flat
bathroom	often a euphemism for toilet
coeducational/coed	mixed (male and female)
condominium/condo	flat which can be bought outright
dormitory	student hall of residence, usually with single rooms
duplex	an apartment occupying two floors
efficiency unit	self-catering apartment, sometimes in motels
elevator	lift
faucet	tap
half-bath	a room with a toilet and sink but no bath
outhouse	outdoor toilet
roomer	lodger
roommate	flat or house sharer, who does not necessarily share the same room
rooming house	a house in which rooms are let
RV	recreational vehicle (camper van or mobile home)
washroom	toilet/bathroom

One of the most regrettable facts for the traveller in North America is that there is nothing comparable to the family-run pensions and cheap and cheerful hotels which can be found in Europe. The cheap hotel you find near the Greyhound bus depot will not be in the same league as the cheap hotel you'll find near French or Italian railway stations. Not only will it be more expensive, but it is likely to be run-down and inhabited by lowlife. Most travelling Americans stay either in modern expensive chain hotels or in motels. Fortunately the network of low-budget hostels is expanding, and those who enjoy a little more luxury can buy vouchers in advance which give substantial discounts at motel and hotel chains.

HOTELS

Chains such as Holiday Inn, Hilton, Sheraton and Ramada provide predict-able clean rooms the world over. The rates, too, are uniformly expensive starting at around $90 per double room per night. But foreign travellers can make substantial savings by purchasing accommodation vouchers in advance when buying transatlantic air tickets. All North American tour operators offer discount vouchers for hotel chains including Days Inn, Howard Johnson and Holiday Inn. Typically a voucher costs £50 and allows up to four people to occupy a room. You may, however, have to pay substantial surcharges to stay in more upmarket places.

Hotel rates in America are quoted per room not per person. Singles — where they exist — are only slightly less than doubles, so it is much more economical to travel with a friend. If you are planning to stay for a week or more, it is always worth asking at the outset for a discount. You can get excellent weekend deals in big-city hotels, as most places slash their rates to attract custom when business people are thin on the ground. They may still cost more than many of the budget places recommended in this book, but should be substantially more luxurious. If you are not on a particularly tight budget and are looking for inns and hotels with character look for the series of accommodation guides called *Country Inns, Lodges and Historic Hotels* to various regions of North America.

MOTELS

Apart from youth hostels (see below) the cheapest and most comfortable accommodation can often be found in motels. These products of the motoring age dot the approach roads of every American city, advertising their facilities: swimming pool, colour TV, air-conditioning and free ice are common. The price of a room will seldom drop below $30; motels without neon signs are usually the cheapest. They are not called motels (motor-hotels) for nothing. Most are awkward to reach by public transport, but if you are driving around the US, they are a sensible (if somewhat predictable) option. The Big 6 chain of motels is about the cheapest, and they make it easy to book a room in your next motel for the price of a call. Also watch for Regal 8 (1-800-851-8888), Super 8 (1-800-843-1991), Days Inn, Red Roof Inns (1-800-THE-ROOF) and Susse Chalet. Howard Johnson (1-800-I GO HOJO) offers more upmarket accommodation for more upmarket prices.

BED & BREAKFAST

American tourists who have for years been smitten with the British institution of bed and breakfast have finally succeeded in importing the idea into their homeland. Most regions of tourist interest and many large cities now have bed and breakfast associations. Unfortunately rates are not at the familiar £30 level, but more like £60 for a double. Although this competes favourably with hotel prices it is by no means the cheapest accommodation available. In many cases, though, it might be the most interesting. Once you've seen one motel you've seen them all, but bed and breakfast homes vary greatly according to the personality and taste of the owner, and they can provide a unique glimpse of middle class American life. You may even get along with the host so well that you are asked to stay longer without paying, or invited back in the future free of charge.

The addresses for B & B registers are given in the regional *Accommodation* sections whenever possible. In addition, most bookshops have directories of local bed and breakfast opportunities. For advance bookings from the UK, contact Home Base Holidays, 7 Park Avenue, London N13 5PG (081-886-8752).

BUDGET ACCOMMODATION

Student travel offices in North America and abroad sell a useful booklet called *Sleep Cheap: North America;* the UK price is £2.

Youth Hostels. Joining your national youth hostels organization (£8 in the UK) might turn out to be the wisest investment you can make in preparation for your American travels. Membership entitles you to stay at any hostel under the auspices of Hostelling International, including those run by American Youth Hostels. And since most of the clientele are young foreign visitors, you'll meet like-minded travellers. A bed in a youth hostel ranges from $10 for a bunk in a simple hostel to $20 for sharing a double room in a superior hostel. You are expected to provide a sheet sleeping bag; if not, you can rent one for $2. There is usually a 25% surcharge during the winter (October 15-April 15) to offset heating costs. Hostellers can expect to have to perform a small chore before leaving. Some larger hostels even offer the option of doing several hours work in exchange for your board, allowing you to stay for free. There are nearly 300 hostels, but unfortunately they are not distributed evenly over the country. Whereas areas like the Colorado Rockies, the San Francisco Bay area and the Great Lakes are amply provided with hostels, many states (Alabama, Arkansas, Oklahoma, etc.) do not have a single hostel. Some hostels are located inside national parks where they often have a monopoly on accommodation.

In addition to the regular hostels operated by American Youth Hostels, supplementary accommodation is sometimes made available to hostellers in YMCAs, church halls, university residences, etc. Beds are normally available to non-YHA members also, but for a higher fee. Another variation on the usual kind of pupose-built hostel is the home hostel, which is simply a private residence open to youth hostellers for the same price as a hostel. Many hostels permit camping on their property for a small fee. All of this specified in the *American Youth Hostels Handbook* available from YHA in Britain (8 St Stephen's Hill, St Albans AL1 2DY; 0727 55215) for £7.50 including postage or $5 from any hostel office in the USA excluding postage.

The AYH national headquarters is at PO Box 37613, Washington DC 20013-7613; tel: (202) 783-6161. To complement the network of AYH hostels, some cities have low-cost hostels without the restrictions on time-keeping, alcohol, etc., that many travellers find tedious.Details are given under the *Accommodation* heading where applicable.

YMCAs and YWCAs. Young Men's Christian Association establishments and the equivalent organizations for women (YWCAs) provide budget-priced accommodation for both men and women. The average is about $35 single and $40 double (though doubles are not always available).

Despite the wholesome reputation of YMCAs — most are complete with swimming pools and fitness rooms — they do seem to attract a number of down-at-heel locals. In cities like Boston, New York and San Francisco — where cheap accommodation is hard to find — it is important to book ahead. You can reserve a room through the Y's Way, a central office in New York (224 E 47th St, New York, NY 10017; 212-308-2899; fax 212-308-3161). Full payment must be made in advance to reserve the room.

Camping. Almost 60 million Americans go camping every year, and that can mean anything from backpacking with a two-man tent to living in comfort in a plush RV. There are almost 18,000 campgrounds serving these campers. Many are in national or state parks and forests. Campers and campsite managers are often funds of information on events and eating places in their area.

Whereas government-run campsites are normally inside designated parks or recreation areas, private sites may be within automobile access of cities and other tourist attractions. The best known network of 700 commercial campsites is called KOA ('Kampgrounds of America') which are not intended for the back-to-nature camper (although tenters are welcome). The cost of a night's accommodation (including TV and games facilities, possibly a swimming pool, etc.) is around $10-$15, so they are not much cheaper than motels. In high summer, they are frequently full. A complete list of sites is available from the KOA Executive Office at PO Box 30558, Billings, Montana 59114 (406-248-7444).

LONGER TERM ACCOMMODATION

College Dorms. If you plan to be in a college or university town for a week or more during the summer months, it is worth writing to the University Housing Office to see whether they let travellers stay in student rooms. Some college residences are allowed to summer schools and conferences, but others are open to itinerants. Booking should be made early. Travelling students may be given preference if rooms are scarce.

Rented Accommodation. If you are staying for a week or more, you might be able to find space in a rooming house, where rents might be as low as $60 a week. Check in the 'Furnished Rooms' column of the newspaper classifieds. You could also try to arrange to sublet a room or a flat during the summer by checking in the personal columns of the campus newspaper. Most ads appear March/April/May. You can also find self-catering apartments often known as 'efficiency units'; enquire at the local tourist office.

House Exchange. If you want to live in an American home and have it all to yourself, you might want to participate in a house exchange. The two main requirements are that you are willing to spend two or three weeks in one place and that you have a house in a desirable location (London, the Cotswolds) which you are willing to trust to strangers. There are several agencies which charge a fee of (around £30) for publishing your house specifications in a register which is then distributed to all members. For some reason thsi has not yet become a big business, and many of the agencies are run by individuals from their homes. Try Home Base, 7 Park Avenue, London N13 5PG (01-886 8752) or Intervac, 6, Siddals Lane, Allestree, Derby DE3 2DY (0332 558931).

Eating and Drinking

a la mode	with ice cream
au jus	with gravy
automat	a restaurant where food and drink are taken from

	coin-operated machines
biscuit	scone
bittersweet	plain (as in chocolate)
bologna	processed pork and beef roll, like luncheon meat
broiled	grilled
brown-bag (vb)	to eat or take a packed lunch
brownie	a heavy chocolate cake, almost like fudge
brunch	late morning meal, often a social occasion
busboy	general restaurant dogsbody, table wiper and water pourer
Canadian bacon	thin gammon steak
candy	sweets
candy bar	chocolate bar (occasionally still called 'Hershey bar')
car hop	waiter/waitress at a drive-in restaurant
carry out	take away
check	bill
chiffon	frothy eggwhite dessert, often used as a filling for pies
chips	potato crisps
cookie	sweet biscuit
cracker	savoury biscuit
diner	basic restaurant which serves unpretentious American food
doggie bag	bag provided by a restaurant for taking away leftovers
eggplant	aubergine
English muffin	muffin (toasted, flat crumpet)
entree	main course
frank	frankfurter (hot dog)
french fries or fries	chips
gravy	seasoned white sauce poured over biscuits (qv)
greasy spoon	basic diner
grits/hominy grits	rural Southern dish of coarsely ground grains, a kind of small-bore tapioca with absolutely no flavour nor other redeeming feature.
gumbo	okra stew or any stew, characteristic of Louisiana
hash browns	chopped potatoes fried in bacon fat and shaped into flat cakes
hot cake	pancake
hush puppy	small deep fried cornmeal cake (Southern)
jello	jelly
jelly	jam
link sausage	a sausage in the British sense, i.e. cylindrical and encased in skin
lox	smoked salmon
maitre d'	head waiter
muffin	leavened cake in the shape of cupcake, often made of bran or with blueberries
munchies	peckishness often arising after indulging in controlled substances
oatmeal	porridge
pastrami	smoked beef with seasoning
popsicle	ice lolly
potato chips	crisps
quick and dirty	a cheap cafe
sack lunch	packed lunch

sausage	a flat, burger-shaped piece of processed meat
scallion	spring onion
scrod	young Atlantic cod or haddock
seafood	any fish (including freshwater)
sherbet	sorbet
short stack	two or three pancakes
shrimp	prawns
succotash	mixture of corn and beans (Iroquois Indian word)
sunny side up	fried eggs which have not been turned
surf n' turf	seafood and steak
take-out	take-away
tenderloin	fillet steak
truck stop	transport cafe
zucchini	courgette

Statistics such as the fact that snacks account for 25% of the average American diet may make some visitors fearful about the prospects of finding a decent meal. Such worries are groundless: eating out, and eating well, are conducted with gusto in the USA. Over five million people are employed in the catering industry to minister to the avid appetites of Americans. Although the kitchen of the average American is equipped with all manner of time-saving gadgets, the owner can regularly be found dining elsewhere. Consequently there is a huge range of eating establishments from basic diners to trendy vegetarian cafes, from authentic Ethiopian restaurants to the ubiquitous steak and seafood places serving 'surf 'n' turf'.

Some ethnic cuisines have flourished in America even more than in their own countries or origin: pizzas can be tastier in Chicago than in Calabria, Dim Sum more appealing in San Francisco than in Shanghai, and the tacos spicier in Texas than in Tijuana. Chefs in the USA have nurtured the French concept of *nouveau cuisine* and serve it in much larger portions, a style becoming known as *nouvelle Americain*. There is also a great deal of over-priced, mass produced, artificial garbage masquerading as food. A brief account of the kind of eating establishments to be found in most urban centres, followed by a run-down of the most common ethnic cuisines, should help the discerning traveller to find well prepared food at a reasonable price.

RESTAURANTS

It is impossible to make many useful generalizations about American res-taurants, since the range of style and ethnic style and ethnic cuisine is enormous. Many do tend to be gimmicky. There will be no understatement on the menu, the decor will be unusual in some way and the staff may be dressed up as if on safari or as characters from a cartoon strip. It seems that the publicity manager and interior decorator are paid more than the chef. One advantage of this corny mentality is that many restaurants will bake a cake for a special occasion if given prior warning and the waiters may even sing happy birthday to your embarrased companion. Often there are dress requirements for customers. Men may be refused admittance, even from fairly modest establishments, for wearing jeans or failing to wear a jacket and tie. Enquire when booking, or turn up prepared. If you book in advance you may be asked for your credit card number. If you don't show up for the reservation your account will be charged to an amount representing the average cost of a meal.

Restaurant service is attentive to the point of being obtrusive, in a way which some visitor find uncomfortably familiar. 'Hi, I'm Ron and I'll be looking after you this evening.' It is tempting to think that this ritual is intended to lead to a generous tip.

Many travellers are bemused by the number of staff clamouring to serve them. You may be seated by the hostess or *maitre d'* (pronounced maytradee), waited on by Ron and the bar waiter and cleaned up afterwards by the busboy. Ron is the only one you should tip, though there is usually a system by which tips are pooled and shared.

Often the price of the entree includes a starter, bread, salad and dessert. Some restaurants offer small helpings called 'petite dinners'. This may well be sufficient since the portions served in most restaurants verge on the obscenely large. If you can't finish your meal and want to save the leftovers for breakfast, ask for a doggy bag. Lunch in smart restaurants is usually cheaper than dinner, even though the menu may be the same. Other restaurants charge less for meals consumed at an unfashionable time of day: many offer 'early-bird specials' for people prepared to eat dinner before 6pm.

Restaurant proprietors are keenly aware of the new fad for healthy living and almost every menu has some appetizing vegetarian choices. Vegetarians will not have to make do with undressed green salads and cheese omlettes.

Fast Food. McDonalds, Kentucky Fried Chicken and Taco Bell are the culmination of the American desire for familiar, palatable food served instantly. Since the first McDonalds opened in the mid 1950s the company has sold billions of burgers. It has also employed, at sometime or other, one in five of the American workforce. And the company claims that in any year 95% of Americans eat at McDonalds. Most fast food outlets are national chains, so the burger you eat in Los Angeles is exactly the same — down to the last gram of monosodium glutamate — as the burger you ate in Boston. With a few exceptions, the antiseptic decor is identical from state to state, the prices and muzak will be the same, and the staff will be wearing the same uniforms and same forced smiles. Americans seem to adore standardization, and these places were flourishing even before Colonel Sanders experimented with his first unfortunate chicken. Most connoisseurs maintain that Wendy's and Burger King are preferable to McDonald's, and the International House of Pancakes offers a more fulfilling dining experience than Taco Bell or Pizza Hut.

Although this kind of meal is not likely to be memorable, it is a cheap and efficient way to eat. A quarter-pounder with all the trimmings, plus large fries and a soft drink won't set you back more than $3. Fast food can also be nutritious: you can order a McSalad rather than a Big Mac. Many fast food outlets have drive-in service. You park your car beside an intercom, relay your order to the staff inside, and wait for a waitress (who may or may not be wearing rollerskates) to bring out a tray, laden with burgers and root beers, and clip it to your car window. Alternatively, you drive round to another window where you pay, pick up your meal and drive away.

Diners. The first diners gleaming steel caravans made in New Jersey, bought by immigrants from southern Europe and driven to suitable roadside locations throughout America. Now the term is loosely used to describe any unpretentious truckstop or city cafe with a long menu and low prices. There is a counter with stools where you can watch your meal being prepared, or chairs and tables where you are waited upon by the blue-rinsed wife of the proprietor. The European influence on proletarian American food lives on only in the names: 'bologna', 'hamburger', 'frankfurter' and 'wienie' (from Vienna hot dog).

Roadside diners are becoming an endangered species due to the growth of 'family restaurants' or 'roadhouses', which are national chains dealing in standardized, portion-controlled meals. But away from the Interstates, on the edges of small towns, you can still find genuine diners. Although they used to pride themselves on their hearty home-cooking (stews, casseroles, etc.) they now have conformed to the tyranny of the hamburger. But the star turn is breakfast. John Steinbeck once said 'I've never had a really good American dinner, but I've never had a really bad American breakfast'. Competition is keen and for as little as $1.99 you can enjoy some of the following, and, for a little more, all of them: cereal, eggs, bacon, toast, jelly, hash browns, pancakes, syrup and unlimited coffee. Don't be surprised if everything (except the coffee) arrives on the same plate. After unsuccessfully trying to keep the syrup from the eggs and the jelly from the bacon you'll give up and eat them all together as Americans do. Brunch, eaten between 11am and 2pm, especially on Sundays, is like breakfast only more so. If you're ordering eggs the waiter will ask you how you want them done. If you want them fried, you'll have to specify if you want them 'sunny side up' (unturned), 'over' (turned) or 'easy over/over easy' (turned but runny).

The lunch special may be stew, bread and Coke and very cheap. You may see signs saying 'no substitutions'. This means you cannot have, say, french fries instead of a baked potato for the same price. To avoid embarrassment and extra expense, stick to the fixed menu.

Coffee shops are upmarket versions of diners with slightly fancy decor. They serve a range of egg dishes, fry ups, toasted sandwiches and pancakes. Many city hotels have a coffee shop on the ground floor which stays open late even all night. Drug stores often have a counter which serves cheap breakfasts and other snacks.

Mealtimes. Americans tend to dine much earlier than Europeans. Lunch is eaten around noon and dinner (usually called 'supper') between 5.30 and 7.30. But in cities you can eat at any hour of the day or night. Some diners and coffee shops advertise breakfast 24 hours a day. You can usually find an all-night drug store food counter, bus station cafeteria or hotel coffee shop. Diners and coffee shops which do not stay open all night generally open at 5 or 6 am and serve breakfast until 11 am.

In small towns, dinner may not be served after 7.30 pm. But there will doubtless be a local fast food joint open later or a 24-hour truckstop on a nearby highway.

Payment. In fast food joints you always pay at the time you get the food. At other places, you get either a computerized print-out or a scrawled bill ('check') to which tax, but not service has been added. You might also find, therefore, a syrupy note from your waiter saying 'It's been a pleasure to serve you — Ron'. At upmarket restaurants you pay at your table. At diners, take the check to the cash desk on the way out. You may find that each member of your party gets an individual bill, which is the management's way of avoiding fraud — it eliminates the problem of a group of diners getting separate bills and paying only one or two. There is no problem paying with a recognized travellers cheque (see *Money*) or cash. Most restaurants also accept credit cards.

Delicatessens. The 'deli' is a mainstay for American consumers, especially busy office workers. Delis usually serve bagels with cream cheese or lox (salmon) and sandwiches prepared from several varieties of bread and a score of fillings. Order as snappily as you can, and don't be put off by the number of questions fired at you about the type of bread, addition of mayonnaise, etc. The two great deli sandwiches are pastrami (smoked beef) and corned beef, served on rye bread with mustard only. These cost about $3.

Street Snacks. The hot dog was allegedly invented at the 1904 St Louis World's Fair. Nearlt a century later it is still going strong. Street vendors positioned at busy corners do a roaring trade in tasty hot dogs at a dollar each, with the American apology for mustard included in the price. They also do side orders of french fries and soft drinks. You can buy a slice of pizza for $1 from street stands. Pretzel vendors are unfamiliar to most northern Europeans. Pretzels are glazed salty curls of pastry and seem to be very popular.

Cheap Deals. Fixed price buffets, normally called 'smorgasbords' in America, are popular especially at Sunday lunchtimes. You can help yourself to whatever you like as often as you wish. A variation found in many restaurants is a serve-yourself salad bar. You are given a bowl and possibly only a single run at the salads on offer. The art is to begin with the densest salad (coleslaw, meats, potato salad) and build up your pile with progressively less dense ingredients. Finish up with lettuce and perhaps a tomato or two to anchor down the construction. To avoid undue spillage, apply dressing to each layer rather than all at once at the end. Many restaurants, particularly pasta joints, have 'all you can eat' specials. For about $7 you are entitled to endless helpings of the day's special dish, usually spaghetti bolognese.

FOREIGN CUISINES

You are probably familiar with American favourites such as steak, fried chicken and fruit pies (blueberry, pumpkin, pecan, banana cream are all delicious) and some of the most familiar ethnic cuisines such as French, Italian and Indian. Although there are a few surprises (e.g. when French cuisine collides with southern influences in Louisiana), most travellers will be able to cope. But there are a number of ethnic cuisines which are rarely found in Britain, yet which are ubiquitous throughout the States: principally Mexican and various Far Eastern cuisines (Chinese, Japanese, Korean and Vietnamese). You might also try a soul food restaurant which will probably feature ribs and cornbread or an American Indian place serving Native American specialities such as *sopapillas* (deep-fried puff bread).

Tex-Mex. Mexican chefs must be intrigued or appalled at what the USA has done to their national cuisine. Tex-Mex is not confined to Texas and can even be found in Alaska. Although often disparaged by gourmets for not being as fiery or as authentic as the original, it has the advantage of superior quality beef and pork, and has contributed some dishes of its own such as chilli con carne.

The basic menu of Tex-Mex is tortilla (flat, unleavened bread made of maize), rice, refried beans (beans which have been boiled, mashed and fried with chillis) and various kinds of sauce made from chilli peppers. Wrapped around meat or cheese, and oven baked, the tortilla becomes an *enchilada*. Fried, folded and filled with meat, cheese or salad, it becomes a *taco*. Toasted and broken up into squares or triangles, it becomes *tostados*, which are served either with a hot chilli sauce or with guacamole (mashed avocado, lemon and a hot green chilli sauce called *salsa verde*). This is enjoyed either as an hors d'oeuvre or as a snack to accompany beer or margaritas (see below). Only a a tourist drinks wine with Tex-Mex food.

To this basic menu has been added stuffed sweet and hot peppers known as *chilli rellenos*; *fajitas*, steak skirts marinated and charcoal grilled; *carne asada fajitas* covered with a sauce of tomatoes, chillis, onions, chopped avocado and cilantro (coriander) leaves, all eaten within a tortilla.

Finally there is the *nacho*; the supreme Tex-Mex snack, which may be purchased at rodeos, baseball games, and other events. In essence, it comprises *tostados* topped with refried beans and cheese, popped into the oven until the cheese melts, and then crowned with a coin-shaped slice of chilli called a *jalapeno*

If your budget allows, start your Tex-Mex meal with a margarita, a delicious and potent cocktail made with two parts tequila (a Mexican liquor made of fermented cactus juice), one part fresh lime juice, a dash of triple sec or Cointreau, shaken over crushed ice, and served in a glass whose dampened rim has been impregnated with salt. Again, if your budget allows it, wash down Tex-Mex with Mexican beer. Sol and Dos Equis are even more popular in the USA than in the UK.

Tex-Mex food with a more Mex than Tex flavour is good value and can be found at cafes and restaurants with a predominantly Mexican American clientele. There are many fast food chains offering Tex-Mex food, the most popular of which is called Taco Bell, though the quality of the food can't compete with small family-run Mexican restaurants.

Chinese. In Britain almost all Chinese restaurants are Cantonese. America is also dominated by Cantonese cuisine, but it is also easy to find Szechuan (setch-*wahn*), Mandarin and even Hunan restaurants. In Szechuan cuisine there is less reliance on glutinous sauces and more use of hot spices. Mandarin cooking (whether the Beijing or Shanghai varieties) uses a great deal of oil. You can tell an authentic Chinese restaurant by the number of Chinese people eating there, the absence of an English menu and the appearance of the soup at any time apart from the beginning of the meal.

Many Chinese restaurants offer *Dim Sum*, a luncheon tradition in which trolleys of small pastry parcels are wheeled to your table and you choose as many as you like. These contain various exotic combinations of meat, vegetables and noodles. Your bill is calculated according to the number of empty dishes at your table. Dim Sum is usually served from 11 am to 3 pm, and is especially popular on Sundays.

Chop suey may sound oriental, but was in fact invented in New York in September 1896. Most oriental restaurants distribute chopsticks but will provide a knife and fork if specially requested. At the end of the meal each diner gets a 'fortune cookie', an edible hollow biscuit containing a slip of paper claiming to tell your fortune but more often contains a piece of solid American philosophy such as 'He who works hard prospers greatly.'

Japanese. There is a strong Japanese influence even in the most American restaurants. Steak or chicken teriyaki have entered the repertoire of American dishes. Whereas originally this meant that the meat had been marinated in soy sauce and rice wine prior to grilling, usually it will merely have been basted with a sweet and sour barbecue sauce.

Eating out in an authentic Japanese restaurant is possibly the most foreign experience you will enjoy in the USA. The meal is served in a long series of courses in no apparent order: it seems to be simply the order in which the cook finishes each item. You will need to allow a full three hours, much of which will be spent drinking *sake* (hot rice wine) while you wait for the next plate of goodies to arrive.

The fish will arrive raw. Although this may sound disgusting, it is in fact rich, tender and tasty. You may also have a bowl of raw egg in which to dip *sukiyaki:* stir-fried beef, bamboo shoots, noodles and bean curd. *Tempura* are pieces of fish or vegetables deep fried briefly in batter.

If a full-blown Japanese meal is too expensive or too daunting, try a snack of *sushi* — small rice-and-seaweed packages decked with morsels of fish, egg or vegetable.

Korean. The delicate flavours of Japanese and Chinese cuisine go out of the window in Korea. Spices are heavy, meat is plentiful and *kimchi* (pickled cabbage with lots of garlic) will sort out who your friends are. Prices are lower than in Japanese restaurants, and you also get to cook the meat yourself on a portable barbecue.

DRINKING

barkeep	bartender
blitzed	drunk
brown bagging	drinking illicitly from a can or bottle concealed in a brown paper bag
BYO	bring your own (bottle)
chaser	long drink (usually beer) to follow a spirit; sometimes vice versa
cold duck	mixture of red and sparkling white wine (also a brand name for a wine made in Ontario)
cordial	a *digestif* such as port or a liqueur
excise laws	licensing laws
fifth	a bottle of spirits (i.e. a fifth of a US gallon)
float	ice cream drink
happy hour	half price drinking period, usually late afternoon and early evening
highball	whisky and soda or ginger ale
hooch	spirits
iced tea	cold tea with sugar and lemon
jag	prolonged drinking binge
loaded	drunk
malted (milk)	drink like a milkshake
Margarita	popular tequila cocktail (see eating: Tex-Mex)
Martini	the American drink: 3 parts gin, 1 part vermouth, served with an olive
Mint Julep	bourbon and mint cocktail associated with Southern planters
Old Fashioned	bourbon, bitters, sugar and fruit
regular coffee	white coffee (sometimes with sugar)
regular tea	tea without milk (often called clear or black tea)
root beer	soft drink
sarsaparilla	soft drink flavoured with the American plant of the same name
set-up	soda or soft drink for mixing with spirits
shot	measure of spirits (not standard but usually about equal to an English double)
soda (pop)	carbonated soft drink
speakeasy	illegal drinking establishment, originally from

	Prohibition
straight/straight up	neat, no ice
suds	slang for beer
tea	could mean 'iced tea', especially in the South
to drink one's face off	to go on a drinking binge
to tie on a bag	ditto
Tom Collins	gin, lemon juice, soda and sugar
warm case	beer sold in bulk and unrefridgerated, therefore cheaper
white lightning	crude, powerful homemade whisky

Social drinking in the USA does not revolve around neighbourhood pubs as it does in Britain. In fact there *are* no neighbourhood pubs, since suburbia is almost entirely devoid of bars. Although is some small towns you can still find a bar which serves as the focus for the local community, this concept barely exists in cities. People tend to go to bars not for a quiet chat with friends, but for an expensive night out on the town when conversation is usually rendered impossible by the noisy crowds and the loud music (often live). The closest equivalent to a place for a quiet drink is the cocktail lounge, where business people and office workers stop for a drink on their way home.

Attitudes towards drunkenness also differ. Displaying the effects of drink is a social misdemenour, and jolliness or rowdiness after a night on the town is regarded with disdain. Leaning heavily on the counter is sometimes enough to earn a reprimand from the bartender. If you don't sit up straight, he'll refuse to serve you, and the bouncer who checked your ID at the door won't hesitate to eject you. Once outside, if you stagger around drawing attention to yourself you'll be a prime target for both police and muggers. But despite all the problems, going drinking is still a good way to see a slice of life or to make friends.

Licensing Laws. The multifarious collection of legislation governing the sale and consumption of alcohol in America, called excise laws, makes Britain's licensing laws seem positively progressive. In some small towns in the Bible Belt, Prohibition has never ended. Getting a drink in Utah requires advance planning and military precision. State drinking laws can be modified by municipal legislation, and frequently are. Alcohol is often banned completely from Native American reservations. The result is a maze of anomalies prescribing what strength of liquor may be sold to whom between which times. The only way to find out is to enquire locally.

As a general rule, bars open at some time between 9am and noon and close between midnight and 3am. Sunday opening, if permitted, is for shorter hours. The drinking age is 21 virtually everywhere in the USA, as a result of pressure from the lobby against drunk driving. Age limits are strictly enforced by both the management and the police, and visitors in their thirties are sometimes flattered and amused to be asked for proof of age, so careful are the proprietors. Always carry your passport or other ID showing your date of birth. There is a considerable trade in unofficial identification cards. You can buy ID over-the-counter at print shops, and the assistant will print whatever you require: a false age, an address in the USA, a false social security number, etc. Note, however, that young people who use these to buy alcohol are guilty of fraud as well as under-age drinking.

Container Laws. These cover the heinous crime of drinking in a public place, an offence almost everywhere in the USA. The laws are not taken terribly seriously. Most Americans — including picknicking families as well as alcoholics — circumvent the law by drinking from a bottle or can concealed in a brown paper bag.

Buying Liquor. Every state except New Hampshire imposes duty on alcohol in addition to sales tax. The rate varies roughly in proportion to the historical influence of the local temperance movement, and is heavier on spirits than beer or wine. Mormon-dominated Utah has the highest prices, but even these are low by British standards. It is much cheaper to buy liquor from shops than to drink in a bar or restaurant. Beer comes in two standard sizes: 12 fl oz and 16 fl oz. Bottles and cans are sold individually or in packs of six. If you are able to shop around, you should find six-packs for $2-$3.

Many states have 'bottle laws' offering a 5c or 10c deposit on returned beer or soft drink bottles or cans (but not usually wine, spirit or fruit juice bottles). The deposit will be added at the check-out in addition to the advertised price. You may get a few pennies for returning aluminium cans, and indeed many down-and-outs scrape a living by collecting them.

The standard size for wines and spirits is the same as in Europe, 750ml, known in common parlance as a 'fifth', i.e. a fifth of a US gallon. Cheap foreign wine costs upwards of $3 per bottle; Californian and other American wine is more expensive. Bourbon starts at around $7 per bottle.

In a few states, you can buy any kind of alcohol at any time of the day or night. In others, beer and wine can be sold at any time while the sale of spirits is restricted to certain stores at certain times. Many states have a monopoly on the sale of liquor: it can only be bought from official State Liquor Stores within restricted opening hours and at standard prices. It is therefore pointless to shop around. There are some counties (particularly in Texas and Utah) where the sale of alcohol is totally prohibited. In West Virginia, drinks are sold only to members in private clubs; however temporary membership of such clubs is exceedingly easy to obtain.

The minimum drinking age applies to purchases of alcohol. If there's any doubt about your age, shops are supposed to ask for your ID. In practice, supermarkets rarely bother. But if a supermarket check-out girl is under age, she will ask an elder colleague (or you) to ring up the price of, say, a six-pack of beer. Otherwise she would technically be in breach of the law by selling you alcohol. (If you consider this to be yet another bizarre American custom you should know that the same practice has been known to happen in Tesco).

Bars. The stereotype of an American bar is not hard to find; look for a plastic-upholstered shell deserted except for a solitary drunk, a pair of desultory pool players and an adulterous couple conspiring in a darkened corner. It will probably have pictures of nude women and baseball stars as decoration. Single women will feel distinctly uncomfortable in such a place. The wild west saloon, with sawdust on the floor and only bourbon behind the bar, has died out more or less completely. The cocktail lounge has established itself as the primary venue for self-respecting drinkers, especially in big cities. Cocktail lounges approximate to British wine bars in style and clientele, but with a little more sophistication: for instance you may find your drink chilled with frozen grapes rather than ice cubes. You are waited upon at your table, and pay after each round or upon leaving. Either way, you'll be expected to leave some change in the waiter's saucer. Singles bars are a special case of cocktail bars. Customers willingly pay high prices for the privilege of eyeing up one another in the hope of finding the perfect partner. Even if you have no intention of doing likewise, the behaviour in singles bars provides an excellent spectator sport.

Many bars double as places to hear music or dance or both. Depending on the quality of the music, an admission fee or cover charge will be levied. Alternatively the price of drinks will be weighted.

Happy Hours. To drink on a low budget, choose a happy hour every time. Happy hours are rarely as short as 60 minutes. Most stretch for two hours or more in the late afternoon and early evening. If you see a sign saying 'Happy Hour Forever', it probably refers to cheap drinks all night rather than in perpetuity.

The simplest form of happy hour is where all drinks are half price. Other variations include 'All Drinks 99c', 'Half Price Draft Beer During Football Game' or 'Two Highballs for the price of one.' There is nothing to prevent you piling up a supply of drinks at happy hour prices as long as you pay upon serving to avoid disputes when settling up.

An added bonus of many happy hours is the range of free food on offer. The more up-market establishments (where you might never be able to afford drinks outside happy hours) often provide free hors d'oeuvres such as guacamole dip or cheese and biscuits. With a little determination and a thick skin it is possible to wolf down a complete meal while you linger over a solitary cocktail.

Free Drinks. Some clubs and bars offer free drinks all evening to single females. They are not necessarily the sorts of places that your mother would like you to visit. Others with music have ladies' nights when women are excused the cover charge but still pay for their drinks.

Tours of breweries, wineries and distilleries are invariably followed by free tastings. The South is best for distilleries; the Midwest for breweries; and Northern California for wineries. Addresses are given under the regional sections.

Beer. Almost all beer sold in the USA is pasteurized, pressurized lager brewed from maize or even rice, rather than from barley; it is invariably served ice cold. America, like other countries, has beer snobs. The best-regarded beers are Canadian (Molson), Mexican (XX, pronounced Dos Equis) and Filipino (San Miguel), rather than the standard American varieties like Budweiser, the best seller, and Michelob. Naturally the foreign brews are more expensive.

Canned and bottled British beers are available at the more up-market establishments, but cost the earth. Drinking Guinness is considered chic. There is a relatively new trend for 'boutique breweries' to start up brewing beers with some character; usually these are not marketed outside their immediate area. Try, for example New Amsterdam Bitter in Manhattan, Cartwright beer in Oregon and New Albion ale in California.

In bars and restaurants, beer is sold by the glass, can or bottle in measures of 12 fl oz, costing $1.50 or more. Many establishments also sell pitchers. These are jugs filled with a quart or half-gallon (32 or 64 fl oz) of draught beer. They provide considerable savings on buying by the glass, with prices starting as low as $4 for a half-gallon jug. Whereas the cost of drinking in a pub in Britain is not much more than buying beer at an off licence, the difference is much greater in the US. As a result, a great deal more beer drinking goes on in private homes in America than in Britain.

It is not considered normal to add lime or lemonade to beer in America. However, some people attempt to pep up Budweiser by adding tomato juice:

ask for a 'Bud and blood', which is not nearly so disgusting as it sounds. A variation on beer is malt liquor, which is simply canned beer without the hops. As a result it tastes sweet and insipid. The leading brands are Colt 45 and Schlitz. Another variation, brought about by the quaint licensing legislation in some states, is 'three-two beer' of 3.2% alcohol, about the same as cheap bitter in the UK but weaker than most other American beers.

Wine. House wine in restaurants and cocktail bars is usually Italian plonk. A half-litre carafe in a typical restaurant might cost $3. Californian wine is highly regarded in the USA and can be extremely good. But it usually isn't as cheap as one might have expected. Decent Italian and Chilean table wines are often cheaper. Look for wine as cheap as $3 a bottle in off-licences. Californian rose or 'blush' wines are popular and reliable, and the cabernet sauvignons (red) and rieslings (white) are occasionally outstanding. Cheap blended Californian wines known as jug wines are a real bargain, for example $5 for a magnum of Gallo red wine. Christian Brothers, Inglenook and Paul Masson (familiar to all Sainsbury's shoppers) are most reliable brands. Some wine is produced in other parts of the USA, notably upstate New York and the excellent soil of Idaho and Washington State. There is an increasing number of cottage wineries producing more varied vintages.

At cocktail bars, a favourite tipple among the diet-conscious is white wine and Perrier. An undiluted glass of wine in a cocktail bar costs at least $3 outside happy hours. Sangria, a mixture of cheap red wine and fruit juices, has been somewhat superseded by 'coolers', blends of rough white wine, juices and sugar. Beware of the effect of coolers (particularly if you plan to drive) and note that the sugar and flavourings added to the poor quality of the wine can lead to an almighty hangover.

Spirits. A fair shot of neat spirit (approximating to a double English measure) costs at least $2. The most popular is bourbon, a whisky distilled from maize, which originated in Bourbon County, Kentucky. Jim Beam and Jack Daniels are the superior brands. Rye whisky, such as Canadian club and Seagrams 7, tastes rather like dubious blend of Scotch. Try mixing it with Seven-up; ask for a '7 and 7'. The genuine article, like Johnny Walker Black Label, can be twice as expensive. Vodka is gaining popularity; American-made Sirnoff is cheaper but weaker than the imported Polish and Russian varieties. Spirits are rarely drunk neat ('straight up'). Usually they are served 'on the rocks' or they form the basis for mixed drinks. The term 'cocktail' originated in Louisiana as a corruption of *coquetier,* meaning egg-cup and is now used as a term for any drink containing a spirit and mixer.

The first cocktail was probably the mint julep, made from bourbon, fresh mint and sugar. Mixing drinks became necessary during Prohibition to disguise the disgusting taste of illegal hooch. The term 'highball' is used to describe simple drinks such as whisky and soda, gin and tonic or rum and coke. Short stiff drinks include Martinis (vermouth — not necessarily Martini — swamped by gin), Manhattans (vermouth and bourbon) and Black Russians (vodka and Tia Maria). The Tequila Sunrise uses orange juice and grenadine to make a longer, less potent drink; beware of the salt which is applied liberally to the rim of the glass. The ever-popular Margarita also relies on Tequila. The Daiquiri is simply white rum and lime, but often comes with crushed banana or strawberries as well. Every cocktail comes with lashings of ice unless you specify otherwise, plus assorted miniature umbrellas, cherries and so on. Before you order make sure that your drink will be freshly made. Some bars sell only pre-mixed cocktails straight from the can. On average a cocktail costs $5.

However you take your poison, you should remember that American spirits are generally stronger than in Britain: 80 or 90 proof rather than 70. And since they are poured by hand, you could seriously underestimate the rate at which you are drinking. You might want to adopt the practice favoured by many serious drinkers in the USA of drinking a chaser (a long drink, usually beer) after each shot.

Soft Drinks. There is no stigma attached to abstaining from alcohol and drivers are socially and legally encouraged to drink in moderation or not at all. There are plenty of non-alcoholic drinks to choose from. Still or sparkling mineral water (usually imported) is sold for about the same price as beer. Bear in mind that in a blind tasting of mineral water, New York tap water was the outright winner among still waters; in the sparkling category, ordinary soda water easily beat some of the top name European mineral waters.

Seven-Up, Sprite, Coke, Pepsi and root beer (a vaguely medicinal-tasting fizzy drink devoid of alcohol) and many other varieties are collectively known as 'soda pop' or 'soda'. They cost about 50c for a 12 fl oz can from vending machines located at every garage, bus station and motel. Soda is the strongest drink you can hope to find at most diners and fast food outlets. It is served in regular (large) or large (enormous) paper cups, along with a small glacier's worth of ice. If you are concerned about your health, choose instead a freshly-squeezed fruit juice or a non-alcoholic cocktail.

Try to pay at least one visit to a soda fountain, a veritable soft drinks emporium. For a dollar or two you can sample a fizzy chocolate and ice cream milk shake (malt). At least it contains real milk: most of the synthetic slush sold as shakes by fast food chains has never been near a cow.

Coffee. American coffee is almost always filtered or percolated from fresh beans and is generally excellent. The 'bottomless cup' — where you can get endless free refills — is standard practice. Coffee is either 'with' or 'without cream'; the term 'white' is not used. Coffee is also either 'regular' or 'Sanka', a brand-name for decaffeinated coffee. The price of a bottomless cup starts at 50c.

Tea. In *The Tea Lover's Treasury,* James Norwood Pratt suggests that the Boston Tea Party episode has given the American people 'a prenatal disinclination for tea.' The American idea of what constitutes a cup of tea is usually insipid and fairly disgusting. You are given a cup of hot water and a tea bag and left to get on with it. Milk or lemon may be supplied if you're lucky. Tea costs 50c upwards, but you only get one cup.

If you ask for tea in the southern states, you'll get iced tea unless you specify the hot version. Iced tea can be a deliciously cooling brew of double strength tea poured over ice cubes, lemon and sugar. Unfortunately, it is sometimes made from powder or served straight from the can, when it bears little relation to the genuine article.

In the words of an overused cliché, if you have an itch, America will scratch it. Whether you want to be frightened out of your wits on a roller-coaster ride or immerse yourself in visual art, the USA can meet your needs. Short on heritage? With little surviving history beyond the past few hundred years, entire buildings and their contents have been imported from Europe, such the Cloisters, a reconstructed mediaeval monastery at the northern tip of Manhattan. Even if you have no strong ideas about what to see or where to go, the streetscapes and scenery are constant sources of surprise and enjoyment.

MUSEUMS AND GALLERIES

The enormous budgets of many American art galleries guarantees a wealth of visual art. You would expect to find collections at the Smithsonian in Washington, the Art Institute of Chicago or the Metropolitan Museum of Art in New York which are equal to the National Gallery in London or the Hermitage in the Russian city of St Petersburg. But many smaller cities, such as St Petersburg in Florida and Malibu in California, also have excellent galleries. Because of their large endowments, many museums are free; others post a suggested donation which you are at liberty to ignore if you have the nerve.

In addition to museums of art and sculpture, there are many eccentric collections, often located in out-of-the-way places, for example the Museum of Fire Engines in New York City or the Balzekas Museum of Lithuanian Culture in Chicago.

America specializes in museums of science and technology. Whereas Europeans excel at preserving and restoring their past. Americans are more future-oriented. Even people with no scientific background or interest find fascination at places such as Space Center Houston and Washington's Air and Space Museum. Many such places are 'hands-on' museums which invite visitor participation.

AMUSEMENT PARKS

Whether internationally famous like the Walt Disney creations, or known only to afficionados of the roller-coaster and Ferris wheel, the multi-billion-dollar industry of amusement parks is for many people the number one reason to visit the USA. A few high-minded entrepreneurs have tried to shift the emphasis towards education-through-entertainment, however, the biggest queues at Walt Disney World in Florida are not for the multicultural Epcot Center but for Space Mountain, an unashamed fairground ride.

The usual practice is to buy an unlimited-ride ticket for around $40-$70 per day. This might seem excessive, but allows for a day of unlimited entertainment. The only restriction on the number of rides is the time taken up by queuing. At peak periods (weekends and public holidays) you can waste half the morning standing in line for the star attraction, though the management takes pains to keep queues informed of the likely waiting time.

Darien Lake near Buffalo boasts a roller-coaster named the Thunderball Express, which turns passengers upside down five times in a couple of minutes. But the title of the biggest roller-coaster in the world has been snatched by Magic Harbor at Myrtle Beach, South Carolina.

The Midwest has more than its fair share of amusement parks but for the best selection you have to go to the Orlando area of central Florida. Walt Disney World, the Disney/MGM movie complex and Universal Studios, not to mention old favourites like Sea World, jostle for business. For a complete rundown of these and other attractions — such as the Grizzly River Rampage in Nashville or the Loch Ness Monster coaster in Virginia — consult *Amusement Parks of America* by Jeff Ulmer, published by Doubleday.

Rodeos. Most rodeos remain loyal to their cowboy roots, with modern-day cowboys competing in bronco-busting, steer wrestling and calf-roping events. Others offer less traditional but equally exciting contests such as barrel racing. Try to see a rodeo in a small Midwestern or Southwestern town rather than at the grander, more commercialized venues such as Buffalo Bill's Wild West show in North Platte, Nebraska or Dodge City Days in the 'Cowboy Capital of the World', Dodge City, Kansas. For a calendar of upcoming events, contact the International Rodeo Association, American Fidelity Building, Box 615, Paul's Valley, Oklahoma 73075 (405-238-6488).

Bungee Jumping. The sport of jumping off structures attached only to an elastic strap was made famous by the Dangerous Sports Club of Oxford University, members of which leapt off the Golden Gate Bridge in San Francisco. Public bungee jumping was popularized in New Zealand, and has now spread to the USA. Most jumps use man-made towers, and you pay around $80 for the privilege of being scared witless.

Other Attractions. Fairs, festivals, jamborees and parades are times when Americans are at their most colourful and gregarious. State Fairs provide a chance to see log-splitting and pie-baking contests and plenty of other esoteric activities. There are Kite Festivals, Garlic Festivals, Apple Blossom Festivals, Blue Grass Music Festivals, Tobacco Spitting Contests and countless others. There are also corn roasts, clam bakes and chilli cook-outs. In addition there is a wealth of ethnic celebrations from Czech to Celtic. Ask at the state tourist office for details of local festivals.

RECREATION

At times you will be tempted to think that America is a nation of joggers. Track suit and running shoe manufacturers have made a killing (not to mention osteopaths and physiotherapists). On the whole Americans are sporty: they ski, sail, waterski and canoe as a matter of course. Most children are exposed to outdoor recreations at summer camp or at their family's holiday home (called a 'cottage'). Although there are many spectacular hiking trails, usually in mountainous areas or parklands, there is no tradition as there is in Britain of simply going for a weekend walk in the country, partly because of the supremacy of the motorcar, and partly because there are very few pedestrian rights of way in rural areas.

There are also many less energetic recreations favoured by Americans. Mini-golf courses and bowling alleys proliferate and are a good place to see American families at play. Golf is a more proletarian sport in America than in Britain, and there are many public golf courses where it is possible to hire clubs and play a round of golf for a modest fee. In prosperous America, it is not surprising to find a high density of swimming pools, skating rinks and tennis courts, which are either free or nearly free. Pool halls provide a less wholesome alternative; take care not to 'foul on the eight-ball' (ask the locals for an explanation).

Every affluent American seems to have a hot tub (large pool which holds up to half a dozen bathers) or a jacuzzi with the additional feature of swirling water. If you don't happen to be invited to share a private one, you can rent one for a few dollars at the more legitimate massage parlours or at a jacuzzi joint in city centres.

barracker	sports fan
bunco game	crooked card game
cotton candy	candy floss
couch potato	television addict
craps	popular gambling game with dice
creamed	soundly beaten
exacta	racing forecast
Ferris wheel	big wheel at a fun fair
field hockey	hockey; by 'hockey' Americans mean ice hockey
first balcony	upper circle in a theatre
high roller	big-spending gambler
hootenany	jamboree, rave-up, often implying a square dance
jock	keen athlete
loge	front of the dress circle at the theatre
mezzanine	dress circle in a theatre or cinema
movie theater	cinema
place (verb)	to come second in a horse race
orchestra	front stalls in a theatre
road team	away team
scalper	ticket tout
show (verb)	to come third in a horse race
stock company	repertory theatre company
summer stock	repertory company which works in resort areas during the summer
taxi dancer	a girl who dances with customers at a dance hall, for a price
Tony Awards	Broadway theatre awards named after Antoinette Perry
twofers	two-for-the-price-of-one theatre tickets

With so much disposable income, Americans spend a lot of time going out and in the process support a massive entertainment industry. Whether your tastes are for Baroque chamber music or naked female mud wrestling, there is much to take in. Of course the big cities have most to offer, but smaller communities also have ways of satisfying Americans' deeply felt need for a good time.

Tickets. You can buy a ticket for almost any musical, theatrical or sporting event anywhere in the country from any branch of Ticketron. This is a national chain of ticket agencies linked by computer, often located in Sears stores. Because the promoters get so much business through Ticketron, often you need pay no surcharge. Ticketron are also worth trying for cut-price tickets for local events on the day of performance. Most large cities now have booths selling half-price theatre tickets on the day; details are given in each regional chapter, but in general the booth is located in the theatre district.

The terminology for the location of seats in auditoria may be confusing: the 'orchestra' equates to the front stalls in a British theatre, while Americans describe the dress circle at the mezzanine.

MUSIC

Serious Music. When rich Americans hear the word 'culture' they reach for their wallets. It is not over-cynical to suggest that the reason why serious music, ballet and opera are so well patronized is because of the desire to impress. For instance Cleveland (not generally noted for its sophistication) boasts an orchestra of world-renown. This pattern is repeated in cities throughout the USA, and in all the arts. Whatever the motives for such bulk-purchase of culture and prestige, serious music lovers should take advantage of prices subsidized by local wealth and patronage. Tickets are by no means cheap — $30 for a concert, $50 for an opera or ballet — but represent a bargain in view of the costs of staging these extravaganzas.

Most of the top orchestras — such as the Boston Symphony, the Chicago Symphony, the Los Angeles Philharmonic, the New York Philarmonic and the Philadelphia Orchestra — have a winter season at their main downtown concert hall and a summer season in a more informal setting such as a park or pavilion.

Popular Music. Whatever your taste in pop music, you will find something to object to in America. The birthplace of jazz, the blues and rock and roll also produced the Muzak Company, purveyor of anonymous background music to be played in lifts, restaurants and supermarkets. There are more radio stations than in any other country and yet many of them limit themselves to repeating identical playlists of oldies or the Dire Straits/Genesis/Bruce Springsteen axis. The mainstream of American music is AOR — 'Adult Oriented Rock' — slick, clean, professional but ultimately uncontroversial music. In defence of this 'product', it does sound rather more acceptable when played loud in an open convertible driving down the freeway on a sunny morning than it does when heard in a bedsitter on a rainy afternoon in Barnsley.

British bands are immensely popular, and relics from 80s, 70s and even 60s rock bands are still doing the rounds. Those with a particular taste, in, say, country and western or jazz-rock should be able to find radio stations, record shops and clubs to cater for their needs; America's vast population means that 'minority interest' groups form a viable market.

Nostalgia buffs stand a better chance of seeing vintage bands such as the Grateful Dead or Crosby and Nash, or Crosby, Stills and Nash, or even (in a good year) Crosby, Stills, Nash and Young in America than back home. People who prefer to look forward musically should check out the free listings papers which can be found in cities as small as Little Rock Arkansas. Bars and clubs often feature free entertainment, some of it surprisingly good.

Opera. The leading opera companies perform in San Francisco, New York (both the Met and the City Opera), Seattle, Chicago, Boston and Santa Fe. There are sometimes substantial reductions for students or for people willing to accept standing room.

Dance. As in many things, New York leads the USA in dance with several excellent companies including the renowned New York City Ballet. The National Ballet performs in Washington DC, and there are also very good companies in Pittsburg, Philadelphia and San Francisco. The two most important touring companies are the American Ballet Theatre and the Martha Graham Dance Company.

THEATRE

Mainstream drama is confined to the 37 theatres of Manhatten's Broadway (the 'Great White Way') plus conventional theatres in most large cities. The latter often survive on a diet of touring companies from Broadway, or provide a testing ground for new plays before they move to New York. Many Broadway plays originate in Britain: at the time of going to press, five shows were playing simultaneously in both London and New York.

For more experimental theatre, you might prefer to visit an 'Equity-waiver theatre'. These are theatres with 99 seats or less, so-called because they do not need to pay union rates. Therefore they can afford to stage experimental material. The best examples are the 'off-Broadway' or 'off-off-Broadway' theatres in New York. Because of their small size, 'Equity-waiver' theatres are chronically short of money. Even after buying your ticket you'll be asked for extra donations before, after and even during the show.

Theatrical life outside the big cities and university campuses includes Shakespearean festivals in unlikely and out-of-the-way small towns (several of which are called Stratford). These can be most entertaining, if only for the spectacle of a Hamlet with a rich English accent playing against minor characters with southern drawls. Many stock companies play in repertory theatres located in summer resort areas. Although they tend to confine themselves to lightweight farces, the quality of the productions can be high.

Tickets for Broadway-standard shows are expensive; $50 for a reasonable seat is not unusual. They can be booked through Ticketron or by phoning the theatre box office direct and paying by credit card. For less popular productions, just go along to the local half-price tickets booth where unsold seats are sold off on the day of performance.

CINEMA

Watching television has not replaced going to the movies and box office receipts at cinemas are showing remarkable resilience.

Cinemas fall into three categories: 'first-run', which approximate to local cinemas in Britain and show films on general release; and 're-run' cinemas, which specialize in showing old classics. Advance booking is necessary only for first-run cinemas, which charge $6-$10 a seat. Many are 'multiplexers' with up to a dozen screens, some of them tiny. Second-run cinemas cost between $3 and $5. You shouldn't pay more than $3 at a re-run cinema, except for all-night sessions, and some cinemas charge only 99c.

Drive-ins. Ever since they were invented in Camden New Jersey in 1932, the huge screens of drive-in cinemas have towered above small-town America. You simply pay at the gate, drive into a parking place, clip a tinny loudspeaker to your car window and watch the movie. They rarely show new releases, nor seldom old classics, but this seems of little concern to the clientele. It seems that adolescent culture in some small towns has not progressed at all since the 1950s. Sadly, videos have undermined the popularity of drive-ins, and many now stand abandoned as reminders of the lost innocence of youth.

TELEVISION

All the stories you have heard about American television are true. There are countless stations, programmes (even live sport shows) are interrupted every few minutes for a batch of commercials, and most children spend longer in front of the box than at school. The average adult watches 28 hours a week. Wherever you are and whatever the time you can be certain of a choice of viewing. Even the crummiest hotel or motel will boast a TV in every room, albeit with numerous dead flies attached to the screen. Airports and bus stations have coin operated televisions built into arms of the chairs.

Having seen a few programmes you may find it hard to comprehend the addiction. British television takes only the 'best' American entertainment; what remains is even more banal than *Baywatch*. Quiz shows are inordinately popular, sometimes with prizes of over $100,000. Most of the questions concern other television programmes. Although news broadcasts and documentaries have occasional flashes of brilliance, serious political analysis is usually sacrificed to the cause of sensationalism. Pictures of violent death are shown in gory detail, then re-run forwards, backwards and in slow motion. Michael Caine once said he could find out more of actual importance in ten minutes of listening to the BBC World Service than from watching three and a half hours of TV in California.

Reception. Programmes are mostly so ghastly that the poor reception experienced in many areas can be something of a blessing. Even when reception conditions are perfect, the image is far from ideal. The USA has had colour television since 1952 and uses a relatively primitive transmission system. There are only 525 lines on the screen, as opposed to the more usual 625, with a consequent loss of definition.

Operation. There are few televisions with simple push-button selectors as found in Britain. Older sets have rotary dials, often showing numbers which bear no relation to numbers of each channel: Channel 3 might appear at '42' on the dial. More modern TVs have remote control handsets with which you can select a channel with repeated button-pushing. The station you have selected is displayed in red digits next to the screen. But again, there is not necessarily any correlation between the number shown and the channel of the station as quoted in newspapers or in the *TV Guide*. If you seriously want to watch a particular programme, accost a friendly local to help tune in.

Networks. Most of the stations which transmit programmes belong to one of the three national commercial networks: ABC, CBS and NBC. The competition between them is intense. Programme ratings are compiled overnight and series terminated abruptly the next morning should they make a poor showing. Heavy self-censorship is practised to avoid outraging vocal minorities: even the mildest swearwords are wiped from the soundtrack of late night movies, and anything resembling a sex scene is cut before transmission. The contents of films are listed in graphic detail in newspapers, with amusing euphemisms such as 'Adult Situations' — meaning 'sex scene'.

This search for mass audiences drags programmes quality down to the lowest common denominator. The result is a diet of dehumanizing game shows and soap operas so dire as to make *Eldorado* seem profound. Should you become addicted to one of these gripping sagas, don't despair if you miss an episode. Several 'dial-a-storyline' numbers will give you an instant

60-second update on the latest goings-on. And if you want to see a game show being recorded, head for Hollywood where they give out free tickets in the streets.

Public Broadcasting. An antidote to the overwhelmingly tasteless networks is provided by the many regional stations that make up the Public Broadcasting Service (PBS). They show documentaries, discussion programmes and high quality foreign drama. Instead of interrupting the programmes with advertising, PBS stations spend a great deal of airtime appealing for donations and displaying messages of gratitude to their commercial sponsors.

Cable. In all but the most rural areas, cable TV offers a supplementary repertoire of 24-hour TV programming. In the large cities, it is not uncommon to find 50 or more channels in addition to the regular network and PBS stations.

To receive these additional channels, viewers pay a monthly subscription fee to the local cable company. These fees reduce the need for advertising, which is part of the attraction of cable TV. Some channels, particularly the movie channels, require an additional monthly charge from the viewer.

There are few restrictions on what may be shown on cable TV. You may watch evangelism or pornography, local council meetings or heavy rock. 'Wayne's World', a movie about a cable show made in a suburban home, was not too far of the mark. The range of channels available depends upon the local cable company and the nature of the franchise agreement it has with the municipality. Many of the channels are transmitted by satellite and are available across the country. They include the movie channels Cinemax, Home Box Office (HBO) and Home Theatre Network (HTN); a Disney channel and a Playboy channel; MTV (rock videos); Country Music Television and the Nashville Network; Cable News Network (CNN); C-SPAN, which is where you'll see news conferences in their entirety; and the sports channel, ESPN, which sometimes shows British soccer matches.

Satellite TV. The USA and Canada are served by about 20 TV satellites, each with a capacity to transmit up to 24 channels. Most transmissions from the satellite are for the exclusive use of local cable TV companies. These act as the middlemen, passing the satellite signal through a cable network to individual subscribers. The contracts between the satellite owners, programmers and local cable TV companies are exclusive, so direct reception of the satellite signals is illegal. Nevertheless a growing number of Americans are tuning in with their own back yard 'dish' antennae realizing that ownership of a dish is legal and that it is virtually impossible to enforce a law that attempts to control the way you convert the satellite signal after it has entered your home. Since the direct satellite owners' expensive attempts to scramble their signals have invariably failed, since the circuit diagrams for descramblers are soon in circulation.

RADIO

Many travellers find American radio a better source of entertainment and information than television. There are 50,000 radio stations in the USA, so you should find something to your liking. As long as you don't anticipate serious programmes of the kind found on BBC Radio 4, you won't be disappointed. If you have access to a short wave radio, you might want to tune into the BBC World Service on the 49 metre band; write to World Service Publicity, PO Box 76, Bush House, Strand, London WC2B 4PH

(071-257 2211) for wavelength and schedule information. In big cities you can find any kind of music at the turn of the dial: MOR (middle of the road), AOR (adult oriented rock — mostly album music), Urban Contemporary (black music); top forty hits, golden oldies, country and western, jazz, gospel, reggae and classical music. The speech content is equally diverse, from the latest West Indies cricket score or Dow Jones Index to ferocious fundamentalist sermons.

The choice of station thins out considerably as you move away from large cities. In vast tracts of Texas and the Midwest you'll find only two or three stations, whose entire output seems devoted to country and western music plus the odd farming programme. Technically, stations range from hi-tech automated affairs (where everything is on tape and the engineer monitors the output on a radio at the local bar) to shoestring stations run by a man, dog and a pile of records. If you want to look around a station, just phone up and ask. Most stations will be delighted by your interest.

Radio stations are classified as AM or FM depending upon the mode of propagation. Some stations broadcast simultaneously on both wavebands, but most use only one. Frequencies are quoted in kHz (AM) or MHz (FM). With a few exceptions, each radio station is identified by a four letter code; for stations east of Mississippi, the first letter is W; in the west, it is K.

FM. Most FM broadcasts are high-quality stereo. Historically, the lower end of the FM dial (below 92 FM) was reserved for non-profit stations, mostly student stations, offering classical music and intellectual discussions. Although this is no longer strictly true it is still a fairly accurate guide. The speech content on these stations is largely community information; meetings, lost cats, ride-sharing etc. The other end of the FM spectrum is occupied by rap, rock and country; it seems to be a rule of the Federal Communications Commission (which oversees broadcasts) that at least one country station is audible at all times.

AM. Sound quality is worse on AM, but the signals travel much further. Although there are no real national radio networks in the USA, several stations cover the eastern half of the country on AM. You are most likely to find news and top forty stations on AM: the phrase 'AM Rock' is widely used to describe modern commercial pop music.

NEWSPAPERS

Once again the USA has earned another superlative, with more daily newspapers (1,600) than any other country. The biggest seller is *USA Today* which is edited in Virginia and transmitted by satellite to printing plants all over the USA. It tends to be bland — some Americans refer to it as *McPaper,* the journalistic equivalent of junk food — but nonetheless it sells over five million copies daily. The only other truly national newspapers are the *Wall Street Journal* and the *Christian Science Monitor*. Other newspapers are either regional (e.g. the Memphis *Commercial Appeal*, serving a small patch of Tennessee). Although it is possible to buy the *New York Times* in Los Angeles or vice-versa, most Americans stick to their local regional paper. Most rely heavily on syndicated features, so you can read the same article on one day in Washington and the next in Chicago.

Most newspapers are broadsheets — the same size as the *Independent* and *Guardian* — and approximate in style, if not in breadth of coverage, to British 'quality' papers. Tabloids are confined to large cities and place more emphasis on sport and sensationalism than serious news.

Papers cost 25c-50c. Sunday editions cost three or four times as much but are truly enormous, containing a dozen or more sections. There are few newsagents as found in Britain; the few Americans who don't get a daily paper delivered buy them from vending machines at downtown street corners and shopping malls. You put in coins to the required amount, whereupon the door opens. You are trusted to take only one copy and to close the door firmly afterwards.

Being highly localized, most newspapers are good at information about what's on. Many cities also have weekly listings magazines which are free and more detailed: these are described in each *Entertainment* section.

Foreign newspapers can be found at specialist news kiosks in city centres. They are usually expensive and out of date: if you have an insatiable craving for the *Times*, expect to pay $3 for a two-day-old copy. The cheapest and most up-to-date British newspaper is the *Financial Times,* printed locally and costing $1. For a free read, try larger libraries or the reading room of the British Consulate, though these will be even more outdated.

SPORT

The most popular way to be idle in the US is to watch sports either on television or live. Try to see a big league game. Even if you don't understand all the rules and strategies, the antics of both players and fans provide ample entertainment. Furthermore, despite the frenzy generated by cheerleaders, music and instant video replays, there is virtually none of the hooliganism (except on the field) that taints some spectator sports in Britain.

Ball Games. The big American spectator sports have few practitioners elsewhere. This is historically because America has had no empire to adopt its pastimes (as Britain introduced cricket and rugby to its former colonies). To gain a thorough understanding of each sport would require a degree course in the subject, but a brief sketch of each game may help.

Baseball is like rounders, only the ball is harder and players wear large gloves. After three fair throws by the pitcher a batter is out. But if he hits the ball, he runs to the first of four bases, and further if he feels he can getaway with it without being run out. The equivalent of hitting a six at cricket is a home run. Each of the nine innings ends when a team has three 'outs' (i.e. loses three wickets in cricketing terms). If there is a tie, the teams go into extra innings. The main leagues are the American and the National, of roughly equal status, each divided into East and West divisions. The baseball season starts in April and climaxes with the World Series in October, when the winners of the American League take on the champions of the National League.

American football is called simply 'football'; to refer to it as American is as strange as talking of 'British cricket'. The aim is to cross the opponents' base line with the ball, a slow process achieved by a series of plays in ten yard stages. Like rugby, the players use hands, feet and shoulder to move the oval ball — and the other team — around. The National Football League is divided into the American and the National Conference, effectively two divisions with no obvious (e.g. geographical) reasons for which team goes where. These are further sub-divide into three regions, East, Central and West, although again this is a less-than-perfect split: Houston is in the Central Division of the American Conference, while Dallas — further west — is in the Eastern Division of the National. The winners of each Conference play each other in a sequence of matches at the end of the season, called the World Series. College football culminating in such famous New Year events as the Rose Bowl in Pasadena and the Orange Bowl in Miami, is followed almost as avidly as professional football.

Ice hockey can also be a vicious game; Canadians are the best exponents: see page 403. Basketball is played from September to March. Although the aims and rules of the game are fairly straightforward, the degree of skill displayed by players is phenomenal. Try to see a major league game. Basketball is organized along similar lines to baseball and football, with American and National Conferences.

Soccer. Many Americans consider soccer to be an inferior import, although this attitude is changing as the USA is host for the 1994 World Cup. The Americans have done extraordinary things to the game in the name of entertainment — instant large screen replays, emasculating the offside rule, etc — and purists will certainly want to avoid the bastardized indoor game. The American Soccer League has Northern and Southern divisions, with five teams in each, and the season runs from November to May. Most league players are foreign, particularly British and Latin American.

Motorsport. As you might expect from a nation where the car is king, motor and motorcycle racing are taken to the ultimate in the USA. Big events are held from spring to autumn. At Easter, half the motorcyclists in America congregate in Florida for the Daytona Beach speedway events, a long weekend of beer and bike racing. Non-enthusiasts might prefer to be elsewhere, since the reputation of the spectators is considerably worse than that of English football fans.

Little trouble surrounds the Indianapolis 500, which is held at the end of May each year, and provides a great spectacle. The 300,000 people who attend make this the biggest single spectator event in the world and pay $10 million at the turnstiles. The race itself lasts three hours, with the winner averaging nearly 170 mph.

The Indy 500 is but one in the 12 or 13 race Indy Series for big-engined single-seater cars. About half the races, which are held around the country, are on tailor-made tracks and the remainder are on street circuits. For times and locations of the big events, consult the racing calendars published in the New York editions of *Motor Sport* magazine. Be warned that accommodation becomes very scarce during race meetings in cities like Indianapolis which are quiet industrial backwaters for much of the year.You need to book up early (and pay four times the going rate), or be prepared to sleep rough along with many other less wealthy racegoers.

For spectacle, the highly professional MASCAR series for stock cars should not be missed. In America, 'stock car' means a highly developed but productin line based vehicle — not an old banger — and Amerias top drivers participate in the series. Demolition Derby and drag racing events are less well patronized. Events are advertised on fly posters and in the local press, and for a few dollars you can see screaming hulks of metal reach 60 mph in the blink of an eye, or knock bits off each other.

Horse Racing. The sport of kings is largely restricted to the flat in the USA, though there is some jumping. Off-track betting is legal in only three states — Connecticut, New York and Nevada. Like high-class greyhound tracks in the UK, the courses are normally surrounded with glass-enclosed grandstands. Racing takes place on most days of the week, usually from noon to 6pm. On race days local newspapers often carry advertisements attracting customers with the lure of a free drink or snack. For a complete list of events and a guide to form, try *The Racing Form,* the American equivalent to *The Sporting Life.*

Admission is cheap: around $5 entitles you to a seat if one is available, and an extra couple of dollars will reserve you a seat. If you get a seat and wish to move around, the accepted custom is to place a sheet of newspaper on the seat to reserve it. If you book a meal you automatically get a seat facing the track, and can place bets and receive winnings without moving. Those without seating are consigned to the 'standees' enclosure'. Unfortunately there are no bookies to add colour to this area.

To follow the fortunes of your chosen steed, you can hire binoculars for about $2. All betting is based on the 'tote' system, in which the total money staked — less the operator's cut — is shared among the winners. There are various booths accepting stakes from $1 to $1,000 or more. Some of the terminology is the same as in Britain, though if you plan to make a study of it, consult the locals. A forecast (first and second in a race) is known as an 'exacta'. To 'place' means to come second, to 'show' means to come third. An 'each-way' bet is a bet on a horse to win, place or show. The types of bet are explained in the official programme, as is the history of horses and riders.

In the three states where off-track betting (OTB) is legal, totalisator bets can be placed at OTB offices. These are identical in appearance, decor and clientele to British betting shops.

The richest event in the racing calendar is the $3 million Breeder's Cup Classic, held at Hollywood Park California in early November. Next most valuable is the Arlington Million, held at the end of August at Arlington Park in Chicago. Other big races are the Florida Derby (Gulfstream Park near Miami, early April), the San Juan Capistrano Handicap (Santa Anita near Los Angeles, mid-April), the Kentucky Derby (Louisville, the first Saturday in May) and the Belmont Stakes (New York, early June). If you like horses, visit the Kentucky bluegrass country. The world centre of the thoroughbred is Lexington, which has a Horse Park complete with farm, racetrack and museum. Several stud farms in the area welcome visitors.

While the best throughbreds are groomed in Kentucky, the top races are held in neighbouring West Virginia. Betting on greyhounds operates in small towns of the Midwest and elsewhere, and attracts surprisingly large interest. The biggest annual event is the $1.5 million Woodrow Wilson Classic at Meadowlands in late July.

GAMBLING

Casinos. Most forms of casino gambling are banned throughout North America. The exceptions are the State of Nevada, Atlantic City on the New Jersey coast and Native American lands in the Midwest. It is extraordinary to see the determination with which Americans dispose of surplus cash in the hope of accruing even more. The gambling industry is so highly developed that there are two ways for visitors to try to make money: the first to gamble; the second (and much more certain) is to take advantage of the extraordinary deals designed to extract as much as possible from gamblers by tempting them with free offers.

The casinos realize that the more punters who can be tempted to the city, the more money will flow into the coffers of the casino operators. Some people will go to any lengths to gamble, but most need an incentive. To tempt the marginal punter, gambling 'resorts' offer low-cost meals and accommodation.

For richer travellers who wish to play the tables seriously, a couple of ground rules follow. Firstly, the odds are always in favour of the casino.

Secondly, the free cocktails that magically appear by your side are strictly an investment on the part of the casino; by dulling your rational senses, they hope to persuade you to part with much more cash than you intended.

Numbers. Americans indulge in many forms of illicit gambling, the most prevalent of which is the 'numbers game'. This is particularly popular in northern industrial areas, where factories employing many blue-collar workers are ideal territory for the operators of this racket. One version works like this: each participant picks a number from 1 to 999 and stakes a dollar. The winning number is the last three digits of a publicly-quoted index, such as the closing price of pork belly futures. If the number comes up, then he wins $500. With a payout of only half the amount staked, this is clearly a mug's game.

Blue Laws	legislation restricting opening on Sundays
cigar store	tobacconist
cut-outs	discontinued records
drug store	chemist dispensing medicines as well as many other items, often with a snack counter
five and dime	downmarket chain store (e.g. Woolworths) which used to sell items for 5c and 10c
jumper	pinafore dress
layaway	putting a deposit on an article to be paid for and collected at a later date
make change	give change
natural tobacco	hand-rolling tobacco
notions	haberdashery
pants	trousers
pantyhose	tights
pocket book	wallet/purse
raincheck	promise of the same article at the same price at a later time
rummage sale/ garage sale	jumble sale
schlock	cheap, crummy merchandise (slang)
sneakers	plimsolls
sweater	jumper
thread	cotton
twofers	items sold at two-for-the-price-of-one
underwear	pants
vest	waistcoat

America is the ultimate consumer society. Americans are spoilt for choice, and it is easy to get caught up in their seemingly endless shopping spree. You can begin at stores bearing familiar names like Woolworth and Safeway before moving on to smart expensive department stores such as Bloomingdale's and Nordstrom, where high quality products can cost a fortune. For those with less exotic tastes, there are thousands of less pretentious stores with vast amounts of good quality merchandise. J.C. Penney has been compared to Marks & Spencer, but with changing rooms.

To meet more basic human needs there are mammoth supermarkets, cut-price stores and plenty of 24-hour shops. The heart of American commercial life, however, is the Mall. The first 'shopping and entertainment complex' was built at Bloomington Minnesota in the 1950s, and it is fitting that the nation's biggest — the Mall of America — opened nearby in 1992. A typical mall (pronounced to rhyme with tall) is a sprawling, covered air-conditioned centrally-heated shopping centre. At one end there might be a large discount department store such as K-Mart; at the other, a supermarket. In between are all manner of shops interspersed with cinemas, laundromats and fast food restaurants. Most are situated on main roads in middle class suburbs, a few miles from the city centre, and surrounded by acres of parking lots plus a gas station or two. Teenagers favour them as hang-outs — community life has moved out to these temples of commercialism in the suburbs.

Surprisingly, some European goods are actually cheaper in the USA than in their country of manufacture. Even if you don't understand the economics, you may want to take advantage of the fact that Shetland sweaters can be cheaper in Dallas than Dundee, and books published in Oxford cheaper than in Oxford bookshops.

Sales Tax. Most states levy a tax on retail sales. The rate is usually 5-8%, and some cities add a couple of percentage points for themselves. Taxable and tax-exempt items vary from state to state; some states exempt shoes and books and others don't. Quoted prices almost never include sales tax. So if you're down to your last $5, don't try to buy something advertised at $4.99. On expensive purchases, sales tax becomes a significant extra, so try to buy in a low-tax state. If you are intending to have a purchase shipped directly out of the state or country, it is always worth asking if you can be exempted from the sales tax. Regulations vary according to the state and the item. It is not worth doing this merely to save the tax, since shipping charges would probably cancel out any saving, but it might be useful to reduce the amount of luggage you have to carry.

STATE SALES TAXES (%)							
Alaska	nil	Illinois	4	Montana	nil	Rhode Island	6
Alabama	4	Indiana	5	Nebraska	3.5	S. Carolina	4
Arizona	4	Iowa	4	Nevada	5.75	S. Dakota	4
Arkansas	3	Kansas	3	New Hampshire	nil	Tennessee	4.5
California	4.75	Kentucky	5	New Jersey	6	Texas	4
Colorado	2.5	Louisiana	3	New Mexico	3.5	Utah	4
Connecticut	7.5	Maine	5	New York	4	Vermont	4
Delaware	nil	Maryland	5	N. Carolina	3	Virginia	3
DC	6	Massachusetts	5	N. Dakota	3	Washington	6.5
Florida	5	Michigan	4	Ohio	5	W. Virginia	5
Georgia	3	Minnesota	6	Oklahoma	2	Wisconsin	5
Hawaii	4	Mississippi	5	Oregon	nil	Wyoming	3
Idaho	4	Missouri	4.1	Pennsylvania	6		

Hours. While there are individual variations, most downtown shops open from 9.30am to 5, 5.30 or 6pm, Monday to Saturday. There is usually at least one late-night shopping evening per week, when stores remain open until 9pm. Suburban shopping malls stay open until 9pm every week night. Sunday opening is subject to state and/or local laws, which often allow small corner shops to stay open, but prohibit the large department stores. In addition, most towns have all-night supermarkets selling food and drugs. Outside large cities, they are often adjacent to 24-hour gas stations. Look for the ubiquitous 7-Eleven chain (so called because they originally opened from 7am to 11pm) which stay open all night in some locations.

Complaints. Depite — or perhaps because of — being the world's number one capitalist country, the USA has a high degree of consumer protection legislation on its statutes. Paranoia about the expensive consequences of law suits meants that a politely worded complaint with just a hint about future legal action will usually be sucessful in getty a replacement or refund on faulty goods. Consumer consciousness has also led to a liberal returns policy, and few questions are asked if you return an item which looks unused. For expensive purchases (over $150), buy with a credit card: you should then be able to claim against the credit card company if the company goes out of business and you are stuck with faulty goods.

Tobacco. Never underestimate the sensitivity of Americans to smoking. State and federal laws make it an offence to light up in virtually any enclosed public place, and there are tight rules on smoking in offices, shops and even some parks. The smoker is rapidly becoming a social leper, and even offering a cigarette to any American may cause offence. The health warnings carried on every pack of cigarettes do not mince words. One example: 'Smoking by pregnant women may result in foetal injury, premature birth and low birth weight'. See *Getting Around* for details of smoking restrictions on aircraft, trains and buses. State and city authorities impose their own rules in addition to federal laws, such as the New York City ordinance which forbids smoking within 20 feet of a hotel reception desk.

The smoker will already be familiar with many American brands, such as Marlboro (the world's biggest-selling cigarette), Camel and Winston. Less well-known abroad are the ultra low tar brands, whose advertising makes you wonder whether they are more satisfying than inhaling fresh air. Try True (less than 0.1mg tar) if you think you'd like to give up. British or European cigarettes can only be found in specialist tobacco shops, and are often blended differently for export; the popular Benson & Hedges brand tastes nothing like its British namesake. Menthol cigarettes are popular: the top-selling brand is Kool.

A pack of 20 cigarettes costs around $2, less in tobacco-producing states such as North Carolina. Imported brands cost around twice as much, so try to acquire a taste for the local cigarettes. The cheapest way to buy cigarettes is in cartons of 200 at supermarkets. For single packs, try gas stations and drug stores: there are few tobacconists as such. Look out for special promotions along the lines of 'two packs for the price of one'. Choosing your cigarettes can be a daunting prospect; you have to decide between 'Regular' and 'Lite' (high or low tar), between 'Regular' (king-size) and '100' (even longer), between 'flip top' and 'soft pack', and between untipped and filtered. Whichever you finally choose, you'll probably end get a free box of matches thrown in.

American and European cigars are widely available, but the import of

Cuban cigars is a federal offence. Pipe smoking has not been promoted in the USA as a less dangerous alternative to cigarettes, and is something of a dying art. But with perseverance you can find decent tobacco and well made pipes.

Few Americans roll their own cigarettes (using what is described as 'natural tobacco'). As a result, Europeans who smoke roll-ups in the USA are frequently presumed to be smoking marijuana. If you wish to avoid embarrassing situations (such as being thrown out of a restaurant) or the the attention of the police, stick to tailor-mades. Furthermore, although papers are sold in every shape, size and colour, good tobacco is hard to find. Some rolling tobacco is soaked in bourbon and tastes disgusting.

Clothing. American factories often have a retail outlet on the premises from which they sell seconds at such good bargains that people drive hundreds of miles to shop at them. Inexpensive new clothes may also be found at 'off-price' stores. Located in unfashionable suburb areas, they pile clothes high and sell them cheap. Try to buy clothes at sale times: shortly after Christmas, in mid-February (around Washington's birthday) and at the height of summer.

Secondhand clothes, clean and in reasonable condition, can be bought cheaply at Salvation Army and Goodwill charity shops. These are usually located in dilapidated areas of many cities. At the other end of the market is the 'preppy wardrobe': corduroy trousers, Oxford cloth shirts, collared T-shirts, Shetland sweaters, etc. Jeans are always a good buy, and Levi 401s can cost as little as $25.

Men's clothing sizes are the same in Britian and the USA, except shoes (see below). Women's dress sizes involve subracting two from the British size: British size 10 is US size 8, British size 12 is US size 10 and so on. Slightly built women should also check under the 'Boys' or 'Teens' department for jeans. Short men should investigate the 'Undergraduate' department for all kinds of clothes. For both men's and women's shoes, sizes vary as follows:

British	3	4	5	6	7	8	9	10	11
American	$4\frac{1}{2}$	$5\frac{1}{2}$	$6\frac{1}{2}$	$7\frac{1}{2}$	$8\frac{1}{2}$	$9\frac{1}{2}$	$10\frac{1}{2}$	$11\frac{1}{2}$	$12\frac{1}{2}$

Books and records. American bookshops are big, bright and packed with thousands of cheap paperbacks. Many stores give a discount on the cover price, and one chain — Crown Books — claims never to sell books at full price. The euphemism 'quality paper' is used to describe respectable fiction, and cost about 50% more than the standard $5.99 paperback. For not a great deal more, you can buy top-selling hardbacks.

Music is almost entirely sold on CD, cassette and DCC, at prices about one-third cheaper than in Britain. Chain stores worth seeking out include Tower Records and Sam Goody's. Cheap records are sold as 'cut-outs', where a lump is deliberately taken out of the cover or case.

Photography. Top-name film costs around $5 for a 24-exposure 135 or 110 cartridge. The one-hour processing services offered at drug stores costs about $10 for 24 prints and you may get a free film or a second set of prints thrown in. Cameras bought in the USA can be considerably cheaper than in Britain, but do not always carry worldwide guarantees. Unless your future travel plans will allow to return the camera should something go awry, the absence of after-sales service may discourage you. Remember that the extreme heat that you encounter in the Southern states can have an adverse effect on colour film.

Spectacles. Even after paying an optometrist for a sight test, a pair of glasses or contact lenses costs much less than in Britain. The cheapest place is likely to be a department store.

Electrical Goods. The American supply is 110 volts at 60 cycles per second. Britain uses 240 volts at 50 cycles per second. This is more than enough to burn out most American electrical appliances. Most audio equipment made in the Far East has voltage and frequency selectors on the back allowing them to be used anywhere. Most American made equipment does not. You can buy a transformer to reduce the voltage, but the difference in frequency means that cassette recorders and record players will run at the wrong speed.

Do not buy a television or video cassette recorder made for the American market: the 525 line system used makes them incompatible with British television equipment. Similarly, pre-recorded video cassettes will not work on machines designed for use in Britain.

The leading chain of stores for all things electrical is Radio Shack (which trades as Tandy in the UK). A fax machine, which can be used in the UK, can be yours for under £200.

Garage Sales. Although Americans may donate clothes to Salvation Army or Goodwill stores, they are likely to dispose of their other superfluous possession at a garage sale and keep the money themselves. Garage sales are phenonenon usually confined to summer weekends. The vendor simply displays his chattels in his garage (or, more likely, on the front lawn) and waits for the eager buyers who learn of the sale through local papers, fly posters, leafletting or word of mouth. All prices are negotiable: anything still around towards the end of the sale is likely to be knocked down cheaply. Even if you don't pick up the bargain of a lifetime, a garage sale is great fun and gives an insight into how American communities operate.

Gifts. America has great scope for gifts with which to astonish your friends and relations. T-shirts with arty, imaginative or outrageous designs are sold everywhere. Trendy boutiques specialize in 'preppy' clothes (a combination of King's Road chic and American college casualness) and designer jeans. A current fad is safari-style wear sold by the Banana Republic chain, whose shops are always enteraining.

Handicrafts are one of the few remnants of Native American culture. Be cautious when shopping on or near reservations unless you are sure you can distinguish tourist trash from the real thing. Shops set up in large cities by the various Native American nations pride themselves on marketing the authentic products of artisans. For specific recommendations on handicraft centres and other unusual ideas for gifts, see the regional chapters.

When buying presents, remember that any purchases above the duty free limit of £32 will attract duty of around 15% upon import to Britain.

Americans benefit from the most sophisticated and expensive health care in the world: 11% of the national income of the USA is spent on health, compared to 6% in Britain. The whole medical industry has a decidedly unhealthy preoccupation with wealth that makes the British health service seem a paragon of care and efficiency. If you arrive without adequate health insurance, ring any office of the ubiquitous Blue Cross for information about visitors' cover.

If you take precautions against the extremes of temperature, the USA is a healthy place to be. You need no vaccinations. Drinking water is safe everywhere, food is usually hygienically prepared and there are few contagious diseases to worry about. As long as you don't run foul of the more threatening varieties of flora and fauna (humans included), there is little to worry about unless you're unlucky enough to get caught in an avalanche, tornado or earthquake.

Emergency Procedure. Dial the emergency number — usually 911 — for an ambulance. (This also alerts the police). The paramedics will take you to the nearest hospital. This is fine so long as you can produce evidence that you are insured, but if your insurance has expired, you face the choice between astronomical hospital bills or finding a free ('public') hospital. Most large cities — but few small towns — have such a hospital, usually run by charity and with highly stretched resources. They will treat you until you are able to leave under your own steam.

Doctors. In Britain, GPs are respected members of the community although not terribly well-paid. In the USA, physicians are right at the top of the professional tree in terms of prestige and wealth. American doctors don't just sit at desks prescribing cough remedies or refering patients to specialists. Their surgeries are miniature hospitals, where X-rays are taken, blood samples tested and full medical screenings take place. For these services they are extremely well-paid by the insurance companies of wealthy patients and the public *Medicaid* and *Medicare* schemes for the poor and the aged respectively.

If you need to see a doctor, you'll have to rely upon a personal recommendation or plough through the Yellow Pages until you find a willing practitioner. If you happen to be in a city which has a British Consulate, ring them for a list of recommended doctors. Night calls and weekend work are usually out of the question, and even during working hours it can be difficult to get an appointment if the doctor has a full workload or is playing golf. The minimum fee will be about $50.

Hospitals. In view of the above, and the fact that most travellers will be seeking instant treatment rather than long-term screening, it is usually best to go for treatment at a hospital. Anyone will direct you to the nearest general hospital. Except in a real emergency, do not go to the accident unit (sometimes called 'Emergency', comparable to Casualty in the UK). Admission charges are high to discourage use by non-urgent cases. Instead, ask at the reception desk to see the duty physician. The policy for charging varies from one hospital to another. At some you may have to pay for minor treatment and prescribed drugs and subsequently reclaim the cost from your insurance company. At others, sight of your policy is sufficient. For essential surgery, no hospital will insist on cash in advance.

Be cautious when seeking treatment. For example if you go to a hospital complaining about abdominal pain, you may find your appendix has been removed almost as fast as you can produce your insurance certificate. This is not entirely due to the greed of surgeons working on a piece-rate system; it is also because of past litigation against doctors who have failed to diagnose appendicitis correctly and whose patients have subsequently died of peritonitis.

Pharmacies. Most over-the-counter drugs are cheaper than in Britain. If you are prescribed medication in a hospital, it will normally be supplied by the in-house pharmacy. Otherwise you need to take the prescription to a drug store. Late-night pharmacies are listed in each regional chapter under *Help and Information.* Prescription medicines are charged for at the full market rate, which can be frighteningly high. Save all receipts for prescription drugs so you can claim the cost from your insurance company.

Dentistry. Your friendly neighbourhood dentist ('orthodontist') has more in common with NASA Mission Control than a simple drilling-and-filling operation. Vast amounts of expensive technology are employed in dental surgeries. Together with the inflated salary of the dentist and his assistants, this means that even a simple filling can cost $100. Crowns and other complications can increase the price tenfold. Don't be tempted to go beyond the bounds of your insurance policy, which is likely to cover only emergency treatment. An achingly-infected tooth constitutes an emergency. If it is driving you wild with pain, oil of cloves is an effective local anaesthetic to tide you over. Failing that, swish a mouthful of whisky around the offending tooth. Don't be tempted to dissolve an aspirin on it, since this will only make your gums sore.

HEALTH HAZARDS

Sunburn. If you travel anywhere in the continental USA in summer, be careful to avoid sunburn. The most effective protection is to stay out of the sun, particularly between 10am and 3pm. The next best precaution is to encourage gentle tanning. Start with less than an hour of sun a day to get your pallid skin used to the idea. Use a lotion with a high protection factor to screen the burning rays, but remember that most of it will wash away if you bathe. Seawater, perfume and after-shave will increase the rate of burning. Aspirin delays but does not reduce the reddening process and thus may increase your suffering. The best way to avoid sunstroke or heat exhaustion is to remain in the shade as much as possible, and wear a wide-brimmed hat. Wear loose cotton clothing for maximum comfort.

If you are like most sun-starved travellers and ignore this advice, treat the resulting burns with cold, damp towels or take a long cold bath. Apply after-sun cream or yoghurt to the affected areas and drink gallons of fluids.

Cold Weather. Americans cope with the cold by eating well, sleeping well, overheating their homes and wrapping up well before venturing outside. Temperatures already below freezing can be reduced dramatically by the wind chill factor. If you're out in the cold, it is essential to stay dry to avoid frostbite or exposure.

Creatures to Avoid. Humans apart, the USA has several lethal species wandering around. Grizzly bears, rattlesnakes and alligators are perhaps the best known. While it is not necessarily pleasant to meet them, they will usually be at least as frightened as you. The simple expedient of walking, swimming or running away normally works and they will probably do the same. A lot of nonsense is also talked about sharks. The closest you'll ever come to one is likely to be at Sea World or the clockwork Jaws at Universal Studios in Orlando. Even if a shark swims up to you while you bathe, a sharp tap on the nose should send him on his way. Many species of snake thrive in the US, especially in the swampy areas of southern states. Ask local park rangers or well-informed locals to describe the dangerous versus the harmless, ones and find out if there is a first aid hut before venturing into the wilds.

Smaller animals can be a bigger nuisance. Dingy hotel and motel rooms in the southern states are infested with cockroaches. Although they are harmless, they can be upsetting. You might be tempted to invest in a cockroach trap known as the Roach Motel — 'they check in, but they don't check out'. Ignore any lizards you may see edging up the wall: they keep the insect population down and are to be encouraged. Mosquitoes are a summer hazard in Alaska and the northernmost states of the continental USA. Use a heavy-duty insect repellent; take local advice on the most effective brand. Malaria is not a problem in the USA, but in the South there is a slight risk of contracting equine encephalitis from mosquitoes; it is usually fatal.

The chigoe fly is fond of sand dunes and beaches. It is an unpleasant creature which burrows into the sole of your foot to lay eggs. The only way to remove it is to conduct a little excavation with the aid of sterilized needle. Scorpions and black widow spiders are a serious nuisance in southern areas; remember to shake out your shoes since they will bite only if you annoy them.

Plants to avoid. Poison ivy, which is unknown in Britain, is widespread in North America. An encounter with it is much worse and longer-lasting than a brush with stinging nettles. It is especially a nuisance for children who find it impossible to prevent themselves from scratching the irritated skin and thereby spreading it. Unfortunately the plant looks like an unassuming ivy, though you should make an effort to learn to recognise the three pointed leaf.

Whereas there are many delicious wild berries unfamiliar to Europeans (boysenberries, huckleberries, wortleberries, etc.) there are also many poisonous varieties. Ask the locals before munching. As in Europe there are dangerous toadstools and mushrooms. There is also an abundance of hallucinogenic mushrooms, especially in mountain areas.

Smog. The chief constituents of smog are ozone, sulphur dioxide and other petrol-engine emissions. Smog is at its worst during climatic inversions. When these occur in Los Angeles or Denver (the worst culprits), a sickly yellow pall hangs over the city. Healthy young people find their eyes watering and their throats burning. Young children, the elderly and infirm suffer greatly. If you suffer from a nasal or chest complaint, you may be wise to avoid the worst cities and to keep a check on smog forecasts in other areas. Weather reports in Los Angeles include the 'eye irritation level' along with routine data on temperature and humidity.

Acts of God. The United States suffers from most forms of natural disaster: earthquakes and volcanic eruptions on the West Coast, avalanches and flash floods in the Rockies, tornadoes in the Midwest, hurricanes in the South and fierce electric storms in most parts of the country. While travelling in danger areas, pay attention to advance warnings of eruptions or tornadoes and don't hesitate to evacuate. If you are caught out in the open during a thunder storm, stay out of water and well away from tall objects which act as potential lightning conductors. Cars are relatively safe places to be because of the insulating effects of rubber tyres. You may also get caught in a sandstorm if you are travelling in desert areas; sit it out in a car if possible.

Fifth Amendment	the right to remain silent when arrested
jay walking	crossing a street not at an intersection
Mann Act	Congressional Act that prohibits men from taking women across state borders for 'immoral purposes'
mugger money	a cache of about $50 which will satisfy a potential mugger and prevent him from searching for more
patrolman	ordinary policeman

Despite the statistic that the United States has the highest rate of serious crime in the world, the dangers of violent attack on travellers are greatly exaggerated. It is true that many ordinary citizens own guns, availing themselves of the second amendment to the Constitution which protects the right to keep and bear arms, and also that there are more murders in Chicago and Miami than in Britain. But the huge majority are internecine killings. According to a recent survey, London is the seventh most dangerous city in the world just below Los Angeles but above New York. Murder of travellers is mostly confined to victims of psychotics and addicts, or more often, those who fail to behave in the accepted manner while being mugged. And mugging is not nearly as widespread as popular reports would have us believe. If you take care in choosing where to go and in comporting yourself correctly, it is highly improbable that you will be mugged. You are more likely to fall victim to a pickpocket, hotel thief or someone out to pick a barroom fight.

The most crime-ridden cities are not necessarily the ones you would expect. According to recent FBI statistics, the top ten cities on the all-crimes index were: Atlantic City (New Jersey), Odessa (Texas), Miami (Florida), Gainesville (Florida), Lubbock (Texas), Bakersfield (California), Savannah (Georgia), New York City, Sacramento (California) and Stockton (California). Miami, Houston and Odessa have the highest murder rates in the country. The most violent state seems to be New York with nearly one violent crime per hundred people per annum; the safest is Nebraska with only 61 violent crimes per 10,000 population. In general the prevalence of violent crime is much higher in the southern states than in the north.

How to avoid a Mugging. Despite the display of ostentatious American wealth all around you, never let it be known that you are worth robbing (unlike the New York bank robber who was mugged on his way to the getaway car). If you count your holiday cash in a crowded bar, don't be surprised if you're attacked on the way home. Leave your expensive watch or jewellery at home, and give some thought to where you'll carry your documents and money. The important rule is not to have all your valuables in one place, so that even if you are robbed or mugged you will have an emergency fund intact.

Find out which areas of a city a native would hesitate to visit. After dark, wherever you are, stick to well-lit main thoroughfares. Always walk purposefully. Don't stop every few yards to peer at a map; work out your route beforehand. Never appear drunk even if you are. And if you are shaking with terror, try to disguise your fear. Stride across the street to avoid the attentions of the gang of malevolent youths who are following you.

How to be Mugged. If you find yourself being mugged, there are several sensible precautions you should have taken to minimize personal danger and loss. Ideally, you should carry $50-$100 in cash. Any less than this, and the villain will become belligerent and search for hidden wealth to make his attack worthwhile.

Most muggers are young males who operate alone. You can expect to be grabbed from behind and threatened by a gun or, more likely, a knife. After your initial spasm, stay completely still and don't try to resist. Muggers can be extremely wound up and will not hesitate to use this weapon if things go wrong; they are highly susceptible to sudden or unexpected movement so do exactly as you are told. Direct your attacker's hand to the wallet or purse. When the mugger has your cash, he may also remove your watch or jewellery and promptly run away into the shadows. You are now at your most vulnerable; trembling with shock and fear, and without the 'mugger money' to pay off subsequent attackers. Stay still and silent until you are sure he has gone. Flag down a cab if you can find one, explain your predicament and ask to go to the nearest police precinct station. It is a rare taxi driver who will refuse you. At the station, your story won't arouse much interest. Collect the number of the police report to facilitate your insurance claim, and ask for a lift home.

The above pattern is the ideal. If, instead, you are set upon by a gang intent upon mindless violence as much as theft, there is little you can do except to protect your head and play dead.

Pickpockets and Bagsnatchers. Theft by stealth rather than violence is a growth industry in the USA. Pickpocketing and bagsnatching are most prevalent at airports in subways and bus stations, where tired travellers are plunged into a frenetic and confusing environment. Money belts and pouches worn next to the skin will foil most pickpockets; avoid moving in crowds and treat unusual events with suspicion. Tricks like dropping a handful of change or spilling coffee on someone are employed by pickpockets to distract attention.

Make sure your luggage is in your sight, if not necessarily in your hands, to deter bagsnatchers. And beware of well-dressed strangers who ask you to watch their case while they visit the toilet. When it comes to your turn to go, don't feel morally obliged to ask the stranger to do the same for you. Travellers who entrust their belongings in this way often find no sign of luggage or stranger upon their return.

Hotel Theft. Burglary is popular in America. Nothing appeals to the burglar more than the prospect of rich pickings in hotel and motel rooms. If you have to relinquish your key when going out for the day, make sure you hand it to the reception clerk rather than leave it lying on the desk. But whatever precautions you take, access to unattended rooms presents few problems to the professional thief. Keep all your valuables in the hotel safe while you're out and about. Even when you're asleep in your room, a burglar may still break in. Most are so stealthy that you won't wake up; if you do, pretend to be asleep to avoid unpleasant consequences.

Be wary of opening your door to callers who claim to be the hotel staff. Some villains simply knock on a door and, when it opens, threaten the occupant with a gun or a knife. You are usually forced to stand in the bath while he goes through your possessions. Fortunately, most room doors are equipped with spy holes through which you can size up the caller. Phone the reception desk to check his credentials if you're suspicious. If your room has no telephone, ask him to let himself in. Most genuine employees (and unfortunately some thieves) have a master key.

Violence. There is a great deal of tension in American society. Although the more overt demonstrations of racism such as those practised by the Ku Klux Klan have largely subsided, there can be considerable conflict between different ethnic groups. When the short fuse of underlying racial tension is inflamed by drink, drugs or unbearably hot weather, the consequences are often frightful. It is not safe for blacks to venture into poor white or Hispanic ghettos, nor for whites or Asians to wander through black neighbourhoods. Furthermore, large tracts of inner-city territory are a battleground for rival gangs, most of them armed through profits from the drugs trade. The character of an area can change dramatically within a block or two. If you are in any doubt, stick to main thoroughfares which are generally safe territory. Even when driving, you should keep all doors locked and windows closed and not hesitate to follow the custom of ignoring red lights if you feel threatened.

You may notice an undercurrent of paranoia in some settings which manifests itself in aggressive behaviour. Bar-room brawls are frequent occurrences, so avoid heated arguments when out drinking. Bars which have lots of souped-up cars and motorcycles parked outside, and large burly men with platinum blondes inside, are best avoided.

Confidence Tricksters. It is not always easy to distinguish between con-artists, religious fanatics and people who are genuinely trying to help. As a rule, the unsavoury characters who hang around bus stations and hotel bars do not fall into the latter category. Any stranger who engages you in a conversation which eventually turns into a suggestion that you should part with some money — to place on a 'fixed' horse race, as a partner in some fabulous financial deal or for a prostitute who subsequently fails to deliver — is almost certainly a con-artist. Smile, explain that you're penniless and waiting for cash to be sent from Europe in a week or so, and walk away.

Never become involved in any illicit street card games such as 'Spot The Lady' or with pool sharks who might let you win the first time to build up your confidence (and the amount you're willing to bet on the game) but will clobber you in the end.

THE LAW

The lawmakers in Congress are supplemented by the legislatures of 50 states and of thousands of counties and cities. The result is a vast amount of piecemeal legislation which makes it difficult for travellers to keep track of the law. For example, few visitors can be expected to know that it is illegal to draw faces on window blinds in Garfield Montana, or that riding on a bus in the Indiana town of Gary is unlawful if you've eaten garlic within the previous two hours. Even without these eccentric ordinances the reams of statutes and civilcase law result in thousands of trials, retrials and appeals which keep the highly litigious legal profession in business. A million 'peace officers', equipped with all sorts of menacing hardware, attempt to keep some sort of order. Yet there are still areas where police fear to tread. In addition to the police force, there are a large number of armed security guards technically without the rights of publicly-employed police, but you are not advised to test this out.

Police. Enforcers of the law fall into four broad categories: city police, state police (who operate the highway patrol), the National Guard and the Federal Bureau of Investigation. Each state has a National Guard, civilian reservists who are called up to deal with civil unrest or natural catastrophe. The FBI concerns itself with major offences and crime across state borders. You are unlikely to become involved with them unless you are a drug dealer or fail to deliver a driveaway car.

A fifth category is the US Secret Service, whose chief function is to protect present and past Presidents. They are easily identified by their ill-fitting gabardine suits with bulges under the shoulder and a hearing aid (actually a radio device) in one ear. Finally, the men with white hats, gloves and holsters are Military Police, concerned only with deserting soldiers and drunken sailors.

When dealing with law enforcement officers, remember that you are in a nation where guns are almost as common as tennis rackets. Any sudden movement, or even slouching with your hands in your pockets, could be misconstrued as an attempt to reach for a gun, with potentially lethal consequences. Don't even think of offering a financial inducement to get out of trouble.

More progressive police forces have devised ideas to enhance their image. In Washington DC, for example, you can tour the headquarters of the FBI. Better still, the capital's Metropolitan Police has a scheme whereby any visitor can ride along with a patrol officer on duty. Apart from being an experience you will never forget, it challenges your views on the police and makes most TV cop shows look thoroughly ridiculous.

Arrest and Summons. Offences are categorised as misdemeanours (dropping litter, smoking marijuana in liberal states) or felonies (robbery, carrying marijuana in conservative states). You are certain to be arrested for a felony and likely to be summonsed for a misdemeanour. In an arrest you are frisked for concealed weapons (just like on TV), possibly handcuffed and 'helped' into the back of a police car. You will have the Fifth Amendment — the right to remain silent — quoted at you (just like on TV). At the station you will be charged before being put in a cell. This is the time to phone anyone who might stand bail for you.

Being summonsed is a lot less traumatic. Legally this is equivalent to arrest and is answerable in court, but it allows you to avoid the cells.

Drugs. Among middle-class Americans, smoking marijuana at a private gathering is considered as natural as drinking beer, and joints are offered round as casually as cigarettes. Many of the country's thrusting young achievers are addicted, at least psychologically, to cocaine. But the laws on drugs are complicated and often extremely harsh. Each state fixes its own penalties. The possession of a small amount of marijuana for home consumption is legal only in Alaska. The drug has been decriminalized in 11 states which means that you will only get a fine if caught with less than an ounce. In all but two of the other states, it is a misdemeanour, but in Arizona and Nevada it is a felony punishable by a lengthy prison sentence. The most common penalty is up to a year in prison and a fine of $2,000. Penalties for possessing harder drugs, including heroin and 'crack', are severe as are those for dealing of any kind. Parents form a strong lobby and maintain pressure for exemplary punishment of anyone who could conceivably be corrupting their kids.

Of course theory and practice are two different things. In many cities, people smoke grass openly (especially in under-policed neighbourhoods) and dealers hang about ostentatiously on street corners with no apparent fear of the law. In the course of a short visit it is unlikely you'll be able to ascertain where it's safe, nor who it is safe to deal with.

Other Laws. Legislation affecting the motorist or hitch-hiker are mentioned in the relevant sections of *Getting Around*. Pedestrians should beware the dreaded jay-walking law. You must cross downtown streets at intersections and never diagonally. If a policeman sees you scooting across mid-block or crossing against a red "Don't Walk' light, he may hit you with a hefty fine.

Strict laws affect minors in many states. If you drive an under-aged person over a state border, you may be committing a federal offence. These laws are designed to prevent kidnapping. In some localities, there is even be a curfew for minors.

biking/bike	cycling/pedal cycle
diamond back	domestic American rattlesnake
dude ranch	ranch style holiday resort
flashlight	torch
garter snake	harmless snake with three lengthwise stripes
parka	anorak (both are Eskimo words)
poison ivy	shrub which gives a painful skin rash on contact
pup tent	low one-man tent
RV	recreational vehicle (camper van)
skinny dipping	swimming in the nude
smudge	smoky fire intended to drive away insects
trailer	caravan
white-out	drifting snow which reduces visibility to zero

Visitors from a crowded island such as Britain have difficulty coming to terms with sheer vastness and emptiness of the USA. Much of the terrain is not merely uninhabited, it is uninhabitable. The stark beauty of the wilderness is in complete contrast to the brash commercialization of the cities. The two extremes frequently collide, when a billboard or diner blots out the landscape, or a neon city like Las Vegas rises out of the desert.

Some Americans have abused their environment shamelessly in pursuit of wealth. Despite the efforts of American entrepreneurs to despoil the landscape, there are still many beautiful places where the traveller can find quietness and solitude on coastal cliffs, in the mountains or on the lakes and waterways. Large areas are protected from exploitation, being designated National or State Parks. the most famous of these (Grand Canyon, Yosemite, Yellowstone) can be appallingly crowded, but many are so large that a day's hike will remedy this. Most have excellent facilities for camping and 'nature interpretation'. They make the best of the Great Outdoors easily accessible and should not be missed.

Many indigenous species of wildlife can be seen while travelling in the wilds of America, from the endearing little chipmunk (an Algonquin word for the North American squirrel) to the grizzly bear. There are many unique small mammals and marsupials such as raccoons, possums, skunks and gophers as well as larger ones like elk and moose. The groundhog (or woodchuck) gives its name to February 2; if the groundhog sees his shadow on Groundhog Day (a fairly safe bet), he returns to his burrow and winter continues for six weeks longer. The decline of the population of bald eagles (the symbol of the United States) seems to have been reversed in the past few years. For a description of dangerous species and ways to remain safe in the bush, see *Health: Creatures to Avoid* (page 106) and *Canada: The Great Outdoors* (page 406).

National Parks. The National Park system includes national monuments, historic sites and national seashores, but the prime attractions are the 37 National Parks. They range in size from the 3,472 square miles of Yellowstone in Wyoming to a single volcanic crater of Haleakala in Hawaii. In all, the Natonal Park Service controls 77,000,000 acreas of land. Common to all these parks is a set of regulations to preserve the environment, such as no smoking in some areas (to prevent forest fires), all garbage to be disposed of, and of course no hunting. But the parks encourage all kinds of outdoor activity and there are excellent networks of trails.

One feature which may take you by surprise is that you have to pay an entrance fee to at least half the parks. The charge for a vehicle and its occupants is usually around $10. There is a free Golden Age Passport for the disabled, giving free entry anywhere in the system and 50% off the regular camping and user fees. Hitch-hikers of course will get in free in any case; cyclists and hikers have to pay a nominal admission of $1.

Another idea which takes some getting used to for people accustomed to wandering freely around the wilderness elsewhere in the world is that some regions off the beaten track are accessible only if you have a permit for 'backcountry' use. The person to approach, by mail or directly, is the superintendent of the park. As well as issuing permits for hiking or camping he and his staff can tell you everything you could possibly wish to know about the geology, ecology and history of the park.

There is normally a choice of accommodation. The larger parks have simple wooden shelters for the use of hikers, and ample camping facilities. For a little luxury there are log cabins or (if you don't mind not blending in with the surroundings) ordinary motel rooms. That said, you should plan ahead if you decide to visit a park. There are crowds at most of them during the summer, and many shut down entirely or offer only limited services in the winter. Facilities are generally in short supply, and bookings have to be made as mucyh as six months in advance. Camping facilities outdoors are usually on a first come, first served basis, so it makes sense to arrive early if you want the better pitches.

Many of the National Parks are mentioned in the regional chapters. For further details ask the USTTA for their free brochure *The Great Outdoors of the USA*, or buy the *Backpackers Sourcebook* by Loelle Liebrenz. American Youth Hostels, PO Box 37613, Washington DC 20013-7613 produces a useful brochure called Discount Storeroom which lists many more specialized books.

If you are interested in donating some of your time and labour to mountaineering footpaths in national parks, you can become a volunteer with the American Hiking Society. You should have some experience as a camper and hiker and be prepared to work hard for ten days in rugged terrain. Food may or may not be provided free of charge depending on the project's finances. For further details, contact Kay Beebe, AHS Volunteer Vacations, PO Box 86, North Sciutate, Massachusetts 02060; 617-545-4819.

For information on camping in the national parks, send for the *Guide and Map: National Parks of the United States* from the National Park Service, Public Inquiries Office, 18th and C Streets, NW Washington, DC 20240; for a complete list of national forests, request the free brochure FS13, *Field Offices of the Forest Services* from the US Forest Service, Office of Information, PO Box 2417, Washington, DC 20013. the National Park Service also encourages campers to use less-visited national parks in its brochure *Lesser Known Areas of the National Park System*, usually available free from local offices of the Park Service.

State Parks and National Forests. Although not quite on the grand scale of some national parks, don't overlook these reserves. With planning, you can cross the USA staying in a different one each night if you're travelling by car. Rates vary from park to park, as does the quality of accommodation, but in general you should pay no more than $7 a night. 'Campground Full' signs are a rare sight.

National forests often border or surround national parks. They are well worth while exploring, although camping in them tends to be primitive. The advantages over national parks is that they are usually free. You'll need detailed maps, and a sense of adventure.

Organizations. For people (particularly first-time visitors) who might feel more relaxed with an experienced guide or other camper, five organizations are worth contacting:

American Forestry Association, 1319 18th St, NW, Washington DC 20036 (202-467-5810).
Sierra Club, 530 Bush St, San Francisco, CA 94108 (415-981-8634).
Nature Expeditions International, PO Box 11496, Eugene OR 97440 (503-484-6529 or 1-800-634-0634).
National Wildlife Federation, 1400 16th St, NW Washington DC 20036-2266 (703-790-4414).
Appalachian Mountain Club, 5 Joy St, Boston, MA 02108 (617-523-0636).

The Sierra Club has branches all over the USA. Their organized outings could unkindly compared to boy scout hikes — you have to take a turn with the camp chores — but many travellers find the trails a good way to explore lesser-known areas and to meet people. Apart from one- or two-week 'Highlight Trips' around the western states, they organize plenty of one day outings which are advertised in local newspapers.

More regimented and rigorous are the 'wilderness skills' courses offered by Outward Bound in various locations in the USA. They are expensive —

$750 for a week — but if you are interested, contact Outward Bound, 384 Field Point Rd, Greenwich CT 06830 (1-800-243-8520; fax 203-661-0903).

Connoiseurs of flora and fauna are in for a treat, since there are many species unique to North America. Buy a field guide such as *Audubon Society Beginner Guides* to birds or reptiles and amphibians or wildflowers for about $4 each. Or join a naturalist tour such as the one operated Questers, 257 Park Avenue South, New York 10010 (212-673-3120). The National Wildlife Federation, mentioned above, has programmes of field trips and classes. Contact the Federation at 1400 16th St, NW Washington DC 20036-2266 (703-790-4414).

WATER SPORTS

Waterskiing. Invented on a Minnesota lake in 1922, waterskiing has been upstaged by windsurfing. But it is still popular on lakes and in calm coastal areas throughout the USA. Beginners' packages are available from many resorts. The prices may be lower than you'd think, but waterskiing is considerably harder than it looks.

Canoeing. Canoeing, kayaking and rafting are various ways of experiencing the inland waterways of the US. Canoes for several paddlers (known in Britain as 'Canadian canoes') are the most popular way to explore the calm lakes and backwaters of the Ozarks, the northern Midwest and so on. You need no experience for this. However if you want to tackle the rivers in a kyak, which in North America refers to a one-man enclosed boat versatile enough to be taken on turbulent waters, you'll need some previous training and practice. There are many canoe rental outlets (about $20-$25 a day) and complete outfitters who supply camping equipment and all the food you will need for a leisurely week canoeing. For a free list of outfitters, write to Grumman Boats, Marathon, NY 13803.

Those who lack canoeing experience can still experience the thrills of the fast rivers of New England, the Rockies and even the Grand Canyon by joining a white water rafting expedition. The inflatable rafts are virtually unsinkable. Many rafting organizations arrange for you to be returned to your point of departure after the trip which lasts a half day, one day or sometimes longer.

Another watersport craze is 'tubing' which means floating down rivers in an inner tube. You can either rent these for $3-$6 a day (which usually includes transport back to your starting point) or you can buy your own at any truckstop for $10.

Swimming. America has produced more Olympic swimming champions than any other country. Like other forms of exercise, it is taken seriously and most children take formal lessons at their local suburban swimming pool. The majority of hotels have pools, which in the summer offer a much needed respite from the heat. University campuses have Olympic-sized pools which may be open to the public for a minimal fee. Municipal pools, though often smaller and more crowded, are often cheaper. But most Americans share their backyard swimming pool as readily as their phone.

Disused quarries, gravel pits and ponds are also popular swimming holes. Lakes and rivers are colder and potentially more dangerous if there are rapids and whirlpools. Subterranean activity in many parts of the country produces free natural jacuzzis. Since most of these are sulphur springs, you will have to take a shower soon afterwards to rid yourself of the smell. 'Skinny dipping' (nude bathing) is popular though on crowded resort beaches it is unlawful to change — you are supposed to use the cubicle provided — let alone disrobe entirely.

Windsurfing and Surfing. Windsurfing was popularized in California by attaching a mast and sail to a surf board. After a few hours of professional tuition (around $20 an hour in small groups) you should be able to start, turn, tack and sail along at a good few knots. Every coastal and inland lake resort will offer windsurfing instruction and hire facilities.

One of the principal entertainments in Southern California and Hawaii is watching and admiring the top surfers. If you're a beginner, be very cautious of the pounding breakers. The Atlantic coast and the Gulf of Mexico provide a gentler introduction to the sport.

For an interesting variation, try landyachting. By putting a set of wheels on a sailboard, you can travel along hard-packed beaches at up to 50 mph. The sport is relatively undeveloped, but enthusiasts can be found on Floridan and Californian beaches.

HUNTING AND FISHING

Hunting and freshwater fishing require permits issued by the state authorities. Hunting licences for non-residents are much more expensive than for residents, ranging from $4 to hunt waterfowl in Oklahoma to $400 to hunt bighorn sheep in Wyoming. Fishing licences are generally cheaper, seldom above $5 for three days. Contact the state government department of Natural Resources (Fish & Wildlife Division) for further information about seasons and where to purchase a licence.

The traveller who has adapted to the bitter winters of the Midwest or New England might wish to try ice-fishing from a 'fish-house'. These are wooden huts erected on frozen lakes around a small circular hole which permits fishing inside the hut. The catch can then be barbecued on the spot. Some temporary ice communities even have their own bars and cinemas. Some states require all fish-houses to be cleared by the last day of February to avoid mishaps on melting ice.

CYCLING

Cycling is enjoying a renaissance in the States because of its economy and health-giving properties. The TransAmerican Trail for cyclists wends its way along 4,250 miles between Oregon and Virginia through national parks, prairies, deserts, farmlands and country towns. Strip maps of the route are available from American Youth Hostels, PO Box 37613, NW Washington DC 20013-7613. Almost every state has marked bikeways, which state tourist offices will be able to tell you about. If you want to plan your own bicycle route, stick to back roads, canal towpaths, abandoned railway lines and beaches with hard-packed sand.

Buying or Renting a Bicycle. Cycle shops offer a selection ranging from one-speed runabouts to ten-speed racers. The best, and most expensive models are French and Japanese imports. Prices are perhaps slightly lower than in Europe: the cheapest ten-speed costs around $150 new, $100 in good secondhand condition. You might want to consider a mountain bike with wide tyres suitable not only for off-road riding but for pot-holed city streets. Some cycle shops hire out bicycles for around $20 per day. A returnable deposit of $100 or more or credit card is required.

There is often a roaring trade in used bicycles, especially on and around college campuses. Because of the high level of theft, anyone with a decent bike removes the front wheel and uses a Citadel or Kryptonite lock to fasten it plus the rest of the bike to an immovable object. Few bicycles are fitted with mudguards since few Americans cycle in inclement weather.

Further Information. There is a wealth of cycle touring information published in the USA, including strip maps of bicycle trails and maps for negotiating city centres. for an overall impression try *The American Biking Atlas and Touring Guide* by Sue Browder, published by Workman, 231 E 51st St, New York 10022. Details of other publications can be obtained from the Cyclists' Touring Club, 69 Meadrow, Godalming, Surrey.

SKIING

There are a few states in the Deep South where skiing is not feasible, but virtually every other state in the Union provides facilities for skiing, even if they have to make the snow artificially. But it is generally accepted that the best skiing is confined to the Western Sierras, the Rockies, Vermont and New York State. There are few package tours to be had, so it is a matter of turning up at a resort and finding your own room, hire shop, instructor and cable car ('tramway'). This can become very expensive; most skiers do not expect much change from $100 a day. People in the Rockies in the spring should look around for late-season ski deals, e.g. $12 lift tickets and 'Women Ski Free'.

To make sure the investment is worth your while, there are several numbers to call for ski conditions: New Hampshire (900) 976-3700; New Mexico (505) 984-0606; Utah (801) 521-8102; Colorado (505) 984-0606; Vermont (900) 976-3740.

One of the advantages of learning to ski or improving your technique in North America is that the instruction will be in English. Most resorts teach the Graduated Length Method (GLM) — the American equivalent of 'Ski Evolutif' — which starts complete beginners on very short skis and allows them to progress to longer skis as their proficiency increases. Experienced skiers may find Ameican resorts a little too regimented (piste stewards equipped with walkie-talkies enforce 'slow skiing' zones where runs converge), but the USA is certainly a good place for beginners.

In addition to basic downhill skiing, the cross country variety is popular. Write to the National Park Service (Department of the Interior, Washington DC 20240) for literature about parks which have cross-country trails, or to the Ski Touring Council (West Hill Rd, Troy, Vermont 05868) for cross country routes throughout the country.

To find untracked snow in higher mountains, a group of experienced skiers can club together to hire a helicopter and take up the increasingly popular sport of heli-skiing. An interesting variation is offered at some resorts where you can balloon up to the top of a mountain and then ski down. Other attractions include renting a Sony Walkman for music while you ski, or an outdoor hot tub for relaxation afterwards. Even out of season, ski resorts are often very good bases for outdoor activities. You can often find golf, tennis, rafting, fishing and horse riding facilities at a single mountain centre, and accommodation is cheaper than during the ski-season. For an annotated list of ski resorts, consult *The Morrow Book of American Resorts* edited by Thomas Tracey.

RANCHES

City slickers get a taste of the great American outdoors on dude ranches, which are popular from Montana to Texas. If the cowboy life appeals to you, you will have to be prepared to pay for it, since dude ranches are usually more like posh resorts than working farms (usually over $500 a week per person). Ask the Dude Ranchers' Association (PO Box 471, LaPorte, Colorado 80535; 303-223-8440) for its annual *Vacation Directory*.

TOURIST INFORMATION

The American government tourist office is called the United States Travel and Tourism Administration (USTTA). Its British office (no personal callers) is at PO Box 1EN, London W1R 1EN (071-495 4466). Its US headquarters is at 14th and Constitution Avenues NW, Washington, DC 20230 (202-377-2000). Call in or write with an outline of your plans. Within the USA you can use the toll-free USTTA Hotline, 1-800-255-3050.

The national tourist office holds only a small proportion of the available travel literature. Most travel promotion is done at state level, so if you know in advance which states you'll be concentrating on, write to the travel offices (all addresses and phone numbers below) or to the city tourist offices given under *Help and Information* for each region.

When you call or write to a state tourist office, mention any special interests such as theatre, cycling or ornithology, since many offices have leaflets on all sorts of subjects. But don't expect a personal reply to your enquiry. And don't expect a detached or discriminating tone in the bumph; be prepared for the hard sell. It is still a worthwhile exercise for the road map and the list of forthcoming events.

Emergencies. If you need emergency medical assistance see the chapter *Health*. For dealing with a financial crisis see *Money*. In the *Help and Information* section of the regional chapters are listed the addresses of the post office, American Express, Thomas Cook and telephone numbers for emergency medical treatment.

Travelers' Aid. This voluntary organisation began life in the 19th century. In the predominantly male West it was popular to advertise for brides in British provincial newspapers. A Chicago lawyer, alarmed at the plight of women who travelled to the USA but took fright upon meeting their potential husbands, established Travelers' Aid to help them escape. This role has decreased significantly. Nowadays the Travelers' Aid bureaux at airports and bus stations cater for any foreign visitors in need of succour. If all your money and documents have been stolen, they will contact the Consulate and a relative at home to help you out. If you arrive at nightfall in an unfamiliar city, they will help to arrange (paid) accommodation and advise you of areas to avoid.

The resources of Travelers' Aid are stretched. It should be emphasized that they should only be used in an emergency. And if you need medical help, go direct to a hospital: Travelers' Aid are not equipped to deal with health problems.

Consulates. There are eight British Consulates-General in the US in addition to the Embassy in Washington. These are located in New York, Atlanta, Boston, Cleveland, Houston, Los Angeles, San Francisco and Chicago. In addition there are British Consulates in Anchorage, Dallas, Kansas City, Miami, New Orleans, Norfolk, Philadelphia, Portland, Seattle and St Louis. Unless you lose your passport, are destitute and want to be repatriated or there is a revival of the American Civil War, you won't need to consult the addresses which are provided in the regional chapters. (If you lose your money, try to have them cash a cheque). If your passport is lost or stolen, notify the police immediately, and go to the nearest consulate. You will be issued with travel documents which will allow you to complete your stay and take a one-way trip back to Britain. It is also worth notifying the local Immigration & Naturalisation Service of the loss, to avoid suspicion of overstaying.

Handicapped Travellers. The American travel industry is highly aware of the problems facing handicapped travellers and makes careful provision for ease of access. Hertz and Avis rent cars adapted with hand controls at normal rates subject to ten days notice. Greyhound Bus Lines and most American airlines allow an escort to travel free with a handicapped passenger. Amtrak provide specially-designed compartments on all long-distance trains. Potomac Tours, 1919 Pennsylvania Avenue NW, Washington DC 20006 (1-800-424-2969) operate escorted rail tours for handicapped groups to various areas of the northeastern USA.

Accommodation presents few problems as long as you book well in advance. Every hotel in the Holiday Inn chain has one or two rooms for handicapped guests. Other hotels specialise in catering for the disabled. For example, the Vista International in New York has 18 rooms equipped with hydraulic lifts for baths and showers, plus a large fitness centre complete with physiotherapists.

PUBLIC HOLIDAYS

Although all holidays are legislated by the state rather than the federal government, in practice most states observe the holidays legislated for federal employees as below. Banks, most businesses and some restaurants are closed on the following days:

January 1:	New Year's Day
January 16:	Martin Luther King's Birthday
February (3rd Monday):	Presidents' Day
May (last Monday):	Memorial Day (except Alaska, Louisiana, Mississippi, South Carolina)
July 4:	Independence Day
September (1st Monday):	Labor Day
October (2nd Monday):	Columbus Day (32 states only)
November 11:	Veterans' Day
November (4th Thursday):	Thanksgiving

December 25:   Christmas

In addition, many other holidays are celebrated, such as Lincoln's birthday which is widely observed in the north and neglected in the south. Details are given in the *Calendar of Events* at the end of each regional chapter.

STATE TOURIST OFFICES

Where a telephone number beginning 1-800 is listed, you may call toll-free from within the USA.

Alabama Bureau of Tourism and Travel: 532 S Perry St, Montgomery, AL 36104; tel (205) 832-5510; 1-800-392-8096 within Alabama; 1-800-252-2262 from outside the State.

Alaska Division of Tourism: Pouch E, Juneau, AK 99811; tel (907) 465-2010.

Arizona Office of Tourism: 3507 N. Central Avenue, Suite 506, Phoenix, AZ 85012; tel (602) 255-3618.

Arkansas Department of Parks & Tourism: 1 Capitol Mall, Little Rock, AR 72201; tel (501) 371-7777; 1-800-482-8999 within Arkansas; 1-800-463-8383 from outside the State.

California Office of Tourism: 1030 13th St, Suite 200, Sacramento, CA 95814; tel (916) 322-1396; 1-800-TO CALIF.

Colorado Tourism Board: 225 West Colfax, Denver, CO 80202; tel (303) 892-1112; 1-800-433-2656.

Connecticut Department of Economic Development: 210 Washington St, Hartford, CT 06106; tel (203) 566-3948; 1-800-842-7492 from northeastern states only.

Delaware State Travel Service: 99 Kings Highway, PO Box 1401, Dover, DE 19903; tel (302) 736-4271; 1-800-282-8667 within Delaware; 1-800-441-8846 from outside the State.

Washington DC Convention & Visitors Association: 1575 1 St NW, Suite 250, Washington, DC 20005; tel (202) 789-7000.

Florida Division of Tourism: 126 Van Buren St., Tallahassee, FL 32301; tel (904) 488-8230.

Georgia Department of Industry & Trade: PO Box 1776, Atlanta, GA 30301; tel (404) 656-3590.

Hawaii Visitors Bureau: 2270 Kalakaua Avenue, Room 801, Honolulu, HI 96815; tel (808) 923-1811.

Idaho Travel Council: State Capitol Building, Room 108, Boise, ID 83720; tel (208) 334-2470; 1-800-635-7820.

Illinois Department of Commerce & Community Affairs: 310 S. Michigan Avenue, Suite 108, Chicago, IL 60604; tel (312) 793-2094.

Indiana Department of Commerce, Tourism Development Division: 1 N Capitol, Suite 700, Indianapolis, IN 46204; tel (307) 232-8860; 1-800-2 WANDER.

Iowa Tourism and Film Office: 600, E Court Avenue, Capitol Center, Suite A, Des Moines, IA 50309; tel (515) 281-3100; 1-800-345 IOWA

Kansas Travel and Tourism Department: 503 Kansas Avenue, 6th Floor, Topeka, KS 66603; tel (913) 296-2009.

Kentucky Travel Development Department: Capital Plaza Tower, Frankfort, KY 40601; tel (502) 564-4930; 1-800-225 TRIP.

Louisiana Office of Tourism: Box 44291, Baton Rouge, LA 70804; tel (504) 925-3860.

Maine State Tourism Office: 189 State St, Augusta, ME 04333; tel (207) 289-2423.

Maryland Office of Tourist Development: 45 Calvert St, Annapolis, MD 21401; tel (301) 269-3517; 1-800-331-1750.

Massachusetts Division of Tourism: 100 Cambridge St, Boston, MA 02202; tel (617) 727-3201.

Michigan Department of Commerce, Travel Bureau: Box 30226, Lansing, MI 48909; tel (517) 373-0670; 1-800-5432 YES.

Minnesota Travel Information Center: 240 Bremer Building, 419 N Robert St, St Paul, MN 55101; tel (612) 296-5029; 1-800-642 9747 within Minnesota; 1-800-328-1461 from outside the State.

Mississippi Division of Tourism: Box 22825, Jackson, MS 39205. 1-800-962-2346.
Missouri Division of Tourism: Truman State Office Building, Box 1055, Jefferson City, MO 65102; tel (314) 751-4133.
Montana Travel Promotion Bureau: 1424 Ninth Avenue, Helena, MT 59620; tel (406) 449-2654; 1-800-548-3390.
Nebraska Tourism Division: Box 94666, Lincoln, NE 68509; tel (402) 471-3796; 1-800-742-7595 within Nebraska; 1-800-228-4307 from outside the State.
Nevada Commission on Tourism: Capitol Complex, Carson City, NV 89710; tel (702) 885-4322.
New Hampshire Office of Vacation Travel: Box 856, Concord, NH 03301; tel (603) 271-2343.
New Jersey Division of Travel & Tourism: CM 826, Trenton, NJ 08625; tel (609) 292-2470.
New Mexico Tourism & Travel Division: Bataan Memorial Building, Santa Fe, NM 87503; tel (505) 827-6230; 1-800-545-2040.
New York Division of Tourism: 1 Commercial Plaza, Albany, NY 12245; tel (518) 474-4116; 1-800-CALL NYS (from north-eastern states only)
North Carolina Travel & Tourism Division: 430 N. Salisbury St., Box 25249, Raleigh, NC 27611; tel (919) 733-4171; 1-800-VISIT NC.
North Dakota Tourism Promotion Division: Capitol Grounds, Bismarck, ND 58505; tel (701) 224-2525; 1-800-472-2100 within North Dakota; 1-800-228-4307 from outside the State.
Ohio Office of Travel & Tourism: Box 1001, Columbus, OH 43216; tel (614) 466-8844; 1-800-BUCK EYE.
Oklahoma Tourism & Recreation Department: 500 Will Rogers Building, Oklahoma City, OK 73105; tel (405) 521-2409; 1-800-652-6552 from nearby states only.
Oregon Division of Tourism: 595, Cottage St, NE, Salem, OR 97310; tel (503) 373-1200; 1-800-223-3306 within Oregon; 1-800-547-7842 from outside the State.
Pennsylvania Bureau of Travel Development: 416 Forum Building, Harrisburg, PA 17120; tel (717) 787-5453; 1-800-VISIT PA.
Rhode Island Department of Economic Development, Tourist Promotion; 7 Jackson Walkway, Providence, RI 02903; tel (401) 277-2601; 1-800-556-2484 (from north-eastern states only).
South Carolina Division of Tourism: Edgar A. Brown Building, 1205 Pendleton St, Suite 110, Columbia, SC 29201; tel (803) 758-8735.
South Dakota Division of Tourism: 221 S. Central, Pierre, SD 57501; tel (605) 773-3301; 1-800-952-2217 within South Dakota; 1-800-843-1930 from outside the State.
Tennessee Department of Tourist Development: 601, Broadway, Box 23170, Nashville, TN 37202; tel (615) 741-2158.
Texas Travel & Information Division: Box 5064, Austin, TX 78763; tel (512) 475-5956.
Utah Travel Council, Council Hall, Salt Lake City, UT 84114; tel (801) 533-5681.
Vermont Travel Division: 134 State St, Montpelier, VT 05602; tel (802) 828-3236.
Virginia State Travel Service: 202, N Ninth St, Suite 500, Richmond, VA 23219; tel (804) 786-4484.
Washington State Tourism Development Division: 101 General Administration Building, Olympia, WA 98504; tel (206) 753-5600; 1-800-544-1800.
West Virginia Travel Development: Building 6, Room B-564, Charleston, WV 25305; tel (304) 348-2286; 1-800-CALL WVA.
Wisconsin Division of Tourism: Box 7606, Madison, WI 53707; tel (608) 266-2161.
Wyoming Travel Commission: Frank Norris Jr Tavel Center, Cheyenne, WY 82002; tel (307) 777-7777; 1-800-CALL WYO.

New York

New York looks like nowhere else on earth. Man-made pinnacles rise threateningly from a hopelessly overcrowded island, concealing the fear and squalor — as well as the glamour and excitement — at street level in Manhattan. Yet the city is not alienating, and its people are not aliens. While New York bears little relation to the rest of the USA, it is certainly worth experiencing, as one of the great world cities.

New York may not have London's grandeur, Paris's romance nor Venice's beauty, but what it does have is vitality. To a New Yorker those other cities with their various claims to greatness don't matter a fig. New York is a place of extremes: it has the best and the worst in every category. New York is no place for the weary or for the poor. You need energy and vitality to match the city's, and enough money to enjoy its opportunities.

New York is known as the 'Big Apple', an expression which originated among the blacks who migrated from the South, to describe anything very, very big. Although the city may not always be equal to the task of feeding, clothing, educating, informing, entertaining, heating, cooling, policing and protecting its seven million people, it tackles the job with great gusto. Somehow, it has enough left over to cope with 20 million visitors as well.

One hundred hospitals and five medical centres cater to New Yorkers' health needs. Seven thousand underground cars carry 1.5 billion riders annually. Two thousand and fifty schools and 91 colleges, universities and technical schools educate the city's young and old. Fourteen thousand sanitary engineers (dustbin men) take away four million tons of refuse annually and keep 7,500 miles of streets clean and free of snow. Fifteen TV stations, plus dozens of cable TV channels, and over 30 radio stations provide New Yorkers with news and entertainment. Theatres, ballets, concert halls, 125 museums, five zoos, a planetarium and an aquarium entertain New Yorkers. Two baseball teams, two football teams, one soccer team, two ice hockey teams and three race tracks make the Big Apple a sportsviewer's (and punter's) paradise. Those into active sports have 538 municipal tennis courts, 13 golf courses, 37 outdoor and 11 municipal indoor swimming pools, and facilities for boating, biking, hiking, riding and jogging.Some 1.2 billion gallons of water must be brought in each day, so that New Yorkers can drink, cook, bathe and launder their clothes. These mind-boggling statistics for pages give an impression of how awesomely huge and splendidly organised the city is.

Metropolitan New York is divided into five boroughs which together cover an area of 300 square miles. The island of Manhattan (almost always called 'New York' by natives and visitors alike) lies in the mouth of the Hudson River and is the place in which the visitor will spend most of his or her time. The other boroughs are Brooklyn, Queens, the Bronx and Staten Island. Their residents are described derisevely by Manhattan people as the 'B & T' (bridge and tunnel) crowd. The Bronx, the only borough which is on the mainland. is mainly known for its slums. Brooklyn and Queens are part of Long Island, which stretches 350 miles out into the Atlantic.Staten Island occupies its own island which is connected to the mainland by one of the longest suspension bridges in the world.

Almost every New Yorker and many non-New Yorkers believe (with some justification) that New York is where everything important happens. To paraphrase Sinatra, if you can make it in New York, you've made it: there is no higher achievment. With such prestige comes gross arrogance and parochialism. As a former Governor of New York, Al Smith, once observed about New York versus the rest of the country, 'When you're west of the Hudson River, you're camping out'.

New Yorkers are quirky, proud and unpredictable. They are products of a defiantly artificial megalopolis whose towering architecture, success/money ethos, and extreme urban style of life can overwhelm all but the most resilient. Most visitors find the place thoroughly exhausting.

THE LOCALS

The city's present and future are, you sense, considered much more important than its history: its discovery by the Dutch in 1524, its acquisition by the British in 1775, the establishment of Central Park in the 1860s, the construction of the famous skyscrapers during the 1930s following the Wall Street Crash and so on. As the visitor soon discovers, many natives believe the history of the city started with their (or their parents' or grandparents') arrival. 'The story of New York' wrote Anthony Burgess, 'is a story of immigrant battling with immigrant', and perhaps it is this continuous battling that makes New Yorkers so hard.

What is not open to question is the fact that sucessive waves of immigration have produced a city with the greatest ethnic diversity of any in the world. Indeed, in New York, the minorities seem to be the majority: over three million blacks and Hispanics make up almost half the population, American-Italians constitute just under 10%, and American-Irish about 7%. Half a million Asians (mainly Chinese, but now including many Vietnamese and Koreans) and some 300,000 German-Americans. Austrian-Americans and Swiss-Americans are also there. On top of that, there are large communities of Hungarians, Greeks, Filipinos and Indians. To complicate matters further,

700,000 people are racially unclassifiable. There are at the least 56 different ethnic origins represented in the Big Apple, because that's how many different foreign language papers are published in the city. Visit the Museum of Immigration on Ellis Island, where all the 'huddled masses' were processed between 1892 and 1924, and which came to be known as the 'Island of Tears'.

The wide ethnic diversity is reflected in the city's numerous religious and folk festivals: you can celebrate Chinese New Year, march in the St Patrick's Day or Pulaski Parades, sing along to the guitars and bongoes of the Puerto Rican block parties on San Juan Bautista's Day, or quietly observe in the company of American-Japanese the solemn rites of the Feast of Obon held on Riverside Drive above the Hudson River.

An ethnic self-consciousness accompanies the ethnic diversity, and this cosmopolitanism contributes in large measure to the Big Apple's fascination. When blacks and Jews and Poles and Chinese don green caps and wave little green flags, singing 'When Irish Eyes are Smiling' on St. Patrick's Day, you may think that you understand the intention or hope of the melting pot theory. But predominant in the consciousness of New Yorkers is the firm belief of not being melted in that pot, of retaining a separate identity.

Class, as well as race, divides New Yorkers. Millionaires, the middle classes, yuppies, 15,000 vagrants sleeping rough (1,000 of whom die unidentified and unclaimed each year) and over one million welfare recipients crowd together in the city, though the gap between rich and poor is seldom bridged. Panhandlers (beggars) are numerous and persistent, but you should quickly cultivate resistance to their approaches. Some shops sell T-shirts reading 'NO spare change'. What unites New Yorkers of all classes and races is simply that New York, for better or worse, is their city, that living within its 300 square miles bestows a unique privilege, burden, opportunity and right to voice an opinion on how it ought to be run. Every New Yorker is an authority on New York; every New Yorker will insist that he or she alone knows the best place to eat, shop, sleep or visit. Ask directions on a street, and two New Yorkers will argue abut the best way for you to get there, and often give two completely contradictory answers. Moreover, each will give you the directions with utter certainty that he or she is right, the other wrong.

On the other hand there are unexpected demonstration of fellowship among New Yorkers. A good example is of a man who arrived at his parked car just as the meter expired and at the moment a traffic warden was about to summon the towing squad. When the warden persisted despite the man's protests, 15 passers-by climbed onto the car to prevent it from being towed away. The spontaneous expression of citizen solidarity could never happen in Britain, and would probably not take so flamboyant a form in any other city in the world.

Making Friends. The reputation New Yorkers have earned for pugnacity is understandable. Being cocksure is often hard to distinguish from being aggressive. New Yorkers also have a reputation for coldness which is simply undeserved. They are the most open of all American city dwellers, open not only to fads, art forms, life-styles and ideologies, but to people. Too self-confident for shyness and to curious for caution, they think nothing of engaging complete strangers in intimate conversations. To their way of thinking, if someone's in a public place, that person wants to talk. This ties in with their exaggerated image-consciousness. Those who find other peoples confessions and self-revelations unwelcome had better avoid New Yorkers.

Exploring new relationships and tasting new experiences are active goals of most denizens of the Big Apple. Suprisingly, it has one of the nation's lowest divorce rates among big cities, possibly because 'meaningful associates' and 'cohabitees' have replaced spouses.

If you can't make friends in the Big Apple, its unlikely you'll make friends anywhere. New Yorkers not only lack reserve, they spend an inordinate amout of time out their homes and flats. Weekends are spend at museums, concerts, poetry readings, or in the city's many parks. Evenings are spent on the town. Following cocktails and dinner, there can be opera, disco, ballet, a concert, nightclub, jazz joint, film, party or bar — anywhere but home.

Clubs are excellent places to meet people, though it's not cheap to hop from one club to another when there may be a $20 cover charge (which does include a drink or two). Many have a short lifetime and fads change. A quick glance at *Village Voice* should give you a few ideas. The singles bars play an even greater role in NYC than in other cities. The highest concentration of singles bars is along 1st and 2nd Avenues between 60th and 85th Streets. Often they live cheek by jowl with ordinary pubs and clubs.

If your main ambition is to see celebrities, you could try lurking outside the Dakota Apartments, Central Park West and 72nd St where many stars have lived, including John Lennon: Strawberry Fields, a garden within Central Park dedicated to his memory, is just across the street.

If your object is not so much sex as a stimulating conversation, there is the regular New York City bar — many of them with a strong Irish flavour.

Except for San Francisco, there is probably no other city in the USA with such a visible gay population. Bars play an important part in the social interaction. The Oscar Wilde Memorial Bookstart is a good place to invest-igatge the gay scene; here you can pick up journals, newspapers and postings of both male and female gay events. Here, too, you can find copies of the *Gayellow Pages*, a listing of goods, and services for the gay community. You can also call National Gay Task Force (741-5800) or the Lesbian or Gay Switchboards for additional information. The gay scene in New York has come a long way from Victorian drawing rooms with men standing around wearing green carnations and making *bons mots.*

Among the places to meet people are the campus and bars, cafes, book-stores and restaurants of the neighbourhoods surrounding the campuses. New York University (NYU) is downtown beside Washington Squre; check in the Loeb Student Center for university events open to the public. Columbia University is uptown not far from Harlem. To get the flavour of the area around Columbia, drop into Marvin Gardens Restaurant, West End Cafe or Green Tree Hungarian Restaurant, all within a five minute stroll of Columbia University.

Those looking to make friends among college people might also appreciate the folks that they are likely to meet in musuems, gallery opening and in the queues waiting to get into concerts, films or plays where common interests are an easy opening to conversation. Or loiter around the Citicorp Center (53rd St at Lexington Avenue; 559-4259) where you and others like you will be entertained by the chamber music or jazz. The free summer concerts of the New York Philharmonic in Central Park (see *Music*) are especially friendly occaisons with a mood of celebration.

You'll notice in most parks baseball and softball games materialize when-ever enough enthusiasts gather for a few informal innings of play. You'll also see rugby, soccer and maybe even cricket played impromtu in the Upper

East Side area of Central Park facing 5th Avenue. It is easy to meet people with similar interests in this way, both New Yorkers and expatriates.

CLIMATE

In general, early spring is windy and rainy; May and June are ideal; July and August are oppressively hot, often going above 90°F/33°C and stiflingly humid; autumn is generally delightful with a surprising range of colour in the foliage; and from December through February, there are snowstorms, icy conditions and slush underfoot which makes walking treacherous. Call 976-1212 for weather information.

When deciding on your travelling wardrobe, remember that the city buildings are over-cooled in summer and over-heated in winter.

ARRIVAL AND DEPARTURE

Air. New York's airports are not the best introduction to the city or the country. Even before you land, your flight is likely to be delayed because of crowded airspace. Once you touch down, you can face a wait of an hour or more to clear immigration and customs, unless you have had the benefit of 'pre-clearance' in the country of origin. In addition, the problems of changing flights or travelling into Manhattan are considerable. For details of airport links, call 1-800-AIR-RIDE toll-free.

Kennedy International Airport (JFK). Most international flights arrive at JFK, about 15 miles east of Manhattan. It is the aviation equivalent of Dante's Inferno, a hateful confusion of terminals caught in a tangle of access roads. It is one of the worst airports in the world for both immigration and customs clearance. The fastest way into the city is by helicopter ($70). A taxi will cost at least $40. To avoid being taken on a circuitous route, ask the driver to use either the Manhattan Bridge (for the south of Manhattan) or the Queensboro (59th St) Bridge; this will give the impression that you know your way around, so a scenic diversion via the Bronx is less likely. Next quickest (at least in theory) is the Carey Transportation bus ($8) running to Manhattan's Grand Central Station and the Rockefeller Center, although services are unreliable.

The cheapest way into the city — and fastest during the morning rush hour — is to take the free long-term parking bus to Howard Beach subway station. Here you buy a subway token ($1.25) and board the A train which runs straight to Manhattan via Brooklyn. You can transfer to virtually any other subway line.

When changing aircraft, note that JFK has five terminals. Each terminal is self-contained, with extensive shopping facilities, left luggage, etc. Check with the airline which terminal you arrive at or depart from, since signposting in the airport itself is appalling. The terminals are linked by a slow irregular shuttle bus which arrives at and departs from the ground level of each terminal and travels anticlockwise: for a faster ride, cross to the inner ring road and catch the clockwise yellow shuttle bus, intended for staff. A direct bus service runs to La Guardia ($7, about 30 minutes), while to reach Newark you need to take a bus or a subway to Manhattan then travel out.

Newark International Airport (EWR). A more user-friendly and accessible international gateway is ten miles southwest of Manhattan. International arrivals are at terminal C, while Virgin Atlantic departures leave from Terminal A. A taxi to New York City involves paying a $10 surcharge plus the toll and is likely to cost $40-$50. More cheaply, you can take the New Jersey Transit bus to Manhattan's Port Authority Bus Terminal, or the Olympia bus to the World Trade Center, Penn Station or Grand Central Station. There are departures every 20-30 minutes. To cut the journey cost to $2, take the local bus to downtown Newark then a PATH train to Manhattan. This will not be a pleasant experience at night.

La Guardia (LGA). This airport is much closer to Manhattan than the other two airports, about five miles east in Queens. It handles domestic and Canadian flights, including the USAir and Delta shuttles to Boston and Washington DC. To reach it by public transport, take the subway to Jackson Heights and connect to bus Q47 or Q33. Alternatively, bus M60 runs every half-hour from 125th St at the top end of Manhattan. Carey Transportation buses run to all La Guardia terminals from the Rockefeller Center and Grand Central Station for $7. A taxi costs $15 or so.

Arriving in Style. For each of these airports there is a spectacular way to the city, involving a little more expense and effort, but well worthwhile if you want to indulge yourself and enjoy the skyline for your first visit. All of these can be undertaken in the reverse direction, but are not nearly so impressive.

Kennedy: take the A train to Brooklyn, then walk along Montague St to the Promenade. Stroll north from here to Brooklyn Bridge and walk across the bridge to south Manhattan.

Newark: take a cab (about $25) to the ferry terminus on Staten Island, which is linked to New Jersey by bridge. From here the 50c ferry ride to Battery Park at the southern tip of Manhattan confronts you head-on with the city.

La Guardia: take a cab to Roosevelt Island tramway station ($12), and fly in ($1.40) from there on the cable car which King Kong removed.

Buying Air Tickets. New York is the best place in the USA to buy cheap international air tickets. Students and those under 26 should try Council Travel, 205 E 42nd St (661-0311). Its sister organisation, Council Charter (same address, 661-0311 or 1-800-223-7402) sells cut-price tickets to non-students on both scheduled and charter flights. For other agencies, check advertisements in weekend editions of *New York Times*.

Bus. Long-distance services arrive at the Port Authority Bus Terminal, 8th Avenue and 41st St (564-8484); the Greyhound number is 635-0800. It is a widely held view that the best pickpockets in the city operate at the Bus Terminal. If you want to excape from Manhattan, the Catskill Mountains are less than 100 miles away; the two-hour bus journey to Monticello on the Short Line Bus System (736-4700) costs about $30.

Train. The two Amtrak terminals are Grand Central (42nd St and Park Avenue) and Penn (34th St between 7th and 8th Avenues). The former is a fine, imposing building (with a splendid oyster bar); the latter is almost entirely subterranean, and difficult to spot from street level. A shuttle bus service operates between the two stations. Grand Central is the terminal some suburban trains, but most fast trains serve only Penn. The Long Island Railroad (739-4200) can take you from Penn Station to Montauk at the tip of Long Island for $15 one way, a three-hour journey. The route along the east side of the Hudson River from Grand Central is also a scenic outing; see page 148.

Driving. Think carefully before attempting to bring a car into Manhattan. Road signs on the outskirts seem designed to confuse; you are offered options of various crossings to Manhattan, or obscure freeway names which are of no use to drivers unfamiliar with the city. On most crossings to Manhattan (but not Brooklyn or Manhattan bridges) a $2.50 toll is levied. The authorities are at present looking for ways to keep cars out of Manhattan and proposals include a $10 per day tax on visiting motorists.

Hitchhiking. Around Manhattan the overwhelming majority of traffic is local, so it is necessary to invest a few dollars on public transport to get away from the city. The closest reasonable proposition for I-80 east and I-95 north is the Manhattan approach to the George Washington Bridge; take the subway to 181 St station and stand somewhere on the tangle of approaches to the bridge, holding a sign and smiling wanly. For I-95 southwest, take a train from Penn station to Metropark New Jersey, close to the suburb of Iselin and with relatively easy access to the Interstate.

Driveaways. Many auto driveaway companies listed in the Yellow Pages. One particularly welcomes foreign drivers; you are invited to call in advance, and the minimum age is 19 rather than the usual 21. It is Dependable Car Travel Services, in Suite 301 at 1501 Broadway (840-6262). Although competition for cars from New York is intense in summer, with patience and persistence you should find one.

CITY TRANSPORT

City Layout. Avenues run north-south, streets run east-west. Broadway traces a crooked diagonal from the south the the northwest. It is relatively easy to navigate in central Manhattan, but you should bear in mind the 3rd and 5th Avenues are separated by three others (Lexington, Park and Madison), and that 8th Avenue becomes Central Park West north of 59th St. Avenue of the Americas is usually known as 6th Avenue. In the south of Manhattan the grid system collapses into disarray around the oldest settlements, exacerbated by the underpases and flyovers leading to bridges and tunnels.

Fifth Avenue runs through the centre of the city and is the dividing line between East and West in street addresses. You will also hear people talking about downtown, midtown and uptown divisions of the city. Downtown or lower Manhattan is the southern tip of the island including Wall Street, Chinatown and Greenwich Village; Midtown extends from roughly 14th St to 59th St, which forms the southern boundary of Central Park, all the way north to the Bronx, including Harlem.

Walking. New York is a pavement town and you are likely to do a lot of walking in it, so bring comfortable shoes or buy jogging shoes with hard rubber studs which are especially designed to save wear and tear on feet in cities. Even the city's yuppies wear running shoes to work.

The pavements of New York are a constant source of entertainment. On Easter Sunday join in the traditional see-and-be-seen promenade along 5th Avenue (near the Museum of Modern Art). Many areas such as Wall Street, Greenwich Village, SoHo, 5th Avenue and Central Park are best appricated on foot. You can walk to or from Brooklyn Heights across the architecturally striking Brooklyn Bridge which offers a vantage point from which to view the harbour and skyline of Manhattan. This is especially stunning at sunrise when you can watch the play of lights on the glass and steel facades of the buildings.

NEW YORK

1 Lincoln Center
2 Strawberry Fields
3 West Side YMCA
4 Central Park Zoo
5 Visitor Center
6 Carnegie Hall
7 Museum of Modern Art
8 Rockefeller Center
9 Times Square
10 Port Authority Terminal
11 Grand Central Station
12 Post Office
13 Madison Square Garden
14 Penn Station
15 Empire State Building
16 United Nations
17 Chelsea Hotel
18 Washington Square
19 New York University
20 World Trade Center
21 South St Seaport
22 Staten Island Ferry

Walking tours are listed in the *New York Magazine*. Adventures on a Shoestring (300 West 53rd St, 265-2663) arranges more off-beat walking tours. If you want to walk on your own, investigate *Flashmaps* at $4.95 each, a well-organized series of individual neighbourhoods.

Bus. The Metropolitan Transport Authority runs buses on all north/south avenues and the most important east/west crosstown streets. Buses have no conductors and drivers won't give change. Board at the front of the bus and deposit $1.25 in coins or an MTA token (which can be bought at booths in subway stations) in the box beside the driver. If you don't have change, fellow passengers will help. Ask for a free transfer if your trip requires changing buses.

Subway. The New York subway is one of the fastest and most extensive (240 miles of track) underground railways in the world. It can also be the most frightening, confusing and unpleasant. Be sure to pick up a detailed map of the system given away at stations and tourist offices, since you cannot rely on finding a map once you have entered the system. Unfortunately the subway map is horribly confusing and even a simple journey requires considerable study and planning. It is also difficult to ask for directions since ticket sellers are shielded behind layers of bullet proof (and sound proof) glass.

The subway map explains some of the peculiarities of the system, whereby express trains miss out certain stations at certain times of day. Find out if your destination is a 'local' or an 'express' stop. If you are still in doubt, ring Transit Information on 1-718-330-1234 and explain where you are and where you want to be.

Originally run by three competing companies, IND, IRT and BMT — names which are still used by many New Yorkers — the system is now run by the New York City Transit Authority. It provides round-the-clock service and a $1.25 token will, if you wish, take you around the entire system. To enter the system, simply drop a token into the turnstile slot and walk through.

Weighed against the advantages of speed and economy is the fact that the subway is filthy, noisy, and especially at night, a semi-degenerate world of its own, unpredictable, potentially dangerous. There is an independent 3,000 strong special police force called the Transit Police. In addition, there is a group of volunteers called 'Guardian Angels', male and female vigilantes in red berets who ride unarmed, relying on their martial arts skills and teamwork rather than weapons. For details about how to maximise your safety on the subway, see the section *Crime and Safety*.

Suburban Trains. The subway extends into the outlying boroughs, but to get across to New Jersey or the northern and eastern suburbs you need to use the suburban train networks. New Jersey is served by the Port Authority Trans-Hudson (PATH) railway, with the main Manhattan terminus at the World Trade Center. Long Island can be reached on the Long Island Rail Road (LIRR), and the northern suburbs on Metro North; trains on both these systems leave from Grand Central.

Car. Don't bother with motoring in the the city: the traffic is frantic; streets are so potholed that axles are always being broken; there is very little legal street parking and midtown garages cost at least $15 per hour. Parking law in the city is so complex that an entire book is devoted to the subject. Glen Bolovski's *New York Alternative Side of the Street Parking Calendar* details all the rules and highlights the 30 days each year when normal restrictions are lifted. The book is available from the author (who no longer drives) at PO Box 2499, Grand Central, New York 10163. If the police take your car to the 'docks', it costs a minimum of $100 to retrieve it, plus a $35 ticket and an unpleasant visit to the pound which is surrounded by armed guards.

You may decide to rent a car for a weekend drive out-of-town. But car rentals in NYC are often twice as expensive as they are in Florida or California. The best deals are booked up early, especially over a holiday period, so make reservations well in advance. Alternatively, take a bus or train out of town and rent a car when you arrive.

Taxis. New Yorkers are inveterate taxi users, so you may find competition stiff, especially in foul weather. Avoid cabs which are not yellow, since these are probably unlicensed, and look for the identity card with a photo of the driver displayed inside. Unlicensed drivers prey on tourists in locations such as Grand Central Station and the Port Authority bus terminal; some purport to have been sent by your hotel. You might be asked to pay $20 after a trip of only a few blocks, and you won't get your luggage back until you pay up. Be especially cautious if you are taking a taxi from JFK. There are many stories in circulation of drivers who will take you to Manhattan via New Jersey, charging upwards of $200. If you are ripped off or have a complaint, phone 747-0930 giving the driver's name and number.

A three-mile journey in Manhattan might cost $5 or $6, plus a dollar tip. You have to pay any bridge or tunnel tolls in addition to the mileage charge. Don't be tempted to smoke in the back of a cab, since this carries a fine of $50.

Cycling. The bicycle courier fraternity takes pride in the fact that one of its number won an Olympic gold medal for speed cycling. Despite the antagonism generated by the couriers' antics, cycling is growing in popularity as a means of getting around the city and there are some demarcated cycle routes. But there are problems: potholes, inclement weather, theft and motorists who just don't seem able to spot cyclists in their rear view mirrors, nor remember to check before opening car doors. If the prospect doesn't frighten you, cycling is a quick and cheap way to get around, and a popular Sunday recreation of New Yorkers. Bicycles can be rented for about $5 per hour or $20 per day, with a deposit of $50 or credit card. Sunday, with its limited traffic, is an excellent day for exploring lower and midtown Manhattan. Traffic is prohibited from Central Park on the weekends, so this is a good time to rent a bicycle and watch New Yorkers at rest and play. Try Metro Bicycles which has six branches including one at 1311 Lexington Avenue at 88th St which is handy for Central Park (427-4450); Loeb Boathouse in Central Park at about 72nd St (360-8111); or Sixth Avenue Bicycle, 545 6th Avenue at 15th St (255-5100), well situated for bicycle forays into Greenwich Village and SoHo.

Ferries. To get an idea of Manhattan from the water that surrounds it, take a Circle Line tour leaving from Pier 83, West 43rd St (563-3200), price $15; the boat tour lasts abut three hours, leaving every 45 minutes. It runs between mid-March and late November.

New York's favourite boat ride is the Staten Island Ferry. At 50c, it must be one of the cheapest water voyages per mile in the developed world. You get good views of the Statue of Liberty and the skyline of Manhattan. There's not much point in getting off on Staten Island so you might has well stay on board and save a quarter. The service runs every half an hour day and night from Battery Park on the southern tip of Manhattan, which is a good place for a pre-ferry picinc.

 Accommodation costs are frightful in Manhattan, and standards lower than you would expect elsewhere in America. Low-budget travellers who are well-organized should book well in advance for one of the hostels listed below; other visitors must expect to pay dearly.

Hotels. As prices for property increased, small inexpensive hotels and low-price rooming houses have all disappeared. In Manhattan, a one-room flat with a bathroom and kitchenette in a good, safe neighbourhood fetches of $1,000 a month. Competition is fierce for any reasonably priced hotel rooms which are still around. It may well be worth while making a transatlantic call to one of the hotels listed below. Otherwise you could trudge the streets of Manhattan for hours or else pay a high price. Add 14.25% sales tax (19.25% for rooms costing $100 or more) plus $2 occupancy tax, and your stay in Manhattan could turn out to be a short one.

Head for the New York Convention and Visitors Bureau, 2 Columbus Circle (397-8222) and pick up the free pamphlet: *Hotels* with addresses, phone numbers and rates. Check the Travel Section of the *New York Times* for hotel ads offering weekend package deals: two for the price of one, sometimes with breakfast or theatre tickets thrown in. The following hotels often participate in the scheme: Bedford, 118 E 40th St (697-4800), Beverly, 125 E 50th St (753-2700) and Carter Hotel, 250 W 43rd St (944-6000).

Below are a few suggestions of reasonably priced hotels, but phone ahead for reservations:

Chelsea Hotel, 222 W 23rd St (243-3700). A bohemian landmark in whose lift Leonard Cohen met Janis Joplin, and the place where Bob Dylan wrote 'Sad Eyed Lady of the Lowlands', $85 double.

Clinton Herald Square Hotel, 19 W 31st St, between 5th and 6th Avenues (279-4017), $50 double

Franklin Hotel, 164 E 87th St (289-5958), $50 double

Rio Hotel, 132 W 47th St (382-0600), $60 double

Hostels. The International Youth Hostel on Amsterdam Avenue between 103rd and 104th Streets (431-7105) is housed in the former Associated Residence for Respectable Aged Indigent Females. It costs around $25 for a bed for a night. The Chelsea Center Hostel (511 W 20th St), close to the other end of Manhattan, is well situated and clean; expect to pay $15-$20 per person including breakfast. Book in advance on 243-4922.

International House, on the Upper West Side (at 500 Riverside Drive at 122 St; 316-8436), is a hostel which was founded by John D Rockefeller Jr in 1924. The atmosphere is cosmopolitan, with lots of foreign students. It is a huge place which overlooks the Hudson River but is some way away from anything else you might want to see. 'Student' rooms (for which proof of student status might be required) cost $25, with reductions for stays of two weeks or more. Two people sharing a 'guest' room pay $65.

YMCA. Ys which accept both men and women charge approximately $25-$30 per person in a double. Try the YMCA Vanderbilt (244 E 47th St, 755-2410), close to Grand Central Station and with sauna, pool, laundry and library; the McBurney YMCA (215 W 23rd St, 741-9226); or the YMCA

West Side (5 W 63rd St, 767-4400) near the Lincoln Center. Bookings for these can be made through The Y's Way, based at the Vanderbilt at 224 E 47th St, New York, NY 10017 (308-2899; fax 308-3161).

Bed and Breakfast. Because of the high cost of other accommodation in New York, bed and breakfast can be particularly good value. Try Urban Ventures (594-5650) or the Bed and Breakfast Network of New York (645-8134).

Longer Term Accommodation. Check the sublet columns in the *New York Times* and the *Village Voice*. New Yorkers are prepared to let out rooms for as short a time as one or two weeks if it will make them a few extra dollars.

Eating and Drinking

Where to eat follows money and precedes sex as a New Yorker's favourite topic of conversation. Recomending places to eat in the Big Apple is both fraught with difficulties and perhaps unnecessary, since there are so many good places and publications galore on dining in New York. Don't feel you have to sit down to eat. Street food like sausages, soulaki and tempura is delicious and cheap. From more than 25,000 eating places, here are some suggestions which have good food served with few frills at reasonable prices. Not all accept credit cards and, unlike pricier restaurants won't expect men to wear jackets and ties. The eating places are listed geographically, moving from downtown to uptown.

Sloppy Louie's 92 South Street Seaport (952-9657) has long been one of the cities most colourful eating spots. You sit at long tables in the company of dock workers, stockbrokers and tourists all devouring fish and shellfish.

Hong Fat 63 Mott St in Chinatown (962-9588) open 24 hours, unspoilt by success and rude waiters. Try shrimp and black bean sauce at 4am, a dish considered by many New Yorkers to diminish the next morning's hangover. There are good restaurants all along Mott St, e.g. at numbers 13, 21, 81 and 113.

Say Eng Look 5 East Broadway (732-0796) in Chinatown. Popular for lunch, specializing in Peking cuisine (try Moo Shoo Pork).

Umberto's Clam House 129 Mulberry St (431-7545) in Little Italy bordering Chinatown, Serves Italian style seafood, outdoor seating in summer, open late, frequented by the local 'Godfather' types. Sit at the counter and watch the squid, conch and shrimps cooking.

Luna 112 Mulberry St (226-8657). Superb family run Italian restaurant.

Ratners 138 Delancey St (677-5588) in Lower East Side. Strictly kosher dairy and convenient for Sunday brunch when you're bargain hunting at the nearby street market on Orchard St. try blintzes (stuffed crepes) or matzo-bri (egg pancakes and matzos soaked in milk).

Ray's Pizza 465 6th Avenue (at 11th St) plus several other locations. Excellent pizzas.

Nathan's Famous (several locations throughout Manhattan). Famous for its hot dogs, french fries, and meat and seafood delicatessen. Good value fast food, and an essential part of the New York experience.

Carnegie Delicatessen 854 7th Avenue (near West 55th St; 757-2245); renowned for its unsurpassed pastrami on rye bread, sour pickles and cole slaw, not to mention its corned beef hash. Open 6.30am to 4am. No credit cards.

V&T Pizzeria 1024 Amsterdam Avenue (663-1078) on the Upper West side. A favourite with students from Columbia University.

Moving up a notch, it is well worth spending a little more to enjoy some truly excellent food. The following restaurants are, at the time of writing, providing excellent food at reasonable prices:

Eat 11 St Mark's Place between 2nd and 3rd Avenues (477-5155). A small (and hard to find) bistro/cafe with consistently good food; vegetarians are well catered for.

Union Square Café, 21 E 16th St (243-4020). Must book several days in advance, reconfirm on the day and expect to wait anyway. In return you get superlative new American food.

Japonica, 90 University Place (243-7752). Top-rate Japanese food at comfortable prices.

Nick's Coffee and Pizza Shop 736 11th Avenue (757-2432). Open all hours except 5am-6am, there is a seemingly infinite variety of pizzas plus excellent home-made yoghourt and baklava.

Cherry Restaurant 335 Columbus Avenue between 75th and 76th Streets (874-3630). From outside it looks like a typical old coffee shop, but you go through to a comfortable eating area with a menu combining New York favourites with Japanese influence. Try Long Island Duck.

The best (or at least the most prestigious) restaurant in Manhattan is the *Russian Tea Rooms* on W 57th St between 6th and 7th Avenues. If you're not famous, the waiters will point out people who are. Expect to pay at least $60 per head.

You need to add about a quarter to all menu prices to estimate the final total: 8.35% tax is added to the bill, and it has become an accepted convention to give twice this amount as a tip (it is also relatively easy to calculate by doubling the tax figure). Some restaurants even add 16.5% to the bill as a 'suggested' service charge.

As well as the obvious areas like Chinatown and Little Italy, New York has numerous concentrations of other ethnic restaraunts. For seafood, go to 2nd Avenue at E 77th St and 3rd Avenue at E 79th St. There is a huddle of Indian, Pakistani and Bangladeshi restaurants on Lexington Avenue between 27th and 28th Streets. W 14th St is the place for Hispanic restaurants, while for soul food try Lenox Avenue around 126th St. South of E 9th Street along 2nd Avenue you will find many Ukranian and Polish places. The best Russian food is at Brighton Beach and Coney Island in the borough of Brooklyn. Still in Brooklyn (but much closer to Manhattan), Lebanese restaurants can be found along Cort St and Atlantic Avenue.

Picnics. As in other great gastonomic cities, the picnic lunch is both economical and delicious, and fixings can be bought at any corner store. For a gourmet picnic or just to drool, visit one of the Big Apple's famous food emporiums. For example, Balducci's (422 6th Avenue in Greenwich Village) has exotic varieties of fresh fruit, cheese (try Monterey Jack from California, a tasty American speciality), sliced Virginia ham, smoked turkey and pastries, which, though not cheap, are fresh and fantastic. Take your picnic a few blocks away to Washington Square Park where there is folk singing, comics trying out their routines (including some talented young comics a bit too raw for TV) and assorted instrumentalists. Then there is Zabar's 2245

Broadway (uptown near 80th Street and the Museum of Natural History) which is famed for its chopped chicken liver on pumpernickel bread and its coffee cake topped with pecans and peach ice cream. For a choice of eight varieties of smoked salmon (among other things) visit the long-established Murrays deli on Broadway.

The recent proliferation of Korean grocery stores is good news for budget picnickers. Most of these stores have a salad bar on the premises, where you can choose your own salad and pay according to weight: $2.50 to $4 per pound is the usual price range.

DRINKING

New York has all manner of bars: cocktail, ethnic, artistic bars, neighbourhood affairs, hard-drinking bars. They are allowed to stay open until 4am every night except Saturday nights when they must close at 3am (on the theory that if you drink up an hour earlier you will be in better shape to spend Sunday morning at church or with the family). Tipping a dollar or two per round is standard, but some New Yorkers don't bother unless they're drinking something other than beer and they have had more than a couple of cocktails or glasses of wine.

One bar definitely deserves a visit. McSorley's Old Alehouse (15 E 7th St) has been called 'more a state of mind than a place'. It is an Irish workingman's bar in a run down Ukranian neighbourhood which serves only beer, dark and light, and cheese. Its slogan 'good ale, raw onions and no ladies' has had to be adapted slightly to the age of feminism, and both sexes are now welcome. Queues form most evenings and every weekend.

Here is a random selection of other bars and a brief summary of their character:

Puffy's, 81 Hudson St at West Broadway.
Roaul's, 180 Prince St..
Cedar Tavern, 82 University Place. Artists' bar.
Kettle of Fish, 114 MacDougal St. NYU student hangout.
West End Café, Columbus Avenue, near W 112th St. Cheap food and jazz as well as 70 kinds of beer.
Riviera Café, Sheridan Square, junction of 7th Avenue S and W 4th St Greenwich village. Best street cafe/bar.
Village Corner Tavern, Bleecker St at La Guardia Place. Free jazz on Sunday afternoons.
Chumley's, 86 Bedford at Barrow. Former speakeasy and literary bar.
P J Clarke's, 915 3rd Avenue at 55th St. Semi-chic old pub with a good atmosphere and tasty salads (but avoid the burgers).
Blue Bar, at the Algonquin Hotel, 59 West 44th St. Established literary chic bar.
Kellers, 384 West St. Grandfather of gay bars.
Andre's, 8th Avenue at 125th St. Biggest and best-known gay bar in Harlem.
Tennessee Mountain, 143 Spring St. Monday night 'barbecue and brew'; for around $20 you get ribs or beef plus all you can drink.
New Amsterdam Brewery, 26th St and 10th Avenue. Barn-like pub-brewery, always crowded and noisy, with several interesting beers and good snacks. Call 255-4100 to join a tour of the brewery.
White Horse, Hudson and Bleecker Streets, Greenwich Village. Dylan Thomas reputedly drank his last drink here, and a bar has been named

after him. The tavern sells draught beer by the Imperial pint ($3) and serves excellent fish and chips.

From the dazzling view at the top of the World Trade Center to the quiet solitude of the Cloisters, at the opposite end of Manhattan, New York is endlessly rewarding. The information in this chapter should sustain you for a short stay in New York, but for longer visits you might wish to invest in a specific guide book. The Michelin *New York City* guide provides comprehensive details on virtually every place of interest, together with good maps.

Le Courbusier called the architecture of New York City 'a catastrophe, but a magnificent catastrophe'. The Empire State Building, immortalized by a love-sick gorrila, is located at 5th Avenue and 34th St (736-3100). Despite its loss of the title 'World's Tallest Building' which it held for 40 years, it is still worth going up to the open observatory on the 86th floor or the glass-enclosed one on the 102nd floor, expecially on a clear night (it's open 9.30am until midnight every day).

The Rockefeller Center lies between 5th and 6th Avenues, and between 48th and 52nd Streets. It has an observation roof which affords a panoramic view of Manhattan unsurpassed even by taller downtown buildings. Check on the tours available by calling at the Information Desk in the lobby or ringing 246-4600. The Center's most famous landmark is the golden statue of Prometheus, floating above a sunken plaza. This space is used as an outdoor cafe in summer, and as an ice rink in winter when a giant Christmas tree is put in place. A tour allows you to take a leisurely stroll through the pedestrian walkways or glimpse the luxurious, over-designed interiors of shops and restaurants. The architectural centrepiece of the Center is the 19-storey RCA Building at 30 Rockefeller Plaza. Completed during the Depression, the socio-realist murals reflect the preoccupation with the shortage of work by exalting it.

Located downtown at Liberty St, the twin towers which make up the major part of the World Trade Center stand 110 storeys high. Two months after completion in 1974, the WTC was replaced by the Sears Building in Chicago as the tallest building in the world. On a clear day visibility extends for 100 miles. The observation deck on the 110th floor of WTC 2 is open except in bad weather. The tower is open 9.30am to 9.30pm daily; the cost is $4.25 (call 466-4710). The Windows on the World restaurant at the top of the WTC 1 is another option: a weekend buffet brunch costs $35, and the view is free.

Close by, the five-block dockland area of the South Street Seaport has rejuvenated lower Manhattan by making it a place to stroll, sit and enjoy concerts, buskers and puppet shows. A restored printers shop offers maps and maritime souvenirs and there are several early vessels including a square rigger docked at the piers, which may be toured for $5. On your way to this area located at Fulton and South Streets, notice the giant mural paintings which cover the side of a brick building in an amusing *trompe l'oeil* of a bridge tower which appears to part of the real Brooklyn Bridge visible above the building.

Apart from these well-documented landmarks, there are thousands of less celebrated buildings: in particular, the worlds's largest cathedral — St John the Divine on 110th St — is a breathtaking construction as well as a lively centre for performing arts. It stages a Bach Festival, a silent film festival, free theatre and dance, and hosts Sunday afternoon concerts.

Museums and Galleries. Manhattan has more museums per square mile than any city in the world. Call ahead for information on special exhibitions. Many of the city's museums are closed on Mondays; some offer free admission on Tuesday evenings and most give student discounts. A number of museums are not allowed to charge admission because of their charter. Instead, they have a 'suggested contribution' of about $5. If you really can't afford to pay bear in mind that New Yorkers have free entry to most of Britain's museums. If you happen to be in New York in mid-June, a stretch of 5th Avenue known as the 'Museum Mile' is closed to traffic while promenaders are allowed to visit the museums within that area free of charge. It's a festive occasion with clowns, street musicians, etc.

More art and antiquities are amassed in the **Metropolitan Museum of Art** than anywhere in the world. With 248 galleries, still only a quarter of the collection is on display at any one time. In addition to the many Old Masters, the American wing is of special interest for its extraordinary collection of furniture and decorative arts from early colonial times (1630) to the nineteenth century. The museum is on 5th Avenue at 82nd St, on the edge of Central Park (535-7710). It opens daily except Mondays from 9.30am to 5.15pm, with late opening on Tuesdays to 8.45pm.

If you would like to get away from the hustle and bustle of Manhattan, you can visit the **Cloisters** and have a picnic in Fort Tyron Park. The Cloisters are accessible by bus number 4 which runs along Madison Avenue, or by a special bus from the Metropolitan Museum ($6 return). Overlooking the Hudson River and George Washington Bridge, this unusual attraction houses bits and pieces from four medieval French monastries, purchased and reassembled on behalf of the billionaire Rockefellers. The park itself has varied terrain with footpaths and a small botanical garden.

The **Museum of Modern Art** at 11 West 53rd St (956-7070) has an astonishing collection of masterpieces from 1880 to the present from Monet's water lilies (stunningly displayed in a room of their own) to household objects of superior design. It opens 11am-6pm daily except Wednesday when it is closed, and Thursday when it opens until 9pm (and you 'pay what you wish from 5-9pm). Usual admission is $7.

Other artistic museums include the **Frick Collection** (1 East 70th St near 5th Avenue, 288-0700) housed in an elegantly furnished nineteenth century mansion, and the **Guggenheim** (5th Avenue at 89th St, 860-1313) in a building designed by Frank Lloyd Wright.

The **Museum of the City** is located on 5th Avenue and 103rd St (534-1672) is as varied as the city it celebrates. It contains dolls' houses, model ships, period rooms, toy collections and multi-media shows. The **Cooper-Hewitt Museum** (2 E 91st St and 5th Avenue, 860-6868) is a working museum of design, including an extensive collection of fabrics. The **American Museum of Natural History** (79th St and Central Park West, 769-5100) has the best collection of dinosaurs in the world, the golf-ball sized 'Star of India' diamond and literally millions of other items. The **Hayden Planetarium** is nearby, with its $2\frac{1}{2}$ ton Zeiss Projector. Call 724-8700 for times and programmes.

The **Brooklyn Museum** is out of the way but worthwhile (Eastern Parkway and Washington Avenue, 638-5000). It contains primitive art from Africa, a highly acclaimed Egyptian collection and early American paintings. For a large collection of Americana, visit the **Museum of American Folk Art** tucked away at 55 West 53rd St (581-2475). You will find patchwork quilts, samplers, weathervanes, whirligig toys and carvings in the folk tradition. For more contemporary objects go to the **American Craft Museum** at 40 W 53rd St (696-0710). If you are interested in native American culture, visit the **Museum of the American Indian** (Broadway at 155th St, 283-2420).

Two hi-tech 'museums' are recommended for excellent hands-on exhibits: the **New York Hall of Science** out at Flushing Meadows in Queens (718-699-0675), and the **AT&T InfoQuest Center** (Madison Avenue and 56th St, 605-5555). One more jewel in New York's crown is the **American Museum of the Moving Image** in Astoria, Queens (35th Avenue and 36th St, 718-784-0077). Located in a redeveloped movie studio, it offers the chance electronically to try on Scarlett O'Hara's dress and to dub the sound effects on a TV commercial. Admission costs $5, and it opens noon-4pm from Tuesday to Friday and noon-6pm at weekends. You reach it on subway R or G to Steinway St, or an N train to Broadway in Astoria.

United Nations. The UN headquarters are spread over several acres on the East River. The entrance lies at 1st Avenue at 46th St (963-7113). Free tickets to sessions of the General Assembly and Security Council are obtainable from the Information Desk before debates begin at 10.30am nd 3pm on a first come, first served basis. Guided tours take place daily from 9.15am to 4.45pm and cost $6. You get the chance to shop at one of the most varied stores in town, and can buy anything from Albanian postcards to Zambian handicrafts.

Statue of Liberty and Ellis Island. The first thing to be said about these sights is that trying to visit them on a weekend is likely to be tedious and frustrating. Crowds are big and queues are long: perhaps half an hour or an hour to get on the boat, with a two-hour wait to ascend the Statue of Liberty. So go midweek, and go early. The combined boat and admission ticket costs $6.

The Statue of Liberty in New York Harbour was the creation of sculptor Barthould and engineer Eiffel, and was given to the city by France in 1884. A lift takes visitors halfway up and then a stairway gives access to the observation platform in the crown. Ellis Island Museum of Immigration is well worth a visit to trace the history of the 'huddled masses' who landed on the island in New York harbour. It looks very much like a Victorian railway station, and sits on a 27-acre artificial island made from the earth hewn from the city's subway system. For 32 years from 1892 it was the main port of entry for new arrivals to the country. Now it is a fascinating museum, with the minutiae of how millions sought a new life. There is also a so-called Immigrant Wall of Honor, paid for by the descendants of those who passed through Ellis Island.

Parks. Central Park had mundane origins, being modelled on a municipal park in Birkenhead on Merseyside. Today, however, it is Manhattan's saving grace, an oasis of calm in the midsts of chaos. It covers 840 acres in the middle of the island, stretching from 59th St to 110th St and bounded by 5th and 8th Avenues. Despite the large number of New Yorkers in serious need of rest and relaxation, it is so big that overcrowding is rarely a problem. One of the most pleasant parts is Strawberry Fields, a gently rolling grassy area dedicated to the memory of John Lennon. It is on the west side of the park, close to the Dakota apartment building where Lennon lived and died. Central Park also offers one of the best views of the awesome scale of Manhattan. Although the top of Belvedere Castle is only 100 feet high, the panorama allows you to marvel at the sheer hugeness of the city.

The *Green Pages* gives details of nearly forty other large parks in New York City, including Fort Tryon Park at the far north of Manhattan (with delightful views of the Hudson and disturbing views of urban decay) and Prospect Park in Brooklyn (which contains Brooklyn Botanic Garden).

Zoos. The zoo in Central Park is a small but well-organized and illuminating place. It is divided into a 'Tropical Zone', 'Temperate Territory', 'Polar Circle' and 'Edge of the Icepack', ranged around a sea lion pool. A noble effort has been made to recreate natural environments but this does not deter hardened New York kids from taunting the animals. With the exception of the sea lions, most of the residents seem to spend their lives hidden or asleep, and so if you visit especially to see a Japanese snow monkey you may be disappointed. Admission is $2 for adults, $1 for children and senior citizens. Central Park Zoo is on the east side of the park at 64th St. It opens daily at 10am; closing time varies according to seson, so call 220-5111. There is a small Children's Zoo adjacent, for which admission is just 10c.

One good reason to venture out to the Bronx is to visit some of the 4,000 residents who dwell in imaginative settings — caves, an island in a lake, hollow trees and meadows — in the 265 acre Bronx Zoo (367-1010). Carefully arranged habitats and camouflaged moats separate the animals from the onlookers; you can also observe the wildlife from the tramway over the 'African Veldt' or take the 'Bengali Express', a monorail to view the Asian Animals. Charges vary according to season, so phone 220-5100. Admission is free Tuesday to Thursday. The zoo is open daily from 10am to 5pm; many outdoor exhibits are closed during the winter. You get to the zoo's entrance at 185th St and Southern Boulevard by subway to Pelham Parkway.

Adjacent to the zoo is the New York Botanical Garden which offers free admission. In the spring, the azaleas and rhododendrons brighten the hemlock woods and the Bronx River rushes through the steep narrow gorge that bisects the garden. A series of Victorian glasshouses, recently restored, contain tropical flora and desert plants. The garden is open from 10am to one hour before sunset. It's not Kew, but it's not far off.

Entertainment

New York has the greatest concentration of entertainment in the world, and it would be an achievement ever to feel that nothing of interest was on offer. Make use of the excellent tourist advice centres which have current schedules of city events. from June through August, leading theatre groups perform shakespeare, jazz, dance, opera, pupet shows, pop and folk music — much of it free — in the parks and plazas of buildings. Phone 755-4100 for daily schedules. For the summer entertainment in Central Park arrive early with a picnic basket and plenty of beer or wine.

The monumental complex for the performing arts is the Lincoln Center at 65th St and Broadway (877-1800). It houses the Met (Metropolitan Opera Company), New York Philharmonic Orchestra, New York City ballet, the New York State theater and the Julliard School of Music whose students sometimes perform free concerts. During the day the central plaza is enlivened by buskers, assorted street characters and outdoor cafes. Tours including some behind-the-scene glimpses of the Opera, are available daily from 10am to 5pm (877-1800, ext 512). The Center is most impressive at night when the buildings and the fountains are brilliantly lit.

In addition to some of the best theatre, music and art in the world, there is plenty of spontaneous street entertainment and free performances in parks and city squares. For example, visit the Citicorp Center at 53rd St and Lexington Avenue. this trend-setting skyscraper, 59 storeys, with a metallic finish reflecting the clouds, blue skies and sunsets, built on stilts delicately straddling a bright couryard with shops (including a gourmet coffee shop called 'Slotnick's daughter'), restaurants and even a church, is a classic Big Apple blend on monotheism and monetarism. In a deal with the city, Citicorp agreed that ground space would be set aside for people to sit, relax, shop, picnic or dine and be delighted by entertainment provided daily — chamber music, jazz, trios etc.

New York Magazine publised on Monday and the *New Yorker* on Wednesday carry comprehensive entertainment listings and witty critiques. The *Village Voice* is an excellent source of what's on in the city.

Music. Apart from the New York Philharmonic, which is among the best orchestras in the world (phone 874-2424 at the Lincoln Center for details), Brooklyn boasts two symphony orchestras, the Bronx has one, and there others in Queens and Manhattan. Performing at the Carnegie Hall represents the highest dream of many musicians (247-7549). Chamber music ensembles are beyond counting. Among the famous are the Guarneri and the Juliard Quartets. For concerts of chamber music go to the peaceful courtyard garden of the Frick Museum on Sundays. A music lover will also find Chinese opera, Jewish choirs, balalaika orchestras and choral groups.

The free summer concerts given by the New York Philharmonic in Central Park two or three times a month are wonderful occasions. As many as 100,000 people gather on blankets to eat picnics (from peanut-butter sandwiches to caviar) and enjoy the music. More modest free concerts are held at the World Trade Center at luchtime in summer and at the IBM Atrium (56th St and Madison Avenue). Branches of the Manhattan Savings Bank employ pianists to entertain them the lunchtime queues of customers, and you're welcome to sit and listen even if you have no business to transact.

Jazz of all kinds is alive and well in the Big Apple. You can hear it in clubs, in first-floor 'lofts' and in college concert halls. try Bradley's (cool), Eddie Condon's (Dixie), Mikell's (informal), Jimmy Ryan's (Dixie), Michael's Pub (cool — where Woody Allen used to play clarinet), Village Gate (bop) and the Village Vanguard (mainly cool). Sweet Basil, Lush Life and Fat Tuesdays are also interesting and reliable. Most jazz joints charge about $12 at the door; if entrance is free, drinks will be expensive and there may be a minimum. (This minimum may be waived if you stay at the bar instead of a table, but the bar is usually noisy.) Most clubs have three sets, the first at 10pm, the second at midnight and the final one at 3am. Call the Jazzline (463-0200) for a daily recorded announcement of what's on, pick up a jazz news sheet at the information Center in Times Square.

Here is a selection of venues for other kinds of music.

Bottom Line, 15 West St (228-7880). Slick but not innovative.
Max's Kansas City, 213 Park Avenue, near 17th St (777-7871). Fascinating clientele.
The Mudd Club, 27 White St near Broadway (227-7777). Rap; crowded.
Dan Lynch, 221 2nd Avenue (677-0901). Blues. No cover.
Tramps, 125 East 15th St near Irving Place (777-577). Blues.
Lone Star Cafe, 5th Avenue and 13th St (242-1664). Country.
O'Lunney's, 915 2nd Avenue near 38th St (751-5470). Country.
The Bitter End, 146 Bleecker St (637-7030). Folk, and first date for Joni Mitchell and Bob Dylan.

For rock music consult the *Village Voice* listings. Big concerts are staged at the Radio City Music Hall in the Rockefeller Center (541-9436) and in Madison Square Garden (563-8300).

Theatre. The Broadway theatre district around the Times Square area has the greatest concentration of theatres in the world. When looking for Times Square remember that it is not really a square at all, but merely a widening of Broadway above 42nd St. Hit shows are usually sold out months in advance, particularly if they are musicals. Tickets can be ordered by credit card (usually with a surcharge) through Tele-Charge on 239-6200, Teletron on 246-0102 or Hit-Tix on 564-8038. Call the New York City on Stage information line on 587-1111 for current productions. Tickets for Broadway shows are expensive, seldom available for less than $20, and more often $45 for plays, $60 for musicals. Try the TKTS booths (at the World Trade Center, with short queues, and in Bryant Park on 42nd and Sixth) for half price tickets on the day of performance. Queues usually form well in advance of the 3pm opening. You will also find ticket touts outside theatres charging exorbitant prices, despite the bye-law which makes it illegal to sell tickets marked up by more than $2.

Both more fun and adventurous is Off-Broadway, a term used to describe smaller theatres beyond the trade union authority and trade union wages. Many a play has started Off-Broadway and made it to Broadway. Tickets cost between $10 and $20. Productions at the Circle Repertory Theater (99 7th Avenue S), the Public Theater (425 Layayette St) and Manhattan Theater Club (321 E 73rd St) are all worth investigating.

Fringe theatre or Off-Off-Broadway theatre may be held in a drab room in a slum district, in a church meeting room or an old loft with crumbling board benches. See the *Village Voice* for details.

Since New Yorkers are theatrical in their everyday lives, check out some theatre in the wider sense of the word. The New York Stock Exchange, at 20 Broad St in the Wall St area, welcomes visitors to watch the frantic activities from the free public gallery overlooking the trading floor. It is open to spectators from 9.20am to 4pm, Monday to Friday; call 656-5168. Or you might like to sit in on a court case at the Criminal Court, 100 Centre St. Trials in the US are highly publicized, even televised, and you might be able to attend one which you have been reading about in the papers. For especially bizarre cases that might have come out of the Mad Hatter's Tea Party, drop into the nearby Small Claims Court and see what people will sue for.

Nightlife. Every taste is catered for, from the most glittering and expensive floor shows to the sleaziest topless bars, from chic discos to old-fashioned ballrooms. And New Yorkers pride themselves on the exotic parties they give in their own apartments or homes.

For a night of dancing try Heartbreak (Varig and Vandem Streets) which is a cafeteria by day and a 60s/80s rock and roll club by night; admission is $15. For something different, try the clubs which serve as training grounds for young comics. Among the best of these are Catch a Rising Star (1487 First Avenue), Improvisation (358 W 44th St) and Comedy Cellar (117 MacDougal St). The humour may be slightly obscure for non-New Yorkers.

There is no legalised gambling in New York City unless you include the racetracks and the State Lottery. If you're into higher forms of wagering — roulette, black jack, craps — head for nearby Atlantic City. Plenty of cut-price bus trips are offered, usually organized through corner drug stores.

Cinema. Manhattan must have served as a backdrop for more films than any other cities, and cinema is taken very seriously in New York. The annual Film Festival, at the Lincoln Center in mid-September to early October, is so serious that in order not to be vulgar and commercial like the Cannes Film Festival, no prizes are awarded. You can see previews of soon-to-be-released Hollywood blockbusters as well as experimental art films. Ring 362-1911 for Festival details.

The Museum of Modern Art has a fine film library and shows films daily, usually Hollywood classics.

Check local papers and magazines for prices and times of new releases. Admission charges start at $7 for a seat during the evenings; matinees are cheaper. As befits a serious cinema-going audience, New Yorkers are especially keen on foreign art films. There are more subtitles in Manhattan than in the rest of the country put together. In addition to the art cinemas like Cinema Studio (Broadway and 66th St, 877-4040) or Film Forum (57 Watts St, 431-1590), many cinemas specialize in revivals. Programmes change frequently. Among the best known are the Cinema Village (8th St Playhouse) and the forerunner of them all, the Thalia (95th St and Broadway).

Special Events. In addition to jazz, film and dance festivals, there are many ethnic celebrations in which to participate. Depending on the lunar calendar, Chinese New Year (known at Tet) is celebrated with week long festivities, fireworks and parades in Chinatown. Phone the Chinese Community Center, Mott Street, for the exact dates in late January/February (226-6280). If you are a fan of fireworks, try to be in New York on the 4th of July, when spectacular fireworks are set off from barges in the Hudson River. Riverside Drive on Manhattan's West Side provides the best vantage point.

Most businesses along 5th Avenue close on March 17th when the annual St Patrick's Day Parade takes place. Regardless of race or religion, everyone becomes honorary Irish and joins the parade past St Patrick's Cathedral and along the edge of Central Park to 86th St. Many marchers head for the ethnic Irish bars on the Upper East Side for green-dyed beer and stronger stuff. Bar-room celebrations can quickly flare up, so avoid political or religious discussions. Beware also of adolescent revellers who often choose this particular day to exceed their capacity.

Other parades include the Hallowe'en Parade through Greenwich Village on October 31, a bizarre affair which starts at dusk just west of Washington Square Park. On the last Thursday in November, Macy's Department Store sponsors the Thanksgiving Day Parade on Broadway from 77th St and Central Park West to their store. Starting at 8.30 am, you can see building-tall helium-filled balloons of Kermit, Snoopy, Bullwinkle and other cartoon characters. Call 397-8222 for further information. The tree lighting ceremony at the Rockefeller Center is held a couple of weeks before Christmas, followed by an (oddly secularized) Christmas carol sing-along. A few weeks later you can join the New Year's Eve revellers in Times Square.

SPORT

Baseball. New York City's two teams are the Mets (National League) and the Yankees (American League). Many home games are played at night under spectacular floodlights. Except during the last few weeks of each season, when teams may be in contention to win division titles and get into the World Series, you should be able to pick up tickets at the box office on the day of the game.

The Mets (National League) play in Shea Stadium in Flushing, Queens (507-8499) which can be reached by subway line 7 to Willets Point/Shea

Stadium Station. The Yankees (American League) play in Yankee Stadium in the Bronx (293-6000) which can be reached by subway lines CC, D and 4 to 161st Street Station. Stick with the crowd when leaving the stadium on your way home by subway since the neighbourhood is decidedly unsafe.

Football. Tickets to the games of both New York City teams are hard to come by because of the many season ticket holders. The Jets play in Giant's Stadium at the Meadowland Sports Complex in East Rutherland, NJ, about six miles from midtown (easily reached by bus from the Port Authority Bus Terminal); if you're lucky enough to get a ticket, dress warmly as Meadowland is notoriously cold and windy in the autumn and winter..

Basketball. New York's team is the Knickerbockers (Knicks for short) who play at Madison Square Garden, 7th Avenue and 33rd St. Tickets are usually available on the night at prices ranging from $10 to $20, unless it's near the end of the season and there's a close race. If you visit Harlem, you will notice a high density of basketball hoops and young lads dribbling and shooting baskets. Because green parks are so rare, the locals have adapted their sports preferences to the concrete jungle.

Ice Hockey. The city's two teams are the Rangers who play at Madison Square Garden (564-4400), tickets $10 and $20; and the Islanders whose games on ice held at Nassau Coliseum on Long Island (516-794-9100). The season lasts from October to April, with availability of tickets fluctuating according to the whims of the fickle fans.

Tennis. The best time of year for tennis is early September, when the US Open Tennis Championships are held at the National Tennis Center, Flushing Meadows, Queens (592-9300). Last-minute tickets are available only from ticket touts at outrageous prices.

Horse Racing. Turf fans will be delighted to hear there is year round flat racing. From October to April you can place your bets at Aqueduct (the 'Big A') Racetrack in Queens (subway lines A and CC), and then from April to October at Belmont on Long Island (Long Island Rail Road); call 739-4200 for special fare and admission deals to Belmont. There is off-track betting (known as OTB) as well as racetrack betting in the state of New York. Dial 976-2212 for results. Trotting, called 'harness racing', takes place as Roosevelt Raceway on Long Island (718-895-1246); take the Long Island Rail Road from Penn Station.

Participation. Get a free copy of the *Green Pages,* a guide to New York City Parks and a source of information on activities ranging from archery to tennis. The *Green Pages* is available from information booths in all main parks. Jogging is undoubtedly the favourite. The most popular venues are Central Park, along the East River Promenade, and, for a vista of the Hudson River and New Jersey beyond (with its gorgeous sunsets thanks to pollution), the West Side Highway below 42nd St.

In October, crisp days and golden foliage make an ideal setting for the New York City Marathon, which starts at the Staten Island side of the Verrazano Bridge and ends 26 miles and 365 yards later (after touching all give boroughs) at the Tavern on the Green in Central Park. The race is run on the third or fourth Sunday of October. A circus atmosphere prevails. Entry is by mail, and only 16,000 applicants are chosen. Write for an application form to the Road Runner Club, PO Box 881, FDR Station, New York, NY 10150, or the club headquarters, 9 East 89th Street, New York, NY 10028 (860-4455).

Cycling enthusiasts have their own annual event, the 50-kilometre Bicycle Challenge held in the second week in July.

During the winter, every snowfall brings out the skiers and tobogganers in Central Park, Prospect Park in Brooklyn and Van Cortland Park in the Bronx. Skis can be rented and instruction obtained at the latter two parks (965-6511 and 543-4595 respectively). You'll be amazed to find how hilly some areas of New York are.

For indoor ice skating year round, try The Sky Rink, 450 West 33rd Street (695-6555) or watch the disco skating Friday and Saturday nights. There's outdoor skating (subject to weather) from October to April at the Rockefeller Center Rink, and the Wollman Skating Rink in Central Park at 59th Street (397-3158).

You can rent roller skates at several locations near Central Park from mobile vans set up along Columbus Avenue between 70th and 80th Street, from the Skate Connection, 349 West 14th St (243-6353). There are also indoor rinks: Village Skating, 15 Waverley Place (677-9690) which is ideal for beginners; and the Roxy, 515 West 18th St (691-3113) for serious disco skaters.

Several beaches where you can sunbathe and swim in the ocean can be rached by subway: Coney Island in Brooklyn (with its famous amusement park); Orchard Beach in the Bronx; and Rockaway and Jacob Riis in Queens (the west end of the beach is a favoured meeting place for gay men; it can be reached by subway line 3 to Flatbush, then bus Q35). The finest public beach is Jones Beach on Long Island, an hour by bus from the Port Authority Bus Terminal. Before you bathe, bear in mind that New York's beaches are periodically closed down due to pollution ranging from medical waste to decomposing rats. For further information on how to reach the beaches and the condition they are in, phone the Parks Department on 360-8111.

SHOPPING

New York City abounds in speciality shops. One sells nothing but seashells, another that sells only kites and a bookshop which carries only mystery novels. But unless you have precise requirements and plenty of time and stamina, stick to the department stores. Start with the top two stores; Macy's (Herald Square, between 7th Avenue and Broadway, 695-4400) and Bloomingdale's (59th St between Lexington and 3rd Avenues, 355-5900). Both stay open late on Thursday evenings and Macy's is also open Monday to Friday evenings and on Sunday afternoons.

At the other end of the price spectrum, two chain stores specialize in leftover merchandise (including some quality stuff) from big-name or bankrupt shops. Weber's (2064 Broadway, 505 5th Avenue and 390 6th Avenue) and Odd-Lot (33 W 34th St and 585 8th Avenue) have everything from cosmetics and clothing to furniture and food at low prices.

Remember that 8.25% sales tax will be added at the cash till except on necessities such as medicines, groceries and infants' clothing.

Flea markets are held between April and November and sell jewellery, antiques, clothes and all manner of junk; visit Sixth Avenue at W 26th St on Sunday, or 8 Greene St in SoHo on weekends.

Clothing. Madison Avenue from about 42nd St north has a wealth of men's and women's speciality shops from the classics at Brooks Brothers on 44th St to the striking designer fashions of Saint Laurent Rive Gauche on 70th St. The clothes are expensive, partly because of the shops' high rents. Also try the famous Fifth Avenue department stores such as Saks, B Altman and Lord & Taylor.

The following two stores cater for both men and women. The Gap (145 E 42nd St near 3rd Avenue) which has one of the widest selections of jeans plus lots of other casuals, and the Unique Clothing Wearhouse in Greenwich Village (718 Broadway near Washington Place) which has trendy, inexpensive clothing, as well as surplus and workmen's clothes. The cheapest jeans in town are sold at the huge Canal St Jeans, which has Levi 401s for around $25. One of New York's most colourful sights is the racks of new clothes being wheeled out of the Garment district (7th Avenue between 23rd and 40th Streets) to stores throughout Manhattan. Film-maker Spike Lee has a store over in Brooklyn, selling all sorts of trendy clothing. It is a corner shop called Spike's Joint, at South Elliott St and De Kalb Avenue.

Charity shops regularly receive donations of fashionable clothing from department stores as well as from individuals. Two within a short walk of each other are Repeat Performance on 3rd Avenue at 84th St and Trishop on 3rd Avenue at 92nd St.

The Lower East Side, a predominantly Jewish area, is at its liveliest on Sundays (closed on Saturday, the Jewish Sabbath). You'll find Orchard St south to Canal St jammed with shoppers bargaining ('hondling') with stall keepers. Open front stores are bursting with merchandise. You may hear of designer clothes and shoes being snapped up from pushcarts for a song, but *caveat emptor;* many of the goods are seconds or shop-worn, though undeniably cheap. Stores here and elsewhere in New York close for Passover in late March, Rosh Hashanah in early September, Yom Kippur later in the same month and Hanukkah in early December.

Americana. For American folk art, such as patchwork quilts, try Spirit of America (269 E 4th St in Greenwich Village) or America Hurrah (316 E 70th St on the Upper East Side). The best place to find American Indian Jewellery is at the American Indian Community House, 849 Broadway; this is shortly to move to new premises. Among their wares may be found Zuni 'squash blossom' necklaces and silver 'concha' belts. For well made artifacts from around the world, visit the UN shop, which also sells UN stamps. Since the UN occupies 'international territory' no tax is levied. A fine collection of New York post cards can be found at a shop called 'Untitled' (159 Prince St).

Jewellery. On 5th Avenue at 57th Street, Tiffany's (755-8000) vies with its great competitor Cartier (5th Avenue and 52nd Street; 753-0111) and other posh jewellery stores for the most stunning eye-catching window displays and opulent interiors. All have some small items at modest cost that recipients back home would be impressed by, such as Tiffany's silver 'snowflake' charm at around $30. Downtown in SoHo and Greenwich Village, shops and galleries sell hand-crafted siler and gold pieces, as well as a large selection of unusual rugs.

THE MEDIA

Leaving aside the numerous New Jersey, Westchester County and Long Island stations, there are dozens of AM and FM radio stations operating in New York City. Try WCBS (880 AM) which broadcasts only news, and its sister station WCBS (101.1 FM) for 'solid gold music'. The Brooklyn-based WKRB (90.0 FM) has probably the best new music. WLIB (1190 AM) is the all black news and information station which broadcasts cricket scores five times daily from 7.15 to 5.30pm, once or twice daily at weekends.

One tour available from the Information Desk in the lobby of the Rockefeller Center takes you behind the scenes of NBC TV studios, another backstage at Radio City Music Hall, home of the precision dance troupe, the Rockettes. You can get tickets to locally produced TV shows from the Visitors Bureau at 2 Columbus Circle. The Museum of Broadcasting, at 23 W 52nd St (between 5th and 6th Avenues), allows the public access to famous old television and radio programmes. There are tapes of the McCarthy hearings and videos of the Apollo moonshots, which you can watch or listen to at playback consoles. Apparently the most popular request is the Beatles on the Ed Sullivan Show in 1964.

The *New York Times* (known locally as the *Times*) is arguably America's best newspaper. The tabloid *Daily News* has been called America's worst, although it boasts a circulation of 1,300,000. *New York Newsday* at first sight seems to be another dismal tabloid, but it's not at all bad. The *Village Voice* is an excellent left-of-centre listings paper whose value to the visitor for recommending entertainment, accommodation, etc. cannot be overemphasized. New York has a flourishing alternative press, e.g. the bimonthly feminist newspaper *Womanews* and the gay guide *NY Native*. The free *New York Press* can be picked up at bars and restaurants; its reviews and listings are surprisingly good for a free newspaper.

Crime and Safety

There are many misapprehensions in Europe about street crime in New York city. Surprisingly, it rates only 16th most dangerous in the crime statistics for American cities; and has the strictest gun control laws in the USA. The theoretical odds are 32,000 to 1 that you will be the victim of one of the 225 daily muggings, and much longer that you will be one of the four murdered on the average day. If you avoid endangering yourself by walking around drunk and disorderly in neighbourhoods you should avoid, the odds rise dramatically in your favour.

Certain sensible precautions such as those described in the introductory section *Crime and Safety* should stave off most dangers. The great majority of residents live in New York without incident, and do not dress in bulletproof fabrics (though there are shops in the city which sell them). On the other hand, there was one fellow who was mugged twice in the same evening. The first time he was reeling home under the influence of too much drink; the second under the influence of too many knocks on the head. If he hadn't been drunk in the first place, there probably would have been no first or second assault. Keep enough money after a pub crawl for a taxi home.

Still, there is no denying that New York is a dangerous town. There are sections of it you simply should not visit. If you want to see the burned out shells of Harlem, go through it in a bus. (Harlem is north of Central Park and between 125th and 156th Streets.) You need only walk a few blocks and you may be in a completely different and possibly risky neighbourhood, even if it doesn't look particularly slummy. It is easier to avoid tough, dangerous, hostile slum neighbourhoods which are known by everyone. There is a depth of ill-feeling you cannot conceive of unless you have been getting the short end of the stick for generations on account of your nationality or colour, so don't go into them. In particular avoid the South Bronx, south of Fordham Road, the Bedford-Stuyvesant area and the Lower East Side (east of First Avenue and south of 12th St.). Also do not go into Central Park after dark. You should exercise caution in Chinatown, the Bowery and the area west of Broadway to the waterfront.

The subways are notoriously dangerous. When waiting at a relatively deserted station, stand in the clearly marked and brightly lit 'off-hours' waiting area which has an intercom to the Transit Police. Travel in the central cars where the guard travels. Avoid isolated cars and deserted exits; stick with the crowds wherever possible. Don't display jewellery or wallets and don't sit next to the doors where pickpockets often operate. Try to memorize your route ahead of time so that you don't betray your unfamiliarity with the system by consulting a map en route.

Drugs. It seems that New Yorkers from all walks of life regard narcotics as the only way to survive the city. Dealers sell quite openly, pedlars hawking openly with pitches of considerable invention: 'I've got the herb that's superb, the smoke that's no joke. Don't pass until you've tried my grass'. At parties you could be offered cocaine. And, if for some reason you're in a slum, crack is available. The possession of cannabis has been all but decriminalized. Using cocaine could mean prosecution, but it's a middle and upper class activity due to the price; the police seldom make a fuss and rarely raid parties in high rent apartments. It is still illegal, and in view of the prison conditions at prisons such as Utica, you will want to do your best to avoid arrest.

Sin. It is no surprise that sin is for sale in New York. The boys and girls operating on the streets in the Times Square area are so tough, say the *cognoscenti*, that their spit bounces. Prostitutes encountered in bars in mid-Manhattan have been known to lead prospective clients back to a mugging ambush. Abstinence is advised, especially in view of the prevalence of Aids and other diseases.

Creatures. Not all of the threats to your safety in New York take the form of muggings. It is reputed that dozens of crocodiles inhabit the sewers of the city as a result of pet owners who have flushed their reputiles down the toilet once they become too big for their aquariums. You are unlikely to escape Manhattan without confrontation with a cockroach; these harmless insects infest even expensive hotels and apartment buildings, and are said to be more numerous than humans. And if you are worried about rodents, be consoled that according to one Police Commissioner, three times as many people in New York are bitten by other people as are bitten by rats.

Help and Information *i*

The area code for Manhattan and the Bronx is 212, and 718 for the other boroughs.

Information: The New York Convention & Visitors Bureau, 2 Columbus Circle, New York, NY 10019 (397-8222/8200). Tourist Information Desks are also located in the Rockefeller Center and in Times Square. If you write in advance stating your specific interest, they will try to put you in touch with relevant organizations.

British Consulate — General: 845 3rd Avenue (752-84).

American Express: 15 East 42nd St (687-37) and nine other offices in Manhattan.

Thomas Cook: 2 Penn Plaza (967-5800).

Post Office: 8th Avenue and 33rd St (967-8585).

Western Union Telegrams: 962-7111.

Medical Emergencies: Bellevue Hospital, 1st Avenue at East 27th St (561-4141).
Dental Emergency Service: 679-3966.
24 hour drugstore: Kaufman Pharmacy, 557 Lexington Avenue (755-3300).
Emergencies: 911.
Fire: 682-2900.
Crime Victim Hotline: 577-7777.
Legal Aid Society: 8 Lafayette St. (577-3300).
Travelers' Aid: 42nd St between Broadway and 7th Avenue (944-0013).
Also in the International Arrivals building at JFK Airport (718-656-4870).
New York Transit Authority: 718-330-1234.
Lost and Found: 374-4925.

New Yorkers believe in the telephone. Not only can you dial Dr Joyce Brothers, the psychologist, for advice on mental problems, you can contact a representative of the Almighty through Dial-a-Prayer (246-4200) or get a laugh on Dial-a-Joke (976-3838).

Don't neglect calling the New York Public Library (340-0849) if you have a serious or not-so-serious question about New York or any other subject. Their reference section is more than likely to come up with a brief answer to any question you have remarkably quickly. For years, bets have been settled by a call to the Library.

Just as some Londoners refer to The North as everything beyond Watford, so native New Yorkers refer to everything above Manhattan as Upstate New York. It matters little to them that this region is only a fraction smaller than the whole of England. It is seen merely as a quaint backwater, a place to visit at weekends. The locals upstate complain bitterly about the invasion of weekending New Yorkers, who have caused land and house prices to soar and who swagger around the small country stores with their fashionable clothes and their loud voices. But there are still plenty of undiscovered places. The ideal guide book for independent travellers who prefer not to rent a car is Theodore Scull's *Carefree Getaway Guide for New Yorkers* (Harvard Common Press, $9.95). It describes excursions from Manhattan using public transport alone.

THE HUDSON VALLEY

Cutting a north/south swathe between the Taconic mountains to the east and the Catskills to the west, the Hudson River provides a splendid antidote to the city. Easily the best way to enjoy the beautiful Hudson Valley is to take the train north from Penn Station to Rhinecliff or Hudson. The train from Penn Station as far as Rhinecliff takes 100 minutes and costs $29 for a day trip at weekends (when the train is far less crowded anyway).

The rail line hugs the river all the way along. The sights are a curious mixture: forested river banks (best in October for the leaf display), yacht marinas, and the industrial degeneration and electricity generation — the Indian Point nuclear power plant gets its cooling water from the river. Some dramatic bridges provide a strong contrast to the natural beauty.

Look out for the guard towers of Sing Sing prison (40 minutes out of New York). An hour north, just beyond the station of Garrison, the buildings of West Point Military Academy cling to the west bank. The isolated hotel-like building, high on the hill, is exactly that. The hostages from Iran were brought here to the Thayer Hotel for debriefing after their release. Bannerman's Castle, on Pollopel Island close to the west bank, is a folly which formerly housed an arsenal; this exploded and caused the damage which is still visible.

The area has visible traces of the origins of the early settlers, mainly Dutch and French Hugenots. The hills are speckled with buildings from another continent: big Dutch barns, elegant houses — not to mention mansions built on strict classical Greek designs.

An excellent place to base yourself is the lovely small town of Rhinebeck, little more than a crossroads in the middle of the Hudson Valley. Alternatively you could centre a visiton Hyde Park, a larger settlement a few miles south. Both options are covered below.

Arrival and Departure. Almost all mainline trains to Albany from New York's Penn Station stop at Rhinecliff station, right next to the river and 100 minutes north of New York City. From here it is a brisk half-hour walk or a $5 cab ride into the town of Rhinebeck.

If you are driving from New York, the most pleasant road north is the Taconic State Parkway, an old 1930s highway from which trucks are banned. It winds laconically from the northern tip of Manhattan through to Albany.

Getting Around. The sole public transport in the area is the Loop Bus. Contrary to its name, it runs on a straight line from Tivoli in the north, through Rhinebeck, Hyde Park to Poughkeepsie. Unfortunately there are only five services a day, and none at all on Sundays.

Accommodation. The Rhinebeck Chamber of Commerce produces a list of Bed and Breakfast accommodation in the area, most of which start at around $60. The motels on Route 9 in Hyde Park are likely to be cheaper.

Eating and Drinking. Rhinebeck possesses the oldest inn in America, a splendid pub on Route 9 just south of the crossroads, called the Beekman Arms. British people will feel at home in the pub-like atmosphere of this rambling old hostelry, in which tall people should mind their heads and everyone should try the Hudson Lager on draught. The Beekman also does good food, for which you should book in advance

The wackiest surroundings and the tastiest food, however, can be found close to the crossroads in Rhinebeck. La Parmigiana (37 Montgomery St, 914-876-3228) is a fine pizzeria in an only-barely-converted church. The bar is where the vestry used to be, the main dining area is the transept and the kitchen has two entrances, which used to be the segregated access for male and female worshippers.

Exploring. The Rhinebeck Historical Society produces a walking tour brochure, free from the Visitor Information Centre, which leads you around this lovely clapperboard town.

Each of the following three historic homes is operated by the National Park Service; details of opening times on 914-229-9115.

Franklin Roosevelt's Home: the birthplace and home of FDR is on Route 9 at the south end of the town of Hyde Park. It opens daily from April to October. President Roosevelt called the house the 'Summer White House'. Here he signed the agreement with Winston Churchill which led to the development of the atomic bomb.

Eleanor Roosevelt National Historic Site, Route 9G (the by-pass), Hyde

Park. FDR's wife established a retreat here at Val-Kill Cottage to escape the constant chiding of her mother-in-law. Because FDR was struck down with polio early on in his political career, his wife acted as his eyes and ears. She provided the support and intelligence which enabled him to implement the 'New Deal' programme in 1932, an almost state-socialist endeavour to restart the economy.

Vanderbilt Mansion, Route 9, just north of Hyde Park (914-229-9115). The Vanderbilt family made their fortune from shipping and railways, and this is one of six family homes. It is outrageously lavish, with Italian marble and French furniture. The best touch is Mrs Vanderbilt's bedroom, with a rail to keep tradespeople away from her bed. The grounds (which you do not have to pay to visit) are wonderful, with lovely views across the Hudson and an exquisite formal gareden.

Millbrook Vineyards: French Hugenots first planted vines in the region in 1677, and some good wines are made in this part of New York State. This is probaly the most interesting of several winery tours to make. A rich ex-State Commissioner, John Dyson, bought an old Dutch farmhouse and converted it into a winery and the fields around it into vineyards. He grows all the classsic French grape varieties. The chardonnay and cabernet sauvignon are excellent. Call 1-800-662-WINE for information and directions.

UPPER NEW YORK STATE

Saratoga Springs. Forty-five minutes north from the dull state capital, Albany, off the Northway, is Saratoga Springs. This once elegant spa town has recently had its downtown and beautiful old hotels and inns restored. In the summer the Philadelphia Orchestra, New York City Ballet Company and other top clasical and popular performers put on two months of stunning entertainment at the Performing Arts Complex. The famous harness and flat race tracks are located 'just around the corner' from the concert area. The flat races take place in August and are attended by the rich and famous. This is your chance to wear your top hat and tails or carry a parasol. There are many fine restaurants in and around Saratoga Springs, but rooms are very hard to find in the summer.

Finger Lakes. I-90 runs between Syracuse and Rochester. South of it, looking rather like dangling beans, are the half-dozen Finger Lakes. In addition to the beautiful scenery, you will find the Finger Lakes area dotted with wineries. After you have been around one or two of them, you may come to share the local enthusiasm for wines produced in the area.

Niagara Falls. Continuing west past the lakes you will come to the large industrial city of Buffalo (where there is an excellent art gallery called the Albright-Knox), and nearby Niagara Falls, which form a boundary between the US and Canada. The view is best from the Canadian side. Many visitors are disappointed by the extent of the tourism industry surrounding the falls, but for all the cliched postcard pictures, seeing 200,000 cubic feet of water spill over a crest 3,172 feet wide every second is worth a detour. Most accommodation around the falls is devoted to honeymooning couples, although the Youth Hostel on the US side accepts non-members for $12 per night.

Catskill Mountains. Visitors to this modest mountain range occupying the area in the southern part of the state between the Hudson River and the Pennyslvania border, find a host of diversions, from vineyard-visiting to hang-gliding. The ski slopes at Hunter Mountain and Plattekill Bowl get very crowded at weekends. The Ice Caves Mountains are a fantastic remnant from the age of the glacier. There is also a renowned Game Farm where 2000 animals and birds roam freely.

The Catskills are sometimes called the Borscht Belt, since this has been a traditional resort area for the East Coast Jewish population: nowadays it is frequented by everyone regardless of religion or money. Big-name entertainers and famous show people have made their start at the clubs here.

The Adirondacks. There are no fewer than 43 peaks over 4,000 feet high in this six million acre state park. This mountainous and forested region takes up the whole of northern New York State. The landscape is not unlike that of Scotland, although the weather in summer is much more predictable. If you get off the principal route, through this genuine wilderness, be sure you have enough petrol and a place to stay when the chilly nights fall.

Whiteface Mountain Memorial Highway leads visitors to one of the most spectacular views in the Adirondacks. But it is better, if you have time, to abandon your car and take to some of the thousands of miles of hiking trails. You will see Park Ranger stations all along the way, where you can seek advice about routes and camping facilities. For information on ski tours to upstate New York contact Sportiva Sporthaus, 145 East 47th St (421-7466). The principal ski resorts are Adirondack, Lake Placid and Whiteface Mountain.

Calendar of Events

early February	Overland Ski Marathon, Panama to Westfield
March 17	St Patrick's Day Parade, NYC
mid May	9th Avenue International Festival, NYC
mid June-mid July	International Festival of the Arts, NYC (even-numbered years)
early August	Harlem Week, NYC
August	Lincoln Center Out-of-Doors Festival, NYC
early September	US Open Tennis Championships, Flushing Meadow, NYC
mid September	Buffalo — Niagara Falls Marathon
October 31	Hallowe'en Parade, Greenwich Village
early November	NYC Marathon
late November	Macy's Thanksgiving Day Parade, NYC
late November	Festival of Lights, Niagara Falls
early December	Tree Lighting, Rockefeller Center, NYC

Boston and New England

Connecticut   Maine   Massachusetts   New Hampshire
Rhode Island   Vermont

Known locally as 'Beantown' and 'The Hub', Boston is the home of John Adams, Paul Revere, a famous strangler (later electrocuted) and perhaps even Mother Goose. The city is also the scene of the famous Tea Party, and is one of several eastern cities that lay claim to the title 'Birthplace of the Revolution'. It is now the second largest financial centre in the nation with a greater metropolitan population of nearly three million and it has what New Yorkers refer to as 'quality of life' in abundance.

Boston's hinterland consists of Massachusetts — home state of the Kennedys — and the five other states of New England. The three southern states of Connecticut, Rhode Island and Massachusetts are dominated by urbanization and big industry, but the cities are more provincial than New York or Washington and the residents more friendly. There is a high concentration of Ivy League colleges in peaceful campus settings. (The Ivy League comprises eight north-eastern universities, including Harvard and Yale, with high academic and social status.) The three northern states represent another contrast, despite weekending New Yorkers. In the far northern woods and mountains of Maine, New Hampshire and Vermont, time is meaningless, and bear and moose are more populous than people.

The austere Atlantic coast starts in Rhode Island and runs up through to Maine — which has more coastline than California. The string of charming seaside towns that dot the coast from Newport Beach to Bar Harbor are the most appealing places, outside Boston, to visit in New England.

151

THE PEOPLE

The most visible ethnic groups are Irish, Hispanics, Chinese, Italians, French Canadians and blacks. Races have segregated themselves geographically. South Boston (known as Southie), for instance, is predominantly Irish. Roxbury has traditionally been black (and poor) but is now being settled by yuppies. Chinatown and the Italian North End are close to the centre of the city.

Including the separate municipality of Cambridge across the Charles River, Boston boasts America's highest concentration of colleges and universities, dominated by Harvard and the Massachusetts Institute of Technology (MIT). The vast student population of 100,000 in the Boston area makes it a young and energetic place with a vigorous intellectual and artistic life.

Making Friends. Boston has its share of bars, singles and otherwise, that might prove suitable meeting places, but it also offers interesting prospects for meeting people. Picking the right spot to eat your meal in Quincy Market, for instance, or spreading your blanket on the Boston Common or the Charles River Embankment on a hot summer weekend, could bring you within talking distance of the man or woman of your dreams. Investing $10 or $20 on a whale-watching trip or deep sea fishing cruise could also bring you into contact with people of similar interests. Look for ads in the local papers or tourist literature, or check through the 'Boats — Excursions' and 'Boats — Charter' headings in the Yellow Pages.

The colleges and universities are the focal points of most social and cultural activities. You can meet people in the bars and coffee houses around the various campuses or at events open to the public. If all else fails, you can always resort to the personal ads in the *Phoenix*. All tastes are catered for, and most of the ads are graphically explicit.

CLIMATE

New Englanders take pride in the region's abruptly changing, unpredictable weather. Surprise blizzards occur as late as May and the most promising sunny afternoon can quickly degenerate into heavy showers. Summer officially lasts from Memorial Day (end of May) to Labor Day (early September), during which you can rely on hot weather most of the time. The city gets stiflingly muggy, on average heating up to 35°C/95°F. Fortunately, it is easy to escape to a nearby beach for refreshing sea breezes; evenings on the beach can be cool, so have a sweater handy. Remember, too, when you plan your beach trips, that most of New England is not touched by the Gulf Stream, so the Atlantic is cold even when the weather is extremely hot. The exception is the coastline of Connecticut and Rhode Island and the southern shore of Cape Cod, where the waters are warm wnough to attract the occasional shark.

From September, expect rapidly decreasing temperatures, often falling below freezing for weeks on end, especially in Northern New England near the Canadian border, and occasionally dropping below -18°C/0°F between December and February. Expect a lot of snow and ice in these months too. Winters are excellent for skiers particularly in the mountainous sections of Vermont and New Hampshire. For Boston weather information, dial 567-4670 or 936-1212.

ARRIVAL AND DEPARTURE

Air. Boston's airport is Logan, located in five terminals (A to E) on reclaimed marshland just three miles northeast of the city. Touching down you get an impression of landing in the water, since the runway protrudes into the bay. Information about flights and facilities is available on 482-2936. Logan prides itself on the range of restaurants, which includes Legal Seafood and a sushi bar in Terminal C.

All international flights arrive at the International Arrivals Terminal. Waits can be long at immigration since most aircraft from Europe arrive during the afternoon.

Logan is second only to Atlanta in terms of easy access to the city it serves. The cheapest way into Boston is to take the free shuttle bus to Airport subway station (number 22 from Terminals A and B, number 33 from C, D and E). From here the subway takes about ten minutes to Government Center, where you can change if necessary for other lines. The standard subway fare is 85c.

By road, the airport is only ten minutes from downtown Boston in light traffic, but the journey can take an hour or more in busy periods. Going north, the airport exits directly on Route 1A, which leads to I-95 for Maine and New Hampshire.

The fastest and most reliable journey into town is on the Airport Water Shuttle, a launch which runs from Logan Dock (a short bus ride away from the airport terminals) to Rowes Wharf on Atlantic Avenue. The service operates ever 15 minutes Monday-Friday between 6am and 8pm, and half-hourly at weekends from noon to 8pm.

Two airport buses are operated by Airways Transportation (267-2981) and Hudson Bus Lines (395-8080) to the downtown hotels; the cost is $3.25 and $4 respectively. Hudson Bus Lines will also take you straight from Logan to other towns in Massachusetts and New Hampshire. If you prefer a taxi, there is also a Share-a-Cab system which you can find out about at a desk inside the terminal. Dial 1-800-23 LOGAN for more details of ground transportation arrangements.

The Boston area, with its huge student population, is well served with agents offering student and youth fares. These places are also worth checking out if you are old and unstudious. STA Travel has offices for cut-price international flights at 273 Newbury St in Boston (266-6014) and 65 Mount Auburn St in Cambridge (576-4623. Council Travel is at 729 Boylston St (266-1926).

Bus. The Greyhound terminal is at 10 St James Avenue (432-5810); the nearest subway stop is Arlington.

Train. The two main stations in Boston (North and South) adjoin subway stops. Amtrak long-distance trains serve South Station, a beautifully restores Beaux Arts building; call 1-800-USA-RAIL for schedules and fares.

Trains leave South Station every two hours to New York, with less frequent services west to Springfield and beyond.

Commuter rail services run from South and North Stations. For information call 1-800-392-6099. The Massachusetts Turnpike (I-90) is the watershed between the two areas of service.

Driving. Among rental companies at Logan airport, the keenest rates tend to be with Budget, American International, Econo-Car and Thrifty. Better deals may be found a five-minute shuttle bus away, e.g. at Ajax, among the suburban rental offices listed in the Yellow Pages, and of course at discount places like Rent-a-Wreck.

Driveaways. You should have little trouble finding a car to Chicago, Denver or the west coast, except at the ends of term. Around November, the biggest demand is for people to drive cars to Florida.

Ride-sharing. The Youth Hostel at 12 Hemenway St (see *Accommodation*, below), has a rideboard predominately offering trips to the West Coast and Florida. Alternatively, look under 'Travel' in the *Phoenix* classified.

Hitch-hiking. Because of the complexity of the road system in and around Boston, a sign always helps to get a lift, even though it may seem obvious where you are heading. The high student population has made hitch-hiking a common, if unpredictable, form of transport even within and between Boston and Cambridge. When heading out of town, natives will probably advise you to pick any suitable downtown ramp on to the urban highway network, but this can be both dangerous and frustrating.

Instead, try the following: going south on Route 3 (to Cape Cod), Route 24 (to Fall River) or I-95 to Providence, take the train from South Station to Route 128 Station, at the Route 128/I-95 intersection. Stand on either I-95 South, or, for Route 3 and 24, on Route 128 south. The westbound I-90 (Massachusetts Turnpike) to Springfield, New York City and all points west and south is only road that is hitchable from a downtown location, namely the Massachusetts Avenue ramp (subway to Auditorium). If you are going north on I-95 (to coastal New Hampshire and Maine), take the subway to Airport and hitch up Route 1A; this leads to Route 1, which joins I-95 at Danvers. Heading north on I-93 (to most places in New Hampshire and Vermont), take the subway to Wellington then bus 100 to the West Fellsway ramp on to I-93. This is the best route to take if you wish to make a pilgrimage to Lowell, home town of Jack Kerouac. There is a memorial to the author of *On The Road*, bearing passages of his writing.

CITY TRANSPORT

The Massachusetts Bay Transportation Authority (MBTA) runs buses, a subway network and, under contract to other companies, a commuter rail service. The entire system, especially the subway, is known simply as the 'T'. The sign for the stations and bus stops is a black T in a white circle.

For route and service information, call 722-3200 or 1-800-392-6100. Route maps are free from the Boston Visitor Center at the Prudential Center and on Boston Common, the MBTA information desk in Park Street Station, the MBTA Customer Service office on the fourth floor at 50 High St, or Waldenbooks bookshops. Bus drivers carry free timetables of their individual routes. Services run from about 5.30am to 1am.

Subways. Boston has an unusual underground railway network. Three of the four lines — red, blue and orange — are straightforward, but the fourth — green — is a glorified tram service. It clanks below street level around the downtown area, then emerges to trundle along Beacon Street. It splits into four separate destinations at the far end, but most visitors do not let this trouble them. Other passengers are an excellent source of advice. The subway system is small enough that many Bostonians have the route map committed to memory.

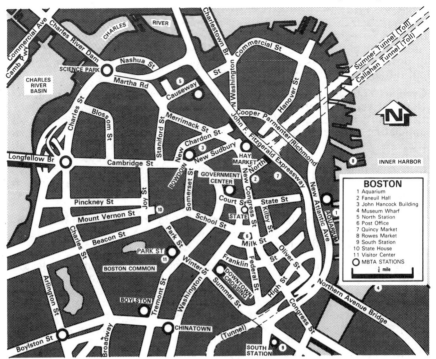

To enter the subway system, you need a token, costing 85c at the desk at the entrance. You ride without a ticket and have unlimited travel until you resurface. Extra fares are charged for travel on the green line west of Reservoir and to the southern extremes of the red line.

Buses. Expresses charge $1.50 or more, but ordinary buses have a flat fare of 60c or an 85c subway token. You place the money or token in a machine as you board the bus, under the watchful eye of the driver. There are no transfers.

Cheap Deals. Children and senior citizens travel at half fare. A number of monthly passes are available depending on how much of the system you want to use — just buses, just subway, both, just one subway line, etc. They are available at banks during the last week of the preceding month. For example, the all-subway weekly pass costs $18. For information about passes call 722-5218.

Car. Boston drivers are among the worst in the world, and the road system is particularly difficult to navigate, with an elaborate one-way system. There are two one-way tunnels leading in and out of the city (Sumner and Callahan respectively), both of which charge a 30c toll.

Parking is so bad in the centre of town that the best advice is to pick a suburban subway station and leave your car there. In central Boston, on-street parking is either metered or restricted in some way, so your best bet is to park in a multi-storey lot for around $12 a day. the most central are on Dalton, Charles and Sudbury Streets.

Taxis. A taxi ride between North End and the Prudential Center, for example, will cost around $8 plus a tip in light traffic; in heavy traffic the fare can be astronomical. For information or complaints, contact the Cab Association of Boston, 253 Sumner St (462-8316). So bad was the reputation of Boston taxi drivers for rudeness and poor navigation that they are being put through a 'Customer Care' course.

Cycling. You can rent bikes by the hour, the day or the week, from the Herson Cycling Company, 1250 Cambridge St, Cambridge (876-4000); or Community Bike Shops, 490 Tremont St, Boston (542-8623). Boston is good undulating cycling terrain, but get yourself a good lock and chain, and learn from the natives who always lock both wheels as well as the frame to an immovable object. Write to the Massachusetts Department of Environmental Management, Division of Forests and Parks, 100 Cambridge St, Boston, MA 02202 for a free series of maps covering ten one-day rides in the greater Boston area, or just pedal along the 18-mile bike path that runs through Boston and Cambridge along the Charles river.

The Tour de Boston is a half-day guided ride around Boston and Cambridge. Call 499-9445 to book the tour, which costs $20 including rental of a mountain bike and helmet.

Ferries. You can choose from a half-hour lunchtime cruise around Boston Harbour for $2, indulge in a few hours' island-hopping in the Harbour, or take a longer trip to Cape Cod for example. Bay State Cruises (723-7800) runs express ferries from Boston to Martha's Vineyard via the Cape Cod Canal. The three-hour trip costs $30 one-way, $50 for a day' return. There are also ferries to Provincetown in Cape Cod from the Commonwealth Pier in South Boston (subway to Aquarium, then the shuttle ferry from Long Wharf). These services operate only in summer.

Accommodation

Hotels/Motels. Expect to pay at least $30 for a single room, $20 per person for a double in a motel on the freeway or in the distant suburbs. Susse Chalet is a good franchise to try, since it has numerous New England locations. Call 1-800-5-CHALET to find the most convenient. In town, barely decent rooms start at about $75. The hotel desk at each terminal in Logan airport is unusually good at helping travellers locate hotels which are offering good deals. The independently owned Park Plaza, in the city centre, often has special offers around $89 double.

Hostels. The Youth Hostel is well located a few blocks west of the Prudential Center near the Back Bay Fens Park. The address is 12 Hemenway St at Haviland (536-9455 or 731-5430). Take the 'T' to Haynes Convention Center, turn left out of the station, cross the freeway bridge then go right at the lights for one block; Hemenway St is on the left. Reservations are usually essential in summer, but if you turn up without one the staff will point you towards other nearby options. A dormitory bed (the only option) costs around $15.

Ys. The YWCA runs the Berkeley Residence at 40 Berkeley St (482-8850), but for women only. It is in a residential area close to Back Bay 'T' station. A 'recession special' single room costs $22, a double $32. Long-term residence, including breakfast and dinner each day, costs around $120 per week, with a minimum of four weeks.

The YMCA at 316 Huntington Avenue (536-7800) accepts both men and women. It charges $40 single/$52 twin, including breakfast.

Guest Houses. For the best prices you have to go out of the centre of Boston; there is a string of them on Beacon St in Brookline. Call in advance since they are often full. Try Anthony's Townhouse (566-3972), Beacon Inn (566-0088); Beacon Street Guest House (232-0292) or Beacon Plaza (232-6550).

Bed & Breakfast. Since advance reservations are advisable in summer, selected addresses and phone numbers are given below. These agencies act as clearing houses for tourists wishing to stay in a family setting. Prices are comparable to hotel room prices. Try: Bed and Breakfast Area Wide, 73 Kirkland St, Cambridge 02138 (576-1492); Bed and Breakfast Associates, PO Box 166, Babson Park, Boston 02157 (872-6990); Bed and Breakfast Brookline/Boston, PO Box 732, Brookline 02146 (277-2292); Country Cousins, PO Box 194, Concord 01742 (369-8416); Greater Boston Hospitality, PO Box 1132, Brookline 02146 (734-0807); New England Bed and Breakfast, 1753 Massachusetts Avenue, Cambridge 02138 (489-9819); and Host Homes of Boston, PO Box 117, Newton 02168.

Longer Term. If you are staying more than a night or two, you might find weekly boarding or renting arrangements, starting as low as $50 a week in the off-season, in the 'Furnished Rooms' section of the *Boston Globe* classifieds, but don't expect a royal suite. You may also strike lucky in the 'Sublets' ads in the *Phoenix* classifieds. for longer term stays (several months), look under 'Housemates' in the *Phoenix*. Places tend to come open at the ends of term in December, May and August.

The Boston University Department of Rental Property Management has a few surplus apartments available during the summer, with monthly rents starting at about $500. Advance booking is required, and you will have to put up a security deposit equal to one month's rent. Call 353-4101 for more information.

Camping. Nothing in the immediate Boston area, but there are campgrounds on Cape Cod and the North Shore (Gloucester, Salem area), both at least one hour's drive from Boston. The *Massachusetts Campground Directory* is free from the Division of Tourism, 1 Cambridge St, Boston 02202 (727-3201).

Eating and Drinking

Boston is renowned not only for its baked beans, but for its seafood which is excellent throughout New England. For traditional New England fare, try clam chowder (made with milk not tomatoes as in the counterfeit Manhattan variety) with a piping hot blueberry muffin. Legal Seafoods in Boston and Cambridge serves outstanding fresh fish *à la carte*. If you're feeling wealthy head out on Northern Avenue and splurge on a seafood dinner at Jimmy's Harborside, 243 Northern Avenue (423-1000). Menus also feature clams, mussels, lobsters and other shellfish. Try a 'Steamer', a huge bowl of steamed soft shell-clams. Fresh fish available includes bluefish, swordfish, scrod (young cod) and shark. One of the best known seafood restaurants (because it is the oldest in Boston) is the informal and bustling Union Oyster House at 41 Union Street (227-2750) near the old city centre. Not only does it serve the best clam chowder in town, it's historic — a French prince lived there once.

If seafood does not appeal, try any of the small lively Italian restaurants in the North End, especially along Hanover Street. The European is a capacious pasta and pizza place — a North End institution. For more sophisticated Italian cuisine go down Richmond Street to Felicia's — Felicia is the chef-owner. Chicken verdiccio is her speciality and always superb. Jacob Wirth's, on Stuart Street near the theatre district, is one of Boston's oldest restaurant's, yet undiscovered by tourists. It's a German pub featuring excellent sausages of various types, saubraten and, of course, beer. Boston has the nation's third largest Chinatown — after San Francisco and New York — but you have to walk through a seedy pornography and prostitution district they call the 'Combat Zone' to get there. Go for *dim sum* at the Imperial Tea House on Beach Street. Along 'Mass Ave' in Cambridge there are dozens of good little ethnic restaurants — Greek, Ethiopian, Middle Eastern, Japanese — which tend to be inexpensive since their primary clientele are impoverished academicians. New Englanders eat more ice cream per capita than anyone, and there are ice cream parlours everywhere. Herrell's and Steve's are the fiercest rivals, both chains were started by the same man — Steve Herrell. Emack Bolio's leads the pack with interesting flavours.

At Quincy Market (the middle building at Faneuil Hall Market Place — Boston's version of Covent Garden) you can invent your own menu by buying food from different vendors, and eat it in a common seating area on a terrace or under a glass roof. At Durgin Park Restaurant, one of the most famous restaurants in the market, a dinner of Yankee roast beef or oyster stew will cost around $25. Sailors have been eating there for over a century.

Go for drinks — not the overpriced, mediocre food — at the Top of the Hub. This is a restaurant with a view, located on the top floor of the otherwise unattractive Prudential Center; until recently, this was Boston's tallest building. (That honour now goes to the nearby John Hancock Building, built in a fit of pique to outdo the rival insurance company's attempt to impress).

DRINKING

Pubs as well as restaurants advertise widely in the *Boston Globe* and *Phoenix*. Those with live entertainment receive a short critique in the *Phoenix* listings column, 'Boston After Dark' section. Bars are open until 1am. All states observe 'Blue Laws' which forbid the sale of package liquor on Sundays. Wine and beer can be sold in food stores as well as in liquor stores in Massachusetts; New Hampshire's state government has a monopoly on liquor sales, but the prices are so low that people drive in from all over New England to stock up.

The Black Rose on State Street in Boston and the Plough and Stars in Cambridge are good basic pubs with the addition of nightly music. Clarke's in the financial district has outdoor seating in fair weather. The city has two good breweries: the Commonwealth Brewing Co, 138 Portland St (tours at 3.30pm on Saturdays, noon on Sundays) and Samuel Adams Brewery, 30 Germania St, Jamaica Plain (tours at 2pm on Thursdays and noon and 2pm on Saturdays; take the Orange T line to Stoney Brook). For Guinness and an Irish ambience, visit the pubs along Dorchester Avenue.

The inspiration for the television series *Cheers* was the Bull & Finch at 84 Beacon Street (227-9605), and the Hollywood studio set version is modelled upon it. It milks its celebrity status thoroughly, selling almost as much merchandise as beer. For British pub atmosphere, try the Staples at

77 Beacon Hill, which has a young unpretentious clientele. Prices are reasonable and there is a good range of beers.

Doyle's, some way out of town at 3484 Washington St (524-2345), has also been a setting for filming. It boasts 21 beers on draft and 17 single malt whiskies. To find it, take the Orange Line of the T to Forest Hill. Walk down the steps to the bus stop and turn left onto Washington St, continuing for three blocks. Doyle's is on the right at the corner of William St.

The standard route for the determined sightseers is the Freedom Trail which links 16 sits and buildings of historic interest. It is marked by a thick red line on the ground and crosses some of the bleakest parts of town as well as some the most picturesque. Pick up the map from the Park Street Visitor Information Center on the edge of Boston Common (subway to Park Street) and set off from there. Free maps of the city, showing public toilets among other things, are available from the National Historic Park Service, in State St.

Excellent views of the city and environs, sometimes stretching as far as the mountains of New Hampshire, may be obtained from the observation floors of the Prudential Center or the John Hancock building. The engineers seem to have solved the problem which afflicted the latter when it was first built, and huge sheets of glass are no longer liable to fall out on a windy day. The old Trinity Church nestling at the base of the skyscraper provides a remarkable contrast of old and new, and makes a lovely photograph.

Museums. Boston has some of the best museums of art and science in the country. Visit the Museum of Fine Arts (465 Huntington Avenue, 267-9377) or the nearby charming Gardner Museum (280 The Fenway, 734-1359) for a comprehensive collection of visual arts. For modern art, visit the Institute of Contemporary Art (955 Boylston St, 266-5152).

Boston has its share of viewer-participation or 'hands-on' museums such as the Museum of Science (723-2500), perched above the water between Boston and Cambridge — it has its own subway stop on the Green line, Science Park. It opens 9am-5am daily, except on Mondays between January and the end of April. Late opening on Fridays until 9pm, and during school vacations to 7pm. Try to start your visit early in the day, since there the excellent hands-on exhibits are swarming with people later in the day. Admission is $6.50, except on Wednesdays between 1-5pm when it is free. Nearby is the Charles Haden Planetarium (Science Park, 742-6088).

To re-visit the scene of the Boston Tea Party, when the early colonists demonstrated their dislike of British taxes on traded commodities by dumping 342 chests of tea into Boston Harbour in 1773, go to Museum Wharf at 300 Congress St (338-1772). You can tour a full-size replica of one of the three ships and even heave a chest of tea overboard (which is subsequently winched up for the next tourist). Close by, the new Children's Museum (adjoining the giant milk bottle on Museum Wharf) takes hands-on exhibits to extremes. You can make computerized rock music or clamber round a replica sewage system. No child on a visit to Boston should be deprived of a day at the Children's Museum.

In the grounds of Harvard University lie half a dozen internationally acclaimed museums. The Fogg and Sackler museums hold the bulk of Harvard's massive art collection. The Busch-Reisinger is dedicated to Germanic art. The Peabody Museum houses artifacts from ancient civilisations and at the adjacent Botanical Museum the celebrated Blaschka glass flowers are displayed. Ring the Harvard operator (495-5000) and ask to be connected with the particular museum to find out opening hours.

The New England Aquarium (742-8870) is a short stroll from Faneuil Hall and well worth it to see the comical penguins and seals, as well as the 1,999 other species of sea-life exhibited there.

All current entertainment is listed in the 'Boston After Dark' section of the *Phoenix* and in the weekly calendar included in Thursday's *Boston Globe*. Tickets for most theatrical and musical events can be bought from Ticketmaster (931-2000) or try the Bostix kiosk at Faneuil Hall (subway to Government Center; 723-5181 for recorded information), which offers half-price tickets on the day of the performance. The kiosk's hours are 11am to 6pm Monday to Saturday; noon to 6pm on Sunday.

Music. For rock groups, Boston, Worcester or Hartford are the usual New England stop on a national tour. In the summer, Boston Common is the location for a series of outdoor concerts. Check the *Phoenix* for listings for upcoming concerts. Tickets for rock concerts can be bought through Ticketmaster (931-2000) or any of the other theatre ticket agencies in the Yellow Pages — the heading to look for is 'Theatre and Sport Ticket Service'.

For local new music in a bar setting try the Rathskellar — known as 'the Rat' near Boston University in Kenmore. Jazz lovers will want to spend at least one evening at Zachary's on Huntington Avenue). Boston is also strong on folk music — the careers of James Taylor and Tracy Chapman took off here.

For classical music, Boston has opera and ballet companies, a symphony orchestra, many chamber ensembles and the Boston Pops Orchestra. The latter, and other groups, give a series of free concerts and dance performances at the Hatch Shell Auditorium on the Charles River Embankment from mid-June to mid-September.

Film. With movies, too, Boston usually gets the pick of the new releases early on. Queues form early so be sure to telephone the theatre to find out when ticket sales start.

Nightlife. Many bars offer live musical or comic entertainment, with some of the best jazz in town being played at corner dives around Faneuil Hall and at Inman Square, Cambridge. The Universities are naturally the focal points of most nightlife. In particular, try Harvard and Kenmore Squares, and check the listings in *The Phoenix*.

Theatre. Drama is alive and well in Boston, and many productions which open here move on to New York's Broadway. Downtown, the Wilbur (423-4008), the Schubert (426-4520) and the Colonial (426-9366), and in Cambridge the American Repertory Theatre (597-8300) are among the most prominent playhouses in the area.

SPORT

Most visitors will be in Boston during the baseball season (April to September). The team is the Red Sox and they play at Fenway Park (MBTA to Kenmore; 1-800-382-8080). At other times of year, spectators go to the

Sullivan Stadium in Foxboro to watch the New England Patriots play football (1-800-543-1776), and to the Boston Garden (MBTA to North Station; 1-800-828-7080 for ticket information) to see the Boston Celtics play basketball or the Boston Bruins play ice hockey. For the homesick, the *Boston Sunday Globe* prints English, Scottish and Irish soccer results. Tickets to all big sports events are handled by Ticketmaster (931-2000), Ticketpro (1-800-828-7080) and many of the other agencies in the Yellow Pages.

Horse racing fans can go to Suffolk Downs (727-2581) in East Boston. Dog racing is held at Wonderland Park (284-1300) in revere. Betting at the track only in both cases.

The Boston Marathon takes place each year on Patriot's Day, the third Monday in April.

SHOPPING

Sales tax of 5% applies to everything except clothes and food (but restaurant and take-out meals are taxed). Regular shopping hours are 9.30am to 5pm but many downtown department stores stay open until 9pm on Mondays and Thursdays. Shopping malls also stay open until 9pm or later every night except Sunday, and some corner stores and supermarkets (such as Purity Supreme or Heartland) stay open 24 hours.

Boston offers many different kinds of shopping experience, form the Dickensian (Beacon Hill) to the ultra-modern (Prudential Center) and renovated-trendy (Faneuil Hall). The main downtown department stores are located on Washington Street. Cambridge's main shopping area is around Harvard Square. New England produces all sorts of high-quality handicrafts, from patchwork quilts to scrimshaw, an unusual folk art of carved or engraved whale teeth, bones or shells.

A trip to Haymarket — two blocks north of Faneuil Hall — makes for a pleasant expedition on a Saturday or Sunday morning when local farmers and fishermen set up stands in a bustling open air market.

An interesting exercise in American capitalism takes place every Monday morning at Filene's Department Store Basement on Washington Street. After two weeks on sale at full price, the cost of an item drops by 25%; after three weeks, by 50%; after four weeks 75%; and after five weeks without a buyer the item is given away to charity.

For good deals on books, records and cameras, check out the Harvard Coop stores (rhymes with hoop) at Harvard Square or on the MIT campus on Massachusetts Avenue in Cambridge, or at 1 Federal Street, Boston. It also has a mail-order service: 1-800-368-1882.

The Harvard Square area in Cambridge is the best place in the USA to shop for books. On Brattle Street, Wordsworth and the Paperback Booksmith carry an impressive array of titles at slightly discounted prices. The Harvard Bookstore on Mass Avenue has a positively mouthwatering selection of new used and out-of-print books. Schoenhoff's, on Mount Auburn Street carries a wide selection of foreign language books.

THE MEDIA

Newspapers. The *Boston Globe* is the leading newspaper, but in the last few years, Rupert Murdoch's *Herald* has been capturing an increasingly larger market share. The weekly *Phoenix* started out as an underground paper and has retained that image despite being taken over by big business. It comes out on Tuesdays and excess copies are distributed free at college campuses a day or two later. for a full range of European newspapers, try Out of Town Newspapers Inc, on Massachusetts Avenue in Cambridge (354-7777)

Radio. The USA's foremost classical music station is WCRB, broadcasting to Bostonians on 102.5 FM. It shares programmes with BBC Radio 3, and transmits concerts from Tanglewood (see *Further Afield*). For good 24 hours stereo rock, try WBCN (104.1 FM) or WFNX (101.7 FM). For top 40, the best known station is WXKS (107.9 FM) which advertises itself as 'Kiss-108'.

At the lower end of the FM end dial are grouped a number of student and other non-profit stations, most noteworthy of which is GBH (89.7 FM) which has a varied menu of classical music and current events programmes. Another good non-profit station is WBOS (92.9 FM) with programming from Boston University. MIT's own station is WMBR (88.1 FM).

The AM dial has little worth listening to. Of historical significance, though, is WBZ (1030 AM), owned by Westinghouse, which in 1921 became the nation's first licensed broadcast station. (KDKA in Pittsburgh, also a Westinghouse station, had put out programmes the previous year, but without a licence). Unfortunately WBZ now offers 24 hours of mediocre music and generally dull chat shows that can be heard across 38 states and the southeast and central portions of Canada. For news listen to WEEI (590 AM) or WRKO (680 AM).

Crime and Safety

Boston has had its fair share of street crime but is not in the same league as New York or Detroit. Boston Common should be avoided by single women at night, and anyone is likely to meet with trouble in the red light district, also known as the 'Combat Zone', around Park Square between Chinatown and the Greyhound station.

Drugs. Possession (though not selling) of an ounce or less of marijuana is no longer an arrestable offence, though you can still be prosecuted.

Help and Information *i*

The area code for Boston is 617.

Information: Greater Boston Convention and Tourist Bureau, Prudential Plaza West, Box 490, Boston 02199 (536-4100). There is a Visitor Center on the Fremont St side of Boston Common.
British Consulate-General: 4740 Prudential Tower, Boylston St (437-7160)
American Express: 10 Tremont St (723-8400)
Thomas Cook: 156 Federal St (267-5000)
Post Office: Post Office Square, opposite northern end of Federal St (223-2246).
American Automobile Association: 141 Tremont St (482-8031).
Medical: Massachusetts General Hospital, Fruit St, (726-2000).
24 hour drug-store: Phillips Drugstore, 155 Charles St (523-1028).
Travelers' Aid: 711 Atlantic Avenue (542-7286). Also at the airport (569-6248) and 312 Stuart St (542-7296).
Police: 145 Berkeley St (247-4200).

MASSACHUSETTS

Historic Sites. Cape Cod and the North Shore have their beaches and recreation areas, but most worthwhile of the day trips from Boston involve cultural or historical sights. Lexington and Concord, now virtually suburbs of Boston, are the sites of the first fighting between British soldiers and the revolutionary 'minutemen'. You can get to Lexington on express bus 528 from Harvard Square in Cambridge. Concord is on the commuter rail line from North Station. On Route 24 just outside of Concord lies Walden Pond where Henry David Thoreau lived. In Concord proper are several museums dedicated to the leaders of the Transcendentalist movement: the Antiquarian Museum — Ralph Waldo Emerson's old house — the Alcott house, among others. The oldest continuing operating inn in America is in Sudbury, a few miles southwest of Concord. The Wayside Inn (443-8846) is the best place in the Bay state to have a traditional New England meal: try the Indian pudding, a sweet gooey delicacy made with cornmeal (ground maize) and molasses. The pilgrims loved it.

Further afield, you can see living history in two restored colonial villages where centuries old skills and crafts are demonstrated. On is Sturbridge Village, about 50 miles west of Boston, near Worcester just off the Massachusetts Turnpike. The other is the Plimoth Plantation in Plymouth about 40 miles south of Boston. Plymouth is the site of the Pilgrim Fathers' landing in 1620. A replica of the Mayflower is on display there.

Cape Cod. If you go southeast from Boston on Route 3, you eventually reach the Cape Cod Canal, marking the start of a hooked arm of land sticking out into the Atlantic. Much of Cape Cod is now a state park featuring over 50 square miles of sandy beaches and dunes. It also has wildlife sanctuaries and is the site of Marconi's first transatlantic telegraph message. At the extreme tip, Provincetown is a lovely quiet resort which loses its charm only when it fills up on summer weekends. The offshore islands of Nantucket and Martha's Vineyard (ferries from Boston, Wood's Hole, Falmouth and Hyannis) are old whaling communities and make for pleasant sea cruises on hot summer days. (Anyone visitor travelling on a Delta or Northwest Airlines standby airpass should note that both islands, plus Hyannis and Provincetown, are accessible). The islands attract artists, writers and Boston's high society, while Cape Cod itself is a much more proletarian holiday destination. You can rent a (fairly primitive) cottage in the Cape Cod National Seashore for $100-$175 per week from the Peaked Hill Trust, PO Box 1705, Provincetown MA 02657. AYH hostels are located at Eastham, Hyannis, Truro, Martha's Vineyard and Nantucket.

Western Massachusetts. The interesting areas begin about ten miles north of Springfield in the Connecticut Valley. There are five colleges and universities in the triangle formed by Amherst (Amherst College, Hampshire College, University of Massachusetts), Northampton (Smith College) and South Hadley (Mount Holyoke). The so-called Five College Community is a miniature version of Boston or Berkeley, with many fine restaurants, bookshops, cinemas, music and an interesting and vocal feminist and leftist community. The colleges are linked by a free bus service.

Basketball began in Springfield, and the Hall of Fame at 1150 West Columbus Avenue (413-781-6500) does a good job of telling the story.

Berkshires. Between the five college area and the New York state border is yet another distinct section of Massachusetts. The old film *Alice's Restaurant* shows the scenery. In the autumn, the gently rolling Berkshire hills have magnificent foliage; in winter, skiing is popular. But the summer is the time the action takes place. The Boston Symphony Orchestra hold summer concerts at weekends at Tanglewood, located in Lenox. Tanglewood is also a music school and you can walk through the beautiful grounds and gardens and take in practice sessions, modern music concerts, etc. Lawn seats for the weekends are about $5. You can attend the rehearsals on Friday and Saturday morning for a nominal charge. There are also popular artists appearing in last August and early September at Tanglewood. Food — but not liquor — can be brought into the grounds. Check the local *Berkshire Eagle* newspaper or listings in the Boston newspapers or telephone (266-1492) for a performance schedule. During July and August there is a theatre festival in nearby Williamstown at the Adams Memorial Theatre at Williams College (597-3408); the Summer Dance Festival at nearby Jacob's Pillow is also worth checking out. Some of the brightest lights of the American stage come to perform.

On route 20 heading into New York state is the Hancock Shaker Village, located in Pittsfield not Hancock. There are the original buildings and continuous demonstrations of various crafts (carpentry, tinsmithing, bread baking, etc.). The beautiful surroundings are gradually being put back under the plough and made agriculturally viable again. If you are going to be in this area for a few days check the schedule in the Visitor's Center of the village. They often have intensive one-day courses open to the public on subjects such as herb cultivation, cane weaving for chairs, etc.

NEW ENGLAND COAST

Starting with New York City's dormitory towns in southern Connecticut, the coastline becomes more interesting as you travel northeast beyond New Haven, site of Yale University. I-95 hugs the coastline within a few miles of dozens of historic fishing and boatbuilding harbours overlooking Long Island Sound.

Mystic, Connecticut, for example, has the largest maritime museum in the USA, at 50 Greenmanville Avenue (572-5315), open 9am-4.30pm daily. The resort's aquarium (536-3323) keeps the same hours. You might also want to visit the colonial-style shopping centre called Olde Mystic.

Newport, Rhode Island is the home of the Regatta and of the Jazz festival; New Bedford and Nantucket, Massachusetts have outstanding whaling museums. Fall River, Massachusetts has two excellent maritime museums: Battleship Cove and the Marine Museum.

North of Cape Cod, the coastline is a patchwork of active ports (Boston, Portsmouth and Bath); very garish seaside resorts (Revere, Salisbury, Hampton Beach and Old Orchard Beach), and the more upmarket Oqunquit; and quaint old towns and fishing villages (Gloucester, Rockport and Newburyport in Massachusetts, the Strawberry Banke district of Portsmouth and Kittery, Kennebunkport and Freeport in Maine). Portland, Maine is a busy fishing and shipping city which has some wonderful examples of what happened to Victorian architecture when it reached the USA. The new Portland museum of Art is surprisingly good, and has a Mona Lisa which some art experts theorize could be da Vinci's original.

The Great Outdoors

Northern New England is an outdoors experience with little in the way of historical or cultural entertainment. the states of Vermont, New Hampshire and Maine have turned their wildernesses into tourist areas offering hiking and camping, hunting and fishing, skiing, canoeing, whitewater rafting, mountaineering, rock climbing or just getting away from it all. The area is perhaps at its best in late September and October when the bright maple foliage is spectacular. There are even 'leaf-peeping' reports on radio stations giving the locations of the most dazzling colours. For the latest information on where to see the best colours, call the following state numbers:

Connecticut: 1-800-282-6863 from mid-September.

Maine: 1-800-533-9595 — 'unofficial' advice until 16 September, when detailed reports begin.

Massachusetts: 1-800-632-8038 instate, 1-800-343-9072 out-of-state, from 21 September.

New Hampshire: 1-800-258-3608 from mid-September to id-October.

Rhode Island: 1-800-556-2484 from late September.

Summer is the time when the mosquitos and other biting insects abound. Spring is the season for tasting maple syrup for which Vermont in particular is renowned.

Inland in Maine, the Baxter State Park is the start (or finish) of the Appalachian Trail, stretching as far as Georgia and is typical of the kind of wilderness area, you will find across the northern reaches of New England. Accommodation for hikers on the Trail is provided in mountain-top huts. The Maine wilderness is on a scale that is unsurpassed in New England. From Greenville to Ashland, a predominantly dirt road winds 120 miles with barely a sign of habitation. If you park your car at a random point on that road and head northwest, you can walk another 120 miles without seeing any sign of human life. Since you can easily lose your way doing this, you should remain on established trails. Maps can be obtained by contacting the Baxter State Park Authority, 64 Balsam Drive, Millinocket 04462 (207-723-5140). Mount Washington in New Hampshire is a peak of extremes. The highest in the highest peak in the northeastern USA at 6,288 feet, scene of the strongest winds recorded anywhere in the world of 320 mph and subject to the worst winter weather outside the Poles. It was described by the showman P.T. Barnum as the 'second greatest show on Earth', but sadly the peak has been spoilt by drab tourist facilities, reachable by any vehicle which can handle 30% inclines. The cog railway is a less terrifying journey.

Whale-watching. The best time of year is October, and the best base is Provincetown at the tip of Cape Cod. Organized trips take about four hours and cost around $25. Operators include Provincetown Whale Watch (1-800-992-9300), the Dolphin Fleet (1-800-825-9300) and the Portuguese Princess (1-800-442 3188).

Hunting and Fishing. Hunters and fisherman should head north to Maine, New Hampshire or Vermont in the appropriate seasons. All hunting and fishing is closely regulated, however, and licences are required. Information on regulations and seasons is available in booklet form from any town or city hall in the state you are interested in visiting. Non-residents always pay more for licences than residents do.

Skiing. Downhill skiing is also big business in the northern states, and

Bostonians are willing to travel to Killington or Stowe in Vermont or Waterville, New Hampshire rather than settle for the lesser slopes of Massachusetts or Connecticut. With the aid of snowmaking machines, the season can stretch from mid October to early June. Northern ski resorts advertise seasonally in the travel pages of the *Boston Sunday Globe*, which also gives weekly reports on skiing conditions in the main resorts. Tourist-conscious New Hampshire has its own information centre in Boston, the Ski New Hampshire store is a 6 St James Avenue (423-7676). Most radio stations give daily ski conditions as well, or can phone toll-free 1-800-258-3608. You might also like to browse in *Roxy's Ski Guide to New England* which describes and compares the downhill ski areas of New England.

Cross country enthusiasts might wish to ski in the orchard of the Nashoba Valley Winery at 100 Wattaquadoc Hill Road, Bolton (799-5521), 35 miles west of Boston. You must provide your own equipment (which can be hired in Boston), but the skiing, winery tour and tasting are free.

Calendar of Events

mid-March	New England Crafts Festival, Worcester Massachusetts
April	Maple Festival, St Albans Vermont
April (3rd Monday)	**Patriots's Day, Massachusetts**
April (last Monday)	**Fast Day, New Hampshire**
early July	Harborfest, Boston
July	Lobster Festival, Rockland Maine
mid-August	Jazz Festival, Newport Rhode Island
September	Oyster Festival, Norfolk Connecticut
mid-December	Re-enactment of the Boston Tea Party

Public Holidays are shown in **bold**.

Washington and the Mid-Atlantic States

Delaware Maryland New Jersey Pennsylvania Virginia West Virginia

Like the Vatican, the District of Columbia is small in area but large in influence. It was designated capital of the United States in 1800 after the southern states insisted upon a more southerly replacement for the original capital, Philadelphia. The title 'District' distinguishes the capital from the 50 ordinary states it governs; it is run by Congress, though one of President Clinton's campaign pledges was to give it full statehood.

Where resides such power and wealth, culture is liable to flourish. So within the five square miles heart of Washington, there are numerous museums, theatres, parks, historical monuments and shopping areas, as well as government buildings. There is enough in this central location to keep the most curious and hardy visitor busy for weeks. Like New York, Washington is hardly representative of the USA, but the District of Columbia is a much gentler introduction to the country than is Manhattan.

Washington is a fulcrum set between two geographical areas: to the north are the industrial and financial centres of America with their hectic pace of life; to the south begins a more tranquil and rural way of life. It is not suprising then that you find an unlikely synthesis of the two in Washington, such as frenetic businessmen with soft Southern drawls and genteel manners.

In 1882, Henry James attributed DC with a charming climate and the most entertaining society in America. The former has never been true, and the latter claim would have been laughable until the 1970s. Until then Washington was provincial. Since then it has come a long way, and while it may not have the glamour of New York, it does have an enormous number

167

of things to see and do. DC may be special because, or in spite, of its being the capital of the United States, but it indisputably exerts a unique charm and fascination.

THE LOCALS

If you define a local as anyone who has lived in the District for more than five years, the locals of DC are comprised of blacks and bureaucrats. Those who came to Washington to find jobs might live in the District with a roommate for a few years. But as soon as they start moving up the career ladder and can afford to move, they buy a house in the city suburbs in Virginia or Maryland. Housing in Washington itself is either very expensive (hence the need for room-mates) or very decrepit, though there is an increasing trend for middle-class whites to buy up and renovate old houses in the north-east part of the town. In the poor sections of the city you will find blue collar workers who cannot afford to move to the wealthier suburbs and poor blacks. The more established and upwardly mobile ethnic communities such as Koreans and Cubans have joined the white commuters in the Maryland and Virginia suburbs.

Making Friends. A book claiming to teach how to 'make friends and influence people' is a perenniel bestseller in the USA. In Washington however, it is easier to make friends if you already influence people. Washington is full of very bright, eager and ambitious men and women in their twenties and thirties. You may not find this stereotyped career-obsessed newcomer to Washington very congenial company. It is the norm for these lawyers, economists, management consultants and lobbyists to work 12-hour days, not to take holidays (only business trips) and to have few interests outside their niche of government.

Since Washington thrives on paperwork, and therefore secretaries, and because gender steroetyping still exists in the capital, there are several women for every man working in Washington. This means that if you are a young man you needn't be wealthy, influential or handsome. The most popular nightspots for this crowd are in Georgetown, about two miles from the White House; the noisiest pubs and bars are on M St and on Wisconsin Avenue, but the lettered side streeted (O and P, especially) off Wisconsin are just as nice and tend to be more discreet.

The District also includes a good number of universities. Between the White House and Georgetown around 20th and Pennsylvania, is George Washington University, Georgetown University (where Bill Clinton studied), the American University and Howard University (predominantly black). These have active social lives, if you can manage to lock into them.

Gay and lesbian listings can be found in *The Washington Blade* available free in many of the bookshops around Dupont Circle.

The Mall, in the geographic heart of the city, is a strip of greenery where the natives come to play frisbee or softball, to attend free concerts, to jog, busk and picnic.

CLIMATE

If you think anything over 85°C/30°F is hot, absolutely avoid Washington during June, July and August. It is unbearable, since the unrelieved heat always brings with it a lot of humidity. Unless you are used to that kind of weather, be sure to get air-conditioned accommodation or, if you plan to rent a car, a vehicle with air-conditioning. Other than those three months, the weather is not too bad, though Americans certianly don't vacation in Washington for its climate. The autumn is chilly and often damp. During the winter you can expect freezing tempertures and a quanity of snow and slush. April and May are the beautiful spring months in DC when the cherry blossoms are at their best. The air is clear and dry, though it may become slightly cool in the evening. Dress warmly for the winter, bring a sweater in the spring, and wear as little as possible during the summer. Bring a raincoat, regardless of the season. For a short-term forecast for DC dial 936-1212.

Getting Around

ARRIVAL AND DEPARTURE

Air. Three airports serve Washington, though none is actually in the District of Columbia: Washington Dulles (IAD) in Virginia, National (DCA — domestic only) also in Virginia and the Baltimore-Washington International airport (BWI — between DC and Baltimore in Maryland).

Most international flights arrive at *Dulles*, 26 miles west of Washington. Call 703-661-8040 for information. The terminal building was designed by Saarinen and is stunning, but the facilities and comfort are minimalistic. It is also slow and inconvenient to reach the capital. The Washington Flyer bus will either take you non-stop to 1517 K St for $15 or take you to the nearest metro station (West Falls Church) for $7. A taxi to to the centre of town will cost about $50.

National Airport is just three miles south of Washington downtown in Alexandria. The usual flight path into National follows the Potomac River so you get a splendid view of Washington as you arrive and depart; the normal configuration means you should sit on the left when flying into Washington. National Airport is in the throes of rebuilding a new terminal, which should open in 1996 and promises to be architecturally startling. It will also be convenient, unlike the present arrangement, struggling among all the building work. Passengers are bussed from the Metro station to the Main or Interim terminals. The Metro Orange and Blue lines stop at National Airport, which makes getting into DC quick (18 minutes), cheap ($1 off-peak) and easy. A bus runs between the terminals and the station, but you will probably find it quicker to walk. Trains leave every ten minutes or so.

BWI is served by Washington Flyer buses to downtown, costing $15 one way, but it is cheaper and usually quicker to go by train. BWI airport station is on the main line between Washington and New York. It is served by MARC trains from Washington's Union station (25 minutes, $2.75). The airport station is a couple of miles away from the airport itself, linked by a free Amtrak Shuttle bus every 20 minutes. This departs from the Ground Transportation point at the middle of the arc which constitutes the airport concourse.

Fares to New York on the Delta and USAir Shuttles (from National Airport) are expensive ($142 one-way), but rates to other US cities can be reasonable. Council Travel in Georgetown (1210 Potomac Street NW; 337-6464) has cut-price charter, student and youth fares for overseas flights.

Bus. The Greyhound Terminal (565-2662) is at the corner of 1st and L streets NE. The closest metro station is only four blocks away at Union Station, but the area is rough and a taxi is advisable if you arrive after dark.

Train. Union Station (484-7549), where the Amtrak trains pull in, is the only railway station in the District. It was recently restored to its original magnificence, and is an attraction in its own right. Union has its own stop on the comprehensive metro system. It is on Massachusetts Avenue, north of the Capitol. There are frequent trains to Boston via New York and Philadelphia. Washington to nearby Baltimore costs about $20, to Philadelphia $68 and New York City $89. Metroliners, the high speed trains which take under three hours to get to New York, cost slightly more, and tickets should be bought in advance. They operate hourly from 6.50am to 7pm, with all but the first departure on the hour.

Driving. If you are travelling by car and want to get into the heart of DC, take the 14th St Bridge coming from Virginia. You may get confused as you approach the bridge because the I-95 and I-495 seem to merge and then split. Follow the I-495. If you are arriving from Maryland, take the Beltway, I-495 and exit at either Wisconsin or Connecticut Avenue. From there it is another 15 to 30 minutes to get into the heart of Washington. Connecticut Avenue will eventually put you within two blocks of the White House; Wisconsin Avenue will take you to Georgetown.

Driving in Washington tests the nerves of even the most aggressive city driver and the jams on the Beltway test the patience of the most serene person. Public transport is excellent in Washington and cars are best left outside it. If you have to bring a car into DC, then stay in a motel and park it there for free as regular car parks are expensive and fines are easily caught. Bear in mind that if you feel incomplete without wheels and intend to drive a vehicle in Washington for two weeks you are supposed to apply for a visitors permit from the Bureau of Motor Vehicles (727-6679).

Unless otherwise marked, you are not supposed to exceed 45 mph on expressways or 25 mph in built-up areas. If a test shows that you have over 0.5% alcohol in your blood, you are considered to be under the influence; twice that is considered intoxication.

Hitch-hiking. It is best to get into Maryland or Virginia first. All the good roads are high-speed (i.e. Turnpikes, Beltways, etc) so it is difficult to hitch within the city. For I-95 north to New York, take the Metro to New Carrollton, Maryland and hitch along I-295 to the junction with I-95 or the Baltimore-Washington Parkway. This may also be sucessful for those heading south. Do not accept a lift to Baltimore unless you actually want to visit the city.

The *Washington Post* classified advertisements list people or agencies wanting cars driven across country. You could also try the universities for lift sharing — in the university newspaper or bulletin board in the student union. All American Auto Transport has its headquarters in DC (347-2000) and should be able to fix you up with a driveaway vehicle without too much trouble in the summer months.

CITY TRANSPORT

City Layout. The District of Columbia is divided into four parts: North-West (NW), North-East (NE), South-West (SW) and South-East (SE). It is important that you use these designations when addressing mail or giving instructions to a taxi driver, if the address is at all obscure. The areas are formed by the intersection of Constitution Avenue and North and South Capitol Streets, where the distinctive domed Capitol Building is located. In practice you will probably spend most of your time fairly close the the Capitol in NW.

Streets which are named by a letter, e.g. C Street, M Street, run east/west and streets which are named by a number, e.g. 3rd Street, 25th Street, run north/south. Thus if you found yourself at the intersection of 3rd and D, NW you would be three blocks and four blocks up from the Capitol. After the alphabet has run its course, the street names revert to the alphabet but become two syllable words, e.g. Adams, Bryant, Channing then three syllable words and so on.

In addition to this grid of letters and numbers, there are streets radiating like spokes which are named after states, such as Connecticut, Massachusetts, Rhode Island. If you can ignore these in your calculations, you should be able to estimate the positions of places from their street addresses; 2030 M St is between 20th and 21st St, while Ford's Theater is at 511 10th St, between E and F Streets — the fifth and sixth letters of the alphabet.

The two main types of transportation to get through this maze are buses and subways (the Metro). Phone 637-7000 for transit information. Whether you use these, taxis or cars, remember that between 7.30am and 9am and between 3.30pm and 6pm you will be competing for space with tens of thousands of civil servants who flood to and from DC every day. In addition, traffic in the centre of Washington is often disrupted by demonstrations.

Bus. Buses run quite frequently between 7am and 6pm from Monday to Saturday. However, the service in the evening and on Sunday is patchy and you may have to wait for an hour for a bus. Unless you have a transfer ticket, you will have to pay your fare with the exact change. Within DC fares are 90c off-peak, $1 peak. Ask for a free transfer if you wish to change to another bus.

Metro. The underground system is still surprisingly clean and quiet, and the air-conditioning works. Like the buses, it runs into the surrounding suburbs in Virginia and Maryland. There are five coloured lines (red, green, blue, orange and yellow) which are shown on a simple schematic map, not unlike those of London's underground. Each Metro station entrance has a large concrete post outside with the letter 'M' in brown and white. Brown is a gentle, subdued colour and so the stations don't actually leap out at you when you are looking for them. Inside the stations are good Metro and local maps, and attendants are always on duty. The train driver will announce each stop (and which side the platform will be), but usually unintelligibly, so look for the station signs. This means of transportation is highly recommended in the summer, when it is exhausting to move around on foot.

The difficulty for the first-time user is the ticket system. The best thing to do — and all tourists do it — is to stand in front of the automatic farecard dispenser and watch someone more experienced use it. The machines accept nickels, dimes, quarters, $1, $5, $10 and $20 bills; be warned that if the notes are dog-eared the machine will spit them out. The basic fare is $1, which covers most stations except during peak hours when you pay more

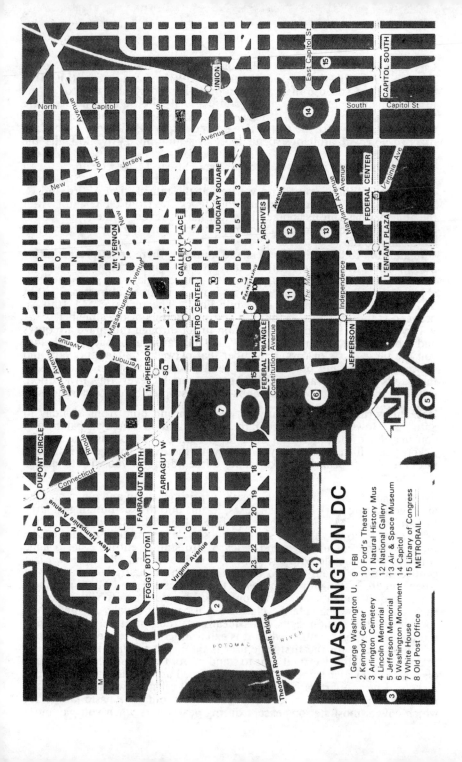

WASHINGTON DC

1 George Washington U.
2 Kennedy Center
3 Arlington Cemetery
4 Lincoln Memorial
5 Jefferson Memorial
6 Washington Monument
7 White House
8 Old Post Office
9 FBI
10 Ford's Theater
11 Natural History Mus
12 National Gallery
13 Air & Space Museum
14 Capitol
15 Library of Congress
METRORAIL

to get to outlying destinations. (Peak hours are 5.30am to 9.30am and 3pm to 7pm, Monday to Friday.) You can buy a one-day travel card, which allows as much travel as you like, after $9.30 for $5. There are also $10 and $20 farecards which give you a 5% and 10% discount, respectively, and can be used on any day until the credit runs out. Help yourself to a transfer from one of the machines to found in metro stations if you want to continue your journey on bus. It is not possible to transfer free of charge from a bus to a metro.

The Metro keeps respectable hours on weekdays (5.30am-midnight), but on Saturdays it starts at 8am and on Sundays at 10am — a problem if you have an early flight or want to start sightseeing early.

Taxis. Instead of meters, fares are calculated by the driver according to the distance travelled as interpreted by a formula baffling to the newcomer. Scope for cheating customers is therefore wide, but most drivers are honest. Fares increase steeply if you stray into Maryland or Virginia. By law not all taxis are allowed to leave the District, so make clear your destination before getting in. All the drivers expect big tips.

Cycling. Bike rentals are available in DC, Maryland and Virginia. Try the Thompson Boat Centre, Rock Creek Pathway and Virginia Avenue NW (333-4861), for bikes by the hour ($4) or the day ($15). For longer rentals check the Yellow Pages for cycle shop listings. Always lock your bike; bicycle theft is rife in the capital, so don't rent anything bright and shiny. Rock Creek Park is a nice place to cycle and has cyclists' lanes. You can get a free booklet called *Bicycle Paths in the Washington Area* from the Metropolitan Council of Governments (1224 Connecticut Avenue NW; 962 3256) or a paperback called *Greater Washington Bicycle Atlas* for $11.95 which is useful for cycling through the mid-Atlantic states. The book is available from Washington Area Bicycle Association, 1819 H St NW, suite 640; 872 9830. Bicycles are allowed on Metrorail trains after 7pm on weekdays and all day at weekends. You need, however, a permit to show you have completed a saftey course; call 962-1116 for details.

Accommodation

The fact that there are so many free things to see in DC is offset by the expensive accommodation. It it is sometimes hard to find accomodation at any price, so book ahead if at all possible. Not only are there tourists but government conferences, conventions, rallies etc.

Motels. Motels in Maryland and Virginia tend to be a bit cheaper and still within 30 to 45 minutes from downtown Washington. The best thing to do is look in the Yellow Pages under hotels and motels and phone ahead for rates. Prices are generally higher in the summer though many places have special weekend or other special deals.

Hotels. If you know you are going to Washington at least 30 days in advance then you can book a super saver rate of $59 a night at either of of the Days Inn. They are at 4400 Connecticut Avenue, between Yuma and Albemarle Streets (244-5600) and 1201 K St NW (842 1020). Other reasonable options for those unable to plan so far in advance are the Howard Johnson Lodge (2601 Virginia Avenue, opposite the Watergate Center; 965 2700; $82 single/ $90 double per night), and the tattier University Inn (2134 G Street, 342 8020) for $57 including breakfast.

Hostels. The best place to stay is the International Youth Hostel at 1009 11th Street (737-2333), three blocks north of Metro Center; $15 for Hostelling International members. You must supply your own sheet (or rent one for $1 a night) and there is a midnight curfew. There are a couple of alternatives; Davis House, 1822 R St NW (232-3196), which is open only to foreign visitors and costs $25 per night. The International Guest House at 1441 Kennedy St NW (726-5808) is a bargain at $25 a night including breakfast and afternoon tea.

The YMCA runs the Harrington at 11th and E Streets NW (628-8140), which charges about $60 single, $70 twin.

Bed and Breakfast. Washington has numerous bed and breakfast agencies. Try Sweet Dreams & Toast, 363-7767; the Bed and Breakfast League, PO Box 9490 (363-7767); and Bed 'n' Breakfast of Washington, PO Box 12011 (328-3510). Double room rates range from $45 to $130, and bookings should be made several weeks in advance.

Camping. Of the six sites in Maryland and Virginia close to DC, the Capitol KOA Campground (768 Cecil Avenue, Millerville MD; 301-923-2771) has the best transport links with Washington.

Eating and Drinking

The range and quality of restaurants in and around Washington is marvellous. Because of the great ethnic mix in the area and a general interest in gourmet dining, you can easily find anything from French to African and Thai cuisine. The Yellow Pages list the restaurants not only alphabetically but by national cuisine as well. A curious feature of Washington's restaurants is that the greatest concentrations are from the world's trouble spots. The best area for dinner is Adams-Morgan, centred on the intersection of 18th Street and Columbia Road, a mile or two north of downtown. The dominant cuisine is Ethiopian, best eaten crouching on floor cushions. Salvadorean is a close second, reflecting the number of refugees from this war-ravaged Central American country. And Peruvian food is just starting to appear, as that country descends further into turmoil.

Many of the Smithsonian Museums have good value cafés. Easily the best of these is in the National Gallery of Art; it is underground between the two wings of the Gallery with a spectacular view of the waterfall-cum-skylight. Away from the Mall but still in a museum is the Palate Café at the National Museum of Women in the Arts (1250 New York Avenue at 13th St; 783-5000) which serves light lunches with a wonderful view of the marble entrance hall.

Going to a railway station to eat when you've grown up with British Rail buffets seems a ridiculous idea but the newly renovated Union Station has a vast selection of excellent eating places, ranging from the expensive Adirondacks (in the former Presidential waiting room) to the better-than-average food court.

Round the clock eating and reading is possible at Kramerbooks and Afterwords café (1517 Connecticut Ave NW between Q St and Dupont Circle; 387-1462). This fascinating book-and-coffee-shop is open from 7.30am to 1am Monday to Thursday and all hours from 7.30am on Friday to 1am Sunday. It serves good food at all times of day, and on Friday and Saturday nights has live entertainment.

Bars in Washington tend to serve drinks only, though some around the

Capitol do good lunches as well. Almost every bar has a happy hour between 4pm and 6pm and many have certain days when women get some free drinks. Both bars and restaurants advertise heavily in the *Washington Post* and local magazines. There are always embassy parties going on, if you can get in. The longest beer list in DC is at the Brickskeller (1523 22nd St NW, 293-1885) which has nearly 600 from 46 countries. The Black Rooster on L St between 19th and 20th Streets is more like a British pub, though in an unBritish fashion it has a happy hour from 4 to 7pm daily.

The number of things to see and do in Washington is extraordinary, and many of the options are free. The best way to approach the question is to decide whether you want to pay for it or not. Most of the sights listed here are regarded as property of the American people, and are therefore free. The sequence below will take you a couple of days and is guaranteed to wear you out. A word of warning: Washington offers many cultural goodies and its easy to overdose. As you wander between planes, printing presses and the Potomac remember that you are allowed to pause in the many museum bookstores and cafés.

Washington Monument. The sky over the capital is pierced by this elegnat needle. It was begun in 1833 and quickly reached 150 feet, but then the money ran out. For the next forty years the stump stood forlornly in the middle of America's capital. Mark Twain dismissed it as 'a factory chimney with the top broken off', and spoke of 'tired pigs dozing in the holy calm of its protective shadow'. After the civil war, Congress voted the money to complete it, and now only tourists rummage around the base. At a height of 555 feet and 5 inches, it is the world's tallest masonry structure, and the queues that snake around the base can easily match it for length (as a rule of thumb allow 40 minutes for each complete circuit made by the queue). In the summer queuing in the sweltering heat can be unpleasant and avoided by ascending the tower in the hours of darkness to see Washington's lights twinkling beneath you, as the summer opening hours are 8am to midnight. When the first lift — a steam hoist — was introduced, women were forbidden to travel in it. They walked, while their menfolk enjoyed food and wine during the 20-minute ride. The current elevator takes 90 seconds. At the top is the best view in Washington, though it is impeded by the scratched plastic windows through which you must peer.

If you can arrange your visit for a weekend, ask to join the 'walk-down' to become one of the few people allowed an inside glimpse of the tower. At 10am and 2pm on Saturday and Sunday, a park ranger escorts a group down the 897 stairs inside, stopping to look at the plaques placed on the walls. The tradition began when each of the states was asked for a contribution to the monument. Arizona said it could afford only a stone conveying gratitude to George Washington, and this started a trend. All fifty states have supplied messages in local stone; the newest is Alaska's, in solid jade.

The White House. It is impossible to ignore the fact that Washington is the seat of government as you walk around the District many of the buildings that house law, order and governance are open to the public. The most famous of them all is the White House. Work on the presidential residence began 200 years ago. The architect was Irish, the masons were Scottish and the troops which attacked it in 1814 were English. The first occupant,

Thomas Jefferson, called it 'big enough for two emperors, one pope and the grand lama'. A century later, President Taft felt it to be 'the loneliest place in the world'. Presumably he had not tried the public tour. The White House is only open for two hours a day and needs careful planning if you really want to see the State Dining Room. One free ticket per person is available from 8am at kiosks on the ellipse (15th St and Constitution Avenue NW), though queues start earlier. When you get to the front of the line you will get a ticket stamped with a tour time between 10am and noon, use the time in between ticket allotment and tour by having a breakfast at one of the nearby hotels to make up for the early start.

The Capitol. At the other end of Pennsylvania Avenue, the Capitol is Washington's tallest and most elegant building. Unlike the Palace of Westminster, the visitor can wander freely around the seat of Congress, beneath the huge dome which imposes on the Washington skyline and the world. To see a debate in the Senate or the House of Representatives, get an International Pass from the crypt — take your passport. Debates are conducted in surprisingly modest chambers, with Senators seated at school-like desks. Tours of the Capitol operate 9am-3.45pm daily; call 224 3121.

The Library of Congress. All but the keenest bibliophile might baulk at the idea of visiting a library while on holiday. But the Library of Congress (corner of 1st Street and Independence Avenue; 707 5000) is no ordinary lender of books. It is the largest on the planet, and a repository for published knowledge in all its forms — from baseball cards to computer games, it has catalogued 100 million items. It opens 8.30am-9.30pm from Monday to Friday, 8.30am-5pm on Saturdays, 1-5pm on Sundays. Guided tours take place at 1, 2 and 3pm daily, plus 10 and 11am from Monday to Friday. In the new facility, you can see the application for copyright of Gone with the Wind, Chuck Berry's sheet music for 'Sweet Little Sixteen' and an 1822 'Atlas of Marriage' showing the Sea of Doubt and the State of Agitation. The recently refurbished original building, the Jefferson, is a wonderfully elegant place.

Bureau of Engraving and Printing. You get no free samples on the tour here, where all dollar bills are made, but you can buy sheets of uncut $1 or $2 dollar bills in the shop afterwards.

The Federal Bureau of Investigation. On the tour of the FBI (E St NW between 9th and 10th Streets) you are told which areas of crime the Bureau are most concerned with, the methods of catching the crooks and a display of their ill-gotten gains. A small display cabinet shows samples of the most popular drugs in a rather-too-appetizing manner. You tour the forensic laboratories where DNA samples are matched and fibres examined. From a single human hair the scientists can determine gender, age, whether it was pulled or fell out — and what sort of drugs the owner has taken. The tour is especially popular with small children. Crowds are best avoided by arriving as close as possible to the 8.45am opening time.

Old Post Office. This curious building is run by the National Park Service, even though it is little more than a gigantic eating and shopping complex. It is on the corner of Pennsylvania Avenue and 12th Street (523 5691). Tower tours operate 9.45am to 5.45pm daily, providing a fine view from the belltower.

National Archive. Alex Haley did his research for 'Roots' in the National

Archives (Constitution Avenue between 7th and 9th Streets; 501-5000; open 10am to 5.30pm daily). Even if you don't have family connections to find you can see the Declaration of Independence, the Bill of Rights and the Constitution. The atmosphere in their cases is pure helium to protect the fragile paper. A 1297 version of the Magna Carta is included, to show where the idea for codifying nationhood began. It was give to the USA by one Ross Perot. The tapes of Nixon's Oval Office meetings, which proved his downfall in the Watergate scandal, are part of the National Archive and are now housed in a warehouse at Pickett St in the suburb of Alexandria. Visitors can take a free shuttle bus from the main Archive (or the Blue Metro to Van Dorn) to savour the undeleted expletives of a world leader in big trouble.

Ford's Theater. The vulnerability of presidents is brought into focus at Ford's Theater, where the American fashion for assassinating leaders. During a performance of *Our American Cousin* in 1865, John Wilkes Booth shot Abraham Lincoln, the president who had led the Union through the Civil War. The theatre itself, and the house across the street where Lincoln died, are open.

Lincoln Memorial. The monument to Abraham Lincoln's memory dominates the west end of the Mall. From the top of the steps of the Lincoln Memorial look down the Mall and see the Washington Memorial mirrored in the reflecting pool at dusk. Within the memorial is a monumental stautue of the assassinated president and the walls are covered with the texts of his two most famous speeches; his second inaugural address and the Gettysburg address.

Vietnam Veterans' Memorial. Close by is the long black granite wall bearing the names of the 58,175 people that died in America's longest war, Vietnam, close to the Lincoln Memorial. The victims are listed 'in the order they were taken from us' from 1959 to 1975. This tragic arc of stone is a chronological list of those who died — and the 1,300 still listed as missing — in the war in Indochina.

Arlington National Cemetery. West over the Potomac is the Arlington National Cemetery which is home to the war dead of American wars from the Revolution to Desert Storm. Something of America's skewed view of the world can be discerned from the huge headstone of a US ambassador to a Central American country, misspelt as 'Guatamala'. The cemetery is a big attraction, with Tourmobile trolleys rumbling through all day. Arlington is best visited in late afternoon, when the crowds have thinned out and the calm matches the serenity of the surroundings. The summit is Arlington House, the former home of Robert E. Lee who led the Confederate South to defeat against Abraham Lincoln's Union.

The grave of Pierre L'Enfant marks the best point for surveying the city planner's elegant creation. The centrepiece of this beautiful park is the flame burning above the remains of President Kennedy. In stark contrast, the grave of his brother Robert is a plain white cross in a nearby corner.

MUSEUMS AND GALLERIES

At the heart of Washington is a two-mile stretch of park from the Capitol to the Lincoln Memorial called the Mall. The first mile of the Mall, up to the Washington Monument, is lined with nine galleries belonging to the Smithsonian Institution. For information about special events call the Dial-a-Museum line 357-2020. Whatever you special interest is bound to have a gallery dedicated to it within the complex. The Castle used to be 'The Smithsonian' and house all the exhibits until the number of objects outgrew their home and the other galleries sprouted to house specialist collections. Now it is an orientation centre to help you decide which of the bits you want to visit.

You can stand right next to the Apollo XI command module, whilst the Spirit of St Louis hangs above your head at the National Air and Space Museum, 6th Street and Jefferson Drive (357 2700). This is easily the most popular museum in the capital, with some justification. Open 10am-5.30pm; free guided tours at 10.15am and 1pm.

Arrive on the half-hour at the National Museum of American History (14th St and Constitution Avenue; 357-2700; 10am-5.30pm daily) to be treated to the spectacle of the flag that inspired the anthem 'Star Spangled Banner' being revealed. Elsewhere in the collection you can see Dorothy's ruby slippers and an exhibition of the role of First Ladies in American life.

All the standard European and American great artists are represented at the National Gallery of Art, the 13th to 19th centuries are in the West Wing and 20th century plus special exhibitions are in the East Wing. Open 10am-5pm daily except Sundays (11am-6pm). Free tours at 11.30am and 1.30pm daily.

You can see the Hope diamond (biggest blue diamond in the world) and a 70-million-year-old dinosaur egg at the National Museum of Natural History. Still part of the Smithsonian, but a couple of blocks away at 8th and F St, is the National Museum of American Art which has a comprehensive collection ranging from early American art, through Singer Sargent to Hooper. Next door is the National Portrait Gallery: subjects are not allowed in until they've been dead for ten years, and so the place is an illistrated guide to American history. The other museums in the Mall area are the Hirshhorn (contemporary art and sculpture), Arts and Industries (made in America), African Art Museum, Sackler Gallery (Chinese art), Freer Gallery (Asian Art) and the Renwick Gallery (American Folk Art) all of which have excellent collections.

Away from the Mall and the Smithsonian there are many other museums. The National Museum of Women in the Arts (1250 New York Avenue; 783-5000), is ironically in a building that used to exclude women — an ex-masonic temple. It now houses a exhibition of women's role in art and has an excellent cafe. The museum opens at 10am daily (except Sundays when it opens at noon), and closes at 5pm daily.

You can tour the Pentagon, the world's biggest office building, by calling 695-1776. Guided tours, lasting an hour, commence every 30 minutes from 9.30am-3.30pm.

Entertainment

Music. Whatever kind of music you enjoy, Washington offers it. The Kennedy Center (800-444-1234) is the major serious culture venue and has an Opera House and Concert Hall with the usual classical output and there is often free music in open spaces. Wolf Trap Farm Park for the Performing Arts (Metro to West Falls Church or, in summer, shuttle bus from the Metro) has two venues; the summer one a 7,000 seater semi-open-air arena and in the winter a much smaller pre-revolutionary barn, both have varied programmes from Opera to Jazz. Big name rock stars would find it difficult to miss the District off any tour tickets are available from the TICKET place, Ticketron (432-0200) or Hecht's Department Store (12th and G St NW). Because of its large black population, DC has always been an important area for jazz and excellent jazz can be heard throughout the District. Most jazz at nightclubs is performed at the weekends; check the *Washington Post* for details. The Smithsonian has free jazz concerts throughout the summer for details ring 633-9176.

Theatre. The Kennedy Center has three theatres as well as the concert venues and half price tickets are available on the day of performance from TICKETplace (842-5387). Ford's Theater has been restored to its full nineteenth century glory, including the Presidential box where Lincoln was assassinated, and now has a full programme except during August and September. Performance art can also bee seen at the Arena Stage, National Theatre, Source Theatre, Hartke Theatre and the Woolly Mammoth Theatre Company (for 'off-beat and quirky productions'). Check *The Washington Post* for details.

Film. The American Film Institute (828-4000) is another part of the Kennedy Center and shows classic films, cult movies and hosts themed festivals. The Biograph (333-2696) shows small independent and foreign films. Mainstream movies are shown in Washington's many movie houses, such as the nine screens to choose from at Union Station (703-998-4AMC).

Nightlife. Georgetown is home to gracious buildings, trendy shops and DC's most interesting eating and nightlife. Bars and clubs can be found off and along Wisconsin Avenue and M St. If you want to see stand up comics go to the Comedy Cafe (638-JOKE); entrance is about $13.

SPORT

After a day traipsing round museums, sitting down to watch a ball game will be welcome relief. The Robert F Kennedy Memorial Stadium, on East Capitol Street between 19th and 20th Streets, is the home of the Washington Redskins. Call 547-9077 for tickets. The Washington Bullets (basketball) play their home games at the Capital Centre in Maryland (347-0200).

Participation. Even in the height of Washington's sticky summer you will see desk-bound civil servants jogging around the Mall at midday. At the weekends they can enjoy a vast array of different sports; check the weekend section of *The Washington Post* for details. To go hiking in and around the District phone the Sierra Club (547-2326), which organizes group rambles of varying arduousness. In the winter you can skate on the reflecting pool in between the Washington Monument and the Lincoln Memorial.

Parks and Zoos. The National Zoo has 5,000 animals, among them Hsing-Hsing and Ling-Ling — the giant pandas that were given to President Nixon. The Panda Café is a good place to sit and wait for the stars to make an appearance, which they usually do at mealtimes between 11am and 3pm. the Zoo is on block 3000 of Connecticut Avenue; the nearest Metro stations are Cleveland Park or Woodley Park Zoo. Gates open at 8am and shut at 8pm in the summer (6pm winter). Entrance is free.

Washington has many parks, Rock Creek Park, site of the zoo, is the largest one and runs right out to Maryland. There are many pleasant walks around the Tidal Basin, the area around the Jefferson Memorial, and the adjoining space around the Reflecting Pool. This area is especially nice in spring when the cherry blossom is out. Strolling along the Potomac from

Georgetown to the Tidal Basin is makes a pleasant outing. Starting from Fletcher's Boat House in Georgetown you can take a barge ride up the Chesapeake and Ohio Canal, or hire a bike and cycle along the tow path. For information about event's in DC's parks ring Dial-a-Park on 485-PARK.

SHOPPING

The main shopping area is in the streets surrounding the Metro Center, including the main department store of Hecht's. Turning obselete old buildings into malls seems to fashionable in Washington, and Union Station now houses many small shops and a food hall. One of the most interesting is Political Americana, selling psephological paraphenalia; it also has a branch in the Old Post Office. Across the street from Union Station on North Capitol between G and H Streets is the Government Printing Office. The bookstore inside has many interesting publications, not only about DC but the rest of the USA as well.

One of the most interesting shops in the Pentagon City shopping complex (across the Potomac, but served by its own Metro station) is the Museum Company, which sells products from hundreds of museum across the USA.

Kramerbooks and Afterwords (1517 Connecticut Avenue between Q St and Dupont Circle), is where Washingtonians will direct you if you ask for a good bookshop. Other bookshops and many small boutiques can be found in the Georgetown area.

Potomac Mills claims to be 'the worlds largest outlet mall' and is the place to go for discount designer clothes. To get there take exit 25 on I-95, 20 miles south of DC.

THE MEDIA

The film *All the President's Men* demonstrates the pride that the *Washington Post* takes in its investigative journalism. It is one of the nation's finest newspapers. The rival morning daily is the *Washington Times*, indirectly owned by the Unification Church. There is also a monthly magazine about the city and its environs called *The Washington.*

All the national public broadcasting corporations are based in Washington and, as you might expect in the seat of government, there is a higher proportion of news and current affairs stations than elsewhere. WAMU (88.5 FM) is one of the few American stations to broadcast radio drama (for five hours per week), complemented by current affirs, bluegrass and big band music. WETA (90.9 FM) plays lots of highbrow music. For news, try WTOP (1500 AM); for sport, WMAL (630 AM). WYCB (1340 AM) is a good example of an all-gospel station of the kind that proliferate south of Washington.

Crime and Safety

Every planned urban creation, from Brasilia to Milton Keynes, has its problems; Washington's most pressing is the highest murder rate of any city in the USA. Most of those who die by the gun are young black men, caught up in the vicious drug wars fought out within sight of Capitol Hill.

Danger is quantified geographically. Washington is divided into four quadrants. The highest crime rate is in the poor black neighbourhoods in the southeast quadrant; trouble can generally be avoided by sticking firmly to the northwestern portion. Be warned that pickpockets are active in the White House and Capitol Hill area. Those busy areas can become empty and spooky at nights. Police patrol on foot and in cars and at night tour the parkland immediately around the Mall instructing pedestrians to clear the area for their own safety. Georgetown is relatively safe (since the streets are thronged at night), though if you're in the northwest quadrant, don't go lower than Washington's Broadway, i.e. 14th St.

Ride-alongs. The workplace tour is common in America, but in the nation's capital you can enjoy a personal guided tour of the law-enforcement industry. Once you've done the White House and the Smithsonian, you can ride along with the law. The Ride-along scheme operated by Washington Metropolitan Police takes tourism to extremes. It isn't intended just for visiting law-enforcers or journalists: ordinary visitors are invited to join a Master Patrol Officer for an afternoon or evening, cruising the streets of the American capital as part of a day's work.

The Ride-along scheme is operated from all Washington Metropolitan Police stations. The First District, based at 415 Fourth Street SW (727-4655), is recommended since it covers a mix of official and residential, safe and dangerous areas. Most Ride-alongs take place in the evening, from 7 to 11pm. Participants should register two days in advance if possible. This involves filling in two forms. One is for personal details, including your reasons for wanting to participate ('interest in seeing another side of Washington' is sufficient). The other is a disclaimer waiving your rights (and those of your next-of-kin) to sue if you suffer harm. Pairs of visitors will be accommodated, but are placed in separate cars. For additional information on the scheme, contact the Community Relations Division of the Metropolitan Police Department, 300 Indiana Avenue NW, Washington DC 20001 (727-4283).

Drugs. Possession of any amount of marijuana is punishable by up to one year's imprisonment and a fine of $100-$1,000. The corner of U and 14th Streets is notorious as a drug dealing spot. Avoid it if you want to be sure not to be involved in one of the occasional shoot-outs here.

The area code for Washington is 202.

Information: visitor information is available from 1455 Pennsylvania Avenue, next to the Willard Hotel, one block east of the White House; call 789-7038. Open 9am-5pm from Monday to Saturday.

British Embassy: 3100 Massachusetts Avenue NW (462-1340)
American Express: 1150 Connecticut Avenue NW (457-1300)
Thomas Cook: 1624 I (eye) St NW (872-8470)
Post Office: Corner of North Capitol and Massachusetts Streets (523-2628). Open until midnight.
Western Union Telegrams: 800-325-6000 (toll-free).
Medical: George Washington University Medical Center, 901-23rd St NW (676-3211).
All Night Drug Store: People's, 1121 Vermont Avenue NW (628-0720) and 7 Dupont Circle (785-1466). Both open 24 hours a day.
Travelers' Aid: Union Station (347-0101) and at National Airport.

Visa Information: Department of State, 515 22nd St NW (632-1972).

Further Afield 61

From the tawdry glamour of Atlantic City to the country roads of West Virginia, there is more to the mid-Atlantic states than domed government buildings. The climate of Virginia, West Virginia, Maryland, New Jersey and Pennsylvania may be roughly similar to that of Washington, but the topography, people and culture vary considerably. So do the accents which change from the 'Noo Joisee' twang to the beginning of a southern drawl. Expect crisp colourful autumns, cold bitter winters, bright warm springs and hot humid summers.

These states are well served by public transport and an extensive road network. There are two main Amtrak routes through the region, plus an extensive network of bus routes, although if you want to get to the more remote mountain areas a car is essential. It is difficult to avoid I-95, the primary north-south route linking New York, Philadephia, Baltimore, Washington, Richmond, and on south to the Carolinas. If you have time, however, take an alternative route such as US 13 through Delaware which eventually leads to US 1 along the coast, or US 209 and State Highway 611 along the Delaware River in Pennsylvania.

MARYLAND

With the rejuvenation of Baltimore as its focus, Maryland has become a more interesting state for visitors. It retains much of its colonial flavour, particularly in Annapolis and on the eastern shore, and its scenery from Chesapeake Bay to the hills and mountains of west Maryland is equal to far better-known areas of the USA. For something completely different visit Barry Parzow's 'Popcorn Circus' in Springfield, where you can choose from over 100 flavours of popcorn.

Once away from Baltimore and the suburbs surrounding Washington (Prince George and Montgomery Counties) the pace of life slows down, the sense of history is strong and you may find yourself spending more time in Maryland than you had planned. Of all the mid-Atlantic states this is the one where it worth getting off the super highways and turnpikes to discover an older but not ossified America.

Maryland represents an interesting cross-section of American life. This is best exemplified in Baltimore, which has the usual middle class, but also strong blue collar sections, traditional Polish areas, poor whites and blacks, a famous university and an important Catholic hertiage. In the rural areas in the extreme east and west of the state, you find an authentic quiet rural hospitality, rather than the more flamboyant and famous southern one.

Annapolis is well worth a visit. It was the first peacetime captial of the United States and has many beautiful colonial buildings, including the US Naval College. Only if you are interested in industrial archaeology and decaying urban landscapes should you take US 1 along the coast.

BALTIMORE

At the end of 1992, it was announced that Baltimore and Washington would henceforth be regarded as a single conurbation, so closely have they merged. Yet Baltimore is pleasingly different from its more celebrated neighbour, and is well worth a day of your time.

Baltimore had a chip on its civic shoulder for years. Compared with Washington, 40 miles south, it has a modest collection of sites. Like many American cities, Baltimore has seen its downtown area deteriorate over the years, with big stores moving out to suburban locations on the Beltway — the freeway which rings the city.

It prides itself on its Irish Catholic roots. It was founded by Charles Carroll, who left his native Ireland because of persecution from the British and moved to America. He established Baltimore — named after a small town in western Ireland - and built the first Catholic cathedral in the USA there. While downtown has some tall and impressive buildings, it will never compete against the likes of New York and Chicago. But that doesn't stop Baltimore boasting about its altitudinal claim to fame, the world's tallest pentagonal building.

The cultural ambitions of Baltimore are evident. Every street bench is marked READING ZONE and subtitled Baltimore: the City that Reads. Baltimore has a number of colleges and universities, the most famous of which is Johns Hopkins, just on the outskirts of downtown, with opportunities to find bars and good conversation.

Arrival and Departure. *Air:* Baltimore-Washington International is ten miles southwest of downtown. The airport has a rail station, on the main line between Washington and New York. It is served by Amtrak expresses from Baltimore's Penn station (15 minutes, $6), and by MARC commuter trains — slower but more frequent and cheaper ($2.75) to Penn Station and to Camden Yards, southwest of the city centre. The airport station is a couple of miles away from the airport itself, linked by a free Amtrak Shuttle bus. This departs from the Ground Transportation point at the middle of the arc which constitutes the airport concourse.

Train: Penn Station is a mile north of downtown, just beyond the freeway between St Charles and St Paul's Streets. This elegant terminal opened in 1911, and many of the original features — such as the Classical marble columns, the wrought iron balcony and Beaux Arts stained glass roof — have survived.

The station is on the East Coast main line between Boston and Miami, with frequent services to Washington (35 minutes) and to New York (nearly 3 hours) via Philadelphia (75 minutes).

Bus: the Greyhound terminal is central, on Fayette at the corner of Park Avenue. There are eight daily services to New York (4 hours) and Philadelphia (2 hours), and frequent departures to Washington (1 hour).

Boat: express catamarans link Baltimore with other ports on the Bay — Annapolis, Rock Hall and St Michaels. Call 1-800-47-FERRY for fares and schedules. Services do not operate between December and March.

Getting Around. The Mass Transit Administration (MTA) runs the bus services, plus the Metro and the Light Rail (tram), both of which have one line each. Call 539-5000 for schedules. The basic fare is $1.10, covering travel on one vehicle within one zone. Travel in all five zones costs $1.95, and transfers (valid from buses, Light Rail and Metro to any form of transport). Exact fares are required. You can save a little money and a lot of trouble by buying a pack of ten MTA tokens for $10.50. Zone and transfer charges must be paid for separately.

The Water Taxi service shuttles between ten stops in the Inner Harbor. You can get on and off as much as you wish in one day for a fare of $3.25. Call 1-800-658-8947 for information.

To rent a bike, try Light Street Cycles (685 2234), 1015 Light St in Federal Hill — two blocks south of the Inner Harbor.

Accommodation. Mount Vernon is the attractive area to the north of the city centre, and a pleasant place to stay. The old YMCA on Franklin between Cathedral and St Charles has been converted into a Comfort Inn. Otherwise pick one of the bunch of three close together in the west of the city centre, such as the Ramada at 8 N Howard St. As well as state sales tax of 5%, the city imposes a levy of 7%.

Eating and Drinking. Baltimore has a long and fine tradition of seafood and quaint bars. Crab eating in the Chesapeake Bay area (in any non-posh restaurant) is a memorable experience. Explore the downtown restaurants, especialy along Charles St and around the Inner Harbor. The huge indoor Lexington Market (Lexington and Eutaw) offers everything from seafood to pizza to German sausages.

Little Italy, just east of the Inner Harbor — on Albemarle and South High Streets — is full of excellent, good-value Italian restaurants. Vaccaro's Pastry on the corner of Stiles and Albemarle is a brilliant place to round off an evening. For a bit more variety, try the Mount Vernon area; Charles St between Madison and Read Streets has everything from Afghani onwards.

Exploring. Baltimore has an eclectic collection of attractions, with two excellent museums devoted to railways and baseball respectively. In the west of the city, it is impossible to drive along Pratt St and not be aware of the B&O Railroad Museum, due to the large number of huge locomotives parked outside. The Baltimore and Ohio Railroad ran the first passenger service from this location in 1830, and went on to become one of America's great railway companies.

Outside, the collection of rolling stock includes the baggage car that carried Dwight D. Eisenhower's coffin to his resting place in 1969, and one of the locomotives ordered by Stalin in 1946 but not delivered because of the Cold War; instead, they were sold to railroad companies in the eastern USA and hauled commuters around Maryland rather than coal around the Crimea.

This was not just America's first railroad, it was the site of the world's first long-distance telecommunication. In 1844, Samuel Morse persuaded the railroad company to help him experiment with a telegraph link between Baltimore and Washington. A cable was laid along the route of the railway, and he sent the first message — an Old Testament quotation, 'What has God wrought?' — using his own code. This was an extraordinary advance, and today's digital communication technology is merely an elaboration on Morse's ideas.

The Museum opens 10am-5pm daily, admission $5.

A few blocks east, at 216 Emory St just south of Pratt (and behind the Far Pavilion restaurant), the Babe Ruth House & Museum is a tribute to the man named Greatest Player Ever by the Baseball Hall of Fame. George Herman Ruth was born here, close to the Orieles stadium, on 6 February 1895 and began playing for the Baltimore Orieles aged 16 — hence the nickname 'Babe'. He became a brilliant striker, and helped his team to great success. The museum opens daily from 10am until 5pm (7pm on match days). This area has some lovely cottages which have survived the redevelopment.

The waterfront has been sensitively renovated: the Inner Harbor is perhaps the finest example of urban renewal in America. It has many small shops and restaurants, whilst the first ship in the US Navy *US Frigate Constellation*, floats on the water. Apart from eyesores like the nearby World Trade Center ('tallest pentagonal building in the world'), it is a pleasant place to wander. The National Aquarium is actually in private hands (with a steep admission charge of $11.50), but includes interesting environmental exhibits. It is on pier 3, and opens daily except Tuesday from 10am to 5pm (until 8pm on Thursdays). Call 481-6000 for further details.

The best view in Baltimore is from the Top of the World (Trade Center), at 401 East Pratt St (410-837-4515). It opens at 10am (noon on Sundays) until 5pm, and admission is a couple of dollars.

Entertainment. There are two good free sources of event listings: *CityPaper* and *Alive!*, both of which are free from bars, restaurants and cinemas and have comprehensive arts listings. The music scene in Baltimore is particularly lively, with lots of good local bands.

The city has two good formal venues in the Morris Mechanic Theater and Lyric Opera House. The fine Peabody Institute of Music often has excellent music recitals which are free.

Sport. The Baltimore Orioles were once perennial winners of the World Series in baseball, but their days of glory have gone. They play at the new Inner Harbor Stadium (301 347 2010). Johns Hopkins University boasts one of the best lacrosse teams in the country. Pimlico Race Track, on the outskirts of the city, is one of the top race courses in the USA. The highlight of the racing calendar is at the end of the city-wide Preakness Festival in mid-May.

Help and Information. The Visitors Center is at the corner of Pratt and Howard Streets, five blocks west of the Inner Harbor. It looks closed even when it is open, which is between 9am and 5.30pm daily.

DELAWARE

Some claim that Delaware is almost feudal, for it is dominated by the DuPont Corporation, manufacturers of chemicals. The northern part of the state is havily industrialized, especially around Wilmington. As you travel south and then east to the beaches, the state becomes increasingly typical of rural,small-town America, not particularly scenic or quaint but leisurely and quiet. Sometimes, when you drive through one of these small towns, you will think you are in a 1930s Hollywood movie set.

The other great industry in Delaware is finance; rather like offshore tax havens, this small state has tailored its commerce laws to make it attractive for companies to place their legal headquarters there.

Delaware is also famous for its locally raised chickens and for its crab dishes. But the main attraction is not the food but the beaches, despite some unappealing names such as Slaughter Beach, Broadkill Beach, Dewey Beach and Rehoboth Beach. These are more 'social' than scenic beaches, especially the latter two which get crowds coming up from Maryland and Washington.

The best museum, and a jolly good one too, is six miles from Wilmington. The Henry Francis du Pont Winterthur Museum, known simply as Winterthur, is in the town of Winterthur. It is a treasure of American folk decorative art from colonial times, including a splendid collection of Pennsylvania Dutch art. There is an admission fee and reservations are necessary for guided tours.

From the port of Lewes, on Highway 1 in the east of Delaware, you can get a ferry across the mouth of Delaware Bay to Cape May; call 1-800-64-FERRY for fares and schedules. This provides a useful short cut to New Jersey.

NEW JERSEY

'The Garden State' has seen better days. Although its population density is the highest of any state (at over 1,000 per square mile), its quality of life leaves a great deal to be desired. Its eastern beaches used to boast genteel and elegant resorts, stretching from Asbury Park to Cape May. Its cities and towns were once safe and solid; now they are full of slums and political corruption. The opening of gambling casinos in Atlantic City was just another nail in the state's coffers. The northern part of the state, within a 75-mile radius of New York City, has adopted all the bad habits of the metropolis without displaying any of its redeeming culture and glamour. Driving through Elizabeth or Newark is like being heaved into the middle of a Bosch painting or a post World War III battlescape. Newark is one of the most dangerous cities in the US; crime throughout the state is serious and increases as you near New York City.

The only genuinely scenic part of New Jersey is the Delaware Water Gap in the northwest corner of the state. The closer you get to Manhattan the more congested and ugly New Jersey becomes. Every road and bridge seems to demand a toll, so carry plenty of quarters. If you must drive through this area, avoid rush hours at all costs. New Jersey has become just a state to pass through as speedily as possible.

Atlantic City. The east coast version of Las Vegas actually does more business than its rival gambling haven. Although not as glamorous as Las Vegas, the wheels at Atlantic City are honest and there's alot of action. The locals hate the gambling for the crime it has brought, but they don't complain about the increased employment and revenue. Apart from the gambling, Atlantic City is also the entertainment centre in the area, with big-name stars and the Miss America Pageant every September. The ocean boardwalk, colour picture postcard, Ferris wheel and amusement pier all made their debut in Atlantic City. Two thousand buses a day arrive from all over the Northeast, so getting to America's gambling mecca is easy.

PENNSYLVANIA

Pennsylvania is nearly as large as England. There are three main areas within this gigantic state: Philadelphia and environs with its financial and historical interests, the middle through which run the Allegheny Mountains dotted with vacation resorts, and the industrial coal-mining west around Pittsburgh. Until recently Pennsylvania was the largest steel producer in the world and served as the gateway to the industrialized Midwest (Ohio, Michigan and Indiana). While Pittsburgh has recently enjoyed something of an urban rebirth, unemployment is rampant in the steel regions of western Pennsylvania. Some may think that the most interesting thing about Pittsburgh is that is virtually the only 'burgh' in the US to retain the 'h', which it did by local legislation in 1894.

PHILADELPHIA

W C Fields mocks Philadelphia from beyond the grave. His tombstone is inscribed 'All in all, I'd rather be in Philadelphia', and this jibe at America's first capital has perpetuated the myth that the city is dull and its citizens duller. Philadelphia is the most historic city in the USA (though people from Washington DC, Boston and Santa Fe might dispute this. The Declaration of Independence was signed and the Constitution was drawn up here, and only insistence fom the southern states that Philadelphia was too far north prevented it continuing as capital.

Philadelphia today is as diverse a city as you will find in the USA. It still has a wealthy population, most of whom live in exclusive suburbs near the city, plus numerous ethnic communities. The many universities and art colleges add a bohemian atmosphere to what has always been considered a strait-laced city. The University of Philadelphia's campus is the focus for small boutiques and quaint restaurants.

Arrival and Departure. Air: Philadelphia International Airport (PHL) is seven miles/11km southwest of the city centre. It is divided into five terminals. International flights on most foreign airlines use terminal A.

The easiest link with the city centre is on the regular train service, at least half-hourly from 6am to 11pm. Each terminal has its own station (although C and D share one) — four stations within half a mile, the densest concentration on any line in the world, but convenient if you have luggage and prefer not to walk too far.

Train: Philadelphia's main rail station is 30th St, just across the river about a mile west of City Hall which marks the centre of Philadelphia, linked by suburban trains and the subway system. It is a lavish Classical temple, and makes a splendid introduction to the city. The station is on the East Coast main line between Boston and Miami, with frequent southbound services to Baltimore (75 minutes) and Washington (2 hours). Northbound services to New York take 90 minutes.

Bus: the Greyhound terminal is central, on Filbert St between 10th and 11th Streets. There are eight daily services to Baltimore (2 hours), and frequent departures to New York and Washington.

Getting Around. The first point to note is that unlike every other US city, Philadelphia does not call its middle 'downtown'. Instead, it calls it just City Center.

The Southeastern Pennsylvania Transportation Authority (SEPTA) runs buses, street cars and the subway system. Philadelphia's subway system is mostly as grotty as New York's, but it will take you to most of the major sites downtown. The subways are integrated with a good bus system. Call SEPTA on 574-7800 for transport information. The flat fare is $1.50. Easily the best plan for visitors is to buy the DayPass, valid for a full 24 hours and allowing unlimited travel within the city plus a one-way ride to or from the airport.

Accommodation. Low-cost accommodation is in short supply. the best located budget option is the Bank Street Hostel at 32 S Bank St (215-922-0222). The Youth Hostel is the 19th century Chamounix Mansion at West Fairmont Park (215-878-3676) and is very popular; try to book ahead between 4.30pm and 8pm. For bed and breakfast call 688-1633.

Eating and Drinking. You can find the entire range of restaurants in Philadelphia, but the one thing you should not miss is a cheese steak at Pat's King of Steaks stall (625-9368) in Reading Terminal Market, on 12th St between Filbert and Arch Streets (now somewhat overshadowed by the new Pennsylvania Convention Center). Pat Olivieri is something of a local celebrity, and his stall has pictures of him with Humphrey Bogart and Abbott & Costello (Pat is not a young man). The cheese steaks themselves are sandwiches stuffed with beef and cheese; vegetarians are catered for with 'vegi steaks', consisting of cheese, mushroom and peppers. Be sure to eat at some of the Jewish delicatessens; the delis here hare just as good as the more famous ones in New York City. And don't leave without trying a hoagie, a sandwich filled with Italian salami, peepers, onions, provolone cheese and olive oil; Philadelphia is there home, and specifically Antionette Ianelli's place. The cheap and trendy place at night is Jim's Steaks (corner of South and 6th Streets), for excellent steak sandwiches and beer.

Chinatown is on 10th St between Filbert and Race Streets; the Vietnamese places in this area are good value. The chic area is South St between 2nd and 7th St, i.e. five blocks south of the Independence Historical Park.

Exploring. The look of the city has changed dramatically in the last ten years. Prior to 1985 no building in Philadelphia could be higher than the statue of William Penn on top of the City Hall. (Tours to the top of City Hall take place at 12.30pm from Monday to Friday.) Now it looks uncomfortably like many other US cities, except in the area around the Independence Historical Park. This claims to be 'America's most historic square mile'. It contains the Liberty Bell and Independence Hall are two of the many buildings in the park. The National Park Visitor Centre on the corner of 3rd and Chestnut St has a good introductory film, called *Independence*, directed by John Huston. The park buildings open 9am-5pm daily, and an early start is recommended. Call 215-597-8974 for further details.

Other attractions include the Philadelphia Museum of Art, the Rodin Museum, the US Mint and the Betsy Ross House where the first Stars and Stripes was sewn together.

Entertainment. The city is home to the excellent Philadelphia Orchestra and there are many venues for classical, jazz and pop music. Check the arts and entertainment pages of the *Philadelphia Inquirer* for information about what's on.

Shopping. The Reading Terminal Market is fascinating. It opens 8am-6pm daily except Sunday, but ideally you should see it on a day between Wednesday and Saturday, when the Amish come in from Lancaster County to sell their produce.

More esoteric shops are located on South St between 2nd and 7th Streets. Condom Kingdom shows what a little latex and a lot of imagination can do, while Tower Books opens 9am-midnight every day.

Help and Information. The Convention and Visitors' Bureau (1525 John F Kennedy Blvd 636-1666) will kit you out with good maps and guides.

The Interior. Go to Lancaster County, about 80 miles inland from Philadelphia, to see the Amish farmers in their own environment. The Amish, like the Mennonites (mentioned in the chapter on Ontario), have clung to their strict traditional heritage ever since they fled religious persecution in Germany in the early nineteenth century. They are often referred to has the Pennsylvania Dutch, which is a corruption of 'Deutsch'. They dress all in black, drive horse and buggies (which they refuse to defile with the fluorescent sticker required by law for slow-moving vehicles) and use traditional farming methods, all of which is very photogenic. Be sensitive,however, when taking photographs as the Amish don't approve of graven images.

They are a wealthy people and their organic farming newspaper is considered to among the best in the world. These early ecologists have kept this part of the country one of the most fertile and productive in the world. Try to sample their produce and Pennsylvania Dutch cooking generally. The food tends to be a bit heavy in the German style (e.g. dumplings and stews), but interesting and fairly inexpensive. Unfortunately the area fills with tourists in search of this anachronistic community, and so prices have been driven up.

Hershey is not only a factory town for America's largest chocolate manufacturer but a huge sweet theme park. You can drive down 'Chocolate Avenue' or stroll down 'Cocoa Avenue' that are lit by street lights in the shape candy kisses. Factory visits are not possible but Chocolate World is just like stepping onto the set of *Willie Wonka and the Chocolate Factory* as a gliding car with its own video monitor takes you on a re-enactment of the manufacturing process from the cocoa bean to Hershey Bar. Things reach fever pitch in February when the Great American Chocolate Festival takes place.

Gettysburg, in the south of the state, has exceptionally pretty rolling countryside and it is hard to believe that more people died here than in any other battle fought in the USA before or since. So many wounded and dead lay untended on the surrounding fields that the state Governor was moved to buy land for a national cemetery — it was at the dedication ceremony four months later that President Lincoln stood up to say the few appropriate words that we know as the Gettysburg Address. An impressive museum and visitors centre has been built that explains the importance of this battle and the background of the Civil War. This can be followed by a 20-mile self-drive tour around the whole site but be warned that the average speed you can make is 5mph is you're lucky, due to the erratic stopping and starting of other sightseers.

VIRGINIA

Virginia is in many ways the home state of America. Britain's colonial capital was here, the first Thankgiving was eaten here, the Revolutionary and Civil wars were fought here and eight presidents were born here. (Arkansas, home of Bill Clinton, has some catching up to do.) The countryside varies from the comfortable Washington hinterlands, to remote mountains and peaceful coast.

Around Washington. George Washington and Robert E Lee both called Alexandria home. Today it a pretty town with cobbled streets, bustling little shops and some interesting museums. It is easily reached from Washington by taking the Yellow Metro to King Street station and best avoided on Mondays when many of the attractions are shut.

Further down the Potomac is Washington's estate Mount Vernon. One of the pleasantest ways of getting there is by boat; *Spirit of Mount Vernon* leaves Pier 4 at 6th and Water Streets SW (554-8000) during the summer months. Woodlawn Plantation lies next to Mount Vernon. It was originally part of the estate but was given by Washington to his adopted daughter as a wedding present, and can visited as part of a block ticket as Mount Vernon.

Fredricksburg lies 50 miles down the I-95 from Washington. It is a lovely little town with a lively Revolutionary past that has been well preserved. A block ticket (the Americans like block tickets) will get you into seven properties around the town, these can be bought from the Visitors Centre (800-678-4748) which is also the place to obtain a free parking pass.

Richmond and the Historic Triangle. The Pilgrim fathers may have landed at Plymouth but it is along the James River that you can see the glories of pre-revolutionary America. The banks of the James River are dotted with many plantations and their grand houses are open to the public. To visit all of them would be like overdosing on National Trust properties in Britain, so chose one or two that appeal. Carters Grove is included in the price of a Patriots Pass to Williamsburg and is a typical example.

At the head of the James River creek is Richmond, site of the first Thanksgiving, capital of Virginia since 1780 and capital of the Confedercy for four years during the Civil War, makes a good base to see the many Civil War sites in the area. There are about twelve trains a day from Washington. A good place to start is the Metro Richmond Visitors Center (804-358-5511). It has an excellent orientation video and can provide maps, tour and accomodation information. Even if you are totally indifferent to the Civil War a visit to the Museum of the Confederacy is a must: it puts into context much of what you will see and hear as you tour the state. Whilst on the Civil War trail, Virginia State Capitol is the second oldest working Capitol in the United States and was the White House of the Confederacy.

A welcome break from history can be had at the Philip Morris Manufacturing Center, where much of the tobacco for which Virginia is famous is turned into cigarettes. After your tour you will be offered a pack of the product.

Williamsburg was the colonial capital between 1690 and 1780. It was purely a seat of government and had no industry to support it, so when the capital moved to Richmond its fortunes foundered and all that remained of its former glory was the College of William and Mary. Then in the 1920s the rector of the Parish Church, Dr W A R Goodwin appreciated the historical significance of the town and convinced John D Rockefeller of its importance. Rockefeller backed his conviction with money and set about buying up and restoring the settlement. The whole site is now a giant historical theme park, you can talk to people pretending to be pre-revolutionary Americans in buildings that have been lovingly reconstrcted from drawings found in the Bodleian library in Oxford. Tickets are available from the Visitor Center (804-220-7645), choose between a basic ticket that lets you see most things for $21, a Royal Governor's Pass for $24.50 or a Patriot's Pass that lasts for a year and gets you into building imaginable for $28. Having bought your ticket you board a bus that takes you to the town. You then set off walking around the site. It is possible to walk round Williamsburg and soak up the atmosphere without paying; you can go into the restored shops and taverns for nothing, and all you miss is going into the houses and seeing the craftspeople at work.

Jamestown was the first permanant English speaking colony in the New World and colonial capital until mosquitoes finally beat the inhabitants inland to Williamsburg. After government had left Jamestown so did most of the inhabitants and it ceased to be even a hamlet. Today you can Jamestown is managed by the National Park Service. You pay $5 entry fee then take a circular bus tour around the swampy island site, seeing archeological remains of the orginal town and recontructions of the ships that bought the first settlers here in 1607.

Yorktown is the third part of the historic triangle and site of the last big battle of the American Revolution. The Colonial Parkway runs between Jamestown and Yorktown, passing by Williamsburg on the way. You can slip from one visitor center to the next having everything explained to you in more detail than you probably want. Indeed you can buy a combination ticket to include Jamestown and Yorktown.

Mountains. Heading west from Richmond you arrive at Charlottesville, hometown to three presidents: Thomas Jefferson, James Madison and James Monroe. It is a pleasant town dominated by its university. In the Blue Ridge foothills outside the town is one of America's most famous buildings: it appears on the back of the nickel and the $5 note. It is Monticello, home of Thomas Jefferson. On the the road up to Monticello is the Mitchie Tavern which has been serving food since 1784. Today you eat as much Southern Fried Chicken as you can for $8.95 — when you've ploughed your way through a full plate, a waitress will appear and ask 'can I get you anything else, white meat, dark meat, with or without the wing' and you can stuff yourself until you're sick.

Whilst on the trail of past presidential landmarks make a visit to Staunton, birthplace of Woodrow Wilson. A tour around his birthplace will make a welcome change from Revolutionary and Civil War history, as the roots of America's ascendancy as the world's economic powerhouse is charted. Staunton itself is everything you ever thought a small American town would be — wooden buildings, a main street, cinema — and somehow it has escaped the blight of out-of-town shopping malls and the subsequent downtown desertion that has hit so many American towns.

West of the Blue Ridge, the Allegheny mountains start in earnest and some of the most quiet beautiful countryside in Virginia can be found. At Warm Springs you can wallow in pools that bubble out of the ground at 99.6°F. Included in the cost is the hire of a Victorian style swimming costume. The area has lots of walking, horse riding and trout fishing opportunities.

The Blue Ridge Parkway and the Skyline Drive both hug the ridges of the first range of the Appalachians. The speed limit is 35 mph and so following either of them far would take forever and test your patience to the limit. The Shenandoah valley snakes for 200 miles beside the mountains. It was here that many Civil War battles took place, and the New Market Battlefield Museum charts the history of American wars from the Revolution right the way through to Desert Storm (pride of place is given to Stormin' Norman's battle fatigues). There are also many caverns in the area; they all have stunning features made by centuries of dripping water and a visit to one of them is well worthwhile.

The pines may be lonesome in the Blue Ridge Mountains of Virginia but the many deciduous trees make all the states mountains a fine place to see autumn leaf colours. Fall reaches its peak on October 15th in this neck of the woods, a few weeks after the much trumpeted and crowded foliage season of New England.

Coast. The Delmarva peninsular is a neck of land between Chesapeake Bay and Delaware bay that is divided between three states — DELaware, MARyland and VirginiA; hence the name. The lower Virginian section has small and pretty towns, excellent seafood and is good cycling terrain. The world's largest tunnel-bridge complex traverses the 176 miles between Cape Charles and Norfolk. You can stop halfway across at the Sea Gull Cafe for a snack and to take in the view.

Norfolk is home to much of America's navy and to one its greatest art collections. Walter P Chrysler donated his collection to the city. It ranges from Renoir through to Rauschenburg taking in Tiffany on the way. Down the coast from Norfolk is Virginia Beach where Virginians come for their sand and candyfloss holidays.

WEST VIRGINIA

There haven't been many tourists in West Virginia since people came from far and wide to see John Brown hanged in 1859. More's the pity, because if a tourist really wants to see traditional America, West Virginia is the place to go. The people are conservative in the best sense of the word: valuing family tradition, love of the land, sense of community, yet still politically liberal. With its mountains and coal mines, there is a resemblance to Wales, although the number of illegal whisky stills might be more remminiscent of Ireland.

Harper's Ferry in the northeastern corner of West Virginia, where the Potomac meets the Shenandoah, was the site of National Armoury in the years that led up to the Civil War. John Brown led a raid on the town in 1859 to try to incite slave uprisings. He failed but 18 months later the Civil War begain in earnest. Because of its industry, Harper's Ferry was caught in the tussle and never recovered. Today it has been restored and is run by the National Park Service. It is an incredibly beautiful site and the roots of the factory mass production as well as the Civil War are well explained.

The highway system is good, but try to spend as much time as possible on the back roads. Drive or hitch through the mountains (West Virginia's popular name is 'The Mountain State') armed with a good state map; the road numbering on the ground bears no resemblance to out of state maps and after a 200-mile detour finding yourself on 'Troublesome Mountain Road' will seem apt. Accommodation and dining are thin on the ground. Try to ring ahead and book your evening's bed. Once you've found somewhere to sleep and eat, chances are that it will be good, plain and reasonably priced. All in all the scenery is beautiful, the people austere but compassionate, and the state an undiscovered gem.

The Great Outdoors

Densely populated and heavily industrialized as the Northeast is, there are plenty of wide open spaces in the Allegheny and Appalachian Mountains which sweep parallel to the coast, rising to nearly 6,000 ft in south-west Virginia. Furthermore they are a good place to escape the city heat and humidity.

Just an hour's drive west of Washington DC is Front Royal, the entrance to Shenandoah National Park and the Blue Ridge Mountains. There are excellent views and good camping facilities throughout these mountain areas which extend along the West Virginia border and beyond to North Carolina and Tennessee.

The more easily accessible the hills and resorts from New York, the more expensive they will be. For example the scenic Pocono Mountains of eastern Pennsylvania, whose deciduous forests are especially attractive in the autumn, are almost prohibitively expensive to stay in unless you have camping equipment. Accommodation is most expensive along the coast, and in mountain resorts. Many state and national parks have various types of camping and cabin facilities.

Ocean fishing and swimming are popular throughout the coastal areas. Assateague Island in Maryland, south of Ocean City, is a dramatic and beautiful strip of land where there are wild ponies and ample opportunities for beach exploration and fishing. Primitive camping facilities only.

All national parks have information booths which will advise on camping, hiking, picknicking, swimming etc. Just as a short drive will take you from Manchester or Newcastle into beautiful countryside, so it is worthwhile getting past the suburbs of Baltimore and Philadelphia to find rolling countryside, horse farms and gardens.

Atlanta and the Southeast

Georgia   **North Carolina**   **South Carolina**

Some of the more attractive and historic candidates for host city for the 1996 Olympic Games were startled and dismayed when Atlanta was selected. Nine-tenths of the capital of Georgia was destroyed when General Sherman burnt it to the ground for the Union cause during the Civil War. Like the rest of the South, it suffered neglect after the defeat of the Confederates, and was for decades regarded as just another sleepy southern backwater.

Its location, astride several important lines of communication, made it stand out from the rest of the crowd, and since World War II it has grown to resemble a tough northern business centre transplanted to the south. When the State Governor became US President in 1976, suddenly Georgia was on the mental map of the world. Downtown development has produced a towering skyline of concrete and reflective glass. Complexes like the Peachtree Convention Center, with its glass-enclosed overhead walkways, and the massive Atlanta Underground shopping and eating development, have brought the American dream of a 100% air conditioned environment a step closer. Given the heavy climate of Atlanta, this is no bad thing.

Outside Atlanta itself, the three states in the region are thoroughly charming and historic, especially near the coast. Savannah in Georgia vies with Charleston in South Carolina for title of prettiest-and-most-traditional East Coast port. Hilton Head Island is another concept altogether, a baffling 'holiday island' where suburban American values are imposed upon a resort.

Inland, whether you head for Jimmy Carter's home town of Plains or the university city of Athens, a combination of Southern hospitality and a certain economic dynamism is sure to make a visit interesting.

THE LOCALS

Atlanta, says the *Financial Times*, 'is run by a cosy alliance of black politicians and white businessmen'. This highlights two truths about the city: first, that black people have long been in the majority, and secondly that most of the money which has developed Atlanta has come from white financiers. Yet the statement conceals another truth: that Atlanta has the wealthiest concentration of black people of any American city. The civil rights movement which championed the cause of black people was driven from Atlanta, birthplace of Dr Martin Luther King Jr.

Only 50 miles north of Atlanta, however, is Forsyth County, long the domain of redneck racists. Black visitors who feel comfortable in Atlanta may not feel so welcome elsewhere in the region.

CLIMATE

With no sea breezes to alleviate the humidity, and plenty of steel and concrete to absorb and then expunge the heat, Atlanta is an often oppressive place to be. Try to visit in early spring or late autumn; winter can be distinctly chilly.

Arrival and Departure. Air: 'When you die and go to heaven', cynics remark, 'you have to change planes in Atlanta'. Hartsfield airport, ten miles south, made its name as an airport with quick and easy connections. Several times a day, waves of Delta aircraft swoop in, refuel and flock out again, offering connection times of as little as 30 minutes despite the size of the airport. Therefore if you want to fly Delta from Miami to Salt Lake City or from New York to New Orleans, it's fairly certain that you'll have to change planes in Atlanta.

Several massive piers are linked with each other and with the main terminal by the airport's own underground railway and walkways. The terminal itself — where baggage is collected — has its own station on Atlanta's subway system, making Hartsfield supremely accessible from the city. Trains run every ten minutes during the day and take just 15 minutes to downtown.

For international air tickets, try Council Travel (12 Park Place South, 577-1678).

Bus: The Greyhound bus terminal (522-6300) at 81 International Boulevard NW (one block from the Peachtree Center) is, like the airport, a hub for transport in the south.

Train: Atlanta is on the main line between New York/Washington and Mobile/New Orleans. The *Crescent* from New York to New Orleans and the *Gulf Breeze* to Mobile (one and the same train as far as Birmingham

Alabama) operates daily in each direction, calling at Atlanta in the morning going south and in the evening heading north. The journey to New Orleans takes 11 hours, to New York 19 hours.

The Amtrak station is at Brookwood, three miles north of downtown at 1688 Peachtree St NW. It is linked by bus 23 to Arts Center station on the MARTA network.

Driving: As may be expected in a city which derives a great deal of its income from convention visitors, there is plenty of choice in car rental. Atlanta Rent-a-Car (763-1160) at 3185 Camp Creek Parkway, three miles from the airport, is one of the best value companies. Motoring around Atlanta is made confusing by the 26 roads and streets named Peachtree (after Georgia's leading fruit crop). The main Peachtree St is a major north-south artery, along with Spring St and Piedmont Avenue. Ponce de Leon and North Avenues are the primary east-west thoroughfares. To add confusion, downtown Atlanta is a jumble of plazas and streets which meet at odd angles and are regulated by a convoluted one-way system. Given the cheap and efficient public transport, a car is an unnecessary encumbrance.

Getting Around. MARTA is an efficient and supremely straightforward underground railway. It has two lines, one running north-south, the other east-west. They cross at Five Points in downtown Atlanta. Each station has a name and code, e.g. Arts Center N5 is five stops north of the hub.

The railway is supplemented by a network of buses. Every bus route begins at one of the 27 rail stations, so having taken a train to the nearest station you can reach your final destination by bus. The MARTA system runs daily from 5.30am to 12.30am.

The flat fare for both buses and trains is $1.25, for which you need the correct change or a token; you get a free transfer if you pick up a ticket when you pay your fare. The TransCard costs $25 for a week (Monday-Sunday), with a Friday-to-Sunday option ($7) or just the weekend ($5). With efficient security and camera surveillance in every station, MARTA is one of the safest urban transport systems in the USA.

Accommodation

Hotels. Atlanta is the convention city *par excellence*. The good thing about such places as far as the individual traveller is concerned is that when the city is not full of delegates from the American Bar Association or the Democratic Party, the spare capacity among its 53,000 rooms is often sold off cheaply. Downtown has some classy places like the Radisson (165 Courtland St, at International Boulevard, 659-6500; 1-800-333-3333 from outside Atlanta), which was offering a Fall '92 rate of $55 per room per night. More dependably low prices are available at the downtown TraveLodge (311 Courtland St NE, 659-4545) where rooms start at $39; the Days Inn at 300 Spring Street (523-1144); and the Ramada Downtown at 175 Piedmont Avenue (659-2727) from $49.

Two distinct styles of accommodation are offered under one roof at Woodruff House, a couple of miles northeast of the city centre at 232 Ponce de Leon Avenue (875-2882). From the front, it is a plush and personal bed-and-breakfast, costing around $70 double, while around the side is the fully-fledged AYH hostel, with dormitory beds at $12.50 each for Hostelling International members. Either way, it is a comfortable and friendly place with good local amenities. To reach it take MARTA North Line to North

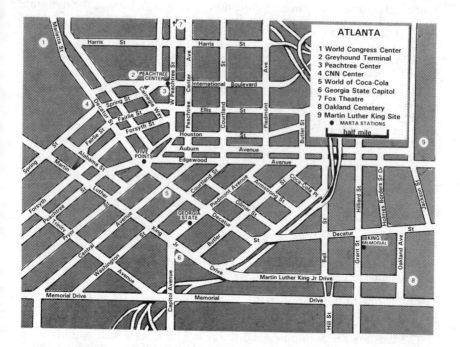

Avenue station, and take the northern exit onto Ponce de Leon Avenue. From here walk five blocks east.

The YMCA is at 22 Butler St (659-8085), but is not a particularly pleasant place.

Atlanta's cheap and efficient public transport makes camping a viable alternative to a dreary hotel or motel room. Try Arrowhead Campsites (948-7362), ten miles west of downtown, or Stone Mountain Family Campground (948-5710), 16 miles east. Both are served by MARTA and have excellent facilities for around $5 per person per night.

For those seeking a taste of the famed Southern Hospitality, two organizations will find you a room in a private guest house: Bed & Breakfast Atlanta (875-0525) who give you a 10% discount to students, and Atlanta Hospitality (493-1930). Most rooms cost $25-35.

Eating and Drinking

One of the best areas for eating is directly opposite the Woodruff House, in the Rio Center mall. In particular, Lettuce Souprise You is good value, with all-you-can-eat soup and salad; it has four other outlets in Atlanta.

The ultimate in glorious American junk food is the Varsity, 617 North Avenue NW (close to North Avenue rail station). This is the world's largest drive-in, with room for 800. You can eat burgers, hot dogs and fries at a school desk in one of five giant television rooms. The Varsity sells more Coca-Cola than any other single outlet in the world.

For more formal eating, Atlanta has hundreds of good restaurants, but many of the most interesting are on or around North Highland Avenue NE, three miles northeast of the city centre. The Mambo Restaurante Cuban (1402-8 N Highland, 876-2626) taints its authenticity by featuring Chinese dishes, but has some good Caribbean food. A stroll in the vicinity will turn up plenty of alternatives.

Downtown, if someone else is paying, go to the state's most acclaimed restaurant: Nikolai's Roof Restaurant, at the top of the Hilton (659-2000). Otherwise choose one of the many cheapish and cheerful places in Underground Atlanta.

For an evening drink, swallow hard and go up to one of the roof-top bars in the hotels around the Peachtree Center. The night-time view of the city (almost) makes up for the prices of the drinks.

 Atlanta is one of the most fascinating cities in the USA to explore. Not only does it have a modest historic area and gleaming new developments, it is dotted with a wide range of specific 'sights' — from the home of Martin Luther King to the World of Coca-Cola.

Get your bearings at the free Atlanta History Center, 140 Peachtree St NW (238-0655) where you can find out more about the city's history and ambitions. An excellent introduction to the city is to take one of the four walking tours provided by the Atlanta Preservation Center (84 Peachtree St NW, 522-4345). The Monday and Sunday tours include the Fox Theater with its fantastical minarets, onion domes and Egyptian art-deco interior.

Until you leave the city centre, it is easy to forget that Atlanta is one of the USA's great black cities. The Martin Luther King Jr Historic Site is a mile east of the Peachtree Center, an interesting walk (safe in daylight) through gradual deteriorating surroundings as white neighbourhoods change to black: faded pictures of King are still displayed in store windows. The site is also served by bus 3 (marked Auburn Ave/MLK) from Five Points. It contains the first home and grave of one of the 20th century's greatest figures, plus a museum (524-1956) and the Ebenezer Baptist church where both King and his father preached, and where his mother was murdered.

In complete contrast, visit historic Buckhead — the city's most beautiful residential district, containing the Greek Revival-style Governor's Mansion. The houses of the Atlanta Historical Society (3101 Andrew Drive NW, 261-1837) show how the other half lived.

For some, Atlanta is synonymous with the struggles of Rhett and Scarlett O'Hara. *Gone With The Wind* fans will wish to see the Margaret Mitchell exhibition in the Atlanta Public Library (Carnegie Way and Forsythe St). She wrote most of the book at her home at 979 Crescent Avenue, which is still standing — it is one block east of MARTA's Midtown station. Ms Mitchell died, aged 49, when she was hit by a car at the junction of Peachtree and 13th Streets. The remarkable writer is buried in the Oakland cemetery, worth a visit not least for its Civil War graves. For those requiring a refresher course, *Gone With The Wind* is shown daily at the CNN Center (577-6974).

Olympic City. No-one was more stunned than Atlanta when it was selected as venue for the 1996 Olympic Games. Barcelona 1992 had the sense of place, panache and passion to stage a world-class event. Seoul 1988 showed how a huge and ungainly city could miraculously become a global venue. And Los Angeles 1984 showed the spectacular results when Hollywood meets the best in world sport.

Atlanta's attributes are as hard to spot as its potential. Arriving at the city by road, rail or air, it simply does not seem to have the potential for what is touted as the biggest sporting event of all time. But Atlanta is out to prove such doubts wrong between now and the Opening Ceremony in 1996.

An Olympic Exhibition of the plans for the Games is open daily from 10am-9.30pm (noon-6pm on Sunday), just east of Five Points station. Basically it is an Olympic souvenir shop, with a hard-to-comprehend display about how the Games came to Atlanta and where events are to be staged: it shows the venues dotted around the city, including the new Georgia Dome. The yachting will take place on the coast at Savannah, while Stone Mountain is the home for archery, canoeing and rowing.

Underground Atlanta. Beneath the streets of the city centre, a lively parallel universe exists — a complete street scene, but buried beneath the roadway. Shops, restaurants, entertainers and thousands of people just promenading make it a terrific place to go, especially in the evening.

The World of Coca-Cola. This is a slick, impressive story of the world's most successful soft drink. At the eastern end of Underground Atlanta, a garish red and white building contains a history of the drink from the 'Intellectual Beverage' created by its founder in 1886 — selling nine glasses a day — to a multinational industry.

It is a study of marketing success, and multi-media exhibits explain how the bottle and logo came to be the most recognized trade mark on earth. Much is made of the company's commercials, and a 15-minute high-definition TV presentation is basically a big long — and impressive — advertisement suggesting how Things Go Better With Coke.

After a stroll through the history of the product, you end up at the tasting room. As well as unlimited free Coke, you can sample the stuff which Coca-Cola sells in every corner of the world. You may well wonder how the Costa Ricans, with so much delicious tropical fruit juices, can possibly have acquired a taste for a sweet and fizzy yellow drink.

The World of Coca-Cola (676-5151) opens 10am-9.30pm from Monday to Saturday, and noon-6pm on Sundays. Admission is $2.50 for adults, $1.50 for children. To find out more about 'the world's favorite soft drink', call 1-800-GET-COKE.

CNN: Headline News is made and broken by Ted Turner's media empire, which includes CNN (Cable News Network) itself, CNN International and the Spanish-language service Telemundo. You can take a 45-minute tour of the newsroom, including the studio set (which just sits in the middle looking distinctly untheatrical). The people who brought the Gulf War to several million homes show their wares to the public. The complex has its own MARTA station (CNN Center). Tours operate 10am-5pm from Monday to Friday, 10am-4pm at weekends, admission $5.

Entertainment

The Arts Festival is held for nine days in the second half of September, and provides for spectacular amounts of visual and perfomance arts all over the city, but concentrating on Piedmont Park (MARTA operates shuttle buses to here from Arts Center station during the festival). Call 885-1125 for details of events.

For the rest of the year, check Friday's *Atlanta Journal-Constitution* for full listings. The main indoor venues are the Woodruff Arts Center, 1280 Peachtree St NE (892-2414) and the Atlanta Civic Center, 395 Piedmont St (523-6275). The newly-restored Fox Theater at 660 Peachtree St (881-1977) is a wonderful auditorium.

In early August in even-numbered years the National Black Arts Festival dominates the cultural life of Atlanta: call 681-7327 for details.

The main rock venues are the Omni, the Fox Theatre, the Center Stage Theatre and the Masquerade (more of an overgrown nightclub). You can preview the bands by getting hold of Saturday's *Atlanta Journal-Constitution*, looking in the Leisure section and finding the Soundline codes. Then you just dial the newspaper from a Touch-Tone phone and select the access number for the band you want to hear. A short selection of their greatest hits will follow. (The same system applies for albums reviewed in the paper.) Tickets for most big events are sold by TicketMaster, 249-6400.

For jazz try the Parrot (571 Peachtres St NE, 873-3165) any day except Monday and Tuesday. For blues, push your way through the crowds into Blind Willie's (828 N Highland Avenue, 873-BLUE) and listen to black Chicago-style blues in a genuinely dark and run-down Chicago atmosphere. Live music starts at 10pm.

The most central comedy venue is the Comedy Act Theatre, 917 Peachtree St NE (875-3550).

Clubs. The most interesting club is the massive Backstreet, on three levels at 845 Peachtree St (873-1986). Uncompromising disco music starts at midnight, but before that the floor is given over to other events: comedy on Sundays, and on other nights events like country dancing for gay couples.

More conventional high-energy dancing takes place at Club Anytime (1055 Peachtree St NE, 607-8050), which is open around the clock, and DC's, out of the centre at 3535 Chamblee-Tucker Road at I-95 (452-9000).

SPORT AND RECREATION

Atlanta was already obsessed with sport before the Olympic decision was announced. The new Georgia Dome at One Georgia Dome Drive (223-9200) is the latest in a line of huge covered sports domes in the USA. Atlanta's version holds 71,500 seats under cover of a dome measuring nine acres. It is home for the Atlanta football team the Falcons, and will host the 1994 World Series. It is to be the venue for basketball and gymnastic events in the 1996 Olympic Games.

The Atlanta Braves baseball team play between April and September at the Atlanta/Fulton County Stadium. You can reach the stadium from downtown on MARTA, but start the journey at least two hours before the game begins. Tickets can be scarce: call 522-7630. If you can't get tickets, watch the match at Jack and Jill's Indoor Sports Bar (112 10th St). It can be just as entertaining to watch the packed clientele of armchair enthusiasts in front of the 60-inch big screens.

Parks. The Oakland Cemetery isn't everyone's idea of a fun day out, but this beautiful Victorian burial ground has 66 acres of park-like setting. As mentioned above, Margaret Mitchell (author of *Gone With The Wind*) is buried there, along with 40,000 other Atlantans.

You can bungee-jump at Lakewood Park near the Amphitheatre, from a height of 200 feet. Jumps operate daily except Tuesday from noon to 8pm. Call 624-1181 for bookings and information.

RADIO

The NPR station is WABE, 90.1FM. News is available on AM on WGST (640), WSB (750) and WDUN (550). Jazz and soul feature heavily on the Clark Atlanta University station WCLK (91.9), while mainstream 'adult contemporary' is available on FM on WMJK (96.7), WSB (98.5) and WALR (104.7).

Atlanta has a high murder rate, but as usual a fair number of killings are drug-related and confined to the poorer areas. Most visitors, whether convention delegates or 'proper' travellers, remain unaware of any problems. Certainly the downtown area is well-policed and safe in the evenings. The areas to avoid are east of I-85 after dark, and a mile or two north of the city centre — it is desolate at night, apart from a few drunks and ne'er-do-wells.

The area code for Atlanta is 404.

Information: The headquarters of the Atlanta Convention and Visitor's Bureau are at Harris Tower in the Peachtree Center (659-4270). A much more convenient location for most people is at street level just east of Five Ways Station.

Post Office: 39 Crown Road (at Hapville St); 221-5307.

British Consulate-General: 225 Peachtree St NE (524-5856).

American Express: Colony Square, 1175 Peachtree Square NE (892-8175).

Medical Emergencies: Crawford W. Long Memorial Hospital of Emory University, 550 Peachtree St NE (892-4411).

Traveler's Aid: Greyhound station, 81 International Boulevard (527-7400). Open 8am-8pm Monday to Friday, 10am-6pm on Saturdays. After hours, dial 522-7370.

Further Afield (61)

Sixteen miles east of the city, on US 78, lies Stone Mountain Park (498-5600), a 3,200-acre recreational area of forests and lakes which includes an antebellum plantation and Civil War exhibition. The main attraction, however, is the world's largest bas-relief sculpture, carved into the side of the granite mountain. There is a stunning laser show against the mountainside each summer night at 9.30pm. Take MARTA bus 120 from Avondale rail station. On weekdays the last bus leaves the park at 7.50pm, although you can easily camp for the night at the park's campground.

To see some of Georgia's more interesting features, follow the direction of Union General Sherman's passage of fire and sword southeastward from Atlanta to the Atlantic, commemorated in the song 'Marching through Georgia' (not sweet music to Southern ears). From Atlanta, I-20 takes you to Augusta via (with short detours) Madison and Washington, all containing fine antebellum buildings spared by Sherman. Augusta is best avoided during the Masters' golf tournament every April: tickets are harder to obtain than for an English Cup Final, and accommodation costs soar.

Savannah. On the coast, the port city of Savannah has, in a rather un-American way, emphasized preservation over development. It has retained its 18th century layout of elegant squares, the wrought-iron clad buildings full of history but many still in use as homes and offices. An interesting sight in the city and throughout the so-called Low Country coastland running up to Charleston, South Carolina is the Spanish Moss which cloaks many trees in eerie grey festoons. Savannah is also the gateway to the Sea Island resorts of Georgia and South Carolina, with their miles of white sand beaches and healthy fun of the sailing/surfing/tennis/golf variety.

You can fly, drive or bus into Savannah from Atlanta; alternatively, it is on Amtrak's New York-Florida route, and just off I-95, the main East coast highway.

The Interior. Other places of interest in Georgia include Franklin Roosevelt's Little White House at Warm Springs, 60 miles south of Atlanta, where he 'took the waters' for his paralysis. Another 60 miles south is the hometown of a more recent president, Jimmy Carter, though today Plains is a shadow of the boomtown it became during his term of office. Mr Carter can sometimes be seen cycling around town.

In the north of the state, you can pan for gold at Dahlonega, site of America's first gold rush in the 1820s, which led the government to drive out the last of the Cherokees. New Echota, on I-75, midway between Atlanta and Chattanooga, was the Cherokee capital, today the site of a restored Indian settlement.

SOUTH CAROLINA

The far west of the state nudges into the spectacular scenery of the Blue Ridge Mountains, but the majority of South Carolina's tourist attractions lie along the coast. Chiefly, they comprise the picturesque and historical city of Charleston and numerous fun-in-the-sun beach resorts.

Charleston. This almost-perfect port has preserved its sleepy Old South charm, and you can tour its historic districts at a suitably leisurely pace in a horse-drawn carriage. The Old Slave Mart museum, now a black crafts centre, is an interesting reminder of the city's earlier principal activity, while Charles Towne Landing, where the first settlers arrived in 1670, is today a delightful park.

A few miles north of the city is Middleton Gardens which are landscaped in a Capability Brown fashion. You may even see huntsmen in pink (a rare sight in America) if you're there on a Sunday.

Charleston comes to life each year for two weeks around the end of May for the Spoleto Festival USA, a wide-ranging arts package of international calibre. You can obtain information on tickets, and accommodation from Spoleto Festival USA, PO Box 157, Charleston SC 29402 (803-722-2764); apply early. If you are not arts-minded, the Festival is a good time not to visit Charleston.

Beaches. Any time from March through October is fine to visit the beaches. Kiawah and Hilton Head Islands are distinctly up-market vacation spots. Hilton Head Island in particular is a strange agglomeration of golf courses, resorts and restaurants. You will search in vain for any real centre to this ten-mile stretch of sand and forest, which caters for rich visitors from the northeast.

Conversely, all tastes and budgets are catered for at Myrtle Beach and the

55-mile Grand Strand running south from there. The Easter break from colleges brings droves of students from the chilly north in search of a good time.

Festivals. Inland, the biggest jamborees are at Darlington, site of the Rebel 500 (mile) stock-car race in April, and the even bigger Southern 500, over the Labor Day holiday weekend at the beginning of September.

The Great Outdoors. There are many state parks in South Carolina, including Edisto Beach Park and Hunting Island State Park. The flora and fauna of South Carolina are particularly interesting and exotic, including scarlet cardinals, egrets and flowering magnolia trees.

NORTH CAROLINA

Rather like Belgium, the 'Tar Heel state' is passed through by many but enjoyed by few. The tourist racing from the bustle of the northeast to the excitement of Florida is in too much of a hurry. North Carolina boasts no great cities: its beautiful island coastline and western mountain ranges are essentially places of quiet and solitude (unless you choose to visit the Great Smoky Mountains National Park on a holiday weekend). Postpone the thrills, spills and queues of Walt Disney World for a couple of days, try a hike through the oaks and pines of the Appalachian Trail or search for wild ponies on Ocracoke Island in the Outer Banks off the coast (see *The Great Outdoors*). North Carolina has the scenic edge on Belgium.

To appreciate the state, take the slow side-roads branching off the Blue Ridge Parkway and talk to the modest, almost indifferent inhabitants of the mountains selling home-made food and craftwork at their roadside stalls. Forget North Carolina if you're in a hurry: finding a place where patience and silence are appreciated in themselves will frustrate someone looking for instant charm or the usual touristic gratification.

Whether or not you have time to get to know the people, stop off in the Burlington/Greenboro area and join the shoppers who come in by the busload from hundreds of miles away to shop for cheap, high quality merchandise, especially clothing and shoes, at the factory outlet stores. Or try a visit at the tobacco auctions and cigarette factories Winston/Salem and Durham, notably the R J Reynolds Whitaker Park HQ off I-40 in Winston/Salem. As befits a state whose economy is heavily supported by the tobacco industry, attitudes to smoking are more tolerant than elsewhere, and cigarettes are cheaper.

Charlotte. Direct flights from Gatwick by USAir make Charlotte a convenient launchpad for exploring the southeast. Walt Disney World is a day's drive south (through Atlanta or Charleston) while the Great Smoky Mountains, Nashville and Memphis lie to the west.

Budget (359-5000) and Dollar (359-4700), among others, operate car rental services at Charlotte/Douglas International Airport (359-4000). The journey downtown takes 15 minutes (cab fare $10, limousine service $4). The downtown Greyhound Bus Terminal (601 West Trade St, 527-9393) offers several buses a day to Atlanta, Savannah and Washington DC (also served by Amtrak, 375-4416).

Unfortunately Charlotte itself has little to offer the tourist. The main throughfare, Tryon Street, with its skyscrapers and plazas is clear evidence of the claim that at $57 billion, Charlotte's banking resources almost outstrip Atlanta's and Miami's combined. This is a mixed blessing for the tourist.

Money generated from businesses has allowed major operations of civic restoration such as Spirit Square and the Victorian Fourth Ward area. Unfortunately, places of interest are dwarfed and squeezed out of the city by downtown development: the old Federal-style US Mint (now at 2730 Randolph Road, 337-2000) was simply taken to pieces, moved three miles, and rebuilt in the northern suburbs to serve as an excellent art museum.

A self-guided tour of historic city sites is available from the Charlotte Convention and Visitors Bureau, 229 North Church St; call 1-800-231-4636 from outside North Carolina, 1-800-782-5544 from inside the state. Don't miss the beautifully renovated Fourth Ward, an area of fanciful wooden homes of the 19th century upper middle classes, two blocks west of North Tryon Street. It is the most pleasant place to stroll in the city, especially in the early evening.

Make sure you visit Ivey's Department Store at 127 North Tryon Street. Its founder, a devout Methodist named J. B. Ivey, balanced his conscience and profession by pulling the blinds of the street level shop windows on Sundays. The young Billy Graham was more forthright. At age 17, he would exhort uptown shoppers from the steps of the nearby First Baptist Church, 318 North Tryon (now the Spirit Square Center for the Arts).

If you have a car, the cheapest beds can be found at the numerous motels on the city outskirts: just follow Tryon St north or south. In town, try the Oxford Inn, 601 N Tryon Street (372-2300) at a more reasonable price than the most motel chains. Travellers jet-lagged by the flight from England, or just seeking genuine Southern hospitality, might contemplate skipping a sterile motel room and staying at The Homeplace, a Victorian wooden house, at 5901 Sardis Road (365-1936), just 15 minutes drive south-east of downtown Charlotte. A double room costs $55-$65 including full breakfast.

The Great Outdoors. North Carolina offers two recreational contrasts: hiking, rafting and skiing in its western mountain ranges, or swimming, snorkelling and fishing on the Outer Banks, a strip of long, narrow islands stretching for 100 miles in a lazy arc as they follow the Atlantic coastline. The islands are linked by route 12, connected to the mainland in the north by US 64 and in the south by a ferry from Ocracoke Island. While hitching is possible, the islands' minimal public transport makes a car or bicycle worthwhile.

Head for two unspoilt southern islands, Ocracoke and Hatteras, both part of the protected Cape Hatteras National Seashore. (A flying visit on the way to the Wright Brothers National Memorial at Kitty Hawk on the commercialized Bodie Island is quite sufficient). As well as the pleasures of sun and surf, favourite activities include birdspotting on Pea Island National Wildlife Refuge at the northern tip of Hatteras Island, and stalking wild ponies on Ocracoke Island. There are official camp sites on both islands (reserve in advance at the Whalebone Junction Information Centre, Bodie Island). While it may not be possible for the authorities to enforce the rule against sleeping on the beaches, the night time beach-buggy races across the dunes may make you think twice.

THE APPALACHIANS

The mountains of western North Carolina are divided into the 'High Country' around Boone, 100 miles north of Charlotte, and the more touristy Great Smoky and Pisgah forested mountains around Asheville, 100 miles to the west. Both towns are just off the beautiful Blue Ridge Parkway (open only from April to November), which winds through the Appalachians to Pennyslvania. The Blue Ridge, Great Smoky, Black, Craggy, Pisgah and

Balsam Mountains are a budget travellers's dream: cheap campsites abound, along with inexpensive (if elusive) Youth Hostels and ski lodges.

Boone. This mountain town, aptly named after the famous frontiersman Daniel Boone, seems to exist solely for rigorous outdoor exercise. For information on the surrounding High Country ask the Boone Area Chamber of Commerce, (264-2225), near the central bus stop, or the National Park Information Desk, Milepost 294 at the Parkway Craft Centre (295-3782).

You need a car to get to the best trail-heads. Hitching in the remoter areas is slow but viable (the normal risks apply). Sometimes the Youth Hostels at Blowing Rock Assembly Grounds (295-7813), or Trailridge Mountain Camp, Bakersville (688-3879), will pick you up from the nearest bus stop along the Blue Ridge Parkway. Inexperienced hikers should consider joining one of the guided expeditions run by Edge of the World, PO Box 1137, Banner Elk (898-9550). Two-day hikes cost around $60 including food and equipment.

Asheville. This is the unofficial capital of the Carolina mountains which surround the city and give it its spectacular panorama. Asheville has several attractions apart from the landscape. The Biltmore Estate (704-225-1700), a magnificent 250-room Renaissance Chateau transported to a New World setting in 1895 by George W. Vanderbilt, is the largest private home in America. More humble but equally interesting is the Thomas Wolfe Memorial, 48 Spruce St, (253-8304). The writer's 'rambling, unplanned, gabular' childhood home is immortalised as 'Dixieland' in Wolfe's first novel *Look Homeward, Angel.*

Asheville celebrates the rich Appalachian folk culture with festivals and craft fairs throughout the year. During the summer, don't miss the Mountain Dance and Folk Festival (1-800-257-1300) or the unique Mountain Sweet talk, a show combining banjo, clog dancing and story-telling. It is performed by the female duo 'The Folktellers' at the Folk Arts Centre Theatre (258-1113) during July, August and the second half of October.

For more information about local events contact Visitors Information, 151 Haywood St (258-3858). The proximity of cheap camping has kept motel prices cheap ($25-$35); start looking on Merrimon Avenue, north of the city. Most approach Asheville on the scenic I-40.

If, however, you wish to by-pass the city and head straight for the mountains, travel along US 64-US 276 between Chimney Rock and Waynesville through the Pisgah National Forest (once part of the Biltmore Estate) and on into the Cherokee Indian reservation on US 19. This is probably the most scenic stretch of highway on the East Coast. The Cherokee Reservation's main attractions are rather tacky, its inhabitants self-conscious tourist attractions without the proud autonomy of the Navajo and Pueblo in the Southwest.

The half-million acres of the Great Smoky Mountains National Park can only be fully appreciated on foot. There is a much greater variety of trees and wild flowers than in the parks of California and Wyoming, and the vistas are best seen as the light gradually changes and mists rise. Arm yourself with the invaluable *100 Favorite Trails*, published jointly by the Carolina Mountain Club and Smoky Mountain Hiking Club, and widely available in Asheville and Gatlinburg. There are plenty of good guided tours and places in Boone and Asheville to buy or hire equipment, so there is no reason to be ill-prepared. Summer nights can be bitterly cold, and even if you don't meet one of the 600 resident black bears, you're sure to meet the resident mosquitoes.

Florida

In the good old days of 1981 when your parents could fly to Miami for £82 courtesy of Freddie Laker and a pound would buy $2.50, the Sunshine State was regarded as an ideal summer destination. Living was almost as cheaply as in Spain, with the bonus that the language was English, McDonald's hamburgers were more reassuring than *paella*, and Walt Disney World was only a short drive away.

What the package tourists failed to realise was that Florida is a winter playground. Nobody save Englishmen and the occasional mad dog goes to Florida in the summer because of the extreme heat and humidity. The other fact about Miami which the tour operators suppressed from their literature was that amid the glamorous world of big yachts, beachfront high society and posh nightclubs has grown an extremely depressed urban area, suffering from drug problems, high levels of racial tension and one of the worst crime rates in the United States. Trafficking and processing drugs, and laundering the money thus obtained, is a major industry.

The first package tourists to Florida discovered these problems for themselves (*Miami Vice* wasn't around at the time), and they began to look elsewhere in the state. The biggest blow to Miami's status as capital of the Southeastern Sunbelt has come from the competitiion of newer Florida resorts like Orlando, Tampa-St Petersburg and Sarasota, which have exploited the state's climate and ambience without suffering much degeneracy.

THE PEOPLE

Florida, the fastest-growing state in the country, expands too swiftly to permit attempts to stereotype or categorize its population. Everyone seems to have come from somewhere else; schools in the area teach children from 114 countries. However, a few general trends in the history of its settlement are worth noting. Miami's boom came with the influx of wealthy North-eastern industrialists, and its composition reflects that period to this day: a large number of its upper class are East Coast WASPs or Jews, who have retained their New York and New England lifestyles and accents.

The fact that Miami is America's chief link to Latin America and the first stop for political refugees and 'boat people', has made it the most significant Hispanic and Caribbean centre of the USA. Over half the population speaks Spanish, and while a fair proportion knows at least some English, most road signs are in both languages. The one-million-plus Cubans comprise the longest-established and most visible Hispanic group in Miami. Most of them have arrived since the 1959 revolution, including 125,000 sent by Castro in 1980, a mostly uneducated bunch — some fresh from prison — known as Marielistas. Many Central Americans arrived during the 80s but the largest number of refugees recently has come from Haiti, though US immigration has sent many back. Those who manage to stay remain without jobs or means of support.

Relations between Miami's natives and immigrants — and between rival immigrant groups — remain strained. Unfortunately, amongst the greatest stresses are those between blacks (making up 25% of the population and the hardest hit by the recession) and the prospering second-generation Cubans.

On the whole, racial tension is latent, and the average visitor is unlikely to be particularly aware of it. More obvious is Florida's status as the East Sussex of the United States, with over a fifth of the state's inhabitants being over the age of 65. Miami Beach is traditionally the favourite place to retire to, though the area's newly-found chic is gradually pricing it out of the pensioners' market.

Making Friends. The first problem is to decide if there is actually anyone you would like to befriend. Blue-rinsed Yankee widows and Spanish-speaking drug dealers might not be your cup of tea, and you would certainly not be theirs. But the pleasure and perils of meeting like-minded people in Miami are not much different from those in other cities. Beaches are anonymous enough for people to feel quite uninhibited about chatting with strangers. As in any American community where neighbourhoods are hacked up by freeways and people isolated by automobiles, singles bars are an important way of meeting people. These range from high-pressure meat-market estab-lishments to cosy lunchtime spots with their regular and amiable clienteles. If such places give you the jitters, the bars around the University in Coral Gables have a more casual atmosphere, though they can be cliquish too.

Anywhere in Florida, the time to meet American youth in its largest numbers is from mid March to mid April, when most of the universities in the Northeast schedule their spring breaks. Undergraduates converge on the state in droves, turning Fort Lauderdale, Daytona, St Petersburg and Jacksonville into month-long beach parties. Most of the students are so wound up about impending final examinations that they're never more than half-sober, and those desiring intimacy with the opposite sex often dispense with formalities.

CLIMATE

Miami enjoys warmer winters than any other city in the continental United States. Even in January daily high temperatures average 76°F/23°C, and lows seldom drop below 50°C. The north of the state is less balmy and more changeable; snow is extremely rare but not unheard-of. Every few winters, storms moving up from the Gulf of Mexico meet cold fronts from the north, causing freezing rain. This decimates the state's vital orange crop and sends tourists home in their thousands.

Nonetheless, barring such flukes, shorts and T-shirts are the order of the day, plus perhaps a jumper for evenings. Average July temperatures peak at 89°F/32°C. June, September and October are the rainiest months, and July and August are often stormy as well. Winter and spring are the best times to visit, for those who can brave the crowds.

The hurricane which destroyed parts of southern Florida in 1992 was unusually fierce, but strong winds and typhoons are familiar elements of the climate in the south of the state. This is the tropics, after all.

MIAMI

Miami used to be America's ultimate goal, an idyll glistening near the tip of Florida's golden finger, washed by warm waters and blessed with warm winters. Then something went horribly wrong, with the city apparently reduced to a state of terminal economic decline and boasting one of the worst crime scenes in the Union. The city's morale was dealt a further blow by the devastating Hurricane Andrew, which struck in 1992.

Yet Miami still draws 13 million visitors each year. Its museums and universities make it the centre of Florida's cultural life, and its beaches appear to have lost none of their appeal. Recently, the city's image has been boosted by the facelift given to Miami Beach and its Art Deco hotels — the epitome of the city's affluence in the 40s, but a decade ago on the verge of demolition. Miami Beach has once again become *the* place to be, and its trendy bars and restaurants do a brisk trade. While Miami is no longer the capital of American resort life, it remains its symbol.

The restoration of Miami Beach has left most districts of the city untouched, however, and visitors shouldn't neglect to venture onto the mainland to get a more rounded picture of what Miami is about — not least for a real taste of the city's Hispanic flavour, which is gradually enhanced as more and more white people move out. Miami can rightfully claim to be the Latin capital of the east coast.

CITY LAYOUT

Dade County refers to Miami, Miami Beach, the surrounding surburban sprawl and part of Everglades National Park.

Downtown Miami is a buzzing centre of commerce and finance, with its focus around the junction of Flagler St and Miami Avenue. You are unlikely to spend much of your time here, particularly in the evening when the area empties. The other main districts of interest on the mainland are south and west of downtown. Coconut Grove, directly south, is the long-established home of artists and writers and is the trendy part of Miami. While the more southerly suburb of Homestead bore the brunt of Hurricane Andrew in this area, Coconut Grove also sustained a lot of damage, some of which is still visible.

At US 1, known as the Dixie Highway, Coconut Grove meets Coral Gables, a wealthy area of leafy boulevards and Spanish-style squares. While

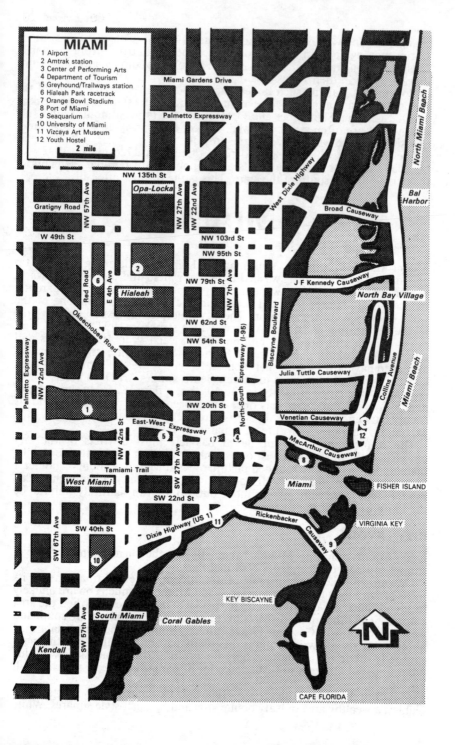

MIAMI

1 Airport
2 Amtrak station
3 Center of Performing Arts
4 Department of Tourism
5 Greyhound/Trailways station
6 Hialeah Park racetrack
7 Orange Bowl Stadium
8 Port of Miami
9 Seaquarium
10 University of Miami
11 Vizcaya Art Museum
12 Youth Hostel

2 mile

Miami Gardens Drive

Palmetto Expressway

NW 135th St

Gratigny Road

Opa-Locka

W 49th St

NW 103rd St

NW 95th St

NW 57th Ave

NW 27th Ave

NW 22nd Ave

Red Road

E 4th Ave

Hialeah

Okeechobee Road

NW 79th St

NW 7th Ave

NW 62nd St

NW 54th St

West Dixie Highway

Broad Causeway

J F Kennedy Causeway

North Bay Village

Bal Harbor

North Miami Beach

Palmetto Expressway

NW 72nd Ave

Biscayne Boulevard

North-South Expressway (I-95)

Julia Tuttle Causeway

Collins Avenue

Miami Beach

NW 20th St

NW 42ns St

East-West Expressway

Venetian Causeway

MacArthur Causeway

Tamiami Trail

SW 27th Ave

West Miami

SW 22nd St

Miami

FISHER ISLAND

SW 67th Ave

SW 40th St

Dixie Highway (US 1)

Rickenbacker Causeway

VIRGINIA KEY

SW 57th Ave

South Miami

Coral Gables

KEY BISCAYNE

Kendall

CAPE FLORIDA

N

the district as a whole lacks great atmosphere, the blocks around the University are lively.

Back towards the downtown area is Little Havana, Miami's famous community of Cuban expatriates. The district is located between SW 12th and SW 25th Avenues, but its heart is 8th St, known as *Calle Ocho*.

Miami's other main focus point lies across Biscayne Bay. It is crucial to realize that Miami and Miami Beach are distinct, geographically as well as culturally. To get from the city across to Miami Beach (a ten-mile long sandbar) and to the Keys of Virginia and Biscayne, you have to cross Biscayne Bay via one of seven causeways. Collins Avenue, which runs the length of Miami Beach, at the southern end becomes Ocean Drive. This is the heart of the newly-restored Art Deco district, roughly between 5th and 20th Streets, and is lined with hotels, restaurants and bars. This area is also known as South Beach, as opposed to the newer North Beach.

In Miami, roads which run north-south are Avenues; those which run east-west are Streets. The key intersection is the junction of Flagler St and Miami Avenue, downtown. Using these axes, the quadrants are prefixed NW, NE, SW and SE. If you ask for directions, people will tell you to head north, south, east or west rather than left or right.

Getting Around

ARRIVAL AND DEPARTURE

Air. A large percentage of the drugs — and not a few exiled dictators and revolutionaries — that arrive in the USA enter via Miami International Airport (MIA), seven miles northwest of downtown. If you are stopped by customs you can expect the official to be extremely diligent.

Once you're through, it's less than an hour's bus ride downtown. Metrobus 7 leaves the upper level of the main terminal hourly from 6am to 9pm, and charges $1.25 (exact change needed, no bills). A 25c transfer, valid for two hours, will take you to all points in Dade County. Bus C serves Miami Beach. Metrobus information is available in the ground level waiting room, or call 638-6700.

The Airport Limousine service (871-7000) is plusher and more frequent, and charges $6 to Miami. SuperShuttle (871-2000) also offers a cheap door-to-door service.

Yellow Cab (885-1111) will take you into town for a flat fare or on a running meter. Expect to pay $12-15. If you can get a flat rate of less than $12 from what looks like a reputable cab, you're doing well. Shared taxis are possible — there's a path where people queue for them — and are often a better bargain than the limousine.

If you find you have time to kill at the airport, go to the eighth floor of Hotel Mia in the terminal (near Concourse E), where you can enjoy the open-air pool, showers and gym for $8.

Miami is the USA's gateway to the Caribbean and Latin America. Bargain fares to Barbados or Bolivia are advertised in the *Herald*.

Bus. Greyhound has six stations in Greater Miami. The downtown terminal is located at 700 Biscayne Blvd (374-7222). Coaches leave from downtown seven times a day for Tampa on the Gulf of Mexico for $43. There is a thrice-daily service southwest direct to Key West from downtown or MIA Airport ($32), leaving downtown at 6.30am, 11.45am and 6.15pm and taking 4½ hours.

Train. After building the line right down the east coast of the USA, the railroad company must have run out of funds a few miles short of the intended terminus, since Miami station is five miles northwest of the centre at 8303 NW 37th Avenue. Bus L runs from the station to Miami Beach.

The *Silver Meteor* to New York via Tampa, Charleston and Washington departs daily at 8.25am and takes 26½ hours. The *Silver Star* to New York (via Orlando) leaves at 3pm and takes an hour less. The inbound trains arrive at 5.50pm and 1.15pm respectively.

Driving. America's two chief east coast highways, I-95 and US 1, pass through the centre of Miami. I-95 is more modern and charges tolls along its entire length within the state. Miami's business areas and tourist attractions are connected by highways; you'll certainly find it easier to get around if you have a car.

Traffic can be difficult on Miami Beach, but in general is no worse than in similar cities throughout the US. Potential trouble spots include the I-95 on-ramps at weekends and the Airport Expressway at rush hour (7.30-9am and 4.30-6pm). If you find the habits of local drivers unpredictable, bear in mind the words of a journalist from the *Miami Herald:* 'When I first came here, I thought: these people *cannot drive.* Now I realise they can but they're obeying the traffic laws of their country of origin.'

Like most American states, Florida has stiffened its drunken driving laws in the wake of a growing number of highway deaths. Fines can reach hundreds of dollars and jail terms are not unusual for second offenders. For lesser offences, you can pay a fine on the spot or have it waived by attending 'traffic school' (where offenders are lectured on good driving techniques).

Cars stopped at red lights used to be easy prey for the hordes of window-washers demanding money in return for a clean windscreen. In response to complaints from frightened residents and tourists, however, the Dade County authorities have made the practice illegal. Culprits can now face a fine of up to $500 or 60 days in jail.

Car Rental: If you arrive by air, there is no point in looking beyond the car rental desks which line the arrivals hall. Competition is intense and the rates are the lowest in America. Downtown, check the listings in the Yellow Pages, but don't be surprised if you find the best deals are at the airport.

Most rental agreements restrict use of the car to Florida and Georgia, and impose high drop-off charges. To overcome both obstacles, ask about the possibility of returning hired cars (i.e. which have been dropped off by other drivers), particularly to the Northeast of the US.

Note that the insurance requirements for hired cars in Florida are lax, so make your own arrangements for extra cover.

Driveaways. Many wealthy Northerners who winter in Florida want their vehicles driven home at the end of the winter, so March is an excellent time to find a car heading north to New York or Chicago. As usual, check Yellow Pages for names of auto-delivery companies.

Hitch-Hiking. Miami's drug and racial problems, and the fact that so many of its deprived areas are located near or underneath freeways, make hitching anywhere near the city inadvisable. Bus fares within Greater Miami are fairly cheap, so you are unlikely to feel the need to hitch locally. And although US 1 carries a good deal of traffic south to Key West, the Greyhound service is excellent. If you must hitch north, you'll probably feel safer taking the bus or train 25 miles north to Fort Lauderdale, and starting from there.

Florida presents other serious problems to the hitch-hiker. In the southern part of the state, many of the cars are too full of vacationing families to have the room or the inclination to stop. In the more provincial north, xenophobia and red-neckism will come into play.

Noticeboards in bars and cafes in Coconut Grove and Coral Gables sometimes carry messages for people looking for rides up North.

CITY TRANSPORT

Bus. Metro-Dade Transit runs Metrobus services in Dade County. Free maps can be picked up from their headquarters at 3300 NW 32nd Avenue, or during working hours from the kiosk at the corner of SE 1st Avenue and Flagler St, in front of the Chandler Shoe Store. Most buses run from around 5am to midnight. The flat fare is $1.25 (exact fare, $1 bills accepted), with transfers valid for two hours costing 25c. Call 638-6700 between 6am and 11pm for route information.

Buses C, K, D and S link downtown with Miami Beach. The latter two cover the most ground, travelling north along Collins Avenue as far as 194th St. In summer, Metro-Dade Transit operates a tourist bus — called The Breeze — along the beach, which runs until 4am; the fare is $1.25.

Roun'Towner: this is a minibus shuttle service linking downtown with the Omni International Mall, a huge shopping centre northeast of Miami on Biscayne Blvd: it starts from Brickell Avenue — just south of the Miami river — and meanders around the downtown area before heading north along Biscayne Blvd. Services run every ten minutes between 8.30am and 5.30pm Monday to Friday.

Metrorail. There is just one train line, linking South Miami to the northern suburbs, with stops in downtown, Coconut Grove and Coral Gables among others. Trains run 6am-10pm, until 7pm at weekends. The fare of $1.25 is fed into machines at each station. To transfer to a connecting bus, you pay an additional 25c.

Metromover: Miami's elevated monorail system has been billed as the 'Downtowner People Mover' (DPM), which the authorities claim 'combines the fun of a theme park ride with the efficiency of above-street-level transport'. The Metromover circular route downtown is worth going on for the ride, though it's usefulness as a means of transport from A to B is limited. It runs 6.30am-9pm Monday to Friday, 8.30am-6.30pm at weekends. The fare is 25c, but you travel free if you have begun your journey on the Metrorail.

Metropass. This permits unlimited travel on Metrobus, Metrorail and Metromover, for the cost of $60 a month. Call 638-6700 for information. Dial 638-6137 to order a map over the phone.

Guides to the Metro-Dade Transit bus and train systems, which you can pick up at stations, include information on the complicated procedure to be followed when transferring between buses and trains.

Car. Parking is difficult and risky in downtown Miami. However, there is plenty of free on-street parking in Miami Beach, from where buses will take you to the centre.

Taxis. The first mile costs about $2, with 35c for each additional quarter; the fare from downtown to Miami Beach, for example, is $8-9. While there is no shortage of cabs on Miami Beach, in Coral Gables or in the business district, you'll have a great deal of trouble finding one in less affluent areas. Cabbies can and will refuse to drive you into many ghettoes such as Liberty City.

Cycling. Florida in general is good cycling territory (there are few hills), but Miami is terrible. Too many of the roads are highways clogged with cars and cut off from the beach by massive hotels. However, there are some cycle paths. Key Biscayne and Coconut Grove are particularly good areas in which to go for rides. You can pick up a free leaflet *Miami on Two Wheels* from the Visitors Centre. Cycle hire charges start at about $3 an hour, $12-15 a day. You'll need $50 deposit or a credit card. Try Cycles on the Beach at 713 5th St at Euclid Avenue.

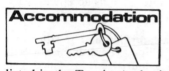

Hotels. Miami's beachfront highrises are mostly astronomically priced. The hotels at the other end of the spectrum are normally in dangerous areas. But there are some places in between, most of which are listed in the Tourist Authority's excellent pamphlet, *Hotels*.

Since public transport is scarce late at night, most people opt to stay in Miami Beach, which is lively and safe in the evening. There are a number of places on Collins Avenue and on the lower part of Ocean Drive which will allow you to cram two or three into a bedroom for about $60. The trendiest place in Miami Beach is the Century Hotel (140 Ocean Drive, 774-8855), but doubles cost from $120.

Downtown Miami is cheaper though potentially less safe than Miami Beach: try the centrally located cheap-but-pleasant Hotel American (273 NE 2nd St, 373-0672) which charges $37 a double. If it's booked up, then try the nearby Leamington (307 NE 1 St, 373-7783), with rooms for $40-50.

Motels The hotel/motel distinction is blurred in Miami. Try the Golden Nugget Motel at 1855 Collins Avenue (932-1445) in a posh section of Miami Beach, with rooms at the comparatively low price of about $60 for a double.

The incoming highways — Routes 41, 441, 835 and US 1 — are lined with motels, though many cater to first-time visitors who overestimate the tightness of the accommodation market in Miami and are willing to pay through the nose during the tourist season. In fact all accommodation is much more expensive between Thanksgiving and Easter. Off-season you can get some real bargains, particularly for longer stays.

Bed and Breakfast. Contact the Bed and Breakfast Company, 105 Mariposa Avenue 233, Miami 33146 (661-3270). Book well in advance.

Hostels. The AYH Youth Hostel is in the historic Clay Hotel at 1438 Washington Ave (534-2988) in old Miami Beach. It's a comfortable place, two blocks from the beach between 14th and 15th Streets. The staff is friendly, and the rates ($10 a night for members in three-bedded rooms) are the cheapest in Miami.

University Residences. Between June and August, call the Housing Office at the University of Miami (284-4505) about the possibility of renting one of their dorm rooms in Coral Gables. This student section of town is lively, safe and pleasant. If there are no vacancies are you're set on staying in Coral Gables, the University Inn at 1390 S Dixie Highway (663-2611) is a good bet, with rooms at about $50 a night.

Camping. The closest site to downtown Miami is the Miami North KOA (14075 Biscayne Blvd, 940-4141). For information on sites elsewhere in the state, call the Florida Campground Association on 1-800-FLA-CAMP.

Eating and Drinking

Miami grew up around ostentatious displays of wealth. As a result the dominant cuisine in its restaurants remains the upmarket staples of the American middle class: steak, seafood, ribs and chops in sauces, and other similar fare. Some use is made of Caribbean and Gulf seafood, with crayfish, conch, fritters and tuna well represented. Stone (or *morro*) crabs — steamed giant crab legs — are available fresh only in Miami. They are in season from mid-October until mid-April. Some of the best restaurants in town are in Coral Gables, though they tend to be pricey. John Martin's (253 Miracle Mile, 445-3777) is a New York-style Irish pub, but serves excellent food.

Don't miss Wolfie's (2038 Collins Avenue at 21st St, 538-6626), a traditional New York-cum-Miami Beach deli famous for its cheesecake, and corned beef sandwiches on rye; it is open 24 hours. The Strand (671 Washington Avenue, 532-2340), also in Miami Beach, is a former deli which now serves excellent meals — a good place to mix with local trendies.

There are also several Kosher dairy cafeterias, specializing in vegetarian dishes such as felafel and noodle pudding. Try Early Bird dinners at cut rate prices if you're hungry at 5 or 6pm. When money is short, fill up with a Key Lime Pie, a pastry filled with condensed milk, lime juice, eggs, sugar and topped with meringue, served cold; it tastes better than it sounds.

Cuban Food. You can eat Cuban food all over Miami, but Little Havana is your best bet for budget dining, since there are lots of small family-run places. The food is mainly lightly spiced meats, vegetables and soups and Cuban pastries and desserts, most notably rich fried *churros* (long thin doughnuts). For a typical meal go to La Esquina de Tejas on SW 12th Avenue (545-5341), which serves up beans and rice *(frijoles negros y arroz),* usually with roast chicken and fried plantains — known as *El Especial del Presidente* ever since a visit of Ronald Reagan in 1983. More formal are Casa Juancho at 2436 SW 8th St (642-2452) and Covadonga at 6480 SW 8th St (261-2406).

For a good Cuban meal outside Little Havana, try La Rumba in Miami Beach on Collins Avenue at 20th St (538-8998). Yuca (148 Giralda, 444-4448) is a much classier place in Coral Gables. Many restaurants serve traditional Spanish dishes as well; of these, La Tasca at 2741 W Flagler St enjoys almost universal acclaim.

DRINKING

Miami suffers from a degree of schizophrenia as far as alcohol is concerned. While much of the city supports the great American lager industry, the areas dominated by tourism (hotels, beachfront singles bars, etc.) have a vested interest in keeping the city's Caribbean image intact, and therefore push drinks like pinacoladas, frozen daiquiris and the like. It should be self-evident that you can do the former sort of drinking more cheaply than the latter. If you're into cocktails, look for a cheap *cuba libre* in Little Havana.

The drinking age of 21 is not enforced quite as rigorously as elsewhere in the USA. You might prefer to take advantage of warm tropical nights to sit on the beach with a six-pack and watch the moon rise.

The social scene in South Beach revolves around its bars, not all of which are prohibitively expensive. The most noteworthy bars tend to be those where you can also here live music too, so see also *Entertainment* below. A more straightforward bar, but currently the hub of South Beach's social scene, is the News Café at 800 Ocean Drive.

Miami Beach. Miami has few attractive areas in which to stroll, but the world's largest concentration of Art Deco buildings is well worth exploring. In particular, the Carlyle and Tides hotels on Ocean Drive and the Delano at Collins and 16th St are eyecatching. You will not be alone: at weekends Miami Beach is invaded by hundreds of 'causewayers', in winter by thousands of tourists.

You might consider joining a walking tour organized by the Miami Design Preservation League (1244 Ocean Drive), beginning every Saturday at 10.30am. You can see more, however, by going on one of the bicycle tours, which depart from Cycles on the Beach (713 5th St at Euclid Avenue) on Sunday mornings; the hire of the bike costs $5. Both tours last for about 90 minutes, and a donation of $6 is expected; call 672-2014 for more details. Wear plenty of sunblock and a hat.

If you aren't into Art Deco architecture or pastel colours, then you can stroll along Ocean Drive and concentrate on watching the rich, famous and fashionable, who lounge on the beach in the daytime and pose in the trendy bars and clubs at night. Or head down the side streets to see how Miami Beach retains its seedy side; in some parts it is not difficult to imagine where the crack dens and brothels used to be (and where some still are).

Little Havana. If you believe everything the tourist brochures says, then in Little Havana you'll expect to find streets full of old men in Panama hats and a permanent carnival atmosphere. The heart of Miami's Cuban community is in fact fairly run-down and surprisingly quiet (at least during the day). Yet it has bags of atmosphere and is well worth exploring — if only to try the famous *café cubano*, the bitter-tasting coffee which sets the heads of the uninitiated spinning.

A stroll down Calle Ocho will reveal a curious array of shops, selling anything from guns to religious trinkets; some display signs saying 'English Spoken', presumably to encourage diffident tourists. The tombstones in the cemetery make interesting reading, though unfortunately the grave of the late President Somoza of Nicaragua (brought to Miami after his murder in Paraguay) is unmarked.

Of the monuments dotted around Little Havana, the most important is the one on SW 13th Avenue, dedicated to those who died during the Bay of Pigs invasion of Cuba in 1961. Not far from here is Máximo Gómez Park (14th Avenue), an open-air domino club; extraordinarily, only men over the age of 55 are allowed to enter. The Cuban Museum of Arts and Culture (1300 SW 12th Avenue at 13th St, 858-8006) is open 1-5pm Wednesday to Sunday.

Little Havana comes alive during 'Carnaval Miami' in March, the largest Hispanic celebration in the States. The carnival lasts a week, culminating in a day-long party on Calle Ocho.

Coconut Grove. Once dubbed a 'sub-tropical Greenwich Village', Coconut Grove manages to mix the Bohemian and the chic, though the latter seems to be in the ascendant. The bad times which have hit the rest of Miami have left Coconut Grove remarkably unscathed, though it is still reeling from the shock of the hurricane. The pavement cafés, particularly the smart joints around Commodore Plaza, are patronized mainly by yuppies and tourists. But while the atmosphere tends towards the quaint, Coconut Grove is a relaxed and safe place to while away the hours. It is also a good place to stroll along the waterfront and gawp at the yachts; some of the humbler boats can be hired.

In mid-February each year Coconut Grove is host to a three-day festival of art. It is one of the biggest in the the country, attracting over 500,000 people. A look around is highly recommended — as much for the wonderful food stalls as for the art. Call 447-0401 for information.

Opa-Locka. This predominantly black area began as an Arabian fantasy, created in the 1920s by a Floridan landowner who had been inspired by *A Thousand and One Nights.* His dream was never completed, and the district gradually fell into disrepair. It has become one of Miami's main drug and sex markets: the district shot to the headlines nationally a few years ago, over the case of a mother who sold her daughter for one dose of crack. The most notorious northeast corner — where Ali Baba Avenue, NW 22nd Avenue and Highway 9 meet — is known as the Triangle, and barriers block access to cars.

Opa-Locka's mayor has spearheaded a campaign to restore the historic district into something approaching its former glory, but progress is slow. While there is little to do in the area, it is interesting to wander through the streets and to see the Moorish-style buildings, with their domes, arches, crenellations and minarets. The steel mesh fences and proliferation of vicious guard dogs lends an eeriness to the atmosphere, even during the day. Be sure to leave by nightfall.

Museums. It is not surprising that a city with as little history as Miami (the place didn't exist this time last century) is short on museums. But the quality of the few museums it does have comes as a pleasant surprise.

The Bass Museum of Art (2121 Park Avenue, Miami Beach, 673-7530) has an extensive collection of European art, with good works by Rubens and 19th and 20th-century artists. It opens 10am-5pm Tuesday to Saturday, 1-5pm on Sunday.

The Museum of Science (3280 S Miami Avenue, 854-4247) includes impressive exhibits of the local wildlife Miami has largely supplanted, but in general the hands-on gadgetry is disappointing by American standards. It is open daily 10am-6pm, admission $3.50.

The Vizcaya Museum (3251 South Miami Avenue, 945-1461), at the northern end of Coconut Grove, is the one you can least afford to miss. It is a collection of continental artefacts housed in an eccentric Baroque-cum-Renaissance style villa that was home to the American industralist, James Deering. The grounds are lovely too. The museum is open daily 10am-4pm (noon-4pm on Sunday).

Newspaper magnate William Randolph Hearst brought one of Spain's treasures to Miami, the 12th-century Segovian Monastery of Saint Bernard — the oldest-known building in the Western Hemisphere. It is now at 16711 West Dixie Highway (945-1461), open 10am-4pm Monday to Saturday, noon-4pm on Sunday. Admission is $4, which includes a guided tour.

Al Capone's House. No self-respecting gangster spent the winter shivering in Chicago. Al Capone, like many of his fellow criminals, flew south to

Florida for the winter. From Miami, drive out towards Miami Beach on the MacArthur Causeway (or catch bus F or K). Take the first turning left, signposted Palm Island. Register at the security gate, then go right towards 85 Palm Avenue (halfway down on the left). The building flush against the road is merely a guardhouse for the main residence, which backs onto the water of Biscayne Bay. It was from here that Capone ordered the St Valentine's Day massacre; he arranged for the local police to call that morning, so his alibi was cast-iron. Ironically, the home led indirectly to Capone's downfall. How, Treasury officials demanded, could a man with no visible means of support buy a $40,000 house? He was arrested, convicted and sent to Alcatraz.

Parks and Zoos. For a city whose cramped urban landscape can easily become depressing, Miami is short on parks. Those that do exist, however, have been imaginatively landscaped, though the parks — like the city zoos — were badly damaged by Hurricane Andrew.

Many people pass an idle hour under the trees in Bayfront Park, by the mouth of the Miami River and near the smart Bayside shopping area; it is also a good vantage point for watching the boats in Biscayne Bay. The North Shore Open Space Park occupies more than 50 acres of oceanfront Miami Beach along Collins Avenue, and is pleasant especially off-season. Hialeah Park, north of downtown, is much larger, but can be spoilt by hordes of tourists in high season.

Zoos: Miami has so ravenously gobbled up the lovely landscape surrounding it, that the only way to preserve local wildlife has been to hide it in pockets of 20 acres or so.

The city's great animal attraction is the 200-acre Metrozoo at Coral Reef Drive and SW 152nd Street (251-0400), which contains animals from all over the world in a setting that has revolutionized zoo-planning everywhere. Here, it is the animals who roam free, while the people move along caged walkways and inside vehicles, viewing the wildlife in its natural habitat. At the time of going to press the zoo was closed until further notice due to hurricane damage; normally, however, it opens daily 9.30am-5.30pm.

The Metrozoo philosphy has been applied at Monkey Jungle (14805 SW 216th Street, 235-1611), where you can walk through a simulated jungle and meet with chimpanzees, monkeys and apes of every description. The centre is open daily 9.30am-5pm.

The biggest attraction is the Miami Seaquarium on the Rickenbacker Causeway (361-5705), where thousands of tourists arrive each day to marvel at trained killer whales, dolphins, seals and walruses. It is open 9.30am-6.30pm. Another attraction is Planet Ocean, also on the Rickenbacker Causeway. The only ocean showplace of its kind in the world, it enables visitors to 'visit' the birth of oceans, touch Florida's only iceberg, and climb into a genuine submarine.

Beaches. With beaches as famous as Miami's, you should go swimming at least once, and possibly take up some watersports too. You can swim from any point along Miami Beach, but you would do better to go to Key Biscayne or the nearby island of Virginia Key.

Key Biscayne is a smart resort but is the closest good beach to downtown: it is within easy cycling distance of Coconut Grove, or take bus B. The northern reaches have been overdeveloped, but there are some lovely quiet spots at the southern end. There is a lighthouse at the tip, where you can buy cheap food or rent a barbecue and cook your own.

Miami and its environs have many public marinas where you can rent any type of boat. Fishing, on-shore and off-shore abounds. The best way to arrange this is to join a group led by a local. You can enjoy a few hours' fishing for less than $20.

Entertainment

Miami's cultural diversity means you can attend anything from a reggae concert to an Oktoberfest-style beer festival. The *Miami Herald* has daily reviews of concerts, exhibitions and shows; Friday's edition includes the most detailed listings of upcoming events. The *Miami* monthly magazine, available from newsstands, also lists events, but is intended more for the geriatric nightclub set. The *New Times*, a free weekly arts and leisure paper, is much better.

Tickets for many events can be bought through TicketMaster: call 358-5885.

Theatres and Cinemas. Miami's large population of expatriate New Yorkers may have brought the frenzy of the Northeast with them, but they are also largely responsible for the number of good theatres in the city (not to mention the exorbitant price of theatre tickets).

The Jackie Gleason Theatre of the Performing Arts (TOPA), at 1700 Washington Avenue in Miami Beach (673-8300), is perhaps the most renowned, and draws the best of local and national talent, theatrical and otherwise, including the Greater Miami Symphony Orchestra; Broadway productions reach here too. Serious drama is also performed at the Coconut Playhouse (3500 Main Highway, 442-4000). Avant-garde productions thrive at the Ring Theater on the University of Miami campus (1380 Miller Drive, 284-3355), and the prices are generally cheaper than those at other theatres.

Ballet Flamenco La Rosa is an excellent dance company which performs at the lovely art deco Colony Theatre in South Beach (1040 Lincoln Road, 672-0552); you can see the Ballet Theatre of Miami at the same venue.

For cinemas, try the Roxy Theater or the Surf Theater, both in Miami Beach, or the Grove Art Cinema in Coconut Grove. For a wider choice, take your pick from the six screens at the Omni shopping complex.

Music and Clubs. Miami Beach is the heart of the city's nightlife. There are several good clubs along Washington Avenue. Club 1235 at (you guessed it) 1235 Washington Avenue is popular, and makes a cover charge of $5-15. The Island Club (701 Washington Avenue) is a bar-cum-disco which plays mostly Caribbean music.

Tobacco Road (626 N Miami Avenue, 374-1198), the oldest bar in Miami, hosts excellent blues bands, both local and national. The Music Room (804 Ocean Drive) has live jazz and a stylish clientele. Good jazz can also be heard at some of the bars and clubs in Coconut Grove. At the Peacock Cafb (2977 McFarlane Road, 936-1994 or 442-8833), for example, you can hear good jazz and blues, plus the occasional comedy act.

For instant music listings call the Jazz (382-3938) and Blues (666-6656) information hotlines. Big rock acts appear at the James L. Knight Center in Miami itself, the Cameo Theater in Miami Beach and at the Hollywood Sportatorium.

SPORT

Miami retains its Southern-ness in nothing as much as its fanatical love of football. Though the local Dolphins are no longer the powerhouse they were in the 70s — when they took three consecutive Super Bowl championships — they remain one of the best National Football League teams. Their fans continue to raise the hackles of their rivals with the gloating way they wave their handkerchiefs after every touch down. The Dolphins play in the enormous Joe Robbie Stadium 16 miles northwest of Miami. For information about tickets call 620-2578; the cheapest go for $20.

The Joe Robbie Stadium is venue for the final of the 1994 World Cup championships, much to the delight of the soccer-loving Hispanic community in Miami.

Professional baseball is an easier prospect for cheap tickets. Florida is where the major teams perform their spring training in March before the actual season starts. You'll find the New York Yankees in Fort Lauderdale, the St Louis Cardinals in St Petersburg, the Baltimore Orioles in Miami. All play exhibition games against one another. Florida has no professional baseball teams, but the university teams at Tampa and Miami are always in the running for the national championships. For basketball, watch the Miami Heat at their downtown arena.

The Hialeah Race Track (entrance at corner of SE 2nd Avenue and 32 St, 885-8000) is open only six weeks of the year from March to May, but it is considered to be one of the most important courses in the USA. Greyhound racing takes place at the Biscayne and Flagler Kennel Clubs.

For something out-of-the-ordinary, watch *jai-alai* (pronounced 'hi-li'), an extremely fast ball game which originated in the Basque region of Spain and resembles a cross between squash and lacrosse. Games take place at the Miami Fronton (3500 NW 37th St, 633-9661), east of the airport, daily except Tuesday and Sunday and usually at 6.45pm.

SHOPPING

The most pleasant area in which to window-shop is Miami Beach's Lincoln Road Mall, a pedestrian street landscaped like a tropical garden, stretching from Washington Avenue to Alton Grove. Prices are more reasonable than you would expect. Browse around the numerous art galleries or the excellent Books and Books store at number 933. North of Lincoln Road is the pricey Bal Harbour shopping area.

Shopping in Miami proper is also mall-orientated. The ultramodern Omni Shopping Complex is at the end of Biscayne Boulevard's prestigious market area, which runs from Flagler to 16th Streets. Flagler Street itself is full of shops and department stores.

Coconut Grove is the quaintest of Miami's shopping meccas, full of little 'ye olde' boutiques for tourists. The Miracle Mile in Coral Gables is one of the country's flashest shopping streets.

For bargains, the Tamiami Trail in Little Havana has plenty of discount shops; and the Tropicaine Drive-In Theatre (7751 Bird Road at 40th St) hosts a large flea market on Saturdays and Sundays. Get there before 9am for the best buys.

THE MEDIA

Broadcasting. All the usual suspects broadcast in Miami: Channel 4 (CBS), Channel 7 (NBC), and Channel 10 (ABC). Channel 2 (WPBT) is the public broadcasting station. For radio news, listen to WIOD (610 AM). The classical station is WTMI (93.1 FM), while WHTE (100.7 FM) is the top rock station. WQBA (107.5 FM) has Spanish programmes.

Newspapers. The *Miami Herald* is the city's daily, and one of the best newspapers in the country. *The Weekly News* (*TWN*) is a gay newspaper, with news, reviews and reports about places of interest throughout Florida.

On average there is one murder each day in Dade County. Miami's crime problems stem from two factors — race and drugs — but this doesn't mean that a sensible attitude to both will guarantee you safe passage. Many of the city's Hispanics and blacks are living below the poverty line and feel themselves ignored by a wealthier white community and beleaguered by a hostile police force. This has left the police understandably nervous, leading to a Catch-22 situation in which the most dangerous areas are the most poorly policed — making it doubly important to avoid trouble spots. These are easy to recognise, and any native will steer you away from them if asked. From the airport bus, you can see teeming slums with some of the most threatening looking street corners in America. The car hire desks at the airports even issue a map of dangerous areas to incoming British travellers.

Be particularly careful around the bus terminal. If you're leaving on a night bus, try to get to the terminal in daylight.

At night avoid deserted areas such as the normally-safe business district west of Biscayne Park. A good rule is to stay near the sea coast resort areas: Miami Beach is generally safe, and the high-rise hotels of Miami are well-lit and extensively policed, often by private security agencies.

Drugs. Given that Miami is America's principal point of entry for illegal drugs, you might think that minor offences like smoking marijuana would be overlooked. It is true that many American states have liberal laws on grass, but Florida is not one of them. Cocaine is treated even more seriously, but is used so widely that police estimate that the average bank note in the city has 35 micrograms of cocaine stuck to it after users have rolled it up to inhale the white powder.

Help and Information

The area code for Miami is 305.

Information: Maps and brochures are available at the Greater Miami Visitors Bureau, 701 Brickell Avenue (539-3000), open 9am-5pm Monday to Friday. For visitor information call 800-283-2707. Information can also be obtained from 1700 Convention Center Drive in Miami Beach (673-7030) or the Metropolitan Dade County office at 140 W Flagler St, downtown (375-5656).

British Consulate: Brickell Bay Office Tower, 1001 S Bayshore Drive (374-1522)

American Express: 330 Biscayne Boulevard (358-7350); or 1221 Brickell Avenue (374-4760).

Thomas Cook: 380 Miracle Mile, Coral Gable (448-0269)

Western Union: 691-7912.

Post Office: 500 NW 2nd Avenue (371-2911).

Medical Emergencies: Mt Sinai Hospital, 4300 Alton Road (674-2200).

All night drugstore: Robert's Drugs, 590 W Flagler St (545-0533).

Gay Switchboard: 35 SW 8th St (358-HELP).
Handicapped Travellers: Center for Survival and Independent Living, 1335 NW 14th St (547-5444)
Weather Forecast: 661-5065.
Helplines: Suicide-Drug Abuse Hotline (358-4357); Rape Treatment Centre and Hotline (549-7273).

Further Afield 61

The big west-Florida cities — Tampa, St Petersburg, and Fort Myers — were the first focus of America's retirement industry and continue to bear the stigma of being towns for the 'newly-wed' and the 'nearly-dead', though this image is becoming less and less appropriate as an influx of young professionals continue to diversify the population. The Florida Keys, especially Key West, have long been a centre for Florida's cultural communities. Lifestyles of the Old South, predominant throughout Florida until a half-century ago, today live only in the northern part of the state particularly in the 'Panhandle' region along the border with Georgia and Albama.

THE FLORIDA KEYS

This string of ever-diminishing islands is connected by 42 narrow bridges and causeways of US Route 1, including Seven Mile Bridge. An air of romance has surrounded the place ever since writers started moving here in the 1920s and 30s. Hemingway lived here, as did Tennessee Williams, and Humphrey Bogart squared off against Edward G. Robinson on Key Largo in the film of the same name. Writers are still attracted to the islands — to Key West in particular — and they have been joined by a motley community of Cubans, gays, drug-smugglers and artists.

Every year millions of tourists pour in. Many come to dive or snorkel, but sport fishing is perhaps the favourite pastime: the campgrounds in the evening are full of happy fishermen frying up their catches. The transformation of the Keys into an international resort, however, has had serious effects on the environment: the coral has been wrecked in some areas, fish stocks are seriously depleted and a frightening number of manatees, an endangered species, are killed by speedboats. On a less serious level, the US Route 1 highway — known in the Keys as Overseas Highway — is flanked by an ever-increasing array of billboards and tacky roadside restaurants, that manage to kill the magic of making such an extraordinary journey out to sea.

The Keys were also badly hit by Hurricane Andrew in 1992, which caused $20 billion dollars in damage, destroying 100,000 homes and leaving 250,000 homeless.

Against all the odds Key West, the archipelago's westernmost town, has managed to maintain its appeal. It should be on the itinerary of anyone who makes it down to Florida.

Key West. Once the home of fugitives and all manner of weirdos and eccentrics, Key West is swamped by tourists in the high season. Yet the permanent residents are a resilient lot. The luxurious and the seedy seem to coexist comfortably side by side, with Key West's continued role as a cocaine town lending an exciting edge to the atmosphere. The pastel-coloured houses enclosed within lush gardens have a taste of New England in the tropics. A walk along Duval St, the main drag now lined with shops purveying tourist tat, can be disheartening. But Key West's side streets have a ramshackle and even Caribbean feel, and the bars are still full of colourful characters. The locals, known as Conchs (pronounced 'konks'), are white fishermen who have lived on the island for generations. They are among the more normal of the people you are likely to get chatting to.

Key West is a lazy, soporific place which is likely to appeal to people who like to eat, drink and simply amble about; or, as one songwriter once put it, to 'waste away in Margaritaville'. It is also the most popular gay resort in the USA; the gay community owns about a quarter of the town. The military owns another quarter: the strategic importance of Key West's location, just 90 miles from Havana, is not lost on the government; missiles were parked here during the Cuban Missile Crisis of 1962.

Arrival and Departure: many visitors to Key West arrive by one of the three daily Greyhound buses from Miami (5 hours, $32 one way); it's quicker in summer when towns are less crowded and stops less frequent. If you're driving and make no stops, you can do the journey in three hours. Hitching should be no problem. The Greyhound terminal in Key West (296-9072) is on Simonton St. Northbound departures are at 7.30am, 11.30am and 4.45pm.

Accommodation. Cheap lodgings are scarce in the high season, when it is hard to find much below $60 a night. However, dorm beds are available. The Pegasus Hotel (501 Southard St at Duval, 294-9323), near the bus station, has beds for $15 per person, plus private rooms for around $70. The AYH Youth Hostel (718 South Street, 296-5719), charges $15 a night ($12 for members), though the dorms are rather cramped. It also rents out bikes ($6 for 24 hours) and snorkel equipment at reasonable rates.

The delightfully named Tilton Hilton (511 Angela St, 294-8697) has simple couples for $35. In the $60-80 range is the Blue Parrot Inn at 916 Elizabeth St (296-0033).

Eating and Drinking: you can eat great Cuban food in Key West — far better than in Cuba itself — and the best place to do this is at La Lechonera, at 900 Catherine St. There are many other good places to eat and drink, including the Two Friends (512 Front St), a noted Dixieland jazz bar; the Green Parrot (400 Southard St), favourite haunt of divers, boating community, hippies and international travellers; and La Bodega (829 Simonton St), a kind of grown-up student café boasting a noticeboard with events and accommodation.

Sloppy Joe's was the name of Hemingway's local bar. It moved to its present location, at the corner of Duval and Greene Streets, not long before the writer died in 1961. The original Sloppy Joe's, now Captain Tony's Saloon (428 Greene St), has changed little since Hemingway's day, and is a much better place to drink and talk to the locals. If you prefer noise, crowds and live music, however, stick with Sloppy Joe's.

Exploring: There's not a great deal to do in Key West besides visiting the homes of the famous people who lived here. Hemingway's house is at 907 Whitehead St (294-1575), where he lived from 1928 to 1940 and did some of his best work. The building is lovely, but virtually nothing inside actually belonged to him; a far better Hemingway Museum exists in Havana, Cuba, where the writer also lived. The most interesting exhibit in his Key West residence has to be the urinal in the garden — originally from Sloppy Joe's and now a drinking trough for a large number of cats. The museum is open daily 9am-5pm, admission $6. Hemingway fans should not miss the festival in honour of the writer, held in July. Among the events is an extraordinary Hemingway lookalike contest.

The home of Tennessee Williams (1431 Duncan St), where he lived 1951-83, is a more humble affair. The former home of naturalist John Audubon (Greene St, 294-2116) is also open to the public and should not be missed. The house and garden are both wonderful. They are open 9.30am-5.30pm, admission $5.

For those who still smoke, there's a Cigar Factory which sells cheap 'Cuban' cigars made by exiled Cubans.

Watching the sun go down from Mallory Square is a Key West tradition, which nowadays is accompanied by a bizarre kind of street circus, where you can encounter anything from performing animals to fortune tellers and even kilted bagpipe players. In winter, there's usually folk music in the streets too.

A couple of good museums illustrate the town's early history, in particular the lucrative trade of the original Bahamian settlers, who lived off treasure saved from shipwrecks: the Wrecker's Museum (322 Duval St) and the Mel Fisher's Maritime Heritage Society Museum at 200 Greene St, containing the booty of a more recent bounty hunter.

Help and Information. The Key West Visitor's Bureau is in the Chamber of Commerce at 402 Wall St (294-2587). The telephone code for Key West is 305.

Island Life and the *Walking and Biking Guide to Key West* are free magazines that you can pick up in hotels and shops; they include useful information and also coupons offering discounts off admission charges.

FORT LAUDERDALE.

Fort Lauderdale (population 150,000) is hardly the 'Venice of America', as the tourist office credits it, but its canals, lagoons, and inland waterways certainly provide a placid and more stately alternative to Miami, 25 miles south.

Rigorous planning laws have kept Fort Lauderdale's six-mile stretch of sandy beach relatively unspoilt, and the fact that there is so little to distract one's attention here makes it more relaxing than its more industrial neighbour to the south. The mansions and life-styles of the nearby Palm Beach area are Florida's stateliest, and the locals would have you believe that the area's natural beauty is pre-eminent as well.

The Fort Lauderdale International House, 3811 North Ocean Boulevard (305-568-1615) has a swimming pool and scuba diving centre. Members of virtually anything from BUNAC to the Youth Hostels Association gets a dorm bed for $12. The official AYH Sol Y Mar Youth Hostel on 2839 Vistamar Street (305-566-1023) has beds for members at similar prices.

Surprisingly enough, Fort Lauderdale is one of the premier dining spots in the United States, with a glut of fine French restaurants. Some of them are beyond young travellers' means, like the gourmet Windows on the Green, overlooking the harbour and Marina. But Wolfie's, 2501 East Oakland Park Boulevard, is one of the best-known Jewish delis in a state full of them, and eminently affordable. Durty Nellie's, named after the original beneath Bunratty Castle in Ireland, is also on Oakland Park Boulevard. It's a bit loud in the evenings, but the hot dogs are free for drinkers. If you're still up at breakfast time, try R Donuts, and be the first in your neighbourhood to talk about doughnuts served by topless waitresses.

Entertainment. Fort Lauderdale is not exactly full of exciting things to do, except during spring break (around Easter) when college students descend on the place for a month of revelry. The Henry Morrison Flagler Museum on Whitehall Way in nearby Palm Beach (655-2833) is an imposing mansion full of china, jewellery, silverware, and other curios. An hour's drive west of Fort Lauderdale on Route 441 is Lake Okeechobee, the largest lake in the United States outside of the Great Lakes region. You can rent canoes for a paddle on the lake at Pakokee Marina (924-7505). Suggestions for other activities and daytrips are available from the Fort Lauderdale Chamber of Commerce, 4201 North Ocean Boulevard (776-1000)

ORLANDO

Few Americans had even heard of Orlando twenty years ago. But since Walt Disney World opened 20 miles to the south, many have come to see the attractions and have been pleasantly surprised by the city. Orlando is indeed handsome, full of parks, rivers and lakes. Although it has been overrun by hucksters and opportunists, and continues to fight against its image as a slightly ramshackle and prefab town, Orlando continues to draw and to impress tourists.

Numerous international flights arrive at the city's overcrowded airport; you can reach the downtown bus terminal for 75c on bus 11. Bus 1 also runs between the airport and the city, but be warned: while many local buses in the USA meander in an odd fashion, Orlando's bus 1 is easily the most ponderous. After travelling from the airport for half an hour you are still only a mile from the terminal, having performed two complete loops, and the overall journey takes 65 minutes (compared with 30-45 for bus 11). Although the rail line cuts through the middle of the city, the rail station is a dozen blocks south and west at 1400 Sligh Boulevard, near Columbia St. The Greyhound Station (843-7720) is several miles northwest on Colonial Drive.

The local buses are reasonably frequent and efficient. The Downtown bus station is at Central Boulevard and Orange Avenue; call 841-8240 for information. The standard fare is 75c, and transfers cost 10c.

The AYH Hostel (843-8888) is the old Plantation Manor at 227 N Eola Drive, at the northeast corner of Lake Eola at the corner of Robinson St; bus 4 runs from the bus station, or you can walk in 15 minutes. The hostel has standard dorm beds for around $12, but also includes an old motel out the back where there are plenty of twin rooms.

The most promising place to find a restaurant is the Church St Market complex, a big shopping and eating complex on Church St between Garland Avenue and Orange Avenue. It includes some busy pubs, such as Phineas Fogg's Balloon Works. Mulvaney's Irish Pub is on Church St at the corner of Orange Avenue.

Walt Disney World. To dismiss Disney World as American tackiness and gadgetry is to miss the point (and the pleasure). It is gaudy, it is primarily child-orientated, but anyone who doesn't enjoy the dozens of dazzling rides and audio-visual presentation must be a real misery.

The older part of the complex, the Magic Kingdom, is a set of six parks modelled on the original Disneyland in Anaheim, California, but on a much larger scale: Tomorrowland, Libertyland, and so on. Main Street USA is where most of the tourist bureau photos of dancing Mickey Mouses are taken; trains leave here for diffrent parks. Space Mountain is probably the biggest single attraction in this part of the park, an amazing roller-coaster ride that simulates a trip through outer space.

The much newer EPCOT Centere was conceived by Walt Disney himself as a model community where new ideas could be tested by scientists, with public viewing and participation. The acronym stands for the Experimental Prototype Community of Tomorrow. Sadly, perhaps, EPCOT has become something of a vehicle for corporate sponsorship: among the miracles unfurled in the Spaceship Earth exhibit (housed in the geodesic dome which dominates the Center) is the telephone, understandable enough the sponsor is AT&T.

EPCOT is divided into Future World — with rides and exhibits such as World of Motion (sponsored by General Motors) — and the Wold Showcase, a series of stylised miniature villages representing different nations grouped around a large lake. For some reason most people visit Future World first and World Showcase in the afternoon, so you should do the reverse. Don't miss the newest addition, the Disney/MGM studio complex. Like Universal Studios in Hollywood, it offers tours which include seeing films and television recordings in progress (Universal is now building its own studios 15 miles away, modelled on its Hollywood complex). After taking in a movie set, a dozen different countries and sensory overload at Future World, don't be surprised if you're exhausted: EPCOT, as they are pleased to remind you, also stands for Every Person Comes Out Tired.

The least busy days at the complex are Thursday, Friday and Sunday. Even for those without the seeminly mandatory Florida hire car, reaching Walt Disney World is easy: there are plenty of bus tours from both Orlando and Miami.

To make the most of your time, get to the complex early; 8.30am is ideal: although the gates do not officially open until 9am, at busy times they have been known to open early. Head straight for space Mountain in the Magic Kingdom to get your thrills before the crowds arrive. Since the Magic Kingdom is open until 10pm or midnight in peak season, you can see everything in a day if you don't mind feeling shattered at the end of it.

Sea World. This is what people came to see in Orlando before Walt Disney World opened. The largest man-made marine environment in the world, Sea World is like Miami's Seaquarium several times over. The killer whales, penguins and dolphins are here, as are the trained seals, but the *coup de grace* is the 150,000 gallon main tank, with a transplanted barrier reef marine environment. Sea World (351-3600) is just west of Orlando on I-4, accessible from the city centre on bus 8.

Universal Studios. Capitalizing on its success in California, Universal Studios has established a movie theme park adjacent to its studios in central Florida (accessible by bus 37 or 40 from Orlando). It is a series of movie set streets linking various attractions. The highlight is the Back to the Future ride, actually not a ride in the usual sense but a brilliantly conceived simulator with extraordinary graphics. The other rides pale in comparison, and the studio tour — say some — is not as impressive as the version in Hollywood.

Spaceport USA. The launch pads and buildings of the Kennedy Space Center spread across miles of swampland east of Orlando on the Atlantic coast. A host of side industries has sprung up to cater for the Center's visitors: in Cape Canaveral you can stay in the Gateway to the Stars Motel, and eat at the Galaxy Station restaurant in Cocoa Beach.

As many Americans have a deep emotional attachment to the US space programme, visitors numbers are steadily growing again after the Challenger disaster in 1986. Dial 1-800-432-2153 (toll-free, Florida only) for launch information.

TAMPA/ST PETERSBURG.

The Gulf of Mexico resorts were developed later than the Atlantic Ocean ones and are noticeably less vulgar and built-up. Flanking Tampa Bay, these two communities complement each other ideally as twin capitals of Florida's Gulf Coast. Tampa is a busy industrial centre, the seventh-largest port in the United States and home to one of the country's oldest Hispanic communities. St Petersburg ('St Pete') is a lush peninsual guarded by the lovely breakwater of the Holiday Isles from the Gulf of Mexico. Started as a retirement community and still one of the largest in the USA, St Petersburg has made a smooth transition into a resort centre. There is no need to worry about bad weather; every day that the sun doesn't shine the local newspaper is given away free, which in 60 years has happened only a handful of times. Taken together, these two communities offer the traveller all the amenities of a Florida vacation with enough history and non-tourist activity to save them from the crass commercialism one finds elsewhere in Florida.

Accomodation. St Petersburg is a more pleasant base than Tampa, and one of the best places to stay in the Detroit Hotel/St Petersburg International Hotel (215 Central Avenue, 813-822-4095). Foreign visitors can get dormitory beds for $10 per night, while double rooms cost $20 per night; there are discounts for long stays.

Eating and Drinking. In addition to the usual range of fast food establishment, there are Tampa's excellent and authentic spanish restaurants. The most famous, the Colombia Restaurant at 2117 East Seventh Avenue (813-248-4961) will set you back at least $15 a head. A couple of doors down, JD's (2029 East Seventh Avenue, 813-247-9683) serves similar dishes at about $5 a plate. For drinks, most of the young people in town flock to the University area, especially to Bennigan's Tavern, 2206 East Fowler Avenue, which serves good lunches as well.

Entertainment. Downtown St Petersburg is not the most likely place to find an exceptional modern art gallery, yet it is the location for the Salvador Dali Museum with the largest collection of the surrealist's work in the world. The new Performing Arts Center in Tampa is also worth checking out. Otherwise, the Tampa/St Petersburg area is not a place for cultural offerings, but for its varied outdoor attractions, especially Busch Gardens, 3000 busch Boulevard (813-971-8282). This is a man-made African jungle on a Disney World scale, complete with wandering elephants and lions, and space-age monorails and conveyance cars. Hillsborough River State Park is a beautifully landscaped grove on Tampa's waterfront, full of tropical flowers and tourists.

St Petersburg is even richer in outdoor attractions. Its Sunken Gardens, 1825 Fourth St (813-896-3186) are one of the best collections of tropical birds and flowers in the United States. Pass-a-Grille Beach is only one of the better of the city's waterfront areas, while Fort deSoto Park, at the peninsula's southernmost tip, is a leafy haven with plenty of campsites.

Shopping. Tampa, like much of Florida, relies heavily on the mall to please its shoppers; the largest is the Franklin Street Mall near the river, a fortunately tasteful project. Nearby is the Nostalgia Market, a restored cigar factory in the Hispanic Ybor city section. With a host of boutiques, ethnic cafes and folk exhibits, it is more typical of America's Northeast, and well worth a vist.

For more information, contact the Greater Tampa Chamber of Commerce (801 E Kentucky Boulevard, 813-228-7777) and the St Petersburg Chamber of Commerce (225 fourth St, 813-821-4715)

JACKSONVILLE.

The biggest city in northern Florida is the second largest in the USA behind Los Angeles in total land area. It stretches from the scenic St Johns River to the Atlantic where Fort Clinch State Park and Little Talbot Island State Park preserve the least uncrowded and developed beaches between the Carolinas and Cuba. It is also the home of the University of Florida where welcoming atmosphere and reasonably priced goods and services are not unlike those found on the campuses of Ann Arbor, Madison or LA for that matter. Students from the U of F make up much of the audience of the Jacksonville and All That Jazz Festival held in mid-October and for which no admission is charged.

The main disadvantage of Jacksonville, however, is the absence of cheap accommodation, especially in the tourist months. Lesser evils include its 9% sales tax added to everything and its dismal public transport which makes travel betwen lodging and the beaches a nightmare. Motels such as the Ambassador Inn (354-5611), Silver Sea Motel (249-1746) and Salt Air Motel (246-6465) will set you back about $20 a night.

You do better with food than lodgings. Ryan's Family Steak House chain will provide fish or steak for about $4 a plate. You can also enjoy all the shrimp you can eat at The Ritespot Restaurant for $7. And at the Center Street Station Restaurant near Fort Clinch, a mere $3.75 will get you a meat and potatoes dinner.

EVERGLADES.

The large swampy areas of southern Florida, known as the Everglades, are further south than Cairo and Delhi. Everglades National Park covers the whole southwest corner of the state and is traversed by Highway 27. Near the park entrance there is a broadwalk over the swampy grasslands where you can see alligators, brightly coloured birds and all manner of subtropical flora and fauna (including swarms of mosquitoes). For a more serious study of this unique area, you can charter a boat and guide who will take you to one of the many backcountry campsites. Camping is free provided you get the permission of the Park Ranger in Homestead, a small town easily accessible from Miami by Greyhound.

New Orleans and the South

Alabama   Arkansas   Kentucky   Louisiana   Mississippi   Tennessee

The South is as diverse and diverting as any region of the United States. While moving fast into a high-tech future, culturally it clings to its heritage — alongside the new, the Old South lives on: white-columned mansions and wretched sharecroppers' shacks are physical evidence of long enduring attitudes and values. The old Confederate flag is widely displayed, and visitors may well come across resentment of 'Yankees'.

Dixie is the name for the Southern states and should not be taken in vain. There are several explanations for its origins; the most common is that in the early 19th century, many of the $10 bills in circulation in the southern states were issued by a bank in New Orleans which printed *dix* on them (French for 'ten'). Dixie should not be confused with the Mason Dixon Line which separated the South from the North in the Civil War.

New Orleans is the supreme attraction of the South, and rightly so. But the region outside the city is not explored nearly as much as it should be — although more and more travellers are discovering the delights of Tennessee's two big cities, Memphis and Nashville; and President Clinton has put his home state of Arkansas firmly on the map. The soul of the South, however, resides in the small towns of rural Louisiana, Mississippi and Alabama, where you can encounter fearful deprivation but are guaranteed a warm welcome — and often the chance to hear some good swamp music.

The excellent reputation of Southern hospitality is deserved. Visitors from the UK are especially fortunate because many white Southerners have British roots of which they are proud. Most of them seem intrigued by the sound of a British accent, which can be a valuable asset in environments ranging from singles bars to police stations. Offers of help and hospitality are frequent and genuine, especially if you strike them as a conservative and law-abiding type.

NEW ORLEANS

Zsa Zsa Gabor, in one of her more perceptive comments, once said that New Orleans was 'the most European of all American cities, not alone for its architecture but also because of the people's attitude towards life.' That the openly racist David Duke only just missed being elected as state governor in 1991 is representative of Louisiana rather than New Orleans. But while the city stands apart from the South, it carries some characteristics of the region to extremes — in terms of food, music, poverty and, occasionally, intolerance.

La Nouvelle Orléans was founded in 1718 as a French colony, then ruled by Spain from 1762 to 1803, when it went back to the French; Napoleon promptly sold it to the US as part of the famous Louisiana Purchase, when the US government paid $15 million for all the land between Canada and Mexico, and from the Mississippi to the Rockies.

While New Orleans has a population of about a million and is the second largest port in the USA, the much smaller city of Baton Rouge, 77 miles upriver, is the state capital of Louisiana. But New Orleans is the pulse of the South, the point at which all that is good or bad about the magnificent Mississippi pours out into the Gulf of Mexico.

The focus of New Orleans — for visitors at least — is the French Quarter, the most perfectly preserved piece of European town planning in North America. Tourism has unquestionably had a deleterious effect over the last decade, and old hands say the city has demeaned itself in the unceasing quest for revenue. But while Bourbon Street has been reduced to a vision of tackiness, the French Quarter's side streets, where grace and sleaze rub shoulders, are still magic.

For lovers of good food, unimaginable cocktails and great jazz, New Orleans is a dream. This is the home of many jazz greats — Louis Armstrong, Jelly Roll Morton, Sidney Bechet, Rix Beiderbecke and Fats Domino among them; and jazz still flourishes in the bars and clubs of the French Quarter. The city also has a long and distinguished literary tradition, and Tennessee Williams wrote several of his books here.

New Orleans has all manner of nicknames, from the 'Big Easy' to the 'City That Care Forgot'. Some of the city police prefer to describe it as a rotten apple, with a lot of the crime problems associated with other, less glamourous cities. The amount of street crime in the city, especially the heavily touristed areas, has increased to worrying proportions. But New Orleans' unique history and culture will always make it worth a visit.

THE PEOPLE

The two most interesting ethnic groups in and around New Orleans are the Creoles and the Cajuns, which are sometimes confused with one another. The term Creole is confusing since elsewhere in the Americas it refers to people of mixed race. In Louisiana, the Creoles are the descendants of the original French settlers who first arrived in 1682, though it is also used more loosely to refer to the descendants of Spanish and other white, non-Anglo settlers. The Cajuns (also known as Acadian people) were French deportees from British rule in Nova Scotia who arrived in the 18th century. Cajun describes not only a people, but also its culture and its cuisine.

The present ethnic spectrum of New Orleans is wider than that of any other city in the States. Almost half the population is said to be black. There are also large Irish, Italian, and German communities. Early English-speaking settlers chose to live further upriver from the French Quarter, in what is known as the Garden District. The Central American community is increasing in size and influence. Honduran immigrants have been joined by fellow Hispanic people from the strife-torn countries of El Salvador and Nicaragua, and New Orleans is becoming for Central America what Miami has long been for South America — a cultural and commercial gateway to the USA.

The principal religious affiliation of the region is the Southern Baptist Church, but there are many less moderate groups which preach their particular visions of salvation with varying degrees of fervour and intolerance. Fundamentalism is widespread. An interesting alternative is the gospel flavour of many churches in the black communities.

Making Friends. Traditional Southern hospitality survives as well as could be expected in a city the size of New Orleans, and people are generally easy to get on with. Making friends requires not much more than the ability to penetrate the Southern drawl so that you'll know what city they are referring to when they talk about N'Awlins. The French Quarter is unquestionably the best place to eat, drink, sleep and meet people. The atmosphere is friendly and the people so gregarious that there should be little difficulty in making contact. People in New Orleans have few inhibitions and enjoy noisy exchanges.

The Mardi Gras festival takes place every year during the two weeks before Shrove Tuesday. It is impossible not to be caught up in the merry-making and this is a great opportunity to make friends.

CLIMATE

New Orleans is normally spared extreme temperatures, with December in the 50s and July in the 80s. A temperature of 70°F/21°C is recorded every month of the year. Because of its sub-tropical delta location, the humidity can be very high at any time and rainfall is occasionally heavy. The best time to visit is between September and the spring, when the weather is cooler and without the threat of hurricanes.

Though New Orleans has not been hit by a hurricane for many years, a 'Tropical Storm Outlook' is issued every day of the summer, and the mayor's office has a 'Hurricane Evacuation Plan'. If a storm warning persuades you to leave the city in a hurry, do not do so by crossing the Lake Pontchartrain road causeway. The lake is only 15 feet deep, so it is not hard to imagine the sort of tidal wave that could be caused by a hurricane.

CITY LAYOUT

One of New Orleans' nicknames is 'Crescent City', owing to the U-bend in the Mississippi River as it flows through the centre. The once shabby riverside scene has changed dramatically over the last decade, with the building of shopping malls, the conversion of warehouses into art galleries and various other developments geared at sprucing up the area's appearance.

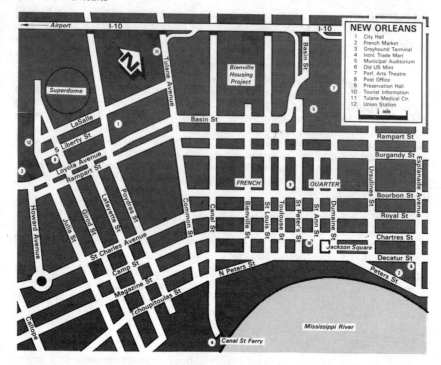

NEW ORLEANS	
1	City Hall
2	French Market
3	Greyhound Terminal
4	Intnl. Trade Mart
5	Municipal Auditorium
6	Old US Mint
7	Perf. Arts Theatre
8	Post Office
9	Preservation Hall
10	Tourist Information
11	Tulane Medical Ctr.
12	Union Station

New Orleans is divided into Downtown and Uptown. The first is made up of the French Quarter and the Central Business District (CBD), with Canal Street as its central artery. The French Quarter, known as the Vieux Carfe, covers 13 blocks between Canal St and Esplanade Avenue; the riverside Jackson Square (along with Bourbon St) is the district's main reference point. When the locals say 'downriver', they mean north of Canal St ('upriver' being south).

St Charles Avenue is the main drag through Uptown. The area of interest here is the Garden District, where most of the prosperous ante-bellum (pre Civil War) mansions are found — concentrated in the area bounded by Jackson Avenue, Louisiana Avenue, St Charles Avenue and Magazine St.

Getting Around

Air. New Orleans International Airport (MSY) is 12 miles northwest of the city centre along I-10. Ring 464-0831 for flight information. Airport Shuttle (522-3500) runs from the airport to hotels in the Central Business District and French Quarter. The journey takes about 30 minutes, and costs $10, compared with a local bus which takes 20 minutes longer but costs $1.10. The taxi fare is around $20.

Bus. There are frequent long-distance services from Houston (eight hours), Miami (24 hours), New York (32 hours) and the California coast (48 hours).

Greyhound's terminal (525-9371) is in the western part of the city centre — behind the Bienville Monument and nestling beneath the freeway as it crosses Loyola Avenue. Most services also pick up and drop off passengers closer to downtown at the corner of Basin and Canal Streets.

Train. More interestingly, you can arrive in New Orleans by train. Amtrak operates from Union Station at 1001 Loyola Avenue, near the Superdome and adjacent to the Greyhound terminal. Call 528-1610 or 1-800-872-7245 for information.

There are three main line services: *The Crescent* (from New York, Washington and Atlanta) arrives at 7.20pm daily after a 29-hour journey which ends by crossing Lake Pontchartrain, with the return journey 7am; the *City of New Orleans* (made fleetingly famous in the song of the same name by Arlo Guthrie) arrives every day at 1.50pm from Chicago and Memphis, returning at 2.40pm; the *Sunset Limited* arrives from Los Angeles via Phoenix, Tucson and El Paso at 7.50pm on Tuesdays, Fridays and Sundays, and departs west on Mondays, Wednesdays and Saturdays at 2.15pm. The journey to LA takes almost two days.

Driving. Although the 24-mile toll causeway which runs north from New Orleans across Lake Pontchartrain is undeniably the longest bridge in the world, it is more a long unimpressive flyover than a stunning piece of engineering.

I-59 and I-55 flank the lake and both enter New Orleans from the north. Outside the city, these join the east-west I-10 which sweeps right through downtown. Drivers wishing to head straight through from Florida to California are advised to leave I-10 at Slidell and use I-12 to Baton Rouge, where I-10 rejoins. This is a shorter journey, and avoids the heart-stopping tension of trying to cruise through on a freeway which also fulfils the role of New Orleans' Main Street.

Hitch-Hiking. I-10 cuts right through the city centre and there are numerous junctions, notably the Canal St intersection, which provide a fair chance of a lift east or west. However, the city police strictly enforce the law against hitching from the roadway and make it clear that they don't like hitchers polluting their city. For a less hazardous start to your journey, take the Canal St bus to its terminus at I-10 heading west, and hitch around Lake Pontchartrain for destinations north and east.

CITY TRANSPORT

Although there are no longer any streetcars named Desire, there is a streetcar named St Charles and a diesel bus named Desire. Buses and the two streetcar lines are operated by the Regional Transit Authority. Ring 569-2700 for route and schedule information, or call into the office in the Plaza Tower, 101 Dauphine St in the French Quarter.

The best way to tour the French Quarter is on foot.

Bus. Buses are identified by the points they serve in the suburbs, e.g. 'Elysian Fields' and 'Desire'. Routes commence from Canal St and mostly run east-west, many until 3am. The flat rate fare is $1 for local buses and $1.10 for expresses. Exact change is required. Transfers are available from the driver. These are also valid on the St Charles streetcar and on the Vieux Carfe minibus. The latter runs around the French Quarter from 5am to 7pm.

VisiTour passes — $3 a day, $6 for three days — allow unlimited travel on all buses and streetcars, and are available from the big hotels.

Streetcars. The St Charles line is a National Historic Monument and claims to be the oldest continuously running street railway in the world. It trundles along St Charles Avenue for seven miles, between Canal St and Audubon Park via Lafayette Square. Taking the streetcar the whole distance — which takes about 90 minutes — is a fun and cheap way to get a taste of New Orleans outside the French Quarter. A new streetcar line links the foot of Julia St, near the Convention Center, with Esplanade Avenue. The flat fare on streetcars is $1.25.

Car. Except during Mardi Gras, the volume of traffic is no more oppressive than in other American cities. A good city map such as that given away at Tourist Information Offices, will help you come to terms with the unusual freeway numbering system (I-610 is actually a by-pass for I-10) and the unpredictable twists and turns of the Mississippi.

Don't try to drive in the French Quarter, let alone park. You can park all day (Monday to Friday) for a few dollars at the Superdome. If the Superdome lot is full, use one of the off-street lots near the freeway, and walk the extra distance. Expect to pay at least $10 for 24 hours of parking.

The alternative is to create your own Park'n'Ride system by parking in a quiet suburban street (e.g. near the western terminus of the St Charles streetcar line) and using public transport to the centre.

Car Rental: for low-cost car hire, try Cheapie Rent-a-Car (3215 Dublin St, 486-3986) or Swifty Car Rental (2300 Canal St, 524-7368). Some agencies require you to have your own insurance.

Cycling. Both City Park near Lake Pontchartrain, and Audubon Park by the Mississippi, are fun to cycle around. Bicycles can be hired from Michael's Bicycle Rentals (618 Frenchmen St) or French Quarter Rentals (410 Dauphine St), and from the AYH Hostel (see *Accommmodation*).

Ferry. The port of New Orleans handles 1,000 ships a month, and exports principally coal, grain, cotton and citrus fruit. Several of the grain tankers are Russian.

For a brief and fascinating glimpse of the port, take *SS Natchez* (a sternwheeler paddle steamer) from Toulouse Street Wharf near Jackson Square. The *Natchez* takes 1,600 people on a two-hour trip down the river to the site of the Battle of New Orleans, where General Jackson slaughtered the British in 1815, and upriver past the site of the 1984 World Fair (which was a flop). Tours depart at 11.30am and 2.30pm, and cost $13.50. Ring New Orleans Steamboat Company on 586-8777.

There are other boats — *Cotton Blossom and Voyageur* — which cruise further, through the swamps and waterways of the bayou country.

For a free ride, take the commuter ferry which travels between the bottom of Canal St and Algiers, the residential area on the opposite shore.

Accommodation

Hotels. Most tourists visit New Orleans primarily for the French Quarter, and accommodation rates reflect this. Cheaper hotels inside the square mile cost $50-60 for a double, those outside at least ten dollars less. During Mardi Gras, rooms are more expensive than ever, and also very hard to find.

The advantage of staying within or very close to the Vieux Carré is not just snob appeal: New Orleans is very much a night-time city, with after dark entertainment focussed sharply on the French Quarter. A long, daunting journey back to a distant hotel, with the added expense of a taxi ride, compares most unfavourably with a short and leisurely stroll home from the bars and bustle of Bourbon St.

Within the Quarter, the friendly Hotel Villa Convento (616 Ursulines, 522-1793) charges $60-70 for a double, with a complimentary breakfast in the palm-shaded Victorian courtyard. Near the Quarter, try the popular St Charles Guest House (1748 Prytania, 523-6556), with doubles for $30-50 and easy access to the Vieux Carré by the St Charles streetcar. Nearby is the Old World Inn (1330 Prytania, 566-1330), which charges similar rates. On St Charles Avenue itself, the Hummingbird at number 804 (561-9229) has doubles for about $20-30 and gives discounts for students.

For longer stays, there are some rooms available in the Quarter starting at about $50 a week, sharing a bathroom.

Bed and Breakfast. Contact Bed & Breakfast Inc (1021 Moss St, PO Box 52257, New Orleans LA70182; 488-4640) or just ask at the Visitor Center in Jackson Square.

Hostels. The AYH Youth Hostel (523-3014) is housed in a gracious pre-Civil War mansion at 2253 Carondelet St, just one block from the St Charles streetcar (get off at Jackson Avenue). The price is $10-13 for members in the summer, with one or two private doubles available for about $30. The hostel is very popular, so it is advisable to ring ahead.

A good alternative is the 'India House' International Hostel (124 South Lopez St, 821-1904), run by and for backpackers. Rates are around $12 per night, or $70 a week. It is a couple of blocks north of I-10, just off Canal St.

The characterless YMCA (936 St Charles Avenue, 568-9622) costs about $20 single, $30 double.

Camping. There are two KOA Campgrounds: one in the west (467-1792) on the Jefferson Highway, which follows the north shore of the river, and the other in the east (643-3850), near Highway 433 on the northeast edge of Lake Pontchartrain. The fee is about $18.

Eating and Drinking

A southern menu might require some interpretation: *hushpuppies* (cornmeal fritters), *grits* (ground corn boiled in milk, like small-bore tapioca) and *chitlins* (the small intestines of pigs, crisply fried and better than they sound) are items which should be tried at least once — not forgetting such better known native crops as peaches, pecans and peanuts.

One of the principal reasons — perhaps the best reason — for visiting New Orleans is its food. Mark Twain wrote that dining here was 'as delicious as the less criminal forms of sin'. There are so many good restaurants that it is hard to go wrong (as long as you avoid the blatantly touristy and/or tacky places). There are only a few places to tempt you out of the French Quarter.

Creole and Cajun cuisines have become blended to such an extent that at times it is hard to distinguish them apart — with more confusion brought by other outside influences: don't be taken aback by restaurants offering Chinese Creole cuisine.

The most common Creole specialities are *gumbo*, a stew of okra and meat or seafood, and *jambalaya*, the Creole version of pilaff, a rice and meat dish. Spicy sauces are an integral part of most dishes. All the tabasco sauce in the world is made under licence from one factory in Avery Island (130 miles west, south of Lafayette), where the sauce was invented about a hundred years ago. Bottles of tabasco in New Orleans are the size of ketchup bottles. Go lightly until you are converted. For a three-hour introduction to Creole cookery visit the New Orleans School of Cooking in the Jackson Brewery (525-2665). Not only is this an education, it also fills you up for the rest of the day, and if the host is in generous mood the free wine may knock you out. The course costs $16.

Cajun food, which has become popular in the rest of the USA and Europe by storm in the last few years, is simpler and more robust than Creole cooking. Meals often centre around fish or seafood, and are hotter than their Creole counterparts.

New Orleans' seafood is superb. Oysters are better eaten cooked; uncooked they are not as tasty as their English counterpart, though they can be found for a little as $5 per dozen e.g. at the Desire Oyster Bar on Bourbon Street. Soft shell crab is delicious, but make sure it is in season and not frozen. A *po-boy* sandwich is cheap and filling and can be found almost anywhere: it is made with French bread and stuffed usually with roast beef and sauteed oysters, hot cream and tabasco.

Johnny's Po-Boys, two blocks from Jackson Square at 511 St Louis (524-8129) is one of the cheapest and best places in town. Avoid the tourists and join the queue of workers at lunchtime for the tastiest fried catfish po-boy sandwich in town: 'Even my failures are edible', boasts Johnny. He also serves some of the most delicious gumbo in town.

The Gumbo Shop (630 St Peter St, 525-1486), in a delightful 18th-century courtyard surrounded by huge cheese plants, is also good value, though touristy these days. Try also Houlihan's at 315 Bourbon St (523-7412), which has a jolly atmosphere and is the sort of place — found only in America — where an omelette is served with hollandaise sauce and fried oysters, and garnished with fresh strawberries. It also offers fried pieces of baked potato skin which, eaten with various hot tomato and horseradish sauces, are delicious.

The most affordable of the top restaurants in New Orleans is Galatoire's (209 Bourbon St, 525-2021), which is well patronized by the locals. You can't make reservations, but the wonderful Creole and Cajun dishes are well worth the wait. Expect to pay at least $20-25.

Party animals and insomniacs need not worry about going hungry. Breakfast is served at The Clover Grill (corner of Dumaine and Bourbon, 523-0904) 24 hours a day, by staff who are refreshingly sarcastic; the burgers are delicious. And you can get coffee and *beignets* (doughnuts) in the riverside French Market at any time of the day or night: Cafe du Monde in Jackson Square is full of tourists but its doughnuts are irresistible, and the chicory coffee compulsory. If the crush is too great go to the Croissant D'Or (617 Ursuline, 524-4663), between Chartres and Royal Streets.

Outside the Quarter. Mother's (401 Poydras, 523-9656), a simple caff with formica tables, is one of the best places in town. The menu includes everything from traditional fry-ups to soft-shell crab and turtle soup; 'debris' consists of the scraps of meat that fall off the joint during roasting.

More of a trek is Uglesich (1238 Baronne at Erato, 523-8571), a seedy joint patronized by a mix of truck drivers and businessmen. Situated beyond the bus and train terminals, it isn't in a particularly safe part of town, so consider taking a taxi. But it's worth making the effort just to taste the oyster and shrimp po-boys.

Further out is Camellia's Grill (626 S Carrollton, 866-9573), one of the great US diners. Situated at the end of St Charles Avenue, it is easily accessible on the streetcar.

DRINKING

The great drink of the south is bourbon, corn-based whisky first produced in Bourbon County, Kentucky. New Orleans, on the other hand, is the birthplace of the cocktail, and you shouldn't leave town without trying at least one ingenious concoction, whether it's a Ramos Gin Fizz, an Absinthe Suissesse or an 'eye-opener' (a local speciality served with breakfast). A mint julep consists of bourbon, soda, ice, sugar and mint leaves and is more pleasant than the sweet Hurricane, which contains rum and passion fruit juice among other things. The latter comes in a glass shaped like a hurricane lamp, which the waiter will try and persuade you to buy.

Bourbon Street abounds with bars, but these include sleazy strip joints and you will find some of the best places down the side streets. Drinking to live music is the norm in New Orleans, so anyone not into jazz or R & B may have come to the wrong city.

The Hurricane cocktail was invented at Pat O'Brien's, a rowdy but fun piano bar at 718 St Peter St (525-4823). Quieter and more civilized are the Absinthe House Bar (400 Bourbon St, corner of Bienville; 525-8108) or Napoleon House (500 Chartres St, 524-9752), where classical music not jazz is played. Around the intersection of Bourbon and Dumaine Streets, most of the bars are gay: the Cafe Lafitte in Exile (901 Bourbon St, 522-8397) is one of the oldest and most popular bars in town, and is open 24 hours.

When ordering you're unlikely to be asked for ID since, unlike most other states, Louisiana imposes no liability on the establishment which unintentionally serves someone under 21; only the drinker gets fined.

Many of the more endearing curiosities of the city will be found by chance or, rather, by walking. You will discover streets with stranger and more enchanting names than perhaps anywhere in the world. The French and Spanish Catholic legacy is responsible for streets such as Annunciation, Assumption, Ascension, Piety; the Greek classical influence for Calliope and Socrates. And who knows the fanciful thoughts that inspired the street names Benefit, Desire, Pleasure, Mystery, Industry, Abundance, Genius, Harmony and Humanity?

The French Quarter. The French Quarter consists mainly of 19th-century buildings, some of which still show Spanish influence, though most of the 18th-century houses were destroyed in the great fires of 1788 and 1794; the continent's oldest apartment block, the Pontalba Apartments, collapsed in 1989. The exquisite ironwork and sheer style of the surviving structures outweighs the abject commercialism of ground-level Bourbon St — look up for the best touches in the city: there are no high-rise blocks in the Quarter (and no traffic lights). At 1140 Royal St, the ghosts of manacled slaves are said to appear on rainy nights.

Jackson Square, where the French Quarter meets the river, is dominated by St Louis, the oldest cathedral in the US. Though not old by European standards (built in 1794) the rest of the Square — with its old government buildings, palm trees, horse-drawn carriages and street artists — is reminiscent of Seville. Visit early in the morning, when pigeons outnumber people and you might hear a lone Creole playing the trumpet to the sky. There is outdoor jazz here on Saturdays throughout the summer, when thousands of locals and visitors throng the shops, bars and restaurants around the Square.

Museums: The French Quarter Museum in Gallier House (1118-1132 Royal St) gives a marvellous taste of what homes in the district looked like in the 19th century. It is open for guided tours 10.30am-3.45pm Monday to Saturday, noon-3.45pm on Sunday.

Louisiana State Museum in Jackson Square (open 10am-5pm Wednesday to Sunday) has a motley collection, ranging from old portraits to musical instruments. Much more fun is the Jazz Museum in the Old Mint (Esplanade Avenue, by the river), with old photographs, recordings and instruments played by some of the city's great musicians. The Mardi Gras display includes a fabulous collection of costumes. Opening hours are 10am-5pm Wednesday to Sunday.

Tours: the guided walking tours of the French Quarter are strongly recommended. The Friends of the Cabildo run two-hour tours, starting at the Louisiana State Museum and costing $7: at 9.30am and 1.30pm from Tuesday to Saturday and at 1.30pm on Sundays. For $8 you can go on a tours in a horse-drawn carriages, also departing from Jackson Square.

The Cities of the Dead. Most of New Orleans is below sea level and the whole of it lies below the high water mark of the Mississippi River. It is easy to understand why graves in News Orleans are built above ground — hence the name 'Cities of the Dead.' The oldest and best graveyard to visit is St Louis Cemetery No 1 (400 Basin St at St Louis Street), on the edge of the French Quarter. The small graveyard is heavily atmospheric, but don't go alone as it is an ideal hiding place for muggers.

Zoos. Audubon Zoological Garden (6500 Magazine St, 861-2537) is one of the finest zoos in the country. Among the biggest attractions are the white alligators and the red wolves, originally native to the region but now extinct in the wild. Admission costs $7, and the zoo opens daily 9.30am-4.30pm. It is close to the western end of the St Charles streetcar, linked to the line by a free shuttle bus. As well as the streetcar, you can also reach the zoo on the Magazine bus, or by catamaran from the Canal St wharf. Don't be tempted to walk, since the most direct route passes through some dodgy territory.

The new Aquarium of the Americas, close to Canal St wharf, is also a must. The simulated rainforest and coral reef are superb, with huge glass tanks containing sharks and other less menacing creatures. It is open 9.30am-9pm daily, admission $8.

Music. It would be unthinkable to go to New Orleans without considering a visit to the Preservation Hall (726 St Peter St, 523-8939). If you're prepared to queue long enough, you can hear the original Dixieland jazz at its best, played by Louis Armstrong look-alikes most of whom are in their 70's. (Most of the younger musicians, who are gradually replacing them, are white.) The bands change each evening, and for $3 you may sit or stand in a room bare of furniture, decoration or a bar, and enjoy great music from 8.30pm until 1am.

To find other venues, the best advice is to walk down Bourbon St and listen: for example at the Famous Door (339), which is one of the oldest and best jazz clubs in town. Check the weekly entertainment papers called *Gambit* or *Figaro*, for details of performers and venues. The *New Orleans Times Picayune* has a special 'What's On' section (the Lagniappe) every Friday. And always ask for advice from the locals.

Don't miss out on the distinctive Cajun music — lively foot-tapping tunes played on fiddles and accordions, with vocals in the incomprehensible bastard French still widely spoken by natives. You can hear some of the best cajun bands — big and small — at Tipitina's at 501 Napoleon Avenue (895-9144); take a taxi home, since this is a dodgy area at night. Devotees should head for Cajun country west of New Orleans — particularly in mid-September when the Festival Acadien is held in Lafayette. The black version of cajun, known as *zydeco,* is well worth hearing. The place to go is the Maple Leaf bar (8316 Oak St, 866-LEAF), five miles west of the French Quarter, where you can also learn the cajun dance-steps. A slightly less frenetic version can be heard at Michael's (701 Magazine St, 522-5517) and Mulate's (201 Julia St, 522-1492).

Festivals. *New Orleans:* Mardi Gras parades have been held in New Orleans to celebrate 'Fat Tuesday' (the last day before lent) since 1837. Mardi Gras is the biggest knees-up in the USA, with 65 parades in two weeks, crowds of over two million and dancing on every street corner. It is an unforgettable experience, but don't forget to stay around afterwards, to see what New Orleans is really like. The carnival season officially begins on January 6, but parades start in earnest two weeks before Mardi Gras day. In 1993 this is February 23; in 1994, February 15; in 1995, February 28; and in 1996, February 20.

The Spring Fiesta takes place during the fortnight following the first Friday after Easter. Some of the 19th-century aristocratic mansions in the Garden District open their doors to the public. For information call 581-1367.

The Jazz and Heritage Festival is an orgy of traditional music, held at the Fairgrounds Race Track at the end of April and beginning of May. You can hear everything from jazz and cajun to Irish folk and Country & Western. Buy tickets on the day.

SPORT

You can see baseball, football and boxing at the Superdome (1500 Poydras St), the world's largest domed stadium. Call 587-3800 for tickets. Most people find the stadium at least as fascinating as the games, and it is well worth going on a tour, particularly if preparations are being made for a big event like a political convention. Look out for the painted seat backs, designed to make it look as though all the seats are full for televised sports events. Tours leave on the hour 9am-4pm; call 587-3810.

Horse racing takes place all the year round, including some Sundays, at the Fairgrounds Track (November to April) and Jefferson Downs (April to November).

According to popular mythology, the driving skills acquired in transporting illicitly distilled 'moonshine' whisky rapidly over country roads produced the early heroes of stock-car racing, today one of the South's most popular spectator sports in spring and summer.

SHOPPING

The colourful French Market is open daily along Decatur St between the 800 and 1100 blocks, by the river. Along with wonderful fresh produce and seafood, you will find a shop called Santa's Quarters, which sells Christmas presents throughout the year and a shop at 536 Royal Street which sells a huge variety of colourful umbrellas and parasols.

Bourbon St is dominated by tacky souvenir shops, but down the side streets you can find shops with names like Chickenheads, selling everthing connected with voodoo. At the Voodoo Museum at 724 Dumaine St, you can learn about the African origins of the cult and buy voodoo kits (dolls, pins and all) for $18. Also try the Witchcraft Shop at 521 St Philip.

The usual selection of glamorous shops can be found in the JAX Shopping Center in the converted Jackson Brewery. The riverside promenade known as Moon Walk, connects it to the French Market.

Legislation in Louisiana allows for overseas visitors to avoid sales tax; it is always worth asking if a store will do this.

THE MEDIA

New Orleans' only daily paper is the *Times Picayune. Gambit* is an informative and entertaining weekly newspaper.

The University of New Orleans station (WWNO 89.9 FM) is part of the National Public Radio network. In addition there are many religious stations and one (WRBH 88.3 FM) for the blind. For news try WWL (870 AM), for classic jazz WWOZ (90.7 FM), for soul Q-93 (WQUE 93.3 FM), for soft rock WLTS (105 FM) and for heavy metal WLMG (102 FM).

Crime and Safety

One of the roles of staff in the visitors center is to write NO in big letters on the maps of tourists worried by the city's reputation for crime. The main no-go area is invariably the Bienville Housing Project, north of Basin St between Canal and St Louis Streets.

The main streets of the Vieux Carré (and to some extent outside it) are well lit and frequently patrolled by police, but the side streets are not so safe. Watch out for pickpockets and tricksters who are drawn to tourist areas everywhere; bagsnatching is particularly popular. During Mardi Gras, as many criminals as tourists flock to New Orleans. Outside the French Quarter, stick to the main thoroughfares after dark. Particularly dodgy areas are around the Superdome and the transport terminals and north of Rampart Street, particularly Louis Armstrong Park.

New Orleans cops are not to be messed with (as throughout the south), and Louisiana justice makes it easy to put someone behind bars.

Help and Information

The area code for New Orleans if 504.

Information: the New Orleans Visitor Information Center is at 527 St Ann St, Jackson Square (568-5661 or 566-5031). Open daily 10am-6pm, 9am-5pm in winter.

American Express: 158 Baronne St (568-8201).

Thomas Cook: 111 St Charles Avenue (524-0700).
Post Office: 701 Loyola Avenue, 70140 (589-2201 or 589-1112), near Union Station.
Western Union Telegrams: 1-800-325-6000.
Medical Emergencies: Tulane University Medical Center (588-5711); emergency entrance at 217 La Salle.
24-hour drugstore: Eckerd Drugs, 3400 Canal St (488-6661).
Travelers' Aid: 846 Baronne St at Howard Avenue (525-8726).
Police: 821-2222.
Louisiana Department of Wildlife and Fisheries: 7612 West End Boulevard (1-800-442-2511).
British Honorary Consulate: 321 St Charles Avenue (524-4180).

LOUISIANA

Plantation Country. For an historical perspective on the society and economy of the South, hire a car and drive along Highway 18, the so-called River Road, which runs along the Mississippi northwest from New Orleans to Baton Rouge and beyond. Scattered along it are old sugar plantation houses, built during the boom prior to the Civil War, many in the style of the Greek Revival popular in Europe at the time. The houses fell into decay following the war, but many have been restored. Most are private homes, but others are open to the public, generally 10am-4pm daily for guided tours; admission is $5-7. It is possible to stay overnight at some of them.

Closest to New Orleans is the 18th-century Destrehan Plantation (764-9315), 22 miles west, which is the oldest surviving example in southern Louisiana. San Francisco (535-2341) in Reserve, 23 miles further along the Mississippi on State Highway 44, dates from 1856; the house is particularly renowned for its exuberance, both inside and out.

One of the most interesting is the Oak Alley Plantation, in Vacherie (523-4351), 60 miles from New Orleans on Sate Highway 18. The house was built in the 1830s and a stunning quarter-mile avenue of evergreen oaks leads down to the river. Visitors are shown around by the servants of the last occupying family, and you can stay overnight in cabins in the grounds. The free Lutcher car ferry which crosses the Mississippi a few miles from Oak Alley permits access to more colonial homes, such as Madewood (369-7151) on State Highway 308, two miles south of Napoleonville; if you have $160 to spare you can enjoy a night in a four-poster bed and wander freely through the house after it has shut for the day.

The huge Ashland-Belle-Helene Plantation (473-1207) is in Geismar, about 20 miles southeast of Baton Rouge; the house contains much of the original furnishings.

An organized tour to a couple of these houses costs about $50 with Southern Tours, 7801 Edinburgh St (486-0604).

Baton Rouge, the state capital, holds little appeal. If you need to make an overnight stop, try the Ramada Hotel (1480 Nicholson Drive, 581-1303), just south of the centre, which charges around $60 for a double.

Cajun Country. Acadiana, or Cajun Country, stretches from Houma, south of New Orleans, west into Texas. The Cajuns seek to preserve the simple lifestyle of fishing, hunting and furtrapping that has been followed since their ancestors arrived in 1755, following the British occupation of their native Nova Scotia. Their distinct culture, cuisine and music has survived, and the latter has grown in recognition since Paul Simon adopted the style in some of the songs on his *Graceland* album.

While renting a car is the cheapest and most convenient way to visit the ante-bellum mansions around New Orleans, the great swampy swathes of Bayou country are best seen on a tour. The bayous consist of thousands of acres of oak and wilderness of backwaters, half submerged trees festooned with Spanish moss and isolated villages accessible only by boat. Bayou country is a haven for birdlife (including egrets and beautiful Louisiana herons), deer and even the occasional alligator. Try to see the film *Southern Comfort* for a vivid, if scary, view of the swamps.

Lafayette: the capital of Acadiana and once a boom town, Lafayette has been badly hit by the oil slump. It is now a sleepy but pleasant place, and ideal for getting to know Cajun country. Acadiana To Go (619 Woodvale Avenue, 318-981-3918) runs tours of the area.

Two excellent museums give a taste of early Cajun communities. Vermilionville (Lafayette's old name) is at 1600 Surrey St (318-233-4077), and is the most accessible. It is very much a living museum, with plays, dancing, cookery demonstrations, lectures, etc. It is open 9am-5pm Monday to Thursday, 9am-9pm Friday to Sunday; admission is $8. The Acadian Village is at 200 Greenleaf Rd (318-981-2364), open daily 10am-5pm, admission $5.

Lafayette is 130 miles northwest of New Orleans, about $3\frac{1}{2}$ hours by Greyhound bus from the city ($22). Cheap accommodation is plentiful, though mostly just out of the centre. Try Lafayette Inn (318-235-9442) and Lafayette Travel Lodge (318-234-7402), or Days Inn (1620 N University Avenue, 318-237-8880), northwest of the centre, which charges $45 for a double. There is a KOA Campground 5 miles west.

As in New Orleans, one of the best things to do in Lafayette is eat. Mulate's (325 Mills Avenue, Breaux Bridge, 318-332-4648) is the most famous place around and consequently fairly touristy; but you can enjoy exellent live Cajun and zydeco music as you eat. More popular among the locals is Prejean's (3480 US-167 N; 318-896-3247), with dancing every night; more humble is Prudhommes Cajun Café at 4676 N E Evangeline Thruway (318-896-7964).

Festivals: there are festivals in Cajun country connected to some kind of activity or appetite more or less year-round; check with the Office of Tourism in Baton Rouge. For example, there is a Boudin Festival every February in Broussard, just south of Lafayette, to honour the Cajun sausage made from ground pork, rice, onions and peppers.

Other dates on the gourmet's calendar include the bi-annual Crawfish Festival at Breaux Bridge, self-proclaimed crawfish capital of the world (early May in even-numbered years), and the bizarre Louisiana Shrimp and Petroleum Festival at Morgan City at the beginning of September each year. Near Shreveport in the northwest of the state, you can attend the Poke Salad Festival held on the second weekend in May to celebrate a plant called poke (or sometimes 'polk'), a vegetable akin to spinach which sustained many local people during the Depression.

MISSISSIPPI

The Old South lingers on in Mississippi — in the cotton fields that once made the state one of the richest in the country (but now its poorest), and in some of the most opulent and well-preserved antebellum mansions in the region. Inequality still persists, and some parts of rural Mississippi are almost like the Third World. The violent struggle between blacks and whites, depicted so vividly in Alan Parker's film *Mississippi Burning*, is a thing of the past, but tension between the races remains.

Mississippi is a valuable state to explore, in order to gain an insight into American history. In addition to the historic towns of Natchez, Vicksburg and lesser-known Holly Springs and Columbus, Mississippi is also Blues Country. The Gulf coast is dotted with resorts, such as Biloxi. This is the least interesting part of the state, although at Bay St Louis, the National Space Technology Center is a free and intriguing introduction to the NASA Space Shuttle.

Natchez. This was once the wealthiest town in the country; nowadays, it is one of the Union's most historic — Greek Revival mansions are as common as muck. The plantation atmosphere, which is strong at any time, is brought to life during the Spring Pilgrimage (March-April), when many historical buildings are open to the public. At other times, only a limited number of homes can be visited.

B & B is available in some of the antebellum mansions, but don't expect any change from $80. A more humble option is Days Inn (109 US Highway 61 S, 601-445-8291), which charges $45; or else camp in Natchez State Park, 10 miles north (601-442-2658), which costs $6-10, depending on the facilities you use.

Natchez Trace Parkway: before the cotton boom, the history of the area was dominated by the Natchez Native Americans. They were responsible for creating the so-called 450-mile Natchez Trace (now known as the Natchez Trace Parkway), which runs diagonally across the state all the way from Natchez via Jackson (the state capital) almost all the way to Nashville. It is an historic highway, and by far the prettiest route north into Tennessee. Information from Natchez Trace Parkway, RR1 NT-142, Tupelo, MS 38801.

Some 200 miles northeast of Jackson, the Parkway passes through the industrial town of Tupelo, best known as the childhood home of the king of rock 'n' roll. The Elvis Presley Birthplace and Memorial Chapel is a diminutive shack at 306 Elvis Presley Drive.

Vicksburg. This town's commanding position overlooking the Mississippi, which afforded great strategic importance in the war, is today one of its attractions for visitors. With steep winding streets and atmospheric riverfront, as well as a generous supply of antebellum mansions, Vicksburg deserves more time than Natchez. A trip on the river is compulsory, best of all on the *Delta Queen* or *Mississippi Queen*.

Reminders of the war between the States are everywhere, recalling the bitter siege of the town, ending with Vicksburg's fall to Union troops on July 4, 1863. About a mile northeast of the town is the 1,700-acre Vicksburg National Military Park (601-636-0583, open daily 8am-5pm). It is a moving place, with well preserved cannon trenches, memorials and 17,000 graves scattered over the hillsides. There is a Visitors Center on Clay St, opposite the park entrance.

Among the cheapest places to stay in town, at $45 a night, is the Economy Inn (4216 Washington St, 601-638-5750). There is a choice of motels near the park, including Scottish Inn (3955 US-80 East, 601-638-5511), which charges from $35.

Blues Country. The 'Delta' actually refers to the flood plain along the eastern banks of the Mississippi. It is an atmospheric land of scorched earth, eerie swamps and lonely shanties, where farmers live in constant fear of flooding from the mighty Mississippi. Highway 61 is the main route through the region, though you'll have to drive along the backroads for the best taste of Delta country.

The port of Greenville hosts the annual Mississippi Delta Blues Festival in September, and has a few good blues joints. But the choice is greater in Clarksdale, 70 miles north. Here there is a Delta Blues Museum (114 Delta Avenue), which has an impressive collection of memorabilia, recalling the lives and music of famous residents, including John Lee Hooker. You may find it hard to find much blues music going on during the week; the best place to go at weekends is Smitty's Red Top Lounge (377 Yazoo Avenue, which has no connection with Alison Moyet).

ALABAMA

Car number plates ('tags' in American parlance) in Alabama proclaim the state to be the 'Heart of Dixie', which accurately describes its location. And it is in many aspects a microcosm of the region — mountains in the north, bayous and Gulf Coast beaches in the south, a major space centre within view of cotton fields little changed since the last century, with a sizeable belt of heavy industry thrown in for good measure.

Alabama shot to the centre of world attention periodically during the civil rights struggle of the 50s and 60s. One of the key campaigns was waged in 1963 in Birmingham, when Dr Martin Luther King Jr was among those put in prison. The brutality used to put down the protests provoked the demonstrations which ultimately led to the Civil Rights Act, banning racial segregation. Progress has been made, and the first black mayor was elected in 1979, but black people's security is continually undermined by the extreme stance taken by white Protestant fundamentalists.

Huntsville. This northern town is a curious amalgam of old and new. After a ride around the historic area of Twickenham, in a trolley or a one-horse carriage, you can head out to the Alabama Space and Rocket Center. This is the home of the NASA space shuttle programme, where the machinery is designed and engineers trained, and also of the Earth's largest Space Museum, which recreates earlier achievements. You can tour the former by bus, whereas the latter invites more direct contact, offering simulated space travel complete with weightlessness, and an Omnimax screen with superb film taken by astronauts. The centre is 5 miles west of town, and opens 8am-7pm daily, 9am-6pm in winter. Call 1-800-572-7234 from within Alabama, 1-800-833-7280 for further details.

Montgomery. The state capital is a city more evidently rooted in the past than Huntsville. It was the first capital of the Confederacy in 1861, and a century later, the scene of early and angry civil rights demonstrations. The 1955 bus boycott by blacks led to the ending of segregation on public transport, but there is still remarkably little racial integration in the town. You can visit the King Memorial Baptist Church at 454 Dexter Avenue (open Monday to Friday), where Martin Luther preached and which was the focus of the 1955 campaign.

Montgomery can offer its own simulated space journeys — at the Gayle Space Transit Planetarium, open for tours on Tuesday, Thursday, Saturday and Sunday.

A cheap place to stay is the Town Plaza (743 Madison Avenue, 205-269-1561), well located near the bus station on S Court St and with doubles for less than $30. For more comfort try the Capitol Inn (205 N Goldthwaite St, 205-265-0541), in the old part of town, which charges around $38.

Selma. Located 45 miles west of Montgomery, on the banks of the Alabama river, Selma was also the scene of some of the most brutal attacks on civil rights campaigners — notably the attack on demonstrators by Governor George Wallace's state troopers in March 1965. Selma makes a good day trip from Montgomery, with its interesting historic district, busy main street and riverfront scenes.

Mobile. It might seem strange to head all the way down to the Gulf simply to arrive at a port full of papermills. But the attractions of Mobile are well-preserved antebellum buildings and fresh seafood. And along the coast are some fine white sand beaches: head either for Dauphin Island or, even better, Gulf Shores on the neighbouring Pleasure Island.

The French, Spanish and English (as well as the Confederacy) have all held sway in Mobile at one time, and they have each left their stamp on the town. You can do little better than stroll through the old streets, though several old houses are open to the public, and there is a History Museum at 355 Government St.

Mobile's ten-day Mardi Gras celebration around Shrove Tuesday is second only to that in New Orleans. This is a good time to see the city, for it also marks the beginning of Mobile's Azalea Trail celebration, centred around the profusion of blooming flowers; it is also the best time to visit the beautiful Bellingrath Gardens, outside the city.

Stay at Red Carpet Inn (Government Blvd, 205-666-7751), or the marginally more expensive Oak Tree Inn (255 Church St, 205-433-6923), which charges $45. For some of the best seafood in town go to Wintzell's Oyster House at 605 Dauphin St (205-433-1004); it closes at 9.30pm.

TENNESSEE

If your taste in music is country, blues, or bluegrass, you're in the right place. Tennessee stretches over 400 miles east to west and contains three distinct cultural regions; in the east it's hillbilly country, fiercely independent villages scattered throughout the mountains and forests of the Great Smoky Mountains National Park; in central Tennessee the landscape levels out into rolling countryside where local farmers' music combined with the wilder eastern hill music to turn a quiet cotton-farming centre called Nashville into 'Music City, USA'. Finally the land flattens out entirely as it meets the banks of the great Mississippi and the city of Memphis. The great river route between New Orleans and Chicago which brought southern gentility to the Memphis upper classes and blues music to the lower classes. It's easy to find things to do in each area and to have a good time; the less interesting the scenery gets, the more friendly the people become.

The area code for Nashville was made briefly famous by the local band Area Code 615; prefix Memphis numbers with 901.

Nashville. If Johnny Cash leave you cold, and you can't see anything special in Patsy Cline's last cigarette lighter, then in Nashville you may experience that occasional panic that *you're* the one who's insane. But even if you take issue with Tammy Wynette's philosophy on life and choice of musical genre, you'll have a wonderful time in Nashville. The city has more to offer than Country music, including a full-sized replica of the Parthenon (complete with imitation Elgin Marbles) and a moderately historic downtown. The

Tobacco Museum is at 800 Harrison St, open 10am-4pm from Tuesday to Saturday (242-9218).

But Nashville is epitomized by Music Row: a street of souvenir shops and 'personal museums' (effectively souvenir shops owned by the stars themselves). Most amusing is the Country Music Hall of Fame, 4 Music Square East (255 5333). Included in the admission price of $5 is a tour of RCA's studio B where Elvis crooned his Christmas albums (each August).

For live music the biggest venues have been purpose-built (with the emphasis on glitter) on the city outskirts. The Nashville palace (2400 Music Valley Drive, 885-1540) dishes it out seven nights a week, and the famous Grand Old Opry (next to Opryland USA, a Country/Disneyland combo) has big names every Friday and Saturday night. It is easiest to find tickets for the matinee performances held between March and September; call 889-3060 for details. The shows are slick, wholesome and footstomping, but probably not ideal if you prefer 'real' Country. There is a trend away from the Nashville sound of digital recordings and orchestral backgrounds, and a return to native bluegrass and more excitingly raw hillbilly sounds.

Cheap accommodation is hard to find in Nashville; try the motels on I-65 or the Tudor Inn (244-8970) on James Robertson Parkway. The best place to enjoy an evening meal is San Antonio's Taco Company, 21st Avenue South (close to Division St). Whatever else you do, make sure you have one meal at the Elliston Place Soda Shop, 2111 Elliston Place. It is hard to say which is its better attribute: the low prices or the perfectly preserved 1950s decor. Elliston Place is the western continuation of Church St from downtown, just past the Baptist Hospital.

The Hermitage, ten miles east of Nashville, is a former home of President Andrew Jackson. It is open 9am-5pm daily.

In Hendersonville, some way northeast of Nashville, you can take in the Johnny Cash Museum (824-5110), Conway Twitty's 'Twitty City' (822-3210) and the Marty Robbins Memorial Museum. Instead you could head southeast to Lynchburg for a tour of the Jack Daniels Distillery (759-7394).

MEMPHIS

This unprepossessing city is the music centre of the USA. It was the birthplace of the blues, the home — and grave — of the world's greatest singer, and artists from Jackie Wilson to U2 have recorded here.

Originally the city's position on the Mississippi made it the hub for the Southern cotton crop, and a boom lasted through the first half of this century. It was to Memphis that Vernon Presley drove with his wife and young son Elvis Aron when he couldn't make ends meet in Tupelo Mississippi in the 1940s. With the decline of the cotton market, two decades of economic and inner city decline set in from which the city is only now recovering. Its improved fortunes are due largely to the influx of white-collar work as corporations move to Memphis, attracted by low prices and its central position in the South.

Memphis has learned from the errors of other cities and is handling its revival by renovating rather than replacing the interesting 1920s buildings with skyscrapers. Despite its large size (the 15th most populous city in the USA), the atmosphere is relaxed and almost provincial. There is a great deal to do and see; Memphis seems likely to become one of the main tourist attractions in the USA in the next decade.

Getting Around. Memphis International Airport, as featured in the film *Silence of the Lambs* is 15 miles south of downtown. There is no airport bus service, and a taxi might easily cost $15. The cheapest way downtown is to take a hotel courtesy bus away from the airport area (when you arrive at the hotel say you'd like to stay but can't afford to), then take a local bus.

Greyhound services operate from the terminal at 203 Union Ave at 4th St (523-7676), two blocks north of Beale St.

The perimeter of the city is orbited by 1-240, from which Poplar Ave and Union Ave run east-west through the heart of the city. Madison Avenue divides the north and south addresses: basically the large black community and the poorest areas are to the south. The Mississippi runs north-south, providing the western boundary to the city and the focal point for much of the new development.

Visitors to Memphis are fortunate in that almost all tourist sites are easily accessible by foot within the downtown area. Even so, the Memphis Area Transit Authority (MATA: 274-6282 for information) runs 'showboats' (ill-disguised buses) on a fixed route between all the major attractions — stops ae marked by red and blue flags. An all-day pass costs $2 for adults, $1.25 for children. Buses run every few minutes, seven days a week. The only sight not covered by the 'showboats' is the greatest, Elvis' Graceland; take bus 13 (marked 'Lauderdale/Elvis Presley') from 3rd and Union Streets (85c each way).

Accommodation. The world's first Holiday Inn is in Memphis, but there are better bargains and more unusual surroundings. As with many cities experiencing regeneration, the downtown area has seen the growth of expensive hotels while more reasonable accommodation requires a car or bus journey. The only cheap downtown location is the TraveLodge at 265 Union Avenue (527-4306 or 1-800-255-3050). Check the rates also at the Days Inn Downtown, 164 Union Avenue (527-4100 or 1-800-272-6232). Both are across from the Greyhound Bus station: when occupancy is low these hotels indulge in price-cutting battles which can sometimes mean doubles for less than $30.

The Lowenstein — Long House/Castle Hostelry (AYH) 217 N Waldren (527-7174) offers both bed and breakfast in a Victorian Mansion as well as rooms in the adjacent youth hostel ($10). The YMCA, 3548 Walker Avenue (458-3580) is nine miles east of downtown; since it is often full, you should call ahead. Bed and Breakfast in Memphis (726-5920) can suggest various local homes for around $40 double or more.

Visitors with a car can try the numerous cheap motels further out along Union Avenue or near Graceland on Elvis Presley Boulevard south of the city. Be warned that rooms are scarce from August 11-17 during the week of commemorating Presley's death in 1977.

Eating and Drinking. Memphis deserves its reputation for good 'soul food' and the best Southern barbecue. For the finest ribs go to the Rendezvous at 52 S 2nd St, in the alley between Union Avenue and Monroe St across from the Peabody Hotel. A measure of its success is that it now sells barbecue ribs by mail order. Other good restaurants include the Marmalade at 153 Calhoun Avenue (522-8800) which has live music, and Leonard's Barbecue Pit, reputedly an old Presley haunt, at 1140 Bellevue Boulevard (948-1581).

Exploring. However much the city develops, Memphis' greatest tourist attraction will always be a surprisingly small house set in a quiet residential district ten miles south of the centre: Elvis Presley's Graceland, 3794 Elvis Presley Boulevard (332-3322; 1-800-238-2000 toll-free from out-of-state). Visitors buy tickets and souvenirs across the road before being bussed up to the house for a guided tour. This has allowed the mansion — itself a Mecca of glitz and tastelessness — to escape the worst ravages of tourism. You can sense the isolation and loneliness behind the mirrored ceilings and stacked televisions. Disbelievers in Elvis' mortality may wish to enquire why the upper floor is out-of-bounds. Graceland opens daily from 8am to 6pm, admission $7. The contrast between the extraordinary

Presley's two greatest influences were the blues and gospel. Explore the restored Beale St, which is to Southern blues what New Orleans is to jazz. Three blocks south of Beale St, in a now derelict area, is the place where Martin Luther King Jr died. On April 4 1968, while staying in Memphis to support a strike by sanitation workers, the great civil rights leader was assassinated at the Lorraine Motel, 406 Mulberry St. It is now the National Civil Rights Museum.

The Sun Studio on Union Avenue is still in working order (U2 recorded *The Joshua Tree* here), though its greatest moments were when Presley and Chuck Berry belted out hits in the 50s and 60s. A tour of the dowdy interior is illustrated with audio clips of the artists in action. This is one of the best tours in a nation which prides itself on catering for visitors. Also try to see a service at the Full Gospel Tabernacle, 787 Hale Road (396-9192), where the Reverend Al Green ('Tired of being alone', etc) preaches. Go south on Elvis Presley Boulevard to just beyond Graceland.

The rest of the city can seem positively ordinary by comparison. Examples of successful restoration well worth a visit include the mansions of the Victorian Village; the luxurious Peabody Hotel at 149 Union St where ducks swim in the central indoor fountain and are ceremoniously escorted to and from the elevator daily at 11am and 5pm; and the historic South Main district (details of a self-guided walking tour from the Visitor Information Center at 207 Beale St, 526-4880).

The most interesting non-musical museum in Memphis is the Mississippi River Museum on Mud Island (576-7241); the island itself is an amusement complex on a former mud bank, connected to the shoreline by a monorail. The museum traces the history of the river from its earliest Indian settlements and on through the Civil War using a combination of standard artefact displays and ingenious full-scale audio-visual replicas. Mud Island also had an open-air scale model of the Mississippi, 800 yards long, flowing into a one acre Gulf of Mexico. Cool off on a hot day by walking in the river, covering several miles with each stride. Admission to all Mud Island attractions plus the monorail ride costs $4.

Other places of interest in the city include the Brooks Museum of Art (722-3500), Libertyland amusement park (274-1776) and the Memphis Zoo (726-4775). Shopping for presents ceases to be much fun after the hundredth souvenir shop selling Elvis Presley baseball caps. Instead, try A. Schwab's store on Beale St which has the catchy motto 'if you can't find it at Schwabs, you're better off without it.'

Nightlife. The city has the best blues scene outside Chicago. Check the 'Playbook' section in Friday's *Memphis Commercial Appeal* or the monthly *Memphis Star* to find out what's on. Rock and jazz concerts are held in summer at the amphitheatre on Mud Island and at the Overton Park Shell. For blues, stroll along Beale St and choose the bar where the music sounds best. Most bars have a disarmingly informal clientele, and are good places to meet people. Except in trendy Overton Square, prices are lower than in most American cities. Try the Rum Boogie Cafe at 182 Beale St, with live entertainment and dancing. When there is not guest band, the house band steps in, often to be joined for a jamming session by a megastar unwinding after a performance on Mud Island.

Crime and Safety. Immediately outside the central downtown area (north of Madison Avenue and south of Linden Avenue) lives a population which has yet to feel the benefits of Memphis' current boom. Crimes committed there against travellers have little to do with drugs but much to do with poverty.

KENTUCKY

The Kentucky Derby is the state's most notable attraction. It lasts for a few minutes each year on the first Saturday in May. Kentucky's other great creation is bourbon whisky, which can be enjoyed every day of the year.

The Derby is the pinnacle of a multi-million dollar horse breeding and racing industry centred on Lexington, which is active year-round. You can visit many of the neat, white-fenced horse farms (free), see horses change hands for huge sums at auction (especially Keeneland, in July), watch them perform at shows, polo games and races, and even race them yourself. Lexington is the centre of Kentucky's bluegrass region, and hosts a festival featuring the music of the same name every June.

Louisville is the home of the Derby, which you might want to attend for the same reason as you would say, the FA Cup Final: both are experiences as much as sports events, and you don't have to care about the result to enjoy the occasion (though a bet does sharpen your interest). General admission to the field costs $10; phone (502) 636-3541 for further information. The city was also the birthplace of Mohammad Ali, 'The Louisville Lip', who has a boulevard named after him. You can visit the Colonel Sanders Museum if you are interested in the history of Kentucky Fried Chicken, or distilleries in Louisville — though you have a wider choice in Bardstown, an hour's drive south. Free samples are not permitted.

Mammouth Cave in the centre of the state, is the world's longest known cave system, 235 miles in length. Indians lived there 3,000 years ago; today you can take tours of varying lengths and depth, and eat lunch in a cafeteria nearly 300 feet below ground. Remember to take a sweater.

Other places of interest in Kentucky include Hodgeville, birthplace of Abraham Lincoln, and Berea, a town and college community preserving the traditional way of life of the Appalachian mountain people. There is a museum and an annual festival (spring) of music and crafts. Another group whose past has been preserved are the Shakers, a sect who seceded from the Quakers and found settlements in Kentucky and elsewhere, where they practised temperence and celibacy. Unsurprisingly, they have virtually died out, though there is a small Shaker community in Maine. If you are passing Shakertown near Harrodsburg, take a look at their restored homes and austere and beautifully-made furnishings.

ARKANSAS

You can break state law by pronouncing 'Arkansas' as it looks. Arkansas is the only state whose pronunciation is governed by statute; an 1881 law requires you to say 'ARK-n-saw'. The old Indian name is all that remains of the original inhabitants. After the Europeans arrived this patch of territory was squabbled over and traded between the French and the Spanish, and was then bundled in as a bonus with the Louisiana Purchase, when the USA bought more land. Arkansas settled into minor-league statehood, with plenty of time for arguments like how to pronounce the name.

For over a century not much happened. In the 1992 presidential campaign, Bill Clinton emphasized his modest roots, drawing attention to this lovely state.

The financial section of the *Arkansas Democrat Gazette* is called 'Business and Farm', which emphasizes the agricultural nature of this small state. Its artery is the Arkansas River, a tributary of the Mississippi. Little Rock is at its centre.

LITTLE ROCK

Initially Little Rock was a frontier town, but as the Quapaw Indians were pushed out it grew up as a trading post. Early settlements were alongside the river, but as the railways developed the centre drifted away from the waterside. Some fine antebellum houses around (but not including) the governor's mansion give it a sense of history. With a population of 200,000, Little Rock is one of the smaller state capitals, but a charming and enjoyable place.

Arrival and Departure. Little Rock is 139 miles from Memphis and a long way from anywhere else — 307 miles from Dallas, 288 from Tulsa and 348 from Oklahoma City.

Adam's Field airport is three miles/5km east of the city centre. Bus 20 operates between the airport and 6th and Center Streets in downtown every hour from 6am to 5pm, taking about 30 minutes.

Getting Around. The local buses are called CATs, and serve all quarters of the city. Most visitors are either noble and walk everyhwere or are lazy and drive or take taxis everywhere (these are not expensive). To call a cab, dial 374-0333 or 568-0462.

Accommodation. The *Little Rock Area Lodging* guide lists 60 places to stay. Two tatty — but cheap and central — motels are next door to each other, a few blocks east of the city centre: the Deluxe Inn, 308 E Capitol (375-6411) and the Diamond Inn, 302 E Capitol (376-3661). For camping, KOA has a site on I-40 west at exit 148 in North Little Rock.

Eating and Drinking. You can get a good steak in Little Rock, but don't expect anything too exotic. Lin's Restaurant is an atmospheric diner forming part of the Deluxe Inn at 308 E Capitol. At Shug's (3421 Old Cantrell Road; 663-2323) you can eat ribs, drink beer and listen to live music which varies from tolerable to terrible.

Exploring. It is natural to want to track down the little rock which gives the city its name, but this is an unrewarding activity. At the scruffy Riverfront Park, a history pavilion explains the settling of the area. The rock itself is a barely discernable outcrop — most of it provided handy materials for the adjacent railroad bridge. To find it you need to circumvent a cluster of freeways. The remains of the rock are just east of the railroad bridge (on its right as you look at the river).

Nearby, at Cumberland and 3rd, the Plum Bayou Log House has taken route. This old sharecroppers' cabin was moved from Scott, 20 miles away, to provide a focus for explaining the frontier existence of Little Rock.

The old State House, where Bill Clinton declared his candidature for the presidency, is a Museum of Arkansas History. It served as State Capitol for 75 years after the state came into being in 1836. It opens 9am-5pm daily except Sundays (1-5pm), suggested donation $1. It begins with an exhibition of first ladies' dresses — the evening gowns of the wives of governors.

Bill Clinton's national headquarters were in the Gazette building, a 1908 gem which housed the oldest newspaper west of the Mississippi, on 3rd between Louisiana and Main. The most attractive 20th century building in town is the old Lafayette hotel, now converted to offices but retaining sumptuous woodwork which you can enjoy without having to go in.

The State Capitol is open 9am-6pm from Monday to Friday, 10am-5pm on Sundays. You can take a tour of this extravagant legislature any day.

MacArthur Park, a mile south of downtown, is both a lovely open space and home to two of the city's cultural asset. At the top of the park, at Sherman and 9th Streets, is the Museum of Science and History. It is housed in the old Arsenal Building, and opens 9am to 4.30pm daily except Sundays (1-4.30pm). Beyond it is Arkansas Arts Center (372-4000)., open 10am-5pm daily except Sundays and holidays (noon-5pm)

Entertainment. The free listings magazine is *Nightflying*. For live music, try Juanita's at 1300 S Main (374-3271) or the Iron Horse Saloon across the river at 2657 K Pike Avenue in North Little Rock (771-0013). The latest-opening club is LA City Limits at 3605 MacArthur in North Little Rock (753-0627).

Help and Information. Arkansas Department of Parks and Tourism dispenses information on 1-800-NATURAL.

The area code for the whole of Arkansas is 501.

HOT SPRINGS

The boyhood home of Bill Clinton is capitalizing unashamedly on its newfound celebrity status. The Hot Springs Chamber of Commerce publishes a guide to his childhood haunts. The president went to church at the Park Place Baptist Church. He also enjoyed the splendid outdoor life around the town. Take the Mountain Trail, a five-mile scenic loop. The best panorama is from the top of the tower at the summit. Bill Clinton's High School on Oak Street, where the Governor learned to play the saxophone, is just a dot in the distance. The foreground is the cleft that contains Bathhouse Row.

All sorts of places, from a suburb of Leeds to a dull corner of Honduras, have been described as 'Little Switzerland', but this part of south west Arkansas has a better claim than most. Dramatic mountainsides and narrow valleys are wreathed in evergreens and studded with cottages. Encroaching upon this enchanted land are ranks of grandiose sanatoria devoted to the reputed healing powers of steamy water. Dozens of geysers bubble from the flank of Hot Springs Mountain, and bathhouses were built to exploit the waters rather than let them just run away down the creek towards Texas.

In the 1920s it was fashionable to take the waters in Hot Springs. The ailing and the curious made a journey to Arkansas which would now be classed as an adventure of epic proportions. The thrill and the custom wore off during the Great Depression of the 1930s, when disposable income evaporated and the bathhouses emptied of water and people.

The Fordyce Bathhouse is a gorgeous confection, recently restored to the prime condition in which it was built in 1915. An exotic plumbing system was installed above a seething spring, sprouting boilers, coolers and tanks, the vital organs of a complex central super-heating system. A spaghetti of pipes laces through the three upper floors, to the Hubbard Tub (a rheumatism treatment) and the electro-mechano room, full of lethal-looking devices to cure ills and ease pains. The bathhouse contains work-out apparatus from a different age when real men didn't wear Nike.

The top end of Bathhouse Row shudders beneath the awesome sandstone bulk of the Medical Arts Building, a neo-Gothic tower decorated in Soviet-style motifs which glorify the working man. The basic design was repossessed from Stalin after he stole the American skyscraper and turned it into an emblem of communism. The tower belongs on a broad, bare avenue in Moscow, not in small-town America. Up above the bathhouses, Promenade Row allows you to peer into the backyards of these curious places, and to be splashed with simmering water from occasional rogue springs.

The Arlington is grandest of all the Hot Springs hotels. Take tea beneath the twin spires of this shrine to sulphur, with decor from Venice via Hollywood. The hotel's Bathhouse opens to the public, so you can submerge in splendour.

You can call the Hot Springs Visitor Center on 501-321-2277, or outside Arkansas on 1-800-543-BATH.

SOUTHWEST ARKANSAS

Southwest of Hot Springs, you reach President Clinton's birthplace, which he referred to in his acceptance speech: 'I still believe in a place called Hope'. Texarkana is split right down the middle. State Line Avenue cuts clean through town, slicing the post office in half and dividing George Bush's adopted state of Texas from Arkansas — formerly governed by Bill Clinton. The third candidate for president, in 1992 Ross Perot, was actually born here. A postcard capitalises on the territorial divide: it shows a donkey on the right, its owner on the left, and carries the slogan 'I'm in Texas but my ass is in Arkansas'. Prohibition persists on both sides of the state line on Sundays.

OZARK MOUNTAINS

Sam Walton opened the first Wal-Mart variety store in Bentonville Arkansas in 1945. The company has grown to become a nationwide chain, and he is now one of America's richest men. The story of how you come to buy a toothbrush in Tucson or a six-pack in Seattle to contribute to his wealth is told in the Wal-Mart Visitors Center, 105 North Main St (501-273-1329).

The gentle, forest-clad Ozark Mountains in the north of the state are the home of some of America's true backwoods people. The Ozark Folk Center at Mountain View is a comprehensive collection of all aspects of this rustic culture — weaving, woodwork, pottery and, above all, music. Ozark music is real downhome hootenanny stuff full of banjos and fiddles and mandolins. Hootenannies are foot-stomping celebrations or jamborees. The highpoint of all this is the Arkansas Folk Festival at the Center, which runs over two weekends in April. The religious side of the mountain people is shown especially in the Passion Play performed five nights in a week in summer at the spa town of Eureka Springs, in the far northwest of the state.

The Great Outdoors Although Southerners are not as geared to energetic outdoor activity as the hyperactive Northerners or the mountain-obsessed natives of the West Coast, there are plenty of opportunities for enjoying the great outdoors while travelling in the Southern states.

Deep-sea fishing is popular in the Gulf of Mexico, and freshwater fishing in the numerous inland lakes and rivers. There is also duck, wild turkey, snipe, quail, raccoon, possum and deer shooting, as well as fox hunting.

In Louisiana you can explore Acadiana west of New It's also possible to rent canoes in many of the small towns, where fishing is always the favourite past-time. No self-respecting general store is without its gruesome tub of live bait.

Arkansas offers a remarkable scope for water sports: water-skiing, sailing, canoeing and fishing. In the north, Mountain Home and Beaver Lake are the major centres; if you are crossing the middle of the state on I-40, Lake Dardanelle near Russellville is convenient and excellent. Experts give high marks to the canoeing on the Buffalo River south of Mountain Home.

The mammoth Tennessee Valley Authority provides facilities for swimming, sailing and fishing. In winter you can ski, skate and toboggan near Gatlinburg, chief town of the Tennessee region of the Great Smokies and full of tourists year round.

Both the Gulf and the ocean coasts are dotted with resorts. The Mississippi coast has been much developed taking advantage of miles of sandy beaches, and offers a full range of resort facilities to suit all budgets. Between May and September you can take a boat from Biloxi or Gulfport to Ship Island, 12 miles offshore, first landfall of French explorers at the beginning of the 18th century.

Calendar of Events

January 8	**Battle of New Orleans Day (Louisiana only)**
January 19	**Robert E. Lee's Birthday**
late February/early March	Mardi Gras Festival, New Orleans
March	Pilgrimage, Natchez Mississippi
late March/April	Spring Fiesta, New Orleans
April	Arkansas Folk Festival, Mountain View
May (first Saturday)	Kentucky Derby
June (first Monday)	**Confederate Memorial Day**
July	Blessing of the Shrimp Fleet, Bayou la Batre, Alabama
mid-August	Elvis Presley International Tribute Week, Memphis
September	Delta Blues Festival, Greenville, Mississippi
October	Pilgrimage, Natchez Mississippi
October	National Peanut Festival, Dothan, Alabama

Public holidays are shown in **bold**

Chicago and the Midwest

Illinois Indiana Iowa Kansas Michigan Minnesota Missouri Nebraska North Dakota Ohio Oklahoma South Dakota Wisconsin

Forget Manhattan. The mightiest buildings in the world, and the greatest architecture in America, rise majestically from the shoreline of Lake Michigan. And Chicago is much more than just an exhibition of the biggest and the best, it is also hugely entertaining city, as sophisticated as it is brash.

Its beautiful setting on the lakeshore should not seduce you into thinking that Chicago is in any way a soft dreamy place. Bustling with mercantile activity, it is 'the city that works' *par excellence.* The oft-quoted description by the poet Carl Sandburg captures the no-nonsense practicality of the Great American city:

> Hog Butcher for the World,
> Tool Maker, Stacker of Wheat
> Player with Railroads and
> the Nation's Freight Handler,
> Stormy, husky, brawling,
> City of the Big Shoulders.

The references to grain, livestock and freight confirm Chicago's role as capital of the Midwest, where the vast region's output is processed and distributed. The strategic location has resulted in its becoming the nation's largest railroad centre, and having the world's busiest airport. Yet despite its importance as a crossroad for shipping, it is self-reliant to the point of isolationism and often parochial in its attitudes and tastes.

252

Sandburg's poem also captures the confidence associated with America's third-largest city (population six million). The nickname 'Windy City' refers primarily to the fierce winds which occasionally blow off Lake Michigan, but also to the hot air and inaction of its politicians, particularly during Prohibition. The city's politics are complex and often scandalous, but always interesting. The claim made by a local alderman that 'Chicago ain't no sissy town' still holds true. His choice of idiom also recalls the famous gangster names associated with Chicago — 'Scarface' Al Capone and 'Baby Face' Nelson.

'Welcome to Chicago — this town stinks like a whorehouse at low tide', is how Sean Connery greets Kevin Costner in *The Untouchables*, the screen biography of Capone. Little evidence remains of infamous exploits; no stone marks the site of the St Valentine's Day Massacre of 1929 (at 2122 North Clark St) and few know where John Dillinger, Public Enemy Number One, was finally gunned down. (The wall outside the Biograph Theater against which he and his gang were shot has been moved to a restaurant in Vancouver, but the seat he occupied is still on display in the Police Museum). Chicagoans are understandably more proud of their achievements in fields other than crime.

The invention of the skyscraper is claimed by the city on the basis of a steel-skeleton building ten storeys high built in 1885. Appropriately, a hundred years later, Chicago added 100 floors to its original record to boast the tallest building in the world, the 110-storey Sears Tower, 1,454 feet high. Another achievement was the reversal of the Chicago River's direction of flow in 1900. By using a series of locks, the river was made to drain eventually into the Gulf of Mexico to prevent the pollution of Lake Michigan. Chicago has always been good at finding innovative and daring solutions to difficult practical problems.

THE NATIVES

The ethnic diversity is almost as extreme as it is in New York. Under half the population is white. There are many charming, plenty of not-so-charming ethnic neighbourhoods. The German and Scandinavian communities are predictably full of immaculately kept houses and gardens. There are more Poles than anywhere outside Warsaw. There are Italians, Lithuanians, Arabs, Koreans, Indians, Vietnamese and Irish. If you are interested in a particular ethnic group, there may well be a museum devoted to them, such as the Balzekas Museum of Lithuanian culture, the Spertus Museum of Jewish artefacts, the Polish Museum of America and the Swedish American Museum. In addition to these communities of European and Asian people, there are large parts of the city dominated by over a million blacks and half a million Latin people. Many of these areas are ghettos, concentrated on the dangerous South Side of town.

White Chicagoans are not renowned for liberalism and racial tolerance, and Chicago has traditionally been a strongly segregated city.

Making Friends. The city is full of young people, partly due to the high concentration of universities and colleges (second only to Boston). The prestigious University of Chicago with 9,000 is one of the smallest; Northwestern, DePaul, Loyola and the Chicago Circle campus of the University of Illinois all have more. A good way to meet people and get fit in the process is to join in one of the omnipresent softball, volleyball or basketball games in any of the lakefront parks. Some groups of friends play regularly, but most games are impromptu and newcomers are welcome.

Rush Street is lined with bars and anyone with an open manner and a full purse should be able to meet fun-loving people. The Division Street bars are for the college-aged crowd, the most famous being Butch McGuire's (20 W Division) home of the Harvey Wallbanger (vodka, orange juice and galliano) and supposedly the first singles bar in the nation. Unfortunately many of the 4,500 who allegedly first met there still seem to be hanging around in pairs. A more open and lively singles bar is the Snuggery (15 W Division).

CLIMATE

The Chicago summer is just as hot and humid as the New York summer with an average temperature of 75°F/24°C and many days over 90°F/32°C. Breezes sometimes have a moderating effect, and it's always cooler by the lake. Violent rain storms can occur over the summer, suddenly interrupting a brilliantly sunny day, but bringing relief from the heat. Spring and autumn are lovely. Winters are bitter with an average January temperature of 26°F/-3°C. The record low occurred in 1982 when temperature dropped to -26°F/-32°C; the wind chill factor took this to -80°F/-63°C, cold enough to make your tear ducts freeze. Call 976-1212 for the city forecast.

ARRIVAL AND DEPARTURE

Air. Despite its tremendous volume of over 50 million passengers, with 2,000 take-offs each day, immigration procedures at O'Hare International Airport are fairly brisk, seldom longer than 45 minutes. Its airport code, ORD derives from its previous name of Orchard Field. For flight enquiries dial 686-2200.

Located 17 miles northwest of downtown Chicago, O'Hare is linked by the Kennedy Expressway. The road journey time varies from half an hour to two hours according to traffic and weather conditions. More reliable is the rapid transit link between the International Terminal and Washington St Station in downtown Chicago. The trains are clean, safe and cheap ($1), and take only 45 minutes to reach Washington St from where you can transfer free to any downtown station.

Continental Air Transport (454-7800) runs frequent buses to suburban and downtown hotels including one located in Water Tower Square. The fare is $6.75. You must first take the free airport shuttle bus to the round entrance building between Terminals 1 and 2. Taxis are plentiful at the airport and charge a fare of about $25. Some taxis participate in a super-saver programme which facilitates taxi-sharing; look for the programme's bright yellow identifying flag. If you arrive on a clear day, you can get your first glimpse of the Chicago skyline from the top of the multi-storey car park at O'Hare. You can also visit one of the observation decks to watch the planes, though the decks are disappointingly spartan and poorly situated. Only a few carriers use Chicago's second airport: Midway (MDW, tel: 767-0500), located on the South Side. Until O'Hare opened in 1961, Midway was the world's busiest airport. You can reach downtown either via the Chicago Transit Authority bus to Jackson Park Station or the minibus service costing $7.50 direct.

Chicago's third airport is Meigs Field (tel: 744-4787), protruding into Lake Michigan from Lake Shore Drive a few miles southeast of downtown.

Cheap flights are advertised in the *Reader* magazine. Council Travel has a downtown office at 29 E Delaware Place (497-1497) and a branch in the suburb of Evanston.

Bus. The Greyhound bus station (781-2900) is very central, opposite the gleaming State of Illinois Center, downtown at Clark and Randolph Streets. There are also direct services from O'Hare airport to eight destinations including Madison and Milwaukee.

Train. Chicago is the Clapham Junction of America. Eight railway lines converge, bringing passengers and freight from every corner of the country. Trains run from the highly imposing Union Station at 210 S Canal St on the corner of Adams St (558-1075).

Commuter services to the six surrounding counties are operated by the Regional Transport Authority and depart from Illinois Central and Nortwestern stations. (Northwestern Station, downtown at Madison and Canal Streets, is a most impressive modern glass structure). A map of services is shown near the front of the Yellow Pages.

Driving. Among the cheapest car hire firms are Econo-Car (70 W Lake St, 332-7785; 850 N State St, 951-6262; and at O'Hare Airport), Dollar Rent a Car (50 W Lake St, 782-8736), Alamo (1-800-327-9633) and Fender Benders (1608 N Wells, Pipers Alley Mall, 280-8554) which claim to have the lowest rates in town. A number of highways leading out of Chicago are toll routes, including I-294, I-90, I-94 and Route 5. Automatic toll booths are quite frequent near the city. Picking the outside lane usually speeds progress. Most tolls are around $1 and enforcement is taken seriously.

Driveaways. Cars for delivery are readily available in Chicago. Check the Yellow Pages and phone the agencies to find out what destinations are on offer and what perks, if any, are included. Auto Driveaway (310 S Michigan Ave 939-3600) is a good bet. Wilson Driveway at the Xerox Center, 55 W Monroe St (236-0445) sometimes needs drivers to deliver cars to comparatively nearby cities, such as Columbus Ohio 300 miles away.

Ride-Sharing. The Metro Ride Board (929-5139) tries to match up lifts to other cities and to the airport. Ride-sharing opportunities are also advertised in the *Reader* magazine.

Hitch-hiking. There have been several reports of hitchers receiving penalties for hitching in Illinois, but most of the time you will just receive a warning. If you're heading west or north take the Howard El-train to Morse or Jarvis and walk north or south respectively to Touhy, which runs east-west to I-94 west. To get on any of the eastbound interstates, take the Dan Ryan El-train to 69th St, though this is not a safe neighbourhood.

CITY TRANSPORT

City Layout. Chicago's street pattern is the conventional grid, with major streets a mile or half a mile apart. The street numbering system follows the compass; State St divides downtown into east and west, and Madison St forms the division between the North Side and the South Side. Once downtown, walking is the best way to enjoy the city. The business and entertainment districts are conveniently close and compact.

The El. Chicago's Metropolitan railway is distinctive for being elevated above ground and having appeared in countless films from *The Sting* to *Dick Tracy*. The downtown business district is known as the Loop precisely

because it is enclosed by a loop in the network, around which all trains on the Ravenswood line pass. The Loop officially consists of an area five blocks by seven, bounded by Van Buren, Wells and Lake Streets and Wabash Avenue.

Trains and buses are operated by the Chicago Transit Authority (836-7000), and comprise a frequent and economical public transport system (the CTA is probably the world's only public transport network whose name has been adopted by a rock group i.e. Chicago, who originally called themselves 'Chicago Transport Authority'). The flat fare on the system is \$1 for adults, with transfers to another bus or train costing 25c. The transfer can be used as a return ticket if it is presented within one hour of purchase. If you plan to stay more than a fortnight, it might be worth buying a monthly pass for $50, which is valid for whole calendar months only. An all-day pass is available for $1.50 on Sundays.

The El operates throughout the night, though many natives consider it took risky to use alone late at night. Like the New York system, it is very noisy, but retains many pleasing characteristics — not least the stunning views of the city from above street level. Get a map of the transit system ($1) from the Water Tower Information Center, the Regional Transit Authority off ice (300 N State St), the Illinois Tourist Information Center at O'Hare Airport or by sending $1.25 and a self-addressed envelope to Chicago Transit Authority, Box 3555, Chicago, IL 60654. Study the map carefully since some lines branch off, just as on the London Underground. Many trains are designated A or B depending on the stops they make; so if it's a B stop you want, be sure to get on a B train.

Bus. Buses are completely integrated with the El, and the same ticket rules apply. For $1.50 you can take the summer Culture Bus which leaves from the Art Institute. Buses run on every main road and some side streets, stopping at most intersections which are indicated by a sign showing route number and details. Although buses operate 24 hours a day, late night services are infrequent and can be dangerous outside the downtown area.

Car. The naming and numbering of expressways in Chicago is confusing. The most famous route is the Lake Shore Drive (US 41), one of the most scenic urban drives in the world. This north/south route passes between harbour, tennis courts and beaches on the east, and the striking city skyline on the west. The Eisenhower Expressway (I-290) approaches from due west, passing through shabby industrial neighbourhoods, until it hits downtown and becomes the Congress Expressway. I- 94, known outside the city as the Edens Expressway, is the main north/south artery. It becomes the Kennedy Expressway at the city limits, until it crosses the Congress Expressway whereupon it becomes the Dan Ryan Expressway. I-90 heads off southeast to become the aptly named Chicago Skyway. For traffic information downtown tune to 1610 AM. Car parks fill early in the downtown area and are generally expensive. One of the more convenient ones is the one on Michigan Avenue just past Monroe St; a cheaper one (about $8 per day) is a few hundred yards further away on Monroe near the lakefront.

Taxis. There are 4,600 cabs in the city, and many run throughout the night. They may be hailed in any busy street and are relatively cheap. Do not expect to find taxis cruising for custom in rough parts of town. If you are at a club in a dodgy quarter, order a taxi to pick you up, well in advance through Checker Yellow (829-4222) or American United (248-7600).

Cycling. An excellent bicycle route runs along the lake front 11 miles north to Evanston, site of Northwestern University. The flat terrain in the northern suburbs makes cycling almost as pleasant. You can rent bicycles from the Bike Stop (4810 N Broadway, 334-3547), the Village Cycle Center (1337 N Wells St. 751-2488), Cycle Smith (2418 1/2 N Clark St, 281-0444) and Spokesmen Inc (5301 S Hyde Park, 684-3737). There is also a bike rental kiosk in Lincoln Park at the corner of Cannon and Fullerton, just north of the Conservatory. Prices start at about $5 an hour or $20 for 24 hours. Look for *Chicago and Beyond: 26 Bike Tours* by Linda and Steve Nash in local bookshops.

Boats. Sightseeing tours are available from Mercury Sightseeing Boats (332-1353), Wendella Sightseeing Boats (337- 1446) and Shoreline Marine Sightseeing Co (427-2900), all docked on the south side of the Chicago River at 102 Wacker Drive. Cruises along the lakefront or on the Chicago River last one or two hours and cost $5-$10. In summer, boats leave from Navy Pier (744-3315) for cruises which include dining and drinking; these cost from $25 to $40.

Hotels. Pick up the *Holiday Package* brochure from the Visitors Center for a complete list of hotels offering cheap two night weekends during the summer and Christmas shopping seasons. Usually rates are around $60 for a double room per night, not including the 9% tax on lodgings. There is no particular area for cheap hotels, although some of the older ones downtown are reasonable. Similarly, there is no central booking service, though the Hotel and Motel Association (27 East Monroe St, Suite 700; 346-3135) will inform you of available vacancies. The Days Inn, 2400 North Clark Street (525 7010) which charges $65 including breakfast, is well placed for North Side entertainment.

The Alton Hotel at 4837 West Cermak Road, Cicero (708-653-0250) is Al Capone's old gambling den and a bit of a doss-house. The nightly rate is $25 (plus $10 for a security box). Only those particularly keen on its historical associations are likely to enjoy a stay there.

Motels. All the approach roads into Chicago are lined with motels, although on I-55 they begin even further from the centre of town than usual. Chicago's Lincoln Avenue motel strip has a large number of motels in a reasonably safe neighbourhood, but the area is visually unattractive and is a 40 minute bus ride from downtown. Try the Spa at 5414 N Lincoln Avenue or the Summit at 5308; both charge around $45 for a room with two double beds. One motel deserves particular recommendation — the Sheridan Chase Motel (7300 N Sheridan Road, 973-7440) located on the North Shore less than half a block from the beach. It is close to the El and other transit routes. The cost is $40, $50 for a maximum of four to a room with savings by the week $225 and $250). Shabby but convenient.

Hostels. The youth hostel is on the North Side at 6318 North Winthrop (262-1011). A summer-only AYH hostel is run by the University of Chicago and located on the campus at 1414 E 59th (753-2270). It is open only between June 1 and September 9. It has the advantage of being just four blocks from Lake Michigan. The youth hostels office is at 3712 N Clark St (327-8114).

YMCA. The Ys in Chicago tend to be frequented by low-lifers and most are situated either in ghetto areas or in far distant suburbs. The most central is the big Lawson Y at 30 W Chicago Avenue (944-6211), which charges about $30 single. The Harrison Hotel is another, much smaller, Y, at 65 E Harrison St (427-8000), charging $50 single/$65 twin.

Bed and Breakfast. Bed & Breakfast Chicago Inc (PO Box 14088), Chicago 60614, 951-0085) is a reservation service which handles a wide variety of accommodation in the Chicago area. The budget rate for two people is $50-$60 per night. A booking fee of $15 must be included with the reservation which is subtracted from the bill.

University Residences. Any student staying from June to August should enquire about accommodation at Northwestern University's dormitories on Sheridan Road in Evanston, a lively and attractive lakefront suburb 30 minutes from downtown. Call the Office of Residence Halls on 649-8514.

Eating and Drinking

Fast Food. Chicago pioneered the idea that meals are more of a necessity than an occasion. The world's first McDonalds is in the northwestern suburb of Des Plaines (pronounced *Dez Plains*). The owner, Ray Kroc was quick to see the potential of a diner stripped to its basics and subjected to ruthless standardization. The first McDonald's was born on 15 April 1955. Kroc reduced the menu at his restaurant to the elements of burgers, french fries and soft drinks, served at a pace which matched the zest of the fifties. As the menu shortened, so the burgers started marching out by the billion. The choice of name avoided the risk of Krocburgers putting customers off.

The first McDonald's no longer serves food, but has been converted into a museum evoking the days when a burger cost 15c. You can reach it by RTA train to Des Plaines, then walking north for five minutes along Lee St/Mannheim Road. Tours operate Wednesday-Friday, but call ahead on 297-5022 to reserve a place. If you're hungry after the tour, a brand new McDonalds is across the road.

The world's third-busiest McDonalds is in downtown Chicago at 600 N Clark St at Ohio St. (It was the world's busiest until recently overtaken by the branches in Budapest and Moscow). Decorated in 1950s and 60s style, it has a couple of excellent juke boxes (one playing 78 rpm records) and some wonderful arcade machines which you can play for free. Only the prices have changed from 1955 — the cheapest burger costs 20 times more, but buys you speaker-to-speaker Elvis and wall-to-wall nostalgia.

For good food and atmosphere, try Ed Debrevic's a block away at Wells and Ontario Streets. Ed's is always crowded and, as the signs say, 'If you think you have a reservation, you're in the wrong place!'. The menu mocks the Chicagoan mania for efficiency: 'If you're not served in five minutes, you'll get served in eight. Maybe twelve ...'.

Street food seems equally popular and you can find decent little hot dog stands on corners all over the city. Also popular are Italian beef sandwiches (around $2) and *gyros*, a Greek sandwich comparable to doner kebabs. On the South Side the word is pronounced *guy-rose*, *he-ross* on the North Side.

Restaurants. The polyglot nature of the city is becoming increasingly reflected in the range of cuisines. Restaurants which offer the most reasonably priced victuals are usually Thai, Mexican and Chinese. The Rogers Park area along N Sheridan St abounds with inexpensive snack shops and restaurants: from Korean bulgogi sandwiches at the Bulgogi Steak House on Morse St to the White Hen Pantry which has takeaway lox and cream cheese on bagels for $1 and chocolate donuts for 50c. The Clark and Belmont vicinity has modestly priced Japanese fare and all manner of Oriental eateries. Other Asian food can be found at restaurants and grocery stores on Argyll St.

One statistician claims that it would be possible to eat out in Chicago every evening and never repeat oneself during a lifetime. The following will last you two weeks:

Chicago Pizza and Ovengrinder Co, 2121 B Clark (248-2570). Leading exponent of the famous Chicago deep dish pizza.

Pizzeria Uno, 29 E Ohio St (321-1000). Original Chicago- style restaurant in a small Italian grotto with friendly relaxed service. If it's full, try the sister restaurant
Pizzeria Due a block away at Wabash Avenue and Ontario St.
Dianna's Opaa, 212 S Halsted St (332-1225). Lively Greek restaurant in which owner Petros often starts up Greek dancing.
Chiam, 2323 S Wentworth Avenue (225-6336). Seating for 500. There are many other Chinese restaurants in Chinatown along Cermak Road and Wentworth Avenue.
Happy Sushi, 3346 N Clark St (528-1225). Reasonably priced flamboyant sushi bar.
Campeche, 7101 N Clark St. Family run Mexican resturant charging $2-$6. Also located at 958 W Wrightwood in Sheffield.
Gaudalaharry's. 1043 N Rush St (337-0800). Food not great but a complimentary taco bar on Wednesdays and a long happy hour (4pm-8pm) most nights.
Nantucket Cove, 1000 N Lake Short Drive (943-1600). Good fresh seafood.
Alexander's American Grill, 914 Ernst Court (944-0265). Crowded and open till 3am, 4am on Saturdays.
The Berghoff, 17 Adams St (427-3170), German food at reasonable prices with good atmosphere. It has its own beer, a delicious brew which is sold elsewhere in the Chicago area, and it's own bourbon.
Leona's, on Sheffield (near Belmont) and North Sheridan (near Morse). Ideal for an Italian binge.
Las Palmas, on Howard St. Great Mexican food, with musicians at weekends.
La Choza, on N Paulina St (near Howard St). Looks like a real dive, but has a lovely hidden outdoor garden and good, cheap food. Bring your own alcohol.
Heartland Cafe, on Lunt St in Rogers Park. Excellent vegetarian food.
Someone had to cash in on Capone. Tommy Gun's, a dinner theatre devoted to the gangster era, is in a renovated garage at 1239 South State Street. Its telephone number is RAT-A-TAT and it boasts the 1928 Ford used in the film *The Untouchables*.
If you want to dine in high style, many of Chicago's fine restaurants offer attractively priced menus at lunchtimes and at unfashionable dining times (5pm-6pm). For example, a small fixed-price dinner at the award-winning L'Escargot (Allerton Hotel, 701 N Michigan Avenue, 337-1717) can be had for $15. You might also like to wander along Devon St, with numerous Indian restaurants which offer interesting buffets. The Billy Goat Tavern, *under* Michigan Avenue near Grand St, was made famous by the American TV show *Saturday Night Live*. It is patronized by rowdy sports fans and has a real live billy goat.
For free food, loiter around the entrance floor of the Museum of Science and Industry and try to catch the eye of researchers from the adjacent Consumer Research Center, who seek out volunteers to taste new foods.

DRINKING

Bars normally stay open until 3am Monday to Friday and 4am at weekends. Rush and Division Streets are full of trendy lively bars, many of which exact a cover charge. On a hot day go to El Jardin's (3335 N Clark St) for one of their 12 ounce killer drinks of tequila, triple sec and lemon juice. More serious drinkers till should head for Resi's Bierstube or Lashet's Inn (2034 and 2119 W Irving Park Road). Locals speak highly of Quenchers (2401 N

Western Avenue). One of Chicago's most famous bars — Frank's 113 Club Tavern (113 E 47th St) — is located in a risky ghetto area, but it is still crowded. The latest trendy area is River North, and you should try Ditka's Citylights at 223 W Ontario St (280-7660), owned by the coach of the Chicago Bears. Many cheaper restaurants are unlicensed and permit you to bring your own booze. Try Sam's Wine Warehouse (756 W North Avenue) for the largest selection of American wines in the city.

 You get superb views from both the Sears Tower and the John Hancock Center; admission is $3.25 and $3.50 respectively. At dusk the view is particularly spectacular. Also visit the ArchiCenter (330 S Dearborn St, 782-1776), an exhibition gallery which features points of interest in Chicago. Among these is the Board of Trade (141 W Jackson Bvld at La Salle St, 435-3590) where you can watch the controlled chaos which contributes trading on the world's oldest and largest commodities futures market.

Buildings of Interest. Anybody with even a slight interest in architecture cannot fail to notice the innovative designs of the Chicago School, culminating in the work of Frank Lloyd Wright. The Chicago Architectural Foundation, dedicated to the preservation of this architectural heritage, gives a number of different guided tours on foot, by bus or even by bicycle from the ArchiCenter. (Hours and tour fees vary so call ahead). The Chicago Loop Tour is intended for people with a casual interest, whereas there are many more in-depth ones, including the Frank Lloyd Wright tour of Oak Park, Wright's home neighbourhood from 1889-1909. The Oak Park Visitor Center at 158 Forest Avenue (848-1500) should be the first stop for devotees of the architect. His own home (at Chicago and Forest Avenues) is open for guided tours daily, as is Unity Temple, his first public building. If you want to walk around Oak Park without a guide to see the 25 buildings designed by Wright, not to mention the house where Ernest Hemingway once lived, take the Lake Street/Dan Ryan El to Harlem or Oak Park Avenue. There are no tours available for the Bach House (Sheridan and Jarvis Streets), but it should not be missed by architecture buffs.

You can take an architectural river cruise from North Pier aboard the *Fort Dearborn* for $10. Some of Chicago's skyscrapers are stunning. Other buildings are simply strange. The former American Furniture Market completed in 1926 has a ghastly blue-topped tower which glows ghoulishly at night and which was originally intended as a mooring for dirigibles (airships). The Tribune Tower is a gothic skyscraper, a temple to journalism, which houses the Chicago Tribune. The facade contains stones from structures elsewhere in the world: chunks of Windsor Castle, the Taj Mahal and the Berlin Wall. Today the radio station WGN has its studios on the tower's ground floor. Watch out also for the twin Marina Towers, a dozen storeys of parking lot topped by 20 levels of apartments. As an elegant contrast, head North on Sheridan Road to the Bahai House of Worship.

Street Art. While wandering around the city, watch for sculptures and mobiles in public places (for information call FINE-ART). At 600 W Madison you will see a 100-foot sculpture of a baseball bat by Claes Oldenburg; outside the First National Bank Plaza is Chagall's 'Four Seasons' mosaic; 'Being Born' is at the corner of State and Washington Streets; and

Picasso's 'Mystery Sculpture' graces Daley Plaza. The lobby of Sears Tower is graced by Alexander Calder's 'Universe'.

Museums and Galleries. The Chicago Council on Fine Arts located in the lobby of the Daley Center Plaza (Dearborn and Randolph, 346-3278) provides information on the city's art exhibitions, of which there are many. The collection of French Impressionists and Old Masters at the Art Institute of Chicago (Michigan Avenue at Adams St, 443-3600; free on Thursdays) is staggeringly vast, and the later works are especially exciting. The shell of the Institute has been described as a Gothamesque Parthenon, and it hoards a world-class collection: from El Greco's Assumption of the Virgin to Warhol's studies of soup tins. You can almost see the lip on Van Gogh's self-portrait curl when visitors pronounce his name to rhyme with Chicago. If you prefer commerce to art, the building takes in the trading floor of the Chicago Stock Exchange — people more interested in pork futures than past glories.

Chicago has many small and interesting galleries. These range from the collection of Eastern European prints at the Jacques Baruch Gallery (900 N Michigan Avenue, 944-3377) and the Photography Museum at 364 W Erie St to the Du Sable Museum of African American History (740 E 56th Place in Washington Park, 947-0600) which traces the history of black people in America.

Most popular of all museums is the mammoth Museum of Science and Industry (Lake Shore Drive at 57th St, 684-1414), housed in a magnificent 1893 building. You can reach it from downtown Chicago on bus 1 (Indiana-Hyde Park) or 6 (Jeffrey Express). The museum opens 9.30am-5.30pm in summer and on winter weekends, 9.30am-4pm during the week in winter. Its 14 acres include replicas of the human heart and a collection of foetuses showing pre-natal development. Admission is free, which is only proper since many of the exhibits are exercises in public relations for American industries, some of the attractions such as a German U-boat and a full-sized model coal mine charge $2 admission.

The Field Museum of Natural History is also enormous and contains dinosaurs' skeletons and much more. It is located on Lake Shore Drive at Roosevelt Road (922-9410), opens daily from 9am to 5pm and costs $2 ($1 for students). Further along at 1300 Lake Shore Drive is the Adler Planetarium (322-0304) whose sky shows 'combine cosmic theater and multi-sensory adventure.' All this for just $2. It opens daily from 9.30am to 4.30pm, with late opening on Fridays to 9pm.

The new Museum of Broadcast Communications has an interesting mix of hardware — a 70-year-old Zenith 'long-distance wireless' and software. You can request archive clips such as the first episode of I Love Lucy, Walter Cronkite's last CBS Evening News, or the Beatles' 1965 performance on the Ed Sullivan Show.

Chicago's gangster past is celebrated at the American Police Center and Museum on Michigan Avenue at 17th Street South. Murals on the walls of the museum depict happy, smiling cops on the beat. Inside, Gangster Alley is a modest exhibit of Chicago's darkest years. Al Capone fought the law and the law won, but only after Eliot Ness and his Treasury team took over from the ineffectual city police. Today's organized criminals are most involved in drug trafficking, and the Horror of Drug Addiction exhibit tried to deter potential customers.

The Capone Trail. An interesting antidote to cultural overdose is to follow in the footsteps of Chicago's greatest gangster. On 14 February 1929, Al

Capone ordered the disposal of the Bugs Moran gang at their booze-running headquarters, a garage in the middle of inner-city desolation at 2122 North Clark Street. Their offence was to ambush an illicit consignment of whisky sent in from Detroit by the Purple Gang, with whom Capone traded during Prohibition. Seven men were massacred at five to eleven on St Valentine's morning. This is now a patch of grass sandwiched between an apartment block and the Chicago Pizza and Ovengrinder Co.

Capone was originally from Brooklyn, but moved to the area to become a bouncer in a brothel straddling the Illinois-Indiana border southeast of Chicago. It was here that Capone contracted the scar on his cheek, and (in a separate incident) the syphilis which ultimately killed him. Prohibition was introduced on Al Capone's 21st birthday, and constituted a coming-of-age present of huge potential. He and his cronies established control of the city's supply lines and, for a time, the city itself.

The streets of Chicago became safer when that rare commodity, an honest mayor, was elected in 1923. The villains promptly hopped beyond the city limits to the suburb of Cicero; skipping across the boundary meant escaping the reach of the city police. Cicero today is scruffy. The Alton Hotel is a filthy rooming house at 4837 West 22nd Street. Sixty years ago it was Anton's Hotel, as the name spelt out in the brickwork testifies. Capone gambled, drank and cooked the books here — the accounts which were to prove his downfall. Capone's headquarters were next door at 4833, now a parking lot.

You can take a southbound bus along Michigan Avenue to the site of the first drive-by shooting at 55th Street. The South Side O'Donnells, who ruled this patch in 1925, objected to Capone's spreading business interests and set out to kill him. He escaped unharmed, but his drivers and bodyguards were injured. These brutal assassinations became the trademark of gang warfare. You needed only a dark saloon car, a machine gun, and a rough idea of the haunts of your prey. Rather than staging a walk-by of the scene, stay on the bus for a ride-by. The area is urban dereliction taken to extremes.

Stay on the bus to the end of the line and transfer to bus 112 picks for the half-hour ride to the place Capone was buried.

Just beyond Morgan Park station on the Rock Island Line, two graveyards face each other across 111th Street. Greenwood is the better of the two — Mount Olivet is for paupers. Capone was penniless by the time his syphilitic brain finally rotted away, and he was buried in the northeast corner of Mount Olivet Cemetery. But he did not rest in peace: his remains were disinterred in the 1950s. Fearing the desecration which afflicts the tombs of the famous and infamous in America, his family moved the gangster's remains to an unmarked plot in Mount Carmel cemetery, 20 miles west. The staff abide by the family's wish not to reveal the precise location of the man who took control of a city and the lives of many.

The most comprehensive source of listing for performance arts, attractions and events is the *Reader*, published each Friday and is free from news stands bookshops, restaurants, etc. *Chicago* Magazine (monthly $1.95) is also useful. The Chicago Convention and Tourism Bureau provides an Eventline for visitors (255-2323) with recorded information about theatre, sports, etc. Both the *Chicago Tribune* and the *Sun Times*

include good entertainment guides, especially the Friday and Sunday editions of the *Tribune*.

Hot Tix Booths sell half-price tickets available on the day of performance for theatre, music and dance events; the downtown booth is at 24 S State St, with suburban branches at 1616 Sherman Ave, Evanston and Oak Park Mall.

Music. For exhaustive listings of the Chicago music scene, consult Section Two of the *Reader*. The Chicago Symphony Orchestra under Sir Georg Solti performs in Orchestra Hall (220 S Michigan Avenue, 435-8111) from September to May. For concert information call 664-0858. Watch for their outdoor performances during the Ravinia Festival in Highland Park (782-9696) which lasts from June to September. The Lyric Opera Orchestra put on free performances at the Grat Park bandshell on certain days in the summer. Free luchtime concerts can be heard at the First National Plaza at Dearborn and Monroe Streets. Major rock artists perform at the Rosemont Horizon (6920 N Mannheim Road, Des Plaines, 635-6600) and outdoor concerts are given at Poplar Creek Music Theatre (W Higgins Road, 426-1222). For forthcoming attractions call 842-5387 and for ticket information 454-6777.

Chicago Music Magazine, free from record stores and bards, is a good source of information about up-and-coming musicians. Electric blues originated in Chicago and thrives there still. One of the original clubs on the South Side, the New Checkerboard Lounge (423 E 43rd St, 624-3240) is still going strong. Take a taxi. On the safe North Side, you can choose between two blues clubs across the road from one another on N Halsted St, B.L.U.E.S. (582-1012) and Kingston Mines (477- 4646). The average cover charge is only $4 with cheap drinks, and they both have the crowded smoky atmosphere appropriate for blues dives. Blue Chicago (937 N State, 642-6261) is a little more upmarket. The style of jazz called 'Chicago' from the 1920s and 30s can still be heard alongside more modern jazz. Try Rick's American Cafe in the Lake Shore Drive Holiday Inn; it features good artists but charges steeply ($5-$10 cover plus very expensive drinks). Try also the clubs on N Lincoln Avenue or one of the following:

The Green Mill at Lawrence and Broadway features 1930s decor (it was one of Al Capone's hangouts) and super music.

Biddy Mulligan's on N Sheridan is a popular place for /blues and sometimes reggae and rock. Low cover charge and dancing.

The Moosehead Bar & Grill on S Michigan (near the Hilton) is the home of Joe Segal's

Jazz Showcase, where a long tradition of jazz is upheld. Phone the Jazz Hotline (666-1881) for details of other events and venues. The Chicago Jazz Festival takes place in late August at Grant Park.

Chicago has one of the strongest folk scenes in the country. The pick of the folk clubs is Holstein's (2464 N Lincoln, 372- 3331) since the venerable Earl of Old Town has been taken over by B.L.U.E.S. For those who maintain 'if it ain't country, it ain't music', there is Nashville North (101 E Irving Park Road, 595-0170) and Sundowners at the R.R.Ranch (56 W Randolph St, 263-8207). Also good for folk music is the No Exit Cafe on Glenview in Rogers Park.

Theatre. Chicago has experienced a boom in theatre over the last few years. The International Theater Festival (held in May and June) is an excellent showcase. There are more than 50 professional theatre groups in the city. Many prominent actors, directors and playwrights have had their debut at the Goodman Theater, housed in the Art Institute Complex. Shows which have either come from, or are bound for, Broadway are put on at the Shubert Theater (22 W Monroe St, 977-1710), at the Blackstone Theater (66 E Balbo Avenue, 977-1717) and at the Arie Crown Theater (2300 Lake Shore Drive, 791-6000). In addition there are many 'off-Loop' theatres on the North Side which present original material.

The League of Chicago Theaters provides recorded messages on ticket availability and brief interviews with critics and actors (977-1755). The Chicago Alliance for the Performing Arts (176 W Adams St, 372- 5178) sells vouchers, often at a discount, to many community theatres. Some theatres advertise in the 'Wanted' section of the *Reader* for volunteer ushers, which is a handy way to see plays for free.

Nightlife. Acid house fans will like the Exit (1653 N Wells St, 440-0535). Dancers with more conventional tastes in music should try Eddie Rocket's (9 W Division, 787-4881) for good value, or F/X (1100 N State, 280-2282) for chic. One of America's most innovative comedy clubs is Second City (1616 N Wells St, 337-3992), where Alan Alda and John Belushi began their careers. It is housed in a converted Chinese laundry; space is limited, so advance bookings are essential. Some comedy fans maintain that Friday and Satuday nights at the Improv Institute (504 N wells St, 782-6387) are better still: even if you don't catch all the local humour, you should learn a little about the Chicago psyche and have a good laugh. Gambling is illegal in Illnois, but serious poker players should find it easy to join a game.

SPORT AND RECREATION

Chicagoans take their professional sports very seriously. Indeed, the quickest way to popularity is to demonstrate some familiarity with their clubs. Generally ticket prices for professional games range from $3 to $12, though hockey is slightly more expensive. The better of the two baseball teams is the White Sox who play at Comiskey Park (35th St and Shields Avenue, 924-1000); however the Chicago Cubs are still Chicago's favourite, playing at Wrigley Field on the North Side (Clark and Addison Streets, 281-5050). The installation of floodlights at Wrigley Field in 1988, following the takeover of the Cubs by the *Chicago Tribune*, was a major national event. Soccer is played quite successfully by the Chicago sting at the grandiose Soldier's Field on S Lake Shore Drive at McFetridge St (558-5425) and, during the indoor season, at Chicago Stadium (1800 W Madison St). American football is played by the Chicago Bears (known as the Monsters of the Midway and featuring William 'Refrigerator' Perry) also at Soldier's Field (663-5408). The Black Hawks play ice hockey and fight at the Chicago Stadium (733-5300). Horseracing and betting take place at the prestigious Arlington Park racecourse 20 miles northwest of downtown Chicago. After a disastrous fire, the course has been rebuilt and is now among the finest tracks in the world. For participatory sports there are numerous tennis courts and golf courses. Despite Chicago's location at the edge of Lake Michigan, there is no point in taking your aqualung. But fishing, swimming, sailing, waterskiing and windsurfing are easily accessible. During a storm, however, Lake Michigan can become very rough and should be avoided.

Parks and Zoos. The Brookfield Zoo can be reached via the Congress El to Forest Park; take the Des Plaines Avenue exit, then transfer to the tiger-striped zoo express bus. The zoo includes species which are extinct in the wilds, some of them in a simulated tropical rainforest. It also has a few koalas, for whom fresh eucalyptus leaves are flown in from a farm in Florida. The zoo is free on Thursdays. The zoo in Lincoln Park is far less impressive, but is free every day and is well- kept. There's also an indoor Conservatory just north of the park. The Chicago Botanical Gardens in the far northern suburb of Winnetka (off Lake Cook Road) are impressive, but afficionados prefer the Morton Arboretum out at Lisle. The world's largest aquarium is the Shedd Aquarium at 1200 S Lake Short Drive (939-2426) which is best visited at feeding times: 11am and 2pm daily, with an extra feed at 3pm during busy periods. The aquarium opens at 9pm (March-October) or 10am (November- February) and closes daily at 5pm. Admission costs $12. Chicago has the longest stretch of beachfront of any major city. Lincoln Park lies along the lake on the North Side, and the beaches and yacht harbours are always crowded. Try Rogers Park, beginning at Pratt Street, where the relatively undiscovered beaches stretch for blocks and are provided with municipal life guards, so swimming is permitted. If you are unwilling to leave downtwon, just head east to Oak St beach.

SHOPPING

The shopping area is concentrated along a one mile strtch of State Street, a pedestrian precinct since 1978. All the major department stores are here, notably the magnificent Marshall Field's, built in 1892 with natural lighting by means of a skylit courtyard (now adapted to the age of electricity). One of the store's most famous employees, a Mr Selfridge, carried on the department store tradition in great style. Explore the whole nine blocks of State Street from Wacker Drive to Congress Parkway. For information about special events and activities call 782-9160. North Michigan Avenue is known as the Magnificent Mile or 'Boul Mich' and has all the fine speciality shops selling everything from antique Oriental carpets to Burberry raincoats.

For less exclusive items, any of the city's 50 Woolworths or Walgreens drugstores should suffice. Men should visit any of the eight clothing Clearance Centers in Chicago: clothes costing less than half retail prices can be found. 'You may go in a loft door and up in a creaky elevator but you get one hell of a buy' (*Newsweek*). At the northern end of the Magnificent Mile is the much vaunted Water Tower Place (825 N Michigan Avenue, 440-3460) which includes a seven-level atrium shopping mall comprising over 100 speciality stores and glass enclosed elevators. The best-stocked book store in town is Kroch and Brentano's on Wabash. For good bargain books, visit Crown Books and if you are feeling homesick, visit Stuart Brent's on N Michigan Avenue, which is modelled after Blackwell's in Oxford. There are plety of secondhand bookshops in the Lincoln Park area on Clark St and Lincoln Avenue.

Sales tax in Chicago is 7% and is applied to all purchases except non-processed food not for immediate consumption.

THE MEDIA

The radio station for classical as well as other kinds of music is WFMT 98.7 FM; listen to the famous programme *Midnight Special* on Saturday nights at 10.15. Soft rock is played on WXRT (93 FM), adult rock on 101 FM and Country on WAMQ 670 AM. The leading black station is on 102.7 FM, while WCKG (105.9) promises 'classic rock and less talk'. For the nearest thing to BBC Radio One, try WLS 89 AM with a moderate teenage-orientated selection (listen to Animal Stories at 9.45am and 5.45pm, a humorous short news programme featuring anecdotes about animals). For serious news programmes tune to 780 AM for WBBM, 670 AM for WMAQ, 92 FM for the National Public Radio Station WBEZ or try to find the Canadian Broadcasting Corporation. On television, PBS can be found on channel 11.

Newspapers. The *Chicago Tribune* was once in the same league as the *New York Times* and the *Washington Post*. Despite a decline in its reputation, it is still a fairly reliable newspaper. The *Sun Times*, formerly a liberal and gossipy newspaper, is now part of the Murdoch group. Both papers cost 35c, $1.25 on Sundays. Try also the *Chicago Defender* for local news that the two main papers don't print.

The fact that Chicago is a tough city should not be underestimated. On average there is a mugging every 15 minutes and a murder every 12 hours. The sound of gunshot is considered commonplace in the rougher sections of town. It is not advisable for tourists to wander off exploring. This is particularly true on the South Side, but also in the unsavoury sections of the normally safe North Side. Certain places such as the Cabrini Green housing project just west of Rush St should be avoided unless you have a police escort. Late night revellers should not wander along Division St west of Clark St, for things change dramatically.

Bus and train travellers should be careful in the vicinity of the terminals. If possible stay north of Roosevelt Road (1200 South) and east of Ashland (1600 West). Do not walk at night in deserted areas and do not venture into the South Side unless your car is mechanically sound, all doors are locked and you have the route firmly fixed in your mind. Tactics popular among villains include deliberately colliding with other motorists, then attacking them when they get out to inspect the damage; other robbers simply smash the windows of stationary cars with baseball bats. (Some South Side locals ignore red traffic lights for fear of sudden attack). Taxis are the best solution. Visitors should ask a policeman, cab driver or even a reasonable looking stranger for advice about safe versus dangerous neighbourhoods.

Law enforcement of drug violations is erratic so do not assume that just because everyone else is doing it you won't be arrested. Dealing even in small amounts of marijuana is taken very seriously by the police. The police are very vigilant in their pursuit of drunk drivers, who face mandatory prison sentences.

Help and Information

The area code for Chicago is 312.

Information: Chicago Tourism Council, Water Tower, Michigan and Chicago Avenues (225-5000). Maps and brochures are also distributed from the Visitor Information Center at 163 East Pearson Street (280 5740) near Michigan Avenue.

British Consulate General: 33a N Dearborn St (346-1810).
American Express: 625 N Michigan Avenue (425-2570).
Thomas Cook: 435 N Michigan Avenue (828-9750)
Post Office: 433 W Van Buren and Canal Streets (886-2575).
Medical Emergencies: Northwest Memorial Hospital, Superior St (649-2000).

Dental Service: 726-4976.
Late night drugstore: Walgreen's Drugs, 1130 N State St (787-7035).
Crisis Center: 929-5140.
Travelers' Aid: 327 S La Salle St (435-4500). Also at Union Station, the
  Greyhound Terminal and O'Hare Airport.

Further Afield

Many visitors simply regard the Midwest as somewhere to be flown or driven over as quickly as possible. To do so is to miss a couple of distinct but fascinating conurbations: Detroit, nuzzling up against Canada and boasting one of the most successful urban regeneration schemes in America, and the 'Twin Cities' of Minneapolis and St Paul, two eminently civilised places which face each other across the Mississippi in Minnesota. These cities are discussed shortly; first, however, it is worth reading a little about the character and characters of the Midwest.

Away from the cities, the massive Midwest stretching from North Dakota south to Oklahoma, and up along the Great Lakes is an area of small towns scattered thinly across flat farming country. There are of course some topographical surprises, but driving across these 13 states does not admit of much variety. If on the other hand you have grown weary of traffic, noise, hurry, expensive bars, beautiful people, and all the other features of urban America, it might be time to expose yourself to one of the sleepy Midwestern towns tenuously linked by miles of straight often deserted roads. People who choose to stop in one town for a while need not worry that they are missing anything new or different in the next town, the next county or even the next state. In *Granta*, Bill Bryson — a native of Des Moines, Iowa — placed his home state 'in the middle of the biggest plain this side of Jupiter' and described the state capital thus:

'A thousand miles from the sea in any direction, 600 miles from the nearest mountain, 400 miles from skyscrapers and muggers and things of interest, 300 miles from people who do not habitually stick a finger in their ear and swivel it around as a preliminary to answering any question addressed to them by a stranger. To reach anywhere of even passing interest from Des Moines by car requires a journey that in other countries would be considered epic.'

On the outskirts of a small town, the population sign separates the monotonous wheat and cornfields from the houses, gas station, post office and shops, whether it's Deadwood South Dakota (population 2,409) or Peculiar Missouri (population 705). Sometimes the town sign offers more information, such as 'Home of the Ottertails', 'Welcome to our Town' or even 'Population 1,863... 1,862 nice, friendly folk and one old grouch'. If you want further information, pull into the gas station where, unless the owner is the old grouch, you will get reliable information about local weather, road conditions, events, the way to the old Methodist church or a shortcut to Pete and Jim's World Famous Bakery. The spirit of the Midwest resides far more in these small, neat communities than in the handful of large cities in the region. Only St Louis, Kansas City, Minneapolis/St Paul, Milwaukee, Cincinnati, Cleveland, and Detroit have populations exceeding half a million. These cities are often the butt of jokes by people from the East and West Coasts: for example, Cleveland is claimed to be the one place in North America where you ask for a room *without* a view. Many state capitals are not the largest cities. Springfield Illinois, Topeka Kansas, Jefferson City

Missouri and, smallest of all with 10,000 inhabitants, Pierre South Dakota, are all thriving hubs of yesteryear.

The Natives. People from the East and West Coasts call the locals 'Flyovers' — because you fly over them on the way from Boston or New York to San Francisco or Los Angeles. The small town Midwesterner does not seek to keep up with city slickers in fashion, taste or income. His spirit of competition is more likely to manifest itself in the energy with which he combats the frightful winters, or at sporting contests between rival small towns. His demands and aspirations are usually modest, and can make a refreshing change from the ambition and agression so evident in most of urban America. You will find the people extraordinarily open, welcoming and delighted (though perhaps a little puzzled) at your choice of destination.

The locals are moderate in most things from their accents (no twangs or drawls, except in the Southern parts of the region) to their politics and religion. Although the local church often plays a central role in small communities, the enthusiastic revival type of worship is uncommon. The Amish, Huttites and Mennonites have communities in Illinois, Ohio and Indiana, but do not impose their beliefs on others. There is much less ethnic variety in these states despite an early influx of Scandinavian settlers, some of whom came to set up utopian communes. On average 93% of the population is white, much higher than in the South or on the coasts. Oklahoma provides an interesting exception. Over 5% of the population is Native American Indian, the highest concentration in America. A high proportion of these people are integrated into society rather than living on reservations. There are many historical sites and museums throughout Oklahoma which allow the visitor to learn about Indian culture. In southern Wisconsin you can visit reconstructions such as Little Norway and the Swiss Historical Village, to learn about early European immigrant life.

Climate. The extremes are cruel, and can seriously impair your travelling pleasure if you are unprepared. Even permanent residents caution each other prior to motoring journeys during the winter. And heatwaves can be very debilitating. It is virtually impossible to rent or buy a car without air-conditioning in St Louis. In Minnesota the average January temperature is a full 15 Fahrenheit degrees below freezing and some people are experimenting with half-buried houses to escape the cold. July temperatures rarely fall below 70°F/21°C even at night. The southern stretches of the Mississippi River valley can become so hot and humid that you might think you were in the tropics. The northern states bordering Canada are much drier. Natural disasters such as tornadoes, floods and dust storms are real possibilities. (In the *Wizard of Oz*, Dorothy's life in Kansas was turned upside down by a tornado). Even if there is no actual catastrophe, storms can have eerie effects on the atmosphere and on the quality of the light. Watch for the Northern Lights which are often visible from the Dakotas, especially in late summer. The natives take all these inconveniences and dangers stoically. They emerge the morning after a blizzard wrapped up like Eskimos, greet their neighbours and set to work cooperatively with shovels to restore normality. Dozens of winter carnivals are celebrated with snowmobile races, sleigh rides, and baseball games in ice.

Eating. Dining in the Midwest is often a basic down-home affair. The larger cities can satisfy the fanciest of tastes but the local greasy spoon is where you will find the residents eating their steaks, hamburgers and french fries in any small town. Summer barbecues are popular. One Midwestern establishment claims to serve the best barbecues in the world (*pace* Texas): Arthur Bryant's Barbecue, located in a rundown section of Kansas City Missouri. And if you're up in Wisconsin, be sure to try the cheese and ice cream produced in America's Dairyland. The central USA is crammed full of McDonalds and a host of other food chains (Country Kitchens are amoung the best). The enormous Gateway Arch in St. Louis (at 631ft the tallest manmade monument in the US) should not be mistaken for the galactic headquarters of McDonalds, although close by is the world's first floating McDonalds.

Drinking. Often there is not much to do in a small town if you don't want to see the drive-in movie, except go to the bar. Unlike sophisticated New York cafes or New Orleans blues bars, these small bars function more like British pubs, with a core of regulars who may look upon their local as a second home. Try to fit in with the customs of the local clientele and avoid initiating any hostility. Ask the bartender to recommend a beer; you may not get the best beer you've ever had but you will have showed your willingness to defer to local practice. Milwaukee Wisconsin is the brewing capital of the USA and is the headquarters for Miller, Pabst, and Schlitz (which 'made Milwaukee famous'). The breweries organize tours which include free samples. The world's biggest brewery, however, is Anheuser-Busch at 1127 Pestalozzi St; St. Louis; call 557 2626 for a free tour. State liquor controls can be strict; for example in Iowa no beer containing over 3.2% alcohol can be sold, which means that Iowans close to state borders shop in neighbouring states before parties. Bars close punctually at 1am, unless the bartender is a special friend. The big cities — Chicago is a special case — have after-hours establishments, often private clubs of dubious character.

Exploring From the state tourist literature you will be able to select the attractions both natural and manmade which interest you. An impressive combination of the two can be found at Mt Rushmore, southwest of Rapid City in South Dakota. Sculptor Gutzon Borglum carved the 'Shrine of Democracy', bearing the likeness of Lincoln, Jefferson, Washington and Roosevelt. Also in South Dakota, the lunar landscape of the Badlands is an area well worth visiting

To compensate for the generally unspectacular scenery in the Midwest, a huge number of man-made attractions can be seen. An excellent guidebook to the weird and wonderful is *The New Roadside America* (Simon & Schuster, $13), which catalogues such wonders as the Spam Museum in Austin Minnesota, Carhenge (an exact replica of Stonehenge constructed entirely from crushed cars), the Tower of Pisa leaning over Niles Illnois, and the Birthplace of Captain James T Kirk at Riverside Iowa. All of these sound more exciting than the Accountancy Hall of Fame at Ohio State University in Columbus.

At one of the world's largest amusement parks, 'Marriott's Great America' in Gurnee Illinois (about 40 miles north of Chicago). Its main attraction is 'Shock Wave', the world's tallest and fastest roller coaster (designed by an ex-NASA scientist). More charming is the Mark Twain Museum and Home in Hannibal Missouri on the banks of the Mississippi, where there are numerous Huckleberry Finn and Tom Sawyer associations. More curious is the Cowboy Hall of Fame and Western Heritage Center in Oklahoma City, though a visit hardly seems necessary in the state where the man-in-the-street often looks and talks like an actor in a cowboy movie. (Try to see these cowboys bareback bronco riding, steer wrestling and calf roping at a rodeo). More restful is the rolling, wooded countryside and large wilderness preserves of Wisconsin and Minnesota. If you hope for something more sophisticated than bars featuring Elvis impersonators, seek out towns with sizeable universities.

Madison has the University of Wisconsin's main campus, which, with 30,000 students, dominates the town. Madison is set between two large lakes and is clean, lively and friendly, with plenty to do. It also provides a good base for exploring the natural beauty of Wisconsin's hills, lakes and forests.

DETROIT

Perhaps Detroit has the best claim as the Midwest's second city. It was also until recently the American city most worth avoiding. Its role as the world centre of motor car manufacturing gave it the appearance of a huge, sprawling Dagenham, then the decline of the industry in the face of foreign competition resulted in a far uglier face, where violence was rampant and the downtown area a slum. The epicentre of soul music (Motown = Motor Town = Detroit) was a crumbling shell, but has been energetically revitalised. While there are still vast areas of the city where it is unwise to venture, the downtown area has been enhanced by gradual gentrification and an efficient elevated railway. Furthermore, it has the largest number of theatre seats in the USA after New York.

Detroit Metropolitan Airport (code DTW) is 20 miles southwest of the city in the suburb of Romulus. It is a strange and unnatural shape, with spidery piers radiating from a narrow spine. Anyone transferring between Continental and Northwest Airlink faces a half-mile walk. The international terminal — where all flights from abroad arrive, and from which British Airways services depart — is detached from the main airport, which itself is divided into the J M Davey Terminal (north and east) and the L C Smith Terminal (south and west). A post office is located in the latter, and between the two is an hotel, whose foyer is built into the terminal.

Detroit's reasonably efficient system of buses is supplemented in the city centre by the Detroit People Mover, an elevated railway with a three-mile circular route and 13 stations. The flat fare is 50c.

The best areas for eating and drinking are all newly restored, such as Bricktown and Greektown just north of RenCen. Bricktown is a corridor of shops and restaurants linking Jefferson Avenue with Monroe St, and the name is derived from the brick facades on the buildings.

Greektown starts at Monroe St. Trapper's Alley in Greektown has Ethiopian and Cajun for people who may have acquired an allergy to lukewarm moussaka.

Close by on Monroe, the International Marketplace has presented Detroit with the world's highest indoor waterfall: 100 gallons of water cascade down the 114-foot drop every second.

The heart of Detroit is the Rennaisance Center, abbreviated by all the locals to RenCen. It comprises seven huge towers, including the nation's tallest hotel — the 73-storey Westin. A beer in the cocktail bar at the top costs only fractionally more than admission to the observation platform two floors lower. RenCen was financed privately by Henry Ford II, who wanted to give something back to the city which gave his family their fortune.

Detroit has all sorts of oddities. As befits Motor City, it has perfected the art of three-dimensional motoring: one city block is occupied by a 12-storey car park. A day could be well spent at the University Cultural Center (which hosts six museums as well as Wayne State University). The Detroit Institute of Art falls short of Chicago's magnificent collection, but star turn include murals commissioned from the Mexican Diego Rivera featuring Detroit industry. The latest area to be redeveloped is Rivertown, a couple of miles east of RenCen on Jefferson Avenue. This is an imaginative mix of converted warehouses, depots and factories.　Tamla Motown fans should brave the badlands and venture out to the Motown Museum, 'Hitsville USA'. Call first (313-875-2264) for an appointment before heading out on bus 16 on Dexter Avenue to the recording studio at 2648 W Grand Boulevard. The Michael Jackson room contains the most interesting exhibit.

Out of town, at Dearborn, the Henry Ford Museum contains a fascinating range of vehicles including the 1961 Lincoln limousine in which John F Kennedy was shot in Dallas in 1963. Bizarrely, the museum also contains the seat from Ford's Theater in Washington DC where President Lincoln was assassinated.

The theatres in Detroit are not just plentiful — they are architecturally exquisite, palaces of the performance arts. The most notable is the Fox Theatre (America's biggest movie house) on Woodward Avenue. It was built by William Fox, a producer with a taste for extravagance: he ordered materials such as black marble, red leather and fine crystal be used. The result was nothing short of lavish, a kind of Oriental art deco, in keeping with Detroit's status as America's richest city. In the 1960s the theatre housed the Motown Revue, featuring everyone you've heard of, from Stevie Wonder to Diana Ross. As Motor City and Motown went into decline, the Fox closed and fell into disrepair. It was recently restored to its former glory as part of the city's urban replenishment.

Two smaller theatres close by are the Gem, which adopts an over-the-t o Romanesque style, and the State — now a leading music venue.

MINNEAPOLIS and ST PAUL

The 'Twin Cities' comprise one of the most pleasant urban areas in the USA, without the frenzy of New York, say, but with a great deal of culture. You can also shop until you drop at the new Mall of America, or just stroll in safe and scenic streets.

An Italian missionary, Father Louis Hennepin, found the falls in the Mississippi River and named them the Falls of St Anthony after his patron saint. Today the 'Twin Cities' are populated predominantly by descendants of Irish, German and Scandinavian immigrants.

Minneapolis

Arrival and Departure. *Air:* Minneapolis/St Paul airport is a well-organized hub for Northwest Airlines. The airport is ten miles southeast of Minneapolis — and ten miles southwest of St Paul.

Bus 7 runs to downtown every 20 minutes or so. It also runs to the Mall of America, in the opposite direction but from the same stop. To complicate matters further, each bus has a suffix after the 7 (e.g. B, C, etc), which defines its exact route. But all downtown-heading 7s go to the city centre. The fare varies from 85c to $1.60 depending on time of day, whether the bus is an express and on the mood of the driver — he or she may not bother to collect the extra quarter due on airport runs. But in any event you will need lots of change because drivers accept only coins. The journey time is between 25 and 50 minutes. You may conclude that a cab, taking only 20 minutes, is an easier option, but expect to pay $20.

The Mall of America is ten minutes away by bus, for a fare of 85c or $1.10.

Train: the local Amtrak depot is in the Midway area, en route to St Paul. Bus 16 stops nearby.

Driving: coming from the east, I-94 cuts straight through St Paul on its way to Minneapolis, whereupon is swerves sharply to run north before veering west once more. Most places in Minneapolis are easily accessible from it or from its branches, I-394, I-494 and I-694. The main north-south route is I-35, linking Lake Superior with the Gulf of Mexico. The freeway splits to the north and south of the city into I-35E serving St Paul, while I-35W slices through Minneapolis.

Getting Around. As indicated above, the bus system is rather complex. The MTC operates a large network of services, and issues a *Transit Guide* map for each city, free from the Transit Store at 719 Marquette Avenue; you can't miss this place because it has a bus apparently bursting out of the window. Call 341-4BUS for automated schedule information — you must use a TouchTone phone. Express services run to St Paul on route 94 and its derivatives (94B, C, D, etc.).

Fares start at 85c but a supplement of 25c is charged for all sorts of things: peak hours (6-9am and 3.30-6.30pm), express buses and crossing a zone boundary. Transfers, however, are free.

You can rent a bike to enjoy Minneapolis's 40-mile/65km network of cycle paths at Bennett's Cycling, a few miles west of downtown at 3540 Dakota Avenue South (922-0311). The first day costs $30, subsequent ones $10 each. Not everyone sticks to the 10mph speed limit on the cycle paths.

Accommodation. Cheap motels are strung out along I-94 and I-35W. Downtown budget accommodation is harder to find. Try the Fair Oaks Motel at 2335 3rd Avenue South (871-2000), some way south of the city (between 22nd and 24th Streets just west of I-35W) but with a free shuttle bus. The Omni Northstar, central at 618 2nd Avenue South (338-2288) has good weekend rates off season.

Eating and Drinking. An area worth investigating is the Mississippi Mile, a development on both sides of the river between Plymouth Avenue and I-35W, walkable from downtown. It has a selection of reasonably trendy restaurants, some of which are not at all expensive.

Exploring. The Twin Cities have the fifth-largest retail sales in the USA, and Minneapolis seems at time to be one gigantic mall. In fact is possesses the largest 'shopping and entertainment complex' in the USA, the gigantic Mall of America near the airport. The Mall has a shop for every day of the year. This quarter-mile-square megalith has four million retailing square feet, seven restaurants, ten 'food venues' and 21 of what Americans refer to unappetizingly as 'food outlets'. The most novel is the Maison du Popcorn (best flavour: pistachio; worst: bacon and cheese). The Mall also has 400 trees, 30,000 plants and a 70-foot waterfall, and a full-scale amusement park — Camp Snoopy — in the middle, a kind of low-rent Disneyland.

Just window-shopping is entertainment enough. At Oshman's Super Sports you can test equipment before buying. It has an in-store squash court and an ingenious rotating dry ski-slope which enables you to try out skis while shoppers stroll by. Benetton, The Gap and the Body Shop also have shops, but impecunious visitors will probably be tempted by Everything's a Dollar, where everything (including the shopping basket) costs $1 plus tax.

Bus 7 runs from the city to the Mall every 20 minutes, fare 85 cents. The shops are open 10am-9.30pm from Monday to Saturday, 11am-7pm on Sundays.

The new mall has had a considerable impact upon the fortunes of Minneapolis' existing stores; the Nicollet Mall, in particular, has suffered. The city centre has a network of 'skyways' which enable you to move around without ever having to venture into the outside air.

Entertainment. Which urban area has most live theatre venues outside New York? Not Boston, Chicago, San Francisco nor Los Angeles, but the Twin Cities. (Note that Detroit has fewer venues but claims to have more seats). The leading Minneapolis auditorium is the Guthrie Theater at 725 Vineland Place (377-2224) but it is supplemented by dozens of smaller theatres. Details of all Twin Cities events — along with news and reviews — appear in the free weekly *City Pages*. Ticketmaster sells tickets for most big events at numerous outlets, or call 989-5151 and pay by credit card.

For comedy, try the Acme Comedy Co at 708 N 1st St (375-1111) any day except Sunday and Monday, or the Comedy Gallery Minneapolis 219 SE Main St (331-5653). Big sporting events take place at the Hubert H. Humphrey Metrodome in Minneapolis (375-1116). The Minnesota Twins have recently been highly successful.

Help and Information. Greater Minneapolis Convention and Visitors Association is on the third floor at 1219 Marquette Avenue, close to the Symphony Hall. Call 348-7000 for information.

The area code for both Minneapolis and St Paul is 612.

St Paul

The information in this section complements that given for *Minneapolis,* above.

St Paul was initially developed by a one-eyed former fur trader named Pierre Parrant who established a saloon on the banks of the Mississippi, and it was initially known from his nickname as 'Pig's Eye Landing'. The town became more respectable when Father Lucien Galtier arrived and built a church dedicated to St Paul. The name was changed to match, and in 1849 it became capital of the Territory of Minnesota — which became a state nine years later.

It has quietened down considerably since the first 30 years of the 20th century. Corruption among city officials enabled criminals to enjoy a kind of sanctuary. All they needed to do was to check in on arrival and pay off the officals, and promise not to commit any crimes within the city limits. Everyone from Kate 'Ma' Baker to George 'Machine Gun' Kelly took advantage of such hospitality. Alvin 'Creepy' Karpis once said 'If you were looking for a guy you hadn't seen in a few months, you thought of two places: prison or St Paul'. Today it is a quiet, handsome and enjoyable city with a fine social life. Just remember to pronounce the name properly — Saint to rhyme with paint, not the truncated 'snt' which many British people use, and Paul not Paul's.

Arrival and Departure. *Air:* bus 62 runs sporadically from the airport to St Paul. If none is due, take bus 4 or 7 to the GSA building — a federal administration facility which doubles as a bus interchange — and get a free transfer to bus 9 to downtown St Paul.

Bus 4 runs virtually due north from the airport along the western edge of St Paul; the most useful point it serves is the Bandana Square complex.

Bus: The Greyhound terminal is central at 7th and St Peter St.

Train: St Paul Amtrak station is a few miles west at 730 Transfer Road in the suburb of Midway, almost midway between St Paul and Minneapolis. Bus 7 goes to within a block of the station.

Getting Around. Bus information applies as for Minneapolis, above. The Transit Store in St Paul is in the American National Bank Skyway at 5th and Minnesota.

Accommodation. The Sunset Inn at Bandana Square is the most unusual place in St Paul. An old locomotive shed has been converted into a comfortable and highly atmospheric hotel. Double rooms cost about $70 a night, but include an evening snack (coffee, juice and doughnuts) and breakfast (ditto). you can reach it from the airport on bus 4, or from downtown St Paul on bus 31.

Eating and Drinking. Two miles from the centre of St Paul, Grand Avenue begins. This has a more interesting range of restaurants than downtown.

Exploring. In St Paul you can take a trail of three domes. The largest unsupported marble dome in the world tops the city's greatest sight, the Minnesota state capitol, at Cedar and Aurora Streets (296-2881). Guided tours are provided 9am-5pm from Monday to Friday, 10am-4pm on Saturdays and 1-4pm on Sundays. You can compare it with the dome of the Cathedral at 239 Selby Avenue (228-1766), which is modelled on St Peter's in Rome and has seats for 3,000.

The Science Museum of Minnesota (30 E 10th St, 221-9400) has a broad range of exhibits, plus a spectacular Omnitheater: films are projected onto a 75-foot domed screen. The theatre is sponsored by the 3M company — the M's stand for Minnesota Mining and Manufacturing. The museum opens 9.30am-9pm from Tuesday to Saturday, 11am-9pm on Sundays and on Mondays in summer.

Entertainment. One of America's leading Black theatre companies is based in St Paul. The Penumbra Theatre Company is based at the Martin Luther King Center, 270 North Kent St, two miles/3km west of downtown (224-3180). Stand-up comics perform nightly except Monday at Comedy Gallery St Paul, 175 E 5th St (331-5653).

The St Paul winter carnival, which takes place in the last two weeks of January, is the oldest winter festival in North America.

Help and Information. The St Paul Convention and Visitors Bureau is Suite 101, Norwest Center, 55 E 5th St, tel 297-6985.

AROUND MINNEAPOLIS/ST PAUL

The Grand Casino company, owned by the Lower Sioux Indian Community, runs gamblers' specials to the casinos at Hinckley and Mille Lacs, about two hours north. The bus ride costs $10, of which you get half back as a $5 roll of quarters. You also get a free 'eat-all-you-can' lunch. For bookings call 449-0057 or 1-800-626-LUCK.

The Minnesota town of Hibbing is famous for three things: the Greyhound Bus Origin Center, where the great mid-20th century phenomenon of long-distance bus travel began; the World's Largest Open Pit Iron Ore Mine, a great big hole in the ground; and the boyhood home of Robert Zimmerman, later Bob Dylan — the great late-20th century folk singer.

The Great Outdoors

Since so much of the Midwest is flat, outdoor recreations have adapted accordingly: jogging, cycling and cross-country skiing are all popular. But the most widely enjoyed activities are boating (Minnesota has more boats per capita than any other place in the USA), fishing and hunting for which you will need a licence. Every small bar in the appropriate areas has a display of enormous antlers or a stuffed walleye, and will be able to give you details about obtaining a licence and when the season begins and ends. Game includes deer, rabbit, pheasant and duck. For a guide to the wilderness areas of the Midwest, consult Bill Thomas's *Mid-America Trips and Trails.* There are excellent opportunities for wilderness canoeing in the Boundary Waters Canoe Area, an area of three million acres of interconnecting rivers and lakes in northeastern Minnesota spilling over the Canadian border. Enquire in Crane Lake, Winton or Grand Marais for information about outfitters and canoe rentals which are available May to October. The Lake of the Ozarks region of Missouri, which begins an hour's drive southwest of St Louis, is a land of high limestone bluffs and caves, of blue heron and wild turkey, beaver and bass; it is perhaps best appreciated from a canoe. Hemingway venerated this part of the country as the true America, and returned through his life for the fishing and solitude.

Calendar of Events

January	Winter Carnival, St Paul Minnesota
February	Chicago Auto Fair
May	Indianapolis 500 motor race
May	Chicago International Art Exposition
June	Detroit Grand Prix
July	Lumberjack World Championship Hayward Wisconsin
August	Ohio State Fair (the nation's largest)
late August/ early September	Chicago Jazz Festival
September	Oktoberfest, St Paul
October	Chicago Marathon
October	Pumpkin Show, Circleville Ohio

Texas

Texas is awesome. Until the admission of Alaska to the Union, it was by far the USA's largest state. Texas is bigger than France, Belgium, Holland and Switzerland combined. Not only is its area immense but the buildings and companies and wealth it contains are enormous. Despite the economic downturn caused by the recession, the number of gleaming skyscrapers in Dallas and Houston testifies to the state's optimism and prosperity.

The size of Texas explains a lot about the state. It is what gives Texas its enormous variety of landscape, weather, flora and fauna, cuisine, sport, art and outdoor activities. More importantly, the immense area gives Texans a different sense of distance and restlessness, pride adventurousness, melancholy and hospitality. It would not be at all unusual for Texans to set off on the spur of the moment to visit a place 150 miles away, and then, if it happened to be in a dry county, drive a further 100 miles to slake their thirsts. They would drive the distance between London and Edinburgh on a whim.

Texas wasn't always a place where the inhabitants could take comfort and security for granted. Five flags have flown over Texas. The first was that of Spain, carried there by the Conquistadores. The second was that of Mexico, from whom Texas won its independence in 1836 at the decisive Battle of San Jacinto, a battle that followed three weeks on the heel of the Americans' defeat at the Alamo.

Texas remained an independent republic until 1845 when it became the 28th state in the Union and the Stars and Stripes was raised. Fifteen years later, Texas and other southern states sided with Confederacy in the Civil War, and the Confederate Flag flew throughout the state. When the Union triumphed, the Stars and Stripes was again hoisted.

After a brief bitter period of reconstruction, Texas began to prosper by raising herds of Longhorn cattle to provide beef for the growing nation's westward expansion. By the turn of the century, oil production was underway and it soon became apparent that Texas sat on top of immense reservoirs of oil. Texas now provides over one third of the USA's oil needs and is home for much of the country's technologically-based industry. In addition to its extensive mineral wealth it is the second largest agricultural producer after California.

CLIMATE

Unless you can cope with really hot weather — 85°-100°F (29°–38°C) — avoid Texas during July and August. It is not unusual for one out of every three days to be over 100°F/38°C. The high humidity especially in Houston is enervating and produces what the natives call 'Gulf weather'. They escape it by resorting to a network of carpeted underground tunnels downtown. The city's annual air-conditioning bill is approaching a billion dollars.

Winters are usually mild — 45°-65°F (7°-18°C) — but there can be sudden drops in temperature to below freezing, and ice storms in December and January are not unknown. The best times to visit are March to May and mid-September to mid-November. Because the extremes of Texas' weather are compensated for by chilling air-conditioning during heat spells or excessive heating during cold snaps, light to medium weight clothing should see you through without pneumonia or heat prostration. For weather information, dial 654-0116 in Dallas, 228-8703 in Houston.

Partly due to the wide range of elevation from sea level to 8,000ft, the rainfall varies from 10-55 inches per year, and the vegetation varies accordingly from desert shrub to thick forest.

THE LOCALS

Texas has a population of 15 million. Nearly every ethnic group found in the USA exists in Tesas: Anglos (i.e. whites) make up 60%, Hispanics 25%, and black people 12%. The population growth was once the fastest in the nation. This was once due largely to a massive migration from the northern United States to the 'Sun Belt'.

Texans are friendly to tourists, if only because it gives them a new audience for boasting about their state and a chance to do some leg-pulling, at which they excel. Beware when they start to tell you the recipe for chilli armadillo on the half shell or that the one-legged crane is the state bird (they mean the building crane). Knowledge of Europe is often comically limited, but they love talking about themselves. You might learn more than you want to about embryo implants in Santa Gertrudis cows, but after enough ice-cold beers even talk of a cherished collection of 100 varieties of barbed wire can become interesting.

Although tourists are welcomed, not all outsiders are gathered to the Texan bosom. Unemployed Northerners willing to work for less than the going wage are resented, and the 'sight of a Yankee in a one-way U-Haul' (a small do-it-yourself moving van) has become a Texan's pet hate. In fact many of those migrating families soon became disillusioned and there is now a stream of U-Hauls going in the reverse direction.

Texans can be even more hostile to each other than to outsiders, and attrition at a rate which appals outsiders in the norm. Most homicides take place in the ghettos and arise out of domestic quarrels. It has been said that

Texans, used to lots of breathing space, get very touchy when crowded together. A further sign of not-so-neighbourly behaviour is the sight of countless pick-up trucks with hunting rifles and shotguns in full view on gun racks mounted behind the driver. Texans are the chief exponents of the citizen's right to bear arms. So avoid the rough neighbourhoods in the big cities whenever possible, and avoid quarrels with stranges and motorists.

Religion Texas is a conservative place. Although many of the newly arrived Northerners spend their weekends worshipping nature or Mamon, Texans are still church-goers. Profanity in front of (or by) females is frowned upon, not to mention kinkiness and pornography. Baptists have the largest religious following, with two million members, followed by Roman Catholics, Methodists and numerous others. The world's largest Methodist, Baptist and Presbyterian churches are all in Dallas.

Texans are work oriented. It's common for a person to work part-time or night, in addition to holding down a regular job: truckers will also drive school buses; law enforcement officers do hotel security work. For many public sector workers, retirement means collecting a pension and starting a new career. You continually meet Texans who have a small business venture on the side: a stall at a flea market; a 'piece of the action' in a bar or restaurant; a mail order deal; or a few video machines sited at a local country club. College students work during their three month summer vacation at amusement parks or children's camps and also part-time during term. Everyone, it seems, is busy.

Making Friends Despite all this, it is not difficult to make friends with the locals. There are plenty of singles bars, clubs and student lounges, especially near the various campuses of the University of Texas. Colleges with a religious affiliation like Southern Methodist University (SMU), Baylor, Rice or Texan Christian University tend to be very staid. But outside these places most Texans have an earthy, if not particularly sophisticated, interest in heterosexual sex.

The biggest gay community is in Houston, where it numbers around 250,000, but a frightening number of Texans are fiercely anti-gay. The spread of AIDS has increased their influence, and verbal or physical abuse of homosexuals is becoming more common. Discretion is advised.

Air. Flying, particularly between Dallas, Houston and San Antonio, can be the cheapest method of transport between cities more than 200 miles apart. Keep an eye on newspaper advertisements for truly silly deals when hostilities break out between competing airline companies.

Bus Greyhound has eight buses a day from Dallas to Houston and vice versa, the fastest taking under 5 hours.

Train There are only two lines in Texas: from San Antonio north to Dallas and beyond, and the southern transcontinental route from Houston to El Paso through San Antonio. The *Eagle* train from Chicago to Los Angeles passes through Dallas, Austin and San Antonio on Monday, Wednesday and Saturday; in the reverse direction Tuesday, Friday and Sunday. The route across the south of the state collects passengers at Houston on Monday, Wednesday and Saturday evenings and deposits them in El Paso the folloowing afternoon. The train in the opposite direction arrives in El Paso from Los Angeles on Monday, Thursday and Saturday afternoon, and arrives in Houston 18 hours later.

Driving Despite the long distances between cities, Texan drives usually observe the national speed limit of 65 mph. A few miles (up to five) over the limit is usually all right, but Texas police enforce the laws. Keep an eye out for the speed trap cops concealed behind low ridges. Seat belts are compulsory for drivers and front seat passengers; the penalty for non-compliance is $50.

Freeways link the major cities, while rural areas are served by 'Farm-to-Market' (FM) and 'Ranch-to-market' (RM) roads; sometimes these are little more than dirt tracks.

Hitch-Hiking Most Texans don't understand it; 'If you can't afford a car, why aren't you home working so you can buy one instead of sweating by the side of the road like a hobo?', is a typical attitude. In a state where the car is a traditional high school graduation present and the murder rate is among the highest in the nation, a lack of sympathy for hitch-hikers is understandable. Hanging around the market, meat-packing area or truckers' gas stations of larger Texas cities like Dallas, Houston, San Antonio or El Paso could turn up a lift with a truck driver who owns his own vehicle and wants some company.

Cycling In the same two words, forget it. Just contemplate those vast distances on inhospitable roads under a fierce sun. Cycle rentals are available in cities for recreational cycling. It could, though, be dangerous: Texans are just not used to sharing roads with cyclist.

Eating and Drinking

Food is cheaper in Texas than in most states. Lower restaurant prices reflect both cheaper labour and lower agricultural produce.

Mexican food, whether or not it is Tex-anized, is wonderful. Highly recommended is the take-away food to be found each Sunday at the 'Tortilla Factory' in every Texan town with a large Hispanic population. Low-priced delicacies include maize and flour *tortillas* (sold in multiples of 10); *menudo*, a tasty tripe stew; *barbecao*, the Mexican barbecue which is closer to a pot-roast than meat broiled over coals or logs; home-made *tostados* (vastly superior to the packaged brands found in shops and supermarkets) and *salsa verde*.

The second cuisine of Texas is the barbecue. Nowhere in the USA is there tastier barbecue. Every Texan has her or his favourite establishment, and taste does vary from place to place according to the type of logs over which the barbecue is cooked, cuts of meat, and most importantly, the quality of the barbecue sauce. Try a combination plate of beef, pork and rings of sausage which go by the name of 'hot links' on the menu. You may wish to avoid the sexist barbecue restaurant in the town of Cut 'n Shoot in eastern Texas, where a sign reads 'Men — no shirt, no service. Women — no shirt, no charge'; the proprietor gives away sandwiches to topless customers.

DRINKING

The sale of alcohol is against the law in 76 of Texas' 254 counties, and only beer and wine can be bought in 14 others. Take-away liquor can be obtained only in state-licensed 'package stores' from 10am to 9pm, except on Sunday.

Beer and wine can be bought in package stores, supermarkets and food shops, between 7am and midnight, except on Sundays, when the sale of beer and wine begins at noon.

Licensed restaurants, bars, taverns and nightclubs in wet counties serve alcohol beverages seven days a week until closing time. However, all sale of alcohol must cease by 2am throughout the state.

It's not illegal to have an opened bottle of liquor, beer or wine in your car while driving. As a matter of fact, it's not illegal to drink while driving. Only being drunk while driving is an offence.

Perhaps the hot climate is to blame for the high crime rate across the southern states (especially Texas) but the fact remains that travelling in the southern US is more dangerous than it is in southern England or southern Canada. Be especially mindful of the advice given in the introductory chapters about exercising caution with fellow motorists and policemen. The person you find yourself confronting in anger may be one of the trigger-happy minority. Although you won't be shot for speeding, you shold be aware that any traffic violations are likely to be noticed by the police.

Drugs. Narcotics are not difficult to obtain in the big cities. Marijuana, smuggled by the private planes and ships from Latin America, is the most frequently used drug with cocaine popular among the young affluent set. Heroin is almost completely restricted to ghetto areas. Although a fine is the most usual punishment for marijuana, jail sentences for anything stronger are by no means rare.

DALLAS

THE LOCALS

The most striking feature of Dallas and Dallasites is their concern for wealth. It sometimes seems that the city exists solely for business, and caters only for success. The average age in 'Big D' is 28. The city proper has a population of 950,000, the metropolitan area 3,000,000. Many thrusting young Dallas residents live in the pristine desirable suburbs, which line the airport road, shop in the smart shopping malls and work in gleaming towers.The gay community is to be found mainly in the Oak Lawn area.

Making Friends It might be worth visiting the campus of the University of Dallas (3113 University Avenue) or the Southern Methodist University (University Park) to meet the outgoing students and check the notice boards.

ARRIVAL AND DEPARTURE

Air. Dallas/Fort Worth International Airport (DFW; 574 6720) lies 17 miles west of Dallas, midway between the two cities.

The size of Manhattan, it's the largest airport in the world. By bus, take the Surtran airport bus (for schedule information, telephone 574 2142). It operates every half hour between 6am and 11pm to downtown Dallas and luxury hotels on the way on a journey taking 35 minutes and costing $10. The taxi ride is at least $30 to downtown Dallas, but ride-sharing could halve this (telephone Yellow Cab 426 6262).

Love Field Airport (DAL; 670 6073), seven miles from downtown Dallas, is for domestic flights. (Don't get the two airports mixed up as the character in a Hank Wangford song did, 'I waited for you at DFW but you must have been in Love'). The frequent flights to Houston 250 miles away costs about $35 one way. By bus, take Transit Bus 38, 70c to downtown Dallas, running every half hour from 5.30am to 10.30pm. Surtran also runs a service for $5. If you want to rent a car, check with Jartan Truck Rental near the airport on 3704 Maple Avenue (526 8496) who rent used cars, free mileage up to 50 miles per day, $18 per day (for a minimum of three days) or $89 per week.

As well as cheap flights to US destinations, Dallas has bargains to Latin America and Europe. Try Council Travel at Suite 101, 3300 W Mockingbird (350 6166).

Bus Greyhound services operate from 205 S Lamar St (741 1481)

Train Union Station is a well restored terminal, full of shops and restaurants, on Houston St at Young St (653 1101).

CITY TRANSPORT

The downtown area is surprisingly small, and is negotiable by foot. On the Dallas Area Rapid Transit (DART) System (979 1111) bus rides cost 70c to $1.50 (exact change required) depending on the length of ride. The Customer Assistance Center, 1501 Main Street, Dallas is open weekdays from 8am to 5pm. The staff are helpful in person and on the phone. Discount passes are available, as are easy-to-read bus route maps.

There is little reasonably priced accommodation in the city centre. There are Y's, however, in Fort Worth, 34 miles east (YMCA: 512 Lamar Street, 332 3281 and the YWCA: 512 4th St). An outfit called Bed and Breakfast Texas Style (298 5433) can arrange rooms in a private house for about $20 a night. Motels ring the city but are inaccessible without a car. If you are a militant non-smoker you might enjoy staying at the Non-Smoker's Inn near the Texas Stadium; residents who smoke in their rooms are fined $100.

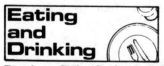

Because Dallas is on the whole full of wealthy residents and visiting businessmen, restaurant food tends to be expensive. Try to stick with Tex-Mex served in ethnic cafes. Try Pepe's (3011 Routh at Cedar Springs) or Rosita's (4906 Maple Avenue) which serves a hearty Tex-Mex breakfast. If you want to sample inland seafood at a reasonable price try S & D Oyster House (2710 McKinney) where you can have seafood gumbo (gumbo is a soup or stew), fried shrimp and raw oysters.

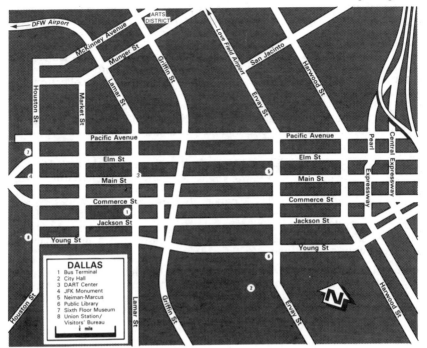

To purchase your own natural food groceries try H & M Natural Food Store (2106 Lower Greenville).

Although beer is the most popular drink throughout Texas, there are outdoor wine tastings for $2 at the Winery (2404 Cedar Springs) on Sunday evenings during the summer. The drinking laws in Dallas are convoluted, since some parts of the metropolitan area are designated 'dry' (which means drinking is only possible in private clubs). Even in 'wet' areas, no strong liquor is sold on Sundays. Licensing hours are liberal, however, and run from 7am (noon on Sundays) to midnight or 2am.

The John F. Kennedy Museum (501 Elm Street, 742 8582) is near the 'grassy knoll' where JFK was killed on November 22, 1963. The building nearby was formerly the Texas School Book Depository where Lee Harvey Oswald hid before the assassination. It is now the Dallas County Administration Building, and 25 years after the President's murder, a small museum was opened on the sixth floor from where the fatal shot was fired.

A less sombre attraction is Southfork Ranch, home of the Ewings in TV's *Dallas*. The ranch ceased to be a private residence in September 1984 and has been turned into a hotel and entertainment complex (442 6536). If you can't afford to stay there, take a snapshot of yourself and companion standing by the gate. Souvenirs include a tiny barrel of real Southfork crude oil and plots of land on the ranch itself (one square inch for $10). Take US 75 north out of Dallas, until exit 30, then follow the Parker Road five miles east to

FM 2551. While in the city, be sure to notice the First National Bank skyscraper which serves as the head office of Ewing Oil on the TV *Dallas*.

Museums and Galleries The new Museum of Art (1717 North Harwood, 922-0220) is part of a planned huge arts complex in downtown Dallas that will eventually include a Symphony Hall, promenade, outdoor restaurants, cafes and art galleries. The museum boasts a fine modern collection and excellent pre-Columbian art.

City Hall (749-4321) on the east corner of Young Street and Ervay Street is a striking building designed by I. M. Pei; the plaza has an enormous Henry Moore sculpture. Free tours take place daily at 2pm.

Consult the *Times Herald* and *Morning News* for city entertainment listings. Note that Friday is the weekend edition. Both papers, but especially the *Times Herald*, give extensive coverage to local and area attractions, forthcoming and past. See also *D*, a monthly magazine on Dallas. Phone Artsline, operating 24 hours a day, for theatre, music, museum events and free public performances (522 2659).

Music Classical music concerts are given at the Southern Methodist University (SMU) Caruth Auditorium (692-3680). The Festival in the Park, held from April to June, includes symphony concerts, opera and ballet, free performances on summer weekends and holidays in the city's park.

Theatre Drop in the W. A. Criswell First Baptist Church (on Ervay and San Jacinto) run by the Reverend A. Criswell, who broadcasts every Sunday morning at 10.30. It's a revelation. For theatre of a more traditional kind, visit the Dallas Theater Center, 3636 Turtle Creek Boulevard (526-8857). Daily tours of the theatre, designed by Frank Lloyd Wright, are available. There are also interesting experimental productions a 15-minute stroll away Theater Three in the Quadrangle 871-3300 July and Augst sees free Shakespeare in the park (954 0199).

Nightlife Try the jazz bar Strictly Tabu (4111 Lomo Alton) which serves excellent pizza, the Tango Disco (1827 Lower Greenville) and for country and western music, which is so popular in Texas, the Longhorn Ballroom (216 Corinth). Greenville Avenue is the trendiest place to be. Lower Greenville caters for younger, more budget-minded people while Upper Greenville is for people with expense accounts.

SPORT

Dallas boasts top collegiate and professional sport: football by the Dallas Cowboys (556-2500) who play at Texas Stadium in Irving (between Dallas and Fort Worth), baseball by the Texas Rangers, (273-5100), soccer by the Dallas Sidekicks (760-7330), basketball by the Dallas Mavericks (658-7068) etc. There's also pro hockey, world class tennis and top track and field. Consult your local paper for events. For those who want something different, head for the Rodeo Kowbell in Mansfield halfway between Dallas and Fort Worth. Rodeo is performed every Saturday night year round (477-3092).

Parks and Zoos A water recreation park called White Water (264-6211) offers a giant 'wave pool' and a terrifying water slide, for which you will need a swimming costume. The admission is expensive (about $12, reduced after 6pm), but it is easy to find on I-30 at Belt Line between Fort Worth and Dallas.

SHOPPING

Going shopping is unlikely to be a problem in a city which has no fewer than 630 shopping centres. The most famous department store is Neiman-Marcus (Main and Ervay) which carries such items as an exercise bicycle with a video screen showing scenes of the Grand Canyon or New York's Central Park. Every year the Christmas catalogue includes something for the couple who has everything, from evening capes made from Russian lynx bellies to a live ostrich.

Bargain shops for second-hand clothes include the Salvation Army Store, on Inwood Avenue. It is open 9am to 5pm and sells off its daily intake of unsold stock from major downtown stores. Also try Linda's Surplus (4323 Maple Avenue) which has inexpensive trendy casual wear for men and women.

The Farmers Market (1010 South Pearl, 748-8582) sells fruits and vegetables in season brought in pick-up trucks by 'old boy' Texans from East Texas farms. It starts at 6am daily.

THE MEDIA

Forty radio stations plus numerous TV channels serve Dallas, so spin the dial until you find something congenial. Note however that a dozen of the radio stations are Christian. There is a Broadcast Museum for the state on 1701 N Market St with displays of early radio studios, famous old programmes etc.

The principal newspaper is the *Morning News*, a staunchly Republican daily. The Reading Room in the public Library (west corner of Young Street and Ervay Street, opposite City Hall) carries newspapers from abroad including the *Times*.

Help and Information *i*   The area code for Dallas is 214.

Information: Dallas Convention & Visitors Bureau, 1201 Elm St, Suite 2000 (746-6702). There are Visitors Centers at Union Station, DFW and Love Field airport.

British Consulate: 813 Stemmons Tower West, 2730 Stemmons Freeway (637-3600).

American Express: 300 North Ervay Street (748-8606); 765 Northpark Center (363-0214).

Thomas Cook: 1801 Commerce St (747-1563).

Medical Emergencies: Baylor University Medical Center, 3500 Gaston Avenue (820-2501).

Pharmacy: Rexall Drugs, 4101 Bryan St (824-4539); Eckhard Drugs, 2320 West Illinois Avenue (331-5466). Both open 24 hours.

Handicapped Visitors: Access Dallas, 4300 Beltway (934-9104).

Suicide Prevention: 828-1000

Post Office: 400 N Ervay St (760-7200)

Telegrams (Western Union): 747-8821.

HOUSTON

THE LOCALS

You won't be in town for long before someone informs you that the first word spoken on the Moon was 'Houston'. The locals are proud of the city's associations with NASA, high technology and the Texas Medical Center. Houston is the fourth largest city in the USA with a population of over 3,000,000 whose average age is 29. An industrial-business complex, it's the most cosmopolitan city in the Sun-Belt with 57 foreign consulates. Huge peacock-coloured mirror-glass buildings give Houston a 'Space City' look and provide a vivid contast to its rougher districts with their massage parlours and sleazy clubs.

As you might expect in a high-technology town, there are plenty of northerners educated at top engineering, business and law schools who have flocked to Houston. Aggressively on the make for power, wealth and status, they lack the provincialism found in cities like Dallas and San Antionio. They also strike visitors as more interested and more informed about what's going on in the world outside.

To get to know a Houston family, contact Americans-at-Home (223-5454), a voluntary organization which arranges visits with friendly locals.

Getting Around

ARRIVAL AND DEPARTURE

Air. Coming directly from abroad, you arrive at Houston Intercontinental Airport (230-3000), 20 miles north of downtown. The Airport Express bus (523-888) goes into the city centre every half hour from 6am to 10.30pm ($7.50). For a cheaper and slower ride into town, follow the signs for 'Economy city Busses' (sic). The same ride by taxi will set you back $40 plus tip. Beware of the 'Solicitation' desk at the airport: charities take turns to use the desk to ask for money for various causes, and the staff seem to be on a percentage of takings judging by their persistence in hounding hapless travellers.

A more 'user-friendly' domestic airport is Hobby (635-6597) only nine miles southeast of downtown. Some airlines use both and it is routine on a foggy winter's day for domestic flights to be diverted from one airport to the other. The limousine service into town costs $5 (644-8359) and serves the Downtown Terminal at the Hyatt Regency on Polk St. A taxi costs around $15.

Bus. The Greyhound-Trailways terminal is at 1410 Texas Avenue (222-1161).

Train. Amtrak offices are located at 902 Washington (224-1577). Union Station is on Jackson St at Prairie. Houston is on the line between New Orleans and Los Angeles.

Driving. More rental cars will be available at the airports than downtown, though many of these will be pre-booked. An economical choice is Thrifty Rent-a-Car (449-0126 at Intercontinental and 644-3351 at Hobby). Another is Rent-a-Heap Cheap at 5722 Southwest Freeway (977-7771).

Houston is notoriously difficult for motorists, who find that along with the heavy traffic on the freeway loop system, the exit numbers and even the

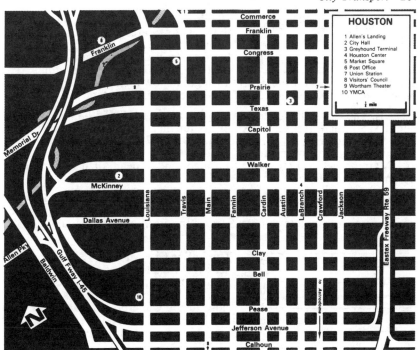

names on signs do not correspond with their maps. For instance, I-45 at the approach to Houston is called the 'Dallas' or 'North' Freeway; south is call 'East Freeway'; west it becomes 'Katy Freeway'. I-610 is the 'Loop' which encircles the city about six miles out; the direction of the road in relation to the city centre is added to the direction you are driving in, thus 'North Loop East'. The Beltways (Texas Route 8) provide another orbital route, about twelve miles out from downtown. For road conditions dial 681-6187).

CITY TRANSPORT

People who naively think it might be nice to 'walk downtown' from the suburbs are likely to get picked up for 'suspicious behaviour' — or for their own protection. Within the downtown area, much of your walking is likely to be underground on the four-mile network of subterranean sidewalks connecting shops, offices and hotels. For an interesting above-ground walk, try the Walking Tour organised by the Greater Houston Preservation Alliance (861-6263) on the third Wednesday of every month.

Houston Transit System, known as 'Metro Buses', is based at 403 Louisiana (635-4000). A 'Shopper's Bus' system allows you to get around the downtown area for only 50c. Other services, alas, are infrequent and the routes in the sprawling metropolis inadequate. Fares are $1; exact change is required. If you don't have a car, you may have to resort to taxis. These are among the most expensive in America. To call a cab, dial Liberty on 695-6700 or United on 699-0000.

Cycling You can get a pamphlet from the Parks and Recreation Department (PO Box 1562, Houston, TX 77001) called *Houston Hike & Bikeways*.

Hotels and Motels. As in Dallas, most of the downtown area is brand new, leaving no room for older budget hotels. Try Fannin Street which as about four blocks west of the Greyhound terminal. The cheaper motels are on the western fringes of town. Alternatively, head out of town towards Galveston Bay for cheaper accommodation.

Hostels. The Houston Downtown Y, 1600 Louisiana St (659-8501— charges about $25 a night (plus 7% tax), but is for men only. There is no YWCA. The clean and friendly youth hostel is at 5302 Crawford St (523-1009). Reservations are recommended. The University of Houston College Center, 101 Main (225-1781) charges $40 a night and is near Allen's Landing, an up-and-coming area.

Bed and Breakfast The B & B Society of Texas, based at Sarah's Bed and Breakfast Inn at 941 Heights Boulevard (868-1130) has rooms at 24 Houston homes costing from $35 double; Sarah's Inn itself costs $50 double.

The Luling City Market (4726 Richmond) near the Galleria Shopping Center has a reputation for the best barbecue in the city, but isn't cheap. Goode's Ribs, also close to the Galleria, is regarded as even better by some of the cognoscenti. The Cortez Delicatessen (2404 West Alabama near River Oaks) has cheap Mex-Tex Food, large portion, lunch counter style; try the *menudo*. Glatzmaler's Seafood (809 Congress Avenue) downtown on Market Square serves a Texas equivalent of fresh fish and chips in a cafeteria style. It's good value, and always crowded. At Otto Barbecue at 5502 Memorial Drive, a plate of beef is about $7. Houston's small Chinatown is around the junction of McKinney and St Emanuel, and is worth a visit for the experience of Chinese cuisine meeting Tex-Mex head on. Quan Tam Luncheonette (1117 Bell) is one of the several cheap Vietnamese eateries that have sprung up and cater mainly for lunchtime office workers. If you're worried about your diet, you can Dial-a-Dietician (827-2458).

Anheuser-Busch runs free tours of its brewery at 775 Gellhorn; call 670-1695 for bookings.

Space Center Houston. The historic phrase 'Houston — this is Tranquility Base. The Eagle has landed' is familiar to anyone who stayed up late in July 1969 to watch the first man on the Moon. Man last took a small step on the Moon over twenty years ago. In the meantime, the entertainment industry has made many giant leaps for Mankind. Space Center Houston balances neatly on the cusp between science fantasy and scientific reality, and between play and hard work.

Space Center Houston is part of the Johnson Space Center, 25 miles southeast of the city centre. The fun starts in a huge hangar where you can see the flight deck of a Shuttle, try on an astronaut helmet and walk through the Skylab trainer — like a cylindrical padded cell. The Feel of Space is a computer game arcade featuring real space invaders: even children versed in the finger-clicking intricacies of Sonic the Hedgehog and Super Mario Brothers find it incredibly difficult to land a Space Shuttle. After ditching your craft, you can examine lunar gems through a microscope and watch lettuces grow on lunar soil. NASA has calculated that a cubic metre of lunar rock contains enough of the right elements to make a cheeseburger with fries and a regular soft drink; until the technology to harvest fast food from moon dust turns up, you can buy a terrestrial burger and chips for $4. In the Silver Moon Restaurant, $9 buys you unlimited slices of a slightly wounded and very bloody Texas steer.

The second stage of your journey into space exploration involves boarding a tram for a ride around the NASA facility itself, reviewing work-in-progress. The buildings look desperately ordinary, like a rather dull trading estate. But behind those blank facades is the stuff of dreams. Mission Control — seen by hundreds of millions during the triumph of *Apollo XI* and the catastrophe of *Challenger* — is on show except when manned missions are in progress. In real life it looks impossibly cramped; only television's wide-angle lenses make it appear bigger than the bridge of Captain Kirk's *USS Enterprise*. It is also almost laughably low-tech, which is hardly surprising since it dates from 1965. The hottest seat is occupied by the Flight Director, him- or herself an astronaut, who has to translate the wishes of the assembled company, such as the Extravehicular Activity Officer or the Flight Surgeon, into commands readily understood by the crew.

Not all the staff are happy about their workplace being transformed from a serious space research centre into an appendage for a theme park. Until Space Center Houston opened in 1992, visitors could tour the site free, but the cost of the new attraction is being recouped with an admission charge of $8.95. Space Center Houston opens 9am-7pm daily.

Museums and Galleries For forty years Dominique de Menil has accumulated one of the finest private collections of art in the world. The Menil Collection is housed in a brash new building in the middle of a genteel suburb, at 1515 Sul Ross Street (525-9400); open 11am-7pm from Wednesday to Sunday, admission free. Detractors say the gaunt, angular structure is totally out of keeping with the neighbourhood. It does resemble a carpet warehouse plonked down in a residential area, but the immense enrichment provided by the contents would justify any town planning atrocity. Exquisite Byzantine relics are displayed ten paces away from some of the great works of art of the 20th century. A couple of Warhol's soup cans, Picasso, Cezanne and van Gogh are all represented in a warehouse in suburban Houston.

A couple of blocks away, at 3900 Yupon St, is the stark Rothko Chapel (524-9839). In 1964 Mrs de Menil commissioned the American artist Mark Rothko to build a multi-denominational chapel. His house of worship is a plain octagon, subdued in the shade of broad cedars. Inside, each face of the octagon bears a grainy black rectangle, reinforcing the aura of sanctity and rejecting the commercial values of the mega-mall along the road. The Rothko Chapel opens 10am-6pm daily, admission free.

The Contemporary Arts Museum on the corner of Montrose and Bissonnet (526-3129) is open Tuesday-Saturday from 10am to 5pm, Sundays noon-6pm, and contains an interesting collection of post World War II American art. The museum shop has inexpensive and imaginative gifts and small toys. The Museum of Fine Art (526-1361), also on Bissonnet at number 1001 has works by Western artist Frederic Remmington, plus collections of Impressionists and Old Masters that only money can buy. The museum lies in an attractive shady sculpture garden, and admission is free.

Entertainment

For current offerings by the Houston Symphony Orchestra, ballet, opera and theatre, phone 227-ARTS or get a free *Performing Arts Calendar* available from the Greater Houston Convention and Visitors Center; or write to Arts for Everyone Inc, 1950 West Gray, Houston, TX 77019 (522-3744 for ticket information). The Wortham Theatre Center (near the river at Smith and Prairie Streets) is worth a visit even if you don't see a show there, since the scale and elegance are impressive. The Center is home to the Houston Ballet (523-6300) and Grand Opera (546-0200), whose seasons run from late September to early June.

The International Festival in March attracts a good range of drama, music and dance companies; call 654-8808. You can see some new movies during the International Film Festival in April (965-9955), while the venue for the Jazz Festival in August is the Miller Outdoor Theatre in Hermann Park (528-6740).

Nightlife. Gilley's, on Houston's southeast perimeter in Pasadena (4500 Spencer Highway, 941 7193), is one of the world's best. The place is outsized, honky-tonk and tops for Western singers and bands. Listen to songs with titles such as 'If You Want To Keep Your Beer Cold, Put it Next to My Ex-Wife's Heart'. NRG at 901 North Shepherd Drive (863-0010) is bigger still, and has a 15,000-watt sound system. Rockefeller's (3620 Washington Avenue; 861-9365) is the best jazz club for name bands, but cover charges range from $10-$15. Cardi's (5901 Westheimer) specializes in folk/rock and is both cheap and friendly.

The Montrose area of town is a multi-racial, tolerant neighbourhood and has a large male gay community. Numbers (300 Westheimer) is a large, long established disco with a friendly atmosphere. Finally there is Escape (8670 South Gessner), a late night mixed crowd disco, open till 4am on weekends.

SPORT

Don't miss the Astrodome, home of the Houston Astros baseball team (799-9555) and the Oilers football team (797-1000). It is situated on the I-610 and Kirby Drive. With a capacity of 66,000 it is the world's largest enclosed stadium. There are daily guided tours that feature a dazzling display on their giant scoreboard; admission $5. It might well be worth putting the money towards a cheap ticket for a baseball or football game instead. For sports events, see *Day and Night* distributed by the Convention and Visitors Center (telephone 526-7220 for ticket information).

SHOPPING

The Galleria, says its publicity, is a unique shopping experience. Located at Post Oak and Westheimer, five miles west of the city centre, this huge complex has luxury stores, restaurants, an Olympic-sized skating rink and even a medical clinic where for a mere $500 you can have a thorough health examination and receive your results the same day.

Downtown Houston has an underground weather-controlled shopping and dining area. Enter the Hyatt-Regency Hotel or at the large banks on the 800 to 1400 blocks of Main Street.

The best buys are to be found at Loehmanns Outlet Store, 7455 Southwest Freeway (777-0164). Also recommended is browsing through *The Underground Shopper-Houston* in any bookstore for specific details on bargain stores of every variety.

For unbeatable flea-market items, try the sidewalks of Montrose. To keep cool in this relaxed, slightly bohemian area, try a peach ice cream at Udder Delight (1521 Westheimer).

Crime and Safety

Houston ranks near the top in almost every category of crime on the FBI table, from car theft to murder. So be even more careful here than in other American city centres, especially after the workers go home to the suburbs and the streets are largely deserted. Strolling is not a safe activity. Many local women drive around with cowboy-hatted dummies strapped to the passenger seat, and the rich employ security guards.

Drugs Illegal narcotics are not in short supply, but neither are members of the drug squad. Caution is suggested. Affluent Houston citizens may be able to afford a $500 fine plus legal expenses better than you.

Help and Information *i*

The area code for Houston is 713.

Information: The Greater Houston Convention and Visitors Council, 3300 S Main (523-5959; toll-free 1-800-392-7722 within Texas, 1-800-231-799 from outside the State). The staff seem to be genuinely interested in helping visitors. They give out free maps, walking tours, a detailed calendar of events, etc.

British Consulate: Suite 2250, 601 Jefferson Avenue (659-6270).

Travellers' Aid: 2630 Westridge (668-0911) and 1410 Texas (223-8946); a desk in C terminal of the Intercontinental Airport is manned during office hours.

American Express: 309 Greenspoint Mall (875-8686); 1200 McKinney Avenue (658 1114); 1000 West Oaks Mall (558-6066); 3435 Galleria (626-5740).

Post Office: 70 San Jacinto (227-1474)

Telegrams (Western Union): 224-1705.

Medical Emergencies: General Hospital, Ben Taub Loop (791-7300).

Pharmacy: Cunningham Pharmacy, 6033 Airline Drive (697-3261). Open 24 hours.

Gay Switchboard of Houston: 529-3211.

Further Afield  **61**

EL PASO

The main business of this large west Texas city (population 600,000) is the building and testing of nuclear missiles, including Cruise and Pershing, but the ending of the Cold War means that El Paso is searching for a new role. Obsolete missiles decorate many buildings including high schools and churches, as well as fulfil practical uses such as bases for goal posts, animal troughs and pot plants. Fort Bliss, close to the airport, trains servicemen from the USA and allied nations to fire the weapons. Its museums (568-2121) show the contribution it makes to 'peace and freedom'.

An interesting aspect of El Paso is the preservation of North American

Indian culture. Visit the Ysleta de Sur Pueblo Museum (869-7718), which traces the history of the Pueblo Indians, or the Tiquas Indian Reservartion where you can see handicraft being made and eat Indian bread with Tiquas chillis.

Nearly two-thirds of El Paso's population is Hispanic, and there is a great deal of traffic across the Mexican border into the city of Juarez. You can eat, drink and sleep much more cheaply across the Rio Grande than in El Paso itself. If you want to remain north of the border, then the International Youth Hostel is in the restored Gardner Hotel at 311 East Franklin St (915-532-3661).

El Paso and environs are on Mountain Time, one hour behind the rest of Texas.

AUSTIN

Texas' relatively small capital city (population 345,000) provides a liberal oasis in the midst of conservative Texas. It has a tradition of tolerance which has attracted artists, writers and artisans. You would not automatically be thought a lunatic here if you happen to be a hitch-hiker. Folk singers croon in many of the bars, especially on Guadalupe Street. Visit the student-oriented area called 'The Drag' where you will find cinemas, book stalls and trendy clothing shops. The friendly relaxed atmosphere of Austin is enhanced by its extensive park system which provides relief from traffic, heat and noise. You might even be invited to join an informal game of baseball.

Assuming you won't be in hot pursuit of memorabilia concerning Austin's 'favourite son', ex-President Lyndon Baines Johnson, you might be interested in the McDonald Observatory, located at Painter Hill and 24th Street. It is freely open to the public every Friday night after dusk. You can even do some homework by phoning 'Skywatcher Reporter' on 471-4478 for a two-minute recorded talk on what stars, planets and satellites are visible.

Austin is surrounded by hills, lakes and reservoirs which offer superb recreational and camping facilities.

SAN ANTONIO

The further south you go, the stronger the Mexican influence becomes. If you are in the laid-back city of San Antonio (population 800,000) you can watch Mexican folk dancing on summer evenings or attend the Mexican version of rodeo called *charreadas* at a local ranch. You must also pay a visit to the state shrine of Texas, the Alamo, where Davy Crockett and other heroes died trying vainly to fend off the much larger Mexican army in 1836. It opens daily from 9am to 5.30pm.

San Antonio is one of the few southern cities where it is not only feasible but safe to walk around. The distances between attractions are easily walkable though there is the El Centro bus around downtown (exact fare 40c). Join the relaxed parade of people on the River Walk and enjoy the sidewalk cafes and outdoor entertainment. There is also a colourful Mexican market, and the Sea World of Texas just northwest of (tel: 512-225-4903) the city. The star is Shamu, a three-ton killer whale, who performs daily in a 4,500-sea stadium. To find out about the people who make Texas what it is, visit the Institute of Texan Cultures in the Hemisfair Plaza (home of the 1968 World's Fair). It opens daily except Mondays, 9am to 5pm, and is free.

MEXICO

You may want to cross the Mexican border to shop in the markets, eat the food, find a cheap *hospedaje* (hostel),see a bullfight or just to say you have been to Mexico. The Mexican officials will want to see your passport, and you will need a green tourist card for visits of 72 hours or more. To return to the USA, make sure you have a multiple entry visa or hang on to your visa waiver.

Tourist cards are available free from any Mexican consulate or in any Texan border town such as Brownsville or Laredo (as well as El Paso). To take your car over the border you will need Mexican insurance which is available from numerous travel agencies on the Texas side of the border. When returning to the USA you may bring back duty free $400 worth of purchases, a litre of alcohol and 200 cigarettes. A little known Texan law prohibits the import of alcohol in containers smaller than a half pint, thereby disqualifying miniatures.

The Great Outdoors

The National Parks and Wildlife Refuges are primarily meant to preserve nature, and are accordingly undeveloped. They are ideal for backpacking and primitive camping. Only three are dealt with here. A comprehensive guide to all the state parks of Texas, including points of interest, phone numbers for booking and camping regulations can be obtained free by writing to Texas Parks and Wildlife Department, 4200 Smith School Road, Austin, TX 78744 (512-479-4800 or from out of state, toll-free 1-800-792-1112).

Big Bend National Park comprises 700,000 acres of desert, remote canyons and mountains on the US/Mexican border. There are excellent hiking trails and free permits for overnight camping. Highly recommended is the South Rim Trail overlooking the Rio Grande (at dawn, you can hear the cocks crowing and donkeys braying across the river in Mexico). Riding and commercial raft trips are available as well as hiking. If you prefer, you can drive around the park on almost 200 miles of adequate roads, but check with Park Rangers first for information on possible rock slides. For details and literature, write to the Superintendent, Big Bend National Park, TX 79834 (915-477-2251). Well worth a detour from the park is a trip to nearby Terlingua which hosts the world famous 'Chilli Cook-Off' in the late autumn.

The second big recreational area is the Padre Island National Seashore. Here visitors will find one of the nation's last unspoilt natural seashores with 80 miles of white sand, excellent surf casting, beachcombing, and numerous shore birds and animals to view. Highly recommended is the Grasslands Trail over the dunes.

The third national park worth visiting is the Guadalupe Mountains National Park. On the New Mexico/Texas border, this 78,000-acre park includes within its boundaries Texas' four highest peaks, deep canyons and an extensive fossil reef. Some of its trails, though, are for experienced climbers only. Highly recommended is McKittrick Canyon with its spectacularly colourful foliage in late October. Camping is permitted only in some areas. For details and literature, either visit Frijole Information Station, Pine Springs, TX, or write to Carlsbad Caverns National Park, 3225 National Parks Highways, Carlsbad, NM 88220 (915-828-3385). From the latter, you can also obtain information on nearby Carlsbad Caverns, famous for the unique flight of bats at sunset.

Camping. Texas also maintains over 90 state parks which preserve much of Texas' historical heritage as well as places of unique rugged beauty and natural phenomena. An annual entrance permit for unlimited visits to any park is $20 and 24-hour tickets can be purchased for $3 each. Camping is encouraged at most parks; RV (Recreation Vehicle, pronounced by the locals Vee-hickel) hook-ups are provided at $5 per day, and at some sites rustic cabins sleeping 4 to 8 people can be rented for as little as $20 a night; this is one of the best bargains Texas has to offer. However, you must book in advance and, in most instances, put up a deposit.

Camping is also allowed in Texas' four National Forests, and some municipal parks offer RV hook-ups. For a free complete list of all campgrounds in the state, write to Texas Public Campgrounds, Travel and Information Division, State Department of Highways and Public Transportation, PO Box 5064, Austin TX 78763. And for a free map of privately owned campgrounds, write to the Texas Association of Campground Operators, 1301 North Watson Road, Arlington, TX 76011.

Lovers of the great outdoors should also take advantage of Texas' small, well-landscaped roadside parks with tables, benches, shade trees and cooking grills. All you need is a bag of charcoal, 'hamburger' meat (ground beef), hot dogs or steaks, tomatoes, *jalepenos*, corn on the cob (you can grill it with husk on which acts as an oven and keeps in the juices!).

Wildlife. In the southwest of the state, there are herds of pronghorn antelope and mule deer, as well as coyotes, jack-rabbits and gophers. Some of the rarer animals, mountain lions and grey fox, can be found in the woodlands of the Big Bend region. Many of the more nocturnal animals — possums, raccoons, and armadillos — are seen only as road casualties.

If you're a birdwatcher, bring a pair of binoculars. Three-quarters of all known American birds are represented in Texas at any time of the year, and the number increases during times of migration. Ivory-billed woodpeckers (once thought to be extinct) and bald eagles can be seen in East Texas, wild turkey in the Central Texas Hill Country and in the south-west, kites and fleet-footed roadrunners (immortalized in a famous American television cartoon). The world's few remaining whooping cranes winter on the coastline at the Arkansas National Wildlife Refuge.

Texas is the only state in which every variety of poisonous snake in North America can be found. Some places even have rattlesnake baiting contests, culminating in a rattlesnake roast.

Traces of long-extinct wildlife also remain in Texas as fossilized skeletons and footprints. Pre-historic Texas was covered by salt-water and lagoons; for the same reason that Texas is rich petroleum products, it has numerous superb fossil sites. Collectors have every chance of finding specimens of sought after minerals, topaz, petrified wood and fossils.

Calendar of Events

January 19	Confederate Heroes' Day
March 2	**Texas Independence Day**
March	Houston International Festival
April	Houston International Film Festival
May	Hot Air Balloon Festival, El Paso
July/August	Shakespeare Festival, Dallas
August	Blessing of the Shrimp Fleet, Galveston Bay
August	Houston Jazz Festival
August 27	Lyndon Baines Johnson's birthday
September	Fiesta de las Flores, El Paso
late September/late October	Texas State Fair, Dallas

Denver and the Rockies

Colorado   Idaho   Montana   New Mexico   Utah   Wyoming

It is often said that the scenery in the USA changes much more slowly than in Europe; but when the plains of the Midwest give way to the Rocky Mountains the contrast is startling, Approaching Denver overland from the east In the space of a few miles, you switch from the laser-straight roads of the Midwest to tortuous tracks winding between snowy peaks. Against the backdrop of the red foothills, Denver is pinched between the prairie and the peaks. Although small by the standards of America (city population 500,000), Denver is the self-appointed capital of the Rocky Mountains. The 'Mile High City' is so-called because it is 5,280 feet above sea level; to be more precise, the 15th step of Denver's Capitol Building is at that elevation. Like most of the city, the Capitol is relatively modern, but it has packed a great deal into a short history since it burst into life with the Gold Rush of 1858.

Some vestiges of the gold mining days remain: restored Larimer Square, the house of Molly Brown (heroic Titanic survivor), and the grave of Buffalo Bill on nearby Lookout Mountain. But the log cabins and tents have been superseded by shiny skyscrapers and sprawling suburbs. Denver is now second only to Washington in terms of federal employees, and hosts headquarters for many energy corporations. Even with this influx of manpower and money, sophistication is not a feature of Denver life. To compensate, the university town of Boulder — half an hour northwest among the foothills of the Front Range — acts as a civilized antidote to the rawness of Denver. Boulder is one of the most politically radical places in the USA — it became twinned with the Tajikistan city of Dushanbe while the old Soviet Union still existed.

Few people come to the region solely to visit the city. Denver's greatest virtue is the proximity of the mountains. Only fifty miles north is a stunning circuit through the Rocky Mountain National Park, Arctic terrain over two miles high. This is just a taste of the marvels of the Rockies as a whole, from the bleak highlands near the Canadian border to the New Age city extraordinary, Santa Fe in New Mexico.

THE PEOPLE

The population of Colorado in general and Denver in particular is mixed: white bureaucrats, some of them descendants of the 19th-century pioneers who tamed the country; a few Indians who survived the taming; Hispanics (about 20% of Denver's population), blacks (about 12%) and, more recently, Asian refugees.

The last 30 years has seen a huge influx from the northern states of middle class immigrants, who viewed Colorado as possessing enormous economic potential. The state government has found it necessary to discourage new immigration; a Boulder city ordinance goes even further by restricting growth to 2% per year. The population of the metropolitan area (which includes Boulder) is 1,750,000.

Making Friends. The leisure sections of local newspapers and magazines are full of listings of the clubs and singles bars frequented by the young and well-off. Most of the action occurs on Leetsdale Drive in Glendale. You can meet young people easily in Boulder, where over 25,000 students (out of a total population of 76,000) are waiting to be befriended. The Colorado Free University runs some extraordinary courses such as 'A Dinner Party for Singles' and 'Exploring Intimate Relationships'.

The large gay population meets in the area to the south of Denver's Capitol Hill and frequents Cheesman Park.

CLIMATE

Along with many aspects of day-to-day living, the weather is affected by the height of the city. Although the altitude of Denver is lower than most of Colorado, it is still much higher than Britain's tallest mountain, for example. The thinness of the atmosphere has some unexpected effects. Water boils at lower temperatures (i.e. about 95°C/200°F) which means that cooking takes longer; there is even a book called *The New High Altitude Cookbook* which tells you how to cope.

The effects on the body take some getting used to. Babies, toddlers and old people are particularly prone to shortness of breath and faintness. Do not over-exert in the first few days. Smokers and drinkers should moderate their habits: smoking may leave you gasping for breath, and the effects of alcohol are exacerbated by the thin air.

As for the weather itself, there is little to fear. Denver makes the unillumin-ating claim that it is the 'climate capital of the world'. It has more hours of sunshine than Florida and Texas, as any of the several hundred solar power companies based in Denver will hasten to tell you. Unfortunately it also has a pallid yellow smog, which clings unpleasantly to the city due to temperature inversions caused by the proximity of the mountains. The internal combus-tion engine does not function as efficiently at high altitude and the by-products of petrol are enough to produce smog which rivals that of Los

Angeles. Every weather forecast includes a smog report with ratings of 'mild' to 'dangerous'. There is little rain to wash the smog away.

The temperature varies from -25°C/-12°F to 38°C/100°F, but the dryness makes even the extremes bearable. From May to September it is usually warm, sunny and comfortable during the day, cooling noticeably towards evening. However, clear summer skies sometimes give way to sudden and violent thunderstorms with dazzling displays of lightning and occasional flash floods. Autumn weather is unpredictable. Snow sometimes falls as early as September 1, but during the autumn warm days are more frequent than crisp and cold ones. December to March is as extreme as winter in any other part of the USA, i.e. bitterly cold. Heavy clothing, boots, gloves and a warm hat are essential. High up in the mountains, the weather is unpredictable whatever the season. Be prepared for any eventuality, and heed official warnings. Denverites take snow conditions seriously and after a snowfall of more than three inches, you can expect TV specials all evening about the heroic efforts of snow-clearing crews. For recorded weather information call 398-3964.

**Getting
Around**

Air. Stapleton International Airport (DEN), is the eighth-busiest airport in the world, and an important hub for United and Continental Airlines. Dial 1-800-AIR 2 DEN for information. It lies within the city limits seven miles east of the city centre, with a direct road link to I-70, making access easy. Buses 28, 32 and 38 cover the journey downtown in half an hour, and buses A/B run direct to Boulder in about 70 minutes. Taking a taxi to downtown Denver will set you back only $15 or so, a bargain compared with most airport journeys. The limousine service to the bus station and the major hotels costs from $6. Go to lower level door 5 to catch a bus, taxi or limousine.

The international concourse is little used, so Denver is a good place to clear customs and immigrations (assuming your papers are in order). Despite the obscure law that prohibits the importation of alcohol from outside the state, luggage is not normally searched on internal services. Flights to nearby resorts such as Aspen are very expensive, but bus services are fast and frequent — shuttle buses depart hourly for the big resorts.

Bus. Greyhound (292-6111) operates from the bus terminal at 1055 19th St, at the junction with Arapahoe St, downtown. Rural bus services in the mountains can best be described as sparse and sporadic; in addition, their inability to negotiate the more interesting mountain roads may persuade you to try an alternative form of transport, such as a four-wheel drive vehicle.

Train. Union Station is at 17th and Wynkoop Streets on the edge of the financial district. The line through Denver runs east to Chicago, and west to Salt Lake City and the West Coast. The run to Salt Lake City, along the former Denver and Rio Grande Railroad line, is spectacular. One Amtrak through-train (the *Californian Zephyr*) runs each way daily: eastbound at 9.20pm, westbound at 8.55am.

Driving. I-25 and I-70 intersect just north of the city centre and provide fast, easily accesible routes for long distance traffic. Many other roads — including US-36 to Boulder — are fast dual carriageways. One road hazard best avoided is the stampede of young, rich inhabitants of Denver, who clog the roads towards the mountains on Friday evenings, and return *en masse* late on Sundays.

Most mountain passes over 8,000ft close completely during the winter, and driving is generally dangerous; some, like Squaw Pass on Highway 103, are not far from Denver. The Colorado State Patrol provides information on road conditions and closures: call 639-1234 for Denver routes west, 639-1111 for I-25 and routes east. Always heed storm and blizzard warnings. During the summer forest-fire season in the mountains, any vehicle using an unnumbered road must be equipped with a shovel, bucket and axe.

Car Rental: most rental agencies are on Colfax Avenue, which runs east-west through the city centre. Rent-a-Wreck is at the junction of Colorado Blvd and W Colfax Avenue, and Cheap Heaps at 16th Avenue at Colorado Blvd (393-0028). Some agencies hire out four-wheel-drive vehicles for the mountains.

Ridesharing. Boulder has a well-used ride board in the University Memorial Center (UMC) on Euclid Avenue. Alternatively, call the Denver-based National Ride Center (837-9738) for lifts anywhere.

Hitch-Hiking. Thumbing in the Rockies is a risky business, particularly for women. It is not unusual for hitchers to be robbed, raped or killed, and many of the nicer sort of drivers do not stop for hitch-hikers for fear they may be armed. Even so, hitchers still manage to enjoy problem-free journeys through the mountains, with a large proportion of lifts in the back of pick-up trucks. To get a ride out of Denver, try any downtown Interstate intersection and use a sign.

CITY TRANSPORT

City Layout. Most of the city is spread out in the familiar grid pattern, except in downtown Denver where rivers and the I-25 highway conspire to upset the pattern. The Interstate snakes around the centre in an arc to the west, roughly following the course of the South Platte River. North of Colfax Avenue the grid pattern becomes tilted to form a diagonal grid on the map. The central business district is contained in this area, which has numbered streets. Numbered avenues are confined to east-west roads north of Alameda Avenue. (Although Colfax Avenue is the main east-west route, the numbering system is based on Ellsworth Avenue). All other roads are named, until you get to the suburbs when numbering resumes. If you become grossly disoriented, just find a local telephone directory, which contains a map and street index at the end.

Bus. The Regional Transportation District (RTD) runs all buses in Metropolitan Denver and the surroundings, including Boulder. The bus service is known as 'The Ride', a slogan liberally plastered over every vehicle, bus shelter and ticket. The system is efficient and well-used, although crosstown journeys sometimes involve two or three changes. Most buses run from 6am to midnight every day, though services dry up in the evenings. For information call 628-9000 or visit the Downtown Information Centre at 626 16th St.

A free shuttle service, the Mall Ride, runs along the 16th St shopping precinct, stopping every 150 yards or so. Other journeys within the city cost 50c off-peak, with one free transfer within 40 minutes. Peak hour services (6am-9am and 4pm-6pm) cost $1, more on the express buses to the surburbs

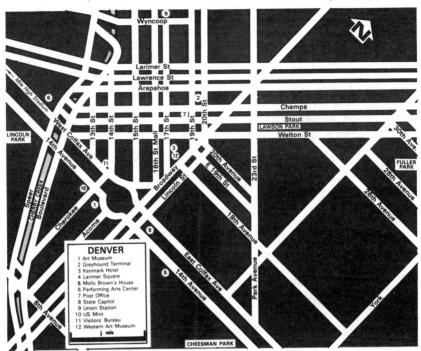

DENVER
1 Art Museum
2 Greyhound Terminal
3 Kenmark Hotel
4 Larimer Square
5 Molly Brown's House
6 Performing Arts Center
7 Post Office
8 State Capitol
9 Union Station
10 US Mint
11 Visitors' Bureau
12 Western Art Museum
½ mile

which run mainly during rush hours. Exact change is required. Outside the city, fares increase to around $2. The Denver to Boulder run operates at approximately hourly intervals but more frequently during rush hours.

Car. Denver is one of the easier large cities in which to drive. To get through the traffic lights in downtown Denver without having to stop at a single red, it is recommended that you travel at a steady 10 mph.

Parking space is hard to find and expensive. Multi-storey downtown car parks cost at least $3 per hour, and meter regulations are strictly enforced by tow trucks. Try to avoid driving in the downtown area after a snowfall. Anyone parking in a designated 'snow route' may be towed away.

Taxi. Do not count on being able to hail a cab. Call Zone (861-2323) or Metro (333-3333) in Denver, or Yellow (442-2277) in Boulder. Expect to pay an initial charge of $1.20-1.40, followed by $1.40 per mile. In serious snowstorms taxi drivers charge by the minute.

Cycling. Denver is mainly flat and so theoretically fine for cycling. However, the numerous potholes on downtown streets can prove dangerous, as can the appalling traffic fumes. The city authorities are actively promoting cycling in an effort to reduce smog levels, by providing special bikeways and smoothing out the streets. For information, contact the Denver Bicycle Touring Club Hotline (794-9443). Bicycles can be hired at I Like Bikes, 4730 E Colfax Avenue, or look in the Yellow Pages. If you prefer to watch, the Coors International Bicycle Classic is based in Boulder in early July.

Accommodation

Denver suffers from hotel overcapacity, so there are plenty of deals around, such as $59 for a good city-centre hotel. The visitors bureaux at the airport and at 225 W Colfax Avenue (892-1112) can book you into moderately expensive hotels. For a lower-priced room try La Quinta (3500 Fox St, 458-1222), which charges from $50, or the cheaper Standish (1530 California St at 38th, 534-3231), with doubles for around $30. Franklin House Bed & Breakfast (1620 Franklin St at 16th St, 331-9106) is homely and well-located, and has rooms for $25 upwards.

The Melbourne International Youth Hostel is at 607 22nd St (292-6386), within easy reach of the centre. Dorm beds cost $10, private rooms $25-30. The International Hostel at 630 E 16th Avenue (832-9996), 10 blocks east of the Greyhound terminal and accessible on bus 15 or 20, charges $8 for a dorm bed. The YMCA (25 E 16th Avenue at Lincoln, 861-8300) charges $20 single, $35 twin. The YWCA is on Tremont St between 15th and 16th Streets.

For cheap motels, head south on Broadway from Colfax Avenue. If you want to be near the airport, stay at the Concorde Hotel (388-4051), with double rooms from $45.

KOA operates two 'Kampgrounds' on the outskirts of Denver. The *Colorado Directory* lists campsites and cabins throughout the state.

Boulder: cheap accommodation in Boulder is hard to find. The Youth Hostel, 1107 12th St at College Avenue, 442-9304 (which boasts a water fountain fed by a glacier) is often fully booked. During the vacations there may be student residences available, but in term-time your best bet is to try to find a cheap motel or go to the KOA Campground at 5856 Valmont.

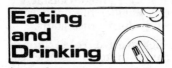

Eating and Drinking

The local specialities are mountain trout and steak, but Denver is a good place to try ethnic fare in a variety of settings ranging from 'nouvelle southwestern' to prime examples of American junk culture. A variety of these options are concentrated in and around Larimer Square, downtown. If you happen to see 'Rocky Mountain oysters' on a menu, you might spare a tear for the young bull so cruelly cut off in his prime to provide the local delicacy.

Thick charcoal-broiled steak (probably from the same young bull) is widespread. The Buckhorn Exchange, 1000 Osage at Santa Fe (543-9505), is the steakhouse of steakhouses, and a local historical landmark — more a restaurant-cum-museum with hunting trophies around the walls; it is celebrated for its buffalo as well as delicious navy bean soup. Lutz's (2651 S Broadway) is less expensive and it boasts one of the best beer lists in town.

Mexican food is to Denver what Indian food is to London: spicy, filling, and cheap. Downtown, La Loma (2527 W 26th Avenue; 433-8307) features authentic south-of-the-border cooking. Try the fajitas (grilled strips of marinated chicken or beef rolled up in a tortilla with peppers, onion, and refriend beans), followed by fried ice-cream for dessert. Cafb Santa Fe (2955 E 1st Avenue) has live music on weekend nights as well as commendable Mexican food.

Denver has some excellent pizza joints: Beau Jo's is a local chain with a branch at 2700 S Colorado Blvd, 758-1519) and one in Boulder (Arapahoe

Avenue and 29th St). You buy pizza by the pound, selecting from a myriad of toppings. The Old Spaghetti Factory is a popular and cheap place for pasta in a converted cable car shed at 1215 18th Avenue at Lawrence St; it is noisy and crowded.

As a rule, restaurants touting 'southwestern cuisine' are as pretentious as they are expensive. Adirondacks (901 Larimer) is no exception but the locals rave about it and you may find yourself tempted to eat there. Look for dishes using native southwestern ingredients, like blue corn.

To economize, stock up with fresh produce at the market on Market St between 16th and 17th Street.

Boulder: Boulder has a phenomenal number of restaurants — at the last count 150, an astonishing number for a modest town. You can eat any cuisine from Russian to Sri Lankan, with a massive choice of non-smoking health food restaurants. The competition means that special deals abound. At the Japanese restaurant Sashi Zanmai (1221 Spruce, 440-0733), for example, you can get cheap sushi at lunchtimes and in the early evening. In early June, the Chili Olympics is held, and you get all the chili you can eat for $10. The *Boulder County Menu Guide* allows you to select a restaurant at leisure.

DRINKING

Beer is easily the most popular drink. Every autumn, Larimer Square is swamped by the Oktoberfest where the participants get as merry as they do in Munich. The local brew is called Coors, made in the suburb town of Golden, 15 miles west of Denver. Tours of the brewery — the biggest in the world — take place at 13th and Ford Streets from 9am to 4pm, daily except Sundays. Book in advance on 277-BEER. RTD bus 16 goes almost to the door. A trip around the brewery is duly rewarded with free beer — up to a two-glass limit. The Wynkoop Brewpub (18th and Wynkoop, 297-2700) has free tours on Saturdays from 1-5pm. So too does the exclusive little Boulder bitter brewery at 2880 Wilderness Place (444-8448), beginning at 11am, 2pm and 5pm.

Another less than erudite course run by the Colorado Free University (see *Making Friends*) is 'Bar-hopping around Denver'. If you wish to teach yourself, note that few bars stay open past 1am. Alcoholic purchases to take away must be concealed in brown paper packages; and open bottles or six-packs cannot be carried in a car, Only '3.2' beer can be bought on Sundays. After eight o'clock on Sunday nights, restaurants may not serve alcohol and they remove unfinished drinks. There are even '3.2 clubs' for people under 21.

Having taken in all this instruction, unwind at somewhere like Ivy's (865 Lincoln, 839-9544) or Brick's (17th and Franklin, 377-5400), which has a good early evening happy hour.

A little of the Colorado gold not housed in the Mint has been used to cover the dome of the State Capitol at E Colfax Avenue and Sherman St. The finest view of Denver can be had from the gallery at the top. Admission is free, and it opens daily except Sunday 7am-5.30pm, while on Saturdays and public holidays the hours are 9.30am-2.30pm. A good way to get your bearings is to follow the walking tour featured in a brochure issued by the Convention and Visitors Bureau.

Museums. An interesting state statute requires that 1% of capital spending must be used to buy art to 'create a more humane environment'. You can best see the results of this law around the Civic Center, at the junction of Colfax Avenue and Broadway. Judge for yourself.

The Art Museum at 100 W 14th Avenue at Acoma St (575-2793) is a fortress-like building which houses a fascinating collection of native art and craftwork. As well as travelling exhibitions, it features a good collection of European art from early Roman to Monet and Picasso. Opening hours are 10am-5pm, Tuesday to Saturday and noon-5pm on Sunday; a donation of $3 is suggested.

Three blocks northwest at W Colfax Avenue and Cherokee St is the US Mint (as distinct from the Bureau of Engravings in Washington). Five billion of the nation's coins are produced here each year and the vaults contain the largest amount of gold bullion outside Fort Knox — hence the machine-gun turrets outside. There are free 20-minute guided tours 8am-3pm every working day (except in late June). Call 837-3582 for information.

Many of the other museums are a little shabby and commercial, or of interest only to connoisseurs of transport, wax and cowboys. Buffalo Bill's Museum (526-0747) is at the place on Lookout Mountain in Golden, where William F. 'Buffalo Bill' is buried. Adults may be more impressed with the panoramic mountain view than the memorabilia, though the view of Denver is obscured by transmitter masts. The museum opens daily 9am-4pm in summer, daily except Monday in winter.

Denver's only other celebrated resident is 'unsinkable' Molly Brown, a survivor of the Titanic, who is credited for saving the lives of dozens of children in that Atlantic disaster. She is honoured at 1340 Pennsylvania (832-4092), her former home now restored in her memory. Opening hours are 10am-4pm from Tuesday to Saturday and noon-4pm on Sundays, admission $3.

For train buffs the Colorado Railroad Museum in Golden (17155 W 44th Avenue, 279-4591) presents a fascinating collection of railroad memorabilia. It is open daily 9am-5pm, admission $3.

Parks. The huge City Park (between York St and S Colorado Blvd, off E Colfax Avenue) is a couple of miles from the city centre; buses bound for the airport pass by it. The park contains the excellent Denver Natural History Museum (Montview and Colorado Blvds, 370-6300), which houses outstanding specimens of Rocky Mountain fauna (stuffed, though), as well as dinosaur fossils and Indian artifacts. It boasts one of the world's largest movie screens in the IMAX Theater, and watching a film ($5) is well worthwhile. The museum opens daily 9am-5pm. In the park there is also a planetarium, which features a laser display, and a zoo where animals are kept in something approximating their natural habitats. Other attractions include a miniature railway, boating and outdoor skating in winter.

Denver has a hundred other parks, including the Botanic Gardens (1005 York St), which lie within Cheesman Park, south of the centre. For those more interested in fun than flora, there are two good amusement parks: Elitch Gardens (4620 W 38th Avenue at Tennyson St), with a huge roller coaster, and Lakeside (4601 Sheridan Boulevard at W 44th Avenue, 477-1621). They open at weekends only in May, then daily in summer. You pay about $10 for unlimited rides.

Entertainment

If you are looking for high culture, you will soon exhaust Denver's resources. But if your tastes are sufficiently eclectic, you should find something to enjoy: the nightclubs and rock venues of Denver or sophisticated student events at Boulder. Tickets for big events are sold through TicketMaster on 290-TIXS.

Music. Free open-air concerts take place in City Park from July 4 to August 18, every night except Monday. Some feature the renowned Denver Symphony Orchestra. During the winter season, the Orchestra is based on Boetcher Hall, part of the Center for the Performing Arts. This is a mammoth complex on 14th St at Curtis (893-4000). Although the Hall seats 2,700, no one is more than 85ft from the stage. Free tours of the Center take place during the day.

Opera buffs should head for Central City, 30 miles west of Denver. In the 1870s residents of the 'richest square mile on Earth' devoted some of its mineral wealth to an Opera House (16th and Tremont Streets). The season runs from April until November.

For information on rock bands check the local press. The bigger bands play at the Rainbow Music Hall at 6260 E Evans Street, one of the several Boulder venues; or at the spectacular Red Rocks Amphitheater (694-1234), 16 miles west of Denver, where U2 recorded its *Under a Blood Red Sky* album — even if the music is disappointing, the scenery makes it worthwhile. Local rock groups can be found in the bars around Larimer Square and in Boulder dives. El Chapultepec at 19th St and Market (295-9126) has live jazz every night. The Arvada Center for the Arts and Humanities at 6901 Wadsworth Blvd sponsors everything from jazz to classical music.

Theatre. In an attempt to rid the city of its image as a cultural backwater, the Center for the Performing Arts (893-4000) has three regular theatres plus an amphitheatre and the Auditorium Theatre. The Denver Center Theater Company can be seen here, along with numerous touring shows and more avant-garde productions.

There are many smaller experimental theatres in the city and in Boulder. These include the Germinal Stage Denver (1820 Market St at 44th, 455-7108) and the Changing Scene (1527 Champa St at 16th, 893-5775).

Nightlife. Downtown Denver has been largely drained of nightlife, but there are several bars offer live music, including some of those around Larimer Square. Comedy Works dispenses jokes every night of the week at 1226 15th St, at Larimer Square (595-3637).

Most nightlife centres on E Hampden Avenue, ten miles south of downtown between I-25 and Havana Street. Here you find nightclubs from the cheap and informal to the chic and sophisticated; there is even a 60s style club complete with Stones, Beatles and other early pop music ... and cheerleaders. The No Frills Grill (7155 E Hampden Avenue, 759-9079) is in the first league — jeans, hamburgers and beer. Dsco action can be found along Leetsdale Drive in Glendale: turn east off Colorado Blvd and choose your venue.

Clubs with no cover charge may seem like a good idea but if you're out to drink rather than dance, beware. Prices can start as high as $5 for a Coke, so ask before ordering. Some clubs have special deals such as 'Ladies Nights', when 'ladies' can have unlimited drink from as little as $5.

Boulder: the nightlife in Boulder is cheaper and less brash. There are bars featuring stand up comics, jazz bands playing for free, and street cafbs which afford a good view of the numerous local posers. Try the Pearl St Mall or the university area. Pleasant, relaxed evening entertainment can be enjoyed in the dozens of smaller establishments that feature folk or country music performers. Check the newspapers.

SPORT

In football, the Denver Broncos (nickname: Orange Crush) have a near-fanatical following. They play from September to January at the Mile High Stadium, 17th Avenue and Federal Blvd (433-7466), which usually has a good crowd atmosphere, great weather and magnificient mountain views. Although the stadium seats 74,000, tickets are hard to come by since most seats are reserved by holders of season tickets (for which there is reputed to be a waiting list of 20,000). The Bears, a minor-league baseball team, share the Mile High Stadium in summer (433-8645).

It is a source of much civic frustration that Denver has been unable to acquire a top-flight baseball team. The 18,000-seat McNichols Arena is the venue for the Nuggets basketball team from October through May, and the Colorado Rockies ice hockey team. The US National field hockey team is based at Colorado Springs. The low oxygen level due to altitude and equable climate of Colorado make the state a favoured training ground for international athletes.

Horse racing takes place at the Centennial Race Track (794-2661), in the southern suburb of Littleton, from May onwards. The dogs race at the Mile High Kennel Club, 6200 Dahlia St from January to March. Off-course gambling, is covert but on-track betting is legal. Rodeos are held at the Coliseum: call 295-4488 for details of forthcoming events. The National Western Stock Show and Rodeo is held in Denver each January.

Participation. There are plenty of venues if you feel like a little exercise yourself. Sports complexes contain some combination of a swimming pool, water slide, bowling alley and, for the more sedentary, a wall of video games. Try the swimming pool in Congress Park. There are hundreds of municipal tennis courts for hire, and half a dozen golf courses.

SHOPPING

The main shopping area in Denver is on and around the 16th St Mall, running from Court Place to Arapahoe St, although prices are lower in the numerous suburban shopping plazas. Expensive boutiques are grouped around Larimer Square. In Boulder, the Pearl St Mall and the university area have the highest concentration of 'New Age' shops this side of Santa Fe.

As you might expect, Denver excels in outdoor gear and equipment. If possible, buy during the end of season sales: January for skis and skates, July for boots, tents and backpacks. There are also numerous Indian art and jewellery shops selling beautiful silver and turquoise pieces.

The highlight of the massive Cherry Creek mall is the Tattered Cover Bookstore, four floors of jacket-to-jacket books.

THE MEDIA

Newspapers. There are two competing dailies, the *Denver Post* (broadsheet) and the *Rocky Mountain News* (tabloid). Both have extensive entertainment and classified sections. The 'Center Section — Friday' of the *Rocky Mountain News* or the 'Sunday Round-Up' of the *Denver Post* are the best sources of listings. The Boulder newspaper is the *Daily Camera*; a free University of Colorado paper called the *Colorado Daily* can be picked up in many shops, bars and restaurants.

Some of the more informative and offbeat weekly magazines include *Denver Downtowner, Up The Creek* and *Westworld,* all of which are free from shops, restaurants and hotels. *Denver Magazine* is available from news stands if you prefer to pay for more complete information.

Broadcasting: among the 35 radio stations serving Denver is KOA (850 AM), which gained fame with a deliberately offensive phone-in host named Allan Berg (who was eventually murdered by an outraged listener). KCFR (90.1 FM) is the university station affiliated with the National Public Radio network, and KDEN (1340 AM) offers NBC news 24 hours a day. KHIH (94.7 FM) dispenses New Age sounds, light jazz and soft rock, while KRFX ('The Fox', 103.5FM) is all adult-oriented rock. KAZY (106.9FM) has classic rock interspersed with syndicated documentaries. For heavy metal try 105.9 FM, and for jazz 89.3 FM) Three other stations offer undiluted country music (e.g. KYGO, 98.5FM), and there are five religious stations. The small town of Oak Creek in northwestern Colorado offers what is claimed to be the world's only wind-powered commercial radio station, as well as good rock programming.

Denver is unusual in having two publicly-sponsored TV stations. In addition to the regular PBS (channel 6), KBDI (channel 12) provides independent local programmes.

Crime and Safety

Denver has one of the highest incidences of rape in the country. Wise women never venture out alone at night nor in the early morning. Avoid the Five Point area downtown and the gangland area around N Federal Blvd after dark. In other situations, be cautious rather than paranoid about street crime. Daylight attacks are rare.

Drugs. Boulder has a justified reputation as the cocaine capital of the Rockies. Along with high pay goes high living, including a large amount of casual drug consumption. Many of the jaded but wealthy younger generation do not find it strange to spend $500 a week on white powder: legislators have made penalties for possession more severe and drug users have made themselves less conspicuous.

Help and Information

The area code for Denver and Boulder is 303. For Central Colorado and Colorado Springs use the prefix 719.

Information: The Convention and Visitors' Bureau of Denver and Colorado, is at 225 W Colfax Avenue (892-1112), across from the US Mint; it has maps and information for both city and state. The bureau also has a branch at the airport. For tourist information in Boulder, visit the Chamber of Commerce, (1001 Canyon St; 442-1044) for free maps and event listings.

American Express: Anaconda Tower, 555 17th St (298-7100), between Welton and Glenarm.

Thomas Cook: 8775 E Orchard Road, Englewood (694-6860).
Post Office: 1823 Stout St, Denver 80201.
Police: 575-2100.
Medical Emergencies: St Joseph Hospital, 1835 Franklin St (837-7111).
    Denver General Hospital, W 8th Avenue at Cherokee St (893-6000).
Travelers' Aid: 1245 E Colfax Avenue (832-8194).

THE ROCKY MOUNTAINS

New Mexico, Utah, Colorado, Wyoming, Montana and Idaho are dominated by the most famous range of mountains in North America, the Rockies. These mountains, so deservedly beloved by environmentalists and other fans of the outdoors, cover an enormous area; in the state of Colorado alone they occupy an area six times that of the Swiss Alps. A feature common to each state (except Utah) is that the Continental Divide runs through them. Ever since pioneering days, the Divide has been of profound significance to Americans. All rivers to the west of the Divide flow eventually into the Pacific: all those to the east, into the Gulf of Mexico or Atlantic.

Unlike other great mountain ranges in the world, the 'roof of America' is accessible. The mountains are traversed by a well-maintained network of roads. Cycling, walking, skiing or canoeing through any part of the Rocky Mountains becomes a great pleasure in the fresh air, hospitable summer climate and stunning terrain. It is one of the most beautiful places in the world. See *The Great Outdoors* on page 313 for descriptions of the main parks.

B & B Rocky Mountain (303-860-8415) offers a free reservation service for guest houses in Colorado, New Mexico and Utah.

Cities of the Rockies. People don't generally travel to the Rocky Mountains for the cities: they go for the rugged mountains and dramatic scenery. Denver is the undisputed capital of the region, and the only other city of significant population is Salt Lake City. But there are other smaller cities that are a better choice for travellers wanting to maximize their time outdoors; AYH hostels are to be found right across the Rockies. The smaller, more obscure towns tend to have lower prices for accommodation and have been more successful at withstanding the homogenizing influence of the rapidly expanding tourist industry.

COLORADO

The USA's most mountainous state is smitten with lust for tourism dollars, and its towns tend to be well-groomed, cosmopolitan and lacking in authentic western charm. You needn't venture far from Denver, however, to find some beautiful spots. Hiking trails lead from the outskirts of Boulder into some beautiful sandstone formations called the Flatirons.

The treacherous Oh My God Road between Idaho Springs and Central City shows real gold mining territory. The 'Keep Out' signs indicate that some of the mines are still active.

Colorado Springs. Seventy-five miles south of Denver on I-25 is Colorado Springs, in the Pike National Forest. While the city is losing what little character it had retained from the Wild West days to rapid high-technology industry growth, it is a good place to visit if you want a whirlwind nature tour. Pikes Peak (14,645 ft), the quintessential rocky mountain, looms ominously in the background. The Pikes Peak Incline Railway runs trains from town to the summit. An hour southwest of Colorado Springs is Royal Gorge, a 1,250ft-deep canyon carved by the Arkansas River. To the south on Cheyenne Mountain is Seven Falls, where a roaring river cascades down a steep, 1,000ft chasm in seven distinct stages. During summer the falls are illuminated at night and can be viewed from a cable car.

Route 24 west of Colorado Springs takes you to the Garden of the Gods — a 940-acre park full of strange red sandstone formations from the Paleozoic era. The AYH Garden of the Gods Campground (3704 W Colorado Avenue, 719-475-9450) rents out cabins to members in the summer ($10 per person), but be sure to phone well in advance. In Colorado Springs itself, reasonably-priced lodgings are abundant, including many bed and breakfast places.

Estes Park. The town of Estes Park, on the eastern edge of the Rocky Mountain National Park, is one of the most heavily visited towns in the Rockies — not least because it is surrounded by stunning mountain pine forests and beautiful scenery. Prices are high, and about the only cheap place to eat in town is the Happy Texans at 153 Elkhorn.

The H-Bar-G Ranch AYH hostel is in the Roosevelt National Park northeast of the town (303-586-3688); it is open in summer to hostel members only.

NEW MEXICO

In ten years New Mexico has leapt to prominence as a clean and pleasant land ideal for the New Age. The terrain is wonderful, from undulating riverside meadows to wide open deserts and majestic high-altitude vistas. A journey through the mountains can take you in minutes from sparse cactus-clad scrub on the sheltered side to majestic firs on the rainward slopes.

Albuquerque. This is easily the largest city (though not the state capital) and a good place to begin a visit. Much is made of the Old Town, founded by the Spanish in 1706, though little remains of the original settlements. More rewarding is the Museum of Natural History (a dinosaurs-meet-Disney journey through time) and the Albuquerque Museum, which provides a good introduction to the culture of the Southwest USA and the history of the Rio Grande valley. Both museums are fronted by impressive sculptures, donated by the city's '1% for Art' campaign which gives a cent in every tax dollar to support public art.

Albuquerque's international airport is one of the strangest in the nation, the only adobe terminal you are ever likely to see. You reach it from Central Avenue downtown on bus 50. Nearby, the Kirkland air force base houses the National Atomic Museum (505-844-8443). A slick film describes the development of the weapons which devastated Hiroshima and Nagasaki. In those Japanese cities solemn peace parks articulate the evils of war. In New Mexico, you get the impression that these massacres of civilians were mere warm-ups before the main attraction, an event for which the militarists are still preparing. In a breathless *Boy's Own* style, the build-up to the detonation of the 'Little Boy' bomb over Hiroshima on 6 August 1945 is described; as is the use of the 'Fat Man' weapon on Nagasaki three days later, with the implied enthusiasm of the bombmakers of New Mexico to test out another plutonium plaything. To enter the base you must obtain and sign a pass at one of the entrances, on Gibson or Wyoming Boulevards; you can reach it on bus 31 or 32. The museum opens 9am-5pm daily.

The sun beams its natural radiation upon New Mexico for 300 days every year, giving hot, dry summers and bright, crisp winters. There is a remarkable quality of light, a clarity and luminescence rather like looking through ultramarine-tinted glasses. The predictably benevolent climate has made Albuquerque into the hot-air ballooning capital of the world, and in the first two weeks of October the skies are filled with thermal-seeking devices, many in shapes so strange that their airworthiness must be questionable. This International Balloon Fiesta is a fine sight; call the Albuquerque Visitors' Bureau on 1-800-321-6979 for details of mass ascents, hot-air balloon races and other events.

Albuquerque has one of the best and cheapest Mexican restaurants in the southwest: the M & J Sanitary Tortilla Factory, 403 2nd St SW. The *carne adovada* burrito merits at least an hour's detour. You can also eat excellent fish in the Museum of Natural History's Café Oceana.

Accommodation: low-priced motels flank the long Central Avenue, including the EconoLodge at number 817 (by I-25). Convenient for the Old Town are the friendly Monterey Motel (2402 Central Ave SW, 505-243-3554), with doubles from $55 and the cheaper El Vado (2500 Central Ave SW, 505-243-4594), which charges from $35. The International Hostel (1012 W Central Ave, at 10th St, 505-243-6101), just south of the Old Town and west of the bus station, has dorm beds for about $10.

Pueblos Around Albuquerque. The Native Americans of New Mexico have fared better than most of their compatriots, but they still live a life twisted by 20th-century civilization. Their settlements (*pueblos*) are traditional adobe villages, but dressed in dust contantly churned up by pick-up trucks. The inhabitants are more likely to be mass-producers of souvenirs than hunter-gatherers. The most authentic of the genre is Sandia pueblo, just 20 miles north of Albuquerque, where no overt exploitation has taken place. Stooping old women shuffle along the dirt tracks, with haphazard TV aerials and adobe workshops used for repairing Japanese motorcycles the other distinguishing features. There are strict rules governing visits to most pueblos, including bans on alcohol, photography and even sketching.

On August 4 the most exciting remaining Indian dance takes place on the saint's day of Santa Domingo Pueblo, 30 miles north of Albuquerque. Festivities last all day, and include 1,000 dancers in the intricate corn dance. The event is for the benefit of the local pueblos, but non-locals are welcome.

Gallup, a small town 150 miles to the west, makes much ado about the Inter-Tribal Ceremonial that takes place there every August. Avoid it like the plague: it is a tourist trap at best and Gallup is really nothing more than a grubby strip of highway. But between Albuquerque and Gallup is Acoma Pueblo, one of the oldest continuously inhabited settlements in America, in this case well over 1,000 years; it is perched dramatically on top of a tall *mesa* (or flat-topped mountain). Intricate silver and turquoise Navajo Jewelry is sold in all the reservations, however the cheapest place to buy good-quality stuff is the pawn shops on Gallup's Main St. Make sure you buy silver that has been initialled by the Indian silversmiths, e.g. GHB — Great Hunting Bear.

Jemez Mountains. While the freeway along the Rio Grande north from Albuquerque takes you through some glorously large-scale scenery, a detour into the Jemez mountains is recommended. Indian communities and one-gas station towns are typicallly New Mexican. Marked temptingly on the local Visitor Guide are some hot springs, confusingly some miles north of the village of Jemez Springs. There is no roadside sign, so you'll need to ask locals for directions. When you park, wait for a regular to turn up and lead you through the valley to the springs. New Age hedonists spend the day 'skinny-dipping' in nature's own jacuzzis, soaking up the sun while inhaling the clear mountain air and the occasional joint.

There is an AYH hostel west off Highway 4, not far from the Springs. It is open all year round. Call 505-867-3294.

Santa Fe. Sixty miles east of Jemez, you reach either Santa Fe or Nirvana, depending on your perspective. Like Key West and Santa Barbara, New Mexico's state capital is a town for lotus-eaters. It boasts 125 art galleries, one for every 200 citizens. There are almost as many estate agents, selling paradise at 7,000ft to refugees from the West Coast hoping to escape crack-dealing wars and terminal smog. Nestled among the splendid peaks of the Sangre de Cristo mountain range, Santa Fe is the one New Mexico city most worth stopping — and shopping — in. In 1992 readers of *Condé Nast Traveler* magazine voted it the world's best travel destination (San Francisco was second). Some local people would not agree that the town has survived the influx of outsiders and the surfeit of speciality shops; some of those who have seen it change resent the new arrivals, and move on to Taos, another 75 mile north.

Founded in the 1540s by Spanish Catholic missionaries, Santa Fe retains its Latin heritage in its architecture and lifestyle. Yet at the same time it has evolved into the centre of southwestern culture. The large colony of artists cohabits the town with the heavily Indian and Hispanic citizenry. Santa Fe means 'holy faith' in Spanish.

The Plaza at the centre of town is dominated by the Palace of the Governors, the oldest seat of government in the USA. Artists lay out their works on blankets under the portal, presumably because all the other prime retail sites have been taken. Opposite is a Woolworth store, the sole survivor from the days when shops sold useful things such as shoelaces and soap. The remainder of Santa Fe's retail trade sells a mix of tourists tat and *objets d'art*; the dividing line is not always clear. Although it is easy to ridicule this trend and other developments such as an adobe multi-storey car park, great pains have been taken to preserve the fusion of Spanish and Indian influences on architecture and atmosphere.

Outside of town, the mountain scenery is some of the best in the Rockies. For information about hiking trails, camping, or picnic grounds, contact the Santa Fe National Forest Service at 1220 St Francis Drive at Alta Vista (505-988-6940).

Accommodation: the problem with Santa Fe is its popularity. The hostel at 1412 Cerrillos Road (505-988-1153), 2km southwest of the centre and $15 per person, is a budget alternative to the motels on Old Pecos Trail and S St Francis Drive. You can call Santa Fe Central Reservations (1-800-982-7669) to book a room in advance.

Eating and Drinking: the cuisine is bicultural. Hispanic dishes have been combined with native American ingredients to produce tasty and nutritious regional specialities — so successfully that Southwestern cuisine is currently America's trendiest. It has always been the most colourful. A prime ingredient is blue corn; it is more a dark grey-green, but made into tortillas it provides an excellent accompaniment to dishes such as huevos rancheros, laced thoroughly with red (hot) and green (hotter) chili peppers. Any morning you can join the queue at Café Pasqual's on Water Street for the best South-western breakfast in the USA.

Exploring: Suitably set up for the day, begin to survey Santa Fe's sights. Among the strangest is the Loretto chapel, which sits humbly in uneasy proximity to the Best Western Inn — a covered walkway from the hotel lobby leads straight into the church. It contains an extraordinary staircase to the gallery, built with no visible means of support by a mysterious carpenter who disappeared the day he finished it. Your financial offerings are sent to the Sisters of Loretta Retirement Fund, presumably a front organization for old waitresses from the Best Western.

Train buffs will be disappointed to learn that the town which gave its name to one of America's great railways has now vanished from the passenger network. Santa Fe rail station is a sad and decrepit goods depot; the only trains which know the way to Santa Fe these days are freight services from Albuquerque. Culture buffs are better served. As well as clutch of small theatres and clubs, there is an Opera House, whose season runs through July and August, and an excellent rock, classical and Indian music scene.

Help and Information: New Mexico Tourism & Travel Division, Bataan Memorial Building, Santa Fe; tel 1-800-545-2040. There is always a wealth of cultural events, high and low, taking place in Santa Fe. For information call the local Tourism Office on 505-827-0291.

Los Alamos. This modern trading estate tucked away outside Santa Fe was the birthplace of the Bomb. You can't travel far in New Mexico without encountering evidence of Robert Oppenheimer's deadly toy. Its pre-eminence as the original (and still the greatest) centre for nuclear weapons research began for no better reason that that Dr Oppenheimer had his summer residence there. He established the National Laboratory devoted to nuclear research. Here the Manhattan Project scientists began their terrifyingly successful mission to increase man's killing power by splitting the atom. Before the War, Los Alamos was basically a boys' private school surrounded by ancient Indian settlements; now it's a modern town complete with shops housing estates and McDonald's, and home to some of America's best physicists.

Taos. While Santa Fe retains its essential dignity, Taos has sold out more or less completely to the sort of people who feel they would like to live in the sort of place where artists and writers are supposed to cluster; there isn't even a Woolworth's. Its eighty art galleries knock Santa Fe's impressive per capita average to pieces. Literary visitors will be most interested in D. H. Lawrence's former ranch, ten miles northwest, which the novelist occupied long before writers' and artists' communities became fashionable. Two miles outside town is Taos Pueblo, which has much of interest — including the oldest continuously occupied house in the USA — but where the people and their culture are exploited through crass and tawdry commercialism. Few Indians seem to live in the village permanently any more, though they all gather for festivals, when they do good business selling crafts. At other times, however, there are usually one or two people making and selling Indian frybread in the streets.

You won't find much in the way of cheap beds in town. The AYH Plum Tree Hostel (505-758-4696) is in the village of Pilar on Highway 68, 12 miles south of Taos. It has dorm beds ($11) and private rooms ($35). Another AYH hostel is ten miles northeast in Arroyo Seco (505-776-8298).

Southern New Mexico. Going south from Albuquerque on I-25 you reach the town of Truth or Consequences, on the banks of the Rio Grande. The town is well-situated for hiking in the hills or immersion in the local hot springs. The AYH hostel (100 Austin Avenue, 505-894-6183) has its own hot mineral baths.

Shortly before the Texan and Mexican frontiers is Las Cruces, devoted to the manufacture of enough nuclear warheads to destroy the planet several times over. Nearby is the White Sands Missile Range, which opens to the public one day each year for visits to the Trinity Site. The atomic age began here in July 1945, when the first nuclear weapon was tested.

UTAH

The semi-desert state of Utah is a curious blend of religious doctrine, salt flats and ancient canyons. What permeates every aspect of life in Utah is the Church of Jesus Christ and Latter Day Saints (often abbreviated to LDS), whose followers are universally known as Mormons. After having a vision of the angel Moroni, Joseph Smith recruited some disciples and set off from the East Coast in search of a settlement where they could practise their religion in peace. Their first choice was Illinois, where Joseph Smith was murdered. His heir-apparent Brigham Young continued the Mormon trail westward, and finally settled in the shadow of the mountains on the banks of Great Salt Lake. The salinity of this lake (second only to the Dead Sea) is due to the dissolved minerals brought by streams from the surrounding mountains. Since there is no outlet from the lake, the minerals are trapped, and evaporation increases the concentration of salinity.

Mormons comprise nearly half the state's population and there is no escaping their influence. From the complexity of the liquor laws to the towering temples of Salt Lake City, the followers of Joseph Smith have made their mark. Utah in general, and Salt Lake City in particular, are extremely rich. This does not stem only from industrial, agricultural or mineral wealth, but from the requirement that Mormons must pay 15% of their earnings to the church. The wealth is reflected in the no-expense-spared architecture in Salt Lake City.

Brigham Young, the first city planner, designated Temple Square as the centre of the city and of the street grid system. It is dominated by the six-spired Temple, which looks suspiciously like something out of Disneyland. The public may attend rehearsals of the Mormon Tabernacle Choir here (Thursday evening) and broadcasts (Sunday morning). Guided tours of the Temple are offered free every few minutes, departing as soon as a modest crowd assembles. Some of the manifestations of Christ have been described by heathens as resembling a member of the Grateful Dead in their early days. After the tour you can search for records of your ancestors on microfiche.

Of particular interest to non-believers are the converted tramsheds of Trolley Square and the Marmalade Historic District around Quince St, where the efforts of British and Scandinavian architects to adapt their building methods to the blistering heat are fascinating. The grave of Hiram BeBee in the City Cemetery is reputed to be that of the Sundance Kid, though the outlaw was actually killed in Bolivia. Two hours out of town lives Robert Redford, who played the film role of the Sundance Kid against Paul Newman's Butch Cassidy; he is owner of the Sundance ski resort in the Wasatch Mountains.

Help and Information: the Visitor Information Station is at 180 South

West Temple St (801-521-2822). Call 801-533-TIPS for recorded event information, and 801-532-BIRD for recorded wildlife information. The *Walking and Driving Tours* brochure (free) details all the main attractions.

Utah Liquor Laws. Alcohol, like tea, coffee and Coke, is forbidden to Mormons. Although you'll have little problem in finding coffee or beer, anything stronger requires a certain amount of planning. If you are staying in one place for a while, take out guest membership at a private drinking club. However, these are not particularly pleasant places, and, furthermore, they do not serve food. If you wish to enjoy your drink with a meal, there are two options. You can either buy alcohol in advance from one of the many state liquor stores (which accept cash only and have erratic opening hours) and order a mixer or 'set-up' at the restaurant; or wait until 4pm (noon on Sundays), whereupon most restaurants will serve miniature bottles of wine or spirits — though you must actually fetch these yourself from the cashier since waiters and waitresses are prohibited from serving spirits. If you are a serious drinker there are many better places to be than Utah.

WYOMING

Set up on a high, barren prairie, the state capital Cheyenne is basically a cattle market surrounded by rundown bars, with a rather Latin air of lethargy. It is only worth visiting during Frontier Days in July, when the city hosts the most prestigious rodeo in the world. Contact the Wyoming Travel Board (1-800-225-5996) for information.

At the entrance to the majestic Grand Teton Mountain range, just east of the state line, the town of Jackson is given over to promoting its 'nouveau-western' image: rather cosmopolitan yet imbued with the spirit of the old west. Scenic hiking trails, lakes, and rivers surround the town. From Jackson you can travel by bus into the Tetons or further north to Yellowstone National Park. In winter Jackson is one of the most chic ski resorts in the Rockies; in other seasons you can ride the ski lift 2,100ft up Snow King Mountain for a panoramic view of the immense wilderness. Each summer Jackson hosts a fine arts festival, summerstock theatre, and symphony, and the dozens of galleries in town buzz with activity.

In spite of the town's trendiness, it is possible to find inexpensive accommodation; and there is an AYH hostel in Teton Village, 12 miles northwest of Jackson (3600 McCollister Drive, 307-733-3415). Private rooms only are available, from $45.

IDAHO

This boot-shaped state is the most obscure of the Rocky Mountain states, primarily because it lacks the accessibility afforded by the bus lines, excellent roads and tourist industries of the other states. Only if you have a car and want to go to a less-frequented, under-deeloped side of the Rckies does it merit a visit.

Ketchum, an old village a mile west of Sun Valley, is the best place to stay. It is within a short drive of the wildlife-rich Sawtooth Mountain Range; the Craters of the Moon National Monument — a vast, ancient lava flow that covers over 100 square miles; and Mount Borah, Idaho's tallest peak 13,000ft. Ernest Hemingway liked Ketchum so much he died there and is buried in the local graveyard. The Lift Tower Lodge (703 S Main St, 208-726-5163), on the main highway, charges from $55.

MONTANA

Montana's Rockies are full of rustic mountain towns whose inhabitants remain untouched by the vitiating impulses of modern life: the rest of America refer to them as 'good people.' Helena, originally known as Last Chance Gulch, is the only city in the Montana Rockies. The richest city in the country during the gold rush of the 1860s, it is now a quiet little capital, convenient to beautiful canyons, mountains, and a sulphurous hot springs. Unlike the rest of the Rocky Mountain states, sightseeing by train is eminently rewarding in Montana. You can board in Helena and journey through some spectacular scenery to Glacier National Park and then east across the north of the state. There are AYH hostels in East Glacier Park, Missoula, Polebridge and Kalispell.

This region of scenic spendour does not rely solely on the mountains for its beauty and interest. Canyons, caverns, craters and geysers and glaciers dot the maps of these six states, mostly inside the boundaries of the 11 National Parks. In addition, National Monuments, Forests, Recreation Areas and Grasslands preserve vast tracts for the lover of the great outdoors. The Rockies are the best place to stop for a while if you're crossing the country. Opportunities for outdoor activities are endless: hiking and backpacking, rafting and inner-tubing, windsurfing and sailing, wilderness trekking with horses (and even llamas), panning for gold (it is still possible to make a little money) and, of course, skiing and snowmobiling.

The environs of Denver contain many places of breathtaking scenic and natural beauty. Only 60 miles southwest of Denver is the highest paved automobile road in North America, which takes you to the summit of Mount Evans (14,262ft) from where there is a fine view of mountains and prairies. Mostly above the tree line, rare alpine flowers and 2,000-year-old bristlecone pines grow. And there are numerous National Parks within relatively easy reach of Denver and the other cities of the Rockies.

PARKS

Rocky Mountain National Park, Colorado. If you visit only one national park in your lifetime, you will not be disappointed if you make it this one. Because of its proximity to Denver and Boulder (less than 50 miles), the park suffers from some commercialism; but it covers such a vast area that the interior remains untouched. Here you can see some of the most exhiliarating scenery in the Rockies, on either side of the Continental Divide which bisects the park.

There are 107 peaks over 11,000ft high within the park's 405 square miles; even the valleys are a mile and half above sea level. The traces of glacial action are so clear that an untrained eye can recognise them. Much of the area is above the tree line with bleak alpine terrain. The weather at this altitude is highly changeable: wrap up well, and never stray from the beaten track in inclement weather. The beaten track in this case is the 50 mile-long Trail Ridge Road — the highest continuous highway in the USA — which follows the course of an ancient Indian track. You can actually look down on 10,000ft mountains. The drive (a toll is payable within the park) takes about three hours, but the hardy can hire a bike in Estes Park and pedal around. Hiking trail maps are available at the Visitors Center in Estes

Park (on US-36, 2 miles north of the town, 303-586-2371) and Deer Ridge Junction. The Tundra Trail at Rock Cut is not too taxing and is highly recommended.

Wildlife is abundant, with elk, deer and Rocky Mountain bighorn sheep. Although coyote, black bear, bobcat and smaller carnivorous animals all live here, they are seldom seen by park visitors. You are also very unlikely to see the 'jackalope' — a cross between a jack-rabbit and an antelope, beloved by Coloradan practical jokers — except on postcards.

The 240-mile drive from Denver via Boulder, Estes Park, Grand Lake (the world's highest yacht club) and Idaho Springs is among one of the most impressive circular routes in the country. From Idaho Springs, take Virginia Canyon Road through the mining hills to Central City. The Argo Gold Mill is still there, but its four-mile tunnel through the hills to Central City is closed.

Mesa Verde National Park, Colorado. Whereas Rocky Mountain National Park is pre-eminent for mountain scenery, Mesa Verde allows the visitor to have a rare glimpse of America's distant history. Mesa is a Spanish word meaning a table-shaped landform; the 'Green Table' in the extreme southwest of the state contains excavated cliff dwellings. Anasazi Indian tribes lived in these caves until the end of the 13th century, when they mysteriously fled leaving behind all their possessions for the delight and bewilderment of archaeologists. The cliff palace is a capacious dwelling 15 storeys above the canyon floor and containing 200 rooms.

The park lies about nine miles east of Cortez on Route 160, and there is a bus service from the town.

San Juan National Park, Colorado. One of the most pleasant and unusual ways to see some of the dramatic San Juan Mountain range is by train on the old Durango-Silverton narrow gauge railway, a relic left over from the mining age. The track winds through some of the most photogenic scenery of the Rockies. The train seats over 400 people, but in summer you still need to reserve a seat about a month in advance: write to 479 Main Avenue Durango, CO 81301, or call 303-247-2733. In summer the trip takes all day and costs $37.50. In winter (no reservation necessary), the trip lasts five hours and costs $32.

North of the Park is the immense Black Canyon of the Gunnison — a craggy, black gorge nearly 3,000ft deep — which you stumble upon in the midst of a bleak plateau. At the bottom of the canyon lies the powerful Gunnison river, a favourite among anglers.

Dinosaur National Monument, Colorado. Situated in northwest Colorado, close to the Utah border, this 325-square mile park has one of the largest concentrations of fossilized dinosaur bones in the world. Nearly 2,000 such bones are on view as a permanent exhibit on a cliff face, and visitors can watch technicians still working to uncover the skeletons of brontosauruses (which are unique to Colorado and Wyoming) and other prehistoric creatures.

The scenery itself is remarkable: there are many narrow gorges with sheer, strangely-carved, red-tinted sandstone cliffs. From Harper's Corner there are spectacular views of the confluence of the Green and Yampa Rivers at Steamboat Rock, over 2,500ft below. River trips lasting between one and five days are available.

White River National Forest, Colorado. This forest in central Colorado was once the hunting ground of the Ute Indians. Within its boundaries lie the Mount of Holy Cross, Glenwood Canyon and the Snowmass wilderness. But most visitors are attracted by the ski resorts of Vail and Aspen. If you are not there during the ski-season, try to attend the music festival in July and August, when the Aspen Music School, Ballet West and the American Theatre Company all perform. Summer visitors may also try white water rafting. River Runners in nearby Salida run reasonably-priced trips on the Arkansas River and have a toll free number to check prices and availability (1-800-332-9100). About 50 miles downriver near Canon City is a remarkable canyon called Royal Gorge, which narrows to 30ft and is spanned by the world's highest suspension bridge (1,053ft).

Carlsbad Caverns, New Mexico. The only National Park in New Mexico features the largest caverns in the world, many of which have not been fully explored. There are over three miles of interconnected chambers. The park is in the southeast corner of the state, accessible off Highway 180 which runs from Carlsbad south into Texas. There are plenty of places to stay in Whites City, the nearest town to the park (on US-180), but you will need your own transport as there are no buses to the caves.

The caves are open for tours daily between 8.30am and 3.30pm, admission $5 (505-785-2233). You can go on either a long or short walking tour, depending on your adventurousness. The longer trip takes you 800ft down (stout shoes with good soles essential), covers two miles and takes in four chambers; it lasts a couple of hours. The other tour (unguided) takes about 90 minutes and involves walking along a well-marked trail and through the Big Room, a spectacular cavern dating back some three million years. Both trips are recommended, but the Big Room is certainly the highlight. Try to hang around till dusk when the thousands of bats which live inside the caves head out to nearby valleys to feed; though maybe even more impressive is the sight of them returning at dawn.

Near Albuquerque, the Basque del Apache National Wildlife Refuge harbours over 300 species of birds, including the gravely endangered whooping crane.

Yellowstone National Park, Wyoming. A whole generation of *Yogi Bear* viewers grew up firmly believing that the correct name for this park is Jellystone. In fact the name comes not from the sandstone which millenia of geographical disturbance have shuffled into a rugged, bubbling wilderness, but rather from the yellow cleft of the Grand Canyon of the Yellowstone River. Beneath the surface of Yellowstone Lake is believed to be the largest single source of geothermal activity. But so large is the lake that it never gets hotter than 65°F. The park has over a hundred waterfalls with a drop of 30ft or more, and some of the best unstocked trout-fishing in the USA.

Yellowstone is the biggest expanse of wilderness in the continental USA, covering an area greater than Wales. Yellowstone was the first National Park, and although a large proportion of its forest was destroyed by fire in 1988 it is still a delightful place. The park is carefully managed and highly organized. An eight-hour tour ($25) covers the main sites, gives thorough explanations and allows about half the time out of the bus. Most visitors — and tour buses — head straight for the huge geyser known as Old Faithful, but it is far less crowded later on in the day. Park rangers can predict its steaming sulphurous eruptions by the intensity and duration of the previous one, and on average they take place every hour — to the delight of the gathered hordes of tourists.

There are other less predictable geysers in the Mammoth Hot Springs area to the north. Once the novelty of geysers wears off, the Yellowstone River has canyons and waterfalls of a less intermittent nature.

The park closes for a month in the autumn, but Yellowstone is becoming more accessible during winter — as long as you are prepared to pay. Snowmobiles and snow coaches (half-track vehicles carrying up to a dozen passengers) transport visitors to view Old Faithful and other sights without the crowds which plague the area in summer. Intrepid cross-country skiers can make the same journey independently. The wildlife is so accustomed to the masses that it is not uncommon to see a bear on the road accepting handouts from passers by.

Grand Teton, Wyoming. Not far from Yellowstone, this park is indeed in the grandest part of the Teton Mountains (the name *teton* is old French for breast, because of the mountains' shape). The glaciated features of the mountains — cirques, valleys and reflecting lakes — contribute to the grandeur. It is the winter feeding ground of America's largest elk herd.

The Tetons are rugged and less-frequented than other parts of the Rockies. They harbour tremendous hiking trails which will lead you to places like Death Canyon — a steep-walled chasm full of wildlife — and the static Peak Divide, the highest point in the park.

Zion National Park, Utah. Zion is an excellent antidote to the commercial excesses of some of the more heavily visited parks, especially Grand Canyon which is only 100 miles away (see page 334). It is on a smaller scale, more easily accessible (a few miles from I-15) and virtually deserted. If you base yourself in the centre of the park — a pleasant grassy area that meanders alongside the river — there is a selection of trails around the peaks and waterfalls. The gentlest stroll would not over-exert even a Los Angeleno deprived of his car; the hardest, an ascent of the Angel's Landing, requires the skill and courage of an experienced mountaineer.

Bryce Canyon National Park, Utah. Although Bryce is only 50 miles from Zion, it is almost a different world. Instead of sub-tropical flora clinging to the rock faces, Bryce has nothing but sandstone. The desert winds have carved this stone into designs which look completely out of place on Earth. It's like walking around caves or catacombs with the roof taken off. There are trails of varying severity, and unobtrusive food and accommodation services.

There are three other national parks in Utah: Arches, which contains giant red sandstone arches and other evidence or erosion; Canyonlands, with extensive evidence of prehistoric Indians; and Capitol Reef, a 70-mile uplift of cliffs dissected by steeply-walled gorges.

Glacier National Park, Montana. The park comprises the larger part of the Waterton-Glacier International Peace Park, which straddles the Canadian border. If you wish to cross between Montana and Canada, note that the border post at Chief Mountain within the park is not open 24 hours: check locally for crossing times.

Glacier is much more difficult to reach than most other parks in the Rockies, and consequently far less crowded during the height of the summer. Like the Trail Ridge Road of Colorado, the 'Going-to-the-Sun' route allows motorists and cyclists to cross the Continental Divide. It is even more rewarding to leave your vehicle behind and take advantage of the 800 miles of hiking trails, in order to see mountain goats, moose and a wealth of wild flowers. The park is at its best from mid-June to mid-September, and even then it is still substantially covered by snow. Hiking in this park is serious business: watch out for grizzly bears and never stray from the trail. Contact Glacier National Park HQ, West Glacier, MT 59936 (406-888-5441) for maps and information.

SKIING

The Rocky Mountain states offer the most reliable skiing in North America, whether in Wyoming's Grand Teton National Park at Jackson Hole, with the best Black Runs in the USA; Idaho's Sun Valley; or in the numerous Rocky Mountain resorts in Colorado, New Mexico and Utah.

Aspen, the ski capital of 'USA, has become so chic and expensive that it has lost ground to skiing 'theme parks' like the twin resorts of Winter Park and Mary Jane, also in Colorado. These operate on a non-profit basis and, among other things, encourage the disabled and very young children to take up skiing. One of the cheapest and least crowded resorts is Loveland Pass about 50 miles west of Denver; head out along I-70 toward the Eisenhower Tunnel. Another good one is Telluride, a working silver mining town until 1972 and still not over-commercialized. Hydro-electricity was invented here. During the summer all manner of informal arts festivals take place.

Two hours west of Denver is Leadville, the town that yuppie skiers bypass on their way to Aspen. Excellent 'bunkhouse' style B&B is available at Jay Jones' Club Lead (719-486-2202), and he hires out skis. A day's skiing at nearby Ski Cooper is $30 for hire and lift pass.

Utah offers excellent skiing at the resorts of Park City and Snowbird for instance, but lousy aprés-ski due to the state's repressive liquor laws.

On the whole, ski resorts in the Rockies have a relaxed and democratic atmosphere. Ski packages are rare and most resorts offer a wide range of accommodation, equipment hire facilities and instruction, which anyone can take advantage of without much prior planning. The season usually starts in late November and runs until late April. Equipment for cross-country skiing is available in all the resort towns.

Calendar of Events

mid March	Winternational World Cup, Aspen, Colorado
late June-late August	Aspen Music Festival, Colorado
late July	Frontier Days rodeo, Cheyenne, Wyoming
late July	Winter Park Jazz Festival, Colorado
August	Colorado State Fair, Pueblo
early September	Taste of Colorado Food Festival, Denver
early September	New Mexico State Fair, Albuquerque
mid September	Oktoberfest, Golden (near Denver)
late September	Oktoberfest, Worland, Wyoming
early October	International Balloon Fiesta, Albuquerque, New Mexico
mid October	Denver International Film Festival.

Los Angeles and the Southwest

Arizona   Nevada   Southern California

Southern California is a freewheeling land of sun, sea and surf. Although the beach parties depicted in the movies of the 1960s are more likely to be private these days, the pleasure-seeking lifestyle persists. Suntanned surfers haunt the beaches in search of the perfect wave and perfect partner.

The reason why visionaries and hedonists are drawn to Southern California is the sheer natural beauty of the surroundings: forests, mountains and deserts. Contradicting nature is Los Angeles, the supremely artificial nerve centre of the southwestern USA. As if making up for its lack of history, LA seems to shape the psyche of its inhabitants: it is less a city than a state of mind.

A great many people have made a great deal of money in LA. It is not a place for disguising your wealth. Rolls Royces (over 6,000 in Beverly Hills alone) and swimming pools (one-fifth of the nation's total) abound. The city's enormous wealth — its GNP is said to outstrip that of India — stems only partially from the film industry. LA is also the country's main manufacturing base.

LA has long had its seedy side, which has only intensified over the last decade. Indeed some observers say that LA is on the verge of breakdown, unable to cope with rapid population growth and rocketing unemployment. The riots in 1992 shocked the world but came as no great surprise to the locals. Sprawling and undisciplined, LA has grown from almost nothing to its current form in less than a century. It has a population of over thirteen million and covers an area about the size of Ireland. Quentin Crisp called

318

it 'New York lying down'. Raymond Chandler described it as '72 suburbs in search of a city'. But suburbs with such evocative names as Hollywood and Beverly Hills help to console the visitor who is disappointed by the lack of a city centre.

The car rules in this straggling city, where 97% of all daily trips are made by car. Walking around the block seems to be anathema to most Los Angelenos. To participate in the spirit of Southern California it is necessary to spend time lane-hopping on the freeways and generally asserting the rights of the individual over society. You are who you want to be in the city where it is safe — even desirable — to be someone you are not. Although some of the glamour has faded from the Movie Capital of the world, this busy, bright and ever-moving city is a bizarre and unique place.

THE PEOPLE

Los Angelenos are as uninhibited as their city's growth pattern. Go to the beachside area of Venice to see amazing street life — drag queens, women pumping iron, even a roller-skating Sikh in full regalia. Or go to one of the haunts of the movie moguls, such as the Polo Lounge in the shocking pink Beverly Hills Hotel on Sunset Boulevard, though star-spotters and unemployed actors usually outnumber the stars; get a friend to page you if you really want to look important. At the Colony and Trancas Supermarkets in Malibu you can rub shoulders with the celebrities who still do their own shopping.

If you are unlucky enough not to see a famous personality, you can safely assume they are seeing their divorce lawyers, plastic surgeons or analysts. But you don't have to be a movie star to be into the study of 'interpersonal exploration'. The old joke — Q. Why does it take 12 Californians to change a light bulb? A. One to change the bulb; 11 to share the experience — is well aimed.

Making Friends. You don't have to wait until your light bulb blows to meet the locals. Go to one of the beaches, rent a surf board and find someone to teach you. Or visit the informal Original Pantry (9th and Figueroa Streets), at any hour of the day or night, where waiters park you wherever there is a free seat, often at other people's tables. A relaxed and open attitude is an asset: at some southern Californian communes you may even encounter the 'hug patrol', always on the lookout for unhappy mortals in need of comfort.

Westwood, home of the University of California at Los Angeles (UCLA), is just to the south of Beverly Hills. This area teems with interesting bars and restaurants frequented by students.

If you make a particularly good friend of the opposite sex, you can take advantage of California's instant wedding industry. Chapels advertise 'no blood tests, no waiting, open Sundays' or offer free champagne to the happy couple. At a pinch you can marry in 20 minutes for $200.

CLIMATE

The casual, outdoor-orientated lifestyle of Southern California is made possible by the climate. The sun shines most of the year (bar the odd week in February or March) and Los Angeles' beaches boast a year-round average temperature of 68°F/20°C. Take advantage of the warm ocean currents because a couple of hundred miles up the coast they are much colder. Downtown LA often has no measurable rainfall from May to August. Dial 213-554-1212 for the Los Angeles weather forecast.

Don't fall into the trap of assuming that LA has an endless tropical climate; inland, frosts become increasingly common as you move higher and further from the coast. Bear in mind that the elevation within the city proper ranges from sea level to 5,000 feet.

The other (literal) blot on the horizon is the murky brown smog for which LA is notorious. The reason is not so much heavy industry as the combination of car exhaust fumes and the lie of the land which traps the air. It is said that God occasionally rolls back the smog to check that LA is still there. The atmosphere is at its eye-stinging worst during the summer, when smog warnings are issued on radio and TV.

Getting Around

Air. Los Angeles International Airport (LAX) has had as many millions spent on facelifts as the city's celebrities. But clearing immigration and customs at the Tom Bradley International Terminal is by no means a streamlined operation. At busy times (early morning and late afternoon) you can often wait an hour or two.

The San Diego Freeway (I-405) passes LAX, but the airport is normally surrounded by traffic jams. If you aren't in a hurry you might be tempted to rent a car from one of the many rental outfits in the airport. Tune into 530 AM, the airport radio station, for up-to-the-minute traffic reports.

Airport buses run from all eight terminals to downtown 24 hours a day. The cost is $12 and the 17-mile journey takes anything from 40 minutes to two hours depending on traffic, terminating at Greyhound Station at 6th and Los Angeles Streets. There is a link by public transport to downtown: catch a combination of the freeway Express 607 and Local 872. For this you need plenty of patience snd lot of change.

Cabs are prolific but not cheap, charging over $25 to downtown. Limousines and vans run to the main suburbs: SuperShuttle (213-777-8000) operates a cheap, 24-hour door-to-door service: charging $12 to downtown and $15 to Anaheim (Disneyland), for example.

There are four other airports in the Los Angeles region. You may find it more convenient — and will certainly find it less stressful — to fly into Orange County's John Wayne Airport (for Disneyland), Ontario or Burbank..

For cheap international flights, check the travel section of the *Los Angeles Times*. Student Travel Network, Suite 507, 2500 Wilshire Boulevard (213-934-8722) has good fares on international flights for normal people as well as students.

For a courier flight to the Far East, call 310-216-1637.

Bus. The Greyhound terminal is downtown at 208 E 6th St (corner of Los Angeles St, 213-620-1200). Conveniently, this is also the terminal for the local Rapid Transit District buses. Inconveniently, it is in a seedy and dangerous neighbourhood. There are many daily services north to San Francisco (8-12 hour journey for $39) and south to San Diego (2½-3 hour journey for $14). A cheaper option to San Francisco is the Green Tortoise service every Sunday night for $30; book in advance on 310-392-1990.

Train. Union Station (800 N Alameda, downtown) would have been even more impressive in the days when it was in full use. Admire the combination of Spanish and Art Deco architecture from the 1930s.

There are eight daily services to San Diego ($24 for the three-hour journey) and one to Oakland/San Francisco ($75 for the ten-hour trip). If you're planning to take the train to Chicago ($205), note that the *Southwest Chief* runs daily and takes 40 hours — this is about 20 hours faster than the *Eagle*, which has a circuitous route via Dallas and runs just three times a week. The *Desert Wind* (daily, via Salt Lake City) comes somewhere in between. For further information call Amtrak on 213-624-0171.

Driving. Given the scale of LA and the uncertainies of public transport, you may want to rent a car even if you are going to stay for only a few hours. In addition to the rental companies at the airport and elsewhere, there are many low-priced outfits: if Rent-a-Wreck doesn't appeal, try Thrifty (800-337-2277) or Avon Rent-a-Car (800-635-7888), where rates start at about $25 a day.

Driveaways. Having your car delivered is a common practice among the locals, and driveaway companies proliferate. Try Auto Driveaway, 3407 W 6th St in downtown LA (213-661-6100) or National Auto, 8235 Sepulveda Place, Van Nuys (818-988-9000). Most cars need to be delivered to the east, but it is worth enquiring about destinations up the Pacific coast.

Hitch-hiking. It is difficult to get a lift out of LA since so much freeway traffic is local. But in view of the high proportion of students and alternative types, it is worth having a go. Just choose any freeway entrance heading in roughly the right direction and be sure to use a sign.

CITY TRANSPORT

City Layout. Distances in LA are daunting: Beverly Hills to Anaheim (for Disneyland) is over 40 miles; and one of LA's main streets, Wilshire Boulevard, is 27 miles long. The main area on which to focus is the zone spreading west from downtown to the sea, the degree of wealth generally increasing the further you progress. Visitors are therefore surprised to find Hollywood directly west of the downtown area. A district where stars used to flit from boutique to boutique is now characterized by homelessness and tacky souvenir shops. Hollywood is also the centre of the sex industry, and boys and girls sell themselves in broad daylight along the more sordid sections of Sunset Boulevard. West LA, incorporating West Hollywood, Beverly Hills and Westwood, fits the more traditional image of Tinseltown, with million-dollar mansions, high security and leafy avenues. Sunset Strip and Melrose Avenue in West Hollywood are the focus of LA's nightlife.

Sunset Boulevard, with some fine Art Deco houses, runs west to the sea and Santa Monica, LA's most elegant beach resort. To the west lies Malibu, where the likes of Madonna and Sylvester Stallone live in paranoid exclusivity. To the south is Venice Beach, the haunt of the young and LA at its most indolent and entertaining, with street shows galore. The more southerly beaches of Manhattan, Hermosa and Huntington are quiet by comparison.

Even if you base yourself between Beverly Hills and Hollywood so that you can walk to both, going any distance on foot is not a rewarding experience. The Los Angeles Police Department zealously enforces the laws on jaywalking) you would be forgiven for thinking (and suggesting) that the police have better things to do, but ignoring a 'Don't Walk' sign can earn you a $25 ticket; and watch out for the taxis specializing in 'kerbing', which involves hounding pedestrians until the alternative to your refusing to get in is a fist in the teeth.

Bus. LA has a surprisingly extensive network of city buses, operated by the

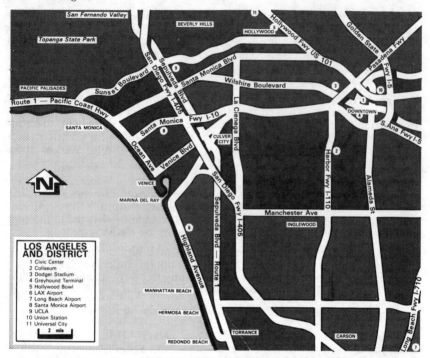

LOS ANGELES
AND DISTRICT
1 Civic Center
2 Coliseum
3 Dodger Stadium
4 Greyhound Terminal
5 Hollywood Bowl
6 LAX Airport
7 Long Beach Airport
8 Santa Monica Airport
9 UCLA
10 Union Station
11 Universal City

2 mile

Rapid Transit District or RTD (213-626-4455). The system is inevitably complicated and buses run infrequently in many cases, but fares are cheap — $1.10 a ride (exact change only) or 10 tickets for $9. There are surcharges on express buses and transfers cost an extra 25c. If you simply want to go in a long, straight line, the service is fine; otherwise a cross-town trip can take half a day.

The best bus service downtown is run by DASH (800-874-8885), which operates frequently during the day Monday to Saturday, just in the downtown area. Having a foreign passport makes you eligible for the tourist pass which permits unlimited travel on the whole system for $2 a day. A monthly pass, valid from the first day of the month, can be bought a week on either side of the day for $30.

Metrorail. LA's fledgling underground railway system so far consists of just the Blue Line, linking downtown and Long Beach. When the network is completed, the frequent services will greatly enhance mobility around the city.

Car. Over half a million cars pour into downtown daily. Two-thirds of the surface area of the business district is swallowed up by streets and parking lots. Even so, parking can be tricky and rush hours are a nightmare. Try to find a residential area behind the major commercial thoroughfares where it is usually possible to park on the street for free — some parking lots downtown charge as much as $2 for 20 minutes. The fine for non-payment is a hefty $53.

If you are going to be in LA for a few days, get hold of a full street directory (about the size of a phone book). It is almost impossible to navigate the hundreds of miles of freeway with tourist or gas station handouts.

Taxis. Taxis are difficult to find except at big hotels. They do not cruise the streets for fares. The initial charge is usually $2 plus $1.50 a mile. If you order a taxi from the Yellow Pages, make sure the company you choose is located in your section of town.

Cycling. You can hire bicycles at the Santa Monica and Venice beaches. From here you can set off along the beachside bicycle path as far as Palos Verdes, 28 miles south. The UCLA campus and Griffith Park, just north of the Hollywood Bowl, are also pleasant places to cycle around. The Los Angeles County Transportation Commission (818 West 7th St) publishes a free bike map, which you can order by calling its Bike Map Hotline on 213-244-6539. The *Los Angeles Times* sometimes features cycle touring maps.

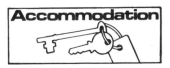

Assuming you do not have the income of Harrison Ford, you will probably not be able to afford the faded splendour of the Chateau Marmont Hotel in Hollywood, hangout of pop and movie stars. You must first decide which area of Los Angeles you wish to make your base. The four main areas to choose from are: downtown, Hollywood, Beverly Hills/Westwood and the beaches.

The disadvantage of downtown is that it is not a safe place to walk around after the offices and shops empty at 6pm. There are plenty of cheap and sleazy hotels from about $12 a night in the neighbourhood of the Greyhound terminal, but these are not recommended for the faint hearted. Hotels downtown offering reasonable rooms and good prices include the LA Huntington Hotel (752 S Main St, 213-627-3186) and the Orchid Hotel (819 S Flower St, 213-624-5855), both of which charge $35-40 for a double.

Hollywood is probably the liveliest area in which to stay, though like downtown it is not particularly safe after dark. About the cheapest rooms you'll find are at Hasting's Hotel (6162 Hollywood Boulevard, 213-464-4136) or the St Moritz (5849 Sunset Boulevard, 213-467-2174), with rooms for about $40/$45 and $25/$30 respectively. In Beverly Hills, the Crescent Hotel (403 N Crescent Drive, 310-247-0505) is up a notch from these, but offers a good weekly rate, e.g. $300 for a double.

On Santa Monica's Ocean Avenue, very ordinary motel rooms go for over $60 a night. Unless you opt for the AYH hostel, you would do better in Venice, which has a good supply of cheap hotels. These include the Venice Beach Hotel directly on the beach (25 Windward Avenue, 310-399-7649), which charges $15-20 (single) or $30-50 double.

Hostels. There are three AYH hotels in LA. The largest is in Santa Monica (1436 Second St, 310-393-9913), a couple of blocks from the pier. The Angels Gate Park hostel is in the South Bay area (Building 613, 3601 South Gaffey St, San Pedro, 310-831-8109). For easy access to Disneyland, the Fullerton Hacienda is ideal (1700 North Harbor Blvd, 714-738-3721), though it has just 15 beds. Advance bookings are usually unnecessary, except perhaps at the height of the summer tourist season.

If these locations are too farflung to suit you, try the YMCA Hostel in Hollywood (1553 N Hudson Avenue, 213-467-4161) between Sunset and Hollywood Boulevards and four blocks west of Vine St, where a dorm bed costs $11, a double room $39. The LA Guest Hostel (1518 Rockwood St,

213-250-7921), near the Civic Centre downtown, has dormitory accommodation for $11 per night; advance reservation is recommended since there are only 16 beds.

There are several hostels in Venice. The Interclub Hostel at 2221 Lincoln Blvd (310-305-0250), 15 minutes from the beach, has dormitory beds for $14. Or, for longer stays, the Share-Tel International Hostel (20 Brooks Avenue, 213-392-0325) has shared apartments from $110 per week.

Bed and Breakfast. Most agencies list B & Bs in both LA and Southern California. Rates start at about $40 for two, but you need to book about a month in advance to secure a cheap room.

Bed & Breakfast International (151 Ardmore Rd, Kensington 94707; 510-525-4569) is the oldest B & B agency in the state and has over 300 listings. There are several other smaller agencies, some of which also impose a two-day minimum stay. Try California Houseguests International (6051 Lindley Avenue £6, Tarzana 91356; 818-344-7878), or Bed & Breakfast of Los Angeles (310-498-0552).

House Exchanges. If you plan to spend several weeks in Southern California, you may want to consider swapping houses with a resident, a practice which is well established in this part of the US. See the introductory section *Accommodation* for details and useful addresses.

Camping. Many of the American families which pour into California camp near Disneyland in Orange County. It is usually necessary to book in advance; this can be done through Ticketron outlets. Get a list of campground addresses from the LA tourist office. All campsites are a long way from downtown. The cost per site is about $15.

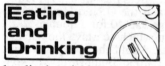

Eating and Drinking

Because of the large Hispanic population (about a third of the total) there are many very good Mexican restaurants and cafés. The greatest concentration of Mexican restaurants and stalls is in the Barrio, a poor but lively neighbourhood east of Union Station. There are some good places on the cobbled Olvera Street, site of the original Spanish settlement. But for a less prettified experience walk along Brooklyn Avenue, where La Parrilla (at 2126) is a favourite — though not for vegetarians.

Chinatown, a few blocks west of Union Station on Hill Street,is small and not in San Francisco's league. Koreatown, further west between Vermont and Western, just south of Wilshire Blvd), is much larger and more exciting, and makes fewer allowances for tourists. Try the Hat Bat Beef Soup (4163 West 5th St), which serves only one dish, and the Ham Hung (809 South Ardmore), a popular noodle bar.

For Japanese food go to Little Tokyo, just south of Chinatown. The cheapest sushi bars and noodle houses are in the Weller Court and Japanese Village Plaza, off South San Pedro St. Try Daisuke Okonomiyaki in Weller Court, which serves stuffed pancakes, cooked at your table.

If you have begun to tire of ethnic cuisine, try Larry Parker's Beverly Hills Diner (206 Beverly Drive, 310-274-5655), where you can get any kind of omelette at any time of the day or night. The best burger in town is reputed to be at Pete's Grandburger, corner of Main and 3rd Streets (213-624-6086), but it closes at 6pm. For sinful hot fudge sundaes go to C C Browns (7007 Hollywood Blvd, 213-464-9726). In West Hollywood is the ubiquitous Hard Rock Café (8600 Beverly Blvd, 310-276-7665).

The Original Pantry (corner of 9th and Figueroa Streets) has already been mentioned as a good place to meet people. Its motto is 'we never close', proved by the fact that there are no locks on the door. Once run by ex-cons, it has lots of local colour. Eat steaks while you marvel at the statistics quoted on fact sheets which circulate, including such fascinating information as the number of celery sticks which have been served since the establishment opened in 1924. Be prepared to queue.

You will need to spend a little more for the chance of seeing a famous actor or actress. One of the cheaper options is to eat breakfast at Duke's Coffee Shop on Sunset Boulevard (310-652-3100) — the working breakfast is said to have been invented in LA). One of Hollywood's classic eating houses is the Musso and Frank Grill at 6667 Hollywood Blvd, which has remained (self-consciously) unchanged for two generations. It goes some way to evoking the old-style Hollywood, and is popular among film crews. The food is mostly fry-ups, but don't miss the clam chowder on Fridays.

Smoking is prohibited in all Hollywood restaurants.

DRINKING

Anyone homesick for the UK should try one of the British-owned pubs, such as the Cat & Fiddle at 6530 Sunset Blvd (213-468-3800) or Ye Olde King's Head, corner of 2nd St and Santa Monica Blvd. Along with your shepherds pie or faggot and peas at the King's Head you can drink Guinness, Sam Smith's and Fullers, and even play darts. Both pubs are full of expats.

LA has numerous offbeat bars, including one — the Beverly Hills Juice Club, 8382 Beverly Boulevard — which sells grass nectar (of the lawn variety) and another which serves nothing but mineral water. Most bars serve the margarita, the drink of Southern California, based on tequila.

While Hollywood is not a great area in which to stroll late at night, there are some likeable bars. Boardner's (1652 Cherokee Avenue, 213-462-9621) is relaxed and unpretentious, though livens up at weekends. Next to the Roxy nightclub at 9015 Sunset Blvd is the Rainbow bar (and restaurant), where Marilyn Monroe first met Joe di Maggio, on a blind date. It has seen many stars since, but now seems to be patronized mainly by exotic-looking women in frighteningly short skirts. Melrose Avenue is a good (and also trendy) place to bar hop. So too is Venice, where Rebecca's (2005 Pacific Avenue) should not be missed. The main concentration of gay bars in West Hollywood is around Santa Monica Blvd and in the Silverlake district.

To rise above the evils of freeways and parking hassles, visit the bar at Yamashiro, on top of a hill not far from the Hollywood Bowl. The view at sunset is superb.

Some bars open as early as 6am, but all close by 2am. Los Angeles is not a late-night city.

While Los Angeles (or at least Hollywood) promotes itself as 'Entertainment City USA', Eastcoasters don't think much of LA's cultural achievements; hence their joke: Q: What's the difference between Los Angeles and yoghurt? A: Yoghurt has culture. But while LA doesn't go in for much highbrow entertainment, the city is by no means a cultural void.

Many visitors to LA feel adequately entertained — and have their prejudices confirmed — by a drive along the 30 miles of Sunset Boulevard (an interesting alternative is to spend a couple of days walking it), or a cruise around Beverly Hills spotting celebrities' houses. A woman on the corner of Sunset Blvd and Mapleton sells Star Maps, to help you in your search.

For the best view of the spectacular suburban sprawl go to Griffith Park Observatory, where James Dean filmed the car scene in *Rebel Without a Cause*.

Museums. Despite the jibes from the East Coast, LA has some excellent art museums; note all of those mentioned below shut on Monday. The Museum of Contemporary Art or MOCA (250 S Grand between 2nd and 4th; open 11am-6pm) is devoted to post-1945 art and is housed in a spectacular building. Also downtown and in a similar vein is the confusingly permanent Temporary Contemporary (152 N Central Avenue), where you can see the likes of Rothko and Hockney. For some less conventional art appreciation, go up to the Hollywood Hills, where you can see how David Hockney has painted his house off Mulholland Drive.

The Los Angeles County Museum of Art or LACMA (5905 Wilshire Blvd; open 10am-5pm) in West LA also has good modern works, while the collection in the Norton Simon Museum in Pasadena (Colorado and North Orange Blvd; open noon-6pm Thursday to Sunday) is broader, stretching from Botticelli to Degas and Henry Moore. The stupendously rich J Paul Getty Museum, housed in a Roman-style villa in Malibu, is worth a visit even if you aren't into classical sculpture and French 18th-century art. It is open 10am-5pm, admission free. To get there catch RTD bus 434 from Santa Monica, 5 miles east. If you go by car, call 310-458-2003 to book a parking space.

One of LA's more offbeat museums is the Museum of Neon Art (704 Traction Avenue) which includes a neon Mona Lisa and elaborate movie house marquees from days gone by. It is east of Little Tokyo between 2nd and 3rd Streets, and is open 11am-5pm (admission $2.50).

Everybody in search of a record contract ends up performing in LA: a staggering one-third of the world's pop and rock music is recorded in the city. The Museum of Rock Art at 6427 Sunset Boulevard in Hollywood is devoted to rock music memorabilia such as album covers and vintage TV shows. It opens noon-4.30pm from Wednesday to Saturday.

At Long Beach you can view the largest aircraft ever to fly and visit the biggest ocean liner afloat — the *Queen Mary*, moored at Pier J. Alongside it is Howard Hughes' flying folly, the eight-engined *Spruce Goose*, built mainly of birch and weighing over 200 tons. The complex (which has restaurants, shops and a tacky 'Londontowne' area) opens 10am-6pm in winter, 9am-9pm in summer; admission is $17.50.

Film and Television Studios. Contrary to popular belief, LA's film studios are not in Hollywood, but are spread around the suburbs. The tours around Universal Studios (University City Plaza, 818-508-9600) are so popular that you must be prepared to queue for up to several hours. Visitors are shown around in 'glam trams', in which you will be attacked by the shark from *Jaws*, besieged by enemy aliens from the Battlestar Galactica and barely survive all manner of disasters including rock slides, collapsing bridges, fire, flood and an earthquake measuring 8.3 on the Richter Scale. *The Star Trek Adventure* is a must for Spock fans. The tour takes four hours and costs $24.95. The studios are open 8am-10.30pm daily, with shorter opening hours in winter.

To see films being made on location, contact City of LA Motion Picture and Video Production (213-485-5324), which issues a daily *Shoot Sheet*, giving a list of which companies are filming and where. The *Daily Variety* and *Hollywood Reporter* newspapers also list film schedules, usually just on Tuesday and Thursday.

Tours of the NBC Television Studios (3000 W Alameda Avenue, Burbank, 310-840-3537) are available for $7. You might get a chance to see a programme being taped. Other TV studios also throw open their doors to the public. Enquire about tickets at the Visitors Information Center, or contact CBS Studios (7800 Beverly Boulevard, 213-852-2455).

If you are interested in movie memorabilia, visit the Chinese Theater at 6925 Hollywood Blvd, where you can see foot, hand, elbow, etc. prints of movie stars in the cement outside. The numerous cinemas along the Boulevard show films all day long.

Theme Parks. Anaheim, 40 miles southeast of downtown LA, is the site of the original Disneyland created in 1955. It should not be confused with the much newer Walt Disney World in Florida. No trip to Southern California would be complete without a visit to this fantasy world. It takes more than a day to see everything, including the magnificent electric parade and evening fireworks display. The Space Mountain ride in which you experience a flight through outer space is worth the hour-long queues, as is the Splash Mountain waterslide and the Captain E/O show, in which Michael Jackson dances in 3D.

The park is open daily 9am-midnight in summer, but closes at 6pm on weekdays during the winter. Note that it is an alcohol-free zone. Greyhound buses from LA take about 50 minutes, the RTD 460 a little longer. The monorail from Disneyland drops passengers off at the licensed Disney Hotel just outside the park.

There are other substantial entertainments in the region. Six Flags Magic Mountain (I-5 north at Valencia) has the Colossus, the world's largest dual track wooden rollercoaster, as well as the Revolution — in which thrill-seekers turn a terrifying upside-down circle in a vast loop. Knotts Berry Farm at Buena Park (close to Disneyland) is another amusement park with a variety of daredevil rides.

The Calendar section of the Sunday *Los Angeles Times* provides a thorough run down of what's on in the city. The *Los Angeles Weekly* and the *Los Angeles Reader* — both free from liquor stores and other outlets — are informative and essential if you want full entertainment listings of alternative things to do.

Music. The 17,630 capacity Hollywood Bowl features a varied programme of classical music from July to mid-September. There is so little rain that in 45 years there have been just three postponements. It is worth going just to sit under the stars and watch the people. The bandshell was designed by Frank Lloyd Wright's son. At the other end of the spectrum are the pop video emporiums, especially popular among teenagers.

In between these cultural extremes, there is an astonishing choice of excellent rock acts. Some of the top venues include several on Sunset Boulevard, such as Whiskey A Go Go (8901), the Roxy (9009) and Club Lingerie (6507), and The Palace (1735 N Vine Street), also in Hollywood.

At My Place in Santa Monica specializes in lesser-known blues/rock performers. For information about traditional blues gigs, look for the black community's paper published on Thursdays called the *Los Angeles Sentinel*. The mecca for country fans and star names like Jerry Lee Lewis and Rick Nelson is the Palomino at 6907 Lankershim Blvd, North Hollywood (818-764-4010), where it is hard to move for cowboy hats.

Many of the bars and restaurants along Ventura Boulevard in the San Fernando Valley feature excellent bands and groups on a regular basis, with no cover charge. For good jazz, try the Blue Note Café at number 11941 (tel: 818-760-3348).

Throughout the summer the open-air Greek Theater (2700 N Vermont Avenue near Griffith Park) and the Universal Amphitheater (Hollywood Freeway at Lankershim Blvd) star big show business names such as Bette Midler. Tickets can be bought at Ticketron offices throughout the city.

Theatre. LA is an important centre for live theatre. Many productions star famous film and television actors tired of celluloid. Try the Mark Taper Forum (135 N Grand Avenue, which puts on alternative productions, or the Westwood Playhouse near the UCLA campus (310-208-5454). Major Broadway productions are staged at the Schubert Theatre (2020 Avenue of the Stars, Century City) and the Music Center in downtown LA.

Nightlife. Your search for nightlife should focus around Sunset Boulevard. In addition to bars and nightclubs of every persuasion, try out the Comedy Store (8433 W Sunset Blvd; 213-656-6225), which features some very talented comedians. Only the young and fit should sample LA's wilder clubs, such as the Scream (Embassy Hotel, Grand St, Fridays and Saturdays at 11pm). The Troubadour (9081 Santa Monica Blvd, 310-247-4890) is a more established club and hosts good bands.

SPORT AND RECREATION

Spectator Sports. Los Angeles can boast more big league teams than any other US city including New York. There are two professional football teams, the LA Rams and the LA Raiders. The LA Dodgers (National League) delight baseball fans at Dodger Stadium in Chavez Ravine (213-224-1400), while the California Angels (American League) play in Anaheim (714-254-3100). Even if baseball is a closed book to you, there is something to be said for sitting in the sun, drinking beer, eating hot dogs and soaking up the atmosphere of the Dodger fans. The cheapest seats cost $6.

The Los Angeles Kings (ice hockey) and the Los Angeles Lakers (basketball) both play in the Forum near the airport (310-419-3182). Since the demise of the Aztecs, there is no longer a professional soccer team in the area, although thee are dozens of soccer leagues.

Horse racing is at the Hollywood Park and Santa Anita tracks, and also at the beautiful Del Mar racecourse, just north of San Diego. Throughout the summer there are volleyball competitions all the way down the coastal strip, and the Championship Surfer Meet at Huntington in September packs the town with spectators.

Participation. A great deal of the social life of Southern California revolves around outdoor activities. After a morning's sunbathing, you may feel inclined to get some exercise on the ski slopes. There are 15 ski areas inland from Los Angeles, offering all types of slope. The season usually runs from November until April.

Ocean sportsfishing services are available at Long Beach, Marina del Rey,

Malibu, Redondo Beach, San Pedro, Santa Monica, Seal Branch, Dana Point and Newport Beach. Marina del Rey is the world's largest man-made pleasure boat harbour, with the number of posh cocktail bars competing with the number of yachts.

Roller skating is another popular form of exercise as well as a means of transport along the boardwalks bordering the beach. Skates can be rented for about $2.50 an hour; additional protection and wrist guards are usually a dollar or so extra, but are a good investment for the amateur.

There are thousands of tennis courts in LA, including private, pay-for-play and free public facilities. Most of them are floodlit for night play as well.

Do not assume that someone who refuses to let you use his or her swimming pool is being unfriendly; so great is the risk of lawsuits, that only close relations or trusted friends are allowed near them. The ocean may not be a perfect alternative, since it is usually chilly — East Coast beaches south of Virginia are warmer.

SHOPPING

If it's not on sale in southern California, it probabaly doesn't exist. Shopping runs the gamut from high-priced quality department stores and trendy boutiques to inexpensive national chain stores. The West Coast's influential garment industry is centered on downtown LA, the city that claims to have invented both the bikini and blue jeans. The stores in this area are shabby rather than glittering and specialize in selling casual and sports clothes at bargain prices. The massive Cooper building (860 S Los Angeles) contains about 80 discount stores, where you can find real bargains amongst the dross.

Beverly Hills — and Rodeo Drive in particular — is for the serious shopper. Visit on a Saturday when the posers are out in full force. Some of the world's most expensive shops, including Gucci's and Hermes, are congregated along Rodeo Drive from Wilshire to Santa Monica Boulevards. Don't try to browse in the ultra-exclusive Bijan — you have to make an appointment. The Beverly Center Mall is less exclusive.

For the trendiest clothing, Melrose Avenue has developed into what King's Road, Chelsea used to be in the Sixties. It is worth a stroll along the street just to see the weird and wonderful clothes of the people out shopping.

If you are fed up with LA, visit Thomas Bros Maps & Travel Bookstore (603 W 7th St) or Maps to Anywhere (1514 North Hillhurst Avenue, Hollywood) to plan your escape.

THE MEDIA

Radio. KFWB (980 AM, 98 FM) gives local and national news 24 hours a day; KMPC (710 AM) is best for sport, KRLA (1110 AM) specializes in old rock music; KROQ (106.7 FM) is the station for the latest hits. KKGO (105 FM) plays virtually nothing but jazz; KFAC (92.3 FM) is the 24-hour classical music station.

For those interested in information about cheap flights across the Atlantic, KFAC (1330 AM) presents a two-hour programme for UK expatriates every Sunday morning, and also plays old British comedy favourites.

Newspapers. The *Los Angeles Times*, the main daily newspaper, is excellent. The *Herald Examiner* has a lot of ground to make up. British papers are on sale at the University City Library (630 W 5th St). *British Weekly* is a magazine for the expat community in and around LA.

Crime and Safety

Los Angeles is one of the most dangerous cities in the world. Random killings are almost commonplace. In August 1992, the worst month on record, 263 homicides were recorded — more than one every three hours. This was a few months after the riots in which 53 people died. Even so, the statistical chances of being involved are tiny. Most crimes involving visitors tend to be thefts from hotel rooms and the occasional purse-snatching in the street.

Avoid south-central LA — particularly Watts — where poverty combines with drug-trafficking, gang activity and general hostility. It is a good idea to avoid Santa Monica Pier and the Venice beaches after dark. The downtown area attracts all sort of wierd and seedy characters at night, and Hollywood and Vine can be similarly creepy; muggings after dark are not uncommon. South and Central LA is the area most notorious for armed battles between rival street gangs. These gangs, which derive their income from drug dealing, have spilled over increasingly into more peaceful suburbs.

Marijuana has been decriminalized in the state of California for quantities under one ounce. Many Southern Californians drive down to Tijuana in Mexico, where medicines which require a prescription in the US are freely available.

As well as the threat from malevolent humans, LA is in constant danger of a severe earthquake. The last serious tremor killed six people in 1987. Seismologists estimate that there is a 50% chance of a massive quake striking the area in the next 30 years. Oddly enough, the massively tall buildings in downtown LA are among the safest places to be during an earthquake due to state-of-the art engineering.

Other hazards which afflict the area are mudslides (winter), brush fires (summer and fall), high einds (fall and winter) and high surf (summer and winter). But most Angelenos survive.

Help and Information *i*

There are two area codes for Los Angeles, 213 and 310; for the San Fernando Valley dial 818. Orange County is 714.

Information: The Greater Los Angeles Convention Visitors Bureau is at 685 S Figueroa St (213-689-8822). There are several branch information offices, including at Hollywood (Janes House, 6541 Hollywood Blvd, 213-461-4213), Disneyland (800 W Katella Avenue, 714-999-8999) and Santa Monica (1400 Ocean Avenue, 310-393-7593). These offices provide maps, calendars of events and tickets for TV shows. Also ring the Info Line (213-686-0950) for a 24-hour information and referral service.

UK Consulate-General: 3701 Wilshire Blvd (310-477-3322), between Barrington and Bundy Streets in West La.

American Express: the Hilton Center, 901 W 7th St (213-627-4800); Beverly Center, 131 N La Cienega Blvd £706 (310-659-1682).

Post Office: the main office downtown is 901 S Broadway, LA 90014.

Medical Emergencies: USC Medical Center, 1200 N State St (213-226-2622).

Dental Service: 213-481-2133.

24 hour drugstore: Thrifty Drugs, 3rd St and Vermont Avenue (213-381-5257).

Traveler's Aid: Greyhound Bus Terminal (213-625-2501) and International Airport (310-646-2271).

Gay and Lesbian Community Services Centre: 1213 H Highland Avenue (464-7400).

Further Afield   61

SAN DIEGO

In terms of population, San Diego rather than San Francisco is California's second city. Just 15 miles north of the Mexican border town of Tijuana, San Diego is blessed with clean air, miles of beaches and weather once voted the most perfect in the USA. Once a haven for senior citizens, the median age has dropped and the city is undergoing a facelift. A $165 million convention centre with a sail-like rooftop structure has already become an architectural landmark on the city's skyline. San Diego has ample attractions including the USA's best zoo, the fascinating museums of Balboa Park and Old Town and an environment infinitely more pleasant than that of LA.

Arrival and Departure. San Diego International Airport (Lindbergh Field) is at the northwest edge of town, across from Harbor Island, and has services from most major North American cities. Fog sometimes delays take-offs and landings. Take San Diego Transit bus 2 downtown for $1.25 or a cab for about $8. You can take a bus to San Diego both by Greyhound whose terminal is at 120 West Broadway at 1st Ave (239-9171) and Green Tortoise (1-800-227-4766). Amtrak rail services terminate at Santa Fe Depot, 1050 Kettner Blvd (239-9021), which is also the terminus for the Trolley to the Mexican border. If you plan to cross into Mexico, see page 260 for details of formalities. The main freeway approaches to San Diego are I-5 which runs down a lovely coast road from Los Angeles, and I-8 which comes in from the desert to the east. Hitch-hiking along either is difficult.

City Transport. Downtown is easy to find your way round because of its grid design of streets: consecutive numbers running north-south, letters A-L running east-west. San Diego is safer than most American cities.

It is easy to reach most areas in the city on the regional transit system. A new bayside trolley line serves the convention centre and downtown. Fares vary: 85c for North County transit routes, $1.25 for local routes, $1.50 for express bus routes, and $2.25-$2.75 for commuter rides; some transfers are free, others are free. Exact change is required. Some buses have bike racks. The Transit Store at 449 Broadway sells a one-day unlimited travel pass for $4, four days for $12.

You can rent a car at standard California rates. Best bargain: Rent-a-Car Cheap at 1747 Pacific Hwy (232-2041) where there are bangers going for $8 a day unlimited mileage plus insurance for another $8 a day. San Diego is cyclist's paradise. Caltrans, 4080 Taylor St (231-24530) provide maps and pamphlets of bike hire shops and paths. Most shops will also rent you skates, boogie boards, and even surfboards.

Accommodation. As tourism is booming, making reservations makes sense. Inexpensive digs can be found in hostels, Y's, and even no-frills motels for anywhere between $13-18 a night for a single. There are AYH hostels at 3790 Udall St (223-4778) and 170 Palm Avenue, Imperial Beach (423-8039). The Armed Services YMCA Hostel at 500 W Broadway (232-1133) has dormitory beds for only $5 a night. The Hotel del Coronado was featured in the Marilyn Monroe film *Some Like It Hot*.

Eating and Drinking. San Diego boasts Afghan, barbecue, Brazilian, Cajun, Greek, Middle Eastern, Mexican, Oriental, seafood and vegetarian restaurants. For 'pure' Mexican (as opposed to Tex Mex), go out to El Tecolote at 6110 Friars Road West in Mission Valley (295-2087). The 'Natural Food' at the Kung Food Vegetarian Restaurant near Balboa Park (2949 5th Ave, 298-7302) in imaginative; the brunch on weekend mornings is particularly recommended. For Chinese, try the inexpensive Hong Kong Restaurant at 3781 4th Ave where Cantonese, Mandarin or Szechuan main dish, soup, rice and eggroll can be had for about $5; for good value, San Diego Chicken Pie Shop at 2633 El Cajon Boulevard (295-0156) where pie, whipped potatoes, vegetables, roll and dessert sets you back a staggeringly slight $4. Go to the Farmer's Bazaar for cheap fresh fruit and vegetables. The best barbecue in California is Gellerosa Ranch at 120 Ash St (232-2838), featuring a wood burning pit, Oklahoma secret sauce, beef, ribs, chicken, hot links and crab salad. You might overdose on protein.

San Diego has plenty of good bars, and some reasonable wineries to visit and sample in the Temecula Valley an hour north. The Princess of Wales pub at the corner of India and Dare Streets sells Double Diamond ale, plus fish and chips.

Exploring. San Diego had some impressive museums, particularly the Museum of Photographic Arts, San Diego Museum of Art and the Timken Art Gallery in Balboa Park, a park larger in area than downtown SD and ideal for picnics. A 'Passport to Balboa Park' gives you entrance tickets to all the museums for $10 (Information Center in the House of Hospitality, 1549 El Prado, Balboa Park, 232-2053).

Entertainment. Like LA, San Diego has a lot going for it with the additional advantage of having it contained within a reasonable area. Don't leave town without seeing the zoo in Balboa Park (234-3153); and visit Sea World at Mission Bay unless you've visited its counterparts in Florida, Ohio or Texas. To find out what's going on, consult the *Reader*, a free weekly paper that lists dates, places and prices. The Times Arts Tix Ticket Center at Horton Plaza on Broadway Circle between 3rd and 4th Avenue features half-price day of performance tickets to theatre, music and dance events, from 10am. In summer, Shakespeare is performed in the outdoor Old Globe threatre in Balboa Park. Twilight in the Park summer concerts are held in the Organ Pavilion from 6.30-7.30pm.

Plenty of music and dance is provided by the San Diego Foundation for the Performing Arts (701 B St, 234-5855), the San Diego Opera (232 7656) and San Diego Symphony (1245 7th Ave 699-4205). Among the best clubs for blues or rock are the Mandolin Wind at 308 University Ave (297-3017) and Diego's Club and Cantina, a surfers' hangout on 860 Garnet Ave (272-1241).

Like most Americans, denizens of SD think they have a comic genius. If you're interested in seeing budding comics, try Comedy Isle at the Bahia Resort Hotel, 998 West Mission Drive (488-6872), the Comedy Store on 916 Pearl St in nearby La Jolla (454-9176) or The Improv at 832 Garnet Ave (232-3121).

Sport. On any weekend at Mission Bay Park, a 4,600-acre acquatic park, countless swimmers, sail surfers, water-skiers and rowers are afloat on the Pacific — despite the danger of raw sewage floating up from Mexico. There's also horseracing nearby and both greyhound racing and jai alai 15 miles south in Tijuana. For those interested in spectator sports, there's the San

Diego Chargers for pro footall, the San Diego Padres for baseball and the San Diego Gulls hockey team. Basketball fans might appreciate one of the best American college teams called the San Diego State University Aztecs. The oddest (and pehaps most enjoyable) SD sport, though, has to be whale watching. There's a free whale-watching station at Cabrillo National Monument on Point Loma, as well as cruises provided by the National History Museum and numerous private companies. However, it's only during winter months that the California Grey Whale and others migrate close enough to shore.

Shopping. The huge Horton Plaza is six floors of shops on Broadway between 3rd and 4th Avenue. Try the Price Bazaar at 1140 Broadway, Chula Vista, where 60 shops include a constantly changing bazaar with handmade items; Clothing Clearance Centers (three locations) with designer men's clothes at discount prices; and the Southpaw Shoppe at 803 W. Harbor Dr, featuring items for left-handed people. Bargains on liquor and Mexican goods may be obtained in Tijuana.

Help and Information. The area code for San Diego is 619.

Information: Visitor Information Center, 11 Horton Plaza (236-1212) and San Diego International Convention & Visitors Bureau, 1200 3rd Ave, Suite 824, San diego, CA 92101 (232-3101). The last-named sends enquirers an excellent package of maps, brochures, calendars and fact sheets.

Post Office: 2535 Midway Dr (221-3310).

American Express: 1640 Camino del Rio N. (297-8101).

Travelers Aid: Airport, 231-7376.

Women's Crisis Hotline: 232-3088.

Lesbian and Gay Men's Center: 692-GAYS.

Apart from the road south to San Diego, there are two principal escape routes from the glitter and glamour of LA. Many people set off on the eight or nine hour drive to San Francisco, preferring to take the very scenic Highway 1 which hugs the cliff-lined coast. There are many worthwhile stop-overs such as the quintessentially Southern Californian lotus-eating town of Santa Barbara where everyone sips cocktails by the pool all day, and Big Sur, once an important hippie landmark. It is possible to sleep rough on the beaches along this coast, though campsites are readily available in the national forests and parks.

The other direction which might tempt you is inland, to visit forests, deserts, Mount Whitney, which is the highest mountain in the continental USA. Place names like Yucca Valley, Cactus Gardens and Palm Desert immediately convey the climate and geography of much of the area. The states of Arizona, Nevada and southern California are very dry and attract hayfever and rheumatism sufferers from all over the country. Palm Springs is the millionaire oasis resort about 120 miles southeast of LA. Not only is every home and public building air-conditioned, but the city planners are working on ways to air condition outdoor areas such as restaurant patios and complete streets. This is not surprising, considering that the average daily maximum between June and September is over 100F.

Death Valley's temperatures are even more horrifying. This enormous area on the border with Nevada is almost intolerably hot in summer (average July high is 115F), and therefore heavily visited in winter. But the coloured landscape and odd rock formations make a visit worthwhile. Be sure to take enough water in the summer (see the section on *Summer Driving* in the Introduction).

For spectacular natural scenery in more temperate conditions, the adjoining parks of Sequoia and Kings Canyon, due north of LA, are worthwhile, the hardwood trees called Sequoia gigantea (after a Cherokee chief) grow to mammoth proportions: the largest is 275 feet tall and 102 feet in circumference.

And for the be-all and end-all in natural wonders, you will want to make the pilgrimage to the Grand Canyon in northern Arizona. Its immensity and beauty are sufficient to compensate for the crowds and commercialism which are never absent from this unmissable tourist destination. All manner of accommodation is available, but must be booked well in advance. Ring the central Hotels Switchboard for reservations (638-2401) or for campsite information try the Backcountry Reservations Office, South Rim Visitors Center (Grand Canyon National Park, Arizona 86023, 602-638-2474).

It is possible to hike to the base of the canyon (which is a mile deep) to the Colorado River, but this should not be undertaken lightly. It is normally a two day trip and accommodation at the base must be secured in advance. It is however a sure way of leaving behind the folks who are continuously disgorged from tour buses.

Strange and striking landforms, abound in these states and it is most worthwhile to take a leisurely drive which takes in the Petrified Forest and Painted desert in eastern Arizona full of colourful geological formations, canyons, caves, sand dunes, meteor craters, mesas (table-shaped hills) and buttes (isolated flat-topped hills). There is also an abundance of interesting flora and fauna. Six hundred species of plants live in the isolation of Death Valley, many of which are unique to the area.

LAS VEGAS

Airline departure boards showing flights to this city call it La$ Vega$, and few visitors to the Southwest can resist the temptation of a stop in Las Vegas. Between Death Valley and the Grand Canyon, this neon-lit monstrosity rises improbably out of the desert. The artificiality and lavishness of 'Glitter Gulch' as downtown Las Vegas is known, is more extreme than anything Los Angeles can offer and is best appreciated after a drive across the tranquil, elemental desert rather than after a flight.

Las Vegas's undisguised vulgarity and hectic commercialism can easily be made into a symbol for modern American life — or at least one important aspect of it — and this alone is a reason to visit. There is very little of historic interest ('Old Vegas', out of town, is a pure tourist trap which was last heard of closed down and looking for new management) although you may care to glance up at the top floor of the Desert Inn where Howard Hughes spent the last ten years of his life. And it is a strange city which has such a thing as a 'topless laundromat'.

Especially after you have bankrupted your own coffers, it may strike you as a morally bankrupt place where the drunken boisterous rabble come only to visit gambling houses, quickie divorce lawyers or brothels. Nevada is the only state in which prostitution is legal, though it has recently been banned in several counties, including Las Vegas County.

City Layout. Since Las Vegas has no good reason to exist in terms of normal human geography, it is not laid out like any traditional city. What would pass for the city centre is around Main St in the north of the conurbation, but the main component of Las Vegas is linear: almost all the hotels and casinos are on this seven-mile-long 'Strip'.

Arrival and Departure. *Air:* McCarran International Airport is an efficient and comfortable facility. Call 261-5743 for airport information. It is close to the southern end of Las Vegas Boulevard. Vans and limousines from here run to hotels on The Strip for $4 or downtown for $5.

Bus: the Greyhound terminal is downtown at 200 South Main St, between Carson and Bridger Avenues. Los Angeles (six hours) is served 11 times a day. Direct buses run to Denver and Salt Lake City. There are midnight and early afternoon departures to Phoenix, taking 8 hours, with a connection at the town of Kingman to the Grand Canyon — 10 hours from Las Vegas.

Train: Las Vegas' Amtrak station must rank as the world's hardest-to-find rail terminal. If you walk through the casino of the Union Plaza at Main and Fremont Streets, you suddenly switch from a glitzy line of excited one-armed bandits to a dull old waiting room and ticket office.

Getting Around. Las Vegas prides itself on its brand-new bus network. The CAT system links all parts of the city with the Downtown Transportation Centre at Stewart Avenue and Casino Center Boulevard. The standard fare is $1. Most routes operate from 6am to 9pm, with some withdrawn at weekends. The Strip, however, is served around the clock on both regular scheduled route 6 and on the Excalibur Express which links the most prominent Strip casinos with each othe and downtown.

Accommodation. In Las Vegas almost every casino is a hotel and vice-versa. If you are driving to Las Vegas, listen to the radio as you approach (e.g. the soft rock station 94.1FM), since hotels often advertise special deals. Bus and train travellers will find themselves deposited close to dozens of places: cheap and tacky motels running south on Main St, upmarket places like Lady Luck in the immediate downtown areas. Leave your bags at the station and check out the best bargains.

Of places on or near the strip, the Aztec at 2200 Las Vegas Boulevard is one of the cheapest, around $30. The Super 8 is around $45. For less than this you should get a good, comfortable room at somewhere like Circus Circus, well placed for the rest of the strip.

The AYH Hostel is midway between downtown and the Strip proper, at 1236 South Las Vegas Boulevard (702-382-8119).

Eating and Drinking. Many hotels offer buffet breakfasts, lunches or dinners for ridiculously low prices, say $1.99, served at anytime of the day or night. There is no admission charge to any casino and you may be offered a free drink as soon as you stroll in. If you stand at a slot machine with a stack of quarters, judiciously inserting one whenever a waitress passes, you may be set up for an evening of free drinks.

Exploring. Las Vegas takes the breath away with its sheer daring. New projetcs are being built all the time, such as the new pyramid-shaped Luxor (owned by Circus Circus) and the MGM Grand Hotel and Theme Park (opening in 1994). There are no 'must-see' sights, but the sum of the parts hovers somewhere between the heroic and the ridiculous.

Entertainment. Most people come to Las Vegas prepared to squander a little (or a lot) along the famous four-mile Strip or in downtown Las Vegas which is some distance away and offers less fashionable and less expensive casinos and hotels. Professional gamblers congregate at Binion's Horseshoe Casino on Fremont St, where the poker World Series is held each Spring. The entrance to Binion's features a horseshoe enclosing one million dollars in $10,000 bills. Among high rollers a 'nickel' is $500, a 'dime' is $1,000 and a 'big dime' is $10,000. Everyone, whether feeding quarters into machines or staking 'big dimes' at the poker table, is hoping for the gold at the end of the rainbow. Three billion dollars are fed annually into the slot machines alone.

Normal self-restraint evaporates in the midst of an atmosphere which intoxicates. Night and day blend together in one long orgy of gambling and pleasure-seeking, for the bars and casinos never close and there are no public clocks. Some casinos provide exceptionally good deals to tempt you in: a couple of people playing the system at Vegas World are guaranteed a profit of $8 each. Check the local giveaway magazines for the best offers. If you want to repeat this, note that the staff are trained to weed out abusers of the incentive system. However the shift changes on the hospitality desk at 8am, 4pm and midnight.

Help and Information. The area code for Las Vegas is 614.

Further Afield. Most of the gamblers in Las Vegas do the region a great disservice, by failing to see some of the stunning scenery within an hour's drive of the city. The Hoover Dam (702-293-8321) — which created Lake Mead — is a wonder of civil engineering. Guided tours operate daily and are well worth the hour's wait and the $4 cost. Visitors are taken through the extraordinarily large and complex piece of civil engineering, which was perhaps the greatest constructional feat of the first half of the 20th century. It straddles the Colorado River at the border between Arizona and Nevada, and carries Highway 93 between the two. If you have come to sightsee rather than to drive straight through, you park you car or leave your bus tour a mile or two before the dam and board a free shuttle bus to the dam itself. You can see an exhibition and view a video of how the dam came to be, but most people are impatient to get on a tour of this startling hydroelectric project.

Still more impressive sights are due west and northwest of Las Vegas, resembling the moon and Switzerland respectively. If you head west on Charleston Boulevard for a dozen miles, you reach the Red Rock Canyon National Recreation Lands, a lunar landscape with strange formations and striking colours. The journey through the canyon is a seven-mile one-way loop, so you need a car, a bicycle or a horse too see it comfortably.

Highway 95 going northwest to Reno takes you to a close approximation to Swiss hillsides: turn left 20 miles out of Las Vegas, where the road to Mount Charleston rapidly leaves the rocky, arid desert behind and climbs to pine-clad hills) The township of Mount Charleston itself is little more than a collection of shacks, but you can turn towards Lee Canyon. This takes you on a beautiful road giving splendid views, and provides a loop to take you back down to Highway 95 to continue north or return to Las Vegas.

Calendar of Events

January 1	Tournament of Roses Parade, Pasadena
April	Tucson Festival, Arizona
early July-early August	Flagstaff Festival of the Arts, Arizona
late August	Reno Basque Festival
July	Hollywood Bowl Summer Festival
September	Mexican Independence Day
late Sept-early Oct	Clark County Basque Festival, Las Vegas
late Oct-mid Nov	San Diego Arts Festival (1-800-245-3378)
late November	Hollywood Christmas Parade
December	Waiters/Waitresses 5km race, Beverly Hills

San Francisco and the Northwest

The Golden Gate Bridge

Northern California   Oregon   Washington

The authorities use Alistair Cooke's sobriquet to describe San Francisco as 'everyone's favourite city'. Its setting is indeed magnificent, with the unmistakable sweep of the Golden Gate Bridge. But it is also devastating. In 1906 the San Andreas fault, on which San Francisco was built, caused an earthquake so huge that it destroyed four square miles of the city. Such a tragedy is not easily forgotten, and San Francisco's architects have broken the city's skyline with comparatively few high-rise buildings. The result is a place that is on a very much more human scale than its southern neighbour Los Angeles. Downtown San Francisco has a population of less than one million.

San Francisco was originally settled because the Bay provided a natural harbour. This was of critical importance prior to the building of the transcontinental railway in the 1860s, since the sea route was the easiest way to the West. The village of Yerba Buena (now submerged beneath Chinatown) was the obvious ocean base for the 1848/49 Gold Rush.

What began as a camp full of drunken goldminers is now the most cultured city on the West Coast. With its good-mannered inhabitants, winding streets, superlative food, cafes full of literary types, San Francisco is traditionally held up as the most European of American cities. The writer Jan Morris once described it as the place 'where all lapsed lovers of America should be taken for refresher courses.' The tolerant and liberal nature of its inhabitants

337

is legendary. It is not a coincidence that the city boasts the liveliest and most overtly gay community in the country. San Francisco is a place to have fun. The nightlife has to be seen to be believed.

When people speak of San Francisco, they often mean the whole Bay Area: the city itself, plus the counties of San Mateo, Contra Costa, Marin and Alameda (which includes the adjacent cities of Oakland and Berkeley). Together they have a population of over four million. Marin County has recently become full of very rich San Franciscans who moved north across the Golden Gate Bridge hoping to enjoy the company of the artists and writers living around Sausalito. Unfortunately, this creative community has largely been dislodged because of high property prices, and many have moved on to Oregon and Washington (where it is popular to subsidize creative talents with a little illicit agriculture).

Oakland has long been regarded as the poor relation of San Francisco, although this reputation is becoming less deserved as the city gentrifies. Neighbouring Berkeley is dominated by the campus of the University of California, once teeming with radical students and drugs, now far more sedate and less opposed to the tenets of yuppie materialism.

Downtown San Francisco, while made up of many distinct districts, is compact enough to walk around. Indeed this is the best way to appreciate the city's architecture, which varies from cosy hill terraces and colonial-style villas to stunning Art Deco creations and dramatic skyscrapers, including the conspicuous TransAmerica pyramid and the 52-storey Bank of America, the largest (but not the tallest) building in the USA. If the hills become too much for your feet, you can take advantage of the most varied urban transport system in North America.

THE PEOPLE

The people of San Francisco take great pride in their city. They never refer to it as 'Frisco', which they consider a vulgar appellation. They are among the nation's richest citizens, with an average income of nearly $20,000.

The population comprises 60% white, 15% Asian, 13% Black and 12% Hispanic. The Asian contingent consists mainly of 65,000 Chinese, who first came to the city during the building of the the trans-continental railway last century. They are crammed into the ever-expanding Chinatown, the largest such community outside Asia. But there is also a substantial Japanese population plus increasing numbers of Koreans and Vietnamese. The city fosters ethnic diversity and the various groups which make up the city's population are remarkably tolerant of one another.

There are no accurate figures for the number of gay people in San Francisco, though it is estimated that one in seven inhabitants is homosexual. Whatever the statistics, the gay community is a large, visible and vocal minority. San Francisco is the only city in the States where the gay community has real political power; gay activists are involved in the whole spectrum of political life, from voter registration to holding office. Even though Aids has cast a pall over life in San Francisco, gays continue to exert a powerful force, and the Bay Area is arguably the most politically radical area of the USA. Mayors tend to be Democrats with liberal persuasions, and an extraordinary range of social welfare laws are in force. Smoking, for example, is forbidden virtually everywhere that the public congregates. Whether you consider this legislation to be evidence of advanced civilization or creeping authoritarianism may indicate whether or not you will feel at home in San Francisco.

Making Friends. San Francisco is an open and friendly place, and meeting people is not likely to be a problem. Attending a ball game at the Candlestick Park stadium (see *Sport*) is one of the best places to strike up conversation. Alternatively, try the bars, bookshops and trendy restaurants in and around Sproul Plaza in Berkeley (once famous for its sit-ins). This is also where you are most likely to find the few hippies left over from the flower power era. Bancroft and Telegraph Avenues are particularly promising. The Berkeley campus attracts foreign students in large numbers, so if you're yearning for a chat with a compatriot then you should be in luck. Even if you don't make a friend instantly, you can't fail to enjoy an espresso and pastry at one of the many street cafés.

Downtown, the singles bars lining the south-eastern half of Columbus Avenue and nearby streets cater for a slightly older and predominantly heterosexual clientele, who will waste no time in striking up conversation with unfamiliar faces. Be prepared for detailed psychoanalytical case histories.

San Francisco's gays meet in clubs and bars throughout the city, with the highest concentrations in the Castro district: see *City Layout.* Check the listings in the *Advocate* for the currently fashionable venues. Most establishments are single sex, usually male.

California is still a stronghold for the Unification Church, better known as the Moonies, though the power of the church has waned. Pairs of religious fanatics prowl the streets, airports and bus stations in search of innocent tourists. However genuine their offer of coffee and a meal may seem, you are advised to be very wary.

To meet more conservative San Franciscans, call 986-1388 for details of the 'Meet Americans at Home' Scheme; at least 48 hours notice is required.

CLIMATE

Mark Twain is quoted as saying 'the worst winter I ever spent was summer in San Francisco'. The city has a reputation for being permanently enshrouded in the mists that roll in under the Golden Gate from the Pacific. Strangely, these arrive mainly in summer. But in fact there are 162 clear days each year, compared with 93 in New York and 57 in Seattle. Between June and August there is virtually no rain, but the fog can keep temperatures low. You must also contend with the hordes of tourists — over eight million a year. Spring and autumn are much less crowded, and it is quite possible to chance upon a spell of fine, sunny weather. There is usually an Indian summer from mid-September to mid- October, which is a delightful time to visit.

Between November and April take a raincoat, but you won't need much heavy-duty cold-weather gear since temperatures almost never fall below freezing. This is fortunate in view of the chaos which would ensue if the slopes of San Francisco iced up. Dial 936-1212 for the latest weather forecast.

CITY LAYOUT

The city's downtown area occupies the northeastern tip of the peninsula separating the Ocean and San Francisco Bay — linked to the mainland by the Golden Gate Bridge to the north and the Oakland Bay Bridge to the east.

The main artery through the centre is Market St. At its northeastern end is the Ferry Building, from which point the Embarcadero runs along the

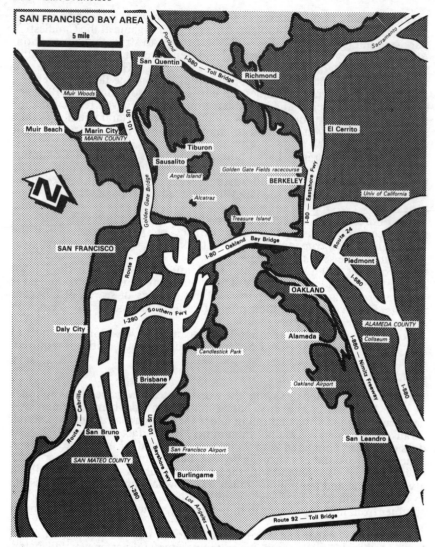

waterfront to Fisherman's Wharf, the city's unabashed tourist area, full of tacky shops and over-priced restaurants and best avoided. The Embarcadero freeway was destroyed after the 1989 earthquake.

To the south of Fisherman's Wharf is North Beach. This is traditionally home to many of the city's Italian inhabitants, though many have moved away. Since the Fifties, North Beach has been more famous as the centre of San Francisco's alternative scene and the birthplace of the Beat Movement. Columbus Avenue, which runs through the centre of the district, is full of buzzing cafes and is a lively at night. Broadway is known as 'mammary lane', though coffee shops and bookstores are scattered among the strip joints.

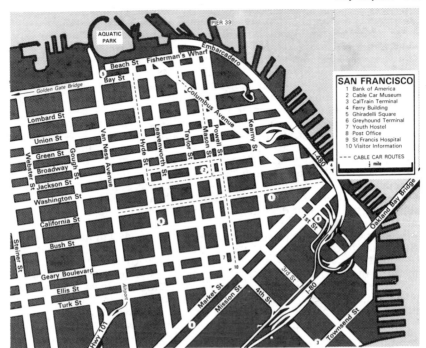

The southern reaches of North Beach are gradually being swallowed up by the ever-growing Chinatown, the gaudy Grant Avenue being the district's main street. In total contrast is the Financial District, to the east, and Nob Hill to the west. The latter might be reminiscent of Montmartre or Hampstead were it not for the proliferation of luxury hotels. Union Square, to the south, is a useful focus point: many hotels are located within a stone's throw of it.

The Civic Centre, to the south, is something of an oasis surrounded by dodgy areas: see *Crime and Safety*. The gay neighbourhood of Polk Street, a few blocks north, has virtually ceased to exist, though boy prostitutes ply a desperate trade.

In South of Market, known as SoMa, clubs and bars jostle for space among the warehouses and old industrial buildings. While there is little to take you here during the day, it is busy at night. Southwest of here is the vibrant Mission district, where many Hispanics live. Beyond that, at the end of Market St, is Castro, the Gay Capital. Golden Gate Park and Haight Ashbury, north of Castro, used to be the haunt of hippies in the 60s. It is now a bizarre mix of street people, yuppies and gays, still with some good bookstores and cafes. The most fashionable area is Lower Haight, where Fillmore and Haight Streets meet. Heading north up Fillmore you reach the more exclusively yuppie district of Pacific Heights, with fine brightly-painted Victorian houses.

Despite San Francisco's coastal setting, it is not a beach resort. Bathing near the Golden Gate is hazardous due to the strong currents flowing between the Bay and Pacific. Furthermore, this part of the West Coast gets the Alaskan current and the water is numbingly cold.

Air. San Francisco International Airport (SFO) lies 15 miles south of the city (761-0800). International travellers arrive at the Central Terminal and connections to onward flights are easy. If your outbound flight is delayed, you could try the sauna (mezzanine floor, South Terminal) or the beauty shop. With any luck, you won't be delayed long enough to need the services of the airport morgue.

The average taxi fare to downtown is $30-35; recommended rates are posted outside the terminal. The SFO Airporter bus (495-8404) links the airport with various hotels in central San Francisco, terminating at the Meridien at 3rd and Market Streets, near Union Square. Departures are roughly every 20 minutes from 6am to midnight. The journey takes 30 minutes normally, an hour in rush hours, and costs $5 one way, $8 return. If there are crowds of passengers waiting for the bus, just walk up one floor to pick up the bus as it deposits departing passengers before descending to the arrivals level.

Express bus 7F will take you downtown for $1.50, as will local bus 7B for $1.25, though the latter makes frequent stops and takes twice as long. Bus 3B runs to the metro or BART terminus at Daly City. These services are operated by SamTrans (508-6200), which allows large amounts of luggage only on specially designated buses. If you're loaded down or just plain exhausted, use the SuperShuttle van service to anywhere in downtown for about $12; call 558-8500 to arrange a pick-up upon departure.

Hitch-hiking south from the airport is feasible: walk straight out of the terminal area to the sliproad leading to US 101 (Bayshore Freeway).

Oakland International Airport (OAK), used by some domestic airlines such as Continental, is across the bay in south Oakland, 18 miles southeast of San Francisco. It is much more convenient for Berkeley and all points east. Many frequent travellers to San Francisco prefer it to the huge SFO, thanks to its compactness and relative quietness. Airporter buses run every half-hour to San Francisco, take 40-50 minutes and charge $6 each way; there is another service to 320 20th St in Oakland. The Oakland Air BART bus (AC57) links the airport with Coliseum/Oakland Airport BART station, a ten-minute ride.

Cheap Flights: travellers looking for a cheap flight to the Far East should check the travel agencies in Chinatown, found mainly in Clay St and Waverly Place; fares to Hong Kong tend to be the cheapest. Low fares to Asia are also advertised in the classified columns of the *San Francisco Chronicle* and the *Examiner.*

Bus. The counties bordering on San Francisco are served by buses from the Transbay Transit Terminal at 1st and Mission Streets. AC Transit (510-839-2882) serves East Bay, including Berkeley, Oakland and the rest of Alameda County; SamTrans (508-6200) runs south through the peninsula to San Mateo County; Golden Gate Transit (332-6600) operates buses across the Golden Gate bridge to Marin and Sonoma Counties, plus ferries across the Bay (see below).

The Greyhound terminal (558-6789) is on 7th St, just south of Market St and close to the Civic Center. Green Tortoise (821-0803) runs sleeperbuses to the East Coast and up and down the West Coast.

Train. The CalTrain depot at 4th and Townsend Streets, southeast of SoMa (800-660-4287 or 495-4546) operates commuter services only, although connections with the Amtrak line to Los Angeles are possible by taking a train to the terminus at San José.

Otherwise, prospective train travellers must take the free Amtrak shuttle bus from the Transbay Terminal to 16th St Station in Oakland (800-872-7245). There is one train daily — the *Coast Starlight* — to both Los Angeles (10-12 hours) and Seattle (22 hours). The *Californian Zephyr* departs daily to Chicago via Denver. Sample one-way fares are Los Angeles $75, Seattle $120 and Chicago $350.

Driving. San Francisco has no Los Angeles-style network of freeways. The road system in this hilly, compact area consists mainly of two or four-lane streets with traffic lights at every intersection. Out of town, the main highways of interest to travellers are State Highway 1, the most spectacular coast road in America, though beware of fog; US 101, a freeway for most of its length as it winds along the coast a little inland (and the road that crosses the Golden Gate Bridge); I-80, straight to New York; and I-5, an eastern by-pass for the city used only by philistines in too much of a hurry to get from LA to Seattle to stop.

Urban freeways reserve the extreme left-hand lane for buses and pool cars. The remaining lanes are crowded and frantic during rush hours, so try to plan your approach and departure at other times. Tolls on the two strategic bridges — the Golden Gate and the Oakland Bay — are charged only inbound to San Francisco.

Driveaways. Because the Bay Area is such a popular destination for settlers, there are more inbound than outbound driveaways available, which can make it hard to find a car out of the city. In addition, there is a large student community and many like-minded visitors all in search of driveaways. Don't bother trying to find one around the end of the university terms, unless you want to try a Sacramento number: 916-371-7227 (demand for cars is lower in the Californian state capital). At other times, try all the companies listed in the Yellow Pages and resign yourself to a long wait. The most likely destinations are Texas and the East Coast; there is little driveaway traffic up or down the West Coast, because the distances are too small.

Ride Sharing. Sharing a car is big business in the environmentally correct Bay Area. Check the noticeboards around the campus at Berkeley, or listen to community radio stations such as KALX (510-642-1111). Los Angeles is by far the most popular destination, followed by Seattle, Vancouver and the East Coast.

Shorter-distance ride sharing is positively encouraged: one of the more civilised aspects of life in the Bay Area is the informal car-pooling arrangements which are a bit like hitch-hiking. Ask around for the local contact point. The deal is simply that you get a free ride, the driver gets to use special car-pool lanes and avoids tolls.

Hitch-hiking. Hitchers may wish to visit 29 Russell St in San Francisco, where Jack Kerouac wrote *On the Road*. Hitch-hiking in the Bay Area is probably better than when he wrote about it: there is a large student population, thousands of motor-borne tourists and a widespread acceptance of the practice.

For US 101 south to Los Angeles, start from San Francisco Airport. Heading north on US 101, try the approach roads to, or the exit roads from, the Golden Gate Bridge. A faster route north is I-5, which you can pick up by taking BART to Berkeley, then the free bus (Monday-Friday only) to

University Avenue. Although often choked with hitchers, no one seems to wait around for long. Berkeley is also a good bet for I-80 east. An alternative is to take BART to Concord, then hitch on I-680 which leads on to I-80.

CITY TRANSPORT

Walking is an excellent way to get around San Francisco. Or you can take advantage of the efficient MUNI public transport system, which includes buses, *Vi* (trams) and the famous cable cars. For information ring 673-MUNI or 673-6864 and tell them which intersection you are near and where you want to go. You can pick up a map showing all MUNI services from their office at 949 Presidio Avenue or from the Visitors Information Centre (where you can also get an excellent general map of the downtown area).

Buses and Vi. Whenever you board a vehicle, pay the driver the flat fare of $1. Always ask for a free transfer: this is a timed ticket valid for two journeys made within 90 minutes on any MUNI service, although return or circular journeys are prohibited. Visitors staying for several weeks are advised to get a Fast Pass, which allows 30 days of unlimited travel on the MUNI system for $32. A three-day pass costs $10.

Buses and Vi operate 24 hours a day, though the service is limited after midnight. Note that some Vi — lines J to N inclusive — run through tunnels in the city centre equipped with proper stations.

Cable Cars. This anachronistic mode of transport is both a National Historic Monument and an integral part of the MUNI system. There is a clause in the City Charter ruling that the cable cars shall run forever.

Looking like a cross between an old railway carriage and a Disneyland ride, each is operated by a crew of two. The driver uses a level-operated pincer to latch onto the cable which runs along a channel beneath the tracks. This pulls the cars up the one-in-six slopes and retards them on the downhill run. He also has a selection of brakes at his disposal (the most effective of which gouges chunks out of the road), tracks and cable to stop the car in an extreme emergency. The conductor collects fares ($3) and issues transfers. The system of fare registration and signalling is a Heath Robinson network of levers, rods and bells.

If there is a queue at the terminus where you wish to join, walk a block or two to the next stop; the conductor ensures that the cars leave with enough room to pick up passengers en route. As benefits a National Historic Monument, there are special rules for riding. When you board, you are supposed to move inside to the spartan cabin. Many visitors ignore the rules (until admonished by the conductor), and cling to the hand rails as the car lurches around corners.

There are three lines: Powell-Mason, Powell-Hyde and California St, which intersect close to the summit of Nob Hill. The cable is driven at a constant 9 mph from the Powerhouse at Mason and Washington Streets, also the site of a free museum (474-1887) describing the building and running of the system.

The Bay Area Rapid Transit — BART. The BART system is San Francisco's above and below ground railway and connects the centre with Oakland, Berkeley and beyond. It serves only a few downtown areas (there are stops the length of Market St), but BART provides a cheap, fast and comfortable means of transport — once you've mastered the method of payment. This involves finding a computer-like ticket machine at the station, pushing the button for your destination, then feeding in coins or notes to the amount shown. At some machines, change is given automatically. The minimum fare is 80c, the maximum $3; most fares are between $1 and $2.

Services start at 6am (9am on Sundays) and run through to midnight. Avoid travelling during the rush hour if possible. There is a handy free bus between the Berkeley BART station and the University campus called the Humphrey Go-BART bus, which operates Monday to Friday.

For information call 788-2278 or 788-BART (465-BART for East Bay). There is an excellent pamphlet called *All about BART*, which explains the whole system clearly. *Fun Goes Further on BART* lists all the attractions in the Bay Area and how to reach them by public transport. Both are available from BART stations.

Car. Rights of way will be asserted by cable cars and streetcars. If you'd like to test your brakes, steering and nerve, then try Lombard Street between Hyde and Leavenworth Streets in the Russian Hill district; ten hairpin bends in a single block, down a one-in- six slope. It is ungrammatically described as the 'Crookedest Street in the World'.

Parking is a constant nightmare for residents, and visitors hardly stand a chance. The whole city is zoned: red means don't even consider parking: an enthusiastic posse of towing trucks roams the streets ready to pounce on offenders (minimum recovery $74); yellow zones permit parking between 6pm and 8am; green means you can park for ten whole minutes during the day, or any time from 6pm-8pm. Even if you do find a street space, you have to ensure your car won't roll away. A city ordinance requires that all cars be left in gear (the 'parking' setting on automatics), with the wheels turned towards the kerb. The best plan is to use a free Park'n'Ride lot (signposted on all approach routes) or to pay the $15 per day demanded by downtown parking lots.

The '49-mile Drive' is a well-signposted circuit of the city and its sights, but it's not worth undertaking during business hours because of the severe downtown congestion.

Car Rental: car hire is among the cheapest in the USA, and you should find a good deal by ploughing through the 14 Yellow Pages on the subject in the local directory. Many firms are gathered around Union Square, among them Thrifty (299 Ellis St, 928-6666), where rates start at $35 a day, with free mileage. Some visitors advocate renting an automatic, so as to avoid a never-ending run of potentially nerve-racking hill starts.

Mopeds. In the last few years numerous moped rental firms have sprung up in the city. You can hire 80cc Honda Elites for about $70 per day; this sounds expensive, but the bikes carry two people, fuel is cheap and parking problems are alleviated. A 50cc Honda goes for $50. A full driving licence is required.

Taxis. Downtown San Francisco is choked with yellow, blue, red, orange and mauve cabs. They congregate outside the major hotels and at the foot of hills, to tempt foot-wary pedestrians. Fares are $3 for the first mile, then $1.50 after that. Away from the city centre, taxis are hard to find; to book a cab, ring Luxor (282-4141) or DeSoto (673-0333).

Cycling. San Francisco is not the easiest (because of the hills) nor the safest (because of the cable car and streetcar tracks) city in which to cycle, although many residents are not perturbed. Golden Gate Park is a popular place to cycle, and there are several bike hire shops on or near Stanyan St, which runs along the eastern edge of the park. Park Cyclery (1865 Haight St, 221-3777) hires out mountain bikes for $30 per 24 hours, $150 for a week.

Cycling maps of the Bay Area are available from Caltrans (due to move to Oakland, address unknown at time of going to press) and show the two dedicated scenic cycle routes. One goes through Golden Gate Park and on to Lake Merced (near the zoo), while the other runs from the south of the city over into Marin County. Riding a bicycle across the Golden Gate Bridge is a splendid experience (it is also possible to walk). There is no special bicycle path across the Oakland Bay Bridge. To take your bike on BART trains, ask for a courtesy pass, valid for one day, from any station agent; permits for longer periods are also available.

Ferries. Commuters from the towns of Sausalito and Tiburon in Marin County avoid the long traffic queues by taking the ferry. Golden Gate Ferries (332-6600) serves Sausalito from the Ferry Building at the foot of Market St for $3.75; the journey takes 30 minutes and the last boat back is at 7.30pm. The Red and White Fleet (546-2896) serves both Sausalito and Tiburon, from Pier 43½ at Fisherman's Wharf.

Even if you don't have an overwhelming desire to visit Marin Country, ferries offer a cheap alternative to sightseeing trips around the Bay.

Accommodation

San Francisco's popularity is reflected in the high cost of rooms. Furthermore, the usual terminology which enables informed guesses to be made about relative prices and facilities is heavily blurred. Some cheap and cheerful hostels call themselves bed-and-breakfast places, as do all sorts of upmarket establishments.

The Visitor Information Center in Hallidie Plaza (391-2000/1) will happily place you in the more respectable hotels. If what they have to offer is too expensive, then there is also a hotel information desk in the arrivals hall of the North Terminal.

Outdoor. The city ordinance which prohibits camping or sleeping out is strictly enforced in the parks and beaches. For official sites, go north to Marin County or south to the environs of Palo Alto. Reservations may be necessary in the summer.

Cheap. Rock-bottom hotels (in terms of both price and standards) are available in San Francisco, but many involve sharing a dormitory or a mattress on the floor.

Hostels: there are two AYH hostels in downtown San Francisco. The oldest is at Building 240 (a former Army dispensary and a registered historic building) inside Fort Mason Park. It lies at the corner of Bay and Franklin Streets, just west of Fisherman's Wharf (771-7277) and costs $13 per night. For a dollar extra you can stay in the new AYH hostel at 312 Mason St (788-5604), near Union Square between Geary and O'Farrell.

The YMCA's main hostel is at 220 Golden Gate Avenue (885-0460). Dorm beds cost $16 (for YH members) and a double room $41. Other hostels worth investigating include the European Guest House (761 Minna, 861-6634), and the Interclub Globe Hostel (10 Hallam Place, 431-0540): both are within spitting distance of 8th St, on the other side of Mission St from the Greyhound terminal, and both charge $15 per person. The Youth Hostel Central, 116 Turk St (346-7835 or 3HO-STEL), is on the grotty side, but has double rooms for $28 (singles $22), with reductions for weekly rentals.

Though not a hostel, Hotel Stratford (242 Powell St, 788-3207) is very cheap, with double rooms for under $30 and student discounts available.

Student Residences: if you are staying for a month or more in summer, then the student residences at Berkeley present an economic alternative. Most are privately owned. Consult the free weekly *Express* or simply look around the streets for a suitable vacation let. San Francisco State University's Housing Office (338-1067) is worth contacting during summer if you're an overseas student. Reckon on $25 per night.

Mid-price. A useful selection of motels can be found along Lombard St between Pearce and Van Ness, the main route in from the Golden Gate Bridge on US101. For a reasonable room in a downtown hotel you must be prepared to pay at least $50 for a double, and $40 for a single. (Note that bed-and-breakfast inns tend to be small and smart rather than private homes, but some 'ordinary' bed-and-breakfast establishments are listed in the *Bay Guardian* annual *Bed and Breakfast Guide to Northern California*, available at news stands.)

The following hotels are all in the vicinity of Union Square:

All Seasons Hotel: 417 Stockton (986-8737).

Ansonia Hotel: 711 Post St (673-2670).

Golden City Inn: 1554 Howard St (255-1110). Further south, in SoMa, but good value, and well located for nightlife.

Golden Gate Hotel: 775 Bush St (392-3702) near the Powell St cable car route. Up a couple of notches, with tasteful doubles and an excellent breakfast of croissants and coffee.

Pensione International: 875 Post St (775-3344).

Upmarket. Sumptuous lobbies do not necessarily mean luxurious rooms. This holds for both the St Francis (335 Powell St, 397-7000) and the Californian at 405 Taylor St (885-2500). But the St Francis, which has a glass lift scaling the outside of the building, offers the best views in town.

Eating and Drinking

The choice of restaurants in the Bay Area is awesome, reflecting the San Franciscans' obsession with eating. The average citizen spends $800 each year on dining out, and there is one restaurant for every 200 inhabitants.

Good-value eateries are listed under all categories, but below are a few miscellaneous places. Ideal for anyone keen to save money are San Francisco's numerous salad bars. At Sizzler (Eddy and Leavenworth Streets, 921-3911), near the Civic Center, for example, you can gorge yourself on avocado, cheese and all manner of fruits and unusual salads for less than $10.

As with other American cities, cafeterias are the bargain basement of eating well; there's no tipping, service is fast, you see what you eat beforehand, and you can get up and go if you don't like what you see. Try Brother Juniper's Breadbox (1065 Sutter St), Manning's Cafeteria (1275 Market St) and Pap Joe's (1412 Polk St).

There is a surprising number of bars in San Francisco where for a $2-3 drink, you can stuff yourself on free hot and cold *hors d'oeuvres*. Favourites include White Elephant (480 Sutter St, 398-1331) and Jay'n Bee's Club

(1223 Polk St, 824-4190). Decadent cakes and chocolates may be found in the cafes and confectioners of Ghirardelli Square (pronounced Gear-ar-delly), the site of an old chocolate factory just west of Fisherman's Wharf. For example, the Ghirardelli Soda Fountain and Candy Shop sells a stupendous 'Golden Gate Banana Split'. Berkeley is renowned for its ice cream parlours: try McCallum's on Solano Avenue, or Vivoli's, which is run by feminists.

San Francisco is an excellent place for do-it-yourself eating. There is plenty of fresh, cheap food, and the famous sour dough bread makes for delicious open sandwiches.

Italian. Don't miss the chance to try a Californian pizza. Kuleto's (221 Powell St, 397-7720), part of Villa Florence Hotel near Union Square, serves pizzas for breakfast, with mascarpone, apple and banana on top. For a cheaper meal, Marcello's (420 Castro St at Market, 863-3900) is recommended.

What is left of Little Italy is centred on Washington Square and offers authentic Italian cuisine as well as Americanized Italian fare. Family-style Italian cooking is available at Capps' Corner, 1600 Powell St (989-2589), a friendly, neighbourhood place. A three-course set menu costs about $10. Little Joe's (523 Broadway, 433-4343), where queues are long but the portions generous, is also a good deal.

In Cafe Tosca, a 1920s establishment at 242 Columbus Avenue at Broadway (391-1244), you can enjoy great coffee and croissants to the sound of classical music on the jukebox.

Oriental. Many restaurants in Chinatown seem to cater purely for tourists who won't ever come back, and standards are accordingly low. If you choose to dine in Chinatown, head away from the touristy Grant St and select a place where Chinese people are eating and no menu in English is displayed. One good place for seafood, Cantonese-style, is Yuet Lee on the corner of Stockton and Broadway. There are some good Hunan places away from Chinatown on Haight and Ashbury.

For lunchtime Dim Sum, try Yank Sing, 427 Battery St (362-1640), near Washington St. Your bill is calculated by the number of empty dishes (around $18 for a filling meal).

Lesser known Japantown (known as Nihonmachi) is around Geary Blvd and Webster St, south of Fillmore. It is less of a tourist trap than Chinatown and makes fuller use of the abundant seafood.

Fish. Naturally, fish figures prominently in the San Francisco diet. The Fisherman's Wharf area is crammed with American fish restaurants, but the same Pacific salmon and Dungeness crabs are far cheaper a few blocks inland. There is a lot of frozen fish around, so beware. One place to find the fresh article is the Tadich Grill at 240 California St (391-1849), in the Financial District. You can tell from the queues outside that this is among the best fish restaurants in town. It opens Monday to Friday only, and does not take credit cards.

Fillmore District. There are some excellent places to eat in this yuppie area, though prices are fairly high. The Elite Café at 2049 Fillmore (346-8668) is a wonderful Art Deco creation, with a great atmosphere and great Creole food. To mix with millionaires — maybe even John Paul Getty — brave the Balboa Café (3199 Fillmore, 921-3944), one of the trendiest and most expensive joints in town. You'll need to spend at least $30 to make the most of it.

On Sundays those who aren't out jogging go to the cafés on Fillmore and Union Streets for brunch.

Mission District. While Mexican restaurants are dotted all over the city, rather than concentrated in a particular area, some of the best are in the Mission District. For cafeteria-style food try La Cumbre at 515 Valencia St at 16th (863-8205) and Taqueria Pancho Villa (3071 16th St), nearby. La Olla, further south at 2417 Mission St, combines Mexican with Nicaraguan and Argentinian dishes.

Berkeley. There is excellent inexpensive ethnic dining in Berkeley's South Campus district, bounded by Bancroft, Dwight, Fulton and Gaby. The entertaining communal eating of Ethiopian can be enjoyed at the Blue Nile at 2525 Telegraph Avenue (540-6777); if Ethiopian honey wine is too sweet for your palate, try the tasty Asmara beer.

DRINKING

Apart from Californian wine and standard North American fizzy beer, the city claims an affinity with Irish coffee for obscure historical reasons. Some bars serve little else and have elevated the drink to an art form. The Buena Vista at 2765 Hyde St (474-5044), near Fisherman's Wharf, claims to have invented the drink. For a more spectacular view while you drink, try Henri's on the 46th floor of the Hilton or the Carnelain Room on the 52nd floor of the Bank of America. Be prepared for sky high prices.

Singles bars are concentrated on and around Union St, in an area known as the Bermuda Triangle (because that's where unattached people disappear). For the ultimate singles bar, go to Perry's at 1944 Union St (922-9022 for details of current happy hours). There is not much difference between Perry's establishment and the East Side bars in New York: advertising executives ogle graphic designers, unemployed actresses chat up accountants, etc.

If you want to spend an evening drinking seriously, away from the singles bars and perhaps with some jazz thrown in, try the bars around Columbus Avenue and Green Street, in the North Beach area. Caffe Roma, Martinelli's or Café Sport are all recommended. Vesuvio's, at 255 Columbus, has long been the haunt of intellectuals. If you consider anaesthesia a good plan, share some murderous Mai Tai with the residents of Chinatown.

Among the most popular of the city's thousands of gay bars, are the Pendulum (4146 18th St, 863-4441). The Castro Station (456 Castro St) is a typical leather bar.

Anchor Steam Beer is one of America's original naturally matured beers. You can tour the 19th century brewery and sample the end product. Red Tail and St Stans (dark and creamy) are recommended; if you call in just prior to Christmas, taste the powerful Old Foghorn brew. Ring 863-8350 for an appointment at 1705 Malpas St.

Those homesick for a British-style pub have a choice. In the city, the Donnington Park is a tolerable English pub at 2301 Folsom (at 19th). Out in Marin County — on Highway 1 at Muir Beach — the Pelican Inn serves excellent beer.

Wine Tastings. A day trip to the Napa Valley is highly recommended (see *Further Afield*). In San Francisco itself, Sonoma Vineyards have a walk-in tasting and sales shop at 2191 Union St, as does the Napa Valley Winery Exchange at 415 Taylor St. The Wine Museum at 633 Beach St does not offer samples, but houses a collection of wine-making equipment dating from Roman times. It opens daily except Mondays.

It's easy to while away several days simply strolling around the streets or sitting in cafés. Yet it would be a shame to overlook the cultural offerings of the Bay Area, which have breadth and depth matched only by New York.

Museums. Until 1963 the island of Alcatraz, standing starkly in the middle of the Bay, was a prison from which reputedly no one ever escaped alive. It is now a museum of penal servitude. The only way to reach the island is to join a boat trip from Pier 41 or 43½; tickets cost $8.50, and be prepared to queue. Call Red and White Fleet on 546-2805 for further details. The excellent but fairly energetic tour includes being locked into a cramped cell — but for half a minute rather than half a lifetime. Other options include trail walks, and cassette tours of the prison narrated by ex-cons and guards. There is a superb view of the Bay from the island. Take warm clothes and stout shoes.

The Museum of Modern Art in the Civic Centre (Van Ness and McAllister, 863-8800) will not disappoint fans of Dali, Matisse or Picasso. Opening hours are 11am-5pm at weekends; 10am-5pm on Tuesday, Wednesday and Friday; 10am-9pm Thursday. Entrance costs $4.50, free on Tuesday and reduced charge Thursday evenings.

The galleries and gardens of the Oakland Museum, 10th and Oak Streets (510-238-3401) feature the history, art and ecology of California. It opens from 10am-5pm, Wednesday to Saturday, noon-7pm Sunday; admission is free.

In Mission district, the first Levi Strauss Factory (250 Valencia) takes visitors on tours. It is open 10am-5pm Monday to Friday, admission free. The Diego Rivera Gallery in the San Francisco Art Institute (800 Chestnut St in Russian Hill district) has among its collection a fine mural done by the Mexican artist in the 1930s. It is open Tuesday to Saturday.

Golden Gate Park. This 1000-acre patch of green was described a century ago as 'a waste of drifting sand', but is now beautifully kept. You can take a free walking tour any weekend between May and October; call 221-3111 to check times. Among the parks's many attractions are the Japanese Tea Garden, the Strybing Arboretum and several museums. The most prestigious of these is the M. H. de Young Memorial Museum (8th Avenue and JFK Drive, 750-3600), which contains American art from the colonial era to the mid-20th century. It opens 10am-5pm Wednesday to Sunday; admission is free the first Wednesday of the month. For greater entertainment visit the Aquarium (part of the Academy of Sciences), which has enormous reptile-filled tanks.

The park becomes the focus of the entire city on Sundays, when it is closed to traffic. If you tire of walking or jogging, rent a pair of rollerskates from the stalls on JFK Drive or hire a bike; or, even better, hire a horse from the Golden Gate Park Stables for a guided tour: call 668-7360 to make an appointment.

Fisherman's Wharf and Aquatic Park. It's worth having a quick stroll around this area, just to see how tacky it is and how contrived the street entertainment. There are usually scores of comedians, magicians, mime artists and buskers — including a human juke box. Sea lions can often be spotted alongside Fisherman's Wharf, and the occasional shark (only three-foot long ones which eat rubbish at the bottom of the water).

Three blocks west of Fisherman's Wharf is the Aquatic Park, where you can fish for free from the municipal pier, no licence required. A footpath runs along the shore from the Park to Fort Point, beneath the Golden Gate Bridge. This makes for a very pleasant walk if you don't dwell too long on the fact that over a thousand people have jumped to their deaths from what is still the world's highest suspension bridge.

Zoo. San Francisco's excellent zoo is at 45th Avenue and Sloat Blvd (753-7061), on the west side of the peninsula. It is particularly hot on primates, containing Gorilla World, Monkey Island and the Primate discovery Center. And don't miss the Penguin Pool. The zoo opens daily 10am-5pm, admission $6.50

Tickets for most events are sold through BASS (762-BASS), which began life as Bay Area Seating Services and has since spread nationwide. For cut-price tickets on the day, visit the STBS kiosks from noon (Tuesday-Saturday) located on the Stockton St side of Union Square. The best source of listings is *SF Weekly*.

Rock. Bands consisting largely of ageing hippies play in Golden Gate Park on summer Sundays. The most popular live bands play at the Opera House or the Civic Auditorium (974-4000) in the Civic Center.

The best venues for less aged rockers include Lou's Pier 47, 300 Jefferson at Fisherman's Wharf (771-0377), which specializes in blues and R&B. The semi-legendary Fillmore West at 1805 Geary (at Fillmore, 922-FILL) has top-line acts. The Warfield (982 Market (between 5th and 6th, 775-7722) has agood mix.

If you fear your hearing has been affected by listening to too much rock music, the Haight-Ashbury Free Medical Clinic will test your ears for free.

Nightclubs are concentrated near the junction of Broadway and Columbus Avenue. To find more jazz, discos and cafes, go to the Haight-Ashbury, SoMa or Castro areas. For gay bars and clubs on Castro St, the main concentration is in the few blocks south of Market St, centred around 18th St. Below is a selection of the best venues.

Cesar's Latin Palace: 3140 Mission St. Watch or dance to the music of big
    salsa bands.
Club DV8: 540 Howard St (777-1419 or 957-1730). An old warehouse in
    SoMa, very popular, good jazz.
I-Beam: 1748 Haight (668-6006). A popular gay club, with a mix of lasers,
    videos, neon, punks and cowboy boots.
Nightbreak: 1821 Haight (221-9008). One of the city's more depraved places,
    with fearful bouncers. Dancing on Friday and Wednesday nights, happy
    hour before 7pm. Has gay nights.
Slim's: 333 11th St (621-3330). Old brick warehouse in SoMa, with cosmo-
    politan clientele and good jazz. Dancing to soul and funk on some nights
    ($5 or free with student card).

Classical Music, Theatre and Dance. The outdoors Midsummer Music Festival, which takes place at Sigmund Stern Grove (19th Avenue and Sloat Blvd), has free Sunday afternoon concerts from late June to August. The San Francisco Symphony Orchestra, one of America's best, plays 'pops' concerts (i.e. light classical music) in the Civic Auditorium in summer. For the rest of the year, the orchestra performs a more serious repertoire at the Louise M Davies Hall in the Civic Centre (431-5400 or 864-6000) at Van Ness and Grove Avenues.

San Francisco doesn't have a great reputation for mainstream theatre. The Geary Theater (Geary and Taylor Streets), also known as the American Conservatory Theater, has a repertory season from October to June, but it is also an established testing-ground for comic actors. For the bigger names in comedy go to the expensive but atmospheric Punch Line (444 Battery St, 397-7573). In both San Francisco and Berkeley there are plenty of Equity-waiver theatres staging largely experimental works. Free Shakespeare is performed in summer at Liberty Meadows in Golden Gate Park.

The Orpheum Theater, 1192 Market St (474-3800) is host to local and travelling companies, plus (for Gilbert and Sullivan fans) the Civic Light Opera from May to July.

The three-month San Francisco Opera season commences in early September with a performance in Golden Gate Park. The remainder of the season continues at the War Memorial Opera House in the Civic Center (864-3330). Each June, the International Summer Festival includes grand opera in repertory. Seats are hard to come by and extremely expensive, although cheap tickets can sometimes be had by queuing on the morning of the performance. Your chances are better at the Theater on the Square (Kensington Park Hotel, 450 Post St, 433-9500). This is the city's main fringe venue, which hosts all types of theatre, including comic opera.

The highly-rated San Francisco Ballet (621-3838) shares the War Memorial Opera House. The season begins each year with Tchaikovsky's Nutcracker Suite in December and lasts through until May. For avant-garde dance, try the Oberlin Dance Collective (3153 17 St, 863-6606), near Shotwell St in Mission District.

SPORT

The 49ers are the local football team and play at Candlestick Park (eight miles south of downtown on US 101; 468-2249). San Franciscans demand good-quality food even at football matches, and alongside the usual hot dogs are vegetarian sausages, salads and other healthy snacks.

The East Bay teams are generally superior to their San Franciscan rivals, particularly in the specialist art of referee-baiting. The Oakland A's (baseball) use the Oakland-Alameda Coliseum (66th Avenue, off US 880, 510-638-4900), easily reached by BART from San Francisco. For soccer, you have no choice but to cross the Bay to see the Oakland Stompers in action. The Golden State Warriors represent the city at basketball.

Horse racing takes place at the Golden Gate Fields (across the Bay at Albany; 510-526-3020) during the spring, and at Bay Meadows (in San Mateo, southeast of the city) at other times of the year. The Grand National is not a race but a rodeo held each October at the Cow Palace (469-6000, ticket office 469-6065), west of Candlestick Park. Bets may be placed on this event and other race meetings on-course; for other forms of gambling you must cross the border into Nevada.

If you feel up to seeing most of San Francisco's sights in a little over two hours, join the city's Marathon in late July, though competition for places is fierce.

SHOPPING

The arcades of Fisherman's Wharf, Ghirardelli Square, the Anchorage and Embarcadero Center are great for window shopping. So too are the shops around Union Square, which include some of the most expensive in the world. The San Francisco Centre on Market St (near the Visitors' Centre) includes the Nordstrom fashion emporium, with an extraordinary spiral escalator which takes shoppers up 150 feet. More ordinary purchases may be made at the department stores on Market St, or the suburbs for cheaper shopping.

If your interests are specialized, head for the Ghirardelli complex (a former chocolate factory), where you will find shops such as Hammock Way, which could provide one answer to an accommodation crisis, and Come Fly a Kite, whose proprietor Diresh Bahadur claims a world *indoor* kite-flying record of over two hours. Just southeast of Ghirardelli Square is a Greenpeace store, where at least you might feel that you're spending money in a good cause. The nearby Cannery (formerly the world's largest fruit-canning factory) and Pier 39 are also worth strolling through, but they are very touristy.

Among the many specialist book and record shops supported by the local community of artists and intellectuals is the avant-garde Citylights books, 261 Columbus Avenue, run by poet Lawrence Ferlingetti and open until midnight.

If you're in the market for used clothing, your best bet is the Purple Heart (veteran's charity) Thrift Store on 1855 Mission St (621-2581). There's a good selection of outdoor clothing, camping gear including sleeping bags ($40), tents and mess kits. Another highly rated shop is the Salvation Army Thrift Store at 1509 Valencia, where you can pick up designer labelled men's shirts and trousers for a few dollars, plus jeans, sports gear, shoes, boots, suits, sweaters, T-shirts ($1), records (99c) and books. While the stock varies at the St Vincent de Paul Society on 1519 Haight (863-3615), the staff are helpful and the clothes very cheap.

When you buy clothes which are not cleaned and pressed, they can be washed and dried for $2 at nearby launderettes.

THE MEDIA

Radio. The prevalent tone of stations in San Francisco has shifted somewhat from the days when KSFO broadcast a 'contraband stock report' listing the current prices for marijuana and prostitutes. But the city still has some innovative stations. KALX (90.7 FM) broadcasts from the University of California at Berkeley. The station specializes in rock music punctuated by community news and information exchange, such as ride-sharing announcements. The numerous other stations serving the Bay Area include outfits which cater strictly for gays, and others broadcasting to the Chinese, Filipino, Spanish and Irish minorities. The nearest equivalent to BBC Radio 3 or 4 is KQED (88.5 FM), which is the public broadcasting station. If homesickness strikes, you can hear BBC programmes on KAWL (91.7 FM). For Country and Western, tune to KSAN (94.9 FM); for black music, KSOL (107.7 FM); and for news, KGO (810 AM) or KCBS (740 AM).

Newspapers. The *San Francisco Chronicle* is the 'quality' daily paper (though it's no *New York Times*), and its listings are fairly comprehensive. *The Oakland Tribune*, while not so good for listings, has excellent news coverage. For complete details of the less formal brands of entertainment, try the free weekly *San Francisco Bay Guardian* or *SF Weekly*; in the East Bay, the freesheet is the *Express*.

Crime and Safety

Tourist haunts in the Bay Area are relatively safe, at least during daylight. At night the main thoroughfares are well-lit and heavily patrolled, but women may be harrassed by kerbcrawlers. You are advised to spend your evenings in lively districts such as North Beach or Castro. While the Union Square area is recommended for its cheap hotels, it is not a place to dawdle at night.

The most notorious area downtown is the triangle enclosed by Market, Geary and Divisadero Streets, including the Civic Center and the Greyhound terminal. Worst of all is the Western Addition (bounded by Gough, Hayes, Steiner and Geary Streets), which is the sort of place that gives inner cities a bad name, and should be avoided at all times. Only marginally less insalubrious is the nearby district known as the Tenderloin — on Ellis, Eddy and Turk Streets, just north of the Civic Center. This is one of San Francisco's main red light districts);

Other areas to avoid after dark are: the panhandle of Golden Gate Park (including lower Haight St), which attracts malevolent loiterers, only some of whom are plain-clothed police; the skid row area south of Market St at 5th and 6th Avenues; Mission district (where street gangs fight out rivalries with guns); and Candlestick Park stadium. Finally, you should be wary of wandering around both Oakland and the off-campus areas of Berkeley after sunset.

Drugs. Marijuana is widely grown in the Northwest USA and is California's leading cash crop. Consequently, marijuana is readily available. The possession of small amounts in the state of California (i.e. under one ounce) will not get you a criminal record, but might get you a fine of $100. Street dealers are often untrustworthy; those on campus in Berkeley are the least unreliable.

The possession and use of cocaine and opium derivatives is still a felony, and buying from street dealers is a highly risky business. LSD is no longer popular among the young, upwardly-mobile set who comprise the major part of the drug-taking community in San Francisco.

Help and Information *i*

The area code for San Francisco is 415; 510 is used for Oakland, Berkeley and certain other parts of the Bay Area.

Information: The San Francisco Visitor Information Center, on the lower level of Hallidie Plaza at Powell and Market Streets (391-2000/1). It is open 9am-5.30pm Monday to Friday, until 2pm on Saturday and 10am-3pm on Sunday. You might also try the voluntary International Visitors Center on the 4th floor of 312 Sutter St, near Grant St (986-1388). In Oakland the information centre is at 1000 Broadway, Suite 200 (839-9000). For fast computer information, find one of the many *Chronicle Videofax* terminals within the city and at the airport. For a recorded summary of the day's events, dial 391-2000. The City Guide Helpline is on 332-9611.

British Consulate: 1 Sansome St (981-3030).
American Express 237 Post St (981-5533); 295 California St (788-4367); 400 21st St, Oakland (510-834-2833).
Travelers' Aid: 38 Mason St (255-2252); also at the Transbay Terminal,

1st and Mission Streets, and on the departure level of San Francisco International Airport.

Medical Emergencies: St Francis Memorial Hospital, 900 Hyde St (775-4321). There is also a 24 hour-clinic at 2339 Durant St in Berkeley (548-2570).

Late night pharmacy: Hub Pharmacy, 1700 Market St. Open 7.30am to 11.30pm.

Helplines: Lesbian/Gay switchboard 510-841-6224; Dial-a-Quake 642-2160; San Francisco Drug Line 752-3400; Rape Crisis Line 647-7273.

Post Office: the main office is at 1076 Mission St, CA 94101 (556-2381).

Legal Aid Society: 864-8848.

The geography of Northern California, Oregon and Washington approximates to a series of north-south strips. Along the coast, a range of mile-high mountains towers precariously above the Pacific. Inland lies a valley containing some of the richest agricultural land in the world. The Cascade Mountains (so called because of the many waterfalls which pour down from the ice- and snow-capped peaks) form the eastern barrier from the huge Central Valley. The rain shadow of the Cascades means that the extreme east of the region is a rocky desert considered fit only for military installations and Native American Reservations. Travel further east, and you reach the foothills of the Rockies. The whole of the coastal area is alive with seismic activity, from the San Andreas fault in the south to the northern volcanoes of unreliable dormancy, of which the most notorious is Washington's Mount St Helens. The eruption on May 1980 has had an effect on the climate of the whole world.

Climate. Rainfall near the coast is heavy throughout the year; Corvallis, Oregon — one of the wettest places in America — is jokingly described as having an English climate. However, the temperature of the sea actually rises as you move north because of the warming influence of the Japanese current, thereby encouraging many coastal holiday towns to flourish. Try one of the oldest: Seaside, in northern Oregon.

NORTHERN CALIFORNIA

Northern California is normally defined as everything north of Fresno, a rather dull market city which does not conform to the Californian image. Economic life in Northern California is a tale of three valleys; the great Central Valley which stretches almost the length of the state and whose fruit supplies much of the western world; the Napa Valley, northeast of San Francisco and California's answer to the Loire in both scenery and produce; and the so-called Silicon Valley, a swathe of land in Santa Clara County south of the Bay, where earth tremors have not deterred the creation of the world centre for microelectronics.

South from San Francisco. The Monterey Peninsula, 80 miles south of the Bay, is a wine-producing area, but the local economy relies more upon the rich and famous who live there and the hordes of tourists who flock to see them. Unlike Beverly Hills, the Peninsula deserves a visit for the charms of its scenery rather than of its inhabitants. The former fishing village of Monterey acts as the northern gateway to the Peninsula. Dating back to the

1770s, the town provides excellent (if overpriced) wining and dining. Its Fisherman's Wharf resembles a miniature version of San Francisco's. Visitors to the Wharf can feed the entertaining (and overfed) sea lions, visit the Bay Aquarium, then dine in one of the smart seafood restaurants such as Rappa's; the clam chowder is excellent, but prices are high, so go for the 'Early Bird Dinner'.

A few miles west lies Cannery Row, where John Steinbeck wrote the novel of the same name. The 15-mile drive south from Monterey to Carmel takes you past some of the most splendid homes in Southern California. The town's most famous resident (and former mayor) is Clint Eastwood. He owns the Hog's Back restaurant in San Carlos St where you can sample such delights as a Dirty Harry burger. It is often busy with diners hoping that Clint might be filling in as a waiter for the eveing. To enjoy the area properly, you need to get out of your hire car and walk or cycle around the Peninsula. For cycle hire try Freewheeling Cycles, 188 Webster St, Monterey (373-3855). The 'Seventeen Mile Drive' winds along the coast to Point Lobos, where you can see otters and sea lions. A $5 toll is charged. Most of the Peninsula's 16 golf courses are open to the public, though they are expensive.

Nearby is Big Sur, an area replete with redwoods, majestic cliffs and beautiful beaches, the most spectacular being Pfeiffer Beach, and the bridge which made the coast road possible. Bixby Creek Bridge on Highway 1 opened in 1932, and opened up the coast to traffic. Big Sur River gets its name from being the larger of the two south-pointing rivers discovered by Spanish missionaries as they made their way north along the Californian coast. It now refers to a 60-mile/100km stretch of coastline where the Santa Lucia mountains drop straight into the Pacific.

Big Sur has a small but lively artistic community, and it is easy to meet people. There are many camping facilities and other inexpensive rustic accommodation. You will find there the quintessential Californian restaurant called Nepenthe, originally built by Orson Welles, which affords a superb view of the ocean.

Just off Highway 1 at San Simeon is the strange and wonderful former vacation home of the late newspaper publisher William Randolph Hearst. Hearst Castle is open for tours every day of the year except Thanksgiving, Christmas and New Year. Its construction began in 1919 and took 27 years to complete. As well as being a newsman, Hearst was also a great movie mogul and would often invite stars to come and stay: Charlie Chaplin and the Marx Brothers were frequent visitors. You can take four different walking tours of the castle, the three guest houses and the gardens. Tour 1 is recommended for your first visit but it is advisable to book: in California call MISTIX on 1-800-446-PARK (from outside the state the number is 619-452-1950). After office hours tickets can be booked at the Holiday Inn in San Simeon.

Continuing south from San Simeon, the friendly town of San Luis Obispo is also worth visiting especially if you can make the Farmers' Market held each Tuesday evening. It is much more than just a market ... barbecued food of every description is available, there are bargain fruit stalls and entertainment from bands, jugglers, clowns and the local radio stations. If your visit does not coincide with a Thursday evening, most of the central coast towns also have Farmers' Markets.

The outstanding views from Highway One continue with interruptions from towns like Pismo Beach where many activities are available including horseriding on the beach, fishing from the pier and surf fishing.

North from San Francisco.

Muir Woods. For those without the time or resources to make the long journey to the Redwoods, Muir Woods to the north of San Francisco offers a scaled-down but rewarding version. Only 12 miles north of the Golden Gate Bridge, off Highway 1, this beautiful and fascinating forest covers an area of 560 acres. The tallest redwood is 252 feet high, and most of the mature trees are between 500 and 800 years old. The park is open all year round, from 8am to sunset. It is cool, shaded and moist all year so jackets are advisable. The forest has six miles of walking trails, details of which are available from the Visitor Center on arrival. You can have an easier walk by starting from the excellent Mountain Home Inn, several hundred feet above the park. Informative tours and night hikes are arranged through the Ranger Station (388-2595). You can reach it by bus from San Francisco: take Golden Gate Transit buses 20, 50 or 64 to Marin City, then transfer to the 63. Picnicking and camping are not allowed but facilities are provided nearby.

The Marin Ridge Trail is a walk through glorious scenery from the north end of the Golden Gate Bridge; call in at the Marin Headlands Visitor Center for a map, or call 331-1540.

Napa Valley. Centred on the small, lively town of St Helena, this area produces some of the best wines in the USA. Most wineries along Highway 29 offer guided tours and free tastings. Christian Brothers Winery (off Redwood Road) is picturesque and generous with tastings. Robert Mondavi in Oakville offers an excellent tour and produces first-class wines. The Sterling Winery in Calistoga is reached by a $5 cable car and provides a splendid view of the Valley. Domaine Chandon is a sparkling wine establishment at Yountville (tel 707-944-2280); it has a good tour, but you have to pay for drinks afterwards. It opens 11am-5.30pm — daily in summer, from Wednesday to Sunday in winter. Take a picnic lunch and visit several wineries. (This is one occasion when hitch-hiking is probably safer than driving). Try to avoid the tourist buses which operate to Napa from San Francisco, unless your idea of fun is supping a thimbleful of wine prior to being herded into the buying room. A tour is especially lively around harvest-time in October; just as in Europe there is a festive atmosphere surrounding the *vendange*. The Valley's annual wine festival is held at the fairground in Napa in early November. For more information, contact the Napa Valley Vintners' Association, 900 Meadowood Lane, St Helena 94574 (707-963-0148).

Californian Redwoods. Giant redwoods abound along the Californian coast north of San Francisco. The coastal scenery and charming fishing villages (actually yacht marinas) through which Highway 1 passes are well worth visiting. You may think there is little to distinguish the attractive villages of Inverness, Bodega Bay and Mendocino from villages along the New England coast, except that the sun sets rather than rises in the Ocean. But as you move further north, the crowds and commercialism fade and the coast becomes more rugged. The highway is line with state parks providing camping facilities and ample opportunities to admire the famous trees, culminating in the world's tallest tree (368 feet high) in Redwood National Park near the Oregon border. The terrain is ideal for hikers, but you'll need strong legs as little public transport exists. Campsites abound, but range from the primitive ($1) with outhouses to the well-equipped ($10) with flush toilets and hot showers. The Redwood Youth Hostel is at 14480 Highway 101 (482-8265) with rooms going for $6.50 a night.

A good way to see the Napa Valley and Redwoods is the Green Tortoise bus. A 'hostel on wheels' when you're not camped out, you can do a six-day looping trip of Northern California for around $250.

Sacramento. The state capital of California (population 275,000) looks remarkably similar to many other state capitals, even though it administers the most populous state in the Union. There is little of interest in the city itself apart from the restored section near the river, but it is a good base from which to explore the '49er territory southeast of Sacramento. Ghost towns like Rough and Ready are all that remain of the 1849 gold rush which led of the opening of Northern California. All the gold has been exhausted, but that does not stop the descendants of fortune hunters from firing out gold pans. Take the appropriately-numbered State Highway 49 from Loyalton south to Oakhurst. This road runs the entire length of the principal gold seam; hence the name Mother Lode Highway.

Yosemite National Park

Anyone familiar with Ansel Adams photographs will not need to be persuaded to visit Yosemite National Park, which lies about 200 miles east of San Francisco. The American photographer has come closer than anyone to capturing the awesome landscapes, though nothing can compete with the reality.

The national park encompasses an area of around 1,200 square miles. At its heart is the Yosemite Valley, a spectacular landscape created by glaciers, walled in on either side by peaks and almost vertical cliffs. Waterfalls cascade to the valley floor, where there are alpine meadows, lakes, gushing streams and groves of giant sequoia (redwood), cedar and fir trees. The valley is eight miles long and just one mile wide.

Bears are among the animals you may be fortunate — or unfortunate — enough to see in Yosemite. The National Park Service asks visitors not to leave their car windows open, and kindly offers the following advice: 'If you see a bear, throw objects towards the bear from a safe distance, yell, clap hands, bang pots together.' We are told that the (unspecified) result is instantaneous.

The millions (literally) of visitors that descend on the park each year are almost as staggering as the place itself. But even Yosemite is vast enough to engulf the swarms that tramp its trails. And by not visiting in July or August, you can avoid the worst of the crowds. The spring and early autumn are both good times to visit, though if you've got good outdoor gear nothing can beat Yosemite in winter, when snow has begun to fall and the park is at its emptiest.

The easy walks are along the valley bottom, to the Bridalveil Falls, for example, or Mirror Lake. These trails are also the busiest, so you must head upwards for the greatest tranquillity and, of course, a whole range of heavenly views. You can, for example, scale the awesome Half Dome, the sheerest cliff in the States: a staircase leads up the back to the top: the 15-mile round trip is no easy climb, and you need to start at dawn. No less dramatic is El Capitan, at the mouth of the valley, which is the largest block of exposed granite in the world.

For those who can't even manage to stroll along the bottom, in summer a free bus does a two-hour circular trip around the valley floor. It stops at departure points for up-hill trails if you should feel a surge of energy. It is also possible to hire bikes.

The finest views of the valley are from Glacier Point, accessible along a road. If you can't face the idea of hiking to the top from the bottom of the valley, take a bus to Glacier Point and walk down.

The park's main attraction outside the Yosemite Valley is the Mariposa Grove to the south, the park's biggest redwood forest. An open-seated 'tram' (actually pulled by a truck) takes visitors from the car park to the grove, though it's not a difficult walk.

Arrival and Departure. The fact that there are so many visitors, reflects the ease with which Yosemite can be reached, at least from the west: it takes about five hours to drive there from San Francisco. In summer there is a never-ending stream of cars, coaches and snazzy campervans (known as 'recreation vehicles' or RVs). If you drive, fill your tank before entering the park, where petrol is scarce and/or expensive.

Access by bus is easiest from Merced, on Highway 99, about 70 miles west of the park. The town is served by about seven Greyhound buses a day from San Francisco ($14 one way), which take 4-5 hours. Buses from Merced to the park are run by Yosemite Via Bus (Greyhound depot, 209-722-0366), leaving daily at 8am and 2.40pm and taking $2\frac{1}{2}$ hours. The fare is $32. The other possible starting-point is Fresno, though buses (McCoys Charter Service on 209-268-2237) run only on weekdays. There is a frequent bus service to Fresno from San Francisco; the fare is $20.

In addition, there are numerous tours available — try Green Tortoise (415-821-0803), with three-day tours for around $220.

Accommodation. One good reason to visit Yosemite out of season is that accommodation prices drop. Cabins are generally cheaper than hotel rooms, e.g. $50 upwards as opposed to $70 upwards. The cheapest places are Yosemite Lodge and Curry Village, whose cabins can accommodate 2-6 people. There are several campsites, the liveliest of which is the Sunnyside Walk-In — probably your only option if you've booked nothing in advance.

In summer you should book in advance by calling Yosemite Reservations on 209-252-4848, whichever type of lodging you choose.

Information. The three roads running into the park converge at Yosemite Village, which is where you'll find food shops, snack bars and also the visitors' centre. General information on travel, lodging and trails in Yosemite is available on 209-372-0264/5.

OREGON

Portland
Oregon's only large city (population 460,000) faces Washington State across the Columbia River, one hundred river miles from the Pacific. Portland originally developed as a staging post for the lumber cut upstream. It got its name after two early settlers — one from Boston and the other from Portland, Maine — tossed a coin for the privilege of calling it after their hometowns. It is now a thriving modern city, divided into east and west by the Willamette River. Despite the mushrooming of shiny office blocks, it remains informal and peaceful. Portland claims to be the 'City of Roses': if you visit between May and late September, you will understand why. The 17-day Rose Festival is held every June. On clear days, Portland is overlooked by Mount Hood, 40 miles distant but over two miles high.

Do not be misled, like some travellers, by the apparent proximity of Canada. The signs pointing across the river to Vancouver refer to a small town in Washington state, not to the city in British Columbia.

City Layout. Portland straddles the Willamette River, a tributary of the Columbia River. The main part of the city is on the west bank of the river, hemmed in by the I-405 freeway. Addresses are classified as SW, SE, NW, NE, depending in whether they are east or west of the river and north or south of the main east-west axis, Burnside St.

Arrival and Departure. *Air:* Portland International Airport (PDX) is six miles northeast of downtown, close to the Washington River. Call 335-1154 for flight information, or 288-PARK for details of parking availability.

The Tri-Met bus to the city centre, number 12, leaves every 20 minutes or so. The journey time is about 40 minutes to 5th and Stark, downtown. The fare of $1.25 includes a free transfer to any other line.

Train and Bus: Union Station, at the north end of 6th Avenue close to the Willamette River in the Old Town, is the city's surface transportation hub. It is the depot for Greyhound buses and Amtrak trains.

Driving: the motorist is not a welcome species in Portland. The city prides itself on an environmentally friendly transport system, so parking is limited downtown and priority given to buses and trams at every opportunity.

Getting Around. First, learn to pronounce some tricky names correctly: Couch is pronounced *kooch*; Glisan is *glee-san.*

Portland has arguably the best public transport of any American city. Tri-Met runs buses and MAX, the local light rail system (Metropolitan Area Express, approximating to a tram system). All public transport is free within the downtown 'Fareless Square' area, bounded by the river, NW Hoyt and the I-405 freeway. Outside this area, there are three concentric zones. A one or two-zone ride costs 95c; all three are $1.25. Fare machines on board take $1 notes as well as coins. You must take a transfer, as it acts as your receipt even if you have no intention to transfer. It must be shown on demand to inspectors.

Most buses are funnelled through the 'Transit Mall', along SW 5th and 6th Avenues. Call 233-3511 for information.

Accommodation. The AYH hostel is on the east side of the Willamette, some distance from downtown, at 3031 Hawthorne Boulevard (236-3380). An organisation called the Northwest Bed and Breakfast, 610 SW Broadway (243-7616) has a list of places starting at $25 a night, but you have to pay an initial $20 to join. There are several comfortable options. The Mark

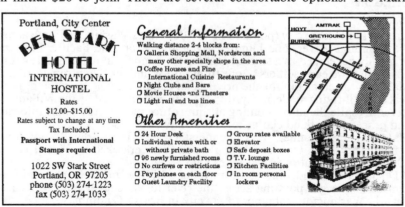

Spencer Hotel, 409 SW 11th Avenue (224-3293) costs around $59 double for a suite, and is good value. The Ben Stark, 1022 SW Stark (274-1223), is cheaper and tattier.

Eating and Drinking. The local speciality is fresh seafood, particularly oysters and Portland salmon. Mother's Deli, a student hangout, at 1802 SW 10th St and Fuller's at 136 NW 9th are best value selections. Portland Saturday Market at 108 W Burnside St (close to the river) has good, cheap fruit and vegetables. Oregon produces excellent wines, and there are 35 wineries just west of Portland.

You can tour the Blitz-Weinhard Brewery (1133 W Burnside St; 222-4351) between 1pm and 4pm from Monday to Friday; call in advance to reserve a place. The microbrewery is alive and well in Portland. Call in for a beer at the Bridgeport Brew Pub at 1313 NW Marshall St (241-7179) and ask for a free copy of the map to the others.

Exploring. Walking around the downtown area is full of surprises. Nancy Macklin's Map of Portland is a wonderful piece of cartography, showing every point of interest from 'an arty nude statue' on SW 5th Avenue to 'Shoe Repair while-u-wait' on SW Alder St.

The world's first post-modernist office block is the Portland Building, enclosed by Main and Madison Streets and 4th and 5th Avenues. It is boldly coloured but ultimately unsatisfying. The 30-foot bronze statue called *Portlandia* is second in size only to the Statue of Liberty.

Close by, Nike Town (SW Salmon St and SW 6th Avenue) is a shop/exhibition devoted to the sport shoe. It has the oddest opening hours of anywhere in America: Monday to Thursday, 10am-7.01pm; Friday 10am-8pm; Saturday 10am-6.52pm; and Sunday 11.25am to 6.23pm.

OMSI is the popular name for the Oregon Museum of Science and Industry, the new riverfront museum at 1945 SE Water Avenue (222-2828). Of interest to more than just thrusting young advertising professionals, the American Advertising Museum (9 NW 2nd Avenue, 226-0000) is the only one of its kind in the world. It opens 11am-5pm from Wednesday to Friday, noon-5pm at weekends.

Entertainment. As well as dozens of cinema screens and bars featuring live music, the Portland Center for the Performing Arts has an excellent repertoire. Consisting of two theatres, a concert hall and an auditorium — plus bars and restaurants — it is at 1111 Southwest Broadway. Free tours of the complex are given on Saturdays and Wednesdays at 11am; call 248-4335 for more details. For event information, dial 248-4496.

Shopping. The biggest bookshop west of the Mississippi is Powell's City of Books, which occupies the entire block enclosed at 1005 West Burnside St (228-4651) and has over a million new and used books. The company also has a branch at the airport and four specialist stores:

Books for Kids: Cascade Plaza, 8775 Southwest Cascade Ave, Beaverton (643-3131).

Travel Store: Pioneer Courthouse Square (228-1108).

Books for Cooks: 3747 SE Hawthorne (238-1668).

Technical Book Store: 33 Northwest Park (at Couch; 228-3906).

Help and Information. The area code for Portland is 503.

The Convention and Visitors' Association is at SW Front and Salmon Streets (222-2223), sandwiched between the blocks of the World Trade Center by the river. There are plenty of free listings papers, plus *The Alternative*

Connection — aimed at the gay and lesbian community. Travellers with disabilities can pick up the free *Oregon Guide to Accessibility* from here.

Further Afield. The only other towns of any size in Oregon are linked to Portland by I-5, part of the Pan-American Highway. Eugene has a population of only 76,000, but the concentration of 16,000 students attending the University of Oregon in such a small city adds a respectable amount of life. Similarly, the state capital Salem has the usual collection of public buildings and bureaucrats but good nightlife thanks to Willamette University. The small town of Ashland (population 12,000) in the south of the state is notable for having a Shakespearean theatre modelled on the Globe. Performances are given year round, outdoors in summer when the weather is always perfect. Despite the occasional but unmistakable disparity between the quality of the star actors imported from afar (usually Britain) and the local cast, the productions are excellent.

The best trip to make from Portland is a loop inland through stunning scenery. Head east along I-84 and Highway 30 from Portland, but turn off onto the onto the Historic Columbia River Highway — part of the original Oregon Trail from the east — which runs to Multnomah Falls. It is well worth the 40-minute ascent to the top of the falls, with stunning views. Continue to Hood River, then head south on Highway 35. Here you are in the lee of Mount Hood itself.   Timberline Lodge is, as its name suggests, at the tree line where forests end and permanent snowfields begin. Jutting from the side of Mount Hood, and reached by a tricky six-mile drive from the main highway, it is a massive ski-lodge which was built from volcanic rock during the Great Depression of the 1930s. In summer, when the wind is still so cold as to keep the huge open fires burning, room rates are surprisingly low; you could stay for as little as $50 double.

You head back to Portland on Highway 26, a relatively dull road enlivened by turnings marked to Orient, Damascus and Boring.

WASHINGTON

Seattle. The largest city (population 500,000) in Washington likes to forget that Olympia is state capital and that Juneau is capital of Alaska, and has assumed de facto responsibility for both states. Puget Sound, upon which it lies, is the southern terminus of the Alaska Marine Highway (although this will switch to Bellingham in 1990), and the Alaska operations of many corporations are based in Seattle. The sheltered harbours have turned the city into an important international seaport. The Space Needle provides a 605-foot panorama of the city. Puget Sound and Mount Rainier in the Cascade Mountains. It is a solidly middle-class city thriving on the lumber and aircraft industry, neither of which is much evidence in the city centre. Seattle also regularly tops polls of USA holiday destinations.

Arrival and Departure. *Air:* Henry M Jackson International Airport (known as Sea-Tac, short for Seattle-Tacoma) is one of the least fraught American gateways for international air travellers, even if there is a large sign up in the Customs hall warning travellers not to make jokes with the officers. After passing through customs, you are whisked under the runway to the main terminal building. Bus 194 (with some express variants) takes 35-55 mintes to Pike St and 2nd Avenue downtown.

Bus: the Greyhound station is a little north of the city centre at Stewart St and 9th Avenue. There are eight daily departures to both Vancouver and Portland, six to San Francisco and two to Los Angeles.

Train: Amtrak's station is south of the city centre at King St and 4th Avenue. the *Coast Starlight* runs daily to Los Angeles via Portland and Oakland, with additional services on the *Mount Rainier* and *Pioneer* as far as Portland.

Sea: the Washington State Ferry Terminal is at Pier 52. Services to Vancouver Island sail from Pier 69.

Getting Around. Buses are free within the 'Magic Carpet' zone, bounded by the freeway and the waterfront. Outside this area, fareas are cheap, $2.50 buying you an all-day pass. One peculiarity: on buses heading out of the city centre, you pay on leaving the bus; on inbound buses, pay on entry as normal. For information, ring Metropolitan Transit (Metro) on 624-7277.

A monorail links Westlake Mall (in the centre of the city) with Seattle Center, site of the 1962 World's Fair. Departures are every 15 minutes from 10 am until midnight and the fare is 50c. The journey takes one and half minutes.

Accommodation. Cheap accommodation is not hard to find in Seattle: try a couple of blocks inland from the port. There is a good AYH hostel at 84 Union St (622-5443).

Eating and Drinking. Eating cheaply in Seattle is not difficult either. The Market Cafe at 1523 1st Avenue (624-2598) gives you a $3.50 breakfast that keeps you going all day; the Manila cafe at 624 S Weller 682 (223-9763) has delicious but cheap Filipino food; the Fran-Glor's Creole Cafe at 511 South Jackson has an immense gumbo from $4.50, with free Dixieland jazz thrown in; and the feminist The Cause Celebre at 254 E 15th Ave (323-1888) has sensational ice cream and baked goods.

Exploring. There is little in Seattle that cries out for the visitor's attention, but it is a comfortable and friendly place to be. The beaches are excellent (if a little breezy for much of the time, the inland walks fun and the museums entertaining. Furthermore the University is a frenetically lively place, with all sorts of good places to hang out on University Boulevard — known as 'The Avenue'. Seattle was the home of rock guitar legend Jimi Hendrix, who died in 1970. He is commemorated only at the city's Woodland Park Zoo. Overlooking the African Savanna habitat is a rock marked as the Jimi Hendrix Viewpoint.

Calendar of Events

late January/early February	Chinese New Year celebrations, San Francisco
late March	Festival of Jazz, University Portland
April	Cherry Blossom Festival, Japantown, San Francisco
May	Northwest Folklife Festival, Seattle
early June	Rose Festival, Portland
August	Washinton State International Air Fair, Everett
late August	Oregon State Fair, Salem
early September	San Francisco International Stand-up Comedy Competition
September (2nd weekend)	San Francisco Blues Festival
mid September	Monterey Jazz Festival
October	Festa Italiana, San Francisco

Hawaii

The fiftieth state to join the Union is a string of tropical islands jutting out of the Pacific Ocean 2,500 miles from the Californian coast — halfway to Japan, and containing what sometimes seems like half the Japanese population on package tours. Nowhere in the USA is the swing of the economic pendulum in favour of East Asia more evident, and the commercial and cultural consequences are fascinating — not least, the chance to browse in some spectacular Japanese shops and to be submerged in Japanese culture.

The most populous and popular island is Oahu, which is dominated by Honolulu, the state capital (population 800,000), and the adjoining excesses of Waikiki — according to some, the best urban beach resort anywhere. Next most important in terms of tourism is Maui, midway between Oahu and Hawaii. Maui is lively and commercialized, but it lacks the plastic paradise image of Oahu and is frequented by a generally younger and trendier crowd; the waters off its west coast also offer some of the best whale-watching in the world. Hawaii ('the Big Island') is the largest of the group, also giving its name to the whole state; it is the best for the great outdoors (although very wet). The only other islands of significance are Molokai, Lanai, Kauai and Nihau. The smaller islands offer a degree of peace and tranquillity.

Although the state has some fishing and farming, the vast majority of the population depends to some extent on the tourist industry. For millions of Americans and Canadians, the islands of Hawaii provide the same mixture of sun, sea and sin that has Europeans flooding to the Mediterranean. And just as on the Mediterranean, travellers can either succumb to the pleasures of mass tourism or stray away from the beaten track to find more unspoilt attractions — which, in this case, take the shape of magnificent volcanic landscapes.

The excesses of Hawaii extend to the price you must pay to enjoy it. In the late 80s even regular visitors from the USA — the mainstay of the state's tourist trade — were deterred by the astronomical resort prices. Be warned that Hawaii can be extremely expensive if you don't go as part of a package tour. As in the former Soviet Union, tourism in Hawaii is geared towards visitors on organized holidays. For around $400 you can get a return flight from the West Coast of the USA, a few nights in a beach motel and a hired car. To make the same trip independently could cost much more: the air fare alone is about $400, motel rooms booked by private individuals cost upwards of $50 per night — unless you camp, or get a bed at a hostel — and regular car rental rates are high. If you plan to go it alone, take advantage of the good bus services and cheap hostels on Oahu, and consider buying a packaged side-trip to another island: these cost as little as $100.

THE PEOPLE

Hawaii's population consists of indigenous Polynesian inhabitants, Asian immigrants (mainly Japanese and Filipino), American settlers and the mixed-blood offspring of combinations of these. Most of the 1.3 million residents are friendly and approachable, as you'd expect from a state which depends for its prosperity on pleasing visitors. You can hardly turn around without having someone greet you with 'Aloha' and put a *lei* (wreath) around your neck — commercial but fun. British visitors seem particularly popular, and Hawaii likes to emphasise its links with the United Kingdom: the state flag bears the Union Jack in one corner, and Honolulu is one of the few places in the USA with anything approaching a decent cricket pitch.

At the start of 1993, however, there was controversy during the centenary of the overthrow of Hawaii's last monarch, Queen Liliuokalani — an action assisted by US Marines. Activists among the 200,000 indigenous Hawaiians are calling for a degree of self-government and some independence from a federal capital 5,000 miles away, and are aiming for the kind of nation-within-a-nation acquired by other native American groups.

The Hawaiian language has the shortest alphabet in the world, which explains why place names appear to be indistinguishable combinations of the letters a, e, h, i, k, l, m, n, o, p, u, and w. Hawaiian Scrabble must be a very dull game. Fortunately, everyone speaks an approximation of American English, though embellished with some native and Asian vocabulary. Since the Hawaiian language is largely phonetic, you shouldn't have too much trouble getting your tongue around place names: practise with Likelike (lee-kay-lee-kay) and Lahaina (la-hyena).

Making friends. You are most likely to make friends with fellow travellers. Should holiday romance blossom, you can take advantage of Hawaii's liberal and imaginative marital laws. Family court judges will perform a marriage for $30 (book a ceremony on 548-2075). Weddings can be arranged almost immediately, and some state religious authorities specialize in unusual ceremonies. Marriages have taken place 50 feet under water and while jogging along a cliff path. Divorce is not so easily arranged.

CLIMATE

Hawaii is the only state in the Union which falls within the tropics. The climate is predominantly hot and damp, though the heat is moderated by

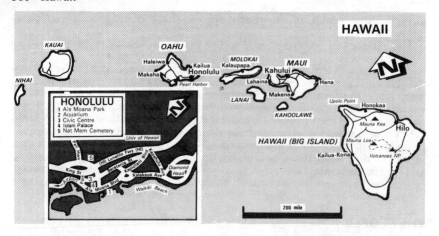

ocean breezes and the wet can be minimised by choosing your location and timing carefully. For example, you will want to avoid Mount Waialeale on the island of Kauai, which is one of the wettest spots on the earth (rainfull record 486 inches a year). But the average rainfall is more likely to be 20-50 inches, and the consistently balmy temperatures (70's in winter, 80's in the summer) make up for the occasional downpour.

The only time you are likely to need warm clothes is for high altitude journeys. A mile or two up in the mountains, the skies are often heavy with cloud and the conditions changeable. The summits of Mauna Kea and Mauna Loa on the Big Island have snow in January and February.

Nothing stands between this chain of volcanic islands and thousands of miles of unpredictable Pacific Ocean weather. The damage caused by Hurricane Iniki in 1992 to the small island of Lihau is distressing.

ARRIVAL AND DEPARTURE

Unless you arrive by cruise liner or wangle your way onto a freighter from the West Coast, you'll arrive in Hawaii on an aircraft bursting at the seams with tourists, businessmen and a few travellers en route to the Far East and Australasia. The majority of flights arrive at Honolulu (airport code HNL) on Oahu. Most of your fellow passengers will be herded on to charter buses or will head for the car hire desks. Local buses 19 and 20 run to downtown Honolulu and Waikiki Beach, leaving every 20 minutes and taking just over half an hour; no large packs or suitcases are allowed. If you have a lot of baggage take the Airporter or Waikiki Express door-to-door service, which charge $5. Both companies will also pick you up from your hotel for the return journey. Taxis will charge around $18 to take you to Waikiki.

GETTING AROUND

Oahu, Maui and the Big Island have the most substantial road networks. Most tourists seem to rent a car, so hitch-hiking is usually easy. If you opt to hire a car yourself, you'll find that rental companies are most particular about where their vehicles may be taken, so don't stray too far from the beaten track. The *Drive Guide* is a free magazine with maps and other information about Oahu.

Buses are virtually non-existent except on Oahu, where services are cheap and fairly efficient, running daily from 5am to midnight. You can pick up the *Hawaii Bus and Travel Guide* (by Milly Singletary) for $2.50, which outlines routes and also includes more general information. Taxis anywhere in are expensive.

Inter-island flights are very frequent, with a staggering 200 flights a day between Honolulu and Kahalui (on Maui). If you approach the airlines direct you'll find fares are high, e.g. $100 between Honolulu and Hilo on the Big Island; but most travel agents sell discounted tickets or can offer a package tour including a car and accommodation for no more than the cost of a return flight.

ACCOMMODATION

Resorts devoted to package tourism tend to be expensive for independent travellers, and Hawaii is no exception. In the summer low season, however, you might be able to strike a good deal. Most budget accommodation is near the waterfront in Waikiki. The choice of accommodation is much reduced outside Honolulu. Bed and Breakfast Hawaii (PO Box 449, Kapaa, HI 96746; 822-7771) has about 75 host homes charging $50-100 for a double room and breakfast.

Honolulu and Waikiki: there are two AYH hostels in Honolulu. One is near the University (2323A Seaview Avenue, 946-0591), which has dorm beds only — $10 for members, $13 for non-members. The Hale Aloha Hostel (2417 Prince Edward St, 926-8313), near Waikiki beach, is open to members only, with beds for $15 and also private rooms. In Waikiki, hostel-type accommodation is also available at the International Network Cotel (2051 Kalakaua Avenue), with dorm beds for $14, and the Waikiki Hostel (2413 Kuhio Avenue, 924-2636), which charges $15 per person, or $45 for a double. Men could also try the YMCA at 401 Atkinson Drive, Honolulu (524-5600), where a single costs about $30. Don't be surprised to encounter the odd cockroach in these cheaper places.

Haleiwa: this old town on Oahu's north shore is the main hangout for surfers, and caters for independent travellers as well as the more mainstream tourists. The Backpackers Vacation Inn and Hostel (59-788 Kamehameha Highway, 638-7838), accessible on bus 52, charges $15-20 for a bed, $40-50 for a double (with good weekly rates). On the same street is the North Shore Hostel (59-784 Kam. Highway), with similar rates.

Wailuku: this is the best base from which to explore Maui, and it has a reasonable choice of cheap places to sleep and eat. Try the Northshore Inn (2080 Vineyard St, 242-8999), which is popular among travellers and surfers, and charges from $20 per bed or $50 for a double. Slightly cheaper is the Banana Bungalow (310 Market St, 244-5090).

Camping. If money is *really* short, the best option is to camp, though there is a curious trend for vandalism at some sites. The authorities in Honolulu operate a number of beach parks where you can camp free for up to a week. Contact the Department of Parks and Recreation (650 South King St, Honolulu, 523-4525) well in advance, since reservations are invariably required. See also *The Great Outdoors*.

EATING AND DRINKING

Tropical fruits of all kinds, especially pineapples, and macadamia nuts are cheap, plentiful and delicious. But most other foodstuffs are imported at great expense from the mainland. Because of this and because of the inflation caused by wealthy tourists, eating out can carve huge holes in your budget. The way to eat most cheaply is to stick to coffee shops and fast food joints, though for a splurge you might go to a Polynesian or Japanese restaurant. Avoid the restaurants in Waikiki, though the much-touted tourist trap Wagonwheel International Market Place — serving food from around the world to the accompaniment of country and western music — can be a laugh.

Local staple dishes include *saimin*, noodles and fish cake in broth, and *maunapua* (large dumplings). Ono Hawaiian Foods (726 Kapahulu Avenue, 737-2275) is a neighbourhood restaurant in Waikiki, serving authentic dishes and patronized primarily by locals; it opens 11am-7.30pm. Helena's (1364 N King, Honolulu, 845-8044), west of the centre near the junction with Houghtailing, is a cheerful place, also serving Hawaiian specialities at reasonable prices. Perry's Smorgy has several branches, offering eat-all-you-can buffets, for breakfast, lunch and supper: one is at 2380 Kuhio Avenue at Kanekapolei (926-0184) in Waikiki. Honolulu's Chinatown, northwest of the Iolani Palace downtown, is pan-Asian and fairly spread out, though there is a concentration of restaurants along N King St. You can find cheap Japanese noodle stands dotted all over the city.

One of the best places to stock up for a picnic is the Celestial Natural Foods Supermarket at 66-44 Kam. Highway in Haleiwa (637-6729). The best place to buy macadamia nuts is at the Hawaii Country Store at 2201 Kalakaua Avenue, the main shopping/tourist street in Waikiki.

Drinking. Contrary to popular opinion, not everyone in Hawaii drinks only piñacoladas (rum, pineapple juice and coconut milk). Most of the locals stick to beer and American or Japanese whisky. Prices are higher than in comparable bars and restaurants on the mainland, but most places have a happy hour (usually 5pm-7pm), with half price drinks and free snacks. Waikiki and Honolulu's bars are disappointing, with little to distinguish between them.

EXPLORING

Many visitors, including those from Japan, visit Pearl Harbor, site of the 1941 Japanese attack which dragged the USA into World War II. The harbour, located a few miles northwest of Honolulu, is still an important naval base. It also has a Visitor Center and offers guided tours around some of the scenes of destruction. A free shuttle boat runs daily except Mondays between the harbourside and the Arizona National Memorial, which is on the hulk of the sunken ship of the same name. Sadly, you cannot escape regimentation even at this sombre monument, and after 12 minutes studying the submerged wreckage and reading the names of those who died, visitors are herded back onto the boat. Next to the Visitor Center is the Pacific Submarine Museum (open 8am-4.30pm), offering tours around the USS Bowfin.

At the other end of the city, the walk to the rim of Diamond Head is highly recommended except for claustrophobes and the vertiginous: it involves some steep drops and a narrow tunnel on the way to the summit of this dormant volcano. You should really take a torch, though this is not essential. The reward is a fine view along the rocky coast, across the incongruent highrise hotels of Waikiki, and on clear days to another island or two. Take bus 22 or 58, or drive right into the crater, from where it is about half a mile up to the rim. Start early to avoid crowds.

At the base of Diamond Head is Kapiolani Park, with the Honolulu Zoo (151 Kapahulu Avenue), which boasts a magnificent collection of tropical birds. It is open 8.30am-4pm daily. Across Kalakaua Avenue, by the sea, is the Waikiki Aquarium (923-9741), also worth a visit — particularly for the sharks. Few visitors to Hawaii imagine spending much time in museums, but the Iolani Palace is definitely worth a visit. It is the only royal palace in the USA, the 19th-century residence of King David Kalakaua. It is at King and Richards Streets in downtown Honolulu, and visitors are taken on guided tours between 9am and 2.15pm, Wednesday to Saturday. The other place to visit is the Bishop Museum (1525 Bernice St, 847-3511), northwest of downtown off Likelike Highway, which has a good collection of Hawaiian and Polynesian artefacts. It opens 9am-5pm and is accessible on bus 2 from Waikiki.

For a cheap day out simply take a local bus right around Oahu (55 and 52 both take circular routes). This will give you the chance to see some of the other resorts and won't cost more than a couple of dollars.

ENTERTAINMENT

Although there is a Honolulu Symphony and Hawaii Opera Theater (521-6537), the state is not renowned for its high culture. Live entertainment revolves around nightclub cabarets, often with a hackneyed Hawaiian slant: steel guitar renditions of old pop songs accompanied by garlanded dancing girls whose origins are just as likely to be in South Dakota as the South Pacific. There is also a very wide range of special events from Buddha Day in April to a Ukulele Festival held each July in Waikiki.

SPORT AND RECREATION

Sport in Hawaii usually means participation, and surfing in particular. You can buy, borrow or rent a surfboard, the latter option setting you back about $12 an hour, plus $25 for some tuition. Oahu is one of the world's surfing headquarters, and many beginners like the gentle waves of Waikiki. More advanced surfers prefer Makahana Beach on the northwest coast, where 20-foot waves are not uncommon. Wherever you surf, always take note of weather and tide warnings; the ocean that produces titanic waves can easily drag anything or anyone out of reach. One of the best beaches for swimming is Kailua, northeast of Waikiki, which is suprisingly quiet — unlike Hanauma Bay, to the south, which is the main place for snorkelling — the reef is so close to the shore that even the most diffident of snorkellers can have a great time. Beaches and bays on the neighbouring islands offer a wide range of surf to suit both the novice and the thrill-seeking expert, and are not as commercialized and crowded as Waikiki.

Other water sports, such as deep-sea fishing and windsurfing are almost as popular as surfing and are easy for the beginner to dabble in. Equipment and lessons are available on popular beaches, or at one of the various Ocean Activities Centers. Golfers and tennis players flock to the islands for their annual vacations because of the year-round balmy weather andy excellent facilities. A round of golf at a mid-range course might cost about $60 per person, including hire of clubs and a buggy; most golfers in Hawaii are too lazy to search hard for lost balls, so you can find plenty.

SHOPPING

Reasonably-priced shops can be found in downtown Honolulu, away from the waterfront, and at the 155-shop Ala Moana shopping mall on Atkinson Drive, between downtown and Waikiki Beach. If you are a souvenir collector, go for sun hats woven from palm leaves or brightly printed fabrics sewn into *muumuus* (loose-fitting dresses for women) or *aloha* shirts for men. Hawaii is paradise for the collectors of kitsch.

HELP AND INFORMAION

The Hawaii Visitors Bureau is at 2270 Kalakaua Avenue, Suite 801, Honolulu HI 96815 (tel 923-1811, fax 922 8991). You can also pick up endless free magazines and leaflets in the main hotels and shopping centres.

The area code for the state of Hawaii is 808, but calls from one island to another are expensive, around $2 for three minutes. Unless your holiday postcards are destined for Sapporo or Sydney, they will take at least a week to reach addresses abroad.

THE GREAT OUTDOORS

If you head inland, away from the strands of tourist development along the ocean shores, you can easily find true wilderness on any of the islands. Mountain hikes should not be undertaken casually, however, since the weather is unpredictable, the terrain varied and many of the trails are tough going. But at least there are no snakes. A useful companion is Hilary Bradt's *Backpacking in Hawaii*. Also contact the State Forestry Division at 1151 Punchbowl St (587-0166), near the Iolani Palace, for free maps showing the trails on all the islands; it is open 7.45am-4.30pm Organized group hikes are advertised in the newspapers. Most visitors make for one or both of the National Parks.

Haleakala National Park. The smallest National Park in the USA contains the largest dormant crater in the world. Haleakala ('House of the Sun') dominates the island of Maui, and on a clear day you can see almost all the Hawaiian islands from the volcano's summit (10,023ft). The oblong crater is awesome, measuring over seven miles long — about the size of Manhattan island. The terrain is mainly bare volcanic lava, but is fascinating to geologists and interesting to laymen because of the colourful streaks which successive eruptions have produced.

A Visitor Center at the southwestern entrance to the park explains the ecology and geology of the volcano, and offers lectures and guided hikes; it also makes free reservations for one of the three crater cabins. In addition, there are four free campsites dotted around the park, all of which are fairly primitive. A favourite day trip is to join a cycling group to freewheel down from the crater rim to sea level. It costs around $100 including meals and hire of a mountain bike.

Hawaii Volcanoes National Park. This reserve, about 30 miles south of Hilo on the Big Island, is much larger and grander than Haleakala, and consists of tropical jungle clinging to the sides of two volcanoes. Kilauea, unlike Haleakala, can put on a dramatic performance, its erupting side vents sending out streams of hot lava down to the sea. The higher is Mauna Loa, over two and a half miles above sea level, which requires an arduous three-day climb to reach the top.

One of the cheapest places to stay in Hilo is the Hilo Hotel (142 Kinoole St, 961-3733), with rooms for $45-55. Another good one is Arnott's Lodge, 98 Apapane Road — close to the airport. It has the advantage of a toll-free number — 1-800-368-8752.

Camping. Camping is so popular in Hawaii that state and federal campsites are very often full, whatever the time of year. Sometimes places are allocated by a lottery held two months prior to the requested dates; so unless you are very organized, you might not get your first choice or none at all. It is more difficult to obtain a cabin than it is to find a place to pitch your own tent, especially in view of the fact that cabins are completely — or virtually — free.

There is no central reservation service covering the entire state, so you must contact the Parks Division of the island you wish to visit.

Calendar of Events

January/early February	Narcissus Festival (Chinese New Year)
March 17	St Patrick's Day Parade, Honolulu
March 26	**Prince Kuhio Day**
late March/April	Cherry Blossom Festival
May 1	Lei Day
June 11	**Kamehameha Day**
August (3rd Friday)	**Admission Day**
September	Aloha Week Festivals
October 12	**Discoverers' Day**

Public holidays are shown in **bold**

Alaska

Barrow Inuit Settlement

Alaska is radically different from the 'Lower 48', as the residents refer to the other states of the Union. Its unique weather, wildlife and frontier ethos make a visit highly rewarding, despite the expense. Alaska is full of bush pilots, trappers and prospectors — taciturn but colourful characters, who belong to a distinctively North American pioneer tradition which breeds legends and heroes. (It also has a lot of people running away from unhappy romances or unpaid fines.)

Alaska belonged to Russia until 1867, when the Americans bought it, for a famous 2c per acre. The purchase of such inhospitable territory was more than amply rewarded when gold was discovered at the end of the century, heralding the 1898 Gold Rush. Russian architecture and old mining towns recall the state's history, but Alaska's greatest attractions are not manmade. Most spectacular of all are its glaciers — of which it has more than half of those found in the world.

The fact that Alaska has a population barely exceeds 500,000 is no surprise given the environment. But the human spirit seems to flourish in a terrain and climate as hostile as Alaska's. The supreme test of frontier endurance takes place every March in the form of the 1,049-mile Iditarod Trail Race of husky-drawn sledges between Anchorage and Nome. Even the six-mile Seward Mountain Marathon, held each Fourth of July, is demanding. It is claimed to be the second oldest race in America (the oldest being the Boston Marathon), and involves running up a 3,000-foot mountain and back.

The 20th century has left scars on Alaska, not least the despoilation of suburban life in Anchorage — indistinguishable in places from any American town. Far more serious, however, was the impact of the oil spill from the *Exxon Valdez*, which ran aground in Prince William Sound in 1989. Despite a $500-million clean-up operation (notorious for its bad organization), the effects of 11 million gallons of crude oil on the environment are likely to be felt for decades. The fishing industry, already in decline, has been badly hit; tourism provides an increasingly important source of income.

THE PEOPLE

Just as fortune hunters once came north after gold, many 'state-siders' (migrants from the Lower 48) have poured into Alaska in search of the riches to be made from oil and fish. Oil was first discovered at Prudhoe Bay on the Arctic Ocean at 3.18pm on February 18, 1968. The pipeline, completed in 1977, runs between the extraordinarily inhospitable north and the now dispirited port of Valdez (pronounced Val-deez), near Anchorage. Many 'johnny-come-latelys' — most of them people of vigour and enterprise — are zealous converts to the northland, and will sing its praises to a responsive visitor. With an average age of 27, the state is very welcoming to young travellers.

The true natives of Alaska are the Eskimos and Indians; they are the descendants of the earliest inhabitants of the American continent and their way of life has changed little since those times. Their numbers have been much diminished in the past few centuries, and they now constitute only 15% of the state's population. The main groups are the Inuits, Aleuts (ruthlessly persecuted during the period of Russian rule and now very few in number), Athapascans, Haidas, Tlingit and Tsimpshian. Their folk tales can be riveting: listen for the one about the Eskimo girl whose lover is killed, only to return to her as a mosquito. Or the modern legend of the Eskimo youth whose headless body was discovered on the snow next to his snowmobile, supposedly having been decapitated by the dropping curtain effect of the northern lights.

Making Friends. Eskimos are a very friendly people. Although there is some latent ill-feeling towards Americans (as a result of US government deals which deprived them of their land), they show great curiosity about Europeans, and the British accent fascinates them. Almost all Eskimos speak English, though they are fiercely proud of their heritage and retain their native languages. Getting along with the Eskimos is easy, providing you behave as a guest in their country.

If you visit an Eskimo Village, first seek out the head man and ask for his permission to stay, which he will not hesitate to give. Your arrival will interest the local community, which will turn to its head man for an explanation. He will be embarrassed and lose face if he can't satisfy the people's curiosity.

The pace of life is generally laid back in the villages, except during the salmon runs in July and September. Don't get in the way at such a time, but offer to help if you feel you can make a contribution.

CLIMATE

Alaska is not a frozen waste all year round. Anchorage, the state's largest city, is hot and dry during the summer, with temperatures sometimes reaching the 80s and 90s. The southeastern panhandle towns of Ketchikan, Sitka and Juneau (the capital) are warmed by the Japanese Current and

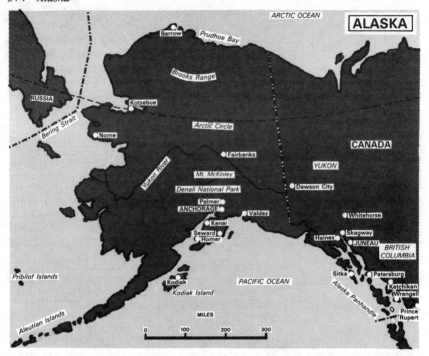

have a relatively mild climate, akin to that of the Western Isles of Scotland. This region, however, is extremely wet; in Ketchikan, which has 235 days with precipitation a year, if it hasn't rained for three days they call it a drought.

Winters can be spectacularly cold. From late October to early May the rivers are frozen over, and most of Alaska is buried under snow. Tempertures of -40°F are commonplace. Without properly insulated footwear, headgear and clothing, you will not survive — let alone enjoy — a winter visit. The lowest temperatures in the world have been recorded deep in the interior near the Yukon border. Between the Brooks Range of mountains and the Arctic Ocean (site of the oil wells), blizzards bring the worst windchill factors in the world apart from the South Pole. Winter visitors who fly to Nome, which is not very far from Siberia, are lent the necessary parkas by the airline.

A summer visit is recommended not just because of the balmy temperatures, but because of the midnight sun. The Arctic Circle, which is defined as the line north of which the sun never sets on midsummer's day, passes north of Fairbanks. Even many miles south of the Circle, night consists only of a brief twilight during the early hours of the morning.

ARRIVAL AND DEPARTURE

Air. *International Flights:* for decades Anchorage was an aerial crossroads linking Europe with the Far East. But its use as a refuelling stop ceased as soon as jet aircraft made it possible to fly non-stop from London to Seoul or New York to Tokyo, bypassing Alaska. New links are being forged with

Russia, however, and you can fly direct to Vladivostok and Kharbarovsk in Siberia. Several European airlines, including British Airways, still serve Anchorage once or twice a week. Clearing immigration and customs at Anchorage International Airport is probably easier than anywhere else in the USA: so few passengers disembark that you would be unlucky to wait in line for more than a few minutes.

Domestic Flights: the main air link between Alaska and the 'lower 48' is the 1,445-mile hop between Anchorage and Seattle, with numerous daily flights each way; there are also non-stop services to Chicago and Minneapolis/St. Paul. Fares, however, are sky-high, and it can be cheaper to fly from Anchorage to New York via London than to fly direct. There are no cheap flights between the continental USA and Alaska, and the best you can hope for is a 25% reduction for taking a night flight: this brings the Anchorage-Seattle round trip down to around $600. Look at airpass options, particularly those offered by Northwest (1-800-225-2525 in the USA, 071-629 5353 in the UK), to cut the cost of reaching Alaska.

Bus. The Coachways System (part of Greyhound) runs as far north as Whitehorse on the Alaska Highway in Canada's Yukon Territory. From Whitehorse, Alaskon Express (run by Gray Line of Alaska) operates buses to Haines, Skagway and Fairbanks, usually twice a week; this service is available only between late June and early September. Note that the Greyhound's Ameripass is not valid in Alaska. The one-way fare for the 600-mile journey to Fairbanks is around $140; to Anchorage $150 and to Skagway $60. The main Gray Line of Alaska offices are located as follows:

Anchorage: 547 West 4th St (277-5581).
Fairbanks: Westmark Inn, 1521 S Cushman St (456-5816).
Haines: Wings of Alaska, 2nd Avenue (766-2030).
Skagway: Westmark Inn (983-2241).
Whitehorse: Bus Terminal, 3211A 3rd Avenue (403-667-2223).

Train. The only railway route into Alaska from Canada is the narrow gauge White Pass-Yukon track, originally built for the Gold Rush, terminating at Skagway on the Panhandle. Trains run for tourist purposes, in summer only.

Driving. The motor trip along the Alaska — or Alcan — Highway, which officially starts in Dawson Creek, British Columbia, is beautiful. While the highway is in a far better state than a few years ago (when much of the road was unpaved), spring floods can still cause delays. Using the route is still very much an adventure, and the highways of Lower 48 seem positively dull in comparison. The total length of the Alaska Highway from Dawson Creek to Fairbanks, the state's second largest city, is over 1,500 miles.

Ferries. The Alaska Marine Highway ferry system is the primary mode of transport to many Alaskan towns — and for hundreds of tourists in summer. In 1990 the southern terminal was moved from Seattle to Bellingham, quite a coup for this pleasant Washington university town near the Canadian border. Ferries travel up through the Inland Passage, making calls at Prince Rupert on the coast of British Columbia, and Ketchikan, Wrangell, Petersburg ('Halibut Capital of the World') and Juneau, all in the Alaska Panhandle. The service continues up the fjord (always ice-free) to Haines — which is linked by road to the Alaska Highway — and Skagway. The whole trip takes 60 hours and costs about $240 deck class. If you are coming from Canada, you can travel by land as far as Prince Rupert (or take a British Columbia ferry from Vancouver or Vancouver Island to Prince Rupert) and catch the Alaska ferry there. The 24-hour trip from Prince Rupert to Juneau costs about $120.

For information on ferries call the Alaska Marine Highway on 465-3941 or 800-642-0066.

GETTING AROUND

Alaska covers an intimidatingly large area, over twice that of Texas. Ease of access helps narrow down the list of places to visit. Bus and train services are very limited. While ferry systems provide vital communication between coastal communities, many places in the interior are accessible only by plane.

Air. Flying is often the only practical way of travelling around the great expanses of land. Residents of remote communities do not think twice about flying into the nearest centre on a shopping expedition. There are more private aircraft per capita in Alaska than anywhere in the world.

The two main airlines are Alaska Air and Markair. Small aircraft, which are equipped with floats in summer and skis in winter, can be easily chartered. Many of these operate as shared taxis, and you may have to wait until there are enough people going in your direction. Otherwise, simply sign up for one of the many tours on offer.

Bus. Public road transport is extremely limited, but there are several locally-based companies which offer scheduled services. Alaska-Yukon Motor-coaches (236 F St, Anchorage) covers several routes, including the Anchorage to Fairbanks route via Denali National Park. Some services are integrated with the ferries. Bus services are curtailed between November and March.

Train. The Alaska Railroad (265-2494 or 456-4155) operates from Anchorage to Fairbanks, 11 hours into the interior. It is extremely important as an all-year communication. There is a departure daily at 9am from both Anchorage and Fairbanks, and all trains call at Denali. The one-way fare is $120, which allows a stopover at Denali. Even if you don't get off at Denali, you will be able to admire the twin peaks of Mount McKinley from Milepost 279. *Aurora,* the crack express which is equipped with vista domes and diners, runs year round. Among the worst headaches for engine drivers are the moose, which prefer to move along the tracks than across the exhausting muskeg.

The only other railway route in the state (not counting the Skagway tourist train), connects Anchorage with nearby Whittier (a port of call for the ferries).

Driving. The network of roads in Alaska is neither dense nor well maintained. However, motor-home touring is very popular and there is a choice of rental outlets in the cities. Discount car hire firms like Rent-a-Wreck, Rent-a-Dent and Cheepie Auto Rental have all penetrated to the last frontier. Rentals are more expensive than elsewhere because of harder wear and tear on vehicles. And despite the abundance of oil which flows through the pipeline to Valdez, petrol is expensive because all the oil leaves Alaska to be refined in the south.

Before setting out on any long journey call 243-7675 for the latest road conditions.

Hitch-hiking. Many travellers have found Alaska to be one of the most rewarding places in which to hitch. Perhaps because of the slow pace of life and frontier hospitality, residents and visitors seem more prone to pick up hitchers. Long distance lorry drivers tend to be 'characters'. For ride-sharing advertisements, check the classified section of the *Anchorage Times*.

Sleds. Motor-powered sleds are a popular means of transport during the winter, though for limited journeys only. The one-man version is called a skidoo. These are sometimes available for hire, so enquire locally.

Ferries. There are three main ferry systems: the Southeast System joins up towns on the Panhandle, and the South Central System operates between towns near (but not including) Anchorage, such as Whittier, Homer and Valdez. Surprisingly, there is no ferry link between the two systems, although they are both run by the same company. Services are increased in the summer. The Southwest Ferry connects the Kenai Peninsula and the Prince William Sound to the Aleutians.

ACCOMMODATION

Motels, hotels and inns throughout Alaska are more expensive than in the rest of America. Standards are high, however, especially when compared to those in neighbouring Yukon. While budget accommodation is scarce, there are a fair number of AYH hostels, and a few older hotels have affordable rooms. In addition, most towns have bed and breakfast associations in most towns, where rates start at about $35 for a single room. Many facilities in Alaska operate only in summer, a season whose starting date is indeterminate. Some hostels in remote locations do not hire out bedding, so you should take your own.

Accommodation is non-existent or fearsomely expensive in most small towns, so a tent is essential if you plan to travel in remote areas. Summers are warm enough to permit comfortable camping, though you should be mindful of potentially dangerous wildlife. The fee for a private campsite is around $12-15. The state government operates a number of free campsites in parks and along highways. Write to the Alaska State Division of Parks for details (Suite 210, 619 Warehouse Avenue, Anchorage, AK 99501), or visit the Alaska Public Lands Information Center (opposite the main Visitors Bureau) in Anchorage.

The US Forest Service operates a number of primitive cabins, usually equipped with wood-burning stoves and outside toilets. These cost about $20 per party, but are often booked up six months in advance. Write to the District Ranger, PO Box 10-489 Anchorage, AK 99511.

EATING AND DRINKING

The cost of living is high throughout Alaska and this is particularly noticeable when buying food. Expect to pay nearly twice as much for meals in Alaska as in California. Even the best agricultural areas of the state have growing seasons for only 120 days, and therefore most produce must be imported at great expense. Fortunately, state taxes are minimal due to oil wealth.

Salmon, both smoked and fresh, is very cheap indeed. Many towns have salmon bakes at which you can typically eat as much salmon barbecued over an open fire as you want, plus sourdough bread and salads, for not much more than $15. McDonalds has found its way to Alaska and fast food restaurants abound. Relatively cheap diners often stay open 24 hours a day.

Meat and fish are the staple diet of the village natives. Moose is popular and tasty, similar to beef in taste and appearance. Traditionally, a great deal of fish and meat were eaten raw, but nowadays that diet survives only among the elders living in remote areas. Sun-dried meat is often a staple on hunting expeditions.

Drinking. Drinking in an Alaskan bar is not much more expensive than elsewhere in the US; a bottle of beer costs about $2.50 in Anchorage. Most sizeable bars supply a free floor show of topless or naked dancers (many of whom are supplement their income in other ways).

Although alcohol is widely available in the big towns, its sale is controlled in Eskimo villages. Like the native Indians of North America, Eskimos have difficulty coping with alcohol, although they have borne up well in most other respects under the relatively sudden 'American invasion'. Most Eskimos will drink whatever is offered and regularly pass out after over-indulging. While it is fine to offer the village head man a drink, if you let it be widely known that you have large amounts of alcohol, you can expect a continual stream of visitors until your entire supply has been consumed. Too much alcohol often transforms the normally placid temperament of Eskimos, and violence and unpleasantness can ensue.

THE GREAT OUTDOORS

Wilderness backpackers and canoeists flock to some of the more accessible natural wonders of the state. The abundance of flora and fauna, which appears when the snows melt, makes Alaska a naturalist's paradise. A fair amount of the wilds are 'organized', such as the USA's largest natural wilderness reservation, the 8.7 million-acre Wrangell/St Elias National Park.

Even if your time is short, and you are restricted to the environs of Anchorage, there are good opportunities for exploring. The most heavily travelled route from Anchorage (much favoured by backpackers and Japanese tour groups) is north to the spectacular Denali National Park and Mount McKinley. The adventurous, however, may want to head further afield e.g. to the distant islands in the Aleutian archipelago, to watch birds or go fishing. These islands are most easily accessible by chartered or scheduled flight, though there is a ferry service.

Short cruises from Juneau or Valdez take you past floating glaciers, which occasionally crack and split in front of you. The vibrations set off by loud noises (such as a ship's horn) often induce ice avalanches. Whales and porpoises sport alongside the boats in summer.

For the ultra-adventurous, the Brooks Range sweeps across northern Alaska and contains some of the largest unexplored regions remaining on earth. Almost as remote are the Pribilof Islands, which are the summer breeding ground for one and a half million fur seals.

The best source of information about Alaska's parks is the Alaska Public Lands Information Center in Anchorage.

SPORT AND RECREATION

Skiing takes place at the Alyeska resort, south of Anchorage, from the end of November until the end of April. Equipment can be hired locally, and a daily lift pass costs about $30. Although the resort failed in its bid to host the 1994 Winter Olympics, facilities are improving all the time.

The fishing is tremendous throughout Alaska. King salmon can run to 70 pounds or more. Trout and pike are plentiful, as well as a local species called 'shee-fish', which can be found throughout the year in the Yukon

River. Tackle can be hired in the tourist centres, but Eskimos in remote places will view someone fishing with anything but a net as slightly mad. Permits may be needed, so enquire at the local fisheries office.

Swimming, windsurfing or boating can be fun in the quiet backwaters, but unless you are of Olympic standard, stay out of the Yukon River (the third longest river in North America). Its powerful currents and 70ft depths can be dangerous. The water level of Alaskan rivers tends to fall gradually as the summer wears on, and a safe course between the sandbanks and rocks one day may not be safe the next.

ENTERTAINMENT

Only Anchorage, which has several theatres and arts centres, has much cultural life. Alaska is so out-of-the-way that few major performers appear. Even so, bars in the biggest towns often feature some very talented rock bands. Folk, blues and country and western are all given a good airing. Many eskimos are remarkably adept at blues guitar.

If they are not strumming guitars during those long nights on the tundra, they are playing cards. Eskimos have an affection for gambling, and both men and women are shrewd card players. In the outlying areas it shouldn't be too difficult to get in on a game. Pool is popular all over Alaska, but mainly in large towns where big-money games are often played, and you must watch out for hustlers.

In the more touristy areas shows of traditional native music and dance are put on. Special entertainments commemorate the history of Alaska: performances of Russian folk dance in Sitka, for example, or the Ragtime Revue in Juneau, which recreates the atmosphere of a Gold Rush saloon.

Shopping. Because the cost of shipping to Alaska is so high, everything in the shops is very expensive. Village stores often get away with charging what they like. For example, a set of fishing tackle might cost five times as much as it would in Britain. One of the few bargains is salmon, and most shops will pack it with ice for an extra dollar or so, which will keep it in good condition for several days.

Native crafts are on sale throughout the state. There are many cultural centres at which native artists carry on old traditions of wood carving, silverwork, beadwork and spinning from musk ox wool. Eskimo arts flourish best in the Far North, in communities like Kotzebue and Barrow.

The Media. Anchorage has thorough news programmes as well as music for everyone. Folk, blues and rock are all found somewhere on Anchorage radio, as well as coverage of the British music scene. In the more remote areas, the choice is limited, and the radio is somewhat monopolized by religious programming between the news and music. Radio disc jockeys in Nome are renowned for trying to convert their listening audience between records.

There is a surprisingly wide range of television stations in and around the big cities. As with radio, the choice of programmes is small in remote regions, though most Eskimo homes have a television if there is good reception. British movies, old and new, are watched with avid interest out on the tundra.

CRIME AND SAFETY

Alaskan cities have their fair share of street crime, but you can usually identify dodgy areas by the preponderance of seedy bars.

Drugs. The smoking and possession of under four ounces of marijuana is legal. Many native Eskimos, especially in areas where alcohol is scarce, use marijuana as socially as Europeans use alcohol. As in the rest of the USA, harder drugs are strictly illegal.

Natural Disasters. Earthquakes are a risk in many parts of the state. Anchorage was devastated by an earthquake in 1964, and the old town of Valdez was wiped out by an earthquake and tidal wave a few years before the coming of the pipeline; a small new city was erected close to the old site.

Health. In the outlying places, medical facilities can be sparse. Victims of serious accidents or illness are flown out to big centres, so make sure your insurance covers such an expensive contingency.

CB radio is slowly being superseded by the cellular phone, but it is still a way of life in Alaska, where most trucks, cars and village homes are equipped with one. A portable CB should be borrowed if possible for unguided walks in any desolate area. A special channel is kept clear for emergency calls only; enquire locally and make sure you remember it.

Wildlife. It is not advisable to wander about in the wilderness without a knowledgeable guide; two people were eaten by bears in separate incidents in July 1992. You can buy a can of bear repellent called Counter Assault for $40 from sports shops in the state. If confronted by a grizzly, stand your ground and talk to it in an even tone. For tips on how to avoid contact with wolves, porcupines, etc. see the Canadian introductory section on *The Great Outdoors* on page 405.

Mosquitoes are the most annoying natural hazard, and you are guaranteed to meet them in the summer. Every portion of exposed flesh must be covered with repellent; locals recommend a product called 'Cutter'. Although they are not a serious problem in built-up areas, the pests can make a visit to the tundra, where they swarm in their millions, a downright ordeal.

EXPLORING

The Alaska Panhandle extends for over 500 miles down the coast which should logically belong to British Columbia. Taking a boat up the Inside Passage — flanked by snow-capped and forested mountains, down which glaciers descend to the sea — is an awesome and unforgettable experience, offering glimpses too of rusting gold mines and even the odd whale. Some of the state's most picturesque towns are scattered amid the dramatic scenery — some with incongruous Russian architecture, but each with pale, clapboard houses and a story to tell.

Ketchikan. The island town of Ketchikan is the first stop for anyone coming up from the south by boat. It is Alaska's salmon city, and in summer you can witness the amazing sight of the fish jumping up the falls as they head upstream. Ketchikan's other great attraction are the totem poles, carved by the local Tlingit tribe: the Totem Heritage Center (Deermount St) has an impressive collection, but don't fail to go also to the nearby Totem Bight and Saxman Totem parks (best visited on a guided tour).

The AYH hostel is at Grant and Main Streets, but it is closed in summer. At other times try Gilmore Hotel (326 Front St, 225-9423), which charges $60 for a double, or the cheaper but less central Alaska Rainforest Inn (2311 Hemlock St, 225-9500).

Juneau. The capital of Alaska (population 26,000) is connected by neither road nor rail to the rest of the state, so the ferry service is vital. Tourism-induced prettification has not succeeded in ruining the beauty of Juneau, or its stunning location in the shadow of the steep-sided Gastineau Channel.

Juneau played an important part in the Gold Rush, whose legacy is still very much in evidence (and vital to the local tourist industry). There is a mining museum and you can visit the nearby Treadwell Mine, one of Alaska's most productive. The Alaska State Museum (395 Whittier St) has good Eskimo exhibits among the mining memorabilia. Out of town the main attraction is the nearby Mendenhall Glacier, which is 12 miles long and 300ft high. It is served by hourly buses from Juneau, and there is a visitors' centre and a campsite.

Glacier Bay, where tidewater glaciers reach 600ft, is a much more awesome spectacle. Located 50 miles northwest of Juneau, however, it is accessible only on a comparatively expensive tour. Whale-watching is possible from May to September: write to the Glacier Bay National Monument, PO Box 1089, Juneau for information.

The Visitors Bureau is at 369 S Franklin, Suite 201 (586-1737).

Accommodation: the AYH hostel (614 Harris St, 586-9559) is among Alaska's better ones, and is open all year. For more privacy stay a the old Alaskan Hotel (167 S Franklin St, 586-1000), a Victorian place with a lovely bar and double rooms for $45-65. Similarly priced rooms are available through the Alaska Bed & Breakfast Association (3444 Nowell St, 586-2959).

Franklin St is the best place to look for food and refreshment. The most touristy bar in town is the Red Dog Saloon on S Franklin St; raunchy Gold Rush songs are performed in the shadow of a hideous stuffed grizzly bear. It's worth a look before heading elsewhere.

Sitka. Accessible by boat from Juneau (or by plane), Sitka is situated on an island in a lovely spot below Mount Edgecumbe. Many travellers leave it off their itineraries, but Sitka is a fascinating place. The legacy of the Russians is strong, evident in the buildings, among which is a neat clapboard church with onion domes. The AYH hostel (303 Kimsham St) is open in summer only.

Skagway. Northeast of Haines (in a magnificent setting but without the history of the other Inland Passage towns), Skagway is the northernmost settlement on the Inland Passage. The 100-mile journey north from Juneau up the Lynn Canal is staggeringly beautiful, with sightings of killer whale and sea lions common.

At the end of last century, the port of Skagway became the main starting point for prospectors en route to the gold fields from the south. At one time the largest and roughest town in Alaska, Skagway is now the most picturesque of the panhandle ports, with a population of just 700. It is a perfect town of the Klondike, preserved almost intact from the Gold Rush days. The result, however, is a slightly unreal, gingerbread town, with horse-drawn carriages, saloons, raised boardwalks, reconstructed miners' camps and gold panning demonstrations. While still an active port, Skagway's main source of income is the tourists, brought in their hundreds by cruise boats in summer. But Skagway is well worth exploring before you head off to do some compulsory hiking.

Information and maps are available from the Visitors Bureau in the city hall (983-2854).

Accommodation: the AYH hostel (456 3rd Avenue, 983-2131), open all year round, offers by far the cheapest accommodation in town. In the historic district, try Irene's Inn (983-2520) or the Skagway Inn (983-2289), both of which charge around $60 for a double room with shared bathroom. Irene's Inn is closed in winter. There are three private campsites in Skagway. For reservations, call 983-2454.

Eating and Drinking: most bars and restaurants are scattered along or near Broadway. The focus of local nightlife is the Red Onion Saloon (2nd and Broadway), a former brothel and now a buzzing pub; it serves excellent food in addition to tasty local beer and live music. Eat-all-you-can joints are particularly good value; try the Prospectors Sourdough on Broadway between 4th and 5th streets.

The Chilkoot Trail: the steep and rugged Chilkoot Trail is popular with hikers who want to follow in the footsteps of the original gold prospectors. It stretches 33 miles from Dyea near Skagway to Lake Bennett in Canada; en route you pass stunning landscapes, peppered with relics of the mining era. It is a well-trodden but tough three to six day walk. Take everything you'll need in terms of supplies and equipment; there are many campgrounds along the route, but the cabins are usually booked up months in advance. In summer, trains from Lake Bennett take walkers along the old White Pass-Yukon railway back to Skagway.

Anchorage. Well over half the population of Alaska lives in Anchorage. Visitors tend to slag it off, but the city should be forgiven for its rather spiritless appearance; the predominantly modern architecture and the gaunt landscape immediately around Anchorage are the result of a devastating earthquake in 1964. The urban atmosphere comes as a shock for those fresh from the quaint towns of the Inland Passage, but it gives a more accurate picture of what life for Alaskans in the 1990s is really like. The nearby mountains are a reminder of the pleasures that lie beyond the city boundaries.

Anchorage is a useful — if not very agreeable — base from which to explore further afield. In the city itself, visit the historical museum (121 W 7th Avenue) or, on Saturdays, watch a sled dog race at the Tudor Racing Track.

City Transport: Anchorage airport is six miles southwest of the city centre. If you are not too laden down with luggage, ignore the taxi drivers ($12-15 to downtown) and the shuttle minibus service, which costs $5. Instead, look for the People Mover bus 6, which costs 75c.

The People Mover bus network around Anchorage is fairly cheap and efficient, but not particularly frequent. The flat fare is 75c, and free transfers are allowed. Most buses arrive and depart from the Downtown Transit Center at 6th Avenue between G and H Streets. For bus information ask here or call the Rideline on 343-6543. Note that only a skeleton service operates on Sundays, and that no buses at all run on public holidays. In winter the schedules are sometimes put out by heavy snow: dial 786-8205 for a recorded report of delays and cancellations.

In addition to the People Mover system, there is an independently operated double-decker bus service linking downtown Anchorage with Lake Spenard and the University. For a flat fare you can stop off anywhere en route and continue your journey on a later service.

Accommodation: the AYH Anchorage International Hostel, open all year round, is downtown at 700 H St (junction with 7th Avenue, 276-3635); the nightly rate is $12. The Inlet Inn (539 H St, 277-5541) has basic doubles for $50 a night. For bed and breakfast accommodation call Alaska Private Lodgings at 1236 W 10th Avenue (258-1717).

Eating and Drinking: Anchorage doesn't have a bad collection of restaurants. For the best (and most expensive) seafood try the places overlooking the Inlet. The most authentic native food is served at the Tundra Club, part of the Alaska Native Medical Center at 250 Gambell St (278-4716); you can reach it by bus 45 from downtown. As well as a cheap set lunch, you can sample *agutak* (Eskimo ice-cream), Indian fry-bread and reindeer sausage. It opens 7am-3pm from Monday to Friday. The best salmon in the Anchorage region is served at Max's, south of the city near the Alyeska ski resort.

The most popular bar and live music venue is Chilkoot Charlie's (Fireweed Lane and Spenard Road, 272-1010), whose motto is 'We cheat the other guy and pass the savings on to you'. For more high-brow entertainment go to the Performing Arts Center (5th Avenue and F St, 263-2787)

Help and Information: the area code for all of Alaska is 907.
Anchorage Visitors Bureau: 546 W 4th Avenue at Front St (274-3531).
Parks and Forests Information Center: 540 W 5th Avenue.
American Express: 333 W 4th St (263-6250).

Around Anchorage. The Sierra Club (276-4048) runs numerous hikes, bicycle tours and canoe trips from Anchorage. There is plenty of scope for independent travel too.

Several glaciers are within reach of Anchorage. While the spectacular Columbia Glacier must be visited on a tour, the Portage Glacier, 53 miles south, is served by train and buses. Get to the glacier sooner rather than later, since it is expected to have receded from its valley by the year 2020. The Girdwood Hostel, in in the nearby Alyeska ski resort (783-2099), is open all year; there is no hot water, but you can take a sauna instead.

The Chugach National Forest, covering almost 500,000 acres, has an extensive network of trails through fantastic mountain scenery. It is less than 30 minutes' drive from Anchorage, but is not served by public transport.

The Kenai Peninsula: extending south of Anchorage, this peninsula is the preferred playground of Alaskans, and is therefore crowded. There is an AYH hostel at Snow River (276-3635) near Seward, which is open all year round, but very busy in summer. For more deserted wilderness, take the ferry from Homer or Seward to neighbouring Kodiak Island. This huge island is the home of the world's largest carnivores, the giant Kodiak bears. It is also where the huge 20 or 30 pound King Crabs are caught, a delicacy favoured above salmon.

Denali National Park: the favourite trip from Anchorage is north to Denali and Mount McKinley, the highest mountain in North America: Denali, the Eskimo name for the mountain, means 'The Great One'. Its summit — shrouded in cloud much of the time — rises nearly four miles above the 900-foot elevation of the Tokositna Glacier below. The surrounding wilderness is indescribably beautiful.

To hike to the top of McKinley will take a month, but there are shorter trails within the park. It is possible to hire horses and in summer a free bus operates the 84-mile journey between the park entrance and Wonder Lake. Free buses also run in high season to the various campsites. Ring 683-2294 for information about camping, trails etc. The Denali National Park Hotel near the entrance (276-7234) charges over $100 a night.

Buses and trains travelling between Anchorage and Fairbanks stop at

Denali, giving access to the mountain. Several minibuses also run between Anchorage and the park, including Denali Express (274-8539).

Fairbanks. Lying about 350 miles north of Anchorage and 130 miles south of the Arctic Circle, Fairbanks is America's northernmost city. Its frontier atmosphere does it few favours, and the boom brought by oil in the 70s has made the city expensive. But while Fairbanks has few permanent attractions — apart from the excellent University of Alaska Museum (5 miles northwest), with its fine collection of Eskimo arts and crafts — it hosts some of the state's best festivals. It is well worth making the trip north to catch the World Eskimo Olympics in August, with competitions such as tossing the blanket. In March, ice-carvers from around the world gather to take part in the Ice Festival, when sled dog races are also held. In winter, however, the greatest influx of visitors is for the spectacular Northern Lights.

The Fairbanks Hotel (517 3rd Avenue, 456-6440) charges $60 for a double and $40-45 for a single. The six-cabin Aurora Motel (456-7361) offers a similar deal. For campsite reservations call 451-2695.

Calendar of Events

January	Winter Festival, Ketchikan
early February	Iditaski cross-country ski race
February	Festival of Native Arts, Fairbanks
early March	Iditarod Trail Sled Dog Race
mid April	International Music Festival, Anchorage
May	Crab Festival, Kodiak
mid June	Midnight Sun Marathon, Anchorage
June (third week)	Spirit Days
early August	Alaska Scottish Highland Games
late August/early September	Alaska State Fair, Anchorage
late September	Equinox Marathon, Fairbanks
December	Christmas Boat Parade, Sitka

CANADA

THE PEOPLE

The world's third-largest country (after Russia and China) is a thinly populated geo-political eccentricity. It also has a staggering diversity of landscape and people, and is an often-welcome antidote to the excesses of the USA. That is not to say that it is not firmly under the Americans' cultural and economic yoke, but a visit to the fringes of settlement — whether Prince Edward Island or Newfoundland in the Atlantic provinces, or the Great White North — show how far it is possible to get from American culture.

Politically, Canada is an aberration. The head of state is the British Sovereign. Ultimate political power is exercised by the throne through the monarch's representative, the Governor-General, who has two residences: one in the capital Ottawa, the other in the heart of Québec City — the centre of French influence. The current debate is about what it is to be a Canadian, in a world where old political certainties are disintegrating. In the mid-1990s it is by no means certain that Canada will survive intact through to the next millenium.

Most visitors confine themselves to the cities and countryside of the southern belt — Vancouver, Toronto and Montréal are all within a few degrees of latitude, almost straddling the US border. They each have an individual character and are surrounded by natural wonders. But to see the best of Canada, the visitor should try to reach the fringes, such as the Maritimes in the east or remote parts of British Columbia in the west.

THE PEOPLE

In mid-1992 there were 27,334,100 Canadians. The fastest way to antagonize one of them is to mistake him or her for an American, and then to say 'well there is not much difference anyway'. It is difficult to avoid confusing the American and Canadian accents unless you have an ear attuned to the sound 'ou' which Canadians say in a short clipped way, almost like 'abote' for 'about'. Or listen for the characteristic 'eh?' at the end of sentences. (Apparently, there is a computer installed in Ottawa which invites commands with 'eh?'). But once it is revealed that you are addressing a Canadian, you must instantly acknowledge that you have committed a gross error.

Canada is heavily dependent on the USA both culturally and economically. This is not too surprising considering that 80% of the Canadian population lives within 200 kilometres of the US border. And yet your average Canadian will fiercely defend Canada's uniqueness. There is considerable anti-American sentiment in schools and in the media which became particularly evident during the 1988 federal election, in which the controversial North American Free Trade Agreement was the central issue. Although in some ways the differences between the two countries are ones of degree rather than kind, in other ways they are fundamental. For example televised political debates in Canada are genuine debates and therefore quite unlike their American counterparts.

The reputation of Canadians as being cautious, conformist, humourless and dull inspired the writer Saki to say 'Canada is all right, really, though not for the whole weekend.' The strong influence of Scottish puritanism during the early days of the colony persists, and the work ethic and a wholesome boyscoutishness continue to hold sway. The fact that Canada is the most heavily insured nation per capital in the world does suggest that the people lack a certain flair.

On the positive side, they are less brash than their American neighbours, not as noisily self-confident. Because they do not take themselves quite so seriously as Americans they are more prepared to laugh at themselves, so you can risk a few good-natured insults. Your overwhelming impression will be that people both in public office and private business are efficient and polite.

A quarter of the population — 6,800,000 Canadians — claim French as their mother tongue. The highest concentration of French-speaking people is in the province of Québec (over 82% French) though large numbers of French-speaking people live in the Maritime provinces, Ontario and Manitoba.

Canada is nearly as ethnically diverse as the USA, but without a large black population. With Italians and Germans numbering half a million each, Ukrainians and Chinese over a quarter of a million each, plus large populations of Greeks, Portuguese and Koreans, no one can complain that Canadians are all alike. One in five Canadians was born outside the country. Canada prides itself on being not so much a 'melting pot' as a 'salad bowl', though second generation immigrants seem to assimilate thoroughly. Since immigration is declining steeply (because of stricter government measures in the face of dire unemployment), the ethnic mosaic may not be as colourful in future generations.

Politics. The biggest political issue is the conflict between the French — who feel their culture is being swamped — and the English-speaking majority, who regard separatism as a threat to the socio-economic integrity of what is a young and thinly populated nation. Québec, with a 'national assembly', already seems well on the way to independence. In a bid to reduces the stresses once and for all, an accord was signed at Charlottetown in the Maritimes in 1992; the Québec-Canada Agreement recognizes Québec as 'a distinct and unique society', and bestows a wide range of new powers covering immigration, the right to opt-out of federal programmes, the right of veto to changes in the Supreme Court (where it is guaranteed three of the nine seats) and other federal institutions, and the right to adopt an individual cultural policy. Unfortunately it was roundly rejected by a referendum in October of that year.

The defeat raises many questions about Canada's nationhood. If Québec goes her own way, then the Maritime provinces — with few ties to Québec —

would probably try to join the USA; after all, New Brunswick is firmly attached to the American state of Maine, and Boston already acts as a kind of commercial gateway for the Maritimes. The second act of this scenario sees British Columbia, pinched betweeen the states of Washington and Alaska, peeling off the join the USA, followed by the Rocky Mountain provinces. This leaves just the central rump, the southern parts of which (cynics would say) are already indistinguishable from America anyway.

Even if Canada remains intact, there a fears about the effects of the new North American Free Trade Agreement which removes commercial barriers between Canada, the USA and Mexico. Already there are signs that unskilled jobs are moving from Canada to Mexico, and worries that any new investment will be channelled south rather than north of the USA.

Language. Everything is almost painfully bilingual. All packaging, government documents, street signs, etc. must by law be in both languages across Canada — except in Québec, where they *must* be in French but need not appear in English. Government employees, from switchboard operators to politicians, are supposed to be bilingual, though in many cases they have no more than a smattering even after attending compulsory immersion courses. Railway conductors have been known to announce first in English 'The train is arriving in Montréal' and then in their French version, 'the train is arriving in Mon-ray-all'. French as spoken in Canada is very different from the language used in Paris. A free tourist handout in Québec recommends that if you want to say how much you've enjoyed your stay, you should pronounce *j'ai beaucoup aime mon sejour* as 'jay bocoo emmay mo sayjoor'. *Vieux* (old, as in Québec), is pronounced 'voo' rather than 'vyer'.

NATIVE PEOPLE

There are only 300,000 Dene (Native Canadians) and 23,000 Inuit (Eskimos) left in Canada, comprising less than 2% of the national population. The majority live on reservations in Ontario and the four western provinces (especially Saskatchewan) where poverty and unemployment are rampant and the levels of alcoholism and crime are alarmingly high. Although Canada has a better record than the US — for example the 'Indian wars' in Canada ended in treaties rather than military defeat — the disadvantaged position in modern Canada of the native peoples reflects their early mistreatment.

The situation has been improving over the past 20 years. Many Native Canadian groups have negotiated settlements for mineral development on their lands held by treaty, substantially improving their standard of living. The federal government has encouraged and funded native rights lobbies to present their cases, though most groups continue dissatisfied. The new constitution is intended to restore rights to the Native people, as well as formalising the relationship between Quebec and the rest of Canada.

Few Native Canadians have integrated into modern Canadian society. Although the rare individual becomes a lawyer or an accountant, the ones who move away from the reservations can often be seen standing on city street corners, usually outside the liquor stores passing a bottle. Unemployment is high, and most Native Canadians have little choice but to live on federal subsidies. At the same time as they are unable or unwilling to integrate, they have also lost many of their traditions. Few dress in their traditional costume except for the benefit of tourists who seem happy to pay a dollar or two to photograph them. Only a handful speak their own languages.

Because Native Canadians no longer rely on their traditional means of livelihood — hunting moose, caribou and buffalo, fishing for salmon, etc. — many of their practical skills are disappearing. Furthermore many of their ceremonies were banned by law, notably the potlatch during which hereditary privileges are passed on. As a result many of the traditional arts and crafts were jeopardized. But with government support, there has been a revival in Native Canadian culture in the past couple of decades. Arts such as mask-carving on the west coast, the folk songs of Shingoose, and the ancient vocal music of the Inuit called Katadjait, throat songs which reflect things in the environment from babies to boiling water. Belatedly money is being poured into Native arts centres where the old arts of carving totem poles and ritual painting can be passed on to younger artists.

In a further effort to prevent the cultural erosion, there are summer wilderness camps where Native Canadian children (who, like most Canadian children, are avid television-watchers and junk food eaters), are taught the ways of their elders. It is even possible for foreign visitors to work as volunteers on such camps and to participate in local events such a moose, bear and porcupine roasts. There are also opportunities for volunteers to help on building projects lasting two months in remote northern Native communities over the summer. (Contact Frontiers Foundation, 2615 Danforth Avenue, Suite 203, Toronto, Ontario M4C 1L6). Inuit communities have not altered as much, since their contact with white society is often limited. (See the chapter on the *Great White North).*

Hunting and fishing lodges are often on Native Canadian land and it is possible to hire a Native guide to take you fishing or hunting. Unfortunately the remote locations of these wilderness retreats make them prohibitively expensive for many people.

To experience the life of Canada's original inhabitants at second hand, the books of Farley Mowatt are highly recommended. His descriptions of the traditions and customs of the people of the Far North, as in *People of the Deer* and *The Snow Walker,* are especially evocative.

CLIMATE

Although Canada's climate has its flaws, it is often wrongfully maligned. It is not unknown for an American tourist to drive over the border in July with a pair of skis strapped to his car roof, only to find the temperatures in Calgary higher than those in San Francisco and warmer in Ottawa than in Massachusetts. If you travel around Canada in July and August you will be almost as hot as you would be in the States, with the exception of the West Coast where summer temperatures remain a little cooler, though still very balmy. The majority of shops and public buildings are air-conditioned. High summer is ideal for enjoying the Great Outdoors (give or take the odd swarm of biting insects), though it can cool down considerably in the evenings. Although there can be heat waves in June and September, they are the most comfortable months in which to travel. As for the proverbial Canadian winter when temperatures hover around 0°F/-18°C, you really will have to acquire a warm and waterproof pair of boots, woollen hat, scarf and mitts and a down or woollen coat. But even in Canada, you are not guaranteed a white Christmas.

WEIGHTS AND MEASURES

One difference between the USA and Canada which will immediately strike the visitor is that Canada has 'gone metric'. Road distances and speed limits are all in kilometres (pronounced *kill*-o-meet-ers), petrol is sold in litres, temperatures are quoted in centigrade and butter is sold in grams. The programme is well advanced now and most Canadians have made the adjustment. There were a few dodgy moments in the early stages, for instance when the tank of an Air Canada 747 was filled with litres instead of gallons of fuel, and the pilot had to make an emergency landing. (He was promptly fired).

Occasionally, groceries are labelled in both Imperial and metric, but in most cases you will have to do a lot of mental arithmetic if you are interested in comparing Canadian prices with those in the States or at home. The chart below provides some useful approximations. Failing this, you can apply the conversion technique used by Canada's two backwoods humorists Bob and Doug MacKenzie who multiply the metric measure by 2 and add 30 to arrive at the Fahrenheit temperature. Unfortunately this also had them going 90 mph in a 30 km/h zone and getting 42 metric bottles of beer for the price of a six-pack.

Length

1 centimetre = 0.4 inches	1 inch = 2.5 cm
1 metre = 3.3 feet	1 foot = 30 cm
1 kilometre = 0.6 miles	1 mile = 1.6 km

Weight

1 gram = .035 ounces	1 oz = 28 g
1 kilogram = 2.2 pounds	1 lb = 45 kg

Temperatures

$$(°C \times 9/5) + 32 = °F \qquad (°F - 32) \times 5/9 = °C$$

Volume

1 litre = 2.1 pints (Imperial)	1 pint = .47 litres
1 litre = .22 gallons	1 gallon = 4.5 litres

Red Tape

Immigration. British and Commonwealth citizens do not require visas to enter Canada as tourists. (If you are from Greenland you don't even need a passport). To work or study legally in Canada, you must obtain the appropriate visa before you leave your home country.

If you are arriving as a tourist, you will probably be granted a stay of 90 days. If you intend to stay longer than three months, you may argue your case (in advance) to the Canadian High Commission in London (Immigration Division, MacDonald House, 38 Grosvenor Street, London W1X 0AA; 071-629-9492). Failing this, you should declare your intention at the port of entry, giving reasons and, providing you can show a return flight and sufficient funds, you may be granted up to six months.

Those who arrive for more than a couple of weeks holiday may be asked to show a return ticket and enough money to support themselves without working. A couple of credit cards and the address of a Canadian relative or family friend should clinch your case. As long as you look like a regular tourist you should have no problem. Canadians on the whole are suspicious of eccentrically dressed people. People under 18 travelling without an adult may be asked to show a letter of permission from their parent or guardian, to check up on runaways.

Many European travellers enter Canada via the USA. If you plan to return to the States it is important to have a multiple entry visa for the USA, since the letter of the 'Visa Waiver' law means that in some circumstances you could be denied entry. Although it is possible to apply for a visa at any of the eight American consulates in Canada, you will find it easier to persuade the US Embassy in Britain to issue a multiple entry visa in the first place.

CUSTOMS

Purportedly because of Canada's anxiety about animal and plant diseases, there is no red and green channel system in airports. All incoming travellers must fill out a form declaring the potentially dubious contents of their luggage, e.g. plants, firearms, alcohol, tobacco and gifts. The customs inspector looks at the form before you reclaim your baggage, so if he trusts your form (and your face) you will escape having your luggage searched. You may bring in as many gifts as you like duty free provided none has a value of more than $40.

The duty free alcohol allowance is 1.1 litres (40 ounces) of liquor or wine, or 8.4 litres of beer. You cannot import liquor unless you have reached the legal drinking age of the province of entry. The minimum age is 18 in Prince Edward Island, Quebec, Manitoba and Alberta and 19 in the rest. If you want to bring in more than your allowance (as you might find it worthwhile to import fine wines or Scotches unavailable in Canada) you are allowed to bring in up to 9 litres more provided you pay the duty at the port of entry.

People 16 or over may bring in 50 cigars, 200 cigarettes and 1 kg (2.2lbs) of tobacco duty free.

There are restrictions on the import of some food products in certain provinces. Fruits and vegetables which are grown commercially in Canada may be prohibited depending on where they come from. For example, peaches, plums and apricots must be sprayed before they are allowed into British Columbia, and apples are prohibited. Vegetables from certain parts of the US (mainly southern and mid-western states) are not allowed in. Better to eat your apples and carrots before arriving at the border. You may bring in as many tropical fruits as you like, since these are not grown in Canada and therefore don't present an agricultural threat.

HEALTH AND INSURANCE

Canada's reputation as a safe and clean country may tempt you not to worry too much about potential health hazards. But a simple fall on the ice in winter, or from a jetty in the summer might necessitate hospital treatment. And with basic hospital care running at $1,000 a day, you will rue the day you decided to skimp on insurance.

Foreign visitors can buy last-minute insurance by the day called 'emergency cover' from Blue Cross, represented in most cities across Canada (e.g. 418-429-2661 in Toronto). You pay about $5 ($9.50 for a family) for every day you want to be covered and can pick up the forms from Canadian drug stores such as Boots and at information centres. You can then pay for as many days as you need at any bank. You are not eligible to apply if you have been in the country for more than ten days. The maximum period of cover is six months. A cheaper alternative is the Hospital Medical Care plan offered by John Ingle Insurance, 710 Bay Street, Toronto (418-597-0666). For extensive medical cover they charge around £35 for 15 days increasing to $150 for three months.

You sometimes get the impression while travelling around the less prosperous parts of Britain that every second lorry driver, secretary and shop assistant dreams of a centrally heated home in the land which they have heard praised by their relatives who emigrated in the 1960s.

But alas it is no longer easy to work in Canada. In reaction to the high levels of immigration and a worrying unemployment rate, the Canadian government has actively promoted a 'Canada-only' policy. Not only are there strict measures regulating foreign workers but they are strictly enforced, and deportation for working illegally is a real possibility. However Canadians are hospitable and eager for visitors to like their country. Even the immigration officer who deported one of our contributors expressed regret that the offender had not had a chance to see more of Canada.

VISAS

To work legally in Canada, you must obtain an Employment Authorization before you leave home. For the past 5 years, the Canadian government has allowed a certain number of foreign students to work temporarily in Canada, partly in response to a sudden increase in the number of unfilled summer vacancies at the end of the 1980s. Despite increasing unemployment, the programme continues, though the quotas fluctuate and there is no guarantee from year to year that the scheme will continue. Interested students should obtain the general leaflet 'Student Temporary Employment in Canada' from the Canadian High Commission (Immigration Section, Macdonald House, 38 Grosvenor St, London W1X 0AA). All participants in the official work exchanges must be British citizens aged 18-30 years and must have proof that they will be returning to a tertiary level course on their return to Britain.

Students who already have a job offer from a Canadian employer may be eligible for 'Programme A'. They can apply directly to the High Commission in London for an employment authorization (reference 1102) which will be valid for a maximum of 5 months and which is not transferable to any other job.

The other and more flexible possibility is to obtain an unspecified employment authorization (reference 1295) which is available only through BUNAC

(16 Bowling Green Lane, London EC1R 0BD; 071-251 3472). Its 'Work Canada' programme offers about 1,000 students the chance to go to Canada for up to 6 months and take whatever jobs they can find. The only requirements are that applicants have $1,000 in Canadian funds (or $500 plus either a letter of sponsorship from a Canadian relative or a job offer) and a return ticket. Until recently all Work Canada participants had to have a medical examination with a doctor from a designated list at a cost of £80-100, to cover the possibility that the student will find a job in food-handling or childcare. However as of March 1992, this is no longer compulsory (though the employment authorization will clearly state that these categories of employment are prohibited). The programme fee is £65, and compulsory insurance £85. Participants may take a BUNAC flight (approximately £370) or arrange travel independently. Applications must be in by the end of April, to allow time for the processing of forms.

Certain special categories of work may be eligible for authorization, such as for qualified nannies who are in great demand but must stay for a minimum of one year (see *Domestic* section below) or for the tobacco harvest (see below).

BUNAC produces its own Canadian job directory for members. Most of the jobs listed are in hotels and tourist attractions in the Rockies which is a beautiful part of the world in which to spend a summer. British university students have an edge over their Canadian counterparts in this sphere of employment since they don't have to return to their studies until the end of September or early October rather than early September. Additionally, BUNACAMP (see *page 31*) places students as counsellors in a variety of summer camps throughout Canada.

Australians should write to the Canadian Consulate in Canberra, Sydney, Melbourne or Perth and request an application form for a working holiday visa which is an open employment authorization valid for a year from the date of issue, available to young people aged 18-30. The quota is allocated in January and is usually filled by June, so the best time to apply is November/December. Processing normally takes 12 weeks. Provided they have support funds of A$2,000, they might prefer to participate in the Student Services Australia package to Canada; details from SSA/SWAP, P.O. Box 399, Carlton South, Melbourne 3053. All participants of approved student schemes can benefit from the advice of the Canadian Federation of Students, including on possible exemption from tax, provided they work less than 183 days and earn at least 90% of their total annual income in Canada.

Some people decide not to struggle against the bureaucracy. Although casual work is available, the lack of an employment authorization or Social Insurance Number (the SIN is comparable to the American social security and the British national insurance) is a perpetual thorn in the sides of itinerant workers. Without them, you will have to steer clear of official bodies such as Canada Employment Centres, tax offices, etc. and many employers will be unwilling to consider you.

If you decide to work without proper authorization, you should be aware that you are breaking a law which is taken seriously in Canada. If you are working in a job known to hire large numbers of foreigners (e.g. tree-planting and fruit-picking in BC), there is a chance that the area will be raided by immigration control (rather than the police whose jurisdiction does not include immigration offences). If you have insufficient funds you may be deported. Otherwise you will be given a 'departure notice' which allows you to travel to the USA.

Wages are fairly good in Canada with statutory minimum wages (e.g. $6 per hour in Ontario and $5 in most of the other provinces). Last year the average weekly wage earned by BUNACers in Canada was $300 with only $80 being spent on food and lodging. Most hotel/catering staff are paid the minimum wage which, as in the US, can be doubled or trebled by tips. Furthermore jobs in holiday resorts come with staff accommodation and meals. As ever, youth hostel notice boards are recommended for information on jobs. Despite the recession, job opportunities abound in the main cities of Toronto (where nearly a half of BUNACers work), Calgary, Edmonton and Vancouver.

The Rocky Mountain resorts of Banff, Jasper, Lake Louise, Sunshine Mountain and Waterton are among the best places to try both summer and winter. Banff seems to absorb the largest number of foreign workers as catering and chamber staff, trail-cutters, etc. It is an expensive town in which to job-hunt but if you are prepared to walk you can find free campsites out of town and up the mountain-sides. The huge Banff Springs Hotel alone employs 750 people.

Other popular holiday areas are the Muskoka District of Ontario centred on the town of Huntsville (comparable to England's Lake District) and the shores of the Great Lakes, particularly Lake Huron. Since most of the holiday job recruitment in Ontario is done through Canadian universities, and the resorts are so widely scattered that asking door to door is impracticable, it is advisable to concentrate your efforts in the west. A possible exception is Niagara Falls, honeymoon capital of North America.

Harvesting and other outdoor jobs proliferate in the spring and summer, especially tree-planting. The interior of British Columbia and around Prince Rupert BC are among the most promising areas. The season normally lasts from the end of March to the end of July. The work is just as hard as any farming or construction work but is also very well paid. Novice planters should be able to earn over $100 a day and by the end of the season $200+, with camp living expenses amounting only to $15 a day.

The Okanagan Valley of BC is a destination famous among travellers looking for fruit-picking work, though wages tend to be low ($30-$40 a day) and the risk of discovery high. The best crop is apples which are picked after the soft fruits, i.e. in September and October. There is also an important apple harvest around Annapolis Royal in Nova Scotia.

Still in the Maritimes, tobacco farmers in eastern Prince Edward Island are major employers of planters in May/June. Opportunities for tobacco pickers in Southern Ontario (around Aylmer and Strathroy) have diminished in recent years with the drastic fall in the demand for tobacco worldwide.

For brief spells of employment investigate special events. The 1994 Commonwealth Games at Victoria in British Columbia is likely to create all kinds of vacancies.

Gone are the days when Canadians could proudly claim that their dollar was stronger than their neighbours' dollar. At the time of going to press, the Canadian dollar was worth about 70 US cents, and living costs are lower by a similar degree. In other words, prices are about the same in figures — car rental for $40 a day, say, or $25 for a cheap double room in a modest city hotel — but foreign currency goes further in Canada than in the States.

Both Thomas Cook and American Express issue travellers cheques in Canadian dollars which you will have no problem cashing and which can usually be used in hotels, restaurants and major stores as cash. American and British currency or travellers cheques can be negotiated at any large bank though a hefty commission is often charged. US currency is accepted in many establishments, but you are unlikely to receive as favourable an exchange rate as at the bank.

Automatic teller machines almost invariably belong to one of the big networks, so with an ATM card or two you should rarely find yourself short of cash. Banking hours are normally 10 am-3 pm Monday to Thursday, and 10am-5pm on Fridays. Trust companies (loosely analogous to building societies) offer services similar to banks, and are open longer hours including Saturdays. If you arrive in Canada with a large sum of money, you might consider opening a bank account in Canadian dollars. You can open an account on the spot providing you have two pieces of identification, preferably showing a local address. An account holder at Canada Trust, one of the leading trust companies (which stays open 9am-9pm six days a week), can withdraw money across the counter instantly, from any branch across Canada. If this system appeals to you, get a list of the branch addresses beforehand, to make sure you will have access to your money in the places you want to visit.

The bright colours of Canadian notes (bills) and the smiling face of the Queen may come as both a shock and a relief after American greenbacks. The $2 bill is pink, the $5 blue, $10 purple, $20 pale green and $50 orange. The terminology used for low-value coins is the same as in the US: penny, nickel, dime and quarter. Although there are 50c coins, you will not often see them in circulation. The handiest for parking meters, telephones and vending machines are quarters and the eleven-sided $1 coin, known as a 'loonie' because of the picture of the loon, a water bird, on the reverse.

Taxes. Canada has a Goods and Services Tax (GST) of 7% which is added to provincial taxes at around the same level. Non-residents can ask for a GST refund for most goods purchased in Canada for use abroad (with exceptions) and for paid accomodation (of short duration). Complete information is provided in a pamphlet printed by Revenue Canada. Call 1-800-668-4748 (Canada) or 1-618-991-3346 for more details.

Telephones. The Canadian telephone system outflanks the American one for efficiency and economy. There are many aspects which are similar such as the dial tone, toll-free numbers and dial-a-joke service. Local calls from a private phone are free, so it is quite permissible to ask in a restaurant or store if you can make a quick local phone call. If you are staying in a private home, you need feel no compunction (from the financial point of view) in chatting for hours on the phone to a person on a nearby number. Local calls from payphones cost 25c. A three minute long distance call (e.g. Toronto to Vancouver) costs about $6.50.

Post. Canada Post, a crown corporation, is notoriously slow and inefficient. Canadians you meet will be amazed to hear about the British system, and green with envy of next-day delivery including Saturdays. Post offices are not as numerous as they are in Britain (which admittedly has the highest ratio in the world). In cities there is often a postal counter in the foyer of shopping malls where you can buy stamps and send parcels. An ordinary letter or postcard within Canada costs 42c and to Europe 84c for the first 20 grams. Poste restante mail should be sent c/o General Delivery, City, Province. Items are held for just two weeks.

Faxes and Telegrams. Faxes can be sent from main post offices and from thousands of commercial concerns — copy bureaux and the like. You can dictate a telegram over the phone to CN/CP Telecommunications and charge it to a telephone bill. If you don't know anyone whose number you can use for this purpose, send your message in person from any CN/CP office (address in phone book); these are distinct from the post office.

Getting Around

AIR
Competition in Canada is weaker, and fares are higher, than in the USA. Fares can be reduced by a third by buying Visit USA tickets before arrival in North America (see page 20). Students with ISIC cards can obtain cheap one-way fares (e.g. $250 from Toronto to Vancouver) at offices of the Canadian student travel organization Travel CUTS. The two main carriers are the government-owned Air Canada, and Canadian Airlines International. Fares and conditions on both are identical.

Before leaving Britain, you can get information and make bookings through Air Canada (081-759-2636) or Canadian Airlines International (081-667 0666). Several small carriers act as feeder comanies for these airlines. Independent carriers have made several attempts to break what they see as the duopoly's stranglehold on Canadian aviation, the most recent being Emerald Airlines which at the time of going to press was promising a fare of $125 one-way for turbo-prop flights between Montréal and Toronto.

One-way air tickets are sometimes sold privately through the 'travel' classified ads of major newspapers like the *Toronto Globe & Mail* or the *Vancouver Sun*. Watch for last minute adverts such as 'One way Vancouver-Montréal. Female. $190 obo (or best offer)'. The reason gender is specified is that airline tickets are non-transferable. Although the airlines don't bother to check your identity, they might feel obliged to make a fuss if they see that your sex does not match the one stated on your ticket. As long as you are flexible enough to travel on the date specified, you can get a bargain.

All airports in Canada are coded to begin with Y and bear no relation to

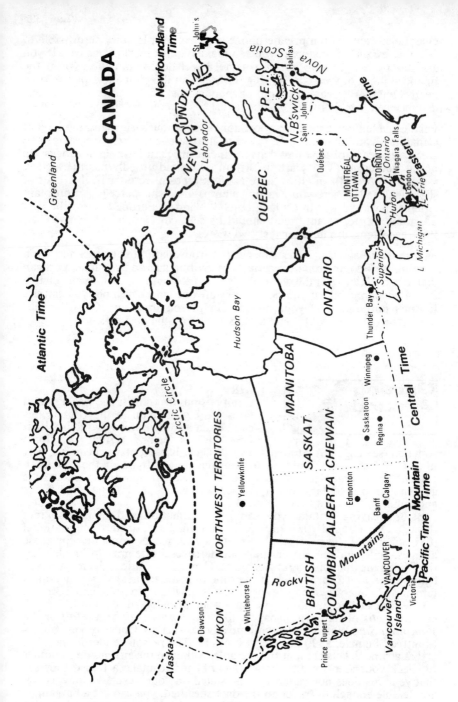

CANADA

Newfoundland Time

Atlantic Time

Newfoundland Time

St. John's

Nova Scotia
Halifax

P.E.I.

N.B'swick
Saint John

Québec

MONTRÉAL
OTTAWA

TORONTO
Niagara Falls
London
L. Ontario
L. Erie Eastern Time
L. Huron

L. Michigan

Greenland

NEWFOUNDLAND
Labrador

QUÉBEC

Hudson Bay

Arctic Circle

ONTARIO

L. Superior
Thunder Bay

MANITOBA
Winnipeg

NORTHWEST TERRITORIES

Yellowknife

SASKAT CHEWAN
Saskatoon
Regina

Central Time

ALBERTA
Edmonton
Banff
Calgary

Mountain Time

BRITISH COLUMBIA

Rocky Mountains

VANCOUVER
Victoria

Vancouver Island

Pacific Time

Prince Rupert

YUKON
Dawson
Whitehorse

Alaska

the place name; Toronto's main airport, for example, is YYZ, Montréal's Mirabel is YMX. Following the lead of a number of US airlines, Air Canada and Canadian now issue air passes for tourists. The price and conditions are similar and both offer a cheaper version — 20% off — for travellers willing to fly standby.

The best bargain for the western half of the country is the Western Canada AirPass sold by regional carrier AirBC (an offshoot of Air Canada). Its network stretches from Winnipeg in the east to Prince Rupert and Campbell River, taking in most places in between and extending south over the border to Seattle and Portland. The tax-inclusive price is £119, £169 and £245 for seven, 14 and 30 days respectively. AirBC's UK office is at 15a Church St, Reigate, Surrey RH2 0AA (tel 0737 226881; fax 0737 223590).

All these air passes are valid throughout North America and must be purchased outside the continent. Canadian and VIA Rail offer a Skyrail pass which allows three sectors of air or train travel. The pass costs £225 (£45 less for travellers flying to Canada on Canadian), with extra sectors priced at only £22.50 each.

Some smaller airlines sell regional passes whic represent excellent value. Late in 1992, for example, Air BC was offering unlimited travel in central and western Canada for a week for £99.

BUS

Greyhound Lines of Canada offer the greatest number of services, especially in Western Canada, though there are dozens of smaller operators such as Voyageur Colonial. For a copy of the *Official Bus Guide* which provides schedules for services throughout Canada as well as the USA, contact Russell's Guides Inc, PO Box 278, Cedar Rapids, Iowa 52406 (319-364-6138). Greyhound's Canadian headquarters are 877 Greyhound Way SW, Calgary, Alberta (403-265-9111). Greyhound's transCanada *Scenicruiser Service* takes the better part of four days to go from Toronto to Vancouver.

In the past, a number of companies have cooperated to offer discounted one-way or return excursion fares but it was not certain that these would be repeated. The maximum single fare between a point in Ontario and anywhere in the four western provinces is around $150 one way. The Canada-wide maximum is about $199. So the 4,250 mile trip between Halifax and Whitehorse could work out at a mere 5c per mile, and allow unlimited stopovers within a 30-day period.

The Greyhound Ameripass (described in *Getting Around USA:* Bus) is valid only for brief forays into Canada including around Ontario and Quebec on Voyageur and Voyageur Colonial Lines. It is not valid for trans-Canada travel. A Canada-only version of the Ameripass, the Greyhound Canada pass, cost £105 for seven days, £155 for 15 days and £175 for 30 days. There is also on All Canada Bus Pass which costs £185 for 15 days and £225 for 30 days in the high season. Both types of passes can be bought in advance from Greyhound International in the UK (0342 317317). Finally, Voyageur Colonial offers a ten-day bus pass for around £100, valid on routes in Ontario and Québec. Buy it locally or through NAR Ltd (0344 890525).

TRAIN

The building of the railway across the country plays a large role in the popular imagination and the national identity. The Canadian poet EJ Pratt wrote an epic poem called the *Last Spike* and Gordon Lightfoot's opus magnum is *The Canadian Railroad Trilogy*. The trans-Canada rail trip on the Canadian is one of the classic railway journeys of the world. The epic three-and-a-half day journey Toronto to Vancouver is an attractive alternative to the flight, but is expensive. Stopovers are permitted. It is sometimes possible to negotiate a discounted berth once you're on the train if these are available; ask any of the porters. Apex return fares which must be purchased at least two weeks in advance often represent considerable savings. There are also worthwhile savings to be made if travelling during the low season (January to early April and mid-October to mid-December).

The terrain through the Prairies and the wilderness of Northern Ontario can become monotonous (as can the food in the dining car). But the section through the Rockies is spectacular. Occasional glimpses from the domed observation car of a herd of elk or moose stampeding away from the tracks or of a lonely little Ukrainian Orthodox church, generate enough interest to keep most travellers happy.

The most dense network of rail services is in the Ontario-Quebec Corridor which connects Montreal with Windsor. VIA Rail (pronounced *Vee-ah)*, which runs most of the passenger services in Canada is heavily subsidized by the government and is under constant pressure to axe services. (One of their economies was to close their London office near Trafalgar Square). Via has introduced some futuristic new trains called LRCs (Light, Rapid, Comfortable) and is doing its best to compete with airlines. This has some advantages for travellers (computerized bookings, deluxe service) but some disadvantages (e.g. the necessity of reserving a seat in advance instead of simply buying your ticket and boarding your train). The express services in the Corridor are called 'Rapido' and are equivalent to the InterCity 125 service of British Rail. The 325-mile/523km journey between Montréal and Toronto takes less than five hours on a Rapido. If you are travelling on or near a holiday period, be sure to book a seat.

You can purchase a rail pass called a Canrailpass from any VIA station. Prices vary according to the age of traveller and region of the rail network. You can get a 15-day pass for the whole network or eight-day passes for the Maritimes or the Eastern or Western regions. Youth discounts of 35% are available to those under 24.

DRIVING

Dependence on the automobile is just as rampant in Canada as it is in the USA. A Canadian without a car is an eccentric Canadian. If you plan to travel around any sparsely populated regions such as the Maritimes or the Northland, a car is virtually essential.

Car Hire. A small car might cost a $40 with unlimited distance, or $220 a week. Camper vans may be hired for about $900 a week. Remember that general and provincial sales taxes will be added to the bill, and that these are not refundable under the government tax reimbursement scheme. The minimum rental age is 21 in most cases.

Petrol. Fuel is sold by the litre across Canada and the variation in price is extreme, from about 50c to 95c per litre. The average should be not much over £1.50 per Imperial gallon.

Rules of the Road. Driving laws are made at the provincial level, so rules and practices vary from province to province. For example you can drive with your UK licence for only 30 days in the Yukon but for six months in

British Columbia. You can turn right on a red light (after stopping) in every province except Quebec. The speed limit in built-up areas across Canada is 50 km/h (30mph) except in Prince Edward Island where it is 60 km/h (37mph). On the open highway, the limit varies from 80 km/h (50mph) in rural areas to 100 km/h (62mph) on major arteries. All limits are clearly and repeatedly signposted in kilometres only.

The minimum driving age across Canada is 16 except in Newfoundland where it is 17. Seat belts are compulsory everywhere except Yukon and the North West Territories.

There are some rules which apply in all provinces. For instance, you must stop for school buses no matter in which direction you are travelling; and driving with over 0.08% alcohol in the blood is a serious offence. After a first offence, your licence will automatically be suspended for at least three months and you will normally get a $150-$300 fine. Speed traps are frequently set up by the police. Approaching motorists will often warn you by flashing their headlamps.

Insurance. Visiting drivers must have full liability insurance. The minimum cover is $200,000 in all provinces and territories except Québec, where it is £50,000. Information is available from either the Insurance Bureau of Canada (181 University Avenue, Toronto; 416-362-2031) or from the Canadian Automobile Association (1775 Courtwood Crescent, Ottawa; 613-226-7631). The CAA is affiliated with the AA and RAC and will provide maps, itineraries, an emergency service, etc. to members of both organizations. The highway map issued by the tourist office is as detailed as most people require for long journeys.

Winter Driving. If you're visiting Canada during the winter, you'll have to have nerves of steel to drive. White-outs and black ice are common, even on the main highways. Police will normally block a road if it is considered too dangerous to navigate. Listen for warnings on the radio. If you are driving in rural areas, you are advised to carry a shovel, sand, flashlight, flares, extra clothes, a blanket, ice scraper and a candle placed inside a tin can. (A candle gives off enough heat in an enclosed space to sustain life for a considerable length of time). If you do get stranded stay in your vehicle and wait for help. Cautious drivers wait out storms in private houses or hostelries on their route. There is even a Canadian word for this: people talk about being 'storm-stayed' for several days.

Driveaways. Under the heading Automobile Delivery in the Yellow Pages you will find a selection of driveaway agencies, just as you do in the USA. From the west coast, cars need to be delivered to California or Ontario; from Toronto, most of the traffic is destined for Florida or western Canada. You should have no difficulty finding a driveaway car during the winter, but there may be delays in the summer.

HITCH-HIKING

There are fewer crazy drivers in Canada than there are in the USA, and hitching is less dangerous in Canada than it is south of the border. There is a large measure of hostility to hitchers among the more conservative elements of society, but on the other hand there is a strong pro-British feeling which should work in your favour if you sport a Union Jack on your luggage. Just as in the USA it is difficult to hitch out of big sprawling cities. but hitching is an accepted practice in country areas, especially in summer. In winter, only the brave or foolhardy would want to try.

As in the USA, most budget travellers choose from youth hostels,cheap downtown hotels (often attached to a bar) or motels. Hotel addresses given out by tourist offices or hotels associations tend to be expensive, at least $45 for a double. Try asking for guest houses or tourist rooms which will be cheaper. Similarly, bed and breakfasts are often interesting places to stay but rarely cheap. Consult *John Thompson's Country Bed & Breakfast Places of Canada* if you're interested. Double rooms in motels start at $35, though you must take into account the additional cost of commuting into a city centre. Also look for signs on residential homes 'Approved Accommodation' which indicates a private guesthouse.

Youth Hostels. Canada is not especially well-endowed with youth hostels, considering its size, but those that there are provide good value to Hostelling International members. The Canadian Hostelling Association (CHA) has a total of 80 with a concentration in the Rockies and in Nova Scotia. Charges vary from $8 to $21 depending on the degree of luxury. Some are primitive, but many of the city hostels — plus those in Banff and Lake Louise have been recently upgraded.

A list of hostels is available from any hostel shop or from the CHA National Office, 1600 James Naismith Drive suite 608, Gloucester, Ontario K1B 5N4; tel 613-748-5638, fax 613-748-5750.

A second network is gradually extending across Canada. The Canadian headquarters of Backpackers International Hostelling Association are at Longhouse Village, RR13, Thunder Bay, Ontario P7B 5E4 (tel 807-983-2042; fax 807-983-2914). The organization can provide details of its independent hostels, mainly in BC and Ontario.

College Accommodation. University residences are usually open to visitors out of term, i.e. mid-May to late August. There may be restrictions such as a minimum stay of one week or priority for visiting students. For a list of universities in Canada offering residential accommodation to travellers, contact the Conference/Facilities Office, Ryerson Polytechnical Institute, West Kerr Hall, 350 Victoria St, Toronto, Ontario M5B 2K3. Enquiries should be addressed to the University Housing Officer of the university of your choice as far in advance of your visit as possible. Charges are about $20 a day single, with reductions for longer stays.

Camping. There are many government and privately-run sites nationwide. Given the climate, you should expect them to be closed from mid-September until the start of June, though some keep slightly longer seasons.

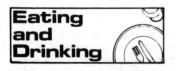

You have to go out of your way to find uniquely Canadian dishes. Any you do find are regional specialities, from the famous French Canadian meat pie called *tourtiere* to fried cod's tongues in Newfoundland. Occasionally a restaurant will serve pemmican (originally a Cree word describing meat which has been dried and pounded with berries), bear and groundhog, but this is very rare. Freshwater fish are delicious and best enjoyed over a lakeside fire a few hours after having been caught. British

Columbian salmon is famous and cheaper than Scottish salmon. Many west coast households own their own salmon smoking devices with a choice of wood flavouring. The most famous Canadian food product is maple syrup, preferably enjoyed with a plate of fluffy pancakes. A small tin of maple syrup is one of the tastiest souvenirs of Canada you can take home.

Apart from a few regional specialities and the excellent French cooking available in many Montréal and Québec City restaurants, eating out in Canada is almost indistinguishable from eating out in the US: fast food franchises, coffee shops, delis, steak and seafood restaurants and a huge range of ethnic restaurants in the big cities. And if you want to eat in rather than out, you can have food such as pizza or Chinese food delivered to your door. Check the Yellow Pages for the restaurants that deliver.

Tipping. As in the US, a 10-15% tip is usual in restaurants. Canadian waiters and waitresses may not display their wrath quite as openly as their American counterparts if you undertip, but they will certainly feel it.

DRINKING

Canadians consume more alcohol than the British and the Americans, most of it in the form of lager-style beer. As in the US, more beer drinking takes place in front of the TV than in public. But beer drinking, like all alcohol consumption, has been declining. As an expensive marketing ploy to revive the habit, some brewers have replaced the characteristic stubby bottle with a taller American-style bottle.

Canadian beer has long been held in high regard not only by nationalistic Canadians but by Americans too, for being slightly stronger and considerably tastier than American beer. It is therefore surprising that American beers have penetrated the market as effectively as they have over the past few years, especially Miller and Budweiser. The Canadian company Molsons brews a version of Löwenbrau to compete with the American imports, though it tastes more like ordinary Canadian beer than the stuff brewed in Munich. However, the three principal Canadian breweries continue to dominate: Carling, Labatt and Molsons, all of whom brew a range of beers. Most beer drinkers buy a 24-pack or 'two-four'. A deposit of about 10c is charged in bottles and cans. Domestic bottled beer costs about $3.50 for a 20oz bottle, $5.50 for an import. The most unusual brews are Carling's Buckeye, Labatt's IPA and Molson's Brador. If possible sample some of the beers brewed regionally. Some, like Moosehead which is brewed in the Atlantic provinces, have become well known, but there are other small breweries known only to a local clientele.

Many people are surprised to learn that a country associated with snow blizzards produces wine. The industries of both British Columbia and Ontario are expanding and producing more mature wines. Some examples are given in the relevant chapters.

Canadian whiskey is drier than American bourbon but quite different from Scotch. Browse in a liquor store for some unusual indigenous liqueurs, for instance Yukon Jack or a liqueur made from maple syrup.

The minimum drinking age is 18 in Alberta, Manitoba, Quebec and Prince Edward Island, and 19 everywhere else. ID must often be produced when purchasing alcohol just as in the US. Hours of opening vary from province to province and are dealt with in the regional chapters. Due to the puritanical influence of the early settlers, the sale of alcohol is strictly controlled by the provincial governments. Government-run off sales usually keep normal shop hours (9am-5.30pm) and so a certain amount of advance planning is necessary. It is also illegal to drink alcohol in public and you may well witness the spectacle of police officers emptying can after can of the demon drink at the entrance to beaches, stadiums, etc.

Most bars fall into one of two categories: rough hang-outs or expensive neon antiseptic haunts where you are constantly hassled to buy another drink, since the staff are trying to supplement their meagre wages with tips. There are also increasing numbers of replica British pubs which never quite come off.

THE ARTS

Canada is less paranoid about its culture than it once was. For years, talented Canadians in every field have drifted over the border for recognition in the US, people like Oscar Peterson, Joni Mitchell, Neil Young, Donald Sutherland and William Shatner. In an effort to stem the tide and to promote Canadian Culture, the government has legislated a minimum level of Canadian content in radio and television broadcasting. There is also a strict Hire-Canadians-Only policy. Xenophobic immigration and employment laws have made it difficult for theatre companies and orchestras to hire British and American stars as directors, conductors and players. The hiring of less well known Canadians in favour of foreign celebrities often results in bitter controversy.

The generous government subsidies of Canadian talent have complemented private patronage to boost the arts. Toronto, Montréal and Vancouver have a great deal to offer the theatre-goer, opera lover, music buff and balletomane, both mainstream extravaganzas (some shows are imported from the US it must be admitted) and experimental works. The Royal Winnipeg Ballet and the Canadian Opera Company regularly tour the country and every city has its own symphony orchestra. The Canadian Film Board is known internationally for the quality of its shorts, documentaries, animations and, more recently, for a controversial anti-nuclear film *If You Love This Planet* which was banned in public cinemas in America. On the whole, though, the Canadian film industry has lagged behind the Australian one; it has produced only two or three films which have achieved some international recognition such as the film *The Decline of the American Empire* and the brilliant *I've Heard the Mermaids Singing.*

Cinema seats cost about $8, with half-price tickets on Tuesdays, while tickets for mainstream theatre and concerts start at about $15. Watch for 'rush-seats', unsold seats which are sold at a discount on the day of performance.

The splashy new National Gallery in Ottawa, the Art Gallery of Ontario in Toronto and Vancouver Art Gallery have international art collections and have visiting exhibitions from Europe and the US. In every town there is a regional gallery which displays art and artefacts from both early and contemporary Canada, which can be fascinating to visitors from the Old World.

Popular Music. Although famous musicians like Bryan Adams and Ian Tyson are Canadian in origin, they have gone to the US for recognition. Artists who remain in Canada normally depend on a regional following. Toronto based bands are often unknown on the west coast and vice versa. For the newest and best, you'll have to ask the locals or guess from listings in the alternative press.

Folk music thrives across Canada and any of the annual folk festivals are very worthwhile attending, especially Mariposa in Ontario and the Vancouver Folk Festival (see regional chapters for details). Quebec has a strong and unique tradition of French folk and popular music which is continued by home-grown *chansonniers.*

Television and Radio. The strict laws which prescribe a minimum of Canadian content in the media mean that programming in Canada is quite different from that of the States. Almost all Canadian households have cable TV which allows them to pick up programmes on all three American networks plus Public Broadcasting. The Canadian Broadcasting Corporation shows some American drivel, but also some worthwhile drama series and documentaries (some bought from the BBC).

The CBC schedules of radio programmes are listed in the monthly magazine *Radio Guide.* Many Americans close to the border tune in to the CBC news, since it is reputed to be more impartial and international than American radio news. The Corporation operates two national English language services. Many stations across the country devote all or part of their schedules to ethnic programming. Some northern broadcasts are in Indian and Inuit languages. For more details about programming, contact CBC Audience Services, Box 500, Station A, Toronto.

Newspapers. As in the US, Canadian newspapers are bulging with advertisements. When you see the size of an average city daily, you will understand why the forests of Canada, vast as they are, are being depleted faster than they can be replaced. Overall circulation of newspapers is exactly half of Britain's (219 per 1,000 people as opposed to 441). The only newspaper which can justifiably claim to be a national paper is the *Toronto Globe & Mail* which is published in a western edition as well. Even so, the circulation is only 312,000, so its influence is limited. The price of the newspaper varies between locations. In Toronto the Monday-Friday editions cost 50c while the Saturday edition cost $1.50; elsewhere in Ontario the price is 75c every day.

SPORT

Canadians are even more avid sports fans than their American neighbours. Extensive media coverage, especially of ice hockey (always called hockey), guarantees that most Canadians are familiar with stars' names and team standings. As in the US, the baseball season takes place in summer, football in the autumn and hockey throughout the winter.

Hockey. It is the rare Canadian who does not learn to skate at a very early age. By about the age of nine, most children — predominantly boys — play hockey either informally or in a local league. In former days, boys would gather on any frozen river or lake with their portable nets, hockey sticks and puck and play for hours until their extremities were numb with cold. These days, most hockey is played in indoor arenas, and when those aren't available, the neighbourhood kids dispense with skates, get together on the road, strap old telephone directories to their shins to act as protection, and take shots at each other's goal. Hockey is ingrained in the national consciousness. There is even a Canadian novel about the game called *The Last Season* by Roy MacGregor.

In the good old days (pre-1967) the National Hockey League consisted of six teams, the Toronto Maple Leafs, Montréal Canadians, Chicago Black

Hawks, Detroit Red Wings, New York Rangers and Boston Bruins, all battling for the top prize, the Stanley Cup. Despite the American location, any Canadian would have told you with pride that the vast majority of the players were Canadian. To the great satisfaction of Canadian fans, the Stanley Cup passed back and forth between Montréal and Toronto during the 1960's. But then the league expanded, eventually to embrace 16 more teams including such unknowns as the New Jersey Devils and Buffalo Sabres. Although many fans lamented the dilution of the league, they don't seem to have become any less fanatical.

The game itself is fast, exciting and easy to follow. If you're in Canada during the season (October to April) and can't see a live game, try to see one on television. One aspect of it that may take you by surprise is the fisticuffs which regularly develop. It is a strange sight to see a heavily padded sportsman trying to pull the opponent's jersey over his head while balancing on skates. Regrettably, the fans love it.

Lacrosse. This indigenous game was adapted from a Native Indian ball game called bagataway. Early explorers reported that games involved as many as 1,000 players, and that broken bones and even death regularly ensued. Although the modern version is not played on so massive nor so violent a scale, it is a fast and rough game, well worth the effort of tracking down.

GAMBLING

Gambling in casinos is legal only in BC and certain parts of other provinces. The minimum age is 19, and the main games are blackjack and roulette.

Perhaps because most Canadians have always been deprived of the pleasures of gambling, lotteries are amazingly successful. If you like to spend time dreaming about what you would do with a prize of $20 million then by all means buy a ticket. Most stationery and newspaper shops sell them.

In a country whose capital means 'buying and selling' in an Indian language, it is not surprising to find an obsession with commerce. The inventor of the shopping mall is reputed to have been a Canadian (who went south to Minnesota to make his fortune). The rate at which suburban shopping complexes continue to spring up makes the casual observer wonder how there can possibly be enough consumers to go round.

The principal department stores are Eaton's, Simpson's, Woodwards (in the West) and the Bay, descendant of the original Hudson's Bay Company. With a few exceptions, these department stores are found downtown. The major discount department stores like Zellers, K-Mart, Woolworths and Canadian Tire are found in suburban plazas. The Bay carries high-quality merchandise including the distinctive Hudson's Bay blankets.

Tax. Sales taxes are the bane of the shopper's life. A General Sales Tax (GST) is levied on almost anything sold anywhere in Canada, and is hardly ever included in advertised prices. In addition, provinces are entitled to levy a tax too. These range from from zero in Alberta, the Yukon and the Northwest Territories to 12% in Newfoundland.

Visitors are able to reclaim tax paid on goods bought in Canada and taken abroad, and the form can be obtained from duty-free shops and border crossings. The procedure is painless and cash refunds can be obtained within Canada itself.

A number of shops allow youth hostel members a discount, so hostellers should obtain the list of participating merchants.

Most shops open from about 9.30am to 5.30/6pm with late night shopping on Thursdays and Fridays. Many shops (including convenience stores such as Mac's Milk and Beckers) open on Sundays.

Clothing and shoe sizes are identical to those in the USA (see page 102).

The Great Outdoors

For many people, the reason for a trip to Canada is to explore the wilderness. Pleasant as Canada's cities are, the forests, mountains and lakes are what give the nation its special appeal. Although the distances between city and undeveloped countryside can be large, every visitor should make the effort to leave the cities. In a country where raccoons and skunks are periodically spotted in southern Ontario backyards, and where the Northern Lights *(aurora borealis)* can occasionally be seen from city parking lots, the call of the wild is not far away.

The trouble with all that virgin wilderness is that it can be inaccessible, and inhospitable once you get there. Dense forests criss-crossed by rivers and dotted with lakes make difficulties for the uninitiated backpacker. The dream of a coast-to-coast National Trail is still a long way from realization. Most hikers head for maintained trails, usually in national and provincial parks. Ironically, these can become crowded. In order to control the numbers, park authorities are now insisting that you book ahead for some of the most popular trails. The reservation is not for a specific campsite but simply for the right to hike. Make enquiries to the park ranger well ahead if you are interested in doing a specific route (addresses of individual parks available from provincial tourist offices or the regional office of Parks Canada). There is no such restriction on day hikes. Topographic maps costing from $7-$10 (including postage) are available from the Canada Map Office, Department of Energy, Mines and Resources, 615 Booth St, Ottawa K1A 0E9 (613-952-7000). A free index of maps will be sent on request.

Parks. In addition to a host of provincial parks, there are 34 national parks in Canada from the Pacific Rim in the far west to Terra Nova Newfoundland accounting for 50,000 square miles (about the size of England). Each park has a distinctive feature such as a glacier, a herd of roaming bison, geological formations or rare flowers and plants. They all offer access to Canada's backcountry as well as tamer opportunities to join organized hikes, rent canoes or attend a naturalist's slide show. You have to pay for vehicle admission, typically $5 for a single day's admission to a national park, $10 for four days and $30 for the whole season (usually May-September). Camping fees range from $8 for a primitive site to $20 for a deluxe site with electricity, showers, etc. Firewood is normally supplied at a cost of $2. Campsites cannot be booked in advance, so you have to take your chances when you arrive. You can't stay longer than two weeks at any one campground, and many are open only in the summer. Consider carefully what provisions you take into a primitive campsite, since you'll have to carry all your rubbish out again. In many parks, tins and bottles are completely banned. Occasionally parks are closed when there is an exceptionally high risk of forest fire. For a guide to the national parks write to

Parks Canada, Ottawa, Ontario KIA 0H3 (819-994-2534). The five regional addresses have been listed in the regional chapters.

Wildlife. Seeing a spouting whale off the Pacific coastal trail or a bewhiskered Rocky Mountain goat high on a crag or hearing the haunting morning call of the loon (a diving bird) could be the highlight of your whole trip. On the other hand confronting swarms of mosquitoes or a bear might be the low point.

If you plan to go into the bush, make sure you take all the anti-bear precautions you can. Most bears attack because they are suddenly frightened or because their cubs appear to be threatened. So it is advisable to make a lot of noise as you hike; some people even wear a special bell called a bear-scarer around their necks. Bears tend to wander along the same route every day, creating shallow trenches which a native guide will probably be able to recognize. At night always hang your food from a tall tree branch; never keep it inside your tent. If you would rather watch a bear from the safety of a car, visit a rubbish dump in northern areas just after sunset. Sometimes the local council even erects a sign at tips warning bear-watchers to stay inside their cars. Polar bears are seen in increasing numbers in Churchill, Manitoba, where a special hotline — 675-BEAR — has been set up to warn of sightings. Climatic changes mean that the bears' usual diet of seals has diminished, and they have taken to breaking into homes to steal food. Sometimes they just eat the first person they see.

Wolves are much less dangerous, since they rarely confront a human, though an injured person left alone could be in danger. It is a good idea to carry a whistle to blow in an emergency, both to notify potential rescuers and to frighten away animals. Porcupines are commonplace but present no threat unless you try to handle one in which case you will find a mass of sharp needles embedded in your hand. Skunks (from the Algonquin word 'segonku') are a nuisance. When frightened they spray a very offensive odour which lingers not only on the victim but in the air for days. The remedy for an afflicted human (including clothing) or pet is a bath in tomato juice.

Insects. One of the worst trials to the outdoors-person is the succession of biting insects. The mosquito season is said to begin in earnest in June; however it is possible to be driven wild by them in May. The blackfly season also lasts for the months of June and July. Blackflies are tiny insects with a vicious bite. You must apply a strong evil-smelling repellent at regular intervals. Look for a brand which is composed of 100% active ingredients viz. diethyl toluamide, colloquially known as DEET. Experienced hikers also recommend eating lots of garlic which apparently offends insects as much as humans. Make sure there are no holes in your tent. Another way of avoiding the pests is to plan to take a trip after the first frost which usually occurs in late September. For instance if you choose the Thanksgiving weekend in mid-October, you may find yourself camping either in hot sun or in snow, but at least there won't be any bugs.

Equipment. Canada is as good a place as any to purchase good quality camping equipment, though prices are no lower than in Britain. It may also be possible to hire rucksacks or tents in places like Banff, or from university co-op shops. Some addresses are included in the regional chapters. Certainly skis and canoes can easily be rented from private outfitters or at resorts.

It is ironical that in a country as heavily forested as Canada, there are often restrictions on the use of wood by backpackers to build fires. Forest fires are a very serious problem and although many of them are caused by lightning, a few are caused by careless campers. When firebuilding is permitted, the rule is that you can burn only dead wood and fallen branches. Along heavily travelled trails, you may have to penetrate deep into the bush to find enough wood. So unless you are carrying your own stove (as most campers do) be sure to start setting up camp well before dark.

A waterproof container for matches is often essential, since downpours can be very heavy. One solution is to use a film canister and glue the striking surface of the match box inside the lid.

Hunting and Fishing. All non-residents must purchase provincial hunting and fishing licences. Fees range from about $10 to $25 for a licence lasting a few days. To shoot migratory game birds you need a special federal licence available from post offices. Hunting rifles or shotguns may be imported into Canada without a permit. Whereas hunting is not allowed in Canada's national parks, fishing permits are available for a small sum from any national park office and valid in all parks. For information about licences, equipment and species, contact either the provincial tourist office (addresses listed below in *Help and Information*) or the provincial government division of Fish and Wildlife.

Canoeing. The placid lakes found throughout Canada are ideal for the beginner. There is also plenty of whitewater for the more adventurous. The cost of an organized trip will be at least $60 a day including log cabin or tented accommodation.

Crime and Safety

Although the population of Canada is one-tenth that of the USA, it has only about one-fiftieth of the number of violent crimes. It is not only the statistics which are reassuring, but also the atmosphere. Walking alone at night is not nearly as terrifying in Ottawa as in Washington nor as dangerous in Montréal as in Memphis. Even in the biggest cities, there are virtually no areas which you need to avoid. You should of course exercise caution just as you would at home but, on the whole, there is little cause for anxiety. People who have hitch-hiked around North America report that their heart rate drops as soon as they cross into Canada. One explanation for the lower level of violence is that there is far less racial tension, and no history of segregation in Canada. Although the Native Canadians' resentment against the white man occasionally flares up in barroom brawls, you are unlikely to be involved.

As in the USA, laws vary from province to province. Some provinces have a dial-a-law telephone number which will provide the basic legal facts about such topics as drugs and immigration. There are also several levels of policing, from the federal Royal Canadian Mounted Police (who are more associated with synchronized riding than with tracking the Mafia) down to municipal policemen who sometimes seem like glorified traffic wardens.

If you decide to work without proper authorization, you shold be aware that you are breaking the law. If you are working in a high-profile job, you may well be raided by immigration control (rather than the police whose jurisdiction does not include immigration offences). If you have insufficient funds you may be deported. Otherwise you will be given a 'departure notice' which allows you to travel to the US. If caught you should contact the nearest legal aid lawyer whose services are free.

Drugs. The drug laws in Canada are federal rather than piecemeal by province. Possession of marijuana is a criminal offence under the Narcotic Control Act, despite the fact that one national organization estimates that over four million Canadians indulge. The penalty for a first offence is a fine of up to $1,000 and/or six months in prison. It is to be presumed that a traveller would not be so foolish as to put himself in the position of committing a second offence, whereupon the penalty is a $2,000 find and a year in jail. Importing and exporting is punishable by up to life imprisonment, but not less than seven years. Incredibly the penalities for marijuana are identical to those for heroin and other opiates. Despite this, the cultivation and use of marijuana by average people of all social backgrounds is just as widespread in Canada as in the US.

Help and Information *i*

The provincial tourist offices publish many informative and useful leaflets, so it is worth writing to them. (Half of them have only a box office address). Their addresses are listed below, alphabetically according to province. Toll-free numbers are valid within North America only.

Travel Alberta: 10025 Jasper Avenue, 15th Floor, Edmonton T5J 3Z3; 1-800-661-8888.

Tourism British Columbia: Parliament Buildings, Victoria V8V 1X4; (604) 683-2000.

Travel Manitoba: Department 7020, 155 Carlton St, 7th Floor, Winnipeg R3C 3H8; 1-800-665-0040.

Tourism New Brunswick: PO Box 12345, Fredericton E3B 5C3; (506) 453-2377. Toll free: 1-800-653-6353.

Newfoundland Tourism: PO Box 2016, St John's A1C 5R8; (709) 576-2830. Toll-free: 1-800-563-6353.

Nova Scotia Tourism: PO Box 130, Halifax B3J 2M7; (902) 424-5000..

Ontario Ministry of Tourism: 77, Bloor St W, 9th Floor, Toronto M7A 2K9; (416) 965-4008. Toll free: 1-800-268-3735.

Prince Edward Island Tourism: PO Box 940, Charlottetown CIA 7M5; (902) 892-2457.

Tourism Quebec: C.P. 20,000, Quebec G1K 7X2; (514) 873-2015.

Tourism Saskatchewan: 2103, 11th Avenue, Regina S4P 3V7; (306) 787-2300. Toll free: 1-800-667-7191.

Northwest Territories: (TravelArctic): Yellowknife X1A 2L9; (403) 873-7200.

Tourism Yukon: PO Box 2703, Whitehorse Y1A 2C6; (403) 667-5340.

Travelers' Aid. The few offices which Travelers' Aid maintains in Canada are in financial difficulty. You may discover that their offices, usually located in downtown railway stations, are closed due to shortage of staff.

High Commissions and Consulates. The British High Commission is at 80 Elgin St, Ottawa K1P 5K7 (tel 613-237-1530, fax 613-237-7980). There are also consulates as follows, going from east to west across Canada:

St John's (Newfoundland): tel 709-364-1200, fax 709-364-3550.
Halifax: tel 902-429-4230.
Montfeal: tel 514-866-5863, fax 514-866-0202.

Toronto: tel 416-593-1290, fax 416-593-1229.
Winnipeg: tel 204-783-7237, fax 204-774-4053.
Edmonton: tel 403-428-0375, fax 403-426-0624.
Vancouver: tel 604-683-4421, fax 604-681-0693.

PUBLIC HOLIDAYS

There are ten statutory holidays celebrated across Canada plus a few holidays unique to some provinces:

January 1	New Year's Day
March/April	Good Friday
	Easter Monday
May (Monday preceding May 25)	Victoria Day
July 1	Canada Day (formerly Dominion Day)
September (1st Monday)	Labour Day
October (2nd Monday)	Thanksgiving
November 11	Remembrance Day
December 25	Christmas Day
December 26	Boxing Day

In addition, most individual provinces observe additional public holidays as shown below; Quebec's festival on June 24th is also known (significantly) as Fête Nationale, while Newfoundland has no less than five provincial celebrations.

March (second Monday)	St Patrick's Day (Newfoundland only)
April (fourth Monday)	St George's Day (Newfoundland only)
June (third Monday)	Discovery Day (Newfoundland only)
June 24th	St John Baptiste Day (Quebec only)
June (last Monday)	Memorial Day (Newfoundland only)
July (second Monday)	Orangemen's Day (Newfoundland only)
August (first Monday)	Civic Holiday/Heritage Day (*not* Quebec, Atlantic Provinces or Yukon)
August (middle Monday)	Discovery Day (Yukon only)

Toronto and Ontario

Ontario is the richest and most heavily industrialised of Canada's ten provinces. For this reason and because Southern Ontario is geographically buried in the central USA, it is sometimes thought to be more 'American' than other parts of Canada. In many ways it is envied and resented by the other provinces for being the most powerful and sophisticated. Certainly there are giant Ford assembly plants and huge American-style agri-businesses in Southern Ontario, not to mention sprawling suburban shopping plazas and neon-lit motel strips. But there are also charming country towns like St Mary's and Fenelon Falls, gracious farming communities, thriving Mennonite markets and thousands of square miles of forest, parkland and even some Arctic tundra — all of which are as yet uncontaminated by minigolf courses and fast food joints. Ontario is an interesting place to start your holiday.

Toronto is many travellers' first taste of Canada. With a population of 3.2 million, it has recently overtaken Montréal as the leading city in Canada. Toronto is renowned throughout North America for its cleanliness and low crime rate, and for its lack of a wasteland between downtown and suburbs, so characteristic of North American cities. Much of its architecture and atmosphere are glossy and new, and yet it has retained many of its old neighbourhoods which lend the downtown area some character. You will probably confine yourself to the pleasingly dense downtown, most of it negotiable by foot, before setting off to explore the rest of the province.

The rest of Ontario has much to offer for lovers of the outdoors. Just a short distance from Toronto there are ski hills (admittedly not very spectacular), and a further hour away are the lakes and forests which are one of the main reason people come to Canada in the first place. With its 1.75 million acres, Algonquin Provincial Park is the best-known destination for canoeists and campers, but there are many others — 130 other provincial parks to be exact.

If you are not as keen on wilderness solitude as on picturesque landscapes, you can enjoy cycling through Prince Edward County west of Kingston to the shore of Lake Ontario; or take the ferry across to the very rural Manitoulin Island, where fishing and blueberry picking seem to be the main activities; or visit Point Pelee National Park, the most southerly point in Canada, to see the exotic birds and flowers. Any Ontarian will be very happy to recommend his or her favourite out-of-the-way discovery, and you cannot do better than to take that advice.

Ottawa, on the border with Quebec, is a rather dour capital city, but it has one of the finest museums in North America, and is easy to get around if you are just passing through.

THE LOCALS

Ontario is the only province of Canada whose urban population is over 80% of the total, and the people seem more sophisticated and fast-living than in the other provinces. Ethnic communities thrive in Toronto and the Italian, Chinese, Portuguese and German populations are numerous and culturally strong. You can attend United Church services (the largest Protestant denomination in Canada) in Korean, Hungarian and many other languages. You can watch soccer being played by Greek and Portuguese teams, admire chess being played by old men in an Austrian club and buy Armenian newspapers.

Outside Toronto, there is a small but influential religious group of people called Mennonites. Originally they were German settlers, and they continue to dress only in black and drive horses and buggies. Their celebrated produce and cuisine is available at markets and specialist restaurants in the Waterloo area of Toronto.

Making Friends. Judging from the number of singles bars and lonely hearts advertisements, Toronto must be full of people in search of a partner. They seem to favour the bars and singles clubs, such as The Spruce Goose, near the corner of Yonge and Eglinton (sometimes dubbed Young and Eligible). The popular singles night is Thursday. Bars at the University of Toronto are few and dismal, but there are plenty of lively off-campus places which students can recommend.

CLIMATE

Although Toronto is on the same latitude as Nice, don't expect a balmy winter. Toronto has a typically Canadian climate which specialises in extremes. The average temperature in July is 70°F/22°C, and it can feel particularly hot and muggy during the summer. Most public buildings are air-conditioned and many private houses have at least one air-conditioned room.

In January the average is 24°F/-4°C. There is an annual snowfall of 141cm (55 inches), but snow is promptly removed from sidewalks and roads so a pair of snow shoes would look distinctly out of place. You may, however, need a pair of waterproof boots to wade through the slush caused by melting snow. Between December and April the ice and slush make cycling not only unpleasant but dangerous. All buildings are heavily insulated and centrally heated, often to about 70°F/21°C which can seem uncomfortably hot to visitors from Britain, where the legal maximum in public buildings is 68°F/19°C.

Rain falls in some form on 134 days of the year. Although July and August are the wettest months, heavy rains are infrequent and unlikely to be a serious nuisance. Watch out for the winds, which swirl around among the skyscrapers of downtown Toronto and occasionally succeed in knocking people flat on their faces.

The best months to visit are probably May and September. In Toronto, recorded weather information is available on 676-3066. In Northern Ontario, the summers are not as hot as in the south of the province, the winters are colder and longer and the snowfall considerably more.

Getting Around

ARRIVAL AND DEPARTURE

Air. The Lester B. Pearson International Airport is named after the Nobel Peace Prize-winning Prime Minister, who led the country during the 1960s. The airport is at Malton 30km/18 miles northwest of the city centre. The recent addition of a third terminal has improved conditions in the airport greatly.

Express airport buses, operated by Gray Coach (351-3311), run between the airport and the ends of the public transport system or between the airport and downtown. Buses from the arrivals level of both terminals (leaving every 40 minutes from 6.20am-12.40am) take passengers to the Islington subway stop near the western end of the Bloor subway line, or to the Yorkdale station on the Yonge line (pronounced Young); the one-way fare is $6 and $6.50 respectively. The third destination is York Mills subway station which costs $7.50, though there is no advantage in using this service unless you are staying with people who live in that area.

For $10.75 you can be taken right downtown. The Airport Express Downtown Service runs every 20 minutes between 6.45am and 12.45am. Travel time to the Royal York Hotel (opposite the main railway station) is about 30 minutes unless it's rush hour. The cost of the taxi ride is about $35.

The cheapest way to get to the city from the airport is to take the TTC (Transport Tourist Commission) bus. For $2 (exact change), Bus 58A will take you to Lawrence West Station. (At the station, be sure to ask for a *Ride Guide*, which is a map outlining all subway, bus and streetcar routes in the city.) To return to the airport take the TTC bus route 58 to the Airport Holiday Inn (the last stop before Highway 427), and then take the free hotel shuttle bus to the airport.

Commuter flights to Ottawa and Montréal operate from the STOL-port (short take off and landing) on Toronto Island, and from the Hamilton Civic Airport. The Buttonville Airport located northeast of the city, operates flights to both of these destinations as well as to New York City.

For low-cost onward flights, contact Travel CUTS at 187 College St (979-2406), or YHA Travel at 217 Church St (862-0226).

Bus. The Bus Terminal is located on Bay St, north of Dundas St, around the corner from Toronto's Chinatown. It is Canada's busiest bus terminal. Information is obtainable on 393-7911 between 7am and 11.30pm. Gray Coach (351-3311), as distinct from Greyhound, operates most of the routes within Ontario, although the Ottawa-based Voyageur Colonial operates the services between Toronto and Kingston/Ottawa/Montréal.

Buses leave for Montréal and for London and Windsor/Detroit about a dozen times a day. There are five buses daily to Huntsville, a small town four hours north in the heart of the scenic Muskoka region. The cost of bus travel works out at about 8c per kilometre (13c per mile).

Train. There are two rail routes from the USA to Ontario. Amtrak runs a daily service from New York's Grand Central Station, departing at 8.45am and arriving in Toronto at 8.10pm. The one way fare is $116 (in Canadian dollars). Customs formalities take place at Niagara Falls. You may decide to break your journey if you want to spend some time admiring the famous waterfall.

Union Station, at the southern extremity of the subway line, is a Beaux Arts architectural delight which was saved from the wreckers' crane in the 1970's. You may even recognize it from the final scene of the *Silver Streak*, when an incoming train fails to stop and ploughs into the station wall. Union is very close to the O'Keefe Arts Centre and the St Lawrence Market, and is only a 15-20 minute walk from the Bus Depot.

The trans-Canada service, called *The Canadian,* arrives in Toronto Union Station at 7pm, three days and eight hours after leaving Vancouver. The train operates three times per week, with the westbound train leaving Toronto at 12.45pm. Information about all rail schedules and prices is available on 366-8411. Some sample single fares from Toronto are $65 to Ottawa, $45 to Sarnia, $18 to Niagara Falls and $77 to Montréal. If you book your seat at least 5 days in advance, you'll receive a 40% discount. As a very rough guide, the normal price of a single ticket is 10c per kilometre (16c per mile). If you want to go to Moosonee in the far north via the Polar Bear Express (a classic train ride), you will have to spend $200 on a return ticket; the journey there takes 16 hours.

Rapid commuter services called 'GO Trains' (Government of Ontario) feed into Union Street from other towns in the Toronto conurbation. They go as far east along the shore of Lake Ontario as Whitby and as far west as Hamilton. Ring 665-0022 for information.

Driving. Entry into Toronto by road is well sign-posted and comparatively swift. Drivers coming from Detroit/Windsor in the west or Montréal and Kingston in the east will approach via Highway 401, now cumbersomely renamed the Macdonald-Cartier Freeway. This is a typical North American highway: straight, wide and not very scenic, with a speed limit of 100km/hr (62 mph). The highway from the south (Niagara Falls) is the Queen Elizabeth Way (QEW to the locals) which cuts off the western tip of Lake Ontario and no longer charges a toll. From the east you'll approach downtown on the Don Valley Parkway, whose traffic jams can be so bad that that locals call it the Don Valley Parking Lot. The standard speed limit on Ontario highways in the 400 series (400, 401, 402 ...) is 100 km/hr.

To reach many of the scenic highlights and lakeside parks in Ontario, you will have to rely on a car, whether as a hitch-hiker or as a driver. The road heading north out of Toronto is highway 400. Avoid this at the beginning and end of summer weekends, because it gets clogged with city-dwellers escaping to their summer cottages.

Petrol in downtown Toronto costs about 57c a litre ($2.60 a gallon), though price wars can bring this down. Prices are usually highest on the highways. In cities, Canadian Tire gas stations usually charge a low price.

Car Rental: there are many rental offices for Budget and Tilden in Toronto, both charging about $50 a day and often including a set amount of free mileage. Tilden's weekend rate is $30 per day. Some weekend specials include unlimited free mileage, so its best to phone around. You can drop the car off in another centre but this is expensive. For example one-way rentals are available from Budget at the airport for $50 a day including 100 free kilometres. Rent-a-Wreck is at 374 Dupont St (961-7500), close to downtown. Also try Discount on 961-8006.

Driveaways. Although there are driveaway companies in Toronto, they almost never need drivers for destinations within the province. Most of the traffic is to Florida or to the Canadian West in early winter or back in the spring. You are allowed four days to get to Florida and eight days to Vancouver. In winter they are so desperate for drivers that some companies even pay for the gas. Try the Auto Delivery Company, 5803 Yonge St (225-7754).

Hitch-hiking. Hitchers heading west should take a GO-Train from Union Station to Mississauga, an outer suburb, and stand on the ramp approach to the 401. Waits can be long here. People heading east usually have better luck; stand on the Ajax ramp, also accessible on the GO-Train. It is technically illegal to hitch on the highways themselves.

CITY TRANSPORT

City Layout. Like American cities, Toronto is based on the grid pattern, though the streets are named not numbered. The main north-south street is Yonge St which, according to the *Guinness Book of Records*, is the longest thoroughfare in the world at 1,700km. Bloor Street is the main east-west artery through the city.

When trying to locate a specific address, bear in mind that all east-west numbering begins at Yonge St. So Dundas St is called Dundas East or Dundas West, according to which side of Yonge you are referring to. The further away from Yonge, the greater the street number. An added trick is that on east-west streets, the even numbers are on the west side. Street signs are yellow for east-west streets and blue for north-south; they are clearly visible at night thanks to helpful lighting.

Toronto Transit Commission. The TTC is credited with being the safest, cleanest and most efficient public transport system in North America. It runs an integrated service which includes subways, buses and street cars. It successfully transports 1.3 million passengers a day, from all backgrounds and income brackets. Information about all routes and times is available by ringing 393-4636. Free copies of the TTC *Ride Guide* are available from most subway stations, and at the TTC Transit Information Centre in the Yonge and Bloor subway station.

The flat fare of $2 (and rising) allows you to travel on any one or a combination of these networks, as long as it's a one-way journey without stopovers. It is more economical to buy your tickets or tokens (small aluminium discs) in bulk: five cost $6.50. A Metropass is valid for unlimited travel for a month and costs $67 plus a photo charge. A Sunday or public holiday pass costs $5 and can be used by up to two adults and four children. A day pass costs $5 Monday-Saturday; this is good for one person only and can be used on all regular TTC routes after 9.30am on weekdays or all day on Saturdays.

If you start your journey above ground, you must have the exact fare,

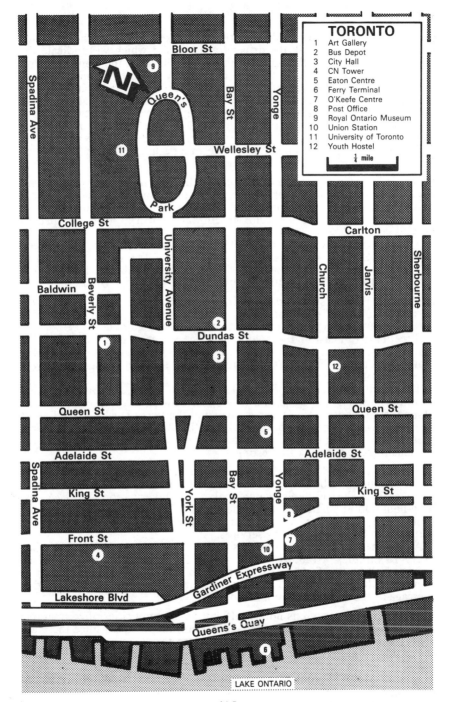

TORONTO

1 Art Gallery
2 Bus Depot
3 City Hall
4 CN Tower
5 Eaton Centre
6 Ferry Terminal
7 O'Keefe Centre
8 Post Office
9 Royal Ontario Museum
10 Union Station
11 University of Toronto
12 Youth Hostel

¼ mile

Bloor St
Spadina Ave
Bay St
Yonge
Queen's
Wellesley St
Park
College St
Carlton
University Avenue
Church
Jarvis
Sherbourne
Baldwin
Beverly St
Dundas St
Queen St
Queen St
Adelaide St
Adelaide St
Spadina Ave
King St
York St
Bay St
Yonge
King St
Front St
Gardiner Expressway
Lakeshore Blvd
Queens's Quay
LAKE ONTARIO

either $2 in cash or a prepurchased ticket or token. If you intend to switch onto another vehicle, ask the driver for a transfer which will indicate the time of purchase. You then present this to the driver of the connecting bus or streetcar, or to the ticket-taker at the subway stop. If you have to use a third vehicle, show the transfer to the second driver but hold on to it.

If you start your journey on a subway, pay the ticket-taker (who can give change) or use a token in one of the automatic gates. Just past the barrier, you will find an automatic transfer dispenser. If you need to continue your journey above ground, push the large red button. Transfers are not needed if you simply want to change on to the other subway line at Yonge and Bloor. If in any doubt at all, take a transfer.

Subway. The subway lines are built under the two main streets Yonge and Bloor, forming a simple cross shape. The Yonge line has been augmented and loops around Union Station and up along University Avenue to bisect Bloor again at the Royal Ontario Museum and north to form the Spadina line.

The system is easy to master. Most stops are named after the cross street, unlike the London underground or Paris metro. Trains start running at about 6am and continue until after 1am. The last subways leave Union Station at 1.40am. Exact times are given in the TTC *Ride Guide.*

Street Car. Electric streetcars were first introduced to Toronto in the 1890s and have flourished ever since. A few of the old model cars from the 1940s are still in use, though they are scheduled to be phased out.

Street cars run east and west along College Street, Dundas, Queen, King and St Clair Avenue, all of which correspond with subway stations on the Yonge Street line. The north/south streetcar runs along Bathurst, four subway stops west of Yonge.

The Harbourfront Light Rapid Transit is a street car route servicing Toronto's waterfront. Streetcars leave from Union Station and run west along the lakeshore from Queen's Quay and the Ferry Docks to the foot of Spadina Avenue. On a warm day, take the LRT to Spadina, and then walk east back to Queen's Quay. There are lots of boats, shops and small beer gardens to keep the walk interesting.

Bus. Buses ply most of the other main roads and provide a more frequent service to the suburbs. Many downtown buses are trolley buses, powered by an overhead electric cable which makes them very economical. A few long-haul suburban trips fall outside the TTC's jurisdiction. Name your destination to the TTC operator on 393-4636 and they will give you a further number for connecting services.

A basic network of routes operates all night, including a Yonge Street bus every 15 minutes, a Bloor/Danforth bus every 30 minutes, and the King, Queen, College and St Clair streetcars. Each TTC bus and streetcar stop is marked with its own individual telephone number which carries a recorded message of the schedule 24 hours a day.

Car. Downtown parking is not as difficult as in many cities of comparable size. Avoid parking in a 'tow-away zone' (normally 4-6pm) since these are rigidly enforced. If driving on a road with streetcars, you must not pass on the inside while passengers are getting on or off, unless there is a cement island on which waiting passengers can stand.

A stiff Metro Toronto programme called RIDE (Reduced Impaired Driving Everywhere) means that random breathalyzer tests to find drivers over the .08 limit are common.

Taxis. You can usually hail a taxi in the downtown area, but it is easier to find one at Union Station or by phoning ahead. You pay about $2.20 as an initial charge, plus about 65c per kilometre. One of the biggest taxi companies is Metro Cab on 363-5611, though there are plenty of others listed in the Yellow Pages.

Cycling. Cycling has become very popular and you will see plenty of locals out on their racing bikes or trail bikes. There are miles of cycle paths, many of which stick to some of Toronto's 354 parks, following ravines which are invisible from the road. The Martin Goodman Trail is a paved route which runs along the waterfront from the area known as the Beaches in east Toronto to Ontario Place in the west. Conditions for cycling can be hazardous in winter (see *Climate*) and downtown beware of letting your wheel slip into the groove of streetcar tracks.

Bicycles may be rented for $14 a day or $42 a week from Brown's Sports and Cycle, 2447 Bloor St West, 763-4176 (nearest subway station is Jane), or from North Bathurst Cycle and Hardware, 3549 Bathurst, 781-6333 (south of Wilson) for slightly more.

Ferry. Although Toronto has a fairly important commercial harbour, there is not much picturesque shipping to observe. Scenic boat trips are offered from Queen's Quay, but these are not much better than the ordinary ferry ride to the Toronto Islands. Between June and September ferries leave frequently from the bottom of Bay St to one of the three islands just ten minutes away. Foot passengers pay $2.75 return; bicycles travel free though there are some restrictions to Centre Island at very busy periods.

The islands are a favourite Torontonian retreat from the heat, since there are beaches, ice cream vendors and lake breezes. Centre Island is the most popular, though it is best suited to young children who enjoy the funfair atmosphere and the McDonalds cuisine. Instead try Ward's Island, which is partially residential but has a secluded beach on the lake rather than the city side, and small canteens serve an interesting range of snack foods. Hanton's Point has a quiet park setting with lots of walking trails.

Hotels. A modest hotel room will cost at least $35 single, $45 double. Many of the cheap hotels are also bars and clubs and may be very noisy. Cheap downtown hotels include the St Leonard, Selby, Isabella and Catnaps, all on Sherbourne St, a few blocks east of Yonge. The Victoria (corner of Yonge and King) and the Strathcona (York and Wellington) are more expensive with doubles from $70. One of the cheapest is the Rex Hotel at 194 Queen St West, which charges $31.50 single, $45 double.

For details if other budget hotels, contact Accommodation Toronto (34 ross Street; 596-7117), a free service operated by the Hotel Association of Metro Toronto. The provincial government imposes a sales tax (5%) on transient accommodation though out-of-province visitors may be exempted, so enquire when checking in. If you are visiting Toronto between December and February, ring 979-3143 for information on hotel discounts.

Tourist homes and guest houses tend to be cheaper (from $35 double) and less central than hotels. A good area to head for is King St W, where you will find the Candy Haven at number 1233 (532-0651) and Grayona Tourist Home at 1546 (535-5443). A more central bargain is the Karabanow Guest House, 9 Spadina Road near Bloor (923-4004).

Hostels. The Toronto International Youth Hostel (368-1848) is at 223 Church St (3 blocks east of Yonge just below Dundas) and costs $14.29 for members, $19.29 for non-members. The regional hostelling office is adjacent, so if you are not already a member, you can join here for $25.

The YMCA runs an emergency shelter for men aged 16-29 who may stay up to seven nights for a pittance. The YWCA (80 Woodlawn E near the Summerhill Subway, 923-8454) charges about $41 for a single, and $56 for a double (women only).

Bed and Breakfast. Bed and Breakfasts are catching on in Toronto and there are several B & B organizations. The Metropolitan Bed & Breakfast Registry (615 Mount Pleasant Road, Suite 269; 964-2566) publishes a free list.

Also try Bed & Breakfast Homes of Toronto on 363-6362; All Seasons Bed & Breakfast (383 Mississauga Valley Blvd, 276-4572), whose houses are less central but cheaper; and the non-smoking Downtown Toronto Group of Bed & Breakfast Guest House, PO Box 190, Station B, Toronto (690-1724).

University Residences. University residences are good value if you are looking for accommodation out of term i.e. mid-May until late August. The University of Toronto Housing Service (214 College St, 978-8045) can provide a list of residences along with their rates. Bookings should be made directly to the residence of your choice as far in advance as possible.

University of Toronto (known as U of T) residences are centrally located and cost $30 a day, $145 a week. York University, also in Toronto, keeps residences open in the summer. Ring 736-5020 for details. Singles cost $32-$37, twins $50-$55, suites $60.

There is a popular 'college-hotel' called Neill-Wycik at 96 Gerrard Street (977-2320), also open only in the summer. Expect to pay $35-40 for a room with breakfast.

Motels. Motel accommodation is not usually any cheaper, and of course is less central. The two main strips of motels stretch along the Lakeshore Boulevard heading west to Hamilton (Inn-on-the-Lake, North American, Westpoint, etc.) and on the road to Kingston.

Camping. Campgrounds are generally open May to September. A directory of sites is available free of charge from the Ontario Travel Information Service at Eaton Centre (Level 1; tel 314 0944). It shows which campsites take reservations.

Two campsites in Scarborough fall within the city limits: Woodland Park (282-1270) and Glen Rouge Park (392-2541). There are seven other campgrounds within reach of downtown, including two KOA sites; check the Yellow Pages.

Ring 1-800-ONTARIO (or 963-2992 locally) in July and August for campground vacancy reports, covering 53 southern Ontario parks. Private campsites will charge between $10 and $18 per site depending on the facilities available. The camping fee in provincial parks is $12-$18 depending on whether there is electricity.

Eating and Drinking

Eating out in Toronto is a delight. If you have become bored with the ubiquitous hamburger, you may wish to avoid the many fast food outlets. But because of the large ethnic mixture in the city the alternatives are endless.

There are over a quarter of a million Italian-speakers in Toronto, the largest Italian-speaking community outside Italy, and a correspondingly large number of Italian restaurants — as the 14 Yellow Pages under 'pizza' will attest. (Most listed will deliver a pizza to your door for a small extra charge). Try the gourmet pizzas at Pat and Mario's (Church and Front Streets), which also has a dance floor. For a more informal atmosphere try the Old Spaghetti Factory at 54 The Esplanade near the O'Keefe Center (864-9761).

Chinatown, one of the largest in North America, flourishes along Dundas Street west of Bay and north along Spadina. You get a range of regional Chinese cooking, so that a Szechuan place will be next door to a Mandarin, and Cantonese next to Hunan, not to mention Vietnamese and Korean variations. Spadina Avenue south of College, offers an excellent choice of Asian restaurants. Try the Lee Gardens (358 Spadina), where long queues attest to its quality. If the decor is mostly formica and the menu is written only in Chinese characters, you can be assured of some authentic oriental cooking.

Explore the Kensington Market (west of Spadina and south of College) for Portuguese, Brazilian, Jewish and Jamaican restaurants. Hungarian, Japanese, Indian and Middle Eastern places are scattered liberally throughout the city. Greek restaurants are concentrated 'out the Danforth' as Torontonians refer to the eastern extension of Bloor St, while the Indian quarter is on Gerrard St E (take a College streetcar heading east).

Good cheap and cheerful places include Fran's at 2275 Yonge St at Eglinton, 21 St Clair West, or 60 College St (at Yonge). For upbeat cafes, try the Queen Mother at 206 Queen West or the Kensington Kitchen on Harbord St, west of the University, though there are many others.

In the moderate to expensive category try the Bangkok Garden on Elm St just west of Yonge (977-6748), or La Bodega (30 Baldwin St), which for many years has been serving creative French cooking (though it's run by a Brit). Consult the monthly magazine *Toronto Life* (available at newsstands) for further inspiration.

DRINKING

Drinking is generally less fun than back home, despite the licensing hours of 11am to 1am. Sundays are dry unless you're dining. Downtown bars tend to be either ritzy, expensive and not very lively, or just plain seedy. Some places now have special pub licences, which means you can buy a drink at the bar and thereby avoid being served by a tip-hungry waitress. In most bars you are served at a table and pay for each round as it arrives, in others you run up a bill. If you are eager to continue drinking after the bars close at 1am, cultivate the friendship of a waitress or bartender who knows where to find a speakeasy, usually located in a disused warehouse.

There has been an influx of imitation British pubs, such as the Elephant and Castle in the Eaton Centre. They are meant more for fashionable Torontonians than for homesick Brits, who may baulk at paying $5 for a pint of Double Diamond. The Artful Dodger at 12 Isabella St is another place for Brits in search of a taste of home; it serves good food and stocks Conners and English draft. If you're looking for a friendly place to meet young Torontonians, try the Loose Moose Tap and Grill at 220 Adelaide St W (971-5252). The Unicorn at 175 Eglington Ave E is a popular pub-style bar, with good food and live bands at weekends. For a huge selection of international beer visit the Amsterdam at 133 John St; be ready for a very loud but friendly atmosphere.

Sports bars are popping up all over Toronto, with Don Cherry's Grapevine at 56 Peter St being one of the most popular. It's located just minutes from the Skydome, Toronto's newest stadium, so be prepared for a big crowd gathering here after major sports events.

The trendy place to drink in the summer, when tables line the sidewalk, is Yorkville, north of Bloor between Avenue Road and Yonge. It's more expensive than most but the beer is still affordable — and *tapas* are sometimes thrown in. Ontario Place, open May to October, has several beer gardens.

If you want to combine a cocktail with a view of the dramatic night-time skyline in Toronto, go to the bar at the top of the Manulife Building (Bay and Bloor) or the Park Plaza Hotel (Bloor and Avenue Road), but the price of the high-rise view will be included in your drink. For the most expensive drink of all, make the pilgrimage to the CN Tower, the tallest free standing structure in the world. The elevator costs $12 (return) and a bottle of beer at 1,150ft will cost $4.50 — the price you pay for being able to say you have been up the tallest building in the world.

Liquor Laws. The sale of alcohol is controlled by the provincial government and neither beer nor wine is ever available from grocery stores. Beer must be bought from the Brewers Retail outlets, and wine and spirits from the LCBO (Liquor Control Board of Ontario). Most LCBOs now display their wares on open shelves, but you may still encounter some where you must choose from a catalogue and fill out a slip which you hand in at a counter. The catalogue rates the sweetness of wine from 0 (very dry) to 23 (Sacramental Jewish wine). Brewers Retails are usually open Monday to Thursday 10am-9pm and Friday/Saturday 10am-9pm. Some LCBOs are also open 10 till 10 but most close at 9pm.

The drinking laws are barbarous in many respects. Strictly speaking, it is illegal to transport liquor anywhere except between the place where it was bought and your home, though this law is hardly ever enforced. However, you may not consume liquor in any public place, which means that wine at picnics is sometimes consumed from tea cups and poured out of a thermos flask. You cannot carry alcohol except in the boot of your car and it must be unopened.

Wine. Ontario wines are grown around Niagara and are improving in quality. Avoid the pop-like Baby Bear and Cold Duck, and try Inniskillin Brae Rouge ($6). Unfortunately, Canada does not encourage its own wine industry as Australia does and there is almost as large a mark-up on domestic wines as on imported wines. For a larger choice of imported bottles than is available at your run-of-the-mill LCBO, try the Rare Wines and Spirits store at 2 Cooper St, off Queen's Quay.

Beer. Enthusiasts should try Conner's beers, brewed in Toronto, including a bitter, an ale in the Scottish style and a hoppy Pale Ale, available at many Brewers Retail stores. Though more typically Canadian in character, Upper Canada ale is also worth trying.

Museums and Galleries. The Art Gallery of Ontario (corner of Dundas and Beverley, 977-0414) has a small international collection. This includes the world's largest collection of Henry Moore sculptures and several rooms of Canadian art, as well as some excellent special exhibitions. There is an admission charge of $7.50 (free on Wednesday evenings) and an excellent book and card shop.

A better representation of Canadian art, including native work, can be found at the McMichael Collection at Kleinburg (893-1121) which is outside the city limits but accessible by a combination of TTC and Vaughan Transit: take the subway to Islington, transfer to Islington bus 37 north to Steeles, and then take Vaughan Route 1. Ring 832-8527 for bus times and fares. Admission is $5.

The Royal Ontario Museum (or ROM) has an outstanding general collection, including some exhibits on native cultures. The imposing building stands on the corner of Bloor St W and Avenue Road. Next door there is a planetarium which puts on interesting shows of the constellations.

Parks and Zoos. The Metro Zoo covers over 700 acres and is well worth a day trip, despite the apparently hefty admission fee of $9. Take the subway east to Kennedy and transfer to Scarborough bus 86A.

Cross-country skiing (you can hire equipment) is popular in winter. Swimming is less popular, at any time of year. Several beaches are located along the eastern area of the lakeshore, but Lake Ontario is fairly heavily polluted. The health department runs a summer hotline at 392-7161 for enquiries about beach closings due to bacterial water pollution. To avoid ear and skin irritations that often accompany a swim in Lake Ontario, ring the pool hotline on 392-7838 for information about indoor and outdoor pools.

Amusement Parks. Ontario Place, on Lakeshore Boulevardd West, caters for everyone, young and old. Attractions include a waterslide, pedal boats and mini-golf, as well as a six storey movie screen and various space-age pavilions. You can eat until fast food comes out of your ears, while admiring the picturesque views over the small marina and Lake Ontario. The easiest route to travel to Ontario Place is to catch streetcar 511 at Bathurst station.

Canada's Waterland (832-2205) is a massive theme park located just north of the city in Maple. It features a variety of rollercoasters, rides and waterslides, as well as live shows with dancers and sea lions. The park is clean and extremely well maintained, with a wide choice of restaurants offering foods from around the world. The park is open from early May to early September, and admission is $26 for unlimited rides. Plan to spend the entire day and evening here, as the park is more than large enough to keep you fully occupied. Gray Coach runs buses to the park several times a day from York Mills and Yorkdale subway stations. Ring 351-3311 for departure times and fares.

There is no shortage of music, theatre or film in Toronto. The key to Toronto's entertainment scene is the guide called *NOW* published on Thursdays and available from many downtown shops and newspaper stands. Also check the Saturday edition of the *Star*, an excellent guide to what's on, or the Thursday and Saturday editions of the *Globe and Mail*, for reviews and listings. The *Varsity Student Handbook*, produced by the University of Toronto, contains good advice about bars, clubs and entertainment. Visit the Varsity office at 92 St George and ask for a free copy, though stocks run out fast. Also look for the free *Exciting Toronto by TTC* brochure.

The established theatre, ballet and opera venue is O'Keefe Centre on Front St (393-7469). Tickets to mainstream cultural events will not normally be less than $12 unless you get student standby tickets. Ring the box office for details. Last minute ticket booths (called Five Star) , comparable to the one in Leicester Square, are located outside the Eaton Centre (596-8211). They sell discounted tickets on the day of performance, but the choice is usually fairly poor. Tickets for the big shows can be purchased through TicketMaster (872-1111) or TicketKing (872-3333).

Harbourfront is an entertainment complex offering everthing from theatre and music to antique markets and food. Although open year round, it is best in the summer, when most of the entertainment takes place in the open air. Take Spadina bus 77B from the Spadina subway station or from Union Station, or the new Harbourfront Light Rapid Transit line.

Music. The Toronto Symphony plays at the dazzling new Roy Thomson Hall (593-4828) near King and University. Parking was such a problem that the whole structure was lifted while an underground car park was built, but this does not appear to have affected the remarkable acoustics. Concert tickets start at about $13.

For rock and blues, try the El Mocambo on Spadina, the Hotel Isabella on Sherbourne, the Brunswick (Bloor past Spadina), or the Rivoli (334 Queen St W). Jazz may be heard at Bourbon Street (180 Queen West), George's Spaghetti House (290 Dundas St E) or at the after-hours jazz club at Meyer's Deli (185 King St W). Folk is performed at the Free Times Cafe (320 College), and at the Spadina Hotel at 460 King St W. The Bamboo at 312 Queen St W specializes in reggae and calypso.

The Waterland theme park (see above) has a stadium where internationally known bands play; tickets are available from Ticketron.

The Mariposa Folk Festival, at one time the best known folk festival in the Americas, is held in the middle of July at Molson Park near Barrie, an hour's drive north of the city. Phone 769-3655 for details of ticket prices, camping arrangements, etc.

If you're looking for a night of dancing, try the Big Bop at the corner of Queen and Bathurst Sts. This club has a $10 cover charge, but once inside you can visit three different floors, each featuring a different type of music. The once famous 99c Roxy Cinema (Danforth and Greenwood) has now become an alcohol-free nightclub open until 3 or 4am on weekends.

Theatre. The Royal Alexandra Theatre on Adelaide St mounts Broadway productions at Broadway prices. But there are plenty of smaller, more experimental theatres; consult *NOW* for times and locations. The well-established Tarragon Threatre (30 Bridgman Avenue; 531-1827) puts on Sunday afternoon productions on a PWYC — Pay What You Can — basis.

The Shakespeare Festival in Stratford (a two-hour drive southwest of Toronto) is internationally acclaimed. The lavish productions are well worth the effort of getting to this quiet, scenic little town. Phone 363-4471 in Toronto, or 1-800-567-1600 for details. Similarly, there is a Shaw Festival each summer in Niagara-on-the-Lake, not far from the famous falls. Ring 1-800-267-4759 for information.

Cinema. Along with New York and Los Angeles, Toronto is the third city in North America where films are likely to premiere, especially during the Toronto Film Festival held in September. The price of a ticket at a downtown 'movie theatre' will usually be $6.

There are several repertory cinemas, such as the Bloor Cinema (506 Bloor

St W) and the Fox Beaches (2236 Queen St E), which show a good selection of films. Tickets cost $6, though if you become a member ($5) the cost falls to 99c. Free films are shown at Harbourfront; ring 973-3000 for details. The Cinesphere at Ontario Place (314-9900) offers box office smash movies on an IMAX screen which is six stories tall. Tickets are $14 and available from the Cinesphere box office or TicketMaster. For the budget-conscious, Cineplex Odean Theatres sell all movie admissions on Tuesdays for half price (about $4.25)

Special Events. The most longstanding summer event is the Canadian National Exhibition, called CNE or the EX (393-6000), which takes place during the last two weeks of August and the first of September. It is located near Lakeside Blvd by the stadium, and consists of lots of rides, junk food, good food, international exhibits, circuses and big name entertainers.

Caravan takes place in late June, during which ethnic pavilions are set up by the local communities around the city and serve up their native food and entertainment. Canada Day (July 1) is celebrated by a picnic at Queen's Park (the provincial legislature) with 5c hot dogs.

Toronto's annual Caribbean Festival, Caribana, takes place for 2 weeks during the end of July and beginning of August. The festival features reggae and calypso music, authentic Caribbean cuisine and a huge parade. Ring the Caribana headquarters at 925-5435 for details.

SPORT

The performance of Toronto's one-time champion hockey team, the Maple Leafs, has become so abysmal that 'fans' have taken to pelting the players with rubbish and abuse. Even so, tickets still often sell out, so it is wise to enquire as soon as you arrive in Toronto if you are interested in seeing a game. Matches are played at Maple Leaf Gardens (Carlton east of Yonge, 977-1641). Tickets cost from $18 (cheapest seats and standing room) to $53. Scalpers (i.e. ticket touts) are always hanging around outside offering tickets at inflated prices. Failing this, you can watch a hockey game on TV three or four nights of the week between October and May.

The Toronto Argonauts play football (not soccer) at the Skydome, as do the Toronto Blue Jays, comparatively recent but formidable members of the American Baseball League. In fact Torontonians have become passionate about baseball and to make friends with a local, just ask about the Jays. For ticket information and the schedules of the Argos call TicketMaster on 595-1131; for the Jays, ring 341-1234. It's worth going to a game just to see the Skydome (Front St W at Bremner Blvd), which is one of the most controversial buildings in Toronto. The stadium houses a retractable roof, as well as an expensive hotel featuring rooms with views of the playing field. You can take a tour of the complex — call 341-3663.

The thoroughbred racing season opens in Mid-March at Greenwood, culminating in the Queen's Plate in mid-July (698-3131). The Canadian national sport of lacrosse is more popular in small Ontario towns such as Owen Sound and Peterborough than in the big cities.

Participation. If you want to have a crack at ice skating, you will have to buy or borrow a pair of skates, since rinks don't hire them out. If you simply want to watch, go to the outdoor rink at the foot of the striking Toronto City Hall, at the corner of Bay and Queen.

SHOPPING

Shopping hours in Ontario are generally 9am-9pm Monday to Friday, until 6pm on Saturday and noon-5pm on Sunday. The ubiquitous Beckers, 7-11 and Mac's Milk corner stores are open 24 hours in many cases, but at least 7am to midnight.

The multi-level Eaton Centre in downtown Toronto is one of the best examples of a lavishly appointed North American shopping complex — a veritable cathedral to consumption. It is claimed to be the most popular tourist attraction in the country. You can buy anything from choice quality Florida fruit to Algonquin Indian carvings. This is not a place to find bargains. The stunning architecture can best be appreciated on a Sunday when the shops and most of the restaurants are less busy; they open from noon to 5pm.

There is an alarming number of posh indoor shopping malls in the downtown area, many of which contain chain stores. Chic stores also abound on Yorkville, just north of Bloor west of Yonge. You will even find a shop called Lovecraft (63 Yorkville Avenue), which sells edible underwear. For a more down-to-earth experience, stroll along Queen St West between University and Spadina.

The large vigorous ethnic communities are often responsible for the quality and abundance of food available in the markets. The best markets are the Kensington Market (near Spadina and College) with its wonderful range of fish, tropical fruit and wholefoods, and the St Lawrence Market (Front St East), where a lively Farmers' Market is held on Saturdays. The quality of the produce is high, as are the prices.

Sales Tax. The provincial sales tax of 8% and GST of 7% is added onto all goods except children's clothes, shoes under $30, books, magazines and groceries. If you are taking goods out of the province, you can avoid paying tax by arranging for the shop to ship your purchases out of the province. In order to reclaim tax, you should pick up a leaflet from the tourist office called 'Sales Tax Refunds for Visitors to Ontario' and send it, along with proof of export (e.g. a foreign customs declaration), to the Ministry of Revenue, Retail Sales Tax Refund Unit, PO Box 630, 33 King St W, Oshawa, Ontario L1H 8L2.

THE MEDIA

Newspapers. The three main newspapers are the *Toronto Globe and Mail,* the *Toronto Star* and the *Sun.* The *Globe* is the closest thing Canada has to a national paper and its international coverage is the best available, though still not extensive. The dailies are weighty, due mainly to the large number of ads rather than an abundance of incisive articles.

Homesick Brits may want to get hold of a monthly tabloid called *Britannia,* published for UK expatriates (613-399-3634). At least it will tell you the football scores. Toronto also supports its own French-language weekly, *(L'Express). The Times, Telegraph, Daily Express* and the Sunday papers are sold at W H Smith in Toronto Dominion Centre (King and Bay) for a hefty $3-4. *Guardian* readers will have to suffer in silence, though you can consult the *Guardian Weekly* at the Metropolitan Library (Yonge north of Bloor) or the British Consulate at 777 Bay St, although the latter has no reading room. You can buy foreign newspapers at Book City at 621 Yonge St, just north of Gloucester.

Broadcasting. There are many radio stations, both AM and FM, mostly on a par with Radio 2: popular light music and bright chit-chat from the DJs. Students tend to favour one of the FM stations, such as Q-107 or CFNY (102.1), which plays more interesting rock music. The non-profit CJRT FM (91.1) carries the World Service news at 8am. The Canadian Broadcasting Corporation (CBC) runs an FM station which offers a more diverse programme (classified music, jazz, current affairs, etc.) on 94.1. You can find CBC AM on 740 on the dial.

Many hotels equip rooms with a TV. You can tune into one of the Canadian networks — CBC (channel 5), CTV (channel 9), TV Ontario (channel 19) — or any of the American networks available on cable.

Crime and Safety

Toronto has remarkably little violent crime for a city of 3 million. It is one of the few places in North America where the crime rate is actually declining.

Most crimes are hold-ups of corner stores and gas stations in the suburbs rather than muggings on downtown streets. Some lone women have expressed anxiety at walking along the streets running east from Yonge Street south of Bloor, especially in the area known as 'The Track' bounded by Isabella, Wellesley and Church Streets. Gerrard and Jarvis is another district with red light overtones, but there are several luxury hotels in the neighbourhood as well and it's not a particularly dodgy area. Stay on the main arteries rather than the side streets and alleys if you are feeling anxious. Even in tough areas there have been few incidents of violence reported, and for the most part anxiety is unwarranted.

Drugs. Although not as popular as it was ten years ago, cannabis is still favoured by students and young professionals. The maximum penalty in the province of Ontario for a first offence of possession is six months in jail and/or a fine of $1,000.

If you get in trouble with the law contact 24-hour criminal law firm, Neuman & Grant for advice (961-7400) Suite 204, 2 Gloucester St M4Y 1L5.

Alcohol. The police are quick to spot drivers who have been drinking and generally show no mercy. Especially in the weeks preceding Christmas, they administer thousands of breathalyser tests. Their campaign has been fairly successful and as a result the taxi business is booming, while tavern owners complain of a slump.

If visiting one of Southern Ontario's provincial parks between in summer, make sure that you are allowed to drink alcohol. Because of past rowdiness and violence, alcohol was completely banned from 13 parks for a time.

Help and Information

The area code for Toronto is 416.

Tourist Information: Call 368-9821 for Toronto city information. Ontario Travel is in the Eaton Centre, or you can call 314-0944 within Toronto or 1-800-ONTARIO.

Ontario Travel: Eaton Centre (965-4008).

Parks Canada: Ontario Region, 132 Second St E, Cornwall K6H 5V4 (613-938-5866).

Travellers Aid Society: Union Station (366-7788).
Post Office: 36 Adelaide St E (973-9673).
American Express: in The Bay (44 Bloor St E; 963-6060); in Simpsons (176 Yonge St; 861-6091); and at 50 Bloor Street W (967-3411).
Thomas Cook: 2 Bloor St W (922-0804).
British Consulate: 777 Bay St (593-1267).
Metropolitan Police: 324-2222. All emergencies: 911.
Canadian Automobile Association: 2 Carlton St (771-3111). Emergency road service — 222-5222.
Community Information Centre of Metro Toronto — 392-0505 (24 hours).

'Teleguide' terminals have been installed in many public buildings, and shopping centres. You type in the information you require, for example 'Restaurants — Japanese' or 'Shopping — Sporting Goods', and the machine provides a list of names and addresses. The information is far from comprehensive, since only paying advertisers are included, but the machines are fun to play with.

Further Afield 61

THE GREAT LAKES

Western Canada is famous for its Rocky Mountains. Eastern Canada has the Great Lakes. The five lakes are by far the largest bodies of fresh water in the world. The biggest and furthest inland is Superior. Next is Lake Michigan which is entirely in the US, then Lake Huron, Lake Erie and finally Lake Ontario, which flows into the St Lawrence Seaway.

A series of locks and canals between the lakes allows ships to avoid Niagara Falls and other natural impediments, and to penetrate all the way to the Lakehead at the western end of Lake Superior. Thunder Bay, at the Lakehead, is Canada's third largest sea port (in spite of being roughly half way between the east and west coasts). Navigation is not always safer than in the open seas — the size of the Great Lakes means that stormy weather can create large waves, and there have been many shipwrecks.

You can visit some islands including Manitoulin Island in Lake Huron, the largest fresh water island in the world. It is accessible by a long land route via Sudbury or a charming ferry ride from Tobermory.

The shores of Lake Ontario and Lake Erie are more densely populated on both the American and Canadian sites than Huron and Superior. Consequently, those lakes are more polluted. The sight of dead fish along a holiday beach is a shocking reminder of the environmental crimes committed in North America during the 1950s and 1960s. A favourite Canadian ploy is to blame the Americans for this (and many other) evils. In view of the fact that the effluent and petrochemicals in the Cuyahoga River — which flows into Lake Erie at Cleveland Ohio — once caught fire and burned for three days and three nights, there is some justification for the complaint. Measures are now being taken to clean up the lakes and Toronto's beaches remain open, except during long hot spells when the algae builds up.

Lake Superior is the least developed lake, and its north shore consists of virtually unmolested wilderness. Not surprisingly, it is also the least accessible. To reach Lake Superior Provincial Park, just north of Sault (pronounced Sue) Sainte Marie, involves a 500-mile (800km) drive from Toronto.

The largest lakes are several degrees colder on average than the smaller

Erie or Ontario. They are all too large to freeze solidly, though skating along the shores is a favourite winter recreation. Sometimes the ice is thick enough to take the weight of cars, and at night you can enjoy the strange spectacle of seeing headlights far out 'at sea' — between, for example, Kingston and Wolfe Island, a mile or two offshore.

Niagara Falls. The sight which few tourists have the courage to miss in Niagara Falls. The mighty falls are located on the Niagara River which connects Lake Ontario and Lake Erie, 85 miles/140km south of Toronto. There are four trains a day to and from Toronto, or you may find it easiest to join a tour: the day trip offered by Toronto Tours (869-1372), for example, costs about $80 including lunch.

Any self-respecting Canadian will assure you that the view of the 176ft drop is much more spectacular on the Canadian side than on the American. A trip on the *Maid of the Mist* boat or a walk down tunnels cut from the rock behind the falls both allow you to experience the pounding noise and spray of the Falls at close range.

Tacky tourist sights abound in Niagara Falls town. Devotees of junk culture will have a field day in the Honeymoon Capital of North America. If you are eligible, you can get a Honeymoon Certificate from the mayor of Niagara Falls. Try to visit nearby Niagara-on-the-Lake, a charmingly reconstructed 19th-century town, home of the Shaw Theatre.

A good place to stay is the Falls View Tourist Home, 4745 River Road (416-374-8051).

OTTAWA

The Canadians have Queen Victoria to thank for choosing Ottawa as the country's capital. It sometimes seems that Montréal and Toronto are still reeling from the shock of the snub. They can at least relish the capital city's reputation as the epitome of dullness.

Life in Ottawa revolves around the government, and there is little action in the streets after 5pm. Great efforts have been made by the authorities to increase the city's appeal to visitors. But the apparent attempt to turn Ottawa into the cleanest place on the planet (even the Mounties are spotless) has done little to enliven the atmosphere. Far more effective have been new developments such as the Byward Market, which succeeds in tempting at least a few of the city's 750,000 inhabitants out after dark: Ottawans by nature prefer a quiet night in. Even so, if you are looking for excitement, you would do well to visit Ottawa at the weekend. But whatever day you decide to come, don't overlook the Museum of Civilization, a cultural centre in a class of its own, which alone makes a trip to Ottawa worthwhile.

City Layout. The city of Ottawa and the Quebec town of Hull face each other across the Ottawa river. Downtown Ottawa is split in two by the Rideau Canal. On the west side is Upper Town, with Parliament Hill as its focus; to the east is Lower Town, bounded on the far side by the Riveau River. Hull is linked by several bridges to its southern neighbour; while there has been a certain amount of integration, the town's identity remains strictly French.

Arrival and Departure. *Air:* Ottawa International Airport (998-3151) is about 30 minutes south of downtown. Rather than take a taxi to the centre and pay at least $15, use the Carleton airport bus, which charges less than half that. Alternatively, catch the local bus from outside the airport compound;

this won't take you right into town, but ask for a transfer and change. When returning to the airport, pick the Carleton bus up outside the luxury Chateau Laurier Hotel (1 Rideau).

Bus: Voyageur Colonial Bus Lines (238-5900) runs long-distance buses, connecting Ottawa with all the main Canadian and several American cities. Services run hourly to Montréal ($25, $2\frac{1}{2}$ hours) and six times a day to Toronto ($53, 5-6 hours). The Voyageur station is about 20 blocks south of Parliament Hill, on the corner of Catherine and Kent Streets. Bus 4 runs downtown.

Train: Ottawa is accessible by rail daily from Montréal (standard fare $30 for the 2-hour journey) and Toronto ($65, 4 hours). Trains arrive at the station on Tremblay Road, 3 miles southeast of the centre. Bus 95 runs downtown; when returning from the centre you can catch the bus on Slater St. For train information call VIA Rail on 244-1660 or 244-8289.

Driving: from Highway 417 follow the red maple leaf signs, which will lead you eventually to Confederation Boulevard downtown. Note that the Transitway (which runs west-east through Upper Town and then south through Lower Town) is reserved for buses only.

Parking is limited to three hours in the city, unless stated otherwise; watch out for Ottawa's zealous traffic wardens.

Getting Around. *Buses:* city buses south of the river are operated by an authority with the curious name of OC Transpo (294 Albert, 741-4390). All routes converge at the Rideau Center on Rideau St, near the Mackenzie King bridge. STO (819-770-3242) runs services north of the river, interconnecting with OC Transpo buses in Ottawa along Wellington and Rideau Streets.

Buses run 6am-midnight. Try to avoid travelling in rush hour (6-8.30am and 3-5.30pm) since fares are higher at this time, i.e. $2 as opposed to $1.30. Buy tickets on the bus (if you have the right change) or at convenience stores. Transfers, valid for an hour, are free. The $2 Minipass gives unlimited travel after 9am during the week, all day at weekends; you can buy this at museums and information centres.

Taxis: you can't hail taxis, but there are ranks outside the main hotels and busiest nightspots, e.g. Promenade du Portage in Hull. Rates are fixed at an initial charge of $1.90, plus 10c for each 90 metres. To order a taxi call Blue Line on 238-1111.

Cycling: Ottawa is one of the most cyclist-friendly cities in North America, with numerous and well-maintained cycle paths. For information and routes contact Ottawa Bikeways (1740 Carling Avenue, 722-4470). Rent-a-Bike on Mackenzie Avenue, behind Hotel Chateau Laurier (233-0268) charges around $20 for a day's rental, depending on the bike, and around $50 for a week; it also sells maps and equipment.

Accommodation. There is a glut of hotels around Parliament Hill, but most places charge at least $70 a night. One of the few cheaper places is the Doral Inn (486 Alberta, 230-8055), which charges $60 for a double room.

The Richmond Plaza Motel in West Ottawa (238 Richmond Rd, 722-6591) offers good value to motorists, with units for $40-50.

Hostels: The Nicholas Gaol International Hostel (75 Nicholas St, 235-2595), is housed in an old county jail which was in use right up until 1971. It is just south of Rideau, accessible on bus 4 from the corner of Arlington and Kent; a bed costs $15 a night in peak season ($19 for non-members). In summer, dorm accommodation is also available at the Carleton University Residence (1233 Colonel By Drive, 788-5609) or at the University of Ottawa (100 University St, 564-5400), which has a residence at 100 Hastey St in Lower Town. You can even camp downtown, at Camp Le Breton (Fleet and Booth Streets, 239-5565).

Bed & Breakfast: B & Bs are increasingly popular, and generally charge $40-50 single, $50-60 double. Among the most central are the Laurier Guest House (329 Laurier East, 238-5525), with doubles from $35, and the more expensive O'Connor House (172 O'Connor St, 236-4221). If you plan to spend your evenings in Hull, it would be worth staying on the north bank: try Couette et Croissant at 330 Champlain (771-2200). Several agencies specialize in finding bed and breakfast rooms for visitors, e.g. Ottawa Bed and Breakfast at 488 Cooper (563-0161).

Eating and Drinking. The best place to eat in Ottawa is in the Byward Market. Located just north of Rideau in Lower Town, this has been a market for fresh produce since the 19th century, though now there are also many craft stalls. In addition, you will find a multitude of restaurants and bars which are, unlike most of the city, busy throughout the day and into the evening. Cafe Bohemian (89 Clarence, 238-7182) serves good, inventive food and Bagel Bagel, nearby at 92 Clarence, is cheap and open 24 hours. Zak's Diner (16 Byward Market, 233-0433) at the corner of York, is a buzzing 50s vision in chrome.

Rideau Mall, further south, has a more lowly range of fast-food joints. Yesterday's (235-1424) in Spark Street Mall — a pedestrian area between Elgin and Bank — is also good value. One of the most popular places in town is Mama Teresa at 300 Somerset West (236-3023), where you can eat exquisite pasta for around $10.

Pubs and bars are required by law to supply small snacks with alcholic drinks, so those with small appetites can fill up without having to pay for a proper sit-down meal. Ottawa has several English-=style pubs. Among the best is the Royal Oak (360 Bank) in Upper Town.

Exploring. *Parliament Hill:* the Parliament Buildings, which command a fine position on a hill overlooking the river, are open to the public. Free guided tours are available around several of the buildings, including the Centre Block, home of the Senate and House of Commons. To reserve a place on a tour, which run 9am-8pm on weekdays, until 4pm at weekends (until 4pm daily in winter), go to the Infotent east of the Centre Block. The entrance to Centre Block is through the Peace Tower, which provides the best view of Ottawa and its environs.

The public is also admitted to parliamentary debates, which are much more entertaining than a straight tour. The best time to go is for the afternoon Question Periods in the House of Commons, held Monday to Thursday. For information on days and times of sittings call 992-4793.

Anyone hankering after good old British traditions, should stick around for the Changing of the Guard. Dressed in their full regalia — bearskins and all — the Ceremonial Guard marches up Elgin St to reach Parliament Hill at 10am. This bizarre anachronism-cum-tourist gimmick runs only from the end of June to the end of August.

Museums: the Musée Canadien des Civilisations was described by its creators as 'a prototype museum of the 21st century' when it opened in 1989. With its domes and swirling contours, the musuem is impressive enough from the outside. Inside, the displays offer all the lastest hands-on computer technology, as well as drums to play on, canoes to paddle in, etc.

The sheer scale of the place is staggering. The Grand Hall, which contains the world's largest collection of totem poles, is five storeys high and has a massive floor-to-ceiling window overlooking Parliament Hill and the river. The History Hall traces Canadian history beginning with the Vikings, with all manner of replicas from a logging camp to a Chinese laundry. For $7 you can also enjoy one of the world's great cinematic experiences; the Cinéplus theatre not only has a standard Imax screen, but also a massive semispherical Omnimax screen, which extends over the heads of the audience.

The museum (100 Laurier St, 819-776-7000) is open 9am-5pm daily in summer, closed on Monday in winter, with late-night opening on Thursday. Admission $4.50, free 5-8pm on Thursday. Take bus 8 from downtown Ottawa.

The National Gallery is downtown Ottawa's most important museum, and is well worth a visit. It provides an excellent overview of Canadian art, and also has some fine works — spanning several centuries — from Europe and the States. The huge National Gallery (990-1985) is on Sussex Drive (one of Ottawa's oldest and smartest streets), not far from Parliament, at Elgin and Slater Streets. Opening hours are 10am-6pm daily, until 8pm Wednesday to Friday, in summer; and 10am-5pm Tuesday to Sunday in winter. Admission is $5, free on Thursday.

The Canadian War Museum: next to the National Gallery at 330 Sussex Drive (992-2774), the War Museum is unmistakable with its array of military hardware outside. It is famous for the car which belonged to Göering, but renamed as 'Hitler's' in a bid to boost the museum's tourist appeal. Open daily 9.30am-5pm, admission $2.50, free 5-8pm on Thursday.

The Rideau Canal: constructed in 1826 as a military supply route, the Rideau Canal connects Ottawa with Kingston on Lake Ontario. It joins the Ottawa River beneath Parliament, with the help of a flight of eight locks. Nearby is the Bytown Museum (open May to November, 10am-4pm), which traces the history of the waterway.

In winter the canal is partially drained and when frozen over becomes the world's longest ice rink. On weekdays you can enjoy the unusual sight of commuters in woolly hats and briefcases skating their way to work, stopping off for hot chocolate and muffins along the way. If you want to join in, you can hire your own skates and go all the way down to Dow's Lake. Call 232-1234 for ice conditions. If you prefer to watch, you can stroll or bike along the tow path.

Gatineau Park: this huge, rugged park covers 356 square kilometres, beginning a few miles west of Hull. There is an extensive network of trails, and cross-country skiing is popular in winter; you can also rent snowshoes. There is no public transport, but a cycle track runs all the way from Hull. If you are driving, take exit 12 off Highway 5. Aim for the village of Old Chelsea, which is near the park entrance and has a Visitor Centre (819-827-2020), where you can pick up maps and other information. There are several campsites in the park.

Entertainment. The National Arts Center in Confederation Square (53 Elgin, 755-1111) is Ottawa's main venue for opera, ballet and theatre. Student standby tickets (which cost at least $10) are available for some shows, from 2.30pm on the day of performance. The Great Canadian Theatre Company (910 Gladstone Avenue, 236-5196) in Upper Town also shows good quality plays.

Jazz is popular, and you can call the Ottawa Jazzline on 232-7755 for listings of jazz and blues in the Capital Region. One of the best venues for blues is the Rainbow Bistro (76 Murray, 594-5123) in Lower Town. You can see bands free at the New Live Penguin (292 Elgin, 233-0057), though it is overcrowded at weekends.

Québec stays open later than its southern neighbour, so party animals always end up in Hull. Nightlife here consists mainly of heaving discos with laser shows and high-decibel music; most bars and clubs are ranked along Promenade de Portage.

Help and Information. The area code is 613 for Ottawa, 819 for Hull.
Tourist Information: Canada's Capital Information Center (14 Metcalfe St, 239-5000), opposite the Parliament Buildings, has information mainly on Ottawa and Hull. For information about Ontario go to the Visitor Centre in the National Arts Centre at 65 Elgin St (237-5158). Both offices are open all year round, daily 9am-9pm in summer. Free maps and a detailed city guide are available, as well as a free accommodation booking service.
Tourist Information Line: 692-7000 (24 hours).
British High Commission: 80 Elgin at Queen (237-1530), opposite the National Arts Centre.
Post Office: 59 Sparks Street Mall.
Medical Emergencies: St Anne's Medical Centre (500 St Patrick, 238-1552), in Lower Town.
Gay Information Line: 233-1324. *GO Info* is free and has the best gay listings.

The Great Outdoors

In addition to the Great Lakes, with their much-visited provincial parks, sandy beaches and holiday havens, there are thousands of smaller lakes in the Ontario hinterland. Travelling north from Toronto you should head for the Haliburton Highlands or the Muskoka District, centred around the towns of Huntsville and Bracebridge. Both these areas give easy access to the 3,000 square mile Algonquin Park. Canoeing, hiking and camping are the favourite ways of enjoying the park in the summer.

Despite the publicity about the pollution by acid rain of many of Ontario's lakes, the water still seems crystal clear and should be safe to swim in for at least another 10 years. The worst form of pollution is the noise of the motor boats.

If you do not want to be bothered with getting camping equipment, you should consider hiring a cottage for a week or more. Study the brochure distributed by the Ontario Ministry of Tourism and Recreation (1-800-ONTARIO) called *Accommodations in Ontario*, which lists housekeeping cottages and fishing lodges as well as hotels and motels. Prices start as low as $100 per week for a small cottage, though most cost $150-200. The long weekend around May 24 is traditionally the time when people 'open up' their cottages after the long winter, and take their first (brief) dip in the lake. The cottage season ends either on the Labour Day weekend (early September) or, more unusually, at the Thanksgiving weekend (mid-October).

If you are attracted by the far north, you can travel on the Polar Bear

Express, a rail service between North Bay and Moosonee, an old Hudson's Bay Company fur trading post. Contact Ontario Northland (805 Bay St, Toronto, 965-4268) for details. From Moosonee, you can take the short boat ride to Moose Factory Island, the original trading post, or a trip by freighter canoe, led by Indian guides, to Fossil Island — a heaven for geologists and other scientists.

Skiing. Although there are no real mountains in Ontario, skiing is extremely poular. The resorts within easy striking distance of Toronto are Chicopee to the west, Dagmar to the east and resorts around Barrie to the north. The resorts popular with more serious skiers are Collingwood in the Blue Mountains or the Huntsville region, several hours north of Toronto.

Phone 963-2911 for recorded cross country ski information and 963-2992 for downhill conditions. A life ticket will cost $20-30 a day and equipment rental about $15. For information about accommodation in ski resorts, ask for the free brochure *Good Times Guide* available from Resorts Ontario, 10 Peter St N, Orillia (705-325-9115). Gray Coach (351-3311) runs buses to the slopes departing Toronto in the early morning and returning in the late afternoon; the return fare of about $40 includes a lift-pass.

There are excellent facilities for cross-country skiing scattered throughout the city and province. Horseshoe Valley near Barrie and Camp Fortune near Ottawa are both superb. You can hire equipment at both. Travel CUTS (187 College St, Toronto M5T 1P1) organizes cross-country ski trips combined with dog-sledding in Algonquin Park.

Montréal and Québec

After Paris, Montréal is the largest French-speaking city in the world. To visit the city and the province is to immerse yourself in a thoroughly different *milieu* than the rest of the continent. For North Americans, a trip to the province of Québec is a convenient (and inexpensive) substitute for a trip to Europe. Visitors are attracted by the old world architecture, the fine restaurants and sophisticated fashions, and also by a distinctly European atmosphere which has little truck with northern prudery. Whereas Toronto was once known as the City of Churches, Montréal was Sin City, where liquor was available during Prohibition (and is still served later than in any other part of Canada), and where art and nightlife were not censored.

Québec's political life is certainly more lively than that of the other provinces. The constitutional talks in 1992 (the Charlottetown Accord) gave the province what many non-French Canadians saw as unfair advantages, so it was no surprise that the voters of Québec passed the referendum approving the new constitution. For more than a decade Québec has been asserting its uniqueness politically and legally. English speakers dominated the province's business and banking — in spite of the fact that a large majority of the inhabitants are French-speaking — so stringent laws on language and labelling were introduced to emphasise the 'Frenchness' of the province. The tension which this created has subsided (partly because many English companies panicked and moved their head offices to Toronto), but Québec is still politically a stimulating place to visit.

One of Québec's most dynamic politicians was Jean Drapeau, mayor of Montréal almost continuously from 1954 until 1986. He was responsible for bringing first Expo 67 (the world fair) to Montréal to celebrate Canada's

433

centennial year and then the 1976 Olympics. These events live on in the Parc des Iles on the site of Expo, and in the Olympic Park, both of which are worth a visit. The impact of the latter also persists in the memory of the city's taxpayers, who had to foot the bills for twelve years after its inception.

So alongside the quaint and charming side of Montréal is the aggressively and lavishly futuristic. The city fathers are proud of their underground city (inspired by an idea of Leonardo de Vinci). Public transport and pedestrians are channelled along separate tunnels, giving access to two train stations, a bus terminal, 1,700 shops, seven big hotels, two universities, 200 restaurants, 45 bank branches, 34 cinemas and art centres, three exhibition halls and several sport complexes. In fact, it is the largest underground development in the world, with 18 miles/29km of subterranean passageways.

THE PEOPLE

Québec has a population of over 6.5 million (25% of the Canadian population), and has an area three times that of France. The Québécois are not just like the French of Paris or Marseille or Toulouse. They are avid hockey fans, they drink bottles of Molsons beer (brewed by a prominent Montréal family), and speak a kind of French which is sometimes incomprehensible to a Parisian.

According to one theory, the French spoken in rural Québec is much closer to the language spoken by the 17th-century peasants who were among the first arrivals in the New World, which has survived relatively unchanged. By now, the Québécois language has adapted many English expressions, such as 'hambourgeois', just as the Québécois people have absorbed many Anglo-North American influences into their culture. Speak French if possible (though Montréalers are no more tolerant than Parisians of hearing their language mangled).

The British defeated the French for control of the region in 1750, but Gallic culture has survived and thrived. Altogether, it is fascinating to visit a place where ethnic traditions have been so vigorously maintained over such a long period, fending off assimilation by English-speakers. St-Jean-Baptiste Day (June 24) is energetically celebrated with fireworks and parades, rather than Victoria Day (late May), which is marked in the other provinces.

CLIMATE

After a certain point you may think that all versions of the harsh Canadian winter become indistinguishable; but the cold is noticeably more extreme in Montréal than in Toronto. Montréalers find the climate-controlled atmosphere of the underground city quite comforting during their harsh winters, when temperatures easily dip down to —25°C or —30°C (—13°to —22°F) on the colder days at the heart of the season. Winters get colder still as you move east to the provincial capital of Québec City, and further towards the Gaspé Peninsula. With the possible exception of Moscow, Montréal gets more snow than any other big city in the world, so dress accordingly if you're visiting between December and April.

The summers are a different matter, hot and still, ideal for sitting at outdoor cafés long into the evening.

Getting Around

ARRIVAL AND DEPARTURE

Air. Two international airports serve Montréal: the original Dorval (12 miles/20km west of downtown) and the much more modern Mirabel, more than twice as far away. Mirabel has one of the largest areas of any airport in the world, and the fewest passengers — or so it seems. Most passengers travelling from points within North America still land at Dorval. Except for its inconvenient location, Mirabel has wonderfully modern facilities.

Connaisseur (631-0026), also known as Gray Line, operates a bus between the principal downtown hotels and Dorval airport; the one-way fare is $8.50. Aeroplus (476-1100) operates from Mirabel, both to downtown hotels and to Dorval; one-way fares are $12.25 and $11.15 respectively.

The suburb of Dorval is on the rail line from Windsor station in Montréal, but the area between the station and airport terminal is a jungle of overpasses, cloverleafs and fast highways. You can try to persuade a taxi driver to take you the short distance to the station, but they usually want to wait until they can get a more lucrative fare all the way to downtown i.e. $35.

Bus. Greyhound buses can carry only international passengers in the province of Québec. They depart from the Port Authority Bus Terminal in New York seven times daily, taking eight hours to reach Montréal. Vermont Transit operates a seven-hour service from Boston.

All bus fares in Québec include tax, which explains the odd-looking figures below.

The domestic carrier is Voyageur, whose depot and head office are at 505 Boulevard de Maisonneuve E (842-2281), at the Berri-UQAM metro stop. There are frequent services into the Laurentian Hills north of Montréal and to the Eastern Townships east of the city. Voyageur buses between Montréal and Ottawa leave every hour on the hour 6am-10pm, and take $2\frac{1}{2}$ hours. The one-way fare is $24.82, a return $49.63; although if you don't leave on a Friday and stay less than 10 days, a return costs $39.73. Buses to Québec City (journey time three hours) leave every hour on the hour 6am-9pm, with an evening bus at 11pm and an additional weekend service at 1am. The fare is $33.80 one way; for a return in less than ten days, leaving on a day other than Friday, the fare is $47.35; otherwise it's $67.55. Smoking is prohibited on all services.

There are five express buses daily from Toronto, taking 6-7 hours. The one-way fare is $55.58, a regular return $111.17. A less-than-five days return fare is $100.10; and less-than-ten days return, not travelling on Fridays and Sundays is $88.97.

If you plan a lot of travelling within the provinces of Québec and Ontario, investigate the 'Tourpass'. This entitles you to ten consecutive days of unlimited bus travel between May and October and costs $165.81. The pass may be extended at a cost of $17.80 per extra day for a maximum of seven days, but the extension must be specified at the time of purchase — you can't decide to extend it halfway along.

Train. There are two stations in Montréal: Central Station at 935 de La Gauchetiere St W, 871-1331 (metro Bonaventure) under the Queen Elizabeth Hotel; and the old and dignified Windsor Station nearby, at the corner of Peel and de La Gauchetiere. Windsor handles more local traffic including commuter services.

The main services are listed below. All return fares are double the single fares. On services within Canada, booking a ticket in advance and not departing on a Friday, Saturday or holiday will give you a 40% discount, but seats at these prices are scarce. The advance notice required is as follows: 5 days (Toronto), 6 days (Québec), 8 days (Gaspé) and 6 days (Ottawa). Cheaper tickets depend on the availability of seats and on departure dates other than Fridays, Saturdays and holidays.

New York: the railway link between New York and Montréal predates the one between Toronto and Montréal. Scenically it is a much more interesting journey, with beautiful views of the Hudson Valley in upstate New York. Amtrak (1-800-USA-RAIL) operates one train each day from Penn Station in New York City called the *Montréaler,* which departs at 5.10pm. The *Adirondack* train to New York City takes about 9 hours and departs from Montréal's Central Station at 10.10am. The return fare is US$101.
Toronto: six trains a day. A one-way ticket costs $72 ($65 for students).
Québec City: three trains a day; the fastest *(Rapidos)* take three hours from Central Station. The one-way fare is $36 ($32 for students).
Gaspé: three trains a week run to Gaspé, over 620 miles/1,000km east of Montréal. This trip lasts 18 hours and costs $100 ($90 for students) one way.
Ottawa: four trains a day. This journey takes about two hours and the single fare costs $30 ($27 for students).

Driving. The road network in and out of Montréal is daunting to the uninitiated, so study your map carefully before entering the fray. On autoroutes (freeways) the speed limit is 100km/h (62mph) maximum and 60km/h (37mph) minimum. On other provincial roads the limit is 90km/h (56mph), in cities and towns, 50km/h (30mph). Both the provincial and the local police use radar to check drivers' speeds. Front and back seat belts are compulsory in the province. Québec is the only province in which it is illegal to turn right at a red light and to overtake in a right hand lane.

Highway 401, the main highway through southern Ontario, continues east from Toronto along the north shore of Lake Ontario and the St-Lawrence River to the Québec border. Here it changes to Autoroute 20 and joins Autoroute 40 from Ottawa, before becoming the Boulevard Metropolitan north of Montréal. To enter Montréal, take exits Decarie, St-Denis or St-Hubert. To bypass Montréal and continue to Québec City, stay on Autoroute 40 by the St-Lawrence.

If approaching from south of the river, you will either be on Highway 15 leading due north from the US border, or on the Trans-Canada (Highway 20) from Québec City. Coming from this direction you will be more aware that Montréal is built on an island since you will cross one of the following bridges: Jacques-Cartier, Victoria, or Champlain.

Car Rental: discount car rental firms were slow to come to Montréal. But now there are many outlets of Rent-a-Wreck in the city, where the company is called Via-route Auto Location. Phone 355-1335 or 521-5221. Tilden, Budget, etc. all charge at least $35 a day. Ask about renting a van at the Complexe Des Jardins. Because of the high provincial tax on gasoline (40%), driving can be an expensive proposition.

CITY TRANSPORT

Finding your way around Montréal is tricky because of the gradual change from English street names to French ones. In particular, the main east-west

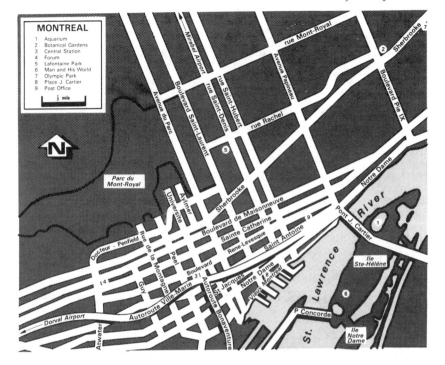

Boulevard formerly known as Dorchester became René-Lévesque some years ago.

Metro. Montréalers are justifiably proud of their metro. The stations all have unique murals and decorations, and the trains themselves run almost silently on pneumatic tyres (unlike the clattering subways of London and New York).

The north-south and east-west lines bisect at the station Berri-UQAM, near the corners of Rue Berri and Rue St-Denis, on Blvd de Maisonneuve. The metro stops which give access to Old Montréal, the best part of town in which to stroll, are Champ-de-Mars, Place d'Armes and Victoria. The metro has been extended across the river to the Ile Sainte-Hélene for the Park des Iles and on to Longueuil on the south shore.

As in Toronto, the metro system is completely integrated with the bus network. Once you have purchased your ticket for $1.50 (a *carnet* of six tickets costs $6.50), you are entitled to complete your journey by presenting the transfer pass comparable to the one offered by Toronto's TTC. For all information concerning public transport, dial AUT-OBUS (288-6287) between 7am and 8.30pm on weekdays, or visit the office at 159 St-Antoine W. The metro starts operating at about 5.30am and stops at 12.30am (1am on Saturdays).

Car. Taking after their Parisian counterparts, Montréal drivers have been variously described as fiendish, maniacal and suicidal. So be prepared to drive aggressively or not at all. (Pedestrians should also be alert and not put faith in signals at crosswalks). Navigating the streets of Montréal, originally laid out by Sulpician monks in 1672, is fairly straightforward, though several of the main thoroughfares are one-way.

As you might expect, parking can be tricky, even if there are 13,127 parking places in the underground city. Parking is particularly difficult in Old Montréal, and the picturesque Place Jacques-Cartier and nearby streets are closed to cars during the summer months. Leave your car at the park by the Champs-de-Mars metro station, and walk from there.

Taxis. Cabs are easily hailed on any downtown street at any time.

Cycling. Bicycles can be rented for $18-30 a day, $58-100 a week (depending on the model) from Cycles Peel, 6665 St-Jacques West (486-1148) or La Cordée, 2159 Ste-Catherine St East (524-1515).

Carriages. You may wish to splurge and have a ride in a calèche or horse-drawn carriage (sleighs in winter) in Montréal or Québec City. Needless to say, these exist solely for tourists and usually come with a guided tour by the driver. Be prepared to spend around $25 for half an hour, or $40 for an hour, though if you are in a group of four (maximum), this may not seem too steep. Carriages park in the Place Jacques-Cartier, Place d'Armes, Square Dorchester (in front of Infotouriste) and Mount-Royal Park in the summer-time. Call Caleche André Boisvert on 653-0751 for more information.

Accommodation

Hotels. John Lennon and Yoko Ono recorded the song 'Give Peace a Chance' in room 613 of the Queen Elizabeth Hotel. Only rich and committed fans are likely to splash out on a night there.

Budget hotels in Montréal are called *maisons de tourisme* or tourist lodges, and tend to be less expensive than their counterparts in the other major cities of Canada. It is always worth asking for an off-season discount between November and April. Double rooms can be found for $25-$35 in hotels around the metro St-Laurent. Other streets to check are rue St-Hubert, accessible from the next metro stop along (Berri-UQAM), and near the bus terminal at St-Denis. Turning left out of the terminal onto rue St-Hubert will bring you to the Hotel le Breton (number 1609; 524-7273), Hotel Kent (number 1216; 845-9835) and Hotel Viger Centre-Ville (number 1001; 845-6058). Rather more upmarket is the renovated Royal Roussillion Hotel at number 1600 (849-3214 or 1-800-363-6057). Continuing north to the next metro stop (Sherbrooke), try the north side of Sherbrooke west of St-Denis for the Hotel Manoir Sherbrooke (number 157; 285-0895) and the Armor Tourist Lodge (number 151; 285-0140), where doubles are all similarly priced in the $30-$45 range. St-Denis St has a number of relatively cheap hotels:

Hotel de la Couronne (number 1029; 845-0901), Hotel des Touristes l'Americain (number 1042; 849-0616) and the Hotel St-Denis (number 1254; 849-4526).

Also cheap and conveniently central are the Vines Tourist Rooms (1208 Drummond; 861-8745) and Maison André (3511 University; 849-4092).

Motels. If you have a car and want to stay in a motel, look along Taschereau (Highway 124) on the south shore, especially around the bridges, or along Saint-Jacques St West. Few doubles will be less than $45. The cheapest is on neither of these roads and quite a way from the city; the Pignon Rouge at 15777 Sherbrooke St East (642- 2131) charges $42 for a double.

Hostels. The province of Québec is generally well provided with youth hostels, and the one in Montréal is particularly popular. If it is full, you may be referred to other temporary summer hostels. It is at 3541 rue Aylmer at Milton (843-3317) near the McGill metro shop. If you supply your own bedding, the cost is $14 per night for YHA members and $19.56 for non-members. Sheet rental costs $1.75. This hostel is open year round (hours 8am-2am), and you are limited to a ten-night stay.

YMCAs. The YMCA is at 1450 Stanley St (849-8393) and offers singles from $33, doubles from $48. The YWCA is a huge building a few blocks away at 1355 René-Lévesque West, at the corner of Crescent St (866-9941). It accepts only women and charges $46 single and $62 double.

University Residences. Several universities and colleges rent out residence rooms between May and August. The University of McGill on Sherbrooke St West offers the best location, so rooms should be booked in advance (398-6367). Singles go for a flat rate of $32.50 a night for non-students; and $24 a night, $110 a week, or $300 a month for students. Much cheaper is the residence of the French-speaking Université de Montréal north of Mount-Royal at 2500 Edouard-Montpetit (343-6531), which has over 1,000 rooms to rent for $23.46 if you have a student card, $34.50 if not. The Concordia University Student Residence at 1455 de Maisonneuve W (848-4755) charges $18/$36 to students, and $24/$38 to non-students. The weekly rate is around $115 a week for anyone.

Bed and Breakfast. In the city itself contact Montréal Bed & Breakfast on 289-9749. Even if you do not have camping equipment you can stay in the country either at a country bed and breakfast or at a farm. Contact Vacances Familles (870 Blvd de Maisonneuve E, 282-9580) or ring *Regroupement Loisir Québec* (4545 Avenue Pierre de Coubertin, 252-3000) for lists of addresses. The guide *Le Gîte du Passant* can be purchased at any CAA (Canadian Automobile Association) branch for $8.50. The average rate at a B & B is $25 per adult, $10 per child occupying the same room. They usually open May to September. The nearest country B & B to Montréal is Coteau-du-Lac 25 miles/40km away.

Vacances Familles can also help you arrange a farm holiday, either staying in the farmhouse itself or in a cottage on the property similar to *gîtes* in France. The cost will range between $245-350 per week, including all meals. Often these rural French families take pride in their dining rooms and serve regional specialities. For example, if you are staying at a farm at St-Urbain de Châteauguay south of Montréal, you can try cheese and yoghurt made from goat's milk.

Camping. People with cars might consider staying just outside the city, rather than in a motel. There are a couple of campsites less than 30 miles/50km away. One is the Pointe-des-Cascades west of Montréal on route 338, just before you cross over to the Island of Montréal. Charges begin at $15, which includes use of the swimming pool. On the south shore there is camping at Côte-Ste-Catherine, 23 miles/37km from downtown on route 132. For around $10 you can pitch your tent or park your trailer and take advantage of facilities for swimming, fishing and picnicking between early June and September.

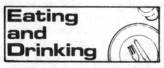

Eating and Drinking

In Montréal, predictably, French is the cuisine to go for. Out of 250 restaurants listed by the tourist office, over a third serve French food. Visit Les Filles du Roy (415 Bonsecours, 849-3535) to find Québécois specialities, such as rabbit pie, *gibolette* fish stew, blueberries, Québec cheese and maple-cured ham.

There are literally thousands of restaurants in Montréal and dining out is part of the Montréaler's way of life. Crêperies, bistros and cafés abound in the inexpensive range, and restaurants serving haute cuisine at the other end of the spectrum. Don't be overwhelmed by the choice; it is difficult to go wrong. You need stray no further than rue St-Denis to keep eating well for months. This is the so-called Latin Quarter of Montréal, attracting students, artists and trendies as well as tourists. Sitting outdoors at one of the many cafés, it is possible to amuse yourself for hours watching the passers-by. Or try the crêperies (most of them licensed), such as Le Triskell at 3470 rue St-Denis. At all these places it is possible to lunch or dine for under $12, and many stay open long into the night. Le Fripon (436 Place Jacques-Cartier) serves *table d'hôtes* starting at $10. Between these casual eating places there are plenty of more formal French restaurants, not to mention cheap Swiss, Moroccan and Asian venues.

If you follow St-Denis as far south as it will go, you reach *le Vieux Montréal.* The dedicated sight-seer will follow the complete walking tour of the historic buildings, but most visitors are distracted by the abundant choice of restaurants, and begin to fantasize about the next meal. In summer Place Jacques-Cartier is filled with tables and chairs — but also tourists, so it can be hard to find a seat. Naturally, food and drink are more expensive here than elsewhere, and more expensive outdoors than in. Still it is also more entertaining than other areas, as it attracts all manner of buskers, hawkers and dawdlers.

Old Montréal also has some of the city's finest French restaurants in elegantly restored old houses near the waterfront. As on most of the restaurant-filled streets of Montréal, there is a choice of prices and cuisines; one fairly expensive ($20-25) but good seafood place is Chez Delmo at 211 rue Notre-Dame (849-4061).

Vegetarians and health good enthusiasts on a budget will enjoy Le Commensal, 680 Ste-Catherine West (871-1480) and 2115 St-Denis (845-0248), where innovative food is sold by weight. Biddles Jazz & Ribs, 2060 Aylmer (corner of President Kennedy, 842-8656) allows the tired traveller to feast on a barbecued chicken and ribs, while listening to a live jazz band. For travellers with money to spare or something to celebrate, the following are pricey, but reliably good. For excellent cuisine, try le Mas des Oliviers, 1216 Bishop St (861-6733). Terrific Greek seafood can be sampled at Milos, 5357 Park Ave (272-3522). Those fond of Japanese food will not be disappointed by Katsura's, 2170 Mountain St (849-1172).

Try the Blvd St-Laurent for many inexpensive restaurants, Polish, Italian, Jewish, Greek and German as well as French. Several good Chinese restaurants are clustered in Chinatown (St-Laurent and de la Gauchetière). Two interesting delicatessens which sell a wonderful range of smoked meats are Main and Schwartz's, both of which have more atmosphere than the more famous Ben's on the corner of de Maisonneuve and Metcalfe, or Dunn's at 892 Ste-Catherine West.

Try to fit in a late-night pilgrimage to the classic St-Viateur Bagel Factory which serves the best bagels with lox and cream cheese in the world (160 St-Viateur E). Or try the trendy Prince-Arthur Street at the base of Mount Royal for Greek, Italian and seafood, where it is customary for restaurants to have a 'bring-your-own' licence. For fast foods, watch for *casse-croutes*, which specialize in hot dogs *(chien chauds)* with French fries and cabbage. A tasty alternative to this standard North American fare is the relatively recent but now firmly established Montréal favourite: a delicious cross between the French croissant and the North American sandwich, served in *croissanteries* throughout the city. When travelling out of town watch for roadside booths advertising excellent *patates frites*.

Provincial and federal taxes total 15.56% on meals over $3.25. It is customary to calculate the 12%-15% tip before adding the tax.

DRINKING

Drinking in the province of Québec can be just as lively as eating, since many bars — as opposed to 'taverns', which stop serving at midnight — are licensed until 3am. (Hence the exodus from Ottawa to Hull in Québec when the capital's bars close at 1am.) Although there is a liquor control board in Québec, it does not have the same monopoly as its counterpart in other provinces. Wine and beer may be purchased from grocery stores *(depanneurs)*, usually for a few cents more than in liquor stores.

Québeckers are traditionally heavy beer drinkers, though wine is becoming more fashionable. Try Québécois cider which, unlike cider sold in other Canadian provinces, is alcoholic — about the same strength as beer. For a really lethal brew try Caribou, a Québécois mixture of red wine and spirit which at its best tastes like cherry brandy and at its worst like hangover-inducing cough medicine. This is the refreshment which is consumed in such quantity at the Winter Carnival in Québec City (see below). Québec imports large quantities of French wine, bottles it in the province and sells it for about $6 a bottle.

Whereas taverns are still male-dominated, brasseries are more mixed and often serve cheap pub food. For a rooftop drink, go to the 36th floor bar of the Château Champlain in the Place du Canada. If the evening is warm, drink on an outdoor terrace at one of the cafés in Old Montréal, St-Denis and Crescent St.

The minimum drinking age is 18.

Cruises on the St-Lawrence depart several times daily from Victoria Pier and Jacques-Cartier Pier in the old harbour of Old Montréal. They are operated by Gray Line (934-1222) and Montréal Harbour Cruises (842-3871), from May to October weather permitting. Jet boat rides through the Lachine Rapids are organized by Lachine Rapids Tours (284-9607) from Victoria Pier. Prices range from $15 to $45.

Museums. Most museums in Montréal close on Mondays.

In addition to the main Musée des Beaux Arts (1379 & 1380 Sherbrooke W), visit the McCord Museum a few blocks east at 690 Sherbrooke St. This museum displays objects of Canadian historical interest including Inuit works of art and Québécois handicrafts.

The Château de Ramezay, 280 Notre-Dame East (861-3708) in Old Montréal, houses a small collection of original native artifacts. The Musée d'Art Contemporain, located on la Cité-du-Havre (873-2878) is Montreal's museum of Modern Art. The Château Dufresne, the city's Decorative Arts Museum, is at the corner of Pie-IX and Sherbrooke (259-2575); it closes on Mondays and Tuesdays. The Palais de la Civilisation, located on Ile Notre-Dame in the former French pavilion of Expo '67, usually hosts several international exhibitions simultaneously. Take the metro to Ile-Ste-Hélène. A shuttle ferries visitors from the station to the museum (872-4560).

Religious Monuments. A number of monuments are well worth seeing. The first is St-Joseph's Oratory which, at 870ft (263m) above sea level, dominates all of Montréal and offers a fine view of the island. It is located at 3800 Queen Mary road. The Basilique Notre-Dame, at 116 rue Notre-Dame W in Old Montréal, dates back to 1829 and is part of the oldest parish of the city. It is one of the city's most striking buildings. Finally, Cathédrale Marie-Reine-du-Monde, on the corner of Blvd René Lévesque and Mansfield St, is a replica (one-third actual size) of Rome's St-Peter's Basilica. All these churches are open daily.

Olympic Park. If you have any interest in sport or architecture, you will want to schedule a visit to Olympic Park, 4141 Pierre-de-Coubertin, site of the 1976 Olympics (metro to Viau). Built at huge and controversial expense (and often referred to as 'The Big Owe'), the scope and originality of the structures are impressive. While you're there, take the funicular railway up to the top of the stadium's inclined tower, from where you get a good view of the city skyline. Hourly tours, costing $7, begin at the Centre d'Accueil Touristique. The pools are open to the public at the cost of $3; phone 252-4622 for details.

Botanical Gardens: across Sherbrooke St from the park (4101 Sherbrooke East, 872-1400, metro to Pie-IX) are the Botanical Gardens, including an Insectarium, open 9am-7pm. Admission to the greenhouse, Insectarium and gardens is $7; but a $12 ticket will allow you to also visit the new and fascinating Biôdome (866-3000). The gardens have 25,000 floral species and the biggest collection of Bonsai trees outside Asia.

Entertainment

Look for the free fortnightly tabloids — *Montréal Mirror* (in English) and *Voir* (in French) — in bookshops, museums and restaurants. Each gives extensive listings. Also check the Saturday *Montréal Gazette* newspaper for a full entertainment section in English.

The Place des Arts (metro stop of the same name) is the central arts complex, hosting symphonies, ballets and operas. It includes the Théatres Maisonneuve, Port-Royal and the Salle Wilfrid-Pelletier. Ring the box office (842-2112) for details of events.

Music. If you are visiting outside the symphony season (September to April), the prestigious Montréal Symphony Orchestra will not be at the Place des Arts; however, it may perform summer concerts at Notre-Dame church.

For traditional Québécois folk music clubs, look for *bôites-à-chanson* in Old Montréal, especially along rue Saint-Paul, for instance Au Pierrots at number 104 (861-1270). These often turn into friendly sing-alongs, which provide a good opportunity to perfect your French accent. For folk dancing in the summer go to the man-made lake in Mount-Royal Park on Monday or Thursday evenings, when the ethnic communities put on free performances of their national dances. The famous Yellow Door Coffee House at

3625 Aylmer St near the youth hostel no longer has folk music, but you might like to check the useful student notice board.

The choice of jazz is especially good during the Montréal Jazz Festival, held on Ste-Catherine St each July for 10 days. But there is plenty of jazz to be heard any time of the year at the bars along St-Denis (e.g. Le Central near metro Mont-Royal) and elsewhere, e.g. Biddles with Oliver Jones at 2060 Aylmer St.

For rock music try the Moustache (1445 Closse St), near the Atwater metro stop. Big name rock bands play at the Montréal Forum in the same area, or at the Théatre St-Denis. Déja-Vu (1224 Bishop, 866-0512) has live rock bands every evening.

Trendy nightclubs abound. In Old Montréal, try Brandy's, 25 Saint-Paul St East (871-9093). Don't forget to admire their twenty-odd giant Tiffany lampshades, each of them unique. Crescent and Bishop Streets, located in the western, 'Anglo' half of downtown, are focal points of nocturnal activity. Winnie's (1445 Crescent, 288-0623) comes highly recommended by resident yuppies, as is the new Hard Rock Café across the street at 1458 (987-1420). The Beaujolais (1458 de la Montagne, 842-8825) boasts both posh interiors and a quiet rooftop terrace, allowing a bird's eye view of the teeming streets below.

Theatre and Cinema. If you are not interested in French films or French theatre, your choice of entertainment will be reduced (films are not always subtitled). Plays in English are staged at the Centaur Theatre in Old Montréal. There is an English language re-run cinema at 2155 Ste-Catherine St (932-1139). The Montréal Film Festival is held annually in late August.

SPORT AND RECREATION

To join in Québec's favourite spectator sport, try to see a hockey game at the Forum (932-2582). The champion Montréal Canadians have won the Stanley Cup two dozen times. The Montréal Expos baseball team plays at Olympic Stadium (metro Pie-IX) between April and September. Call 253-3434 for ticket information.

The seven-mile/12-kilometre bicycle path beside the Lachine Canal can be enjoyed independently or as part of a group tour. There is another along the St-Lawrence River, which begins at the south side of the Victoria Bridge. There are also canoe launching places and cross-country ski trails along the Lachine Canal.

Just as Vancouver has its Stanley Park and Toronto its Centre Island as an easy escape from the downtown bustle, Montréal has its mountain. Mount-Royal Park is the place where the locals can walk along miles of trails, skiing, skating, snowshoeing in winter, and cycling, jogging and sunbathing in summer. Autumn is a particularly good time to explore the park when the maple trees turn brilliant red and orange. There are excellent views of the city from the sign-posted observation points.

It is pleasant to spend a summer's day on one of the largely man-made islands in the St-Lawrence River. Ile Notre-Dame is the site of an enormous floral park. The island has a man-made system of canals and lakes, and a Nautical Pavilion where you can hire boats, catamarans, canoes, sailboards, pedal-boats, etc. Wetsuits and lessons are also available (872-3374).

On Ile Ste-Hélène is La Ronde, a fun fair with some terrifying rides and an Aqua-Park, open only during the summer. In June it hosts an International Fireworks Competition. Admission is $9.50. Another attraction on the island is the David M. Stewart Museum of Discoveries (861-6701), focusing on Canadian history. It can easily be reached from the metro station on the island.

SHOPPING

Normal shopping hours are 9.30am-6pm Monday to Wednesday, with late night shopping until 9pm on Thursdays and Fridays, and Saturday closing at 5pm. The provincial sales tax of 9% is among the steepest in the country.

The main shopping thoroughfare is Ste-Catherine St (near McGill metro), with the city's three major department stores: Eaton's, the Bay and Ogilvy's; only the latter is unique to Montréal. For a high density of fashionable boutiques try Les Cours Mont-Royal, les Promenades de la Cathédrale, Place Ville Marie or Place Bonaventure shopping complexes. The *haute couture* salons and elegant antique stores are found along Sherbrooke St.

There are a number of excellent outdoor farmers' markets in Montréal. Perhaps the best is the Marché Atwater at the southern end of Atwater (metro Lionel-Groulx). Every day of the week from 7am-6pm, farmers sell their produce at reasonable prices. The neighbourhood has some interesting secondhand shops too. Earlybirds should go to the Marché Central Metropolitain at Crémazie and de l'Acadie in the far north of the city, which is reputed to peak at 5am. Also interesting is the market in the Italian district near the Jean-Talon metro shop.

The Canadian Guild of Crafts at 2025 Peel St stocks interesting quilts, textiles, mocassins and carvings. For less expensive traditional arts and crafts try Le Rouet, which has several branches including at Place Ville Marie and 700 Ste-Catherine W.

Québec produces two-thirds of the world's maple syrup. If you are interested in its production, try to visit a maple bush in the early spring when the sap is collected and boiled down. Place Jacques-Cartier is full of boutiques which rely on tourists to buy presentation packs of maple syrup as well as the handicrafts and delicacies which they display.

MEDIA

Most radio and television stations and newspapers are in French. Tours are available of the headquarters of the CBC French network called La Maison de Radio-Canada (1400 René-Lévesque East, 597-7787). CBC-AM in Montréal can be picked up on 940AM and CBC-FM on 93.5FM. Oldies 990 on 990 AM plays music predominantly from the 60's & 70's. Students favour rock and pop on CHOM on 97.7 FM and MIX96 on 95.9 FM. CKMF on 94.3 FM and CKOI on 96.9 FM also play pop/rock music, but links are exclusively in Québécois.

English-speaking television channels available without cable in Montréal are CBC channel 6 and CTV channel 12. The American television networks are all available on cable.

Five of the six Montréal dailies are in French, from the serious *Le Devoir* to the sensationalist *Journal de Montréal.* The English language Montréal daily is the *Gazette.* You can read British newspapers for free at the Municipal Library on Sherbrooke St near la Fontaine Park (nearest metro stop Sherbrooke). Weekend editions are sold at La Maison de la Presse Internationale, at 1393 Ste-Catherine St West.

Crime and Safety

Montreal has a reputation for suffering more than its fair share of organized crime; bank hold-ups are a regular feature and a large proportion of the murders seem to have underworld connections. But innocent tourists can go about their business day or night without anxiety, Montréal is free of no-go zones. Although there are slums in Montréal, they do not seem to nurture violent crime and need not be avoided.

Possession of cannabis is an offence like everywhere else in Canada, and is just as prevalent.

Help and Information *i*

The area code for Montréal is 514.

Tourist Information: Info Touriste, 1001 Square Dorchester (metro Peel) or 174 rue Notre-Dame Est. The Recreation and Sports Federation (*Regroupement Loisir Québec),* is an excellent source of information, not only on recreation and sports, but also on accommodation throughout the province, special events, and general tourist information. Youth Hostel members and International Student Card holders should make a point of contacting Regroupement Tourisme Jeunesse at the same address in order to obtain a list of hotels, restaurants and shops across Canada which give discounts to members.

Parks Canada: Québec Region, 1141 Route de l'Eglise, Ste-Foy Québec GIV 4H5 (418-694-4177).

British Consulate: 635 René-Lévesque W (866-5863).

American Express: 2000 Peel Building, 1141 de Maisonneuve W (284-3300).

Thomas Cook: 2020 University St (842-2541).

Emergency Health Aid (Greater Montréal Referral Center): 527-1375.

Post Office: St-Antoine and de la Cathédrale, Place Bonaventure.

Telegrams: 861-7311.

Weather Information: 636-3284.

Road conditions: 873-4121.

QUEBEC CITY

By North American standards the provincial capital of Québec, also called Québec (population 575,000) is very ancient, having hosted the famous battle between Wolfe and Montcalm in 1759 well on in its history. The church of Notre Dame des Victoires built in 1688 rivals some of the 17th century Spanish missions in the American southwest as the oldest European settlement in North America. Québec City is the only walled city north of Mexico (it was declared a World Heritage Treasure by UNESCO in December 1985), and Laval University is among the oldest universities on the continent.

Unexpectedly the most popular time to visit Québec is early February, when there is a ten-day Winter Carnival. Be prepared for the coldest temperatures you have ever encountered. (Significantly, the advertisement on the inside front cover of the Carnival brochure — 'proud to be associated with such a splendid event' — is for a remedy for chapped lips). Most people who attend the carnival drink large quantities of the local brew (Caribou) to keep warm, in between ice skating on the outdoor rink, going down the giant ice slide on Dufferin Terrace and admiring the snow sculptures at the Place du Palais. Participants from as far afield as China and Morocco, not to mention Inuit from the Canadian Arctic, come to compete in this unique and transitory artistic medium.

City Layout. The suburbs surrounding Québec are hardly different from those around any North American city, except for the fact that every sighpost and hoarding is in French. The real interest begins only when you reach the old part of the city. It is divided into the Upper and Lower Towns, connected by steep and winding staircases, as well as a funicular railway. The narrow and random streets are best explored on foot.

Arrival and Departure. *Air:* Québec's international airport is 15 miles/25km west of the city. When you arrive, signs point optimistically to the bus stop, but unfortunately services ceased in 1992. The remaining options are a taxi ($25 to the old town) or the van operated by Maple Leaf Sightseeing Tours (649-9226), which costs about $8 per person. The journey takes around 30 minutes. To book a taxi to the airport, call Taxi Co-op on 525-5191.

Train: four trains each day make the $3\frac{1}{2}$-hour run to Montrál from the Gare du Palais (692-3940). Another station is located five miles/8km southwest of the city centre in the suburb of Ste-Foy, just of Chemin St-Louis.

Bus: similarly, there are two bus terminals: the main one in the new city, the other out in Ste-Foy. Buses to Montréal (journey time three hours) leave every hour on the hour 6am-9pm. The fare is $33.80 one way; for a return in less than ten days, leaving on a day other than Friday, the fare is $47.35; otherwise it's $67.55. Buses operated by Orléans Express serve Rivière-du-Loup and Rimouski, with a continuing service to Gaspé.

Accommodation. The youth hostel — the Centre International de Séjour — is a rambling old boarding school in the western part of the old town at 19 Ste Ursule (418-694-0755). A bed in a twin room costs $18, in a dorm $15. Services are excellent, and include a fully equipped kitchen, laundry facilities, a baggage check, and a bicycle shed. If it is full, the Manoir directly opposite acts as a kind of overflow facility, charging slightly higher rates. The *patronne* is fussy at times but kindhearted.

Most other places in the old city are twee or expensive or both. L'Hotel de Vieux Québec at 1190 rue Saint-Jean (692-1850) often has promotional rates. La Maison Ste-Ursule, 40 Ste-Ursule (694-9794) is more upmarket. Walking along the streets in the upper part of the old town, you should find a few *Vacant* signs among those reading *Complet*, or either of the old town tourist offices (see below) will let you ring around for free.

The YWCA — catering to both genders — is a mile east of the old city walls at 855 avenue Holland (683-2155).

Camping: the closest site is Beauport Municipal (666-2228), ten miles/16km east of the city centre. Camping Aéroport (871-1574) is around 12 miles/20km west, handy for the airport but noisy. Both sites operate mid-May to mid-September.

Eating and Drinking. The restaurants are renowned throughout North America for their French cuisine. Most offer a reasonably-priced set meal and a good choice of wine. The best plan is to stroll around the old city looking for places which look crowded, but bear in mind that in some cases this just means a busload of tourists is dining. Places on the main drags tend to be more expensive.

Exploring. The atmosphere in Québec City is more quaint and even more French than in Montréal, which is not surprising considering that 95% of its residents are French-speaking and that Québec — not Montréal — is the provincial capital. Significantly, the parliament describes itself as a *national* assembly. You can visit the sumptuous Assemblée Nationale daily from 24 June until Labour Day, or from Monday to Friday during the rest of the year, 9am-4.30pm. The parliament building is at 1025 rue St-Augustin; try to make a reservation in advance on 418-643-7239.

The musée de la civilisation, by the river beneath the Upper City at 85 rue Dalhousie (643-2158), is terrific. This new museum takes five themes — the body, matter, society, language and thought — and looks at them in imaginative ways. In summer (June 24 until Labour Day in early September) it opens 9am-7pm daily. For the rest of the year it opens daily except Monday from 9am to 5pm, with late-night opening on Wednesday until 9pm. Admission is $5 (free on Tuesdays).

Entertainment. Listings (in French) appear in the free weekly *Voir*, available from shops, resturants and the tourist office. The Théatre Capitole, a gorgeous turn-of-the-century building on the edge of the old town, has just been restored and is worth visiting even if you don't see a performance. The Grand Théatre de Québec is more functional but has a good range of performance arts; call 643-8131.

English-language films are shown at several cinemas; try the elegant Cinéma de Paris (next to the Théatre Capitole), Place Québec (525-4524) and Galeries de la Capitale (628-2455). A modest selection of entertainment listings appear in the *Québec Chronicle-Telegraph*, an English-language weekly which claims to be North America's oldest newspaper.

Help and Information. The area code for Québec City is 418.

The Metro Québec tourism bureau is just inside the western wall to the old city, at 60 rue d'Auteuil (692-2491). The provincial headquarters — which also provides information on the city — is on the Place d'Armes.

For detailed information on walking tours, historical background, hotels, restaurants and special events, contact The Quebec Urban Community Tourist Information Center, 60 rue d'Auteuil, Quebec GIR 4M8 (418-692-2471); or the Bureau du Tourisme de Quebec, 12 Sainte-Anne (1-800-363-7777).

US Consulate: 692-2095; *French Consulate:* 688-0430.

Hospital (English-speaking): Jeffrey Hale's Hospital, 1250 chemin Ste-Foy (683-4471); *24-hour doctor:* 687-9915; *24-hour dentist:* 653-5412.

English-language bookshop: La Maison Anglaise, 2635 Boulevard Hochelaga

The Great Outdoors

The Laurentian Mountains north of Montreal, the Eastern Townships southeast of the city, the Gaspé Peninsula 400 miles east along the St-Lawrence River and the vast thinly populated north of the province all provide varied opportunities for outdoor activity. There are two national parks. La Mauricie 130 miles northeast of Montreal and Forillon at the tip of the very rural and French Gaspé Peninsula. Here there are wildlife observation facilities for seeing moose and deer on land, and whales and seals at sea. The Laurentians are particularly beautiful in the fall. Guided bus tours are available in September and October. Contact Gray Line, 1001 Square Dorchester St (934-1222).

The provincial government publishes lists of many types of accommodation. The Ministry of Recreation even sponsors government inns and campsites, and runs a reservation service; in Québec dial (418) 643-3127; or in Montreal dial 374-2417 for province wide information and bookings. Contact the Ministry if you are interested in renting a self-catering cottage for a week or two, some of which are located inside provincial parks. Their detailed list of campsites is most useful; ranging in price from $11 a night for a simple site up to at $22 or $27 for luxury (price varies with the region).

Skiing. Skiing is the most universally popular sport. The ski resorts of the Laurentian Hills are within an hour's drive north of Montreal and are located in such places as Piedmont, Sainte-Adèle, Sainte-Agathe, Val-Morin and Val-David. Gray Line ski buses run between downtown and the Laurentians (St-Sauveur, Morin Heights), Vermont (Jay Peak) or Eastern Townships (Stowe) for $35-40. A day trip to St-Sauveur is around $33, while night skiing from 3pm to 10:30pm is around $27. The price covers bus fare and lift ticket. For more information about destinations and fares, call 873-2015 (Infotouriste) or 934-1222 (Gray Line). Equipment can be rented at all resorts but prices are steep. If you are a foreigner and are boarding a 'ski express' bus to Vermont, don't forget your passport and visa; otherwise, you're likely to spend the day at the border crossing, with the bus picking you up on the way back! The highest peak in the Laurentians is Mont-Tremblant (nearly 3,000 feet/1,000 metres) 90 miles/145 km north of the city. This is part of a huge wilderness park which is also a worthwhile destination for people interested in rustic camping during the summer.

There are also major ski centres within a short distance of Quebec City including the relatively new Mont Sainte-Anne and Stoneham developments. For details of snow conditions phone 861-6670 in Montreal and 827-4579 in Quebec City. Skiing equipment can be rented at any of the resorts.

Canoeing, fishing and hunting are all extremely popular, and there are outfitters and rental facilities in many parks and small towns. If you want to hunt, you must purchase a licence (between $50 and $160 depending on the game). To get this, you will have to have written authorization that you are competent with firearms. Non-residents are not allowed to hunt moose but most other game is available to them.

The Atlantic Provinces

New Brunswick   Nova Scotia   Prince Edward Island   Newfoundland

The 'hospitality industry' outstrips all other sources of revenue except fishing in New Brunswick, Nova Scotia, Prince Edward Island and Newfoundland. Some over-zealous planners have suggested that the Atlantic provinces should be depopulated and turned into a gigantic playground. Fortunately, this futurist dream will never be realized, and Maritimers will continue to pass on their rural lore and their hospitable traditions.

Strictly speaking, the Maritime provinces do not include Newfoundland, since the term was coined well before 1949 when Newfoundland ceased to be an independent British colony and joined the Canadian Confederation. A reminder of Newfoundland's isolation is the fact that it has its own time zone, half an hour ahead in the winter and one and a half hours ahead in the summer of the other Atlantic provinces.

It often seems that the less prosperous a place is, the more slowly it changes. With an average income per capita of about two-thirds that of central and western Canada, the Atlantic region is definitely the least prosperous part of Canada. Change comes reluctantly to this region, and fishing and farming techniques remain relatively backward. Although the people may grumble about the policies of the federal government, they are a peace-loving and traditional people who happily persist with the old ways of doing things.

Whether gentle rolling farmland, dramatic sea cliffs or forested mountains, the changing landscape is always pleasing. Furthermore, the man-made landscape is more picturesque in eastern Canada than elsewhere. White frame farmhouses inland and fishing villages nestling around coves, old-fashioned one room school houses and wooden churches seem to have kept modern ugliness at bay. The scale of distances is more manageable than in the other provinces, so a motoring holiday is not quite the marathon exercise it can become in other provinces.

The other main cities are Moncton and Saint John in New Brunswick, Charlottetown Prince Edward Island (invariably abbreviated to PEI, which often comes out Pea-Eye) and St John's Newfoundland (pronounced Newf'nd-*land)*. These small cities have more charm than sophistication and are worth exploring on foot.

THE PEOPLE

There is a joke about an old-timer Newfoundland fisherman who boasts about how well travelled he is. 'So what did you think of the mainland?' he is asked. 'Oh I ain't ever been to the mainland, but I'se been everywhere else.' Although not every Maritimer is as home-loving as this, they tend to be neither very sophisticated nor cosmopolitan. But they are renowned for their easy going nature and gentleness and you can go for weeks without hearing a voice raised in anger.

The accents of Maritimers are the most distinctive in Canada. Whereas it is impossible to distinguish between a Vacouverite and a Torontonian, a Newfoundland accent can be detected immediately. And because of the lack of mobility, communities within the same province have preserved different kinds of speech. In southern Newfoundland, there is a definite Irish lilt, whereas the north is more English west country. Plus the locals have a vivid homespun vocabulary (such as 'yaffle' meaning a pile of dried fish) and more than their fair share of raconteurs. Try to make the acquaintance of one of these old salts in a local beer parlour, or lounge around the docks when the fishing boats are putting in.

The cultural influence of the British Isles remains surprisingly strong. On Cape Breton Island in Nova Scotia, for example, there are still Gaelic-speaking descendants of Scottish settlers, a Gaelic college and Highland festivals featuring Scottish dancing and bagpipe playing. In fact songs and dances are still performed more spontaneously in this part of Canada than in any other.

There is also a large French population, especially in New Brunswick, where over a third of the population is French. Instead of being concentrated in one part of the province, French communities are scattered among English-speaking ones. So you must exercise a little tact when addressing a townsperson for the first time. These French people are descendants of the early traders and settlers called Acadians. When the land of Acadia (now the Maritimes) was won by England at the beginning of the 18th century, over half the 10,000 French-speaking Acadians were expelled; some went to Quebec, others to New Orleans but many soon returned to the Maritimes. If you are in the area during August, try to attend the Acadian Festival in Caraquet when, among other traditions, there is the Blessing of the Fleet, just as in New Orleans.

CLIMATE

The sea is never far away and provides cool breezes in summer and a moderating effect in winter from the warm currents. PEI has the mildest temperatures. Whereas summer highs are in the range 60°F to 75°F/16°C to

24°C, winter temperatures hover around 32°F/0°C. The snow has usually disappeared by April and medium weight clothing is appropriate thereafter. The Maritimes are comparatively rainy, with some rainfall on nearly half the days of the year and also windier and foggier (especially Newfoundland) than other parts of the country.

Getting Around

Air. The main gateway is Halifax, with good connections from elsewhere in Canada, the USA and Europe. The US feeder airline Northwest Airlink also has a busy network serving Saint John, Moncton and Fredericton in New Brunswick, plus Charlottetown in PEI.

Bus. Because of the low density of population in the Maritimes, the coach services are fairly sparse. Greyhound does not operate in the provinces at all, although the Ameripass is valid in Nova Scotia and New Brunswick but not on ferries or on the two island provinces of Newfoundland and PEI. Details of services are given in the provincial sections which follow this general introduction.

Train. VIA Rail's *Atlantic* leaves Halifax daily at about mid-day for Montréal where it arrives the following morning (cost $90 single). There are daily services between Halifax, Saint John and Fredericton. There are no railway lines on PEI nor on Newfoundland where the only services are on coaches.

Driving. The Trans-Canada Highway links Rivìere-du-Loup in Quebec with Fredericton (the capital of New Brunswick), Saint John, Moncton, Truro and North Sydney on Cape Breton Island. It even continues on PEI and Newfoundland. Although this is the fastest route, it is just two lanes wide for most of its distance. The minor roads are the ones which take you into the picturesque backwaters, though some become difficult to negotiate in muddy conditions. Coastal roads are invariably scenic, in particular the Cabot Trail which runs through Cape Breton Highlands National Park NS. This route is also popular with cyclists. Cars may be hired in any of the cities, though the big firms may be booked up in July and August.

Speed limits are similar to those in the rest of Canada: 100 km/h (62 mph) or 90 km/hr (55 mph) on the Trans-Canada, 80 km/h (50 mph) on other highways and 50 km/h (30 mph) in towns. There is less temptation to speed on these roads than on their much straighter and more boring counterparts in the Prairies. The RCMP patrol the highway and impose minimum fines of $50 for speeding. On the back roads, many of which are gravel, you will have to proceed slowly.

Ferries. In addition to the Canadian ferry between the mainland and the PEI or Newfoundland, there are Marine Atlantic car ferries from Bar Harbor and Portland Maine to Yarmouth Nova Scotia.

For schedules and prices write to Marine Atlantic, 100 Cameron St, Moncton, New Brunswick E1C 5Y6. There are also other ferry routes in the Atlantic provinces, which are marked on the standard road map of Canada.

Accommodation

Bed and breakfast at a reasonable price has flourished in the Maritimes and there is a large choice of charming, inexpensive private homes. You can find double rooms in quiet rural areas for as little as $30, but

GST and provincial sales taxes can add 20% to the total. Self-catering cottages sleeping up to four are priced at about $200 per week. The one drawback of staying in country inns or as guests on farms is that it would be hard to manage without a car, since the rest of civilisation is usually miles away.

Since tourism is such an important business, there is an abundance of facilities with the notable exception of Newfoundland, where prices tend to be higher. Even with a ratio of four visitors to every inhabitant (as there is on PEI), there seem to be enough hotels, bed and breakfasts, campsites, self-catering cottages and inns to go round. Campsites for $9 per tent represent especially good value, and are often near beaches and other recreation facilities. The provincial tourist offices publish detailed lists of campsites.

Eating and Drinking

Fishing is the primary industry in the region and eating seafood is a primary occupation of both locals and visitors. You will notice piles of lobster traps in most coastal towns and lobster appears on most menus. There are also oysters (watch for oyster-shucking contests), scallops, mussels, quahaugs (an Indian word for a kind of round clam), Atlantic salmon and many others. There are plenty of seafood shops from which you can buy shellfish very cheaply to barbecue or cook yourself. An even more enjoyable way to eat the local produce is to attend a 'lobster supper'. These are organized periodically by local communities and held in church halls. Members of the local parish provide all the trimmings. Also watch for strawberry socials in the summer, and also maple syrup festivals in March and April during the sugaring-off season, when the maple trees are tapped for their sap. Many of these local culinary events cost a pittance. Although potatoes are the most important crop on PEI, there are no potato festivals. Delicious blueberries abound near the New Brunswick/Nova Scotia border.

Inexpensive restaurant meals (e.g. under $4 in Nova Scotia) are exempt from provincial sales taxes.

Drinking. The staunch Protestant background of these provinces has resulted in licensing laws which are no more liberal than in other parts of Canada. Off-licences tend to close at 10pm on Fridays, 6pm on other nights. Taverns usually close at midnight, though in some tourist areas their licences may be extended. Cocktail lounges and clubs in cities normally stay open until 2am. The drinking age is 19 throughout the region except in PEI where it is 18. Watch for Moosehead beer brewed in New Brunswick and Nova Scotia, as well as some newer and smaller breweries which brew German-style lagers free of preservatives and additives.

Exploring

With its early colonization and subsequent changes of ownership, the Atlantic region has a long and interesting history. Archaeologists have found Viking remains at the extreme northern tip of Newfoundland and dinosaur remains in western Nova Scotia where a dinosaur museum may soon open. Among other highlights are the Citadel in Halifax, the Fort at Louisberg and the Alexander Graham Bell Museum at Baddeck. You can visit any of the 21 National Historic Parks, ranging from reconstructed fortresses to ruined lighthouses. Contact the Atlantic regional office of Parks Canada for details: Historic Properties, Upper Water St, Halifax B3J 1S9; (902) 426-3436.

Ask tourist offices for lists of events. Look for Gaelic festivities, fiddle contests, country fairs, water regattas, etc. One notable event is the annual Antigonish Highland Games in early July.

NEW BRUNSWICK (NB)

The New Brunswick *Telegraph Journal* wears its view of the French-speaking people on its cover. The left-hand column is headed 'Toronto', with no regard paid to goings-on in Québec, even though the provinces are joined.

Plenty of flights serve Moncton and the capital Saint John, and the Atlantic Canada train line runs through them both. New Brunswick's only coach line is SMT (Eastern) in Saint John (506-658-6500). Both Moncton and Saint John are good bases for exploring the peaceful rural scenery of New Brunswick, which is rich in wildlife.

NOVA SCOTIA (NS)

Halifax, with a metropolitan population of just 277,000, is the largest city of the region and the commercial and cultural hub. Yet the city retains much of its attractive quaintness, because of its situation along seaside bays.

Arrival and Departure. *Air:* Air Canada, Canadian Airlines and Air Nova operate frequent flights from Toronto and Montréal to Halifax, the principal gateway. There are also international flights from London, Glasgow and Boston. The airport is 26 miles/42 km northeast of the city, a distance which can be covered in about 80 minutes on the airport limousine service (873-3525) for $8.

Bus: most services in Nova Scotia are mostly operated by Acadian Lines in Halifax (454-9321) with the service south from Halifax operated by MacKenzie Bus Lines in the nearby town of Bridgewater (543-2491).

Train: Halifax is served direct from Montreal almost daily, taking 20 hours. These trains pass through Moncton; some also call at Saint John.

Eating and Drinking. In the more expensive restaurants you can find some very unusual dishes. For example Newman's Restaurant in Annapolis Royal NS has been known to feature bear stew on the menu.

Help and Information. The area code for Nova Scotia is 902. To call the British Consulate in Halifax, dial 429-4230.

PRINCE EDWARD ISLAND (PEI)

Arrival and Departure. *Air:* the capital Charlottetown is linked with Halifax and Boston, with some flights also to Moncton and Toronto. The airport is on the outskirts of Charlottetown, bus no bus runs there.

Sea: The 45-minute crossing between Cape Tormentine NB and Borden PEI costs about $2.50 for foot passengers and $6.25 for cars. For information call 1-800-565-9411. Northumberland Ferries operates between Wood Islands PEI and Caribou NS takes 75 minutes; schedules and fares from 1-800-565-0201. It is not possible to reserve places on this service, but crossings are made frequently during the height of summer. The ferries stop altogether between December and April.

Getting Around. For the only public transport on PEI, contact the Island Transit Co-op in Charlottetown (892-6167) which operates only during the summer. The car hire desks at Charlottetown airport can offer competitive deals; ask each in turn for their rates. To rent a bicycle, try Red Roads Cycle Tours (628-6218). The office, on Peake's Wharf in Charlottetown (behind the Prince Edward Hotel) is open in summer from 7.30am to 8pm.

Accommodation. The island's top hotel is the Prince Edward by the waterfront in Charlottetown (566-2222). Sometimes it has special rates, e.g $99 double. The Inn on the Hill (894-8572), at the corner of University and Euston Streets, sometimes reduces its rates. In season, there are dozens of places doing bed and breakfast, or you can camp (mid-June to early September) and one of the many sites.

Eating and Drinking. One of the best restaurants in the Maritimes is The Gainsford, an unprepossessing but charming house at 104 Water Street, near the seafront in Charlottetown; try to book on 368-3840. Wash the meal down at the Claddagh Room, a splendid Irish pub at 131 Sydney St (892-9661). It has draught Murphy's stout and Tartan bitter, and good free entertainment. The downstairs area is also a good restaurant.

Exploring. *Anne of Green Gables* is a big attraction to the Maritimes — and to PEI in particular — is the novel by Maud Montgomery of a young woman growing up on the island in the early years of the 20th century. Controversy was caused by a recent proposal to put a picture of Anne Shirley, the red-headed heroine, on licence plates in the province. 'Does PEI have nothing more to offer than the fact that it is the setting for an utterly beaten to death work of questionable literary merit?' wrote one correspondent to the *Charlottetown Guardian*. Anne is fictional but the book is largely based upon the author's experiences. A trail takes you to several settings in the book, and to the places Maud Montgomery lived. Bright River, where the book begins, is in reality Hunter River. Avonlea, where Anne grows up, is really Cavendish, a village 25 miles/40km northwest of PEI's capital Charlottetown.

You can visit the Lucy Maud Montgomery Birthplace Museum (886-2596) at Clifton Corner in New London, across the bay from Cavendish. She was born here on 30 November 1874. The farmhouse where she was brought up no longer exists, but the house in Cavendish which inspired Green Gables has been restored and is open to visitors (672-2211). So too is Park Corner (436-7329), a house on Route 20 five miles/8km northwest of New London where Maud married. This has been converted into the Anne of Green Gables Museum. It opens from 9am to dusk in the months from June to September, admission $2.75. The grounds of the house run down past an old barn to Campbell's Pond, which the author described as the lake of shining waters.

The island has quite a substantial French-speaking Acadian community, centred on the Evangéline region. To meet them formally, contact l'Association touristique Evangéline, Box 12, Wellington, PEI C0B 2E0, or call 854-3131.

PEI's other claim to fame is that the Charlottetown Accord — the basis for Canada's new constitution — was signed here in 1992, even though it was rejected in the subsequent referendum.

Entertainment. Canada's most popular musical ever, *Anne of Green Gables* is performed in Charlottetown every summer. The local newspaper, *The Guardian* ('Covers Prince Edward Island Like The Dew') lists other events.

Help and Information. The area code for PEI is 902, the same as NS. Visitor Information Centres are scattered all over the island, with the main one at Oak Tree Place, University Avenue, Charlottetown. Another good one is the National Park Service office at Cavendish. PEI has toll-free numbers for enquiries: 1-800-565-7421 from within the Maritimes, 1-800-565-0267 from elswhere in North America. By post, write to Box 940, Charlottetown, PEI C1A 7M5.

NEWFOUNDLAND (NF)

The easternmost part of North America is something of a law unto itsel, even to the extent of being half-an-hour ahead of the rest of the Maritimes. A visit here is hard to organize, but can be rewarding. Those in search of social excitement should probably not bother.

Gander airport, a NATO air base on Goose Bay, was one of the regular refuelling stops on transatlantic flights, and some airlines from the old Socialist bloc — Russia and Cuba — still use it. If your starting point is not Havana or Moscow, however, you may have some difficulties reaching Newfoundland. Terratransport Roadcruiser Service (709-737-5900) is the only public transport in Newfoundland. It operates between St John's and Port aux Basques where the ferry from Nova Scotia docks (see below). The 560-mile/900 km journey through such places as Come-by-Chance takes 14 hours.

Bookings are essential on the daily crossing on the *MV Caribou* between North Sydney NS and Port-aux-Basques Newfoundland which is 600 miles/1000km from the capital St John's in the east. The trip takes five to six hours and costs about $65 for a car with two passengers. You can make reservations by calling toll free 1-800-565-9470 within the Maritimes, but you must collect your tickets two hours before the sailing. In the summer months only there is a thrice-weekly overnight service between North Sydney and Argentia, a town just 78 miles (130 km) from the capital St. John's, cutting out the long drive across the whole province; this trip costs $35 one way.

The area code for Newfoundland is 709. For the British Consulate in St John's, call 364-1200 or fax 364-3550.

The Great Outdoors

The wilderness in the Atlantic provinces is more manageable in scale than elsewhere, though there are still vast tracts too remote to be accessible. Except in Labrador, the little-visited mainland part of the province of Newfoundland, there are no mountains over 3,000 ft (900m). The first efforts at conservation in Canada were made in Nova Scotia in 1794 to protect grouse and black ducks.

All outdoor activities associated with the seaside are easy to join in. Whether you take scuba diving lessons, go clam-digging ashore or 'cod-jigging' at sea, swim on any of the supervised beaches or play frisbee, the miles of clean beaches and bracing ocean water should not be missed. Fishing outfittters are very easy to find. If you happen to be in Newfoundland in early July you can catch fish without any equipment during the 'caplin scull', when millions of smelt-like fish called caplin come ashore to spawn and can easily be caught with the bare hands. Cycling is especially recommended because of the relatively high number of back roads and the absence of mountains. There are hire facilities in most towns.

The Prairies

Manitoba   Saskatchewan   Alberta

Most visitors vacationing in Canada — indeed many Canadians — think of the Prairies as 'the land between the interesting places', i.e. the sights of eastern Canada and the Rockies. The bulk of Manitoba, Saskatchewan and Alberta, like Belgium or the Nullarbor Desert of Australia, is something to be crossed as quickly as possible. But the scenery and the people of the Prairies are such an essential part of Canada that it would be a shame to fly over and miss it completely — though walking or cycling would probably be taking things too far. The Prairies are best appreciated by train or car. The miles of wheatfields broken occasionally by a grain elevator or a domed Ukrainian church provide a pleasant contrast with the forests in the east and the mountains in the west. Because of the flatness of the terrain, you will begin to notice and appreciate the magnificent skies.

The main cities of Winnipeg, Regina, Saskatoon, Calgary and Edmonton are, frankly, not very interesting. Readers of *Business Traveller* magazine voted Winnipeg the most boring city in the world. Regina bore the name 'Pile o'Bones' until it was chosen as capital of Saskatchewan late in the 19th century, and renamed in a more dignified vein after Queen Victoria. As a rule Prairie cities are sprawling, crass and lacking in character.

A tour of the main cities is likely to be fairly boring, unless you happen to be interested in provincial legislative buildings or in the history of the Royal Canadian Mounted Police, whose pioneer activities are extolled in several museums. You would be better off leaving the Trans-Canada Highway and visiting some smaller towns. Get a list of events from the provincial tourist offices and seek out some of the rural centres where genuine prairie hospitality prevails. You can choose from the Canadian Open Wellington Boot Throwing Championship in Dugald Manitoba, the World Championship Gopher Derby in Eston Saskatchewan or the Cowpoop Patty Throwing Contest (dried dung tosses) at the Kindersley Goose Festival. Culture, in its traditional sense, is not much in evidence on the Prairies, but since this is cowboy country, there is no shortage of rodeos, whether it be the Canadian Firefighters Rodeo in Virden Manitoba, or the famous Calgary Stampede.

THE PEOPLE

Even by North American standards, the settlement of the Prairies took place very recently, within the last hundred years. Until then the land was shared (not always amicably) between the fur traders and the Indians. Many of the original furtrappers were French, who intermarried with Indians. Their descendants are called Metis and still form a substantial part of the population. There is a much higher proportion of native peoples living in the Prairies than in other parts of Canada. For example there are nearly 150 Indian reservations in Saskatchewan alone.

The land was primarily settled by the British and French, mainly Scottish crofters and French noblemen escaping republicanism and heavy taxation. They were joined by many other nationalities. There are many people of Ukrainian descent and numerous towns have a Ukrainian museum or cultural centre and celebrate Ukrainian festivals with food, entertainment and dancing. The largest Icelandic settlement outside Iceland is in Gimli, Manitoba. Icelanders arrived in the 1870s and still celebrate their heritage every August with food, theatre, poetry contests and music.

One of the most interesting groups are the Dukhobors, who arrived from Russia at the turn of the century. Because of their mystical beliefs and anarchist politics, they were expelled from Russia and with the help of Leo Tolstoy and English Quakers, moved to Saskatchewan, where their practices continue to cause conflicts with the Canadian government. Recently the community began to look for sites in Siberia in which to live, since they feel that Russia provides a more appropriate environment.

Several Prairie cities have ethnic festivals comparable to Caravan in Toronto, when national pavilions are set up around the city, and a 'passport' admits you to all the pavilions. There is Winnipeg's Folklorama in August, Saskatoon's Folkfest in early September and Regina's Mosaic in May. To give an idea of the range of cultural backgrounds of prairie folk, there is a radio station in Winnipeg (CKJS-810AM) which broadcasts in 18 languages from Filipino to Hebrew, Hungarian to Hindi.

CLIMATE

You wonder how the early fur traders and settlers, not to mention the Indians, survived the prairie winters. The provincial tourist offices emphasize the blue skies and sunshine which accompany their winters, but the fact remains that they can be unimaginably cold. Weather reports sometimes provide a measurement in seconds or minutes which lets you know how long it will take before exposed flesh freezes. Waiting five minutes for a bus in Regina or Calgary when it is 40 degrees below becomes an ordeal. The locals dress in down, fur and wool and seem to manage quite happily, moving between their heated homes, cars, offices and stores. Provided you have enough warm gear, you should be able to avoid frostbite.

There is one climatic aberration called the chinook, a warm wind which blows down from the mountains and can raise Calgary's temperature by 30 degrees in a few hours, melting the snow and giving people headaches. (According to the manufacturers of negative ion machines, the chinooks upset the ion balance dreadfully and are responsible for an increase in accidents, suicides and ill health; the solution is to acquire your own negative ion generator). This wind blew uncharacteristically often during the Winter Olympics so that there was much less snow than usual.

A better way of avoiding frostbite than waiting for a chinook is to visit in the summer. But then you will have to beware of sunstroke. The highest temperature in Canada was recorded one year at Regina, 110F/43C. During the summer months (especially July) it is quite usual for the Prairies to get over 300 hours of sunshine in a month, i.e. over 10 hours a day on average. Most motels are air-conditioned, as are the trains. If you are driving, roll down the windows and keep going; air-conditioning in hire cars adds $6 a day to the rental charges. You will not need to worry about sweltering in a traffic jam. Neither do you need to worry about rain, since the Prairies on the whole are very dry. The occasional thunder storm brings some relief from the heat and makes for exciting skies. Summers are so hot and dry that forest fires are a real danger, so be very careful with campfires and heed fire warnings on the radio.

Air. In addition to Air Canada, there are many regional airlines with such picturesque names as Calm Air International and Frontier Airlines which provide frequent services to communities, some of them quite remote, throughout the provinces. There are numerous fly-in lodges in the northern prairies mainly for keen hunters and fishermen. Services are good among the principal Prairie cities. There are, for example, five Air Canada flights a day from Winnipeg to Calgary.

Bus. There are plenty of Greyhound services connecting the Prairie cities as well as more local bus lines serving smaller communities.

> *Regina:* 2041 Hamilton St (306-664-5711).
> *Saskatoon:* 50-23rd St E (306-664-5711).
> *Calgary:* 850-16 St SW (403-265-9111).
> *Edmonton:* 10324-103rd St (403-421-4211).

There are roughly three trans-Canada Greyhounds a day in either direction connecting Winnipeg, Regina and Calgary. The Calgary-Regina trip takes 12 hours, and then it is a further 8 hours to Winnipeg. To get to the northerly cities of Saskatoon and Edmonton which are on the Yellowhead Highway rather than the Trans-Canada, you will have to change. Some sample single fares are Winnipeg to Calgary $80. Winnipeg to Regina $40, Regina to Saskatoon $18, Calgary to Banff $9.

Train. The trans-Canada route is via Winnipeg, Jasper, Edmonton and Saskatoon, so travellers to Regina must transfer to a bus at Saskatoon and Calgary-bound visitors should change at Edmonton. The *Canadian* runs three times each week from Vancouver to Toronto; you can connect to other trains for Prince Rupert at Jasper and Churchill or Lynn Lake at Winnipeg.

Driving. Because of the unendingly flat terrain, the Trans-Canada Highway goes in a seemingly straight line for hundreds of miles. The more northerly Yellowhead Highway is less travelled and just as uninteresting. The construction of some of the highways in the north of the provinces presented very difficult engineering problems; there is a 10 mile/16 kilometre stretch on Provincial Trunk Highway 10 in Manitoba which had to be built over floating muskeg, a Cree Indian word for swamp.

The rules of the road do not differ very much from province to province. The maximum speed limit in Alberta is 100 km/hr (62 mph) by day and 80 km/hr (50 mph) by night; in Saskatchewan it is 80 km/hr and in Manitoba 90 km/hr (56 mph). Littering in Saskatchewan is subject to a $200 fine.

Renting a vehicle is cheaper than in Toronto or Vancouver. Many people fly or take the train as far as Calgary and then rent a car or camper to explore Banff and the mountains.

Accommodation

Except in Banff and Calgary, accommodation in the Prairies is much cheaper than it is in Vancouver or Toronto. Double rooms in downtown hotels in Winnipeg or Saskatoon start as low as $20 a double. And the price of some motels is similarly low. Even in Banff you may be able to find accommodation in private homes for $30 a double (for example 521 Buffalo St). If you are on the back roads, you will find some great bargains like the Rama Hotel in Rama Saskatchewan (population 170) where the five so-called 'non-modern' rooms cost between $9 and $12. All the tourist offices publish complete lists.

Alberta is well supplied with 17 youth hostels as opposed to two in Manitoba and four in Saskatchewan. Prices range from $4-$12 per night. Many of the Alberta hotels in the mountains are humble buildings with wood-burning stoves and few amenities. Even in summer the temperatures can drop at night and so down-filled sleeping bags are a necessity, as is food since there will be no shops or restaurants nearby.

Because of the hot dry summers and the many camping facilities available, camping is very popular. If you are crossing the country on a tight budget, your best option is to make use of the many free campsites. These are free of charge either because they are roadside stop-over places with few amenities, or because they are operated by a generous municipality. There is a fee if you want to camp in a provincial park, ranging from $4-$9, after you have paid the $2 or $3 park admission fee. You can also rent cottages in provincial parks from $18 a night for two people.

Since so much of the economy of the Prairies is based on agriculture, farm and ranch holidays are widely available. Although you are not obliged to help with the chores, there is not much else to do. Prices are from £30-$45 per person per day including all meals. Contact addresses are: Alberta Country Vacation Association, CMH Travel, 217 Bear St, Banff (762-4531); Saskatchewan Farm Vacation Association, Box 24, Bateman (648-3530); and Manitoba Farm Vacations, 525 Kylemore, Winnipeg (475-6624).

Eating and Drinking

Dining on the Prairies is not for the sophisticated. Stick to steaks and you will not be disappointed. Pancake breakfasts are often available and barbecues are popular. Try to sample a berry pie made from indigenous Saskatoon berries.

The licensing hours in the Prairie provinces are normally 9am-1am with some exceptions, such as beer parlours in Manitoba closing at midnight and cocktail lounges in Alberta staying open until 2am. Like the American Midwest, the Canadian Prairies are conservative. Beer and wine advertising was legalised in Saskatchewan less than a decade ago.

The minimum drinking age is 18 in Alberta and Manitoba, and 19 in Saskatchewan. The only beers served are standard Canadian beers. You will not be subsidizing the provincial government when you eat or drink in Alberta, since there is no sales tax in the province — a legacy of their oil boom.

If you are a confirmed urbanite who loves theatre, opera and fine dining, the Prairies would not be an obvious destination for you. Most of the popular music is country and western, though there is a large and excellent Folk Festival held in Winnipeg every July. The cinema listings for a large city like Calgary are very limited, though the University does have an arts cinema series. Your average Prairie native's idea of a good time is certainly not the ballet; it is more likely to be golf, curling (a tremendously popular sport) or watching *Hockey Night In Canada* on TV. You can obtain a free calendar of rodeo events from the Canadian Professional Rodeo Association, 223-2166 27 Ave NE, Calgary, Alberta T2E 7A6.

WINNIPEG

What can one say about the city voted most boring in the world? The Air Canada office is in the Richardson Building at 355 Portage Avenue, and the ride to the airport — just four miles away - costs $1.50. The bus terminal is at 487 Portage Avenue (204-775-8301). If you want or need to stay, the Guest House International is at 168 Maryland St, Winnipeg (204-722-1272).

CALGARY

Sometimes called Cowtown, is the least aesthetically pleasing of all the Prairie cities, and seems to be designed primarily with the car park in mind, as though there is no such thing as a pedestrian. There could hardly be a euphemism more extreme than calling the inescapable expressways of Calgary 'trails', but you will find a Banff Trail, a Bow Trail and so on. Even the frenzy of improvements which preceded the 1988 Winter Olympics could not alter the city's (non)-character. It is now hoped that tourism will replace oil as the next great boom in the economy, though this seems over-optimistic.

The Calgary Stampede features some of the biggest, toughest rodeo events in the world. Among the highlights are the Chuckwagon Races, when four-horse buggies pound around a track. During the ten days of the Stampede, which takes place every July, Calgary becomes very crowded attracting 100,000 people a day, and expensive, so if you hope to see this event, try to book accommodation and tickets ahead, or else arrive as far in advance as possible; write to PO Box 1060, Station M, Calgary T2P 2K8 for information (403-261-0101). Tickets go on sale months ahead and cost between $10 and $50.

EDMONTON

This city is one of the most northerly in the world, and the permeating frontier spirit makes it more interesting than some of the other Prairie cities. Among the 620,000 people are substantial Ukrainian and Asian communities. Edmonton is 2200 feet/668m above sea level, which exacerbates the cold in winter. Summer is the best time to be in Edmonton, with festivals running almost solidly. Late June to early July is the Jazz Festival (433-3333 for information), running simultaneously with The Works, a 'visual arts celebration. In mid-July the Streets Entertainers' Festival takes over. Edmonton Klondike Days is a multi-purpose festival loosely celebrating the Gold Rush days.

August sees, in quick succession: Edmonton Heritage Festival, reflecting the multi-cultural wealth of the city; Folk Music Festival; Fringe Theatre; Country Music; and the Canadian Derby horseracing meeting.

Arrival and Departure. The International Airport is 18 miles/29km south of the city centre. Call 890-8382 for information. The Grey Goose Airporter service shuttles between the airport and the city bus station, calling at the main hotels. The fare is $12 one way, $20 return. For bookings on the return leg to the airport, call 463-7520. Be warned that the circuitous trip can easily take an hour, and sharing a taxi ($35 one way) may be a better option. The Municipal Airport (428-3991) is only two miles/3km north of downtown.

The Greyhound Depot is central, at the corner of 103 Avenue and 103 St. VIA Rail trains depart from the station at 104 Avenue and 101 St.

The Alberta Automobile Association is at 109 St and Kingsway Avenue (474-8601). Call 471-6056 for road reports.

Getting Around. Edmonton's excellent public transport system consists of buses, trolleybuses and the single line Light Rail Transit underground. The standard fare is $1.35, with free transfers, payable in coins only — no change given. The Downtown Information Centre is at 100a St and Jasper Avenue, or call 421-4636 between 8.30am and 4.30pm.

Accommodation. Close to the airport, try the Ellerslie Motel (403-988-6406), which has cheap rooms and a free suttle service. The YMCA is adjacent to the Hilton Hotel on 102a Avenue at 101 St. Moving upmarket, the Mayfair Hotel on Jasper Avenue between 107 and 108 Streets (423-1650, or 1-800-463-7666) is comfortable and good value.

Exploring. Get an overview of the city from the top floor of the Alberta Government Telephones (AGT) building at 10020 100 St— admission is only 50c. Call 493-3333 for opening hours.

Edmonton's greatest claim to fame until 1992 was as location of the biggest shopping mall in the world. The Mall of America in Minneapolis now claims to have outstripped the West Edmonton Mall, but Canada's is still impressive. Covering 48 city blocks, it has hundreds of stores, 110 places to eat, an indoor golf course, a water park, the world's largest indoor amusement park and an exact replica of the *Santa Maria*, the vessel used by Columbus for his first transatlantic voyage. Shops open at 10am (noon on Sundays) and entertainment carries on until late. As you travel west, it begins at 170 St and 87 Avenue.

Fort Edmonton Park is due south of the Mall. It recreates life as it was for the early fur traders. Also south of the river, but much closer to downtown (at 9626 96a St), the Muttart Conservatory comprises four huge glass pyramids, each with a different environment. Studying the flora in the Arid House in the depths of winter is thoroughly confusing. Call 483-5511 for prices and opening times.

The Alberta Legislature is the most imposing building this side of the

Rockies. Inside, the elegant dome towers above a marbled floor imported from Italy, with trimmings of mahogany from Central America. Tours operate daily: from Monday to Friday 9am-6pm, and noon-4pm at weekends.

The Edmonton Space and Science Centre looks like a landed spacecraft. All sorts of hands-on exhibits inform and entertain. It is located at the corner of 111 Avenue and 142 Street (451-7722). Opening hours are 10am-11pm daily from late June to mid-September

A less bewildering place to shop is south of the river from downtown Edmonton. Restored buildings along Whyte Avenue (82 Avenue) between 99 and 109 Streets are the core of the Old Strathcona district. Attractions include the Telephone Historical Information Centre (10am-4pm from Monday to Friday, noon-4pm on Saturdays, closed Sundays, admission $1), the C&E Railway Museum and the Model and Toy Museum. Do not be misled by the tourist publicity into thinking this is a particularly quaint or historic area, but it has some interesting shops (including one selling only Scottish memorabilia) and restaurants.

Help and Information. The area code for Edmonton is 403.

The Visitor Information Centre — reached through the West Door of the Convention Centre at 9797 Jasper Avenue — provides top-quality maps and information. The information centre in the arrivals area of the airport is open 6.30am-10.30pm daily.

American Express is in the Metropolitan Plaza, 10305 Jasper Avenue (421-0608), and in The Bay at West Edmonton Mall (444-1706).

The Great Outdoors

As you move west from Edmonton, the attractions of the country increase. Skiing is being heavily promoted by tourist officials following the Winter Olympics. A sample package costing £250 might include a week's car hire, accommodation and lift pass to several areas such as Lake Louise, Sunshine and Norquay. Hiking remains as popular as ever. Calgarians who find themselves apologising for their city invariably finish by saying 'But it's so close to the mountains'. Although people in Saskatchewan or Manitoba are not very close to mountains, they have taken up cross-country skiing with a vengeance. There are thousands of parks in all three provinces providing the whole range of recreational opportunities from windsurfing to guided nature walks. For example try to visit Oak Hammock Marsh Wildlife Park in Manitoba where thousands of migrating snow geese may be seen in spring and fall.

Banff is by far the most popular resort in Canada, though it is remarkably small and unpretentious (though overpriced). Banff National Park was the first in Canada opened 1887. Jasper, 177 miles/287 km north of Banff is slightly less crowded in the high summer and winter seasons, and in an even more beautiful setting. Banff and Jasper are located inside adjacent national parks, offering hundreds of kilometres of hiking trails and camping facilities both primitive and luxurious. Obviously, such popular tourist destinations get filled up so book ahead or be prepared to spend some time looking for accommoation. There is a privately operated room reservation service operated by Summit Vacations Ltd of Banff (762-5561) and by Take-a-Break Tours Ltd in Jasper (852-5665). Hostelling is probably a better bet.

Vancouver and British Columbia

Confusingly, the city of Vancouver (population 1,300,000) is not on Vancouver Island, but on the mainland. (The much smaller city of Victoria is the main city on Vancouver Island and the capital of British Columbia). The popular image of the west coast is that it is more 'laid-back' than the rest of Canada, that the inhabitants are more willing to experiment with alternative lifestyles. Vancouver is to Canada what San Francisco is to the States. This may not be immediately apparent if you find yourself caught in a rush hour traffic jam on one of the bridges leading to the eastern bedroom communities, surrounded by impatient motorists in business suits. However, a stroll along one of the city's beaches on a sunny day will give you a different impression. It is rewarding to mosey around the streets of Vancouver, sampling the food, music and local atmosphere, to see for yourself whether Vancouverites are as unhurried, tolerant and wholesome as they like to think.

It is more likely to be the scenery than the sociology which attracts you to Vancouver and to British Columbia generally. The forests and mountains for which Canada is so justly famous are easily accessible from the cities of BC. Just a 20 minute drive from downtown Vancouver takes you to the bottom of Grouse Mountain (though there are few grouse), from whence you take a cable car to the top for excellent skiing. Not surprisingly, there is a strong emphasis on outdoor recreation among British Columbians. Wilderness camping, skiing and watersports are all the rage, and you should try to arrange at least one expedition outside the city to experience the rugged terrain. Millions of acres of the province are protected as provincial or national parkland, with trails and campsites.

For the serious adventurer, BC offers intriguing possibilities. The inaccessible and thinly populated north of the province near the Yukon border is a land of unexplored mountains, a place where it is possible for modestly equipped amateur mountaineers to be dropped by a bush pilot in a remote area of the northern Rockies, to go hiking, then successfully submit suggestions for new place names to the Geographical Place Names Committee in Ottawa. Another epic trip which is possible now that the road along the east coast of Vancouver Island has been completed is to cycle its complete length, about 300 miles/500 km.

THE PEOPLE

The citizens of Vancouver are not as ethnically mixed as in Toronto or Montréal. The most prominent racial minority are the Chinese who are concentrated in North America's second largest Chinatown along W Pender St between Abbott and Gore Streets. A few blocks north, there is a smaller but thriving Japanese community. There is also a relatively large (for North America) number of Indians, mostly sikhs.

The alternative lifestyle exerts a great deal of influence in Vancouver and environs, and a large number of unconventional young people were attracted here during the 1970s because of its freer atmosphere. Watch out for some of their more amusing excesses; some expensive alder firewood was advertised as being 'hand hewn by people in the Gulf Islands wearing only natural fibre clothing'. Look for the free newspaper *Common Ground,* which is an amusing source of information on such activities.

Making Friends. With two major universities (the University of British Columbia known as UBC and Simon Fraser), there are plenty of students around. If you want to meet people (and eat cheaply while you are at it) visit the UBC cafeterias open to visitors out of term (May to August). Try the Pit in the Student Union Building, which is the student pub. Another area to find pubs and cafes frequented by students is Kitsilano, where the youth hostel is located.

CLIMATE

By Canadian standards, the west coast has a relatively tame climate. Victoria — just across the water from Vancouver — is the only provincial capital in Canada to have a January mean temperature above freezing, with almost no snow fall. Houses in Vancouver are not as ruggedly built as they are in the rest of Canada; they do not come automatically equipped with double glazing and thick insulation. Although over 20in/51cm of snow are measured in an average winter, it rarely stays on the ground, and the usual winter business of shovelling and putting on snow tyres is not necessary. But there are usually one or two sudden cold spells and every winter a few car owners, who have rashly neglected to use anti-freeze, find their engine blocks have cracked.

Summer temperatures are very pleasant along the coast. The blistering heat experienced in the interior of the country is moderated by the sea to create a potentially ideal climate. That is the good news. The bad news is that it rains a lot, precipitation falling on nearly half the days of the year. Most of the rain falls in the winter, but it is quite possible to have a solid week of rain during the summer. That may be your cue to flee to the dry interior of the province where temperatures regularly soar into the 90s (30c). Once you get past the first mountain range (the Coastal Range) most of the precipitation has been off-loaded, and if you continue into the next valley, you can even find a patch of genuine desert. But on a sparkling sunny day in Vancouver, fleeing will be the last thing on your mind.

ARRIVAL AND DEPARTURE

Air. The approach into Vancouver is very dramatic. After flying over unrelievedly mountainous terrain, you suddenly swoop down over the sea and land on an island. Vancouver International Airport is located on Sea Island, about 8km (5 miles) south of the city on Granville St. The airport is modern and efficient. Luggage trolleys are freely available.

The Airport Express bus (273-9023), travels between the airport and downtown every 15 minutes between 6.15am and 10.30pm, then at 11pm and 2.15am. The fare is $8.25 one-way, $14 return. The best place to get off for the city centre is the Hotel Vancouver at 900 West Georgia. Other airport services are operated by Perimeter Transport (261-2299). The cheapest way into downtown is to take a city bus from the US departure level to 60th and Granville and then transfer to a bus going downtown; the transfer ticket costs $1.25.

Canadian Airlines, Wardair and Air Canada operate services between Vancouver and most cities in Canada and around the province. The VisitUSA fare to Calgary, for example, is $61. The one way fare between Vancouver and Kelowna in the Okanagan Valley is $120 and between Vancouver and Prince Rupert $175. Aircraft operated by Air BC serve smaller centres up the coast (688-5515). Travel CUTS has an office at 1516 Duranleau St (687-6933). For destinations outside Canada, it may well be worth flying from Seattle, a couple of hours south. Belwood Travel (800-284-6366) is one of several agents in Vancouver offering 'cross-border bargains'.

Bus. The Greyhound Terminal is at 150 Dunsmuir St, at the corner of Cambie. Phone 662-3222 between 7am and 11.30pm for information about times and prices. There are many daily departures for Victoria operated by Pacific Coach Lines (737 Humboldt St, Victoria; 662-8074) via the Tsawwassen Ferry Terminal. The trip from Vancouver to Victoria costs $17.50 including the ferry and takes about four hours altogether. Maverick Coachlines (255-1171) operate a through service from Vancouver to Nanaimo on Vancouver Island.

There are four Greyhound buses a day to Banff, and from thence across Canada. The ride to Banff is a wonderfully scenic trip. It lasts 16 hours and costs $85 one way, . If you want to visit towns in the Okanagan Valley, you will have to rely on Greyhound since there is no train line. Six daily Greyhound services run in each direction between Seattle and Vancouver; the express journey takes just three hours. Quick Shuttle also runs a service — call 526-2836.

Train. There are two stations in Vancouver. The VIA Station is at 1150 Station Street at Terminal Avenue; call 1-800-561-8630. The BC Railways Station from which you catch trains to northern BC terminating at Prince George is at 1311 West First Street in North Vancouver (631-350). The Canadian Pacific trans-Canada railway was completed to Vancouver in 1889. You really get the feeling in the VIA Station of being at the edge of a continent, since there are just three departures and three arrivals each week.

The *Canadian* service for Toronto via Jasper leaves on Monday, Thursday and Saturday at 9pm, with the inbound service arriving at 9.30am on Friday, Sunday and Tuesday. The trip to or from Toronto takes 70 hours.

One interesting day trip can be made from Vancouver starts at the North Vancouver Station, a six-hour return excursion by steam train (the *Royal Hudson*) to the logging town of Squamish, which costs about $12 (phone 688-7246 for details), or you can take a combined train and boat excursion for $42.

Driving. If you are approaching from the US border, just 24 miles/40 km from downtown Vancouver, you will be on Highway 99 which turns into Oak Street running parallel to Granville Street, which in turn will take you right across town to North Vancouver, with a few signposted deviations. If you are approaching from the east you will be on the Trans-Canada (Highway 1) which turns into Hastings Street. Since the traffic in the downtown area can get very congested at rush hour, try to avoid those times of the day.

Some discount car rental addresses in Vancouver: Rent-a-Wreck, 350 Robson St (688-0001) plus 12 other locations; McKee's U-Drive Campers, 19335 Number 10 Highway (533-2360). Battered cars from Rent-a-Wreck cost from $35, and a camper van will cost four times as much. Gas costs are in the region of 50c per litre ($2.27 a gallon). There are no toll bridges or roads in BC though highway ferries in the interior of the province charge fees. All drivers must wear seatbelts.

In view of the expense of motoring you may prefer to share a ride. Hitch-hiking is common throughout the province and is uaully very successful, even to remote places. Check in the *Yellow Pages* for drive-away companies. One is Auto Delivery, 1080a Marine Drive, North Vancouver (985-0936). The most common destinations are Calgary, Toronto and Los Angeles.

Recorded reports on highway conditions in BC may be heard on 525-4997.

Ferry. You may want to make the journey between the US and British Columbia by ferry. The ferry service from Seattle to Victoria runs daily in summer ($61 one way, $85 return); the trip takes about four hours. Contact Victoria Clipper (1-382-8100 from Vancouver) for details. Year-round services to Victoria on the *Black Ball* run from Port Angeles in northern Washington state. There are three or four ferries a day during the summer. A car with driver pays US$24 while a passenger with bicycle pays US$6; contact Blacball (1-386-2202).

Ferry information may be obtained from BC Ferries on 669-1211 or for recorded schedules 685-1021. Fifteen ferries a day operate to Vancouver Island during the summer on two routes: between Tsawwassen and Swartz Bay 18 miles/30 km outside Victoria, and between Horseshoe Bay in West Vancouver and Nanaimo.

During high summer both routes are busy and if you have a car, you may have to queue for several hours. The cost is $25.50 for car and a driver, and $5.50 for foot passengers only. Both routes are very scenic looking back towards the Sunshine Coast or threading among the Gulf Islands. Sunrise is a particularly fine time to make the trip, and also the ferries are less crowded early in the morning. There is a ferry from Port Hardy at the northern end of Vancouver Island to Prince Rupert in northern BC ($48 per person one way, $100 for a car). If you want to continue to Alaska, you must switch onto the Alaska State Ferry System at Prince Rupert (see *Alaska*).

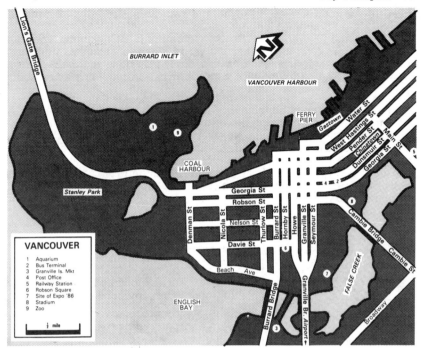

CITY TRANSPORT

Because all of Vancouver's traffic must be funnelled across a handful of bridges, road congestion can be terrible. The Skytrain system — a part elevated, part surface, part underground railway — is the best way to get around.

Car. Drivers should watch the illuminated signs on the Lion's Gate Bridge, since they indicate changes in the direction of the middle lane to accommodate the flow of traffic. Also listen to Radio CHQM which gives rush hour traffic reports. There is an elaborate one-way system on roads which makes navigation difficult. Together with the great pressure on parking spaces, you are well advised to use the public transport system.

Public Transport. The network of buses, Skytrain and the SeaBus to the north shore is fully integrated. Off-peak fares are excellent value. Between 9.30am and 3pm, and after 6.30pm, a flat fare of $1.35 allows travel on all buses, the SeaBus and Skytrain. In peak hours, fares for longer journeys are $2 or $2.75. A free bus shuttles Robson and Chinatown.

Information on all public transport on the lower mainland is available on 261-5100 or you can buy a *Transit Guide* for $1.25 from newsagents. The fare must be paid in exact change when you board and preferably with coins not bills. The trip by seabus across the Burrard Inlet between North Vancouver and downtown takes just 12 minutes, but does permit you a new view of the city and is worth doing even if you have no real reason to go over to the North Shore. You catch the seabus, which departs every 15 or 30 minutes depending on the time of day, from the bottom of Granville

Street. It is also picturesque at night, and you can pretend (for 12 minutes) that you are on a moonlit harbour cruise.

To get to the University of British Columbia (UBC) campus, take bus number 10 from Granville Street. To get to Kitsilano, take bus number 4 from Granville to Jericho Park. A few buses run along the main arteries (Granville, Georgia, Hastings) through the night. Ordinary buses stop about 1am.

Cycling. City cycling is popular in Vancouver, though it can be both hilly and smelly. An obvious cycling destination is Stanley Park, the largest downtown 'wilderness' park in North America. Just opposite the bus loop on Chilco Street inside the park is a bicycle rental shop (681-5581) which charges between $5 and $9 an hour. You will have to leave an additional deposit of $30 plus identification. Bike rentals are also available from Dunbar Cycles, 4219 Dunbar Street (224-2116) and Bayshore Bicycles, 745 Denman St (688-2453). The Bicycling Association of BC has an information hotline on 731-7433.

You can't do better than to use the provincial tourist office's *Accommodations* brochure. It contains details, including prices, of every sort of lodging from houseboats to hotels. The provincial guest tax is 8%.

Hotels. The cheapest hotels can be found in Chinatown around Main and Hastings. In Chinatown, prices can sink as low as $30 for a double but you will be getting no more than you pay for. A few blocks away from Chinatown, try the St Regis Hotel (corner of Dunsmuir and Seymour; 681-1135) or the Dufferin Hotel (900 Seymour; 683-4251). There is also the Niagara (435 W Pender; 688-7574), the Kingston (757 Richards; 684-9024) and the Buchan (1906 Haro Street; 685-5354) just a few steps from Stanley Park. Vincent's Guest House (1741 Grant St, 254-7462) has dorm beds for $10, singles for $20 and doubles $25.

Some of the sleazier establishments rent only by the week ($70 and up). If you do intend to stay in the city for more than a week, it is always worth asking about a discount. Your chances at successful bargaining will be diminished in high summer when there is a shortage of hotel accommodation. Try to book ahead. The Greater Vancouver Convention Bureau (Royal Centre, 1600-1055 West Georgia, 683-2772) runs an accommodation reservation service.

Motels. Motels will cost between $35 and $60 a double. Drive along Hastings East around Exhibition Park, along the Kingsway to Burnaby (the best bet) or along Marine Drive in North Vancouver.

Bed & Breakfast. For more upmarket places to stay, try the establishments listed in *Town and Country Bed & Breakfast* in BC which you can browse through in any Vancouver bookshop. You can try one of the following agencies:

A Home Away from Home: 873-4888
Best Canadian Bed & Breakfast: 738-7207
Old English: 986-5069
Town and Country: 731-5942
Westway: 273-8293

Alternatively try Elsa Schamis in Kitsilano (224-1695) or Lillian Feist (873-0842).

Hostels. Vincent's Backpackers Hostel at 927 Main St (682-2441 or 254-7462) is highly recommended: it has no curfew, free coffee, a central location (close to bus and train stations) and a good atmosphere. You could also try the new Harborfront Hostel at 209 Heatley Avenue (254-0733). The advantage of this place is that rooms for couples ($35) and families are available (a bed in a shared room costs $15) and that is has a comfortable, cosy feel; the disadvantage is that it isn't a brilliant area. The 'official' youth hostel is in the students and bohemian area known as Kitsilano, located on English Bay between downtown and the UBC campus. It costs members $12.50 and non-members $18. Bus number 4 from Granville to Jericho Park stops at Discovery Street, then a ten minute walk. The hostel phone number is 224-3208.

YMCA. The YMCA at 955 Burrard (681-0221) accepts both men and women and charges $23 single. The YWCA further north on Burrard at number 580 (662-8188683-2531) has singles for $31 plus tax and no more dorm beds.

University Residences. Both universities offer summer accommodation to visitors. UBC, about 7km from downtown, opens its enormous Walter Gage Residence from early May to late August (822-1010). There are considerable discounts for students e.g. $20 for a single rather than $28. Ask about availability in other residences on campus, e.g. Place Vanier is only $19. Even better is the nearby Vancouver School of Technology (228-9031) where the spartan rooms are yet cheaper. The Simon Fraser University campus is not as convenient, but it is also strikingly situated, 12 miles/20 km east of downtown Vancouver on Burnaby Mountain. Beds may be available for as little as $12 between June and August. Ring 291-4201 for details.

Camping. If you do have your own vehicle you may prefer to stay in a campground rather than in a motel. There are two campsites within range of Vancouver. Capilano Travel Trailer Park, 295 Tomahawk Avenue in West Vancouver (987-4722) and Timberland Motel and Campground, 3418 King George VI Highway in Surrey (531-1033). The cost of a site will be between $8 and $15 with access to whatever facilities are available, usually showers and launderette.

Longer Term. There are three main areas for longer term accommodation: the West End bordering Stanley Park (which is said to be the most densely populated three square miles in North America), the large East End east of downtown, and Kitsilano near the beach of the same name. You can visit the high rise apartment blocks in the West End to find vacancy notices posted in the entrance halls. The best place to head in the East End is on Commercial Drive around 1st Avenue (the site of Little Italy). Among the alternative establishments are Octopus Books at 1146 Commercial and Sweet Cherubim Health Foods across the road, where shared and cheap accommodation notices cover the front windows especially in the last week of the month. (Meat-eaters and smokers may find that their choice is limited). Kitsilano is one of those areas which has gone upmarket rapidly and so it is not as easy as it used to be to find cheap student-type accommodation here.

If all else fails check the Thursday edition of the *Vancouver Sun* for housing adverts. 'Hydro inclusive' means that gas and electricity are included in the rent.

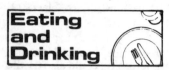

Eating and Drinking

Vancouver is reputed to have some of the most sophisticated restaurants on the continent. Certain areas of town are full of interesting and affordable establishments although, as is the case throughout North America, some are stronger on gimmicky decor and menus than on original cooking. In any case, it is easy to eat well and healthily since Vancouver is as health-conscious as any city in the world.

Gastown is an area which offers lots of choice. Down by the harbour, it was the site of the first settlement of Vancouver. It is not named for any petroleum product but after a colourful and loquacious Yorkshireman who started a pub here in the 1860s and who came to be known as 'Gassy Jack'. In the 1970s extensive renovations transformed the area from a slum into a picturesque area full of pubs and restaurants (and tourists). A stroll along Hastings and Water Streets will allow you to compare a wide variety of menus. You will pass the Old Spaghetti Factory restaurant (which has branches in other North American cities) and the Only Fish and Oyster Cafe, both of which are institutions. You will eventually come to the Harbour Mall where you can indulge in anything from an oatmeal cookie to Lobster Newburg.

Seafood naturally plays a large part in Vancouver menus and the inhabitants consume tons of shrimps and prawns annually. (Pacific shrimp are tiny whereas the prawns are bigger). For a good basic fish and chip restaurant try the Dover Seafood restaurant at 945 Denman, or the simple and inexpensive The Only Seafood cafe at 20 East Hastings downtown. You can sample them straight from the fishmonger if you like. The Granville Island Market fishmongers display their shellfish and other wares most temptingly. This is a gourmet's paradise and so a good place for buying the fixings for a picnic which you can take with you to one of the 150 parks in the city, and also good for general shopping and people-watching.

Another local tradition is to go out for Sunday brunch. Watch for the 'All You Can Eat for $10' type of advertisement. You may prefer the Chinese version of brunch known as *dim sum* which is very good at Ming's (147 Pender SE). For health foods try the Naam (4th and MacDonald). With many ethnic communities, Vancouver's restaurants rival those of San Francisco and Toronto. The primarily Cantonese restaurants may be found along Keefer, East Pender, Gore and Carrall Streets. Try the Ho Ho Inn, the Green Door opposite which is clean, cheap, friendly and bring-your-own, the On On Tea Garden at 214 Keefer, which has become an institution, or Yang's (4186 Main). The best value Chinese restaurant is arguably the On Lok on Hastings past Commercial Drive, which serves large dishes for $3.50-$4. A recommended Vietnamese restaurant is the Saigon on 4th Avenue. Commercial Street has a concentration of Italian restaurants; try Joe's Cafe for wonderful cappuccinos.

One of the most memorable dining experiences you can have in Vancouver is at Quilicum (1724 Davie St, 681-7044) which serves native Indian cuisine such as fernshoots, wind-dried salmon and barbecued caribou. If you like Indian food try the Indian Nirvana Restaurant at 2313 Main St. Excellent Thai food is available at the Thai House on Robson St. For a fast food lunch of ethnic cuisines visit the main building of the Granville Island Market or try the Food Fair at Robson Square (just near the tourist office). There you can choose a Mexican taco, a Ukranian Pyrogy (potato pastry) or a Chinese spring roll for between $3 and $6. You may have to queue at lunchtimes. Delicatessens throughout the city offer cheap and delicious sandwiches for lunch or snacks. Barbecue chicken dinners are cheap and popular with locals.

DRINKING

If you want to combine drinking with The Tourist Experience, then go to the top of the Blue Horizon Hotel (1225 Robson St) to the revolving Sears Tower on Hastings or the bar at the top of the Ramada Inn. It is always better to seek out aerial views just before dusk, so that you can see the city both by day and by night. An opposite drinking experience can also be had on Hastings St (corner of Carrall) where the Funky Winker Beans serves the cheapest beer in town at $1 a glass including a 'meat ticket' for the hourly raffle.

In the 1980's the provincial government finally relented and granted a brewing licence to someone other than the major Canadian brewers (Carling, Molson and Labatts). The best known brewery is the Granville Island Brewing Company which brews an ale and a lager. The Troller pub in picturesque Horseshoe Bay in the west part of Vancouver serves Okanagan lager and stout and good food, though it no longer brews its own beer. There are a number of imitation British pubs in Vancouver including the Elephant and Castle (Pacific Centre off Dunsmuir), the Rose and Thorne Neighbourhood Pub (part of the Kingston Hotel at 757 Richards) and the Dover Arms (961 Denman near the fish and chip restaurant).

There has been a recent and encouraging increase in neighbourhood pubs in Vancouver (as well as in Victoria) which serve imported beers and offer no entertainment apart from dartboards and pool tables. Ask locals for their recommended watering-hole. A new yuppie craze for privately-owned beer stores which are upmarket off-licences has recently hit BC.

BC white wines are improving all the time, leaving the red wines far behind. Try Osoyoos Select white. Most wines cost about $6 a bottle, and like spirits and beer are available only in government liquor stores. There is a greater selection of Californian wines in BC than in eastern Canada.

The legal drinking age is 19. As in the rest of Canada, there has been a very significant crackdown on drinking and driving.

Try to find a copy of the free *Georgia Straight* which is published on Fridays, though it has degenerated slightly since Bob Geldof was involved with it. It contains fairly reliable listings of the music, film and theatre going on during the following week. The monthly *Discorder* is published by UBC students and is geared to more alternative and underground music, theatre and film. There are also several free entertainment guides such as *Key to Vancouver* and *Vancouver Guideline* which has more conventional reviews. Check the entertainment page of the evening *Sun,* especially on Saturdays. Mainstream entertainments can be booked by phone with Vancouver Ticket Centre on 280-4444.

Buildings of Interest. There are many noteworthy buildings in Vancouver. Even the domestic architecture offers more variety and interest than in other Canadian cities. The Law Courts on Hornby St are a stunning example of modern architecture. Even a seemingly ordinary office building like the Marine Building at the bottom of Burrard Street has many attractive 1920s decorative motifs inside and out consistent with its function as a maritime insurer. The Architeture Institute of BC (AIBC) does excellent architectural tours for free during the summer months, for more information contact the AIBC (683-8588).

Museums and Galleries. You should visit the Vancouver Art Gallery (682-5621) housed in the impressive old Law Courts at Georigia and Hornby. Its collection of Canadian art, especially the paintings of Emily Carr, is particularly strong. If you have a special interest in art, check in the foyer the schedule of lecture tours offered by knowledgeable volunteers. The tours are free but the admission to the gallery is $4.25, $2.20 for students and seniors, free on Thursdays 5pm-9pm. It is open Tuesday to Sunday.

If you missed the 'Living Arctic' exhibition on Indian and Inuit life at the Museum of Mankind in London in 1988, you should try to visit the Museum of Anthropology (822-3825) on the UBC campus. Its collection of totem poles, masks, etc. carved by various groups of west coast Indians is very impressive. Admission $5, $2.50 for students and seniors, free on Tuesdays and closed on Mondays. Centennial Museum at Kitsilano Point has more artefacts from the culture of the Pacific Indians.

Music. The music scene in Vancouver is excellent. Unfortunately the proliferation and quality of bands is not matched by available venues and record labels, so very few gain a reputation outside the province. For jazz try the Hot Jazz Society (2120 Main) or the Landmark Jazz Bar (1400 Robson). The Jazz Hotline (682-0706) has information about venues. Rock venues and discos are not in short supply while country and western music has a strong following (prairie cowboys who have migrated west?). The Commodore has a dance floor suspended on springs, while the ultra-modern and trendy Luv Affair in the heart of downtown appeals to some. For folk, try the Soft Rock Cafe (1925 W 4th St). Folk music thrives in Vancouver, especially during the annual Vancouver Folk Music Festival, a three-day event in mid-July. Most who have attended rave about the setting on Jericho Beach, the quality of the music and the general atmosphere. For information and tickets phone 879-2931. There is also now an annual jazz festival in late June.

Theatre and Cinema. The main downtown cinemas are concentrated in the Granville Mall. The Ridge Theatre (corner of 16th and Arbutus) offers cheap double bills throughout the week while the Hollywood (738-3211), Pardsise (681-1732) and Pacific Cinemathque (684-FILM) are also recommended. Films normally cost $6. There is a strong theatre following in Vancouver. Check the Arts Club and the Waterfront Theatre, both on Granville Island, or the Vancouver Playhouse on Hamilton St. During the summer musicals are performed under the stars in Stanley Park (ring 687-0174 for current programmes).

SPORT AND RECREATION

Most visitors catch the outdoor bug one way or another after falling under the influence of the locals. They have built a jogging track in one of the most beautiful settings in the world. And then there is Stanley Park, with its huge trees and fascinating Aquarium with breeding killer whales, lots of locally caught seals and some sea otters. But soon you may find yourself hankering after the real thing; forests out of the earshot of traffic, and whales spouting in the ocean. It is not necessary to participate in strenuous activity;

you can get to the top of Grouse Mountain near Vancouver in a cable car ($13.95), but you may still feel guiltily sedentary when the skiers glide past. Swimming, skating, skiing and hiking are within easy reach of the city. There is a skating rink at Robson Square and a number of city beaches. You need not be a dedicated sporty type to enjoy lounging on Kitsilano Beach or Spanish Banks. As is true throughout the world, beaches are good places to meet people. Wreck Beach is the nude beach, though you do not have to disrobe. There are superb hiking trails open year round, for example a six-mile sea wall around Stanley Park and numerous trails around the University Endowment Lands.

Spectator sports are also popular. The Vancouver Canucks (a slang word for Canadians) ice hockey team play at the Pacific Coliseum and the BC Lions play the Canadian version of American football at the BC Place Stadium, the first covered dome in Canada.

The Canadian Lacrosse Hall of Fame is at 65 E 6th Ave in New Westminster (526-2751). Sports facilities at Victoria on Vancouver Island are being improved rapidly in preparation for the 1994 Commonwealth Games.

A less traditional spectator activity is to watch the harbour. Vancouver's harbour is the busiest on the west coast of the Americas and enormous freighters and container ships are constantly coming and going. You can discover the country of origin and the cargo of the ships in harbour and expected to arrive by phoning 926-7464, which provides a recorded message. You can also visit the Vancouver Container Terminal (Vanterm) to see a port in action. Phone 666-0101 for opening times and tours.

SHOPPING

Vancouver is bursting with boutiques and handicraft shops. Browse in Hill's Indian Crafts at 165 Water St, the Inuit Gallery of Vancouver at number 345 on the same street and the Indian Arts and Crafts Society of BC at 540 Burrard. The standard department stores, Eatons and the Bay, are connected by the underground Pacific Centre Mall while the western department store Woodward's is at 101 W Hastings. The market on Granville Island has an interesting selection of shops which sell books, crafts, toys and souvenirs as well as food. An interesting gift for any gastronomes you may know is wild rice, which may be purchased from one of the gourmet stalls. Upmarket fashions may be found on Robston St while Gastown is good for Kitsch and authentic crafts.

Shopping hours vary from shopping centre to shopping centre but are basically 9.30am or 10am to 6pm, sometimes staying open until 9pm on Thursdays and Fridays. A provincial sales tax of 6% is applied to most purchases with the notable exception of groceries, books and magazines. A new 7% federal tax called the Goods and Services Tax (GST) is added to virtually everything you purchase except groceries. Non-Canadians can apply for a rebate of the portion of this tax paid on accomodation if it is at least $20. Ask for details at your hotel or a duty free shop downtown.

THE MEDIA

The daily *Vancouver Sun* has better coverage of international news than it once did and is very good for entertainment, local news, cheap flights and accommodation, not to mention coloured comics. *The Toronto Globe & Mail* is available in a national edition. The morning tabloid is called *The Province*.

You may consult the *Times* and the *Guardian Weekly* at the Vancouver Public Library at 750 Burrard Street, or at the British Consulate General (800-1111 Melville, 683-4421).

CBC-AM can be located on 690 and CBC-FM on 105.7. There are many local stations carrying all shades of popular journalism. CBC is best for current affairs and CITR, the student alternative station out of UBC, is worth a regular listen.

Hastings Street downtown is considered to be Vancouver's skid row, especially between Main St and Cambie. Also some of the side streets in Chinatown seem quite rough and some locals recommend avoiding these after dark, but on the whole, Vancouver is a safe city.

Marijuana continues to be popular and easily available, especially at music festivals. As in the other provinces you run the risk of being deported if caught, since possession is strictly illegal. 'Campaign O' has resulted in the confiscation of vehicles of anyone crossing the border with any quantity of drugs, including seeds and even paraphernalia such as cigarette papers.

For free general legal information ring 687-4680 or for a referral 687-3221, while the Royal Canadian Mounted Police operate a Tourists Alert numbers (264-3111).

The area code for Vancouver and all of British Columbia is 604.

Parks Canada: Western Region, Room 520, 220 Fourth Avenue SE, Calgary, Alberta T2P 3H8 (403-231-4745).
Post Office: 349 W Georgia, near Homer (662-5724).
Police or Ambulance emergency: 911.
Automobile Association: 999 W Broadway (733-6660).
Recorded weather information: 276-6109.
St Paul's Hospital Emergency Room: 1081 Burrard (682-2344).
British Consulate: 800-1111 Melville (683-4421).
American Express: 1084 West Georgia St (669-2813).

Victoria. The city of Victoria is renowned for being more British than the British. It is the one place in Canada where you might see a cricket game being played or daunting old dowagers in fur stoles (even in summer) munching on cucumber sandwiches at tea in the lobby of the grand old railway hotel, the Empress (provided they don't take their custom elsewhere because of the ambitious renovations taking place at the time of writing). Not many other cities in North America would support a newspaper called *The Colonist.* Because of Victoria's moderate climate, it is very popular as a retirement haven. Characteristically, the most popular tourist attraction on the island is a magnificent garden called Butchart Gardens, set in a former quarry, featuring many ornamental flower displays as well as shrubs and trees. They are located between the ferry port at Swartz Bay and Victoria (admission $6).

Victoria is not altogether geriatric, and has become livelier in the run up to the 1994 Commonwealth Games. Even now it has many big city amenities, such as good restaurants, without the blight of industrialisation. Try for example the late-night Herald St Cafe, Pagliaccis, the Metropolitan Diner or Six Mile House, which are all popular with locals and cost $10-$20 for dinner. There are also some good pubs, such as the Stonehouse in Swartz Bay where the ferry docks, where the beer called Spinnaker's is brewed on site. Altogether Victoria is a charming city. Its Visitor Information Centre is at 812 Wharf St (382-2127).

As the Commonwealth Games approach, employment opportunities are increasing. Several readers have recommended the job of pedicab driving for which the only requirements seem to be a driving licence and a $70 returnable bond. Drivers are virtually self-employed and no one checks documents. The main company is Kabuki Kabs (547 Discovery St, Victoria, V8T 1G8) which allows anyone to lease the cab for about $25 a day and earn whatever he or she can.

The rest of Vancouver Island is well worth exploring especially if you enjoy backpacking. What attracts so many people to the island (after the mild climate) is the wilderness. Vancouver Island is nearly 300 miles/500 km long (the largest island off the Pacific coast of North and South America) and is very thinly populated except in the southeast. Perhaps the most appealing destination is the Pacific Rim National Park, where there is a rugged and beautiful 7-day coastal trail, which was originally used as a way out for shipwrecked sailors. Many hikers are accompanied along their route by spouting whales and sea-lions, herons and humming-birds. One of the most beautiful sections is along Long Beach from Tofino. You can also visit Hot Springs north of Tofino by boat or plane only. Or try the Cowichan Valley, starting at Duncan, which offers canoeing and fishing as well as hiking and camping.

Perhaps the most isolated destination is Cape Scott at the northern tip of the island. Access is not as difficult as it used to be, for it is now possible to drive (or hitch-hike) all the way to the park, though the last stretch is a dirt logging road. Roads used by hitch-hikers are often privately owned by logging companies. Check with the tourist office before setting out because sometimes the logging companies permit access only at weekends. Interesting as the wilderness environment is in these coastal areas, make sure you have tested your camping equipment in Scotland or a tropical monsoon. Cape Scott gets hundreds of centimetrs of rain every year, which sometimes turns the ground into a foot of mud. Still, in good weather, nothing can beat it.

It is also pleasant to spend a day or two in the Gulf Islands (Salt Spring, Galliano, San Juan, etc.), easily accessible by ferry from Vancouver or Victoria, or by Washington State Ferries between Anacortes in Washington State and Sidney 16km north of Victoria. They are covered with wild flowers in the spring and summer and make for excellent walks and bicycle rides. It is easy to visit most of them on a day-trip.

The Sunshine Coast. The Sunshine Coast refers to the 95 miles/150 km north of Vancouver. It looks particularly enticing at sunrise from the ferry to Nanaimo. It encompasses all that is great about Canadian scenery — mountains, ocean inlets, sandy beaches and fishing villages. There is no through road, so if you want to see the northern part of the Sunshine Coast, you will have to take one ferry from Horseshoe Bay to Langdale, another to Earl's Cove about 745km along and then a third one across the inlet to Powell River.

The Okanagan Valley. If you are looking for a good place to relax on your way across the province, the Okanagan Valley is as good as any place. It is world famous for its fruit production, especially its apples, and the millions of acres of blossom in the spring are a wonderful sight. During the summer, roadside fruit stalls are impossible to pass by. The Valley also supports a thriving wine industry. Most of the wineries welcome visitors on tours and tastings. Try Calona Wines in Kelowna (762-9144), Okanagan Vineyards near Oliver (498-4041), Claremont Wines in Peachland, Casabellow Wines in Penticton and Sumac Ridge Winery in Summerland. A further way you might benefit from the Koanagan fruit is that you might be able to earn a little extra money picking it. Ask at the Agricultural Employment Centre offices in Kelowna or Penticton. The whole area fills up with young people and professional transient fruit pickers (especially from Quebec), and it is possible to meet lots of interesting people.

If it is relaxation rather than work you want, the towns along Okanagan Lake are ideal. This is no wilderness, and so camping is a more social activity. Many campsites fill up in summer. Two people in a tent can expect to pay about $13. Windsurfers can be rented in Penticton for about $12 an hour.

Queen Charlotte Islands. Sixty miles off the coast of northern BC, these islands are close to the Alaskan frontier and home of the artistically gifted Haida Indians. The wildlife here is such that researches have called the island 'the Canadian Galapagos'. Birdwatchers will relish the chance to see the world's greatest concentration of Peale's peregrine falcons. Botanists can find unique species such as daisies. Non-specialists will enjoy the grandeur and isloation. Recently the islands have been the focus of friction between the Haida and loggers keen to exploit the Sitka spruce in the south of the archipelago.

Air BC flies from Vancouver to the main town of Sandspit. BC Ferries (604-559-4680) operates a boat from Prince Rupert. For further information — and information on access to more remote areas — contact Parks Canada, Box 37, Queen Charlotte, BC V0T 1S0 (604-559-8818).

The Great Outdoors

Several mountain parks are within easy reach of Vancouver for hiking, skiing or wildlife (watch for bald eagles, deer and bears). For hiking try the relatively tame but scenic Lighthouse Park, or Cypress Bowl for skiing, both about 8km from downtown (take bus 250 from West Vancouver). Slightly further afield is Mount Seymour Provincial Park. Serious skiers will be interested in the world class resorts of Mt Whistler (64 km north of Vancouver), Panorama and big White/Apex Alpine in the interior. There is a youth hostel at Whistler, in a rustic timber cabin on Alta Lake (604-932-5492). Yet another huge wilderness area also 40 miles/64 km away is called Garibaldi Park. Getting from the car park to the campsite involves a full day of fairly serious hiking or cross-country skiing. Admission to provincial parks is free but camping costs about $4. Watch for bear tracks in the mud or the snow. Danger is slight except possibly at the first thaw, when the bears emerge hungry from their winter's hibernation.

The Outdoor Recreation Council of BC publishes a series of recreational maps showing trails, bridle paths, historic landmarks, etc. There are a great many camping and sporting goods shops in Vancouver, so you should not have any trouble getting yourself equipped. You can rent most equipment at Rudy's (3279 W Broadway) and skis are available for hire at the UBC Sport Store in the Student Union Building. The best outfitters are Taiga and Mountain Equipment Co-op which both have notice boards for buying and selling used equipment.

Watersports are also popular; windsurfing takes place off most of Vancouver's beaches. Powell River, 88 miles/142 km north of the city, has excellent diving including wreck diving. Contact the Beach Gardens Dive Resort in the town of Powell River for particulars. You can raft down the turbulent Fraser River for about $70 inclusive. You may prefer to experience the Fraser Canyon, which is a $2\frac{1}{2}$-hour drive from Vancouver, from the safety of a cable car. Oyster collecting is possible along many of the bays and inlets of the Sunshine Coast, particularly in the spring and autumn.

There are many outfitters in the interior of the province who arrange trail riding in the mountains. Trips generally last one or two weeks. A one week trip will cost from $350. Consult Tourism British Columbia for suggestions.

The Great White North

Yukon Territory   **Northwest Territories**

In addition to Canada's ten provinces, there are two thinly populated northern territories which are administered by the federal government. Few visitors reach these parts, but those who do usually receive a warm welcome. Just a glance at the map of Yukon Territory and the Northwest Territories (NWT) demonstrates their uniqueness. In an area as vast as the Northwest Territories (1.25 million square miles), there are just 60 communities with a population of over 20. Some of the place names convey the hostility of the land and the determination of the early fur traders and gold miners to stick it out: Repulse Bay, Fort Resolution and worst of all 'Wager Bay (Abandoned)'. These early traders were, however, only the last in a long sucession of native peoples who have lived in this area for 10,000 years and some find it anything but barren and bleak.

Expanses of land hundreds of miles square, including some islands in the Arctic Ocean, have been designated national park and nature reserves with bird sanctuaries and reindeer grazing reserves. It is common to see large wild mammals such as caribou, moose, lynx and bears as well as a huge variety of birds many of which migrate annually to the most northern parts of the territories. There is a dotted line indicating the 'Northern Limit of Trees'. But even below the treeline, this is forbidding country, and its barren beauty does not appeal to everyone.

Climate. The weather in the territories is even harsher than that of Alaska. The climate between May and August is semi-arid with summer temperatures between 10° and 25°C. Sunlight and insects during this period are abundant.

Extrememly low temperatures combined with long hours of darkness make the winter months harsh. All homes have a wood-burning stove as a back up system in case of a power failure; it must be stoked every two hours to prevent freezing to death. But as in Alaska, summer temperatures are balmy, rainfall is slight, and summer festivities thrive in the near round-the-clock sunshine.

Arrival and Departure. To get to Canada's two Arctic territories, you will have to decide whether to invest time or money. There are daily flights — but few discounts — from the main cities of southern Canada to the Northland, e.g. the excursion fare Vancouver to Whitehorse costs well over $500. If you have several weeks, then you can consider going by land, bearing in mind that the 60th parallel is a very long way from the 49th; the distance between Toronto and the NWT/Alberta border is nearly 3,000 miles/4,800 km. The bus fare from Vancouver to Whitehorse is $270 one way. There are several highways in the territories, the most recent of which was opened in 1983 (the Liard highway linking Fort Nelson in northern BC with the Mackenzie Highway to Great Slave Lake). The Alaska Highway goes all the way from Edmonton, across Northern British Columbia, through Southern Yukon and into Alaska as far as Fairbanks. It a beautiful drive and as of 1992 (50th anniversary of its construction) is entirely paved. The Dempster Highway runs through 700 miles of unpeopled land to Inuvik in the summer the road stops here and a trip to the Artic Circle (Tuktoyuktah) must be completed by air as the MacKenzie Delta makes surface travel impossible. There are two stops for fuel along the way but carry good spare tyres.

Getting Around. Motoring holidays take on a whole new complexion in such terrain. Most roads are gravelled not paved, since the frozen tundra would soon destroy a conventional road. Fuel stops are few and bar between, not to mention regular services in the event of a breakdown. Several of the highways cross major rivers by ferry in summer, by ice bridges in winter, but not at all in the month or so when the rivers are freezing over and then again when they are melting. Traffic on the Dempster Highway is sometimes limited in October and November because of the movement of the caribou herds.

Accommodation. Amenities are, on the whole, scarce: for example there is only one hotel on the 420 miles/657 km Dempster Highway and it costs $110 a double. Camping facilities, open mid-May to mid-September, seem a better idea since many of them are free of charge.

Eating and Drinking. Most of the food served in cafes and restaurants will be expensive, conventional and frozen or tinned. As in Alaska fresh foods are at a premium because of the cost of shipping. You will have to get off the beaten track and become accepted by an Indian or Eskimo family before you will find traditional dishes such as acorn soup, baked skunk or boiled muskrat tails (said to be very sticky to eat). For some very unusual reading about the food prepared in the far north, look at Eleanor Ellis's *Northern Cookbook* which includes one of the strangest recipes of all times for chocolate sauce: the ingredients are simply two pounds of chocolate and a quarter block of paraffin. If you are lucky you may get a chance to taste moose or caribou meat. Salmon can be bought fresh and fairly cheaply in season when it is running.

Exploring. Despite the hazards and difficulties of travel in the Arctic (or perhaps because of them), the government authorities are enthusiastically encouraging tourism. In fact both Tourism Yukon and Travel Arctic (the tourism bureau of the Northwest Territories) provide excellent detailed manuals listing all accommodation (which is sparse), methods of getting around the vast area and events, as well as providing background information on native history and culture. The Klondike Gold Rush spawned a cultural upheaval and invasion of white people at the turn of the century. This remains a key focus for travellers in the Yukon and brings busloads of tourists as well as RV caravans from all over North America and Europe every year. The phenomenon peaks on August 16 which is the anniversary of the discovery of gold in the Yukon and is celebrated with gusto all weekend in Dawson City.

If simple motoring is such a challenge, the two favourite outdoor activities of hiking and canoeing are more so. All travellers intending to venture into the wilderness are requested to register with the local Mounties in case an emergency arises. A car is all you need to be able to access points from which you can embark on a truly 'wild' wilderness trip. Fishing is also good and easily accessible. A recreational fishing licence can be obtained locally for about $15. Less experienced lovers of the outdoors can hire the services of a local guide or outfitter. For local outings in the Whitehorse area, contact the Yukon Conservation Society (Box 4163, Whitehorse). Canoeing on the intricate network of lakes and rivers can be a superb way of seeing the arctic landscape and wildlife. It is possible to hire a canoe from any of the outfitters listed in the tourist literature. In the NWT you can arrange to pick up a canoe at any post of the Hudson's Bay Stores Department, 77 Main St, Winnipeg, Manitoba R3C 2R1.

Culture. One of the highlights of a trip to the Great White North must include glimpsing the life of the Inuit, many of whom continue to live at least partly by their old methods. One way of seeing some of the native traditions is to attend a carnival, jamboree or festival held in most communities, where there may be competitions in tea boiling (i.e. fire building), muskrat skinning, igloo building and harpoon throwing. Other festivals concentrate on the artistic traditions. Yellowknife, for example, stages the Raven Mad Daze on the midsummer solstice in June, and the Folk of the Rocks Festival in the third weekend of July. (For further information write to the Society for Encouragement of Northern Talent, Box 326, Yellowknife, NWT X1A 2N3; 403-920-7806). To see the handicrafts of the native people, visit any of the museums in the region, especially the MacBridge Museum in Whitehorse and the Prince of Wales Northern Heritage Centre in Yellowknife. Dawson City in Yukon sponsors a music festival in the third weekend in July, while Whitehorse stages a Northern Story Telling Festival.